A Passing Game

A PASSING GAME

A History of the CFL

by Frank Cosentino

Bain & Cox, Winnipeg

A Passing Game: A History of the CFL first published 1995 by
Bain & Cox, an imprint of Blizzard Publishing Inc.
73 Furby St., Winnipeg, Canada R3C 2A2
Copyright © Frank Cosentino

Cover photo by Robert Tinker
Printed in Canada by Friesens Printing Ltd.

Published with the assistance of
the Canada Council and the Manitoba Arts Council.

Canadian Cataloguing in Publication Data

Cosentino, Frank, 1937–
   A passing game
   Includes bibliographical references.
   ISBN 0-921368-51-8
1. Canadian Football League – History.
2. Canadian football – History. I. Title.
GV948.C67 1995   796.335'64   C95-920087-8

Contents

Foreword   7

1969 to 1970: Chapter One   9

1971 to 1972: Chapter Two   31

1973 to 1974: Chapter Three   61

1975 to 1976: Chapter Four   95

1977 to 1978: Chapter Five   118

1979 to 1980: Chapter Six   141

1981 to 1982: Chapter Seven   163

1983 to 1984: Chapter Eight   195

1985 to 1986: Chapter Nine   217

1987 to 1988: Chapter Ten   245

1989 to 1990: Chapter Eleven   269

1991 to 1992: Chapter Twelve   301

1993 to 1994: Chapter Thirteen   332

Epilogue   376

Notes   383

With thanks to my parents, Vincenzo Cosentino and Maria Annunziata Sisinni, who travelled the road from San Giorgio Morgeto in their native Calabria to give their children opportunity. They arrived in Hamilton, Ontario, where I met my wife of 36 years, Sheila, always my love and support. The road has continued to Winnipeg, home of our newest grand-daughters, Cecile Louise and Catherine Therese Richard. Winnipeg is also the home of Bain & Cox and Blizzard Publishing. I'm very appreciative of their endeavours regarding this work as well as the great cooperation and hard work of Anna Synenko and Peter Atwood.

Thanks as well to the Winnipeg Blue Bombers and to the Canadian Football League offices for their use of league minutes. A special thanks to the members of the Computer Help office at the Steacie Science Building at York University. Without their help, particularly that of Ms Chris MacDonald, deadlines could not have been met.

Foreword

When the forward pass was adopted in 1931 by the Canadian Rugby Union (CRU), the governing body for football in Canada, the Montreal Amateur Athletic Association (MAAA) unveiled Warren Stevens as its quarterback. Stevens was an American from Syracuse University who had come to McGill to do graduate work and to learn about hockey, which he considered to be the game of the future. The CRU had expected that all teams in Canada would develop their proficiency with the new rule equally; it was new to all Canadians even though the forward pass had been used in the West and the Grey Cup Game in 1929. Stevens was far advanced in the use of the new tactic; the MAAA was undefeated and won the Grey Cup of 1931.

As a result, there was a search for American talent in an attempt to gain an edge, particularly at the quarterback position. It wasn't so much that players were recruited with contracts, football in Canada was still "Amateur" by and large, but players were enticed with jobs in the community. The Sarnia Imperials, for example, won Grey Cups in two of three appearances in the thirties, many of their players, Americans as well as Canadians, were attracted to the team with the promise of a job during the Depression. When the Winnipeg Blue Bombers won the Grey Cup for the West for the first time in 1935, they did so with nine Americans they had recruited from the northern United States at a cost of $7400.

The CRU reacted. It wanted to ensure that a football team was representative of individuals who lived in its area by extending a "residence rule." Ever since 1909, players for a team were required to have lived in the area where they played football (universities were exempted). Most believed that Winnipeg would repeat as the West's representatives; the new ruling would not effect them retroactively, but when Saskatchewan won the west, their Americans were not eligible for the CRU-sponsored Grey Cup, and the

1936 Grey Cup was won by Sarnia defeating Ottawa Rough Riders 26–20. By 1993 Commissioner Larry Smith was stating that the CFL would become receptive to no import/non-import restrictions with the beginning of the 1995 season.

The purpose of this book is to trace the development of the CFL over the last 25 years and the trend towards the Americanization of the game. It will stand on its own or can be read as companion to my book *Canadian Football: The Grey Cup Years* (Musson, 1969).

Frank Cosentino

1969 to 1970

Chapter One

IN RETROSPECT, NO ONE would have thought of 1969 as a watershed in Canadian Football League (CFL) development. The CFL that year was a nine-team affair: the Eastern Conference was made up of the Hamilton Tiger-Cats, Toronto Argonauts, Ottawa Rough Riders, and Montreal Alouettes—the Big Four, as they were known prior to joining the CFL—and the Western Conference included the British Columbia Lions, Edmonton Eskimos, Calgary Stampeders, Saskatchewan Roughriders and Winnipeg Blue Bombers. The East played a 14-game schedule, the West, 16. Play-offs varied between the two conferences. In the East, the third- and second-place teams met in a "sudden death" game to determine who would play the first-place team in a two-game total-point series. In the West, the third- and second-place teams met in a one-game contest, the winner meeting the first-place team in a best-of-three series. The victors would meet the following week in the Grey Cup Game.

On the football field, the 1969 season might best be remembered for a Leo Cahill quote. After finishing with a 10–4 season, the Argonauts' best since 1960, and scoring 406 points, the best in Argo history, and almost every game a sell-out, Toronto fans were thinking Grey Cup (but then, don't they always?). Their hopes were reinforced when the Argonauts defeated Hamilton in the sudden death semifinal 15–9. It was almost a sure thing when Toronto defeated Ottawa 22–14 in the first game of the two-game total-point series. Loquacious Leo Cahill, brimming with confidence, stoked the fires, being so sure that this was the Argos' year. He claimed "it will take an act of God to beat us on Saturday."[1]

When Saturday arrived, an overnight rain and hard frost combined to turn Ottawa's Lansdowne Park into a skating rink. Ottawa wore broomball shoes, their traction was good. Toronto wore conventional footwear, their

9

footing was non-existent. Russ Jackson was in his final home appearance compounding the Argo problems with an outstanding display of quarterbacking. Ottawa scored a 32–3 victory. Cahill's quote had come back to haunt him.

Out West, second-place Calgary defeated British Columbia in the sudden death semifinal 35–21, only to be defeated by Saskatchewan, led by Ron Lancaster and George Reed, by scores of 17–11 and 36–13.

The Grey Cup Game was played on a Sunday for the first time, on November 30, at the Autostade in Montreal. The 1968 Grey Cup Game, played at the Canadian National Exhibition (CNE) Stadium, had attracted a sold-out crowd of 32,655 patrons who witnessed the Ottawa Rough Riders, led by Russ Jackson, defeat the Calgary Stampeders in a hard-fought, well-played 24—21 game. Millions more watched the game which had been telecast in colour. While it was generally believed that Montreal was a Sunday sport city, there were, nonetheless, 15 letters of protest from various groups, most from the west where the time of the game conflicted with church services.[2] It was only the second time that Montreal had hosted the event, the first being in 1931, when the famous Winged Wheelers defeated Regina in a game where the forward pass was featured for only the second time in the national contest. Prime Minister Pierre Trudeau kicked off for the third consecutive year. The game generated income of $556,360, an all-time record to that point.[3] A sold-out crowd of 33,172 braved the freezing weather. A bitter wind blew throughout the game, but Ottawa fans barely noticed. Their team defeated Saskatchewan 29–11.

It was a superb end to a brilliant career for Russ Jackson. He threw four touchdown passes and capped what had been a season of awards. He won the Jeff Russel Trophy as the Most Valuable Player in the East, was voted Most Outstanding Player by the fans and his team mates, was a unanimous choice as the Eastern Conference All Star quarterback for a record seventh time, and for the third time won the double Schenley Awards as Most Outstanding Canadian and Most Outstanding Player. His performance earned him selection as the game's top performer and the gold car which went with it—this in spite of his playing with a separated shoulder from the first quarter on.[4] His performance was all the more remarkable when one considers that threats had been made on his life. Security guards were stationed in and around the park. In those Front de Libération du Quebec (FLQ) days anything and everything was possible.

Off the field, the CFL introduced its new crest in time for the game. It was a stylized football helmet with a red maple leaf and the letters CFL. The old crest had too many colours, making it difficult and expensive to duplicate. It had included an orange, yellow, and green maple leaf atop a brownish football containing the white letters CFL. At the bottom was a blue ribbon containing the words Canadian Football League.

The other major announcements concerned the sale of the Montreal Alouettes and the return of Sam Berger to football. Berger, the former owner of Ottawa, had sold the Rough Riders to Tremblay Realty Company Limited, a private firm owned by David Loeb and his immediate family.[5] Ottawa had been converted to a privately owned club in 1960. It had six directors. In 1966, another six were added, including Loeb. They contributed a reported $50,000 per share. Loeb was reported to have offered each of the other 11 directors $65,000 for their share in order to become the sole owner.[6] It was speculated that because Loeb's money was "IGA money, the groceteria chain may be merely the first commercial chain to buy into the Canadian football picture."[7]

Now Sam Berger moved back into football, purchasing 1,276 of the 1,340 outstanding shares of the Alouettes from owner Joe Atwell. "None of the principals would say what the offer was but it has been reported at between $900,000 and $1,200,000."[8] The remaining 64 shares were retained by Montrealers "who have had a minority interest for years."[9] In a city where the baseball Expos had just made their debut and attendance was dwindling at football games, it was hoped that with the purchase, the league had gone a long way towards solving what Jake Gaudaur, the league's commissioner, had termed its "number one problem."

One of the reasons why the 1969 Grey Cup Game had been played in Montreal was to drum up enthusiasm for football in that city. Everyone seemed to rush in to assist in spite of it being, to some, an *anglais* game with no constituency in the French fact of la belle province. Yet in spite of this and the stadium, which was made up of separate, disconnected sections of stands and was cold and impersonal, the game was a sell-out. Crowds and revenues were at an all-time high. All levels of government cooperated with the CFL, especially the federal government. Prime Minister Trudeau was singled out by Gaudaur for his support and participation. In addition to making his opening kick-off, Trudeau attended a CFL luncheon prior to the game, along with seven cabinet ministers, and appeared at every pre- and post-game function to which he was invited. In Gaudaur's words, "he acceded to every request we made which was necessary to adhere to our very intricate timing schedule."[10]

It was important "that as many federal government representatives as possible be familiar with what Canadian football really is."[11] The league was more than pleased when the prime minister's office requested, and paid for, tickets to the game for 20 Quebec federal members of parliament.[12] Even more remarkable was the fact that this was done while under the threat of violence from the separatist FLQ.

As a franchise, Montreal had become a source of concern to the CFL. In order to have his office monitor developments more closely, Gaudaur commissioned a clipping service.[13] The advent of the baseball Expos indicated that the Alouettes would be hard pressed to average ten thousand spectators a game, in spite of Montreal being the CFL's largest-populated franchise area. The team had received $41,304 in 1968 gate equalization, a formula initiated to have the better-drawing and therefore wealthier teams contribute to the poorer.[14] In 1969, gate revenue declined to $361,622 from $523,454 the previous year. Montreal's share of gate equalization climbed to $78,897.[15] Berger's purchase came at a good time as far as the league was concerned. Montreal's fortunes had to be turned around. In 1960, average attendance was 23,192; in 1962, 21,492; in 1964, 20,627; in 1966, 16,904; and in 1967, 12,129.[16] Baseball or no baseball, the decline in attendance was a gradual development. Some had blamed the ownership by Joe Atwell; the figures proved otherwise. Gaudaur was actively suggesting remedies. He advised Atwell[17] to recognize that French had to play a greater role in the club's marketing approach. Eighty-five per cent of the Quebec population is French, Gaudaur noted, and unless they are a source of fan support, the size of the market shrinks considerably. He suggested "meaningful participation by persons from the French community,"[18] involvement of important French organizations such as la Chambre de Commerce de Jeunes, entertainment by French Canadian groups at half-time, French front-office personnel, and a bilingual approach.

Gaudaur's fear, of course, was that should the Montreal franchise fail, the league would be deprived of one of its major markets. And with Montreal Mayor Jean Drapeau and his agent Gerry Snyder actively courting a National Football League (NFL) franchise, the competition could move in, not only there but into Toronto and Vancouver as well.

Gaudaur had actually concluded an agreement with NFL Commissioner Pete Rozelle to remove that threat—for now. The two leagues agreed that neither would play a pre-season, post-season, league, or play-off game within 125 miles of the exterior corporate limits of the other league's member cities without their authorization.[19] Rozelle mentioned that he did not have unilateral authority to prevent expansion since a required majority of NFL clubs could overrule him, but no expansion was contemplated for at least five years.[20]

Gaudaur further reminded all that "there is a responsibility on the part of the CFL as a whole and particularly the clubs located in the three major CFL markets, Montreal, Toronto and Vancouver, to provide a Canadian football operation which will cause such fans to prefer Canadian football not because it is Canadian but because it is better."[21]

When Sam Berger took over the Montreal operations, he seemed to make a move towards some of Gaudaur's recommendations. Replaced were Big Four and Ottawa legend Tony Golab, Head Coach Kaye Dalton, and Assistant Coach Ralph Goldston, the first black coach in the CFL. Montreal's dynamic duo, Red O'Quinn and Sam Etcheverry, were reunited now as general manager and head coach. Assisting Etcheverry would be Bob Ward and Gene Gaines. All were committed to bring Montreal the Grey Cup.

But first the Cup had to be found. It was missing! On December 20, 1969, someone broke into the Ottawa offices where it was locked in a display case. No other trophies were taken; it was the Grey Cup that the thieves were after.

The CFL commissioner was first alerted of the disappearance by a Canadian Press reporter. A watchman making his Saturday afternoon rounds discovered the break-in. Both David Loeb, owner, and General Manager Frank Clair were out of town. Gaudaur telephoned the Ottawa police for confirmation. On Monday, December 22, Gaudaur informed his CFL officers of the situation. Ottawa Police Inspector Hobbs, who was in charge of the investigation, saw the incident as a prank. Patience was needed. When Gaudaur suggested a reward, the inspector advised waiting until Christmas and in the meantime try the "normal channels." On January 4, 1970, both the Ottawa police and Frank Clair received several telephone messages. The caller knew where the trophy was and was willing to act as an intermediary in its return for a reward from one to five hundred dollars. The following day, January 5, the caller met with Inspector Hobbs; his price was now one hundred dollars and four Ottawa season tickets! "This and a statement by the informer that at the moment the trophy was filled with biscuits in the possession of the thief, led me to wonder whether or not the informer was as full of biscuits as the trophy,"[22] wrote Gaudaur.

As time passed, it became clear that the informer wanted a greater reward. When Gaudaur phoned Hobbs for an update and there was no new news, a reward was actively being considered, as was the decision to manufacture a replica. The original, if it were found, was to remain in the Hall of Fame. "Two Toronto companies offered to reproduce the trophy in silver and present it gratis to the CFL."[23] There was another consideration: whether "something other than the Grey Cup [should] be considered as a symbol of the professional football championship of Canada."[24] At least through all of this Gaudaur retained his sense of humour. "The last four people," he said, "seen with the trophy, photographically speaking, were Prime Minister Trudeau, myself, Russ Jackson and Ken Lehman. I just throw that out for what it is worth."[25]

Fortunately, the Cup was found after a phone call to the Metropolitan Toronto Police Force, February 16, 1970. It was discovered intact in a locker in the basement of the Royal York Hotel. An anonymous caller told police that they would find the key to the lock in a pay phone booth at Dundas and Parliament streets.[26] Metro Police, showing that they also have a sense of humour, stated their claim to the 1970 title. They placed a sticker on the spot reserved for the 1970 winner. It read: Metro Police ETF (Emergency Task Force). In 1972, the league decided to duplicate the trophy. Ever since it had been found, it had been zealously guarded. A decision was made to store the solid silver trophy in a secure place until it could be permanently displayed in the Hall of Fame. In the meantime, the league approved a silver-plated replica at a cost of $550, plus provincial sales tax. The approval was given at the CFL's Executive Committee meeting held June 1 in Regina, the same meeting at which Gaudaur's contract as commissioner was renewed for five more years effective July 1, 1972.

Jake Gaudaur had moved to the office of commissioner from the Hamilton Tiger-Cats where he had been president and general manager. While in Hamilton, he had been associated with Ralph Sazio since 1950. Sazio arrived as a player, became an assistant coach with Carl Voyles and Jim Trimble, and became head coach in 1963. Many believed that his intensity and commitment, as well as the physical presence he portrayed, were responsible for the success of the Hamilton teams in the fifties and sixties. During his tenure as head coach, his teams appeared in the Grey Cup Game four times, winning three. He became general manager when Gaudaur left to become commissioner.

Sazio could become very intimidating when he felt that his best interests were not being served. When Gaudaur took it upon himself to finalize the exhibition schedule because the clubs could not agree by a predetermined deadline, Sazio complained that he was being forced to accept a schedule that was not only unfavourable to Hamilton, but one upon which he had been denied the opportunity to express his opinion. He suggested strongly that the commissioner's action was beyond his authority.[27] This was vintage Sazio and perhaps a bit of a surprise to his new cohorts at the managerial level:

> Something happened behind the closed doors when the Commissioner exercised his prerogative. There was loud dissent and assembled press, radio and TV personnel waiting in the corridor could

hear some of it. Hamilton general manager Ralph Sazio released an outraged bellow and could be heard crashing a huge fist on the table to emphasize his dissent. "Look," he said, "we were willing to take Winnipeg, but it was only on condition that the other part was accepted too."

There was more shouting and table thumping before order was restored. The meeting was extended for another hour before a lunch break was called. It was a grim faced group of general managers that walked out of the room.[28]

A motion was passed to proceed to the Executive Committee to the effect that the commissioner would select only those schedules discussed beforehand by the General Managers' Committee.[29] Less than one year into his tenure, it appeared that Gaudaur was being given the message that the previous commissioner Keith Davey had been given: The commissioner was only there to do the bidding of the member teams. The subsequent meeting of the Executive Committee, however, supported Gaudaur's position by an 8–1 margin.[30]

Throughout the CFL, Ralph Sazio was making his presence felt. "Two years ago," reported Gord Walker of *The Globe and Mail*, "Ralph Sazio was a rookie at the Canadian Football League conference table. This year, he dominated them."[31] Sazio was elected president of the Eastern Football Conference (EFC) and chair of the General Managers' Committee. He was definite in his ideas, continuously balancing off-league interests with his club's. He sought to convince the Rules Committee that there should be an extra official on the field, making a total of six. There were two sides to the suggestion, financial (the extra cost would be about $2,000 and therefore it would have to be passed by the Executive Committee) and technical. Sazio argued that the Canadian field was 50 per cent larger than the American field and the NFL used six officials. In addition, it was necessary to protect the quarterback from late hits, and under the present arrangement the five officials were too busy with the play to do so. Indeed, Sazio said, protection of the quarterback was the main reason for his motion.[32] In spite of Sazio's influence, there was no seconder for his motion, fears were expressed that a sixth official would simply add more penalties since each official, according to league statistics, called three penalties per game. There was no reason to believe that the proposed official wouldn't get in his three calls' worth.

Sazio's preoccupation with quarterbacking was in tune with the league's. Most clubs had a good front-line quarterback but each became a different, weaker team with their starter out of the game. Fortunes rose and fell with the quarterback position. It was the Edmonton Eskimos who prepared the soil for one of the league's most controversial decisions.

During its glory days in the fifties, Edmonton had stability with a group of successful quarterbacks: first with Bernie Faloney and Jackie Parker in 1954, then with Parker and Don Getty until 1962. Edmonton won the Grey Cup in 1954, '55, and '56; the team also appeared in the Grey Cup Game of 1960, but was defeated by Ottawa. After 1962, the team having won 6, lost 9, and tied 1, Parker was traded to Toronto. A succession of quarterbacks was brought in either to work with Getty or displace him in an effort to regain lost glories. Lynn Amadee arrived in 1963 but the Eskimos under coach and former player Eagle Keys were 2 and 14 and finished last. In 1964, new coach Neill Armstrong brought in Jon Anabo and Bill Redell. Getty retired, eventually to become Alberta's premier. The team finished fourth with a 4 and 12 record. Bill Redell and Randy Kerbow shared the quarterbacking in 1965, leading the team to a fifth-place finish with a 5 and 11 record. In 1966, Kerbow and Redell led the team to a 6–9–1 record and a third-place finish and the play-offs. In 1967, Kerbow was converted to a wide receiver, and Redell, Tommy Joe Coffey, and Ed Turek were traded to Hamilton for Frank Cosentino, Don Sutherin, Gerry McDougall, and the rights to Billy Wayte. The Eskimos also signed Terry Baker, a former Heisman Trophy winner who had played with the Los Angeles Rams. His contract for $20,000 translated into constant pressure by the club on the coaches to play him. Sutherin refused to report and was sent to Ottawa which, in turn, made tackle Earl Edwards available to Edmonton. The Eskimos enjoyed their best season since their 10–5–1 record of 1961, finishing in third place with a 9–6–1 record. They were defeated by Saskatchewan in the play-offs 21–5. In 1968, Terry Baker decided to retire. He had started only two games in 1967 and wanted his contract guaranteed before he would return to Edmonton. The club was unwilling. It brought in two American, or import, quarterbacks, Charlie Fulton and Corey Colehour, after the training camp was over. The team again finished third, with an 8–7–1 record, and lost to Calgary 29–13 in the play-offs.

Frustrated by the quarterbacking merry-go-round, Norm Kimball served a notice of motion to the annual meeting of the CFL to introduce a special quarterback category on a club roster without regard to import or non-import status.[33] In recounting his club's experiences in the quarterback area, Kimball stated that "current roster restrictions have limited the opportunity to give a prospect experience in the field."[34] A straw vote indicated that the motion would not pass; five members were opposed and three abstained. Three days later at the Executive Committee meeting, Hugh McColl, the Eskimos' president, introduced the motion stating that a club has a responsibility to develop quarterbacks but, under the present roster regulations, a back-up quarterback has to play another position. Further, he added, the designated import rule did not help since the player who had been replaced could not re-enter the game. His motion called for a basic roster of 31 players, including no more than 13 imports plus three in the quarterbacking category. The proposed total roster of 34 was an increase of two, a source of concern to Hamilton's Ralph Sazio. He could support the motion if rosters remained the same, that is, a basic roster of 30 with not more than 12 imports and two in the special quarterback position.[35] The matter was tabled for further discussion after Bill Clarke of Saskatchewan suggested that the "designated import rule could be adjusted to look after this rule."[36] Subsequently, the general managers voted against the Edmonton proposal at its meeting in Edmonton on April 30,[37] but the seed had been planted. Hamilton and Edmonton traded away their quarterbacks after the 1968 season, one which was disappointing for both teams. Both teams asked that the league by-laws "be amended to permit a separate roster category of quarterbacks, exclusive of import and non-import classification."[38] It was suggested that a designated import modification was the way to effect the change. To that end, a committee consisting of Ralph Sazio, Lew Hayman of Toronto and Earl Lunsford of Winnipeg was struck to bring a recommendation to the next meeting.[39]

When Sazio, Lunsford, and Hayman submitted their report, meant to guarantee stability at the quarterbacking position, they declared that they were unable to agree on a specific proposal. In fact, there were as many opinions as there were committee members.

Proposal A called for an import roster of 14 with one being the designate. If the latter was a quarterback, he would be allowed to substitute freely with the starting quarterback. Only one quarterback would be allowed in the game at one time. If the designate entered at another position, the player replaced must leave the game and could not re-enter. If the designate was not a quarterback, the rule was to be the same as the one in effect in 1969, that is, the replaced player came out and could not return. If the starting quarterback was a non-import and the import quarterback designated, once the import entered the game another import was to come out. This suggestion called for a 13-import playing roster at all times.

Proposal B called for the institution of a special category known as "quarterbacking." In effect, two players would be designated as quarterbacks, similar to goalies in hockey. When one entered the game, the other was to come out but could re-enter. Players' rosters would still be at 32, with 2 quarterbacks, 14 imports, and 16 non-imports.

Proposal C was a variation. It called for 13 imports and a special category of two quarterbacks and an overall roster of 32 players.

Presumably, everyone saw a disadvantage or perceived an advantage for someone else. Discussion revolving around the three proposals was inconclusive. Sazio moved Proposal C. It was seconded by Kimball of Edmonton.[40] It was defeated 4–4 with one abstention.

Ottawa wanted to abandon the whole concept of designation. It was a familiar argument. "Fourteen imports were being paid. Let them all play." The new owners of the Rough Riders thought they were being logical. Others, with a longer involvement in the league, saw where that would lead. Sazio complained that the Ottawa proposal would lead to a creeping increase in the import numbers and therefore more expenses. He reasoned that a club would want "to keep an extra import around in case of injuries, then the pressure will be on to 'play him if you have to pay him.' The coach would play all fourteen imports and disregard non-imports because of the necessity of winning."[41] Both Winnipeg and Hamilton were anxious to retain the present rule of having a designated import and provide an alternative whereby two import quarterbacks could be designated and replace each other freely during the game at the quarterback position.[42] Both teams were prepared to move to that effect. Hamilton decided that it would withdraw its motion in support of Winnipeg's since they were alike. Straw votes revealed that neither Winnipeg nor Ottawa had the two-thirds of the votes necessary to pass the motion. Ottawa had five in favour and four opposed; Winnipeg also had five in favour but only three opposed, with one abstaining.

In 1965, when the CFL decided to do away with the descriptor "Americans" and "Canadians," it settled on the terms "imports" and "non-imports." The decision was partly forced upon it and partly a question of money.

Traditionally, the American player was at the top of the pay scale, the Canadian at the lower end. However, things weren't quite that simple. There were degrees of Americanization. There was an American-born, American-trained citizen of the United States—perhaps a former collegian or an ex-NFLer, although he might also be neither (Willie Bethea and Dave Fleming of the Hamilton Tiger-Cats come to mind). The American player was at the top of the CFL pay scale, the attraction around whom tickets would be sold, publicity generated, and systems of play developed. He was in a class by himself, at various times in the league's history one of as few as five or as many as 16 as rosters increased from 28 to 36.

Occasionally, clubs sought to sell the talented American on carving out a career in Canada. After all, this was one of the advantages of playing in the Great White North. Traditionally, practices started at 5:00 PM or later.

Unlike the NFL where football was a full-day occupation, with meetings and practices stretching from morning into the early evening, the CFL allowed the player to develop a career simultaneously. The player became a member of his community all year round, which enhanced his presence among the public. Not only that, he supplemented his football income and, in the process, took some pressure off the club in maintaining his highest pay status and prepared himself better for the day when his playing days would be over.

The CFL encouraged this, seemingly aware that a community base meant more fan appeal and wider support. American players were encouraged to apply for Canadian citizenship after having been in the country for five years. That being the case, the dictum that Canadian talent was the chief factor in a team's success took on a renewed meaning as a result of franchises making concerted efforts to convince their American talent to settle in the community and apply for citizenship. It seemed to be a win–win situation. In a nation of immigrants, the community benefitted from this influx of usually well-educated people who were involved in the community; the spectators were convinced that they were seeing a better brand of football. After all, there were now more "Americans" on the team, whether or not they were labelled "Canadians." To have the American connection was an automatic measure of quality.

Clubs sought to stock up on this new source of Canadians for a number of reasons: there were only thirty-five universities in Canada fielding football teams; the few junior teams across the country were not able to turn out the quality of player needed; senior football was fast becoming non-existent.

One of the most successful teams of the fifties and sixties was the Hamilton Tiger-Cats. It was no coincidence that at various times their "naturalized Canadians" included key performers such as John Barrow, Hardiman Cureton, Angelo Mosca, Ellison Kelly, Garney Henley, Ralph Goldston, Vince Scott, and Tommy Joe Coffey. Simultaneously, there was a concerted effort to uncover players born in the United States of Canadian parents, thus holding dual citizenship. Again, Hamilton had a plethora of such players: Bronko Nagurski, Jr., Gerry McDougall, Ron Ray, Ted Page, and Billy Wayte. But to restrict these categories of players to Hamilton would be misleading. Naturalized Canadians included some of the league's leading exponents, giving new meaning to the term "Canadian Content": Jackie Parker, Bernie Faloney, Ron Lancaster, Nobby Wirkowski, Billy Shipp, Dick Shatto, George Reed, Jim Reynolds, and Roger Nelson, to mention only a few.

"American" was a synonym for "good." Teams searched for the American connection in the Canadian context. If naturalized Americans were not available, the search was directed to those with dual citizenship—although both avenues continued simultaneously. Failing to uncover those who had that connection, clubs would send high school graduates from their "territorial area" to an American University, to play football while, ideally for the individual, gaining an education and returning to the CFL and his "sponsoring" club that had the CFL rights to the territory in which he resided.

As a result, by 1965 there were five categories of "Canadian," each having a corresponding salary scale. From lowest to highest, they were: the non-university (junior, intermediate, or senior background) player; the Canadian university-trained player; the American-trained Canadian; the dual citizen American/Canadian player; and the naturalized Canadian player. It was a time when the game rosters were set at 32, 13 of whom could be Americans. The Canadian aspect of the payroll—all five levels of it—was increasing dramatically.

Some were to argue that the quality of the game was too, but there was no correspondingly dramatic increase in revenue. Clubs were still dependent upon gate receipts. Something had to be done and when it was, it set off a storm of protests. The CFL decided in 1965 to limit each team to 14 imports and three naturalized Canadians.[43]

The announcement was at once vociferously protested in many parts of the country. This move was made by the CFL in an effort to decrease the rising cost of operation but was immediately seized upon by many as being discriminatory. "According to this recent legislation, a naturalized citizen is discriminated against because he is a professional football player," stated the Montreal *Gazette*.[44] The coaches were not happy either: "I and the other coaches had absolutely no inkling that such changes were even contemplated. There's no question that this hurts a coach's chances of fielding a first class team,"[45] said Dave Skrein. The players were not pleased: "'There's no protection now,' said Angelo Mosca, the big American-born tackle of the Tiger-Cats, 'If I'd known this was going to happen I wouldn't have changed my citizenship.'"[46] Other affected players such as Billy Shipp and Dick Shatto also denounced the legislation. Shipp said that he had considered playing in the American Football League (AFL) when that league was formed but he hadn't done so because he believed he could prolong his playing career by remaining in Canada and becoming a naturalized citizen. Shatto inquired whether a naturalized citizen in Canada was only a secondary citizen. The CFL legislation was also discussed in the Ontario Legislature. John Yaremko, Provincial Secretary and Minister of Citizenship, labelled the ruling "reprehensible to the say the least. It is repugnant to the very basic principle we are striving for in the development of our Canadian way of life—the principle of equality."[47] Three players, Milt Campbell of the Toronto Argonauts, Kaye Vaughan of Ottawa, and Angelo Mosca of Hamilton, announced that they were filing a grievance with the Ontario Human Rights Commission. The application was later withdrawn.

As a direct result of the CFL's attempt to limit the number of naturalized Canadians on each team, the CFL Players' Association was formed. Such an association had been mentioned as early as 1961 when the Ottawa Rough Riders named Bobby Simpson and Gary Schreider as players' representatives. The two players were "to dicker with the club management on issues, including payment for exhibition and Grey Cup games, accommodation, public appearances and training camp conditions."[48] The Ottawa club was mainly dissatisfied with the arrangements regarding remuneration for Grey Cup appearances. Both competing teams at that time received $500. In 1962, another effort to set up an association was made by Ted Duncan, a Calgary lawyer. A problem in setting up such an association had always been that it was perceived as benefitting only the Canadian player; the higher profile athlete, that is, the American, did not have the same concerns as the "home-brew." By 1965, however, there were enough high profile players who had become naturalized Canadians or were thinking about it, that the time was ripe for the association to take root.

The CFL Players' Association became a reality as a result of meetings held at the Constellation Hotel in Toronto on May 15 and 16, 1965. At those meetings, the following were present: Montreal, Clare Exelby and Ralph Goldston; Hamilton, Zeno Karcz and Frank Cosentino; Calgary, Don Luzzi; Edmonton, Tommy Joe Coffey; Regina, Reg Whitehouse; Vancouver, Norm Fieldgate; Toronto, Dick Shatto; Ottawa, Gary Schreider; and Winnipeg, Norm Rauhaus. Gary Schreider was elected president, Norm Rauhaus, vice-president, and Dick Shatto, secretary treasurer. John Agro, QC, a Hamilton attorney who was present at the meeting, was appointed the legal advisor for the association.

As a result of all the adverse publicity it had received over its attempt to limit the number of naturalized Canadians on each team, the CFL reviewed the legislation and decided to base the distinction between an import and a non-import on football playing experience rather than nationality. According to the new ruling, the following players would be classified as imports:

1. A player who has received training in football outside Canada by having participated as a player in a football game outside Canada prior to his 17th birthday.

2. A player who has received training in football outside Canada by having participated in a football game as a player outside of Canada after his 17th birthday but who has received no football training in Canada prior to his 17th birthday.[49]

In an effort to mollify the concerned, the CFL declared that the new regulation was not to be imposed on anyone who had been previously classified as a non-import or anyone who had acquired Canadian citizenship prior to July 20, 1965.

Nonetheless, a number of seeds had been planted. The Players' Association became a reality but, more importantly, the perception had been planted in the public's mind that Americans were deemed to be important, Canadians, "non-important." Through the years, many league decisions confirmed that view, particularly after the 1969 season.

As the discussion revolving around the quarterbacks went on, it was necessary for Gaudaur to leave the meeting to convene a pre-arranged press conference. The matter was still unresolved. The clubs continued to discuss the situation. Ottawa decided to withdraw its motion which would have allowed all 14 imports to play with no designated import regulation, leaving the door open for a Winnipeg thrust. During the press conference, "CFL secretary-treasurer Greg Fulton arrived breathlessly with a penned message for Gaudaur. When Gaudaur had time later in the conference, he read that 'the Winnipeg resolution passed 7–2. Now for what that means, I'll turn you over to Greg.' Fulton thereupon interpreted the cryptic message."[50]

It meant that 32 players could dress for a league, play-off game, or championship game. Not more than 14 could be imports; prior to the game (a) one would be designated as a substitute who would be permitted to replace another import player on the understanding that the player he replaced could not re-enter the game or (b) two import players would be designated as quarterbacks who would be permitted to alternate at any time at the quarterback position exclusively. The rule went on to say that the duties of the quarterback position could include punting, place kicking, or holding the ball on convert or field goal attempts. Such a quarterback could enter the game in another position only under the conditions of (a) above. The addition of the (b) section of the rule was to have a far-reaching effect on the development of the game. It virtually ensured that non-import and quarterback would be mutually exclusive.

The perception that a club needed an import (an American) at the quarterback position in order to win was becoming more ingrained in the CFL. It had received its impetus in 1931 when Warren Stevens was imported to lead the Montreal Winged Wheelers to their Grey Cup victory, in the process giving a fine display of the forward pass as a tactic. Four years later, in 1935, it became more solidified with Winnipeg's victory, the first for the Western Conference. Their nine imports (Americans) caused other teams to look south and, as a direct result, legislation limiting teams to the use of five Americans became necessary.

Coaches, the majority of whom were more likely to be American than Canadian, would not have to worry about developing a non-import quarterback; there were many to choose from in the United States. Canadians had become unimportant, not needed at the quarterback position. Yet, this was not something that was readily apparent at the time this new legislation passed. The Calgary Stampeders, having traded for Winnipeg's first draft choice, selected Wayne Holm, quarterback from Simon Fraser University.

The topic of imports and non-imports seemed to be at the heart of every discussion that the CFL had at its various meetings. When the Rules Committee met to discuss and review new and old approaches to the game, the topic could surface there, as it did at the meeting at the Biltmore Hotel in Los Angeles, California, on January 7, 1969. Chief among the agenda items to be discussed was the rule permitting blocking on punt returns. It had been deferred from the 1968 meeting. At that time, punt returners were still being given a five-yard cushion before making contact with the ball but once having done so, they were on their own; there was no blocking allowed to assist them in their return. It was one player against twelve.

The CFL coaches, who met among themselves to suggest rule changes, through their spokesman, Frank Clair, advised that none of their group had favoured a complete switch to the U.S. rule with its fair catch. Nor were they convinced that the Canadian Intercollegiate Athletic Union (CIAU) rule, with its unlimited blocking and a five-yard restraining area, was the way to go. The unanimous feeling of the five coaches in attendance was that the receiving team should have at least three players at least 25 yards downfield from the line of scrimmage. One would catch the ball; the other two would be eligible to block. It was reasoned that 25 yards would give the officials a clear line of demarcation. As to what would happen on a shorter kick, there was no agreement. Clair also believed that the wider field would continue to aid the returner but also increase the probability of clipping, or blocking from the rear.

There was a resistance to change; some preferred to go with what they knew to be the case rather than conjecture. Rogers Lehew of Calgary reasoned that the punt rule, as it stood currently, required no specialists (most teams put a Canadian, a non-import, in the punt returning positions since he had been conditioned always to return punts and would not suffer a lapse and call for a fair catch.) Deep down, as well, there was a fear that the team did not want to risk injury to one of its important players as a result of 12 members of the opposition seeing him as fair game. A change in the rule might cause coaches to request more players, thereby increasing the rosters and costs. Saskatchewan's Ken Preston felt that a club would have to use its best personnel on the punt return, perhaps detracting from the game rather than adding to it. For Hamilton's Ralph Sazio, however, himself only one year removed from the coaching ranks, the coaches were going at the rule from the wrong direction. He suggested that only the two widest flanked players on either side of the centre for the kicking team could go downfield at the snap of the ball. All other offensive players would have to wait until the ball was kicked. Toronto's Lew Hayman moved and B.C.'s Denny Veitch seconded Sazio's proposal. The motion that passed included a penalty of five yards, down repeated (only to apply to punt returns, not to missed field goals), or the option to refuse.[51]

Pressure to increase the number of imports allowed each team was a recurring league topic. Montreal felt a continual need to strengthen its roster. They wanted to clarify the status of a British soccer player who had tried out with Kansas City. Montreal wanted to sign him as a non-import but the new regulations would not allow it. It was pointed out that while "rules and regulations will always create areas of hardship for persons just beyond the arbitrary cut-off point, it was agreed that however unfortunate for this particular player, the ruling should remain undisturbed."[52] The Alouettes then proposed that the import quota be increased from 14 to 16 with a corresponding decrease in non-imports from 18 to 16.[53] The proposal did not meet with immediate rejection on principle. Denny Veitch felt that strong member clubs should help weaker ones who were below standard in the non-import category.[54] Norm Kimball of Edmonton feared a decrease in the spectacle if more imports were added, since coaches would most likely place the extra imports on defence.[55]

Montreal's reasons for proposing the increase of imports were partly based on the fact that few schools in its territory played Canadian football. Therefore it was at a disadvantage compared with other teams who sent Canadians to American universities. In addition, two stalwart imports, tackle Bob Minihane and linebacker Al Ecuyer, were retiring. The club felt that in order to be competitive it required an increase in imports. Perhaps the piece of information that ultimately led to the defeat of the motion was provided by Calgary's A.G. Burton. He suggested that it would be "untimely to consider any legislation that would decrease the participation of Canadian players in Canada's only national professional sport in view of the pending report of the government's Task Force Report on Sport."[56] The report, commissioned as a result of an election promise by Pierre Trudeau, was to investigate sport in Canada as a result of the country's lack of success in the international arena, particularly in hockey and the Olympics, but also to probe sport at all levels of competition. The CFL in general was lauded for its approach. Its option clause as opposed to the reserve clause of the NHL, the fact that all of its teams were in Canada, and the Report's extolling of the CFL and its Grey Cup Game as a force for national unity, caused some task force members to call for the league's submission to be made public, feeling it would be "enlightening to many people who currently consider the league's motivations to be something other than the actual case."[57]

While the league was attempting to refine its playing rules, its Players' Association was continuing its thrust to improve the lot of its players. The association sought and received standardization of subsistence allowances and fringe benefits, in many cases because of a perceived strike and subsequent loss of revenue by the clubs. Within the league administration itself, some saw the association as a threat, while others could work with it for the betterment of the league. The CFL General Managers' meeting of May 26 in Winnipeg recommended to the Executive Committee that it entertain a proposal for compulsory membership in the association in return for a covenant not to strike against the league or a member club. That motion was carried 7–1 with one abstention. When the committee met two days later, it voted down the motion and relayed the decision that "such a request not be used as a negotiable item in future discussions with the Players' Association."[58] That same meeting of the Executive Committee sought to assuage the players by fixing pre-season allowances at $10 per day when room and board was not provided and $2 when it was. The decision, approved by an 8–1 vote of the clubs, was turned down by the association.

The Players' Association, recognized since 1965, was becoming a force with which to be concerned. Among the requests that it made were that there be compulsory membership—at the time it was voluntary, with 90% of the players being members—revision of the injury clause in the standard player's contract, and an increase in Grey Cup money, to $2,000 for each player on the winning team, and $1,000 for each player on the losing team. Currently, the players were receiving $1,250 and $750 respectively.

The league increased the winning team's per-player share to $1,500, the losers' to $1,000.[59] In addition, each member of the Grey Cup winning team was given a miniature Grey Cup, the value of which was not to exceed $50. Ralph Sazio felt that the league should continue the practice, which had begun in 1964, because of the intrinsic value which the player wouldn't appreciate until his later years.[60] The other two association requests were turned down.

There was a new militancy about the Players' Association. When it was first formed in 1965, the players, in an attempt to attract high-profile members as well as soothe league fears, decided that it would negotiate without the threat of a strike. In 1969, with the Argonauts' Mike Wadsworth as president, the threat to strike was reinstated. League officials did not like it. When the Players' Association requested league permission to hold an All Star game, Denny Veitch of the B.C. Lions recalled that league approval had been given in principle when relations between the two groups were good. He asked whether the approval was still binding now that the association was making "implied threats." Further, he suggested "unlimited imports as an answer to a hostile association consisting in the main of non-import players."[61]

Some players refused to be intimidated. While the association was attempting to have uniformity, for example, a $5,000 minimum salary and equalization of fringe benefits throughout the league, individual clubs were willing to take matters into their own hands. In the matter of training camp and exhibition games, there was no uniformity of approach. Players had to settle for whatever their club offered. In Toronto, players requested $50 a week training-camp expenses for all and payment of $100 for exhibition games, of which there were four. Since payment for exhibition games was against the league rules, the request was later modified to $100 per week for everybody at training camp. A third modification was offered by the players who were due to attend the Argonauts training camp at Aurora, Ontario. They would accept $60 per week for everybody for the duration of the training camp; the 32 players selected for the final roster were to receive $40 per week retroactively.[62]

The Argonauts, who had paid $50 per week to out-of-town candidates only, offered $60 per week to players as long as they were on the roster. The difference of about $8,000 was enough to cause a players' strike by the Argos. Leo Cahill, having met with the club owners and hearing their dire threats of wholesale fines, suspensions, and replacements, informed all that he would start fining "at $50 per day and work up to $100."[63]

The players were firm. They held their own practices at a high school in Port Credit, Ontario where linebacker Peter Martin taught.

Cahill requested a meeting with the players at their workout and made his plea for them to return. They refused. Only when John Bassett intervened and offered to satisfy their demands did they return.

In Hamilton, a similar eruption was averted only at the last moment. There, players who attended two practices per day (those who worked at another job were allowed to attend only one workout) were paid $50 per week if single, $60 if married. When the club was ready to leave for a four-day western exhibition swing, the Tiger-Cats deducted the cost of meals which had been included in the stipend, reasoning that meals would be provided by the club on the trip. "In effect, we would be paying them twice for meals and we're already paying twice for hotel rooms. It would amount to paying them for exhibition games and that is against league regulations," said General Manager Ralph Sazio. Single players received $15 and married players $19, down from their normal $29 and $39. They had received the regular rate for such exhibition games in the past.[64] The players were demanding their $20 or they would strike. After two meetings prior to a team practice, the players reluctantly took to the field, determined to resolve the situation at a later date. Similar problems occurred in B.C. and Calgary. It was clear that the problem had to be addressed by a united front by all.

Adding to the solidarity of the players was the All Star game in Ottawa. It represented an opportunity for them to come together to meet and support each other face to face. A strike was again mentioned. The league met in an extraordinary session and while it did, Gaudaur and the players' counsel, John Agro, convened separately to hammer out an agreement. Both Agro and Gaudaur were from Hamilton. They had known each other for years. In no time, they had resolved the crisis. Players were to receive $10 per day or $70 per week if not living in training camp facilities provided by the club, each player to provide his own meals. When living in camp, or on the road for exhibition games when the club paid for all meals, players were to receive $3 per day.[65] The settlement, while an increase for most clubs, was actually a loss for the Argonaut players. As a result of their strike in 1969, the Argos had been receiving $60 per week while attending their training camp at Aurora. That was decreasing to $21. Despite the decrease, "they were willing to go along with the settlement because they thought it would benefit players on other teams. Some clubs did not pay for training camp labours in other years."[66]

The association continued to work on behalf of its players. A pension plan was put into effect, with allowances made for some retroactivity. Those who had played at least three games in the 1965 and 1966 season and had spent a total of five years in the league, could contribute $300 per season or at least indicate by August 1, 1970, that they wished to participate in the plan.[67]

In addition, it requested that someone, the league or the Saskatchewan Roughriders, make "improvements to the end zone barriers in Regina's Taylor Field."[68] Numerous players had been injured or feared injury while playing there. The most infamous incident occurred in 1967. The corners of the end zone dead-ball area were ringed with a knee-high fence of 2x4s. Hamilton's "Garney Henley had gone after a touchdown pass in the third quarter at Regina. He had launched himself flat out in mid air and flown head first into a post of that kitty corner end zone fence, broken the post off, dropped like a rock, spread-eagled on the ground and lay so horribly still. Not a sign or a heave of agonized breath even."[69]

When improvements to the field were made, it was announced that they were being made "not as a consequence of the association's request, but as a result of continuing representations by the Saskatchewan club to bring the stadium up to the highest possible standards."[70]

The continued pressure of the Players' Association was enough to rile Lew Hayman who "viewed with alarm the fact that the association would make such a demand. 'What would happen,' he asked, 'if the players took such a liking to artificial turf that they refuse to play on natural turf?'"[71] Aside from his reactionary outburst, Hayman had chosen his example with deliberation. The B.C. Lions had announced during the February meetings that the possibilities were good that Empire Stadium would have artificial turf in time for the 1970 season.

The All Star game played in Ottawa on July 2 was a "royal" success. It was the first opportunity for Ottawa fans to see their Rough Riders perform without their "king" Russ Jackson. However, British royalty was in attendance in the person of Prince Charles, who, in addition to watching the game, rode around Lansdowne Park at half-time in a limousine. Ottawa fans got to pass judgement on the other heir apparent, Gary Wood, and saw a good contest, won by the All Stars 19–14. In the process, the Players' Association benefitted from the game by some $33,000. While the bulk of it went into the players' pension plan, the association also contributed $1,000 to the Football Hall of Fame, under construction in Hamilton, and $1,000 in trust for the children of the late Ernie Pitts, a former player with Winnipeg and B.C.[72]

The players also shored up one more item as a result of the Gaudaur and Agro meeting which took place under the threat of a strike. Effective July 6, the players on a CFL team roster for the last league or play-off game of 1969 were to receive an advance of $10 per day for each practice day up to the club's first regularly scheduled game. The money was to be deducted from a player's contract at the rate of $50 per game for the first three games, the balance at any time during the 1970 season. If a player was released prior to the advance being paid off, the clubs were willing to write it off.[73]

And so, the 1970 season began with some optimism. The league and the players were in harmony, albeit with a healthy tension. Fan interest was high; new faces were generating renewed interest in the game. In the Eastern Conference, the Hamilton Tiger-Cats finished in first place with 17 points, Toronto in second with 16, and Montreal in third with 15. In the Western Conference, Saskatchewan was far out in first-place with 28 points, and Edmonton and Calgary were tied with 18 each. In the eastern sudden death semifinal, the Alouettes prevailed 16–7 over the Argonauts, Sonny Wade passing to Tom Pullen for the winning touchdown. In the Hamilton-Montreal two-game total-point final, Hamilton took a quick lead of 14–0, only to lose the first game at Montreal's Autostade 32–22. In the return match at Hamilton, Joe Restic, the Hamilton coach, decided to use Garney Henley both ways in an effort to overcome the 10-point deficit. It didn't work. The Alouettes defeated Hamilton 11–4 to take the series by 17 points and earn a Grey Cup berth.

In the West, Calgary pulled a major upset and defeated Saskatchewan after first eliminating Edmonton 16–9. The score in the first game was Calgary 28, Saskatchewan 11. The second game, played on a Wednesday, saw Calgary behind by a 4–3 score in possession of the ball on Saskatchewan's 24–yard line. The Stampeders opted for a pass rather than attempt a field goal. It was intercepted by the Roughriders' Ed McQuarters who returned it for the touchdown and an 11–3 victory. The third game was played on a Sunday in Saskatchewan in a gale, with wintry conditions and a wind chill temperature of -40°F. Larry Robinson kicked a last-play field goal to win the Western Conference football title for the Calgary Stampeders "in arctic weather suitable only for demented ptarmigan mushing toward the pole."[74] The 15–14 win was the Stampeders' fourth game in two weeks. The Grey Cup Game was to follow in only six days. Some called the Stampeders, many of them frostbitten, "survivors of the Western Conference rather than its representatives."[75]

In the midst of the Grey Cup celebrations, *Canadian* magazine selected its All Star Grey Cup Team of the sixties. On offence, were ends, Hal Patterson, Hamilton, and Farrell Funston, Winnipeg; tackles, Clyde Brock, Saskatchewan, and Frank Rigney, Winnipeg; guards, Kaye Vaughan, Ottawa, and Ellison Kelly, Hamilton; centre, Ted Urness, Saskatchewan; halfbacks, Leo Lewis, Winnipeg, and Ron Stewart, Ottawa; full back, George Reed, Saskatchewan; flanker, Tommy Grant, Hamilton; quarterback, Russ Jackson, Ottawa. On defence were ends, Billy Joe Booth, Ottawa, and Herb Gray, Winnipeg; tackles Ed McQuarters, Saskatchewan, and John Barrow, Hamilton; linebackers, Wayne Harris, Calgary, Ken Lehman, Ottawa, and Tom Brown, B.C.; deep backs, Garney Henley, Hamilton, Bill Munsey, B.C., Joe Poirier, Ottawa, Gene Gaines, Ottawa, and Don Sutherin, Hamilton.[76]

At the Grey Cup meetings, three new members of the Hall of Fame were announced in the Builder's Category: Ken Montgomery of Edmonton and players Johnny Bright of Calgary and Edmonton and Norm Perry of the 1931 Grey Cup Montreal Winged Wheelers. As well, other awards for the season went to Ron Lancaster as the Outstanding Player in the CFL, Wayne

Harris as the Outstanding Lineman, and Jim Young as the Outstanding Canadian Player.

The year was almost at an end when the B.C. Lions announced that they had hired Eagle Keys away from the Saskatchewan Roughriders. He was given a five-year contract, effective January 1, 1970, worth a reported $35,000 per year.[77] Jackie Parker was elevated to the post of executive general manager, leaving "Lions' Denny Veitch out in the cold. Veitch had been told of the appointments and had agreed to take a paid leave of absence until January 1."[78]

At the 1970 Grey Cup Game, once again Prime Minister Trudeau performed the ceremonial kick-off at Exhibition Stadium. However, this time another politician performed kicking duties during the game. George Springate, a member of Quebec's National Assembly, was also Montreal's field goal and extra point kicker. On this day, 32,669 spectators saw the Alouettes win their fourth consecutive post-season game after their third-place finish, defeating Calgary, 23–10. Springate kicked two converts and a field goal. Ted Alflen, on a pass from Moses Denson, Tom Pullen, on a reverse, and Gary Lefebvre, with a pass from Sonny Wade, were the Montreal scorers. Hugh McKinnis, with a touchdown, and Larry Robinson, with a field goal and convert, provided all of Calgary's points.

It was a great climax to Montreal's renewal. "Considered a relief project"[79] by the CFL a year ago, the Alouettes not only won the Grey Cup, but they had drawn a total of 169,127 fans for their seven home games for an average of 24,161. That compared with a total of 84,156 and an average of 12,022 in 1969.[80] Even at that, officials were to report that an attendance of 25,000 was needed to break even at their average ticket price of $3.70 per seat.[81]

1971 to 1972

Chapter Two

IN 1971, THE CFL WAS THRIVING. Despite a slump in the Canadian economy, overall attendance of the league games had increased by 149,888 over 1970. Percentage capacity was also on the increase. In 1968, clubs were playing to 77% capacity; in 1969, to 80.4%; and in 1970, it had jumped to 88.8%. Toronto and Vancouver were still the main contributors to the gate equalization program, $60,000 being Toronto's share in 1970 compared to $59,400 in 1969 and $41,304 in 1968. British Columbia's share had grown to $50,897 in 1970, up from $42,970 in 1969 and $31,120 in 1968. Meanwhile, Hamilton had moved from being a net contributor of $589 in 1968 to receiving $2,882 in 1969 and $14,919 the following year.[1]

Much of the increase in attendance was due to Montreal. In spite of the higher numbers attending and the increased revenue, it declared itself to be still operating under a high expense load. Sam Berger had stated that his total operating costs were in the neighbourhood of $400,000 even though he submitted a figure of $165,000 for the seven home games.[2] The league declared that only two items were valid for deductions: direct taxes related to ticket sales and park rental for league games. The other eight clubs, realizing the importance of Montreal and the significant turnaround orchestrated by Berger's team, allowed Montreal to use the highest amount payable by any club for stadium rental after direct taxes for the 1970 season.[3]

Players' salaries continued to grow. From the 32 contracts for each team filed with the commissioner's office at the end of the year, the average import player earned $16,072 in 1970, up from $14,765 in 1969 and $13,942 in 1968. The average non-import salary was $10,920 in 1970, $9,748 in 1969, and $9,337 in 1968.[4]

On the surface, it appeared that football in Hamilton was in decline, since it was becoming a net receiver from, rather than contributor to, the equalization fund. However, in spite of that perception, it seemed to be as well entrenched as ever. The playing field's name had been changed from Civic Stadium to Ivor Wynne after the former McMaster University football coach and Physical Education head. (Some visiting teams would refer to it as Never Win Stadium because of the success enjoyed by the Tiger-Cats.) A new North Stand had been erected, increasing seating capacity to more than 36,000. It was only the second field in the league to have synthetic turf installed.[5] In addition, the team would have a new coach for the 1971 season. Al Dorow, a former quarterback with the B.C. Lions in 1958 and the Argonauts in 1959, replaced Joe Restic who had resigned early in 1971 to accept a head coaching position with Harvard University.

Revenue has always been important to the CFL, particularly from its attendance. The league published 1968 figures for its members to show where they were relative to each other and league hopes.

1968 League Attendance and Gate Revenue[6]

	Attendance	% of stadium capacity	% of league attendance	Total gate revenue
Montreal	111,119	57	8.0	$523,455
Ottawa	162,149	84	11.7	$596,119
Toronto	197,519	85	14.3	$787,073
Hamilton	165,282	82	11.9	$629,620
Winnipeg	103,206	57	7.5	$403,801
Saskatchewan	141,022	82	10.2	$524,652
Calgary	158,156	87	11.4	$612,642
Edmonton	141,365	84	10.2	$561,423
British Columbia	205,809	78	14.8	$700,254
Totals:	1,385,627	78	14.8	$5,339,038

Television was still a long way from providing the type of revenue that could free the league from wild swings in attendance. There was no interest from American networks to broadcast CFL games. Furthermore, cable TV and community antennae were said to be pirating CFL signals. The league was spending $5,000 for legal fees to appeal to the Canadian Radio-television and Telecommunications Commission (CRTC) to remove that source of irritation. The CFL signed a one-year deal with CTV for the 1969 TV rights to the Grey Cup Game realizing $199,000, slightly more than the $193,000 from the previous year. Conference rights were negotiated by each division, the East receiving $475,000, the West $310,000.[7] The league would have liked to have realized more revenue from television but the major stumbling block was "the CFL's demand for increased blackout areas to thwart Cable TV companies ... Ottawa [took] a strong stand on blackouts, maintaining they will reject television revenue completely rather than see their home games beamed into Montreal and Kingston from where Cable TV picks them up and shoots the action back into Ottawa. Western teams feel almost as strongly."[8]

Financial support continued for the Canadian Amateur Football Association (CAFA), not because of any special feelings for developmental sport but because of the agreement made when the Canadian Rugby Union (CRU) turned over trusteeship of the Grey Cup to the CFL in 1966 and changed its name to the CAFA. The CFL continued to exact conditions, however. They wanted the CAFA to concentrate on junior football and ignore senior, promising not to support it financially. On those conditions, its grant to the CAFA for 1971 was $37,500[9] in spite of representation made by a one-day seminar in Ottawa to revitalize senior football. The seminar approved two resolutions: to develop a submission to the CAFA to present to the CFL and federal and provincial governments; to use the CAFA services to meet senior football needs including a national championship, regional play-offs, and funds for the development of clinics and junior and senior football teams.[10] The president of the Ontario Rugby Football Union (ORFU), at one time a competitor for the Grey Cup, sought to find out "why the CFL isn't interested in senior football—do they think we're beer hall boys or what?"[11]

It was obvious that the CFL had decided to throw in its lot with the universities. Firstly, it cost them nothing, and secondly, the more intensive training was developing more and better players each passing year. The league approved an Edmonton motion that, effective with the 1973 draft, clubs would be allowed exclusive signing privileges for two of their territorial non-imports attending American schools; all others would become part of the universal draft.[12] It was another attempt to promote a league rather than a club perspective.

In an effort to make the league more competitive within itself, Ken Preston of Saskatchewan was asked to investigate the Canadian draft system. At one time, only the four eastern teams participated in the common draft. By 1956, all nine teams were involved. However, even in 1969 Canadians who attended American schools were not included; they were part of each team's "territorial exemptions." According to Preston's report, the number of these Canadians attending American schools were: Ottawa 26, Toronto 25, British Columbia 22, Hamilton 20, Saskatchewan 14, Calgary 12, Edmonton 11, Winnipeg 9, and Montreal 8. Canadians represented 56% of the league's players. Seventy-two (or 42%) of these players had been trained in American schools, 44 were from Canadian universities, 41 from minor football and 11 were naturalized.

Preston noted the trends. Ten years ago the percentage of Canadians entering the league after having attended U.S. colleges had been 10%. In 1969, it was 42%. He predicted that by 1974, it would be 60%, surmising further that naturalized Canadians would be practically eliminated, that the number of players entering the league from minor football was decreasing every year as the calibre of the league rose with the improving players from the university systems. By 1974, he predicted, in addition to the 60% from the American colleges, 35% would be generated by the Canadian universities and only 5% from minor football.

In view of all of this, Preston's report proposed that there be a common draft for all Canadian players, except for three players who could be protected within each club's territory in 1970, two in 1971, and one thereafter. The report, along with Simon Fraser's request not to be involved in the draft, was received for consideration, a decision to be made later.

Simon Fraser made the request because it played among American schools. And since they were not included in the league's draft, the Canadian university felt that its players should continue to be exempt and have the same bargaining power as its competitors.

The 1971 Grey Cup Game was held on Sunday, November 28, in Vancouver's Empire Stadium. It featured the Argonauts and the Stampeders. The defending champion Alouettes were unable to rise above a fourth-place finish, their fate seemingly predicted when only 9,000 spectators turned out to watch them play the All Stars in the Autostade, the Alouettes losing 30–13. In the West, the Saskatchewan Roughriders beat the third-place Winnipeg Blue Bombers 34–23 to win the right to play Calgary in the best-of-three finals. The Stampeders won in two games, 30–21 and 23–21. Unlike the previous year, they would have four extra days to prepare for the national championship.

In the East, Hamilton defeated Ottawa 23–4, gaining the right to play the Argos in the two-game, total-point series. The Toronto team—constantly reminded by the media of 1961 when the Argonauts team, with an 18-point lead after the first game, lost the second by a 48–2 score—won the round by defeating Hamilton 23–8 in the first game and tying the second 17–17. It was to be Toronto's first appearance in the Grey Cup Game since 1952. To some, it seemed the culmination of what had been an exciting season. New quarterbacks Joe Theismann and Greg Barton had responded well to Leo Cahill's strategy of alternating them on each series of plays. Leon

McQuay had been an exciting addition complementing Bill Symons. Dave Raimey was raising eyebrows, having made the transition to corner back. Danny Nykoluk had "unretired" for one last shot at the Cup and Leo Cahill had been named Coach Of The Year.

Calgary had been defeated by the Argos during the season, but Jerry Keeling, the Stampeders' quarterback, did not play because of an injury. Keeling's experience was typical of the Stampeders who were playing in their third Grey Cup Game in four years. Their fans were getting restless for a win. Players such as Keeling, Gerry Shaw, Herm Harrison, Wayne Harris, and John Helton had raised their spirits. They were convinced that this was their year: "Football isn't just a game out here in the foothills. It's a disease and there are a lot of people with barked shins and bumps on their heads from falling off the Stampeder bandwagon, or should that be chuckwagon."[13]

True to form, it looked as if the Calgary fans would again be denied. Having taken a 14–11 lead with less than three minutes remaining, Jerry Keeling, deep in his end, threw a pass which was intercepted by Dick Thornton. He returned it to the Calgary 11-yard line, tackled there by former defensive back Keeling. The sky was overcast; a grey drizzle fell on the already slick artificial turf. The gloom seemed to mirror the Calgary fans' mood. Toronto fans had visions of 1952. Theismann sent McQuay on a pitch wide to the right for a four-yard gain. It was the second down. Theismann called a sweep to McQuay to the left, partly for field position in case the play did not gain the first down. A field goal would tie the game but that was the last resort; they were going for the first down and touchdown. As McQuay glided to his left, he spotted middle linebacker Wayne Harris taking the angle to cut him off. In an instant McQuay instinctively decided to cut up-field. In so doing, he slipped, the ball coming loose when he contacted the ground. It was recovered by Calgary defensive back Frank Andruski. Calgary had hung on to win the 1971 Grey Cup. Leo Cahill was to say later, "When Leon McQuay slipped, I fell,"[14] a reference to his being fired by John Bassett the following year."

Cahill had probably been on shaky ground since he had expressed that he had been undercut by John Bassett during the players' strike of 1969 and his (Cahill's) later decision to trade quarterback Wally Gabler, a personal favourite of Bassett, and retain Tom Wilkinson.[15] Cahill had found out from newspapers that the Argos were looking for a general manager. When he questioned President and Chief Executive Officer (CEO) Lew Hayman about it, Hayman said that the first indication that he had of it also came from the newspaper reporters. It was obvious that the operation of the club was in transition. The search for the general manager was to be conducted by the three sons of the senior directors of the club: Johnny F. Bassett, Len

Lumbers, Jr., and Michael Burns, son of Charlie Burns. When John Barrow, prominent Hamilton Tiger-Cats defensive tackle, was mentioned as a possible candidate, Cahill was unbelieving and scoffed at the idea: "To imagine Argos looking toward a Hamilton football player when they wanted a general manager, you have to imagine that Pierre Trudeau would try to get Robert Stanfield into his cabinet or that President Nixon would ask Ted Kennedy to clean up the White House."[16] Cahill was to write later that "Barrow told a TV broadcaster, who told me, that the minute he signed with the Argos, I was as good as gone."[17]

The victory capped a banner year for Calgary. It ended with a net profit of $40,485 compared with $15,521 in 1970. The profit from operations "boosted retained earnings to $385,430." That did not include the $90,422 it received "from investments and its annual $100 a plate dinner. The dinner and investment revenues were credited directly to a "reserve fund for capital expenditures" which "increased to $254,366." The club had a "record gross revenue of $1,066,776" from having sold "98% of the available McMahon Stadium seats for a record attendance of 243,234 … [and] the club was now looking for additional seating."[18]

The 1971 Grey Cup Game occurred at the end of a week of CFL meetings. Among other items, Don Jonas, the former Argo quarterback who had been traded to Winnipeg prior to the 1971 season, was awarded the Schenley Award as the Most Outstanding Player in the CFL; Wayne Harris from Calgary was selected the Most Outstanding Lineman; and Terry Evanshen of the Alouettes was chosen as the Most Outstanding Canadian. In addition, former players Hal Patterson and Jackie Parker were inducted into the Hall of Fame, as was Hamilton Team Manager Len Back as a Builder.

Hamilton was to be prominent in the news. It would host the 1972 Grey Cup Game and open the Football Hall of Fame during that year. But perhaps the most surprising item about Hamilton occurred early in January in Hollywood, Florida. The CFL had gathered for its annual Rules Committee meetings held in conjunction with the American coaches' convention. The CFL was anxious to maintain cordial relations with American universities and their coaches, hoping to keep open the flow of players to the Great White North. The league sponsored an annual dinner at the National Collegiate Athletic Association (NCAA) coaches' convention. There, the latest Grey Cup film was shown and a traditional Canadian wild-game dinner was served. For 1969, however, the fowl from Saskatchewan was not available; only the salmon from B.C. was. It caused the league to advertise it as a Canadian buffet.[19] Beef Stroganoff replaced the previous year's moose stew.

Much of the change was due to cost control. In 1966 in Washington the cost was $13,517.31; in 1967 in Houston, $11,902.98; in 1968 in New York, $10,623.88; and in Los Angeles, $7,000.[20] Gaudaur stated that the $7,000, less than $2,100 per club, was "the most economical and effective U.S. promotion plan that the league can indulge in."[21]

The discussions and the rule changes serve to indicate the wide range of agenda items. Two were a direct result of a game played between Hamilton and Toronto in 1971. In that game, Hamilton's Bobby Taylor wandered off toward the sidelines, helmet off. Hamilton had the ball and it appeared as if Taylor was leaving the field. Cahill noticed that Taylor, a former Argonaut who was not on the best of terms with his one-time coach, was still on the field. Recognizing the ploy as a "sleeper" play, Cahill sent Jim Corrigal out onto the field as a 13th player. Taylor caught the pass and took it down to the five-yard line. It was called back because the Toronto Argonauts had too many men on the field. As a result, the Rules Committee declared that for the 1972 season, a sleeper by team A should not be affected by substitution by team B, and that a player was required to wear his helmet on the field of play. There was still some dissatisfaction with the punt return rule and, even though the CIAU rule was brought forward as a model, the status quo was retained.

Other motions suffered the same fate. Not seconded were motions for a two-point conversion by pass or run; bump and run tactics by the defensive backs; a sixth official; and a penalty against the home team after three successive attempts to put the ball into play failing because of excessive crowd noise. There were some attempts to modernize some rules, to bring them up to date with current practice. At one time "coaching from the sidelines" incurred a penalty. The rule book still had a regulation calling for a penalty if the coach was sending in plays from the sidelines. On the suggestion of official Paul Dojack, realizing that coaches wanted more control over a team's actions, the practice of sending in messages from the sidelines was legitimized.[22]

There were other attempts at clarification. A suggestion to introduce a rule which would allow ineligible pass receivers to block after a pass was caught downfield was similarly not entertained because of the want of a seconder, nor was a suggestion that when team B committed a foul after team A gained a first down, the penalty be applied from the point where the ball was declared dead. The rule regarding ball contact with the goal post was also clarified; it was decided that any ball which contacted the goal posts was "dead," the only exception was on a field goal attempt if the ball proceeded through the uprights after the contact. In that case, it would still be worth three points.

During the 1971 season when the league was alerted to the fact that some players were spraying their uniforms with a substance that caused them to slip out of an opponent's grasp, a directive was issued against the practice. The 1972 Rules Committee agreed that "such a ruling could stand as a precedent and need not be incorporated into the rule book."[23] Ineligible receivers were entitled to wear any number from 40 to 69. Previously, centres were numbered in the forties, guards in the fifties, and tackles in the sixties. The committee also declared that diagonal line markings in the end zones were no longer necessary. The official's horn was also under review. Each official had a whistle, a horn, and a flag. The horn would continue to be used whenever a flag was thrown during 1972; its use would be reviewed after the 1972 season.

All of these rules generated discussion since they had been part of the league and game for years. But when Hamilton moved that four downs be instituted to make ten yards and, in addition, that the one-yard restraining area between the opposing lines of scrimmage be eliminated,[24] there was what can only be described as stunned silence. Nobody seconded the motions; there was no discussion.

At the General Managers' meeting, still in Hollywood, Florida, the subject of the designated quarterback came up. It was brought up by Winnipeg General Manager Earl Lunsford. Perhaps not coincidently, Winnipeg had drafted University of Manitoba quarterback Bob Kraemer as its first choice in the 1971 draft. It promptly converted him to a defensive back. The discussion at this meeting revolved around why the designated quarterback could not participate in the kick-off. Lunsford moved, seconded by Sazio of Hamilton, that "the duties of the quarterback may include punting, place-kicking, kicking off or holding the ball on converts or field goal attempts."[25] The motion was carried unanimously.

The league was somewhat preoccupied with expenses or at least wanted to be certain that money was being spent in the most beneficial way. It encouraged all teams to contact their Air Canada office to ensure that their representative accompany them on each away game and that only jet aircraft with the best rates be used. In addition, with the increasing number of parks being converted to artificial turf—Toronto's CNE Stadium was set for 1972, Ottawa and Winnipeg next—the need for shoe banks was rescinded. When the B.C. Lions announced that the Empire Stadium would have artificial turf for the 1970 season, it was a league first. It posed questions for the member clubs, the main one being, "who should be responsible for supplying the special footwear for the visiting teams and officials?" The B.C. Club thought it had the answer. The artificial surface was to be the 3M product, Tartan Turf, rather than Astro Turf, thus allowing for "normal footwear," although it was found that multi-cleated soccer-style shoes were even better since they lowered the incidence of knee injuries.[26] The turf was also inflammable. Smoking had to be prohibited, particularly in the bench area where it was still common among some of the coaches in the league. Over General Manager Denny Veitch's objections, the Lions were instructed to open a shoe bank. Veitch had countered that there was no requirement for prairie clubs to provide special footwear for frozen fields in November. When that logic was not accepted, he asked "whether such an expense would be a legitimate deduction under the gate equalization formula."[27] That decision was deferred until May when the Executive Committee decided that the B.C. Lions' shoe bank would have to provide "100 pairs of shoes, equivalent in make and value to that used by the B.C. club; not later than June 12, 1970, each club to advise the B.C. club of the 32 shoe sizes it requires; the shoe bank to be in effect prior to the first exhibition game, each club to be given a complete inventory list; member clubs will be responsible for their own requirements not available from the bank; the shoe inventory will be in a condition acceptable to the other clubs. The financial arrangements were handled by assessing each visiting club $100 for the use of shoes for 1970 and 1971. At the conclusion of the '71 season, the residual value of the inventory shall remain the property of the B.C. club."[28]

There had always been a rumour that "taxi squads," the keeping of players not on the playing roster, were being maintained by some teams, especially the wealthier ones who could afford the extra expense. It put pressure on the financially weaker teams who, when suffering an injury to a player, had to scurry to track down a replacement; the wealthier ones who could afford to carry the expanded roster scarcely missed a beat. Their replacement had practised with them, knew the system, and was available at a moment's notice. The Argos' John Barrow and Hamilton's Ralph Sazio were selected to review the problem among the eastern teams; a similar committee struck for the west and the commissioner would check the "applicable legislation in the NFL"[29] and advise.

They had much to investigate. Perhaps because of the nature of the game or more likely the pressures of fielding a competitive team, some teams were constantly stretching the rules. In theory, taxi squads were not legal. Similarly, if a player was placed on the injury reserve list, he had to remain there for 30 days or miss four games, whichever came first.[30] Leo Cahill's teams were among the most innovative in finding loopholes. He was able to "loan" Mike Eben to Edmonton for the 1970 season, where he made the Western All Star Team, and take him back for the 1971 session. Eben had been there "for what were termed 'future considerations.' The future considerations in this case were that he would get the hell back to Toronto in one year."[31] It was all down on paper in a deal worked out with Norm Kimball. The same year that Eben returned to Toronto, Cahill wanted to keep running back Ed Williams around in case of an emergency, but without putting him on the roster. He would have to be waived through the league first. Knowing of Winnipeg's interest in him, Cahill offered to send Paul Markle, a good developing tight end, to the Blue Bombers in return for their promise not to claim him. He negotiated a similar deal with the B.C. Lions. Cahill wrote later:

> They knew what I was trying to do: put him on waivers, have everyone pass on him, then make a deal to pay him not to play for anybody else that year. I'd get him to sign a piece of paper to that effect, then sign him to a contract for the following year. In court it might be binding but we wouldn't take it to court because it was actually illegal as far as the Canadian Football League was concerned …We did that with several guys … it wasn't a cut rate deal; we agreed to pay him his whole contract just as if he was playing.[32]

Rules were stretched in other areas as well. Rather than putting players on an injury reserve list and therefore playing with fewer imports for one month or four games, Cahill, like other coaches, used the suspension list. Some players, such as Ed Harrington, were said to be refusing medical treatment or not wanting to fly.[33] Montreal placed Moses Denson on its suspension list for refusal to accept treatment; Montreal also suspended Bill Massey who, it was said, failed to report an injury from two years previous; Ottawa suspended Dennis Duncan similarly. It was only when the Commissioner's office asked the players to sign affidavits to verify their reported intransigencies that the loophole was plugged.

Montreal successfully exploited the non-import rule as well by declaring world class American sprinter John Carlos, of the 1968 clenched-fist Olympic salute fame, a non-import. Since he had never participated as a player in a football game outside Canada prior to his 17th birthday, he satisfied the letter of the law. So said Montreal, and played him as a non-import. Not all were amused: "It is too much to hope, one supposes, that Commissioner Jake Gaudaur will insist that the CFL owners tighten their ludicrous rules. That would take all the fun out of hanky-panky."[34]

Because of Montreal's use of John Carlos as a non-import, there was some agitation to change the definition of the classification. Gaudaur solicited the opinion and advice of Dan Hill, chairman of the Ontario Human Rights Commission, and John Sopinka, the legal counsel of that body. Three Ontario clubs were affected by its jurisdiction. The commission had received a complaint that the CFL was circumventing the Ontario Human Rights code "which provides that an employer cannot withhold employment because of the nationality of the employee."[35] Hill and Sopinka opined that it would be "unwise to apply for any changes in definition of training at the time."[36]

Edmonton proposed that the number of imports be increased to 15 on the 32-man roster. The designated import status would be applied to the 15th while one fewer non-import would be on the roster. After much discussion, the motion was carried 6–3. Ottawa, Winnipeg, and Saskatchewan voted against the motion. Ottawa said that it was afraid that costs to the club would be increased; Saskatchewan had found the use of local talent an important selling feature of its club, and Ken Preston was not looking forward to informing Roughrider supporters that one less non-import would be carried. However, Rogers Lehew, of Calgary, offered the opinion that no more scouting expenses would be incurred—one more of those recruited would be kept. Furthermore, he said, at one time a club could carry 16 imports; he didn't anticipate any adverse reaction. Gaudaur offered the insight "that the original limitations on imports was based on economics rather than nationalistic reasons. Members should be guided by what is collectively best for the league at this time."[37]

What might have been best for the "league at this time," at least as far as the owners were concerned, was arguably making sure that the players, particularly the non-imports, got the message that they were pushing too hard too fast. It was reported: "there seems to be general agreement that the CFL is in a prosperous state until teams sit down with the CFL Players' Association."[38] Indeed, the new import addition and the subsequent drop in the number of non-imports was "interpreted by some as a rebuke to Canadian players who have been demanding more money than some general managers think they're worth."[39]

The league also decided to accede to a request by the Players' Association to decrease the size of the ball. The maximum girth allowed for the ball had been 21 1/2 inches; the minimum 21 1/4. League officials stated that these were the same as the NFL measurements except that the American league had been "sticking to the minimum requirements whereas in Canada we have been operating on the maximum."[40] The association, in advocating the change, suggested that "the guys can handle a smaller ball better in rough weather. We feel that it would cut down on fumbles and fumbles spoil the game."[41] It made sense to the clubs for another reason. They were recruiting Americans, specifically quarterbacks, and paying them high salaries because of their demonstrated ability to pass a football. Why handicap them by asking them to learn to throw an unfamiliar football in the CFL?

The Players' Association continued to press for further concessions. While many requests were turned down, some were accepted; the league was still treading gingerly in this new relationship with the players. The 1971 Grey Cup bonuses were increased by $500— up to $2,000 for the winning team, and $1,500 to the losing team. The association had also asked the league for approval in changing the date of the All Star game from Wednesday, June 30, to Tuesday, June 29. The game was to be played in Montreal where in the past there had been political demonstrations on the eve of Dominion Day, July 1. George Springate, the coordinator for the game, advised the playing of the game one day earlier.[42]

Throughout all of these negotiations with the players, the CFL was not pleased. There was always the threat of a strike or the need to come up with more money, which it said it did not have. The CFL was especially determined not to be put into a position where it had to agree to all of the players' demands on the eve of the All Star game as it had the previous year.[43] The original league recognition of the association was granted in 1966 on the "condition of covenants by the Association neither to strike or conduct negotiations during the season which included the pre-season training period."[44] It was further noted and reported to the players that the league had contributed $275,000 to their pension plan over a four-year period.[45] Pensions were on the owners' minds. The league later approved pension plans for Commissioner Jake Gaudaur and Secretary Greg Fulton.[46] New Toronto General Manager John Barrow, himself only shortly removed from the playing ranks, expressed his view that "ten per cent of the Association are militant, another ten per cent do not understand while the other eighty per cent are only interested in clause 3 (salary)"[47] and would go along with any proposal which might increase their pay. He expressed the opinion that the players as a whole were unaware of the league's problems and what the association executive was doing. The league was not about to agree to a closed shop, that is, that the players had to be members of the association. However, it was decided that clubs would "cooperate by withholding dues from the player upon proper authorization for payment to the Players' Association."[48] It also cooperated by agreeing to purchase a table for the All Star dinner. It represented 10 tickets at $15 each.[49]

The league also attempted to be prepared in the event of an emergency—a strike. A committee of Rogers Lehew, Lew Hayman, Ralph Sazio, Ken Preston, and Jake Gaudaur, was struck to determine what constituted a strike and what was to be done in the event of one. A strike was deemed to occur "if eight or more veteran players, that is [a player] who was on the active roster or injured reserve list of a team at the end of the year, withhold their services other than by *bona fide* retirement."[50] If one or two clubs were on strike, the roster of each club will be reduced to 30 players, of which not more than 14 would be imports eligible to play without restriction. For every two non-imports on strike, a club could add an extra import. If three or more clubs were on strike, rosters would be reduced to 30, of whom not more than 20 could be imports."[51] While Ralph Sazio suggested that the various managers "have a frank discussion with the players' reps to explain the league's position on these matters," the committee was asked to remain intact "to continue its deliberation on two other matters: a strike in the pre-season and a technique for stocking a new franchise, should the league expand."[52]

Players' salaries continued to grow. From the 32 contracts for each team filed with the commissioner's office at the end of the year, the average import player earned $16,072 in 1970, up from $14,765 in 1969 and $13,942 in 1968. The average non-import salary was $10,920 in 1970, $9,748 in 1969 and $9,337 in 1968.[53]

The Montreal Alouettes were having trouble trying to sign their tight end, non-import Peter Dalla Riva. He had played out his option and was technically a free agent as of June 1. Montreal felt that their offer to keep Dalla Riva as an Alouette was a good one; Dalla Riva, on the other hand, considered it to be much below his value to the team. In the back of their minds, the general managers were somewhat reluctant to pay high salaries to their non-imports since they could sign an import for less. While Dalla Riva could technically sign with another team in the CFL, Red O'Quinn, general manager of the Alouettes, stated after leaving a meeting of the CFL Executive Committee: "Everyone thinks our offer is more than fair. If he does become a free agent and signs with another club for more money, it will mean someone has gone back on their word at this meeting." [54] So-called "gentlemen's agreements" were a fact of life in the CFL, although their existence would always be denied by the league.

Gaudaur's impartiality was sought after in the area of "free agency." A player had always had the right to "play out his option." That is, every contract signed had a specific term plus one year following, the so-called option year. By choosing not to re-sign, a player indicated that he wanted to become a free agent. First, however, he had to play that year without signing a new contract; he could not sit out. He was reimbursed by not less than 90% of the worth of the previously signed contract. When the option year was finished, the player was technically free to negotiate with any team in the league. In practice, however, the player was ignored by other teams since there was a fear that the signing of these "free agents" would encourage athletes to play out their options and flock to teams with the most money at their disposal. Because, art, artists, and athletes followed the money, the feeling was that the Grey Cup could be bought. Thus the player was more likely to head south and try his luck with one of the American teams. However, the notion was developing that these players, many of whom were of high calibre, should be kept in the league under an arrangement which was similar to what was being done in the NFL. Like his American counterpart, Gaudaur was given the role of final "arbiter in deciding compensation to be paid to a team for a player who plays out his option year and moves to another Canadian team as a free agent."[55] In other words, there was no free agency. If a player was "free" from contractual obligations with club A and wanted to join club B, the latter had to arrange compensation with A because it was losing the player. If the two clubs could not agree, it was up to the commissioner to impose the compensation. Peter Dalla Riva was reported to have signed a three-year pact with the Alouettes within days of Red O'Quinn's comments.[56]

O'Quinn went on to tell reporters that an extra import "gave CFL teams two alternatives. They now can replace what was the 18th Canadian with a young import for 'say $5,000 more in salary and naturally get a better ball player' or get a 'good American and pay him less than a Canadian who has outpriced himself.'"[57] Teams would go to great lengths to sign an American rather than recognize a top calibre Canadian. At the best of times, the signing of an import to play in Canada was precarious. Quite naturally, he preferred to play in his own country before his own fans, who followed his career in college, and if possible in the NFL, the recognized epitome of football in the United States. If the NFL were not an option, new leagues such as the American Football League (AFL), the United States Football League (USFL), or the World Football League (WFL) were struggling for recognition. In the United States, that could mean television recognition and money for a player. Consequently, when a coach came to the U.S. seeking a player, there was a sense of wariness that the import would use the Canadian team's offer as a bargaining lever with the American club with which he was negotiating. Toronto's recruitment of Joe Theismann offers a case study in the "gymnastics" a club might go through in signing a top-line import.[58]

Leo Cahill and his coaching staff had first become aware of Theismann's talents during visits to the spring training camps of the Big Ten schools during 1970. Jim Rountree, Cahill's assistant, telephoned Cahill to tell him of the Notre Dame quarterback, who had the "quickest feet" he had ever seen. The Argos placed Theismann on their negotiation list, consisting of 20 names of imports with whom only they, among CFL teams, could negotiate. Phone calls during the year and a visit by Cahill into the dressing room after a Notre Dame game followed. Theismann was making quite a name for himself. He led Notre Dame to an upset victory over Texas in the Cotton Bowl. His university public relations department continually issued releases that Theismann rhymed with Heisman, the trophy awarded to the most outstanding American collegian each football season. More visits by Cahill followed in the new year. He took the young quarterback and his wife to dinner, creating a friendly and sociable atmosphere. Meanwhile, the Miami Dolphins of the NFL had drafted him in spite of having their own young and dynamic quarterback, Bob Griese. During a visit to Toronto in early spring, Cahill arranged for Theismann to be hosted by a sports buff who also owned a car agency. He was taken to a dinner where he met the club directors. John Bassett made a concrete offer to Theismann who appeared to be somewhat awed by the attention he was beginning to attract. Still, he owed it to himself and his wife, he said, to listen to Miami and their coach Don Shula on March 17—one wonders whether the date March 17 was chosen purposely in keeping with Miami's intent to sign the quarterback of the "fighting Irish." On the next day, March 18, a press conference was called by the Dolphins to announce the signing of Theismann. His wife, Sherri, feeling that Toronto should learn of the news from them, phoned Cahill to let him know. Cahill thanked her, wished them both luck, and told her that he was sure that Joe would be a success. In other words, he was keeping all of his options open in the event that things did not work out for them, so much so that Theismann later told Cahill that his wife said she "hated to say goodbye to Coach Cahill because he's been so nice about the whole thing." On March 19, newspapers carried the story of Theismann's signing with Miami. Cahill concentrated on signing his other quarterback prospect, Greg Barton.

As it turned out, Cahill received a phone call from the automobile dealer who had hosted Theismann's visit to Toronto. He had spoken to a friend in South Bend, Indiana, and, by coincidence, Joe Theismann was there. The two spoke. Congratulations were offered on Theismann's signing. He seemed doubtful about whether he was doing the right thing. Once Leo Cahill heard of this perception, he phoned the young quarterback. Yes, he had signed but he had not mailed in the contract. The door was open a crack. Theismann wanted to see Toronto's contract so that he could compare them. Cahill, who had seen other players use Argos' contracts to bargain for more money or benefits with an American team, would not send it. But, sensing an opportunity, he invited Theismann to Toronto to read over the contract together with him.

Cahill, and Argonaut lawyer Herb Solway, met the couple the following Sunday at the airport. They drove through the most scenic and appealing parts of Toronto to the Solway residence. It was a warm and cosy meeting.

They were later joined by John Bassett who dropped in to say hello. While Sherri Theismann and Elaine Solway socialized, Leo and Joe went into the study to discuss the contract. Cahill's major thrust was: "if it was only you and I were in your position, I'd go to Miami and give it my best shot. But if you want to think about future security, the kind of outside career you can build here and the overall picture of your family, Toronto's offer is much better."

The other item that appealed to Theismann was the assurance that he would definitely play if he signed, whereas in Miami he might languish behind a good Bob Griese. Further, after two years were up, he could decide whether to stay in Canada or take a shot at the NFL where his status would be enhanced as a result of the experience gained in Canada. Cahill left the room; Sherri went in. After 30 minutes, they emerged. Sherri stated: "we can always go to Miami for a visit." Joe still wasn't completely sure. His plane was leaving shortly for South Bend. Could he take the contract with him? Leo said "no." If Theismann was going to sign with Miami, Cahill said that he'd wish him luck; if he wanted to sign with Toronto, now was the time. Theismann signed with the Argos. No terms were announced but it was published, and not denied, that the deal amounted to $200,000 over three years.

There was still a mystique associated with import players. An inexperienced import might be more likely to be put into a key situation than an experienced non-import. For example, during a game in 1972 between Hamilton and Saskatchewan, a preview of the Grey Cup Game, Lewis Porter, an import better known for his offensive skills, was placed at defensive back, the first time he had played that position since high school, seven years previously.[59] Saskatchewan quarterback Ron Lancaster noticed the inexperience of Porter and threw a play action pass in his direction, beating the inexperienced defensive back by 15 yards for a touchdown. As it turned out, Porter redeemed himself by running back the ensuing kick-off 80 yards to the Saskatchewan 28-yard line. Hamilton kicked a field goal to win the game by three points, 20–17.

The situation was such that a sociology professor at the University of Victoria, Donald Ball, presented a paper at a symposium on Sport, Man and Contemporary Society at Queen's College of New York City University. He said that "Canadians suffer from discrimination or at least benign neglect in the Canadian Football League and that Canadian players tend to be excluded from the more rewarding and desirable positions in the CFL and receive lower salaries than imports." The professor's paper and his use of the term "white niggers" to describe Canadians set off a predictable reaction within the league. "Anybody who uses a term like 'white nigger' shows what kind of mentality he's got," said Edmonton's Norm Kimball. Earl Lunsford was as adamant: "guys who talk in ignorance should keep their mouths shut. Some Canadian players in starting positions receive the highest salaries in the league." Lunsford said that Russ Jackson, retired quarterback of the Ottawa Rough Riders, was the highest paid ballplayer in the country and a native Canadian. Jackie Parker of the B.C. Lions stated that he thought that Ball "was using facts of ten years ago." The general managers seemed to agree with Kimball's assertion that it was "typical of the type of things professors sitting in ivory towers at a university say about something of which they know nothing." Other university products were, however, in demand. The CFL held its annual draft of college players. Larry Smith, a running back from Bishop's University, was the first draft choice of the league and the Montreal Alouettes.[60]

The CFL was in somewhat of a quandry. On the one hand it wanted to keep its options open in attracting good American talent. On the other, it had to be aware of public opinion should it be perceived that Canadian players were being overlooked. Being seen as "professional" and "big league" had its cost, and money was hard to come by. The CFL spent some ten thousand dollars on a dinner for American college coaches to sell them on the merits of Canadian football as a viable alternative to the professional game in the United States; spent a further $400 on a dinner for Canadian intercollegiate coaches; produced, with Labatt's, a film of the 1971 Grey Cup Game "with an American oriented script" at a cost of $6,000 and "which had been sold in the United States for approximately $2,000 above the cost"; and served a luncheon during the Grey Cup week "limited to 150 at a cost of $1,152, excluding gratuities."[61] It had also decided on an outlay of $4,000 to a computer firm, Sy-Dec, to prepare the 1973 schedule, something which Greg Fulton had normally done in the league's office but which now, because of the increasing number of variables, had to be generated by computer.

Corporate sponsors were becoming increasingly important to the league. In addition to the luncheon provided during Grey Cup week, to which major sponsors were invited, clubs were allotted 10 tickets for distribution to those important to their franchise. Press representatives for the Grey Cup Game numbered 386. In addition, CEOs from "Labatt's, General Motors, Mennen, C.P. Air, Electrohome, Imperial Tobacco, Schenley and presidents of both CBC and CTV, received personal invitations"[62] from Jake Gaudaur.

Corporate sponsorship also figured prominently in the other news—the sale of the Argos. The three major owners, John Bassett, Charlie Burns, and

Len Lumbers, agreed to sell their shares at the $200 per share offer extended to all shareholders by Baton Broadcasting, owned jointly by the Bassetts and the Eatons. Of the 11,564 outstanding shares, the three directors owned approximately 9,314—Bassett and Burns approximately 3,500 each and Lumbers 2,200. The sale, said to be worth $2,312,000 was to be closed by August 31, 1971,[63] and brought before the league's Grey Cup meetings for approval. A previous session, held on October 28, considered the sale but it was not approved by the Executive Committee until its November 23 meeting. There, it was moved, seconded, and approved by an 8–1 margin that the "CFL approve the request of the Argonaut Football Club Limited to transfer the majority of its shares to Baton Broadcasting, Inc. subject to the execution by the Toronto Argonaut Football Club, Baton Broadcasting, Inc., Telegram Corporation Ltd., and John W. H. Bassett of a document which would provide that the Argonaut Club and Baton Broadcasting will designate said John W. H. Bassett personally as the agent representative and attorney of the Argonaut Club in all matters involving the League."[64]

With the signatures of Lew Hayman of the Argos, John W. H. Bassett for Baton Broadcasting, D. S. Perigoe for Telegram Corporation, and John W. H. Bassett for John W. H. Bassett, the Argos became part of a conglomerate which included the *Telegram*, which ceased publishing in October of 1971, CFTO-TV of Toronto and CKLW-TV of Windsor, and, of course, the Eaton enterprises.

To attract corporate sponsors and to make them happy, however, might be two different things. Whereas in 1970 half-time entertainment cost the league $4,226, the 1971 Grey Cup Game was underwritten for $6,000 "for a show which cost $5,850 on the stage. The sponsors (Players Cigarettes) were satisfied with the quality of the show but not satisfied that they received full value because we required their association to be subtle and planned television 'mentions' were not forthcoming to the degree they felt was necessary to make the expenditure worthwhile."[65]

It was a difficult time to be in the business of sport. New hockey franchises were springing up all over North America; communities that previously had the CFL as their only professional sport now had a World Hockey Association (WHA) hockey team to compete for the public's dollars and sports-page space. Where money was the criterion, to many, for gauging how "professional" players were, Bobby Hull's one million dollar contract to jump to the Winnipeg Jets from the Chicago Black Hawks spoke volumes. Not only were the Olympic Games in Munich and the subsequent shooting of the Israeli athletes competition for the media's attention, but so too, and even more so, was the Team Canada–Soviet series of September. Football was put on the top shelf and when it did emerge, it was just as likely to be the focal point because of a new league which was rumoured to be developing with teams in the United States and possible spill over into Canada.

There was a rush everywhere to be part of "big time" sport. The Montreal Expos had provided it with baseball; teams from New York, Los Angeles, Chicago, and other American cities testified to the fact that Montreal was in the "bigs." The National Hockey League (NHL) provided a similar sense to fans in Toronto, Montreal and Vancouver. The WHA was attempting to weave the same spell with its franchises in Edmonton, Winnipeg, and Ottawa. The CFL, with all of its franchises in Canada, seemed to be caught in its own definition of itself. It was a different style of football, different from the American game; it had quotas limiting the number of imports (Americans) and insisting on a specified number of non-imports (Canadians). In a world where "big time" and "big league" were defined according to the number of Americans, where the American Way and the pulse of Broadway were important, the CFL was fighting a battle which would be part of a continuing war of perception, not unlike the nation as a whole. It all seemed to be coming to a head in 1972.

Gaudaur addressed the problem in the 1972 Grey Cup program. "The Canadian Football League," he said, "would continue to exist as a meaningful big time sport so long as a clear majority of Canadians prefer our game." He stated that most Canadians have an understandable inferiority complex, living next door to the U.S. which guards the free world, provides the vast majority of movies and television programs, puts a man on the moon, etc. As a result, in many cases, the Canadian comparing any product, Canadian or American, assumes that the American is better. Whereas attendance of most Canadian games was in the 20,000 range, occasionally 30,000, attendance at an American game was in the range of 60,000 to 100,000. Not only that, but many Canadians were exposed to American football on the U.S. TV networks and through the CBC which was also carrying NFL football at the time. The combination of exposure and relative attendance figures served to reinforce these perceptions "and if so, it would naturally follow fewer and fewer will regard the CFL as 'Big Time.'"

The Montreal situation was a case in point. The Alouettes, sitting in a market of three million people, were as well financed as any in Canada and averaged an audience of only 24,000 per game. Baseball, with all American teams coming into the city, averaged a similar 24,000 but over a much greater number of games, more than 80. The same was the case with hockey. The Forum was sold out for all of its home games, close to 50. There, all but two of the incoming teams were American. Gaudaur's fear was that if the WHA got off the ground and was considered "big time," areas such as Hamilton,

Winnipeg, Calgary, and Edmonton would be in trouble because at a time when they were trying to attract interest in season ticket sales, those clubs would be facing competition for the entertainment and leisure dollar.[66]

As with any business, the bottom line was profit. There was an unpredictability about the future. Gaudaur saw the following as key items which had to be addressed:

1. A balanced league was a fundamental prerequisite. It was incumbent upon the league to "continually re-examine the existing forms of equalization" to ensure that they address "the wide economic disparity of fan potential among the clubs."

2. It was imperative that each club operate professionally on and off the field to ensure that they attracted their fair share of leisure dollars in their community.

3. The willingness of the communities in which the franchises are located to attach enough importance to the team that they offer up-to-date stadium facilities "commensurate with the increasing sophistication of their citizens who are fans at a cost within the means of the club."

4. The influence of the WHA teams in attracting money at a time when CFL teams sell season tickets.

5. The formation of the new AFL type league, particularly if it enfranchises cities in Canada.

6. The willingness of the CRTC to preclude TV signals by cable operators into areas where another CFL game is being played.

7. The recognition by Consumers and Corporate Affairs in the Combines Act, that balanced competition is the essence of the CFL and "practices of the league which are restrictive in nature, are necessary to the continuation of the league."

8. The continuing acceptance by Canadians and the media that the league which restricts participants is truly "big time." There is no doubt that expansion to large U.S. cities would increase revenue and if so there would be no doubt that more cities would want to come in, leading to perhaps more revenue for a fewer number of Canadian clubs.[67]

It was this last point that was the major bone of contention among the CFL clubs in 1972. In an era of proliferation of sport franchises, there was agitation to expand, preferably to the United States. There was no question that football was riding a crest of popularity in North America. Indeed, one study found that "the game character exemplified in a professional football team is an essential resource for an industrial society."[68] In the United States,

NFL, AFL, and college football popularity were high. Plans were being made for new leagues since no extensive expansion of the major professional franchises was likely to occur. The CFL received requests from interests in Tampa Bay to play a post-season game in that city. It was anxious to acquire a franchise somewhere. While the proposal was entertained seriously, in the end it was denied. The publicity created by such a game would be desirable; undoubtedly, there would be a large crowd. Interest was high there because of the huge number of Canadians who wintered in that part of Florida and also because of the Argonauts' recent signing of Leon McQuay, the University of Tampa stalwart who decided not to return to school. In the end, however, the CFL declined, the fear being "that it might reasonably be considered to be the infringement of NFL territory and lay itself open to more serious retaliatory measures."[69]

Expansion had been a much debated topic in 1971 as well. Groups from London, Ontario, Halifax, Nova Scotia, San Antonio, Texas, Detroit via Windsor, Ontario, and New York all expressed an interest in joining the CFL. The Detroit via Windsor group was an interesting variation since it came about as a result of the NFL's Detroit Lions moving to a new stadium in Pontiac. It meant that the older Tiger Stadium was vacant. Detroit interests behind the bid hoped to "attract people from the Canadian side with whom they would combine to apply for a franchise."[70] Privately, the CFL commissioner was expressing concern about entering an NFL franchise area.[71] Publicly, Gaudaur expressed the view that the CFL's reluctance was based on history. Expansion to the U.S. was frowned upon "lest it lead to the same path of evolution as it did for professional hockey. As pro hockey expanded in the U.S., smaller Canadian centres fell by the wayside until there were only two franchises left up here."[72]

Two more expressions of American interest surfaced in November of 1971, one from Chicago, the other from New York. The latter was particularly enticing. It included a cheque for $25,000 and had the backing of Robert Schmertz, part owner of the Portland Trail Blazers of the National Basketball Association (NBA), and a "financier with a net worth conservatively estimated at $50 million."[73]

CFL owners were divided. There were those who feared for the Canadian game, the import/non-import ratio, the possibility of the NFL moving into Montreal, Toronto, or Vancouver, and the subsequent falling by the wayside of the smaller Canadian cities. Others saw the business side of it, the opportunity to make money. Franchise fees were "tentatively set at $2 million"[74] to be divided among the existing teams. A decision was made to set up a committee to look into expansion. It included Pat Mahony of Calgary, Sam Berger of Montreal, Lew Hayman of Toronto, and Jake

Gaudaur. They were to consider the question of expansion both inside and outside Canada. It caused one newspaper to state that "such money obviously spoke louder than Gaudaur for the moment."[75] Compounding the problem was the fact that while some did want to expand within Canada, if indeed the league was to expand, there was also the knowledge that the only proper application on hand was from New York City's Robert Schmertz, "a person with substantial means who is prepared to enter on the League's terms."[76]

The recommendation came forward that the league "should be receptive to and encourage any meaningful and viable application from within Canada." Further, "that although substantial revenue would accrue because of a club having its franchise outside Canada, the league should not approve such a franchise at this time because the committee believes that the strength of the league derives from its unique character attributable not only to its distinctive playing rules but its geography."[77] Not all members of the league were in agreement with the decision. David Loeb, speaking for the Eastern clubs, said that they had discussed the committee's report but were not in agreement. This wasn't surprising. There had always been a certain amount of friction between East and West. Indeed, the Grey Cup blossomed under it. This difference related to the financial approaches taken by the two conferences. The Western Conference was made up of community-owned teams; the Eastern Conference was privately operated, the money earned flowing directly into the owners' pockets. Generally speaking, the West was more attuned to the game; the East saw it as a business venture.

The Western Conference, with its community-based teams, ploughed all profits back into team operation. Its sentiments were shared by a letter writer:

> The choice to be made is one of ideology rather than practicalities. Quite simply, the CFL owners must choose between either a sense of national community and the wishes of many fellow citizens or a narrow self-interest and the almighty dollar. For several of the owners, I'm sure an additional consideration is the increase in prestige in having American associates in the league. How sad it is that unlike the people of Winnipeg, Regina, Calgary and Edmonton, they don't seem to realize that if it's American, it isn't necessarily better.[78]

Club owners were aware of the consequences either way. If the application from New York were not accepted, a new AFL-type league could be formed, threatening the CFL's survival. If it were accepted and successful, there would be additional pressure to award new franchises to the United

States. Also, how would the federal government, the CRTC, the Players' Association, and the NFL react to the expansion to the U.S.? Various briefs to the government had always stressed the league's contribution to national unity and the CFL's identity as being the only professional league with all the teams in Canada. Gaudaur and the expansion committee had not sought out the aforementioned organizations, suggesting that they would not give out any firm commitments beforehand but would wait to see the public's reaction. B.C. Lions' Dr. Wes P. "Bill" Munsie was disappointed that the NFL hadn't been consulted. After all, there had recently been an agreement that each league would stay away from the other's franchise areas for exhibition games or expansion. Not only that, B.C. was feeling vulnerable. It would cease to have exclusive rights to Empire Stadium after the 1974 season. There were those in Vancouver "who would seek and likely obtain a franchise in any new forum."[79]

Saskatchewan's Al Sangster found that his club would be the first affected by expansion to the U.S. The Roughriders depended on their Canadian identity to market the club throughout the province. Could it compete with a New York team, with their Mayor Lindsay's support and the huge concentration of media eventually clamouring to do away with the category of non-imports and simply have the "best available"?

Memories were long and vivid in the west of another time, another sport. Gordon Burton of Calgary recalled how prairie teams in the Western Hockey League had been sold in their entirety, their franchises shipped south as the NHL expanded and again when "prairie teams had been forced out of western hockey some fifteen years ago when it expanded to California."[80] If expansion were to take place, it should occur in Canada, he said, an opinion shared by the president of the league, Bill Clarke, also of Saskatchewan. He urged the members to take a positive view of the league's future in Canada and help realize that potential."[81]

The ping-pong match of opinions continued. Lew Hayman, of the Argos, stated that while he was personally opposed to expansion outside Canada, "the position of the Toronto Club was the expansion committee should remain active and continue to obtain more facts."[82] It was an opaque reference to the way Argonaut owner John Bassett, a market-driven free trader, was looming over the discussions at the time. Winnipeg was firmly opposed to expansion outside Canada. Its president Gordon Muirhead felt that "the league is at the footsteps of a major breakthrough in its present set up and has the moral support of all levels of government because of its Canadian character which cannot be valued in U.S. dollars."[83] Hamilton was in sympathy with Saskatchewan's position since, for years, the Tiger-Cats had dreaded the possibility of NFL expansion to Toronto, Hamilton's arch rival and biggest draw at the gate. Then too, there was the fear expressed by Edmonton's J.J. Healy: according to the commissioner's report, a new American league seemed inevitable. What if the CFL expanded to the United States and the new franchise failed to gain acceptance? What then of the damage done to the CFL at home, let alone in the U.S.? According to Healy, "whatever the decision, the CFL should emerge looking as strong as possible. If the vote is in favour of rejection, the reason given should be the desire to remain Canadian with faith in the future of the league within Canada."[84]

Following a brief adjournment allowing for informal discussion among the members of the Executive Committee, the group reconvened. In a motion apparently designed for effect, a result of the caucus of the Eastern clubs, Ralph Sazio, with the support of Ottawa's David Loeb, moved, seconded by Vancouver's Bill Munsie, "that in view of the recent sale of the Toronto franchise for $2,500,000, that the application for the New York franchise be approved, conditional on payment of the franchise being at $9,000,000." It seemed to be a variation of the statement, "We've already established what you are ... what we're arguing about now is the price." After some discussion, the motion was withdrawn with Loeb's and Munsie's concurrence. It was then moved by W. R. Graves of Calgary, seconded by Muirhead of Winnipeg, that the "application by Robert Schmertz for a franchise in New York City not be accepted at this time."[85] It was carried 8–1, the Toronto club being the lone dissenter.

But the matter refused to go away. At an extraordinary meeting of the CFL Executive Committee in Winnipeg on November 16, Bassett continued to pursue the issue. He stated that he favoured expansion strongly. Not only did he want to admit New York, but he wanted to move to other United States cities as well. He wanted a viable league and, in his opinion, expansion would make it so. It was a business proposition. At the moment, he felt, some franchises were being propped up by the league. New sources of revenue were needed. It was doubtful whether gate receipts or television revenues could provide them. Bassett said that the Argonauts' lease on CNE Stadium at the moment did not allow another professional football team to play there. However, that lease was due to expire in three years. In addition, there was talk of a new stadium being built. Entrepreneurs wanted to bring in another pro football franchise. The CFL, said Bassett, must make the first move "while it can dictate the terms regarding franchises and TV contracts."[86] He insisted that smaller centres such as Regina would have a better chance of survival if the league expanded now, rather than with the consequences of United States expansion of football into Canada. If the CFL wanted to increase its revenues through a U.S. television contract, it was necessary to have U.S. identification.

The real fear among the CFL teams was that the larger centres of Toronto, Montreal, and Vancouver would become targets for expansion of a United States league, with all of its "big time" connotations serving to seduce the public. B.C. lent some credence to that theory. Dr. Munsie noted again that the lease of Empire Stadium would expire in 1975. He had doubts that the exclusivity clause would be renewed. In his opinion, B.C. people were more south/north oriented than east/west. Vancouver, he felt, would be most receptive to competition with American clubs. In fact, he said, it had almost happened in 1960 with the formation of the AFL. There were certain Vancouverites who wanted to move Vancouver into that league. Edmonton went on record as favouring expansion once the CFL dealt with its own problems such as putting more people in the stands, firming up "soft spots" such as Montreal, improving play-off attendance, and lobbying to prohibit the CBC from promoting the NFL with its telecasts.

The expansion question refused to go away. Meetings continued to be called to react to new circumstances. The extraordinary meeting in Winnipeg had been called in reaction to Robert Schmertz's advice to Gaudaur "that he was thinking of forming a new league if the CFL didn't want him. He gave the impression that Toronto and Montreal might possibly be members of the new league."[87] In the meantime, the government of Canada had become a player in the deliberations. Health and Welfare Minister John Munro, the MP from Hamilton East and a long-time supporter of the Tiger-Cats and Canadian football, and whose portfolio included responsibility for sport, came out flatly opposed to expansion into the United States. When the news emerged that John Bassett had proposed two notices of motion to the CFL regarding expansion, Munro requested that Bassett and Gaudaur come to Ottawa to meet with him. The notices of motion were "that the Canadian Football League approve the principle of expansion of the league through granting new franchises which would be organized for purposes of operating football clubs in the United States of America at such times applications are deemed acceptable to the league; that the Commissioner be empowered to meet with Robert Schmertz to negotiate the terms of application for a CFL franchise for New York City, such application to be submitted to the league for approval to be operative in the football season of 1976."[88]

The Ottawa meeting with Gaudaur and Bassett was held in Munro's office, with his deputy ministers, Joseph Willard and Lou Lefaive, in attendance. Bassett had some facts and questions. He presented figures that the Argonauts had contributed $400,000 in equalization payments over the last four years. He further stated his opinion that projected revenue over the next four years was not enough to maintain the league. Did the minister have an alternative to expansion to the United States to generate funds? Would the government be prepared to make grants to community-based teams in the west and allow eastern clubs to continue the present equalization payments among themselves? Bassett informed the minister that he would not take any action which would conflict with government policy, but certainly it must have been a grating experience for the staunch market forces conservative who was dealing with the Liberal government and its interventionist approach.

Even with that being the case, the meeting did not take on a confrontational atmosphere. In denying that Munro threatened the CFL, Gaudaur stated that "Munro did say, with a conversational background, what steps the government could take to preserve the CFL ... there was no threat atmosphere."[89] Munro sounded very tough when he spoke with reporters at a Hamilton-Ottawa game. He said that "expansion to the United States would represent an erosion of Canadianism. The government must act to stop such a possibility. We must consider all the options." He further suggested that his government would make "representations to the U.S. Congress to prevent the CFL from losing its Canadian identity." Suspecting that the possibility of a third league would represent the "linkage that could connect our three biggest cities, Vancouver, Toronto, and Montreal, to the NFL," Munro suggested that "the government might have to consider built in restrictions. Any federal funds that go to build an Olympic Stadium in Montreal might have to carry a restriction which would be that only Canadian teams be allowed to use the stadium when the Olympics are over." He also suggested that similar to publishing, an industry that received government protection at that time, "a foreign football owner wouldn't get any tax breaks." To Munro, the Grey Cup Game was "a national institution and no fooling, but if Toronto left the CFL, the economic base of the CFL and the Grey Cup would be fragile indeed." Munro recommended that the CFL consider Halifax, London, and Quebec City instead of the United States expansion sites, "which would be deplorable."[90] He was also quoted as saying that television and immigration were two areas where the government could make it difficult for the CFL, should it decide to expand into the U.S.[91]

To Munro's dictum that the CFL should expand to Halifax, Gaudaur countered that the stadium there would only seat seven to eight thousand. And now that he had the government's attention, Gaudaur suggested that any financial assistance the government in its role as a supporter of Canadian football could give, would be much welcomed. He noted that "the government spends about $8 million annually on sport but that only $15,000 of it goes to amateur football."[92] Further, would the government replace the CFL as benefactor of the Canadian Amateur Football Association?[93] Gaudaur then invited Munro to address the CFL meetings in the new year to listen to their comments. Munro declined. His portfolio was changing; he would be replaced by the new minister, Marc Lalonde, who would continue to lean heavily on the "Munro doctrine" in subsequent deliberations.

The December 1st meeting of the league ended with Bassett withdrawing the notices of motion. It was academic anyway. Bill Clarke, president of the CFL, had stated that unanimity was required and at least four teams, probably Edmonton, Calgary, Saskatchewan, and Winnipeg, were unalterably opposed.[94] It was replaced with a new motion by Bassett, seconded by Vancouver's Munsie, that "the league President and Commissioner visit as soon as possible with the new Minister to see whether the government is prepared to accept certain responsibilities."[95] The "certain responsibilities" were not mentioned.

The CFL Players' Association also declared its opposition to expansion into the United States, saying that it would occur "at a cost of Canadian identity and Canadian football players."[96] The announcement, made by President-elect George Reed, suggested that Canada should be the first area of expansion. It had an ally in the NFL Players' Assocation (NFLPA). Their spokesman, Ed Garvey, stated that NFL players are unalterably opposed to expansion into Canada: We are not against the CFL moving into the U.S. and would welcome it.[97] The Canadian Players' Association also selected its representatives. They were: Trevor Ekdahl and Ted Wheeler, B.C. Lions; Fred James and Lanny Boleski, Calgary; Ed Molstad, Charlie Turner, and Bobby Taylor, Edmonton; George Reed and Bill Baker, Saskatchewan; Joe Critchlow and Paul Robson, Winnipeg; Pete Martin and Bill Symons, Toronto: Rod Woodward and Bob McKeown, Ottawa; Jon Hohman, Bill Danychuk, and Al Brenner, Hamilton; Barry Randal and Ed George, Montreal; Gerry Patterson was the executive director, John Agro, QC, legal counsel, George Reed, president, Gregg Findlay, past president, Oscar Kruger, treasurer, Ed Molstad, Western vice-president, and Bill Danychuk, Eastern vice-president. Oscar Kruger and Mike Wadsworth looked after pensions. The Players' Association also made it clear that it wanted to be a player in the talks of expansion into the United States; that it wanted to meet with the government to review the situation and, in addition, recapture the nine non-import positions which had been lost while keeping the nine import ones gained. They would ask the league officials to increase the size of the rosters. In addition, they would seek to enter into a closer relationship with the NFLPA.[98]

Meanwhile, two of Montreal's long-established footballers, Red O'Quinn and Sam Etcheverry, parted ways with the Alouettes. O'Quinn was fired at the beginning of the season, replaced by J. I. Albrecht; Etcheverry, "tired of living in a pressure cooker,"[99]resigned at the end of the Montreal season. The team had ended the year in third place and was defeated by Ottawa by a 14–11 score in the sudden death play-off to determine who would go against first-place Hamilton. Etcheverry was the second coach to lose his job. Leo Cahill, his team dropping from the heights of Grey Cup finalists to last place in the East, was fired shortly after by John Bassett, and was serenaded by 35,217 fans in Hamilton singing: "Goodbye Leo … So long Leo."[100]

There was a different result for the third-place Saskatchewan team in the West. They defeated Edmonton on the strength of Jack Abendschan's leg by an 8–6 score for the right to play a single game with Winnipeg for the Western championship. It was the first time that the format had been used in the West. Both Winnipeg and Edmonton could be excused if they wanted to return to the old system. Saskatchewan defeated Winnipeg 27–24 to represent the West in the 1972 Grey Cup Game.

In the East, the two-game total-points series was still very much alive, much to the delight of Hamilton. The Tiger-Cats suffered a 12-point loss to Ottawa, 19–7 in game one. It was time for the community to show its support:

> Two nights before the second game, the city staged a pep rally for the team on King Street in the middle of downtown Hamilton. Police later estimated fifteen to twenty thousand people had jammed the street. By a quirk of fate—could it have been planned?—the whole pep rally, the band music, the cheers of the crowd, the whole crazy scene, took place directly outside the Riders' hotel.[101]

Riding on the crest of emotion supplied by their fans, the Tiger-Cats clawed their way to a 23–8 victory in the second game to win the round by three points and represent the East.

For only the first time in 28 years, the Grey Cup Game was being held in Hamilton. The last time was in 1944 when the St Hyacinthe-Donnacona Navy defeated the Hamilton Wildcats by a 7–6 score. This was to be the fifth meeting between Hamilton and Saskatchewan, and the prairie club had yet to win. Hamilton was the victor in 1928, by 30–10; 14–3 in 1929 when the forward pass was first used in the Grey Cup Game; 25–6 in 1932; and 24–1 in 1967.

For five days, the Grey Cup festival took over the city. Events were held in the Armouries, gaily festooned for the occasion, in Jackson Square, named after former mayor Lloyd D. Jackson (Wasn't it wonderful, deadpanned one of the masters of ceremonies, what the city has done in recognizing Russ' accomplishments?), the Connaught Hotel, Holiday Inn, and of course the refurbished Ivor Wynne Stadium. Business meetings, the official opening of the Hall of Fame, the Miss Grey Cup Pageant, the Schenley Awards, and a demonstration of hang gliding or "kite flying" as it was called and sky divers as part of the half-time entertainment were all part of a week-long celebration which was the focal point of the whole community. Governor General Roland Michener would perform the ceremonial kick-off, the ball to be held by the sixth Earl Grey, who had been invited to Hamilton by Mayor Victor K. Copps on a visit to England. Gaudaur later recounted how the kick-off party had been finalized. It was an election year and the results were close. First it looked as if one party would win, then the other. Because the prime minister would not be determined until October 31, Gaudaur invited Pierre Trudeau, David Lewis, and Robert Stanfield to perform the ceremonial kick-off if they were elected prime minister. Because of the uncertainty about the election, it was decided, with the permission of all, to invite the governor general to do so. Mr and Mrs Michener along with the other dignitaries were invited to a private luncheon in a small room at Ivor Wynne Stadium. With the Governor General, his wife, and Lord Grey, were Premier William Davis of Ontario, Premier Blakeney of Saskatchewan, Mayor Copps of Hamilton and Mayor Baker of Regina. When Gaudaur had been told by David Loeb of Ottawa that the Governor General had been disappointed that there had been no function after the 1971 Grey Cup Game for him to attend, Gaudaur invited all those who had participated in the ceremonial kick-off, plus Robert Stanfield and his party, to his home in Burlington after the game. It was an informal get-together. It "appeared to be well accepted and enjoyed by the Governor General, his wife, Bill Davis, and the others who dropped in."[102]

The 1972 Schenley Awards were hotly contested. Hamilton's Garney Henley was selected the Most Outstanding Player over Winnipeg's Mack Herron; Chuck Ealey, the Tiger-Cat quarterback, was chosen as the Rookie of the Year over Saskatchewan's Tom Campana; the Best Canadian was awarded to B.C.'s Jim Young over Ottawa's Gerry Organ; and Calgary's John Helton was chosen the Outstanding Defensive Player over Toronto's Jim Stillwagon. Miss Grey Cup stood to gain an abundance of prizes. She was to be crowned by 1971 winner Deborah Barbagallo from Montreal and would receive a new car, a vacation to Mexico, a snowmobile, trailer, snowmobile suit, colour TV set, cosmetics, luggage, and a one-year membership in a health club. Miss Blue Bomber, Maria Gulyas, was crowned by the Master of Ceremonies, Lorne Greene.[103]

Other major announcements were made while football held such prominence. CBC had outbid CTV for the television rights for the 1973 season. CTV had held the rights for 1972, having paid $1,145,000. CBC was reported to have paid $1,200,000 for the upcoming year which would be at least one game shorter as a result of the East having decided to do away with the two-game total-point final, as was the case with the West.[104] There was no question that inflation was influencing the economy. Some suggested that the Grey Cup itself could be used as an indicator of that. When it was manufactured in 1909, it cost $48. The Grey Cup "miniatures," first presented to winners in 1964 by the league cost $55 each. When the Grey Cup was returned from Montreal to be presented to Calgary for the 1971 game, the cost to clean it was $115.[105] The 1972 silver plated replica was reproduced at a cost of $550.

The 1972 Grey Cup Game was played before 33,953 spectators and came down to the last play of the game, a 34-yard field goal kicked by 19-year-old first-year player Ian Sunter. It was only his third appearance in the game. He kicked an extra point and two field goals and earned the Canadian Player of the Game Award, renamed the Dick Suderman Award, after the Calgary player who lost his life in October. The game's Most Valuable Player was selected as Chuck Ealey. The winning players were awarded $2,000 each, the losers, $1,500.

> It was a glowing finish to an exceptional football year in Hamilton. With the addition of AstroTurf and a new east side stand [*sic*], which converted shabby Civic Stadium into immaculate Ivor Wynne Stadium, the city was awarded the Grey Cup game, put on an amazingly successful show. The Cats ran up a 10 game winning streak, won the Schenley with Henley, and the Rookie award with Ealey and won two player awards in the final game. All that and the Grey Cup, too. It will be a hard act to follow.[106]

1973 to 1974

Chapter Three

IN MANY WAYS, the major news stories about the CFL in 1973 revolved around off-field events. Rule changes in the game were minimal. Montreal, gate equalization, and John Bassett continued to be the major topics of discussion.

In Montreal, there were rumours that the club was for sale "to a group whose ultimate goal was to use that as a vehicle for the importation of an NFL franchise."[1] Interspersed were reports of dissension between certain players and coach Sam Etcheverry. The club also conducted a poll. Questions were asked of two groups; one poll was taken at the stadium, the other by phone at home. The poll was also broken down according to French and non-French (English) correspondents. At the stadium, 55% of the French said that Montreal should have an NFL team. Among the English, 37% were in favour of an NFL team, 62% were opposed. By phone, 42% French were in favour, 36% opposed, and 22% undecided. Of the English, 23% were in favour, 65% opposed, and 12% undecided. Significantly, a survey by P.S. Ross and Associates indicated that whereas the Expos drew 45% of their support from French-speaking people outside Montreal, the Alouettes by contrast drew 7%. The survey also showed that there were "400,000 potential football fans in Metropolitan Montreal."[2] One of the poll findings was that if the club were to "get some long established players, attendance would increase."[3]

The CFL had allowed Montreal to have a rental deduction based on the highest club rental in the league. In 1970, the 15.15% rates paid by Calgary were the highest; in 1971 and 1972, the 16.39% and 16.89% rates paid by Hamilton were the highest. Montreal's actual share of the gate equalization was to be recalculated for each of those last two years using Hamilton's rates as a percentage of the gross gate less direct taxes, with the sum of the differences being paid to the Montreal club. The total cost to the league was to be shared equally by the eight other clubs.[4]

The plan to assist Montreal was passed unanimously by the Executive Committee at its meeting in Winnipeg, where it discussed all of these matters. At the same time, however, there was a great amount of searching being done as to how clubs could generate more revenue and how they could keep a greater share of those dollars earned.

The new Minister of Health and Welfare was Marc Lalonde. He represented a Montreal riding where the Olympic Stadium was being built. The Montreal Olympic Games, due to be held in 1976, were becoming a political football. Stadium costs were seen to be exorbitant; taxpayers throughout the country were alarmed at the possibility of their having to subsidize it. Lalonde was seen as having to walk a fine line.

At the same time, some owners felt that the government had acted in a heavy-handed way in denying expansion to the United States. They had written to the Minister of Health and Welfare and some bad press had resulted. It appeared to some that the league was looking for handouts. John Bassett had written and received a reply on January 2, 1973. He sought relief for the league from its obligations to minor football. Marc Lalonde's reaction was to make it "quite clear that any grants to minor football will be contingent on the CFL continuing its financial support."[5] Lalonde also revealed that the so-called "Munro doctrine" had not been discussed at the cabinet level and lent his support to the Autostade's lease being reviewed.[6] Sam Berger felt that this was just so much talk. He wanted action. He wondered whether the federal government was proceeding with caution "because of unfavourable publicity surrounding possible federal support for the Olympics?"[7] He further ventured the opinion that "the league's only hope for survival in Montreal lies in a government imposed condition of exclusivity to any federal government grants to Montreal to build Olympic facilities."[8] Bassett was more to the point: "The only chance to keep the NFL out of Montreal depends on the failure of the Olympics to get under way. If Montreal gets a major league stadium, the mayor will approach the NFL with a proposition it could not refuse."[9] He pointed to Expo '67, the resultant Expos baseball team and their "tax concessions gained from Ottawa permitting write-offs of the purchase price of players." Regarding the claim that federal funds would only be used for non-stadium facilities, the politically astute and aware Bassett was convinced that if that were the case, "the province of Ontario will build a stadium in Toronto for an NFL franchise."[10]

In effect, the Executive Committee meeting took on the tone of a strategy session, the object being to realize, in a tangible way, the benefits which could accrue to the league because of the government's intervention. Gauduar suggested that he should attempt to convene a meeting with both Munro and Lalonde present in order to clarify or attempt to reconcile the respective views.[11] Berger suggested that since the Olympic Stadium was being built in Lalonde's riding, the minister "was aware of the public clamour for the best of everything which, in its mind, would include the NFL."[12] Edmonton delegates mentioned that federal and provincial governments had already promised funds for its Commonwealth Stadium for the 1978 games. Perhaps the objective should be to have the federal government adopt a policy of updating stadiums and sports facilities across the country rather than concentrate in Montreal. Ottawa's David Loeb wondered whether a commitment should be obtained that support for the Olympic Stadium by the federal government should be "contingent upon CFL occupancy."[13] Calgary's Rogers Lehew was all for pressing the attack since the government had made the first move: duties could be lifted on artificial turf, something which appealed to Winnipeg since it was contemplating adding turf to its stadium.

The bottom line was money. Bassett wanted the league to find a way "which would permit the Toronto Club to participate more fully in the revenues which it generates."[14] Since 1968, Bassett stated, the Argos had generated more money for the league, $500,000, than it had for itself, $250,000. Changes had to be made. If they weren't, Bassett was prepared to take steps "within the framework of the constitution" to retain more of the club's earnings. He mentioned three courses of action: he could negotiate a new stadium lease which required a 50% kickback in other areas; he could reduce the net ticket price to subscribers and replace the difference with a service charge which would not be affected by equalization; the selling of television rights would be dependent upon purchasing the half-time show which would be marketed as a separate item. His complaint was that some of the Western clubs were able to generate revenue which was not shared with the league, for example from their $100 a plate dinners. The only private source his club had was the radio rights. Bassett was convinced that the Argos' contribution to the CFL was greater than that of any other club—but it could not go on.

Bassett, an impressive speaker, appealed to his fellow executive committee members that no team should contribute more than 20% of its gross gate. He had been holding up the league's wish to go to a single-game format for the Eastern Conference finals, arguing that it would be too costly to give up the revenue from a play-off game. He offered a deal. If the league approved Ralph Sazio's proposal that the schedule be expanded to give everyone an extra home game and, as Sazio suggested, that the receipts of that game not be added into the equalization pool, he would withdraw his objections to the play-off change.[15]

Bassett's bargain was accepted; the roadblock was removed. "Everybody was very nice to me but nothing has changed," said Bassett of his league cronies. "The Argo owner had described himself as 'the most disliked man in the CFL' because of the opposition among Western Conference teams to his expansion proposals."[16]

What Jake Gaudaur termed "landmark decisions,"[17] flowed directly from Bassett's compromise. It enacted the COOL (Committee On One League) Report from 1969. The CFL announced that its Eastern Conference members would play a 16-game schedule, the same as in the Western Conference, beginning in 1974. In addition, the two extra games, "a compromise settlement of an Eastern request for some extra working capital,"[18] were to be played within the Conference. "The extra home game for each of the Eastern teams will in effect be free from the gate equalization pool."[19] The Western Conference clubs "demanded their pound of shekels in return ... clubs from both conferences would only report seven-eighths of their home gate for equalization."[20]

The new arrangement was to be for a three-year trial period. Its year of implementation, 1974, would be the first time in the CFL that the same number of regular season games and a standard play-off scheme would occur. When the West went to the single-game format in 1973, they raised ticket prices; the result was that the one-game final was more profitable than the two-out-of-three series. The East, in following the same format for 1973, set its ticket prices at $10, $8, and $5 for the semifinal and $12, $10, and $6 for the final.

The CFL Players' Association had been in favour of the uniformity. In fact, Gaudaur noted that there "had been a general commitment to the Association to adopt it if it had proved successful in the 1972 Western Conference trial."[21] Financially it meant that the first-place winners received a bye into the final and $600 per player. That was the same amount awarded to the winners of the semifinal game. The losing team earned $500 per player. The winners of the conference finals were to receive $800, the losers $600 each. Added to the Grey Cup money, the winner was to receive $3,000 plus the $1,400 already earned for a total of $4,400; the loser $2,000 plus $1,400 for a total of $3,400. Players' season salaries, of course, were suspended with the end of the regular season, meaning that the league stood to earn much of its revenues from the play-offs because of higher ticket prices, increased revenues, and lower than season salary costs.

In the name of uniformity, the CFL annual meeting approved a number of other items. It was the first time that players attending schools outside of

Canada were included in the draft. Each team was allowed to protect two of its territorial prospects; the rest were put into a common pool for selection by all clubs according to a predetermined process. Of the 18 protected exemptions, 13 were in attendance at American schools. The first round of the universal draft saw five of the nine selected from Canadian universities.

The overriding concern was that the league be seen to be professional, that all were moving in the same direction to maximize league benefits, that is, money. There was also an announcement about television. Conference games and the 1973 Grey Cup Game rights had been sold to the CBC for $1.2 million, an increase of $55,000 over 1972. In addition, the CFL had accepted a bid from Ralmar Corporation for "$150,000 for TV rights for a minimum of 10 games to be put on a U.S. network ... $50,000 more than was paid last year."[22]

Not all were happy with the sale to the American corporation. During 1972, there had been a lack of advertiser interest. The broadcasts were dropped. Gaudaur stated that for 1973, the problem had been eliminated. Advertising rates had been restructured and efforts to increase the market coverage were being made.[23] Dr. Tom Casey, former Hamilton Wildcat and Winnipeg Blue Bomber and then a resident of Syracuse, NY, addressed the annual Blue Bomber fund raising dinner. He had a distinctly Canadian message; he spoke out against expansion. "You may not realize it but Canadian football is your most important asset. To you, its more important than your ore, your lumber or anything because it's truly Canadian and something you can identify with." He said that the CFL must "ensure that all its franchises remain Canadian owned." Casey was very critical of the CFL decision to telecast its games into the United States. He paid particular attention to former NFL lineman Alex Karras, the colour commentator whose comments Casey found "insulting."

> They made fun of the Canadian game. The way they went about it was a disgrace. Every time somebody made an error or a mistake, it was interpreted as sloppy football. I don't know what the CFL is gaining financially, but I have to wonder how much you are giving up for what. In my opinion, you're selling out by allowing people in the power market to make comparisons and present your game as second class football.[24]

Like any business, the CFL has always felt it necessary to explore all areas of possible revenue. Its small markets in a wide geographic expanse have always exerted pressure on clubs to refine ways of improving cash flow. Licensing of trade marks was one such way. They had to be copyrighted and registered.

The costs for each team were: Montreal $1,483,Ottawa $792, Toronto $1,090, Hamilton $899, Winnipeg $1,134, Saskatchewan $1,105, Edmonton $1,215, Calgary $1,240, and British Columbia $1,138.[25]

There had been complaints from CFL Properties, the league's licensing arm, that clubs were changing their logos, helmet symbols, uniform colours, and design without advance warning. It meant that a licensee might have out-of-date inventory without having had a chance to merchandise it; sales would be undercut by the club's unanticipated changes. Again the commissioner referred to the NFL model where a team was required to give three years' notice of any proposed changes. Gaudaur suggested that "at least one year's notice should be established as the time for a member club to advise the league of such matters."[26] Because of the lateness of the situation, the clubs were given until December 31, 1973, to notify the league offices of their changes for the 1974 playing season.

The commissioner also ventured the opinion that the clubs, collectively, had not been professional in the matter of players' pictures. Bubblegum card photos were being taken for the O Pee Chee Company but the CFL offices did not have photos of the players in the league. It was moved, seconded, and carried unanimously that "each club be required to file with the league office the necessary negatives from which there may be reproduced, in quantity, 35mm colour slides, black and white head and shoulder pictures and full body photos for each player on the club roster."[27] The league was also anxious to establish uniformity on the playing field. There were complaints that some players' white pullover stockings were so high that the team stockings were hardly visible. Then there were players who insisted on wearing a non-team-coloured jersey underneath their club's short-sleeved sweater, exposing a clashing colour below the elbow. The league decided to address the situation "with the use of posters in the teams' dressing room prescribing the proper dress for a game."[28] Later in the year, realizing that public relations was becoming more recognized for its importance to a professional league, the CFL hired veteran *Globe and Mail* reporter Gord Walker as director of information. He would be kept busy in 1974. One of his first tasks was to standardize club information such as press and media books, releases, and players' pictures.

Meanwhile, the league was sending out the message that there were proper ways of behaviour. Mack Herron, the runner-up for the Schenley Award as the Most Valuable Player in the CFL for 1972, and his team-mate, Jim Thorpe, also an outstanding receiver, were waived out of the CFL by Winnipeg. Both were charged with illegal possession of marijuana and cocaine.[29]

Sports operations are extremely sensitive about such things ... Not long ago, Hamilton signed All American Steve Wooster and he was convicted on a dope charge. Ralph Sazio dropped him immediately and he was waived out of the league without a ripple ... [one has] to wonder though whether the unseemly haste of the business with Herron and Thorpe, before conviction, was a decision rooted in emotion and conviction at the expense of wisdom.[30]

To some, the league seemed to be sending out mixed messages. On the one hand, it was waiving players prior to their being found guilty of any "crime." On the other, the Montreal Alouettes had recently signed Johnny Rodgers, the "ordinary superstar." Rodgers had won the Heisman Trophy in 1972 as the top player in the United States collegiate ranks despite objections from some who campaigned against him by publicizing "his jail sentence in 1970 for a gasoline station hold-up and his brushes with police over traffic violations."[31] The inconsistency was not lost on at least one reporter who chastised the CFL Players' Association for honouring "the CFL's unofficial blackball of Mack Herron in the annual All Star game, in Hamilton, June 27 ... [even though] he has not yet been tried or convicted ... Frontier justice?"[32]

When the CFL All Star game was played in Hamilton, under the chairmanship of former Saskatchewan Roughrider, Pat Santucci, it was hoped to improve on the record $83,000 it earned at the All Star game in Calgary in 1972. The '71 game in Montreal had generated $6,700 for the players' pension fund; there was $33,000 from the first contest held in Ottawa in 1970. As part of its program, the Players' Association presented Humanitarian Awards to George Reed and Al Brenner. Reed, the 10-year veteran of the Roughriders and president of the association, was cited for his "fundraising for the Muscular Dystrophy Association, the Special Saskatchewan Olympics for Handicapped Children and Honourary Chairman of the Regina United Appeal in addition to numerous personal appearances across Canada for charitable organizations." Brenner, having lived in Hamilton as a Tiger-Cat for only two years, was "director of the Youth Service Centre, [who] organizes benefit baseball and basketball games and is involved with crippled children programs as well as appearing for charitable groups."[33] The dinner itself raised $5,000 for the Sertoma Club of Hamilton and Burlington; the game attracted 24,765 spectators who saw the All Stars defeat the Tiger-Cats by a 22–11 score.

As a result of regular season play, the Edmonton Eskimos represented the West in the 1973 Grey Cup Game. They finished in a tie for first place with Saskatchewan, which, under the tie-breaker formula, was awarded second spot. They earned the right to play Edmonton in the final by defeating the British Columbia Lions 33–13 in the semifinals. In the Western championship game, Edmonton defeated Saskatchewan 25–23, the victory preserved by John Beaton's interception of a Ron Lancaster pass with only 12 seconds left and the Roughriders moving into field goal position. Beaton's runback of 51 yards assured the victory which had been shaped by the foot of Dave Cutler who kicked six field goals to tie his own CFL record.

The Ottawa Rough Riders represented the East. They, too, finished in first place and waited while the Montreal Alouettes defeated the Toronto Argonauts, in overtime, by a score of 32–10. In the Eastern final, Ottawa defeated the Alouettes 23–14.

It was to be a replay of the 1960 Grey Cup Game, a different cast of players but the same teams. Both had controversy surrounding their quarterbacks. In Edmonton, Tom Wilkinson was vying with Bruce Lemmerman for the starting position. Each had his followers. There were stories that some players performed for Wilkinson but not for Lemmerman. Prior to the game, all seemed verified. News was published of a fight, which broke out in a Saskatchewan hotel room, between Edmonton flanker Bobby Taylor and quarterback Lemmerman.[34] The feisty Edmonton receiver accused the quarterback of ignoring him in games, even when he was the only receiver out on a pattern. After the fight, Edmonton coach Ray Jauch released Taylor, the official reason given that Taylor had lost a step and was "too slow."

Wilkinson generated his own controversy within the league. He was continually accused of using an "unnatural head motion to draw the defence offside." Frank Clair, the Ottawa general manager, was echoing what other teams were saying, as well as alerting the officials to keep their eyes on Edmonton. "I'm not saying that Edmonton designs the play for Wilkinson but when we, Ottawa, went up against them, we went offside 5 times just because of him and we don't go offside."[35]

Meanwhile, Ottawa was having its own problems at the quarterback position. Its two leaders, Jerry Keeling and Rick Cassata, were being pilloried by the public. Keeling, the former Calgary defensive back and quarterback, had been dubbed the "reject." Cassata, in spite of his role in leading Ottawa to an 11–3 record in 1972, was branded the "retard." Keeling had suffered a knee injury in Montreal; there was a distinct possibility that he might not play in the Grey Cup Game. It was reported that "if the 'reject' can't start, they'll stand a better chance with the equipment man than the 'retard.'"[36] In the end, Cassata did play and "stifled the boo-birds" in leading Ottawa to a 22–18 victory.

Edmonton's chances were said to have disappeared "at 10:23 of the first quarter when a Rider defensive end broke a couple of Tom Wilkinson's ribs."[37] The game, played at Toronto's CNE Stadium, attracted 36,653 spectators, most of whom paid the top price of $17.50 a seat to raise a gate of $571,242.50.[38] Gaudaur had also authorized the installation of bleacher seats, for the first time in a Grey Cup Game at the stadium, at a cost of $3.50 per seat. They were priced at $13 each.

Originally, the game had been scheduled for Sunday, December 2. With some foresight, however, the league office recognized the possibility that because of byes in the schedule and the play-off structure, the team with the open date ending up in first place could have "a four week gap between its last game of the regular schedule and the final conference play-off game."[39] The game was moved back one week to November 25. It necessitated quite a bit of adjustment on the part of many, including hotels. The Royal York "agreed to approach and change the reservations of many individuals and organizations who had already been confirmed during the regular week of November 19–25."[40] In retrospect, the decision was a good one. Ottawa had, in fact, ended the season with a bye in the last game of the season and in first place.

The 1973 Grey Cup Game was a successful end to a successful season. The total of all salaries was $4,811,450; the average import earned $19,925, while the average non-import earned $13,875.[41] The figures were only a guide since they did not include signing bonuses, except to veterans, performance or play-off bonuses, nor salaries to injured players.[42]

Dignitaries continued to be hosted at the game. They included: Governor General Roland Michener and Mrs. Michener, Ontario Premier William Davis, Alberta Premier Peter Lougheed, Ottawa Mayor Pierre Benoit, Edmonton Mayor Ivor Dent, Toronto Mayor David Crombie, Metro Chairman Paul Godfrey, Minister of Finance John Turner, Health and Welfare Minister Marc Lalonde, Postmaster General Andre Ouellette, CBC President Laurent Picard, CTV President Murray Chercover, Labatt's President Peter Widrington, Air Canada President J.C. Gilmer, and President of Datsun, M. Miki. During a pre-game luncheon, hosted by Ottawa's David and Mrs. Loeb, Jake Gaudaur presented Governor General Michener a 1973 game ball, mounted on a stand with a plaque, to commemorate his last Grey Cup as a governor general.[43]

In expressing his satisfaction with the event, Gaudaur stated that his approach to the Grey Cup Game was "to professionalize it to the highest degree possible ... based on our belief that, to a considerable degree, Canadian professional football will be judged each year by this final game."[44]

Simmering beneath the surface of all this success and movement towards professionalism, was the issue of expansion—that of the CFL and its new rival, the United States-based World Football League (WFL). Bob Harris, a London entrepreneur, had sought a CFL franchise for that southwestern Ontario city. He had included a certified cheque for $25,000, a league requisite, with his application. While the CFL ultimately decided that "the financial statements were not in form sufficient for proper consideration,"[45] Harris' application was more likely turned down at that time because Hamilton's Ralph Sazio objected. Since the "City of London falls within the franchise area of the Hamilton Club," Sazio argued that "he should have been consulted before the application was made by the London group."[46] Earlier, the Tiger-Cats, with little fanfare, were sold to Dundas trucking magnate Michael DeGroote.[47] It was the only deal consummated. Maple Leaf Gardens Limited had applied for a second franchise to be awarded in the Toronto area. The Toronto Argonauts had exclusivity there; any such bid needed the unanimous consent of the four Eastern clubs and seven of the nine CFL members. In his reply to Harold Ballard, owner of the Maple Leafs, Commissioner Gaudaur wrote that the first hurdle to clear was obtaining the permission of the Bassett-led Argonauts. Once that was gained, Harold Ballard could re-apply.

Not likely! Ballard and Bassett, former partners and owners of the Maple Leafs, were not on good terms and hadn't been since Bassett had cast a deciding vote to depose Ballard as executive vice-president of the Maple Leafs.[48] Sazio cited this precedent which had been made in dealing with the application from Maple Leaf Gardens for a second franchise in Toronto: "An applicant for a second franchise in an area was first to satisfy the holder of the other franchise in that area."[49] The cheque included with Harris' application was returned.

The CFL meetings were being held at a time when press releases were announcing the new World Football League and its franchise for Toronto. The CFL was presented with a barrage of problems. The WFL team, to be called the Toronto Northmen, was owned by Johnny F. Bassett, son of Argonaut owner, John Basset. Leo Cahill, former Argo coach, was hired to run the WFL team. It would seek to play its games in CNE Stadium where the Argonauts held an exclusive lease. In the initial days of its launch, the new league was an unknown quantity to most, including the CFL commissioner. Not so to Bassett, Sr. The league would "commence operations in 1974 with the team in Toronto." Not only that, "while the Argonaut Club holds an exclusive contract with CNE Stadium, the new Toronto team will be permitted to use it." Bassett further expressed his view that the new team would not be harmful to CFL attendance. In fact, Bassett reasoned, he knew some wealthy people who wanted to have a second team in Toronto. "Under the circumstances, he would prefer to have that second team operated by his son John F. Bassett, rather than by some stranger."[50]

Seven of the nine CFL clubs had agreed that Bassett had a conflict of interest among his various corporate structures. Only Montreal's Sam Berger sided with Bassett.[51] It wasn't because of any lack of effort on John Bassett's part that there were not more owners with him, especially in the East where the four clubs were privately owned and the profit motive, naturally, was important. Bassett, Sr. offered the Hamilton Tiger-Cats and Ralph Sazio, particularly, a piece of the action. Right up until January 20, Sazio was interested in Bassett's "talk of Broadway and bright lights." He started off with an offer of 25% and soon increased that to "35% of the Northmen with no money down."[52] There was the tantalizing talk of continuing the storied Hamilton-Toronto rivalry in the new WFL. Sazio wavered but contacted Gaudaur to share this information with his cohort of 25 years. Gaudaur was aghast: "I think the CFL can survive if we have to share the Toronto market with another league. But there's no way the CFL can make it without Hamilton."[53] Gaudaur requested that he be allowed to address the Hamilton executive. On January 22, Gaudaur, speaking to the assembled Tiger-Cat brain trust, made an impassioned plea. Sazio called it a "hell of a speech … he hit our guys right in their patriotism."[54] The executive, some of whom were for the WFL option, were turned around by Gaudaur's words. Some went so far as to "pledge we'd work 18 or 20 hours per day to beat the WFL or any other competitors."[55] Sazio phoned Bassett to inform him of the Hamilton decision. "He seemed a little cool," said Sazio.[56] Bassett's ploy to divide and conquer had not worked.

The elder Bassett withdrew his involvement from the Northmen and "left the WFL to his son. But through interlocking corporations, a conflict of interest still existed and this remained an issue within the CFL. Bassett, in apparent disgust, put the Argos up for sale."[57]

The announcement was made at the afternoon session of the CFL Annual Meetings at the Royal York, February 21, 1974. It was the same day that Lalonde was presenting a speech on Canadian football in Regina. With John Bassett, Sr., absent, "a written offer was presented to delegates."[58] Bassett was giving the CFL 15 days to buy the Argonauts. Contacted later, he gave his price as $3.3 million. There were two conditions: that he be paid in cash and that he could have six seats to the Argo games anywhere he wanted."[59]

The whole subject was in the process of becoming a political football. The clubs were instructed to meet with their municipal and provincial governments in order to consolidate their own position in the community, the chief caveat being caution "against actions or public statements by clubs which would create an undesirable backlash in certain areas."[60] Throughout it all there was the fear that the NFL would use the WFL as a back-door entrance to Canada and the demise of the CFL.

The majority of people recognized the fledgling WFL as a "minor league." However, the fact that the Northmen had attracted such high-profile players as former Miami Dolphins Jim Kiick, Larry Csonka, and Paul Warfield with million dollar contracts, caused some to speculate that the league would eventually follow the course of the AFL. Sustained by television income, the AFL eventually merged with the NFL. There was a fear that history would repeat itself and Toronto would find itself in the NFL, much to the detriment, it was feared, of the CFL. In addition, the federal government and specifically the Minister of Health and Welfare, responsible for sport, had already spoken out against expansion of the CFL into the United States and of American leagues into Canada. In 1972, that policy was dubbed the "Munro doctrine" after the then Minister John Munro. In 1974, however, there was a new minister, Marc Lalonde. His actions would demonstrate whether Munro's dictum was personal or government policy. He wasted no time in making his position well known.

Lalonde ventured into Regina, Saskatchewan, to the soul of the CFL and addressed the Rotary and Kiwanis Clubs. He launched into a framework for the government's interventionist approach. After praising the sporting exploits of Saskatchewan teams, particularly in curling and football, Lalonde highlighted two major contributions of Saskatchewan, lessons for all of Canada. "Many Canadians have come to appreciate the immense debt we owe to the Province of Saskatchewan for its pioneering experiments in many fields of social policy and legislation. Your strong sense of community, so evident in the way you support civic and provincial enterprises, is known and admired all across Canada."[61] He spoke of the success of Canadian athletes at the recent Commonwealth Games in New Zealand. While credit was naturally due to the athletes, their coaches, and the sports governing bodies, the federal government deserved some praise as well. Since the Report of the Task Force on Sports in 1968, government had assumed a greater role and interest, so much so "that in the wake of our success at Christchurch, the Australian government is now being asked to follow the 'successful Canadian system of financing sports.'"[62] Lalonde sprinkled his message with references familiar to his audience. Lalonde was born on a farm. He suggested that farmers today don't get as much exercise as they used to, "not even rugged Saskatchewan farmers." The experiment of the Participaction Program in Saskatoon demonstrated that the "fitness message can be marketed like most consumer goods."[63] The percentage of the Saskatoon population exercising had moved from 7% to 18% after seven months of advertising. Warming to his topic, Lalonde advanced the notion that

> there are those who say, yes, it's fine for the government to get involved with fitness and amateur sports but we shouldn't concern ourselves with pros. One of the arguments is that pro sports aren't really sports at all, but only a branch of the entertainment industry. The next argument is that entertainment is international and people only want to see the best, regardless of nationality. Oddly enough, that argument is often applied to Canadian football and its quota of American players. I think it's appropriate here in the city recognized as "the football capital of Canada" to clarify the government's position regarding Canadian football.[64]

Lalonde's "Regina Manifesto" continued to heap praise on Saskatchewan. He made note of the province's continual support of its football team in spite of a small population, inclement weather, competition for the entertainment dollar, and rising costs. He praised the decision taken as early as 1948 to give their team a provincial rather than local identity, the $100 a plate dinners, and the supporters, some of whom regularly drove hundreds of miles to see a game. He raised a chuckle when he told of a visiting coach who described Taylor Field as the "world's biggest outdoor insane asylum." Lalonde was sure that his description "contained more than a hint of wistful envy."[65] He added, "All of this suggests that football here in Saskatchewan is a true community enterprise—not so much a game as a way of life. Football—Canadian football—matters. It is not just another form of entertainment. It is *your* game, part of *your* life."[66]

Moving to the heart of his speech, Lalonde suggested that those who downgraded the "quality of our football" were no more than "a vocal minority." In dealing with possible expansion of the NFL into Canada, he suggested that the "NFL expansion talk continues ... even when the NFL commissioner just as regularly announces that his league has no ambitions north of the border." In Montreal, Mayor Jean Drapeau was being urged to make his principal selling point for an NFL franchise the availability of the new Olympic Stadium being built for 1976. Lalonde stated that "Mayor Drapeau was fully aware of the federal government's decision. He understood that we strongly oppose any action that might weaken or undermine Canadian football."[67]

Government policy was restated for the benefit of his audience and news coverage. Expansion of the CFL into the United States and of U.S. leagues into Canada would not be allowed. Growth of the CFL must come from within Canada. There must be "broader support in French Canada ... into the Atlantic provinces ... western Ontario ... a second team in the Toronto area."[68]

He dwelled on this last point. The new league's franchise in Toronto "had the silent assent, if not the blessing of some CFL owners who adamantly refused to consider a second CFL team in Toronto only a few months ago ... even a possibility that the CFL Argonauts will share the use of their stadium facilities with the WFL newcomers."[69]

Lalonde said that the threat was real. It was here. The Toronto Northmen were operating, "hiring coaches long established in Canada." Again, he dwelled on the seeming conflict between the Argonaut owners and directors and their "strange lack of resistance" in allowing the WFL to move "into one of the two or three possible areas into which the CFL could expand."[70]

Toronto may very well be able to support a second team, said Lalonde. "If that is so, let us have a second team that will belong to the Canadian Football League and let us not tolerate the type of behaviour that took place last year ... The future of Canadian football is too large and too important a question to be left to the tender mercies of a few entrepreneurs out for a fast buck."[71]

By coincidence, the CFL Annual Meeting was in progress at Toronto's Royal York Hotel while Marc Lalonde was delivering his Regina speech. The Minister of Health and Welfare's presentation had been pre-released by his department; CFL officials were aware of it when they sat down at their discussions. Expansion of the WFL and Lalonde's intervention were dominant topics. Ralph Sazio suggested that the "league should start a movement to stop the WFL from using CNE Stadium."[72] Ever the pragmatist, his arguments flowed from that position: with two teams from two different leagues sharing the stadium, there would be problems with different field markings and goal posts. Not only that, practice times, dressing room space, and schedule dates could be awkward and would have to be ironed out. Bassett had in fact signed an agreement with his son's WFL team, waiving the CFL team's exclusive use of the CNE Stadium. In spite of new owner Bill Hodgson's doubt that the agreement would stand up with the change of ownership, there was still the possibility of the Argos and the Northmen playing in the same park. Two more factors which had to be taken into account were the annual Canadian National Exhibition, which ran during the last two weeks of August and ended on Labour Day, and the rumoured possibility of a baseball team. They were valid concerns. The Argonauts team was the league's flagship. The team was playing before capacity crowds. There was much to lose.

Montreal owner Sam Berger was practical in yet another way. His big worry in Montreal was the campaign for an NFL franchise. "Now that the

Honourable Marc Lalonde has come out strongly in favour of the CFL, perhaps the time is ripe to ask him to obtain an exclusive lease for the Alouettes in Olympic Stadium."[73] Leases were of particular concern to Berger. He resented paying an "unreasonable rent to a government agency under a burdensome lease"[74] for the Autostade.

Edmonton's Jim Hole, noting that Lalonde had "suggested that the league respond in some manner to the proposed stand which had received the unanimous support of the cabinet," proposed that the CFL send a letter of appreciation to Lalonde for his Regina statements.[75] Gaudaur's response was to be more discreet and less public while waging the battle on two fronts. He suggested approaching various political leaders such as Lalonde, Bill Davis, and Paul Godfrey privately, "essentially to inform the various levels of governments and encourage them to volunteer positions."[76] He also noted his recent discussions with NFL commissioner Pete Rozelle, who led him to believe that the American league was not planning any expansion into Canada and moreover that it was "most anxious to co-operate with CFL clubs ... [and] urged the clubs to establish the best liaison possible with NFL clubs so that the better quality players released from the NFL will come to the CFL rather than the WFL."[77]

Gaudaur was still convinced that the CFL's "number one current problem" was "the lack of fan acceptance in the Montreal area of the Alouettes in particular and of the CFL in general."[78] The situation was such that it merited "*special* consideration of the other eight clubs" in order to build up a good base of season tickets sold."[79] Perhaps prophetically, in view of events that would transpire in the nineties, Gaudaur stressed the importance of cool heads and an open mind to change:

> A sport such as Canadian professional football will continue to be judged in the entertainment market and, as the spenders of leisure dollars become more sophisticated, it will become increasingly important that we not rely solely on our established traditions, particularly with regard to playing rules, and, in so doing, reject out of hand any proposed change without considering thoroughly the probable short and long range implications of either trying, or not trying, something that is new.[80]

To verify that the situation in Montreal was in need of support, contrary to the public image of the improvement which had taken place, Gaudaur produced figures to show that while attendance figures indicated an increase from 99,567 in 1972 to 142,383 in 1973, a differential of 42,816, gross revenue from attendance was up by only $23,121. That "indicated that the attendance figures were exaggerated in this instance."[81] He stressed that actual paid attendance figures were necessary if his reports were to have any validity.

Meanwhile, the WFL team pressed on. The Northmen announced the signing of Miami of Ohio graduate John McVay as their new head coach along with the information that training camp would open June 14 at Upper Canada College.[82] The Northmen, who had already signed Leo Cahill as their general manager, continued to round out their coaching staff. On February 26, they announced that former Argo assistant coach Jim Rountree and Ottawa's former assistant coach Jay Fry would join the new WFL team in similar capacities.

Amid all the swirl of activity, the CNE board of directors approved in principle, but refused to sign a contract with the Northmen. Dated February 22, they preferred to refer the political football to Metro Council Executive for signing. Toronto's Mayor David Crombie and Metro Chairman Paul Godfrey had already come out in favour of allowing the Northmen to stay and play in Toronto. Lalonde, once again, entered the fray. On February 26, he held a press conference in Toronto. Once again, he repeated: "We can't stop them from signing the contract. But we can make it invalid later and we have told them so. It is a national responsibility."[83]

In the meantime, Jake Gaudaur was in the hospital where he was "recovering from fatigue."[84] In his absence, Ralph Sazio and David Loeb investigated the seven bids to buy the Argonauts. It was a touch of irony in that both men had been wooed by Bassett for their support for the WFL. And it was equally ironic that the general manager of the hated Hamilton Tiger-Cats "was screening bids for the Toronto Argonauts franchise."[85] In fact, to some, Sazio was being described as "the current champion"[86] of the CFL's existence. Completely taken with Gaudaur's message, Sazio, the "native of South Orange, New Jersey," declared: "I couldn't agree more with the government that the CFL is a cultural thing, a form of Canadianism that binds our country together. It's worth keeping."[87]

The intense publicity surrounding the events resulted in a quick sale of the Argonauts to Bill Hodgson. One writer estimated that had the CFL been required to pay for the publicity it received from the media, the cost would have been $10.6 million.[88] As it was, the $3.3 million received was said to represent a profit of "$2 million before taxes, when surplus assets are added to the sale price."[89] It was an informal deal made between two millionaires. Hodgson and Bassett had known each other casually for years; they sat beside each other at Maple Leaf games. On at least two other occasions, Hodgson had attempted to buy the Argonauts and was always told the same thing: they were not for sale. This time, Hodgson had been on his way to Panama, heard the news, returned and contacted the CFL.

Its lawyer, George Finlayson, called Bassett. Would he mind speaking directly with Hodgson rather than dealing through the league as a middle man? Bassett agreed: "I called Hodgson. I said: 'Bill let's make a deal.' He said: 'I'll be right over.' I said: "Not until the afternoon. I'm on my way to play some tennis.' He came over in the afternoon. The deal was done in ten minutes."[90]

The peace brought to the turbulence was only the calm before the storm. Within days of the Argonaut sale and resolution of the "conflict of interest," the $3 million figure surfaced once again. With an explosion of media coverage, the Northmen showed no sign of backing down. They announced the signing of three of the NFL's Miami Dolphins' prominent players, Jim Kiick, Larry Csonka, and Paul Warfield, for a salary outlay of $3 million! The figure had a familiar ring. It was $3 million that Bassett, Sr., wanted for indemnification in June of 1973 when Harold Ballard wanted to locate another CFL team in Toronto; it was slightly more than $3 million that Bassett had received from Hodgson for the Argonaut sale; it was again a little more than $3 million that Bassett, Jr., had agreed to pay the newest members of the Toronto Northmen.

Marc Lalonde was not amused. Telegrams and correspondence poured into his office. Whether by persuasion or simply as a result of interest in the developments, mayors, MPs, MLAs, and civic authorities all moved to join Lalonde's crusade. Conspicuously absent from the file put together for distribution by Lalonde's office were any missives from Vancouver, Toronto, and Montreal. These three cities presumably stood to benefit from a possible NFL franchise. Manitoba's Minister of Tourism, Recreation and Culture, Rene Toupin, wrote as part of "an informal House Committee formed for the purpose of developing steps that may be taken to insure the continued operation of the Winnipeg Blue Bombers."[91] The committee, which included former Blue Bomber Steve Patrick, MLA, and Bud Sherman, MLA, endorsed Lalonde's stand. It stated that "the people of Manitoba would not be in favour of developments that would see the intrusion of American football in Canada ... lead to the eventual disappearance of Canadian football as we know it to-day."[92] A similar letter came from Steve Juba, Winnipeg's mayor, who offered his "wholehearted support ... the Grey Cup and all it stands for must be preserved." Calgary's mayor, Rod Sykes, telexed: "strongly support your stand in keeping professional football Canadian. Congratulations." Ottawa mayor, Pierre Benoit, writing that he had "not yet had the opportunity to examine the text of the comments attributed" to Lalonde, nonetheless, offered his "whole hearted support for the position I understand" Lalonde had taken. In his view, "there was no greater single contributor to national unity in Canada than Canadian professional football." While Benoit recognized that "better than 50% of the playing and coaching personnel in the CFL are not Canadian citizens ... Canadian citizens from one ocean to another identify with the CFL as something uniquely their own."[93]

Hamilton's mayor Victor Copps, assured Lalonde of "our solid support on your patriotic stand on this important national issue."[94] Regina mayor, Henry Baker "commended and supported Lalonde's stand." He stated that "our present CFL is recognized as a strong professional organization promoting football in Canada. Amateur sports in Canada and our population cannot stand too many professional sports organizations financially."[95] Ivor Dent, mayor of Edmonton, spoke to the point: "I fully support the preservation of the Canadian Football League. I appreciate your attitude and back your statement made in Regina."[96] The president of the Sports Federation of Canada, Bill McEwen, wired his congratulations on Lalonde's stand, as did long-serving member of Parliament, Stanley Knowles, who wrote to support the telegram sent by the Saskatchewan, Manitoba, and Alberta ministers responsible for sport in those provinces. They offered a "plea that the Federal government do everything it can to preserve the viability of the Canadian Football League."[97]

It was an impressive alliance of public figures from all political stripes and colours. To some observers, however, the issue was greater than football. It was private enterprise versus government intervention; the balance between government interference and "market forces." To some extent, Mayor Pierre Benoit attempted to address this concern. Recognizing that a substantial investment had been made by those who owned the Toronto Northmen franchise, he suggested "that their franchise be purchased or if need be, expropriated, and resold for location other than in Canada in order that private citizens be not penalized as a result of belated government intervention and in order to minimize the cost to the Canadian taxpayer of such intervention."[98]

"Belated intervention" was what many opponents, the Bassetts among them, were calling the government stand. They insisted that there was no previous government policy, that they were being penalized by retroactive legislation. The Minister of Health and Welfare took the offensive; he issued a news release package including press clippings, a 1972 statement from the previous minister, John Munro, and a "special note."

The package seemed to answer all the critics. Press clippings were from the Montreal *Gazette*, November 23, 1972; the Toronto *Star*, November 22, 1972; the Montreal *Star*, December 6, 1972; and the Ottawa *Journal*, December 12, 1972. The "special note" was as follows:

The above documentation is clear evidence as to the consistent policy of the government of Canada respecting the question of preserving Canadian football. The policy was first announced by the Honourable John Munro on November 22, 1972. It has been alleged of late that certain principals in the WFL franchise in Toronto were unaware of this previous policy and have been victimized by a decision of the government of Canada after they had made arrangements to acquire a franchise. These documents ... are prepared to give you the facts in this connection.

Munro, in his own separate press release, took issue with the Toronto Northmen Football Team Inc. brief which stated that "even the government does not allege that it had ever enunciated a policy which would prevent the operation of a Canadian team in a U.S. based football league." Further, their brief claimed that "there was no public record of any public policy of the Government of Canada until Mr. Lalonde's speech in Western Canada a few weeks ago."[99] The newspaper clippings clearly demonstrated the government's position, Munro stated.

The media war continued. Dalton Camp, a syndicated columnist as well as a high-profile Conservative, joined the fray. In a provocative article under the headline, "Canada Loves to Lose,"[100] Camp expanded on his views: "We are a nation of losers ... comfortable with second place, far from disconsolate when we finish out of the money, morose about winning." Canadian athletes, he wrote, after winning and being feted at City Hall were in a short time "slowly being disassembled by the population." He proceeded with a litany of Canadian "winners" and the public's response. "The biggest winner in our lifetime, Barbara Ann Scott ... now lives in Obscurity, MD ... Canadian punters gathered at the rail to protest E.P. Taylor's victories by Canadian bred horses." He wrote of almost daily meetings with those who wished "Pierre Berton would write a worst seller." Noting that Canada's most popular hockey player was Eddie Shack, he said that George Chuvalo is "our kind of boxer—nursing a losing streak that is faithful to our national values." He continued: "losing politicians were revered ... and winning ones suspect." People even spoke well of the defunct *Telegram*. Canadian literature was about the "loser syndrome ... the Irish came to Canada as ballast in the holds of lumber boats returning from hunger stricken Ireland; Quebec was abandoned by France; Acadians were driven from the Annapolis valley; Loyalists fled from the United States; most of us arrived here as losers." Warming to his point, Camp zeroed in. "The question before the Nation is whether Canadian football, a national institution permanently enshrined in a distillery, can survive the invasion of an American football team, representing an American football league (pretentiously nonetheless called the World Football League) in beautiful downtown Toronto."

Detailing the conflict between the federal government and the Bassett franchise, Camp's article continued: "confrontation looms. Canadian football awaits its fate. The issue has become larger than Alberta's oil revenues." Perhaps writing in somewhat less of a tongue-in-cheek manner, he suspected that the "Canadian death wish is hard at work." As a strong "market forces" believer, who circulated among others of similar persuasion, he moved to his conclusion: "I meet no one who does not think Lalonde is right, not anyone who does not long for the arrival of the Northmen." He wanted to see the market take its course in a "fierce and forced competition between U.S. and Canadian football here in Canada to see which would lose." He summarized his view:

> Lalonde is on a losing wicket which may ultimately endear him to history. If he is saying that the grand old game of Canadian football cannot withstand the presence of another team of Americans playing with a different ball on a narrow field, then he only confirms what the Canadian citizen suspects—that the game is over. The dilemma is typically Canadian and so will be the denouement.

In some ways the conflict became larger than the issue of football. There was a difference in political approach; Bassett was a Conservative, the government of the day was Liberal. Bassett had a huge media empire under his control; press conferences and media releases became the order of the day—for both sides. Yet another release was issued from Minister Lalonde's office on March 18, 1974. Lalonde sought to remind people that the Department of Health and Welfare had been involved in sport "for a considerable length of time … [with] a budget in the neighborhood of 15 million dollars annually for this purpose." Then, as if to show that the defence of football was not limited to Liberals, he cited former prime minister John Diefenbaker, a Conservative, who wrote in 1961: "The annual Grey Cup Game is a great national event for all Canadians. It stimulates an interest in sports, for it has become symbolic of athletic competitions. It brings East and West together and contributes to the unity of the nation."

Stressing that "the strength of the CFL rests in the interdependence of its teams … the more prosperous teams share their profits with the less well to do teams," Lalonde reiterated the necessity for the Toronto based CFL team, based as it was in the richest market in Canada, to do well since it affected the "viability of the entire league and each team in it." He reviewed the situation: John Bassett, Sr., moved that the CFL expand into the United States at a CFL meeting, November 16, 1972. There were strong reactions.

With reports of that meeting, John Munro, the Minister of Health and Welfare, at that time, stated the government's position, one of opposition to the proposed expansion, labelling it "an erosion of Canadianism." On November 21, Mr. Munro met with Bassett and Gaudaur in Ottawa. He repeated his views. Munro made a public statement to the press on November 22. At the December 1 Executive Committee meeting, John Bassett formally withdrew his motion as a result of his meeting with Munro. On December 5, 1972, Marc Lalonde, as the newly appointed Minister of Health and Welfare, stated that he agreed with his predecessor's policy. A subsequent meeting between Lalonde, Gaudaur, and CFL President Bill Clarke "reaffirmed the government's position." When articles began to appear in the press in the latter part of 1973 about expansion of a new U.S. based league into several Canadian cities, Lalonde reiterated the government's position in Regina on February 21, 1974. As a result, two meetings were held with the Northmen at the request of John Bassett, Jr., on March 2 and 12, 1974. At those sessions, "the WFL group presented their arguments in support of their case."

For each area of reference mentioned by the WFL people, Lalonde counter-punched. True, free enterprise was to be valued, he said, but "even its most vocal proponents would concede that governments must be prepared to intervene on occasion to protect the legitimate interests of all Canadians." Such areas of government influence in the private sector were banking, foreign investment, and broadcasting communications. As far as the NHL and WHA were concerned, there were always a majority of American teams in those leagues. As a result, there were no strictly Canadian institutions jeopardized by the existence of those two leagues. Indeed, Lalonde could have strengthened his case even more by suggesting that those who don't learn from history are condemned to repeat it. Prior to 1924, the "National" Hockey League meant just that: all the teams were Canadian. When the league awarded its first franchise to an American city, Boston, the door was opened to the point where American teams outnumbered the Canadian in the "National" Hockey League. While Lalonde agreed that the Montreal Expos were a member of the U.S. based National Baseball League, he pointed out "that there is not and has never been a national Canadian professional baseball league. He returned to his point that "the CFL is the only completely Canadian controlled professional sports league in Canada and therefore its existence and identity are worth preserving."[101]

With respect to the charge that the CFL was a monopoly, Lalonde stated that the CFL simply did "not have a competitive Canadian league to contend with." He would have no objection to a rival Canadian league being formed. Pointing out that the rival Bassett franchise was really for all of Canada, he suggested that it would "in fact allow the WFL to totally control its own future expansion and competition." The WFL team had argued that their franchise would allow Torontonians to watch more football. Lalonde suggested that there were better ways of satisfying that objective: expand the stadium facilities or grant another CFL franchise in Toronto.[102] He maintained that government policy was to encourage the CFL to expand into other areas, to bring football to more parts of Canada.

To those requesting compensation for the WFL franchise, Lalonde argued that the government's policy had been known in 1972. The WFL came into being and the Toronto franchise was purchased after that pronouncement; good business practice would have been to consult with the government prior to making a financial outlay. In denying financial compensation, Lalonde ventured to suggest that "this group could easily dispose of their assets' obligations and commitments without incurring a financial loss. In fact, I am advised that the group will realize a profit through resale, if they so wished [*sic*]."[103]

Northmen lawyer, Herb Solway, wrote to Prime Minister Trudeau on the matter. He included a letter and a brief which he proposed to send to all members of Parliament. Jake Gaudaur, CFL commissioner, sprang into action. He rebutted all of Solway's points in his missive to the MPs. Solway responded: "The supposed issue of nationalism is a bogus one. Football is no more Canadian culture than literature, poetry, ballet or music." Gaudaur countered with the question, If these art forms are not culture, what is? The CFL, he said, agreed with the government's Task Force on Sport for Canadians, published in 1969, which stated that "a form of culture which involves perhaps 90% of our people is as valid a field for government interest and support as that which involves perhaps 10%, particularly because sport makes a central contribution to our awareness of ourselves."[104]

Referring to the "Munro Doctrine," Gaudaur stated that it was the minister's "assessment that such expansion would change the distinctiveness of the game by causing the elimination of all but three or four Canadian cities from the league and the elimination of the Grey Cup game as one of Canada's greatest annual national events." In Gaudaur's opinion, Munro's assessment was "correct."

The gloves were clearly off. Solway stated that even after the Northmen franchise was announced in August of 1973, there was no outcry from anyone—not until Lalonde's speech in Regina, in February, 1974. He persisted in maintaining that the Northmen were unaware of any government policy in the matter. Gaudaur was direct and to the point, stating that Canadians were being asked to believe that Johnny F. Bassett did not read newspapers or speak with his father. Further, Gaudaur continued, it was as a result of Bassett's motion of November 16, 1972, to expand the CFL into the U.S. that Bassett and Gaudaur were summoned to Ottawa, November 21, to explain to Munro "why the league was contemplating expanding to the United States." It was mentioned that more than 10 United States cities had contacted the league's office wanting to join the CFL. The fear was expressed that if the CFL did not expand into the U.S. a new league would be formed which would expand into Canada." According to Gaudaur, "Mr. Munro advised both Mr. Bassett and the commissioner that it was Government policy to oppose both the expansion into the United States and American Professional football into Canada. He went on to note that the commissioner and Mr. Bassett met separately that same day, after which Bassett agreed to withdraw his motion. Furthermore, Munro was widely quoted in various media, sections of which Gaudaur attached to his brief to the House of Commons.

Solway brought up the contentious issue of equalization payments. He noted that there was concern about the Argonauts' contribution, fear that it might be decreased because of competition from the Northmen. The Northmen offered to guarantee that the Argonaut payments to the equalization fund would remain at 1973 levels for at least the next 10 years.

Gaudaur set out to dismantle what on the surface appeared to be a conciliatory gesture on the part of the Northmen. He mentioned that the Northmen's notion of the equalization payment was based on a figure of approximately $48,000. Then he proceeded to cast light on the real contribution of the Argonauts. The actual figure for 1973 was $50,602, the lowest amount since 1968. Over the past six years, the average Argonaut pay-in had been $55,2300. When the free-enterpriser John Bassett bought the Argos, he did so on the condition that the Argonauts' ceiling on such payments would be limited to $60,000 per year instead of the $75,000 which applied to other clubs. The new owner, Bill Hodgson, had approved of the $75,000 figure. Gaudaur did not stop there. He listed the Argonauts' financial contribution to all forms of equalization for 1973: pre-season gate, $19,690; regular season gate, $50,601; Eastern Conference play-off, $97,000; television, $153,000; and direct contribution to amateur football, $22,000. This was in the Toronto area and over and above their share of the CFL annual grant of $50,000 to the CAFA. Gaudaur summarized that the Northmen guarantee "in order to be meaningful, would have to be more in the area of $300,000, including the guarantees to amateur football in Toronto."[105]

To Solway's offer that the Northmen were willing to turn over the territorial rights for franchises in the WFL to the CFL, thus preventing expansion of the WFL to any other city, Gaudaur poured cold water on the idea. He cited reports that Vancouver's Jim Pattison, himself seeking a WFL franchise, had stated that the Northmen did not have Canadian rights. Further, even if they did, would new owners, if the Northmen were sold, take the same position as the one Solway proposed? And, Gaudaur noted, there still would be no guarantee that another American league, "the NFL, for example, would follow suit and establish a franchise in Canada."[106]

The Northmen knew of the CFL's dependence upon a television contract to assure the league's viability and, to that end, assured the House of Commons that only a local television contract would be negotiated. Gaudaur wondered if the Northmen could speak for the league. Further, he asked, what would happen if the ownership changed? He suggested that the WFL would follow the same course as the NFL and "simply permit a pickup of their U.S. telecast for national network exhibition in Canada."[107]

Turning to players, the Northmen indicated they would urge the other members of the WFL to refrain from signing CFL players under the same arrangement as that which existed between the NFL and the CFL. At the moment, the Northmen said, "fully 70% to 80% of the present name players" in the CFL would not be playing in that league next year unless the Northmen were allowed to stay in Canada. In that case, they would use their influence with the other WFL teams to keep away from CFL players.

Gaudaur saw this as a form of blackmail. He was quite confident that the CFL contracts would stand up in court as they had in 1960 when Joe Kapp was signed by the AFL while still under contract to the B.C. Lions. Gaudaur hoped that MPs would see through this "naked threat" which might "destroy the CFL if the Parliament of Canada voted in a manner which would preclude the establishment of an American based football team in Canada."[108]

The Northmen offered to play an All Star game between the CFL and the WFL. It would generate income through American and Canadian television. The idea was quickly dismissed by Gaudaur. The CFL players already had their own All Star game, the revenue from which went to the players' pension fund. Gaudaur suggested that the Northmen go back and consult their own players.

While the Northmen concluded in their brief to the members of Parliament that there was "clearly no requirement to introduce legislation," Gaudaur thought otherwise: "their representation indicates quite clearly that there is such a need."[109] He further suggested that the CFL's annual contribution to amateur football was much more than the annual $50,000 grant, more like $150,000 to $200,000 because of direct contributions by various clubs. He asked the members of Parliament to contact the CAFA "to ascertain what impact there might be on amateur football in Canada if there was no CFL to which their players would graduate as professionals. Would the WFL guarantee an equivalent amount to amateur football in Canada?" His opposition was not against the Northmen per se, Gaudaur intoned, it was designed to preserve Canadian football. If the Northmen simply divided fan interest in Toronto to a point where Argonaut attendance dropped off to an average of 24,000 per game, the whole league would suffer from the loss of equalization revenue. That might force the league to reconsider expanding to the United States.

Noting that some MPs may prefer the internationalization of sport, as in the NHL, the CFL advanced another concept, suggesting that there be an opportunity for a professional football team

> in Regina to compete against a team from Toronto, and which each year envelops eastern and western Canada in a healthy competition leading to the Grey Cup game, clearly one of Canada's most important national annual events, which in one way or another, appears to embrace the entire nation.[110]

Gaudaur suggested that if the Argonauts were to compete with the Northmen and win the Toronto fans' support, the Northmen would lose only money. If the contrary were so, the Canadian clubs would lose much more; they would lose a hundred years of Canadian sporting tradition. He finished by quoting Canadian prime ministers John Diefenbaker and Lester Pearson. Both endorsed the concept of East/West rivalry and the contribution of the Grey Cup Game to national unity. Pearson's message, written for the 1964 Grey Cup Game, summed up the feeling:

> And each year it becomes more obvious that in the annual classic, Canada exhibits not only a superb athletic contest but more and more, a genuine National symbol, a force for unity and understanding locking east and west in vigorous, healthy competition.[111]

Marc Lalonde prepared legislation designed to keep the Northmen out. Bill C-22, An Act Respecting Canadian Football, was to receive its first reading April 10, 1974. Known by its short title, the Canadian Football Act was perhaps more than the CFL wanted. The Liberal Bill proposed that after December 1, 1974, roster limits of imports could not exceed 15 or 40% of the total number. Up until December 31, 1974, the limit was to be 15 imports or 45% of the total, whichever was the lesser. In addition, the CFL would be barred from expanding outside the country and foreign-based players would be banned from playing league games in Canada. Similarly, CFL teams could only play exhibition games outside the country. If it appeared that a contravention of these restrictions was about to take place, the Attorney General could apply for an injunction lasting 15 days. Refusal to comply with the injunction could result in a fine or imprisonment of up to two years.

If there were any doubts about Marc Lalonde's resolve before, there were none now. The support of the New Democratic Party (NDP) guaranteed passage of the Bill by the Liberal minority government. The Toronto Northmen, seeing the writing on the wall, made plans to move to the United States. Speculation as to the final destination, which turned out to be Memphis, was a wide topic of discussion. They were sure only of being known as the Southmen. They had lost their gamble. The Toronto *Star* editorialized: "Bassett Has No Kiick Coming."

> There's Warfield, there's Csonka and Kiick,
> One's tricky, one's powerful, one's quick,
> Paul Warfield plucks passes from out of the air,
> Big Csonka leaves tackles in broken despair,
> While Kiick gives them moves like a terrified hare;
> Oh, gee, but the Northmen would look mighty slick,
> With Warfield and Csonka, with Warfield and Csonka,
> With Warfield and Csonka and Kiick.
> But even with Warfield, with Csonka and Kiick,
> Lalonde is determined the Northmen won't stick,
> "Warfield's a flanker perhaps without peer,
> Csonka's well worth it, though frightfully dear,
> And Kiick sure can run but he'll run south of here,"—
> At which Johnny Bassett is quietly sick,
> With Warfield and Csonka, with Warfield and Csonka,
> With Warfield and Csonka and Kiick.
>   Imagine paying three million bucks for three players to play in some place like Charlotte, North Carolina. Whew! It wasn't for nothing that it was suggested that the Liberal slogan in the last election was wrong and that it should have read Lalonde is strong.[112]

In preparation for the second reading of the Bill, Lalonde's office issued a press release of the speech he would deliver to the Commons. He had hoped, he said, that such a Bill would not be necessary, that the WFL promoters would reconsider their move into Canada. Failing that, it was necessary to deal with the immediate and "similar threats in the future."[113] Summarizing the events which led up to the government's introduction of the Bill, Lalonde maintained the importance of the legislation. He invited the rest of Parliament, particularly the Conservatives, to join in its speedy passage. "The only other recent sport issue that has aroused as much public interest and heated debate," he said, "was probably the Team Canada hockey series against the USSR."[114]

Meanwhile, the CFL offices were reacting to the Bill. If it were passed, and the total roster remained at 32, the breakdown for 1974 would be 18 non-imports and 14 imports, a transfer of one player from the import to non-import status. The league did have the option of increasing the roster to 33 which would keep the import number at 15 and the non-import number at 18. The 1975 season represented more of a problem. With the government regulation dictating that the roster be 60% Canadian content, much like radio and television programming regulations, a roster of 32 meant 19 non-imports and 13 imports. To keep the import number at 15 meant that the league would have to move to as high as 22 non-imports.[115]

The CFL's release also addressed the federal government's concern about the blackout of games in the Toronto market. The Argonauts had been selling out their games regularly. It was because football fans had been deprived of seeing the Argonauts play at home by virtue of limited ticket availability and blackouts that moves were made to bring another franchise to Toronto. As a result, the federal government was proposing that Argonaut blackouts be lifted if the game was sold out 48 hours in advance. "As a result, the Toronto Club has agreed to apply to the other CFL clubs to have the right to experiment from the beginning of the regular season in 1974 by lifting the blackout if the game is sold out 48 hours in advance of playing the game."[116] The league was clearly on the defensive and yet, because of the government's intervention on its behalf, there was the perception, shared by many, that it had a debt to pay. "Here again," the league stated, "we would have preferred not to change the current blackout situation because we feel it could have an adverse effect not only on the season ticket sales and attendances but also radio revenue in future years. However, we could be wrong …"[117]

Bill C-22 never became law. The minority Liberal government was defeated on a profiteering issue when the NDP withdrew its support. An election was called; Bill C-22 died on the Order Table. Too late for the Northmen who, once the process towards passage of the Bill had been initiated, moved to Memphis. The Liberals won the election of 1974, returning with a majority. Football was deemed to have played a role in the election. One of the most damaging items of the campaign, as far as the Conservatives were concerned, was a photograph of Conservative Leader Robert Stanfield fumbling a football. Perhaps all the publicity from the sure handed way in which the Liberals had handled the WFL controversy contrasted with that Conservative *faux pas*. In any event, the Liberals won 141 seats. The Northmen issue receded into the background, to surface only occasionally when the commitment of the league to pay off its "debt" was questioned.

When the general managers of the CFL met April 30, 1974, it soon became obvious that there was a split among them. Some felt that Lalonde had gone too far in intervening into the league's matters. When Ralph Sazio "asked whether there would be some merit in announcing that this meeting is recommending an increase in the roster to 33 by adding one non-import ... [to] lend support to Mr. Lalonde and his implementation of the Canadian Football Act," B.C.'s general manager, Jackie Parker, "replied that the B.C. club had not taken a public stand on the matter and he was not certain whether he could support such a resolution. He would agree to the roster increase without the fanfare." [118] During the previous year, the Players' Association had suggested an increase of one non-import; the Eskimos had proposed two. Both had been defeated at the time. Winnipeg's general manager, Earl Lunsford, announced his intention to move an increase of one at the league's semi-annual meeting.

As for the pressure placed upon the league to expand, the CFL looked again at the application from Londoner Bob Harris. League secretary, Greg Fulton, had been asked to develop a financial rationale for the cost of an expansion franchise "over a three year period as a result of admission of a tenth team to the League as a full participating member."[119] He recommended:

(a)	to indemnify nine clubs for three years losses under gate equalization	$81,000
(b)	to indemnify nine clubs for three years anticipated drawings from the pre-season pool	$30,000
(c)	to indemnify nine clubs from three years losses in TV revenues	$450,000
(d)	to indemnify four eastern clubs for three years losses in play-off revenues	$160,000
(e)	to indemnify four eastern football clubs for three years losses in Grey Cup revenues	$180,000
(f)	to acquire the right to draft four players from each of the other nine clubs, to acquire exclusive franchise rights including radio rights in the home area, territorial rights, college draft rights, negotiating list rights, etc.	$720,000
	Total:	$1,621,000.[120]

In preparing these figures, it was assumed that a team based in London "would draw the same net gate as the Ottawa club. The television revenues would increase annually by 10% and the parity plateau would be reached in the first year." It was Edmonton's Norm Kimball who proposed that Hamilton should be compensated to the tune of $400,000 "for infringement of its franchise area." Ralph Sazio suggested that the proposed franchise only be told that the fee was $2,000,000 for the 36 players rather than the breakdown of that figure. Kimball moved, seconded by Parker, that the CFL executive committee "approval in principle be given to the application for a franchise in London, Ontario, upon payment of a franchise fee of $2,000,000."[121] By the time the London group was informed of the price in Edmonton at the May 30 meeting, however, the price quoted was $2.7 million.[122] It could have been higher. David Loeb, speaking on behalf of the Eastern Conference, said that his group had met and "agreed unanimously that the London team could be admitted for a total consideration of $3.7 million." The price was made up of the following: the London group would not participate in gate equalization, television and Grey Cup revenues for three years, a value estimated at $1.2 million, and would make an immediate payment of $2.5 million in cash—$400,000 to Hamilton for infringement of territory, $200,000 to the Western Conference for the 20 players drafted, $1,900,000 to the Eastern Conference for the 16 players drafted "plus compensation for damages to the existing structure of the EFC."[123] Members of both conferences adjourned to consider the figure and half an hour later, when they returned, Loeb said that the EFC had reconsidered. They would admit London for a fee of $2.7 million, distributed as follows: $400,000 to Hamilton for territorial idemnification, $500,000 to be divided equally among the WFC clubs and $1,800,000 equally among the EFC teams.[124]

A plan for stocking the new franchise was outlined by Gaudaur. Each team was to provide a complete roster of all those it had under contract, whether "'on the injured players' list, retired list and league suspension list." From that, each club was allowed to protect 18 players, 10 imports and 8 non-imports, including one quarterback. The new club would choose 2 imports and 2 non-imports from each club's unprotected list to a total of 36 players, not more than two of whom were to be quarterbacks. They would be "selected from different clubs with an overall distribution of 18 imports and 18 non-imports." Territorial rights among the eastern clubs were still to be worked out.[125]

It didn't take the London group long to respond. League President Jim Hole, Ralph Sazio, and Commissioner Jake Gaudaur met with the Bob Harris group to inform them of the league's deliberations. "After a short period of consideration, the London group withdrew its application stating that the franchise fee was beyond its capacity to pay ... it objected to the price."[126]

Gaudaur "anticipated some public reaction in this regard." It was an understatement. Indeed, there was strong reaction; none more so than from Marc Lalonde. He "let it be known that he's fed up with the CFL's two-faced approach in so many areas. And he remained silent when London, Ontario interests vowed to acquire a WFL franchise." Indeed, when the rebuffed Bob Harris and his group announced that a WFL game would be played in London's J.W. Little Memorial Stadium on September 2, there was no reaction or statement from Lalonde. It was reported that he had been "double crossed regularly since going to bat for the league."[127]

The Health and Welfare Minister had fought to save the Canadian identity of the CFL but it appeared that the league was not as "dedicated to nationalism and patriotism as Lalonde was led to believe." If it were, it would have launched a program to make itself more Canadian instead of less and less Canadian."[128]

It was also a controversial year with respect to players' relations. The players in the league were unhappy with the CFL. It had approved, in 1973, a 16-game schedule for the Eastern Conference to begin in 1974. While there was some initial publicity about the move, it was quietly ignored as the season began and continued. Players continued to sign their contracts on a per-season basis, many of them unaware of the two extra games to be added. It seemed like a grab for money by the league at the players' expense.

Tony Gabriel, a tight end with Hamilton,[129] was one player who was disturbed by the CFL decision, so much so that he took his club to court. Gabriel, who happened to be the son-in-law of CFL commissioner Jake Gaudaur, was a Canadian who had been an outstanding performer at Syracuse University before joining the Tiger-Cats in 1971. He was a key performer in the 1972 Grey Cup Game, being on the receiving end of some key Chuck Ealey passes in the dying moments of the game which culminated with Ian Sunter's dramatic winning field goal giving Hamilton its 13–10 win over Saskatchewan. Gabriel was playing out his option during the 1972 season.

When he graduated from Syracuse in 1971, Gabriel had not been drafted by the NFL. Nonetheless, he was approached by a number of their teams, including the New York Giants through their representative, Jim Trimble, to sign as a "free agent." Trimble was a former successful coach with the Hamilton and Montreal teams in the CFL. He offered Gabriel a signing bonus of $1,000, a further $15,000 if he made the 47-player roster, and an additional $5,000 if he was on the 40-man playing roster. Gabriel was also in the Hamilton protected territory; his rights in the CFL belonged to them. He had lived in Burlington, grew up following the team, and had an emotional attachment to them. He decided to sign with them. His contract for 1971 was an $1,800 signing bonus and a contract of $8,400 for the season of 14 games. In 1972, Hamilton offered him a basic contract of $9,000 plus an additional $150 for each game he started at tight end, an extra $2,100 for the 14-game schedule. The Tiger-Cats also presented him with an alternative two-year contract: $9,500 plus a higher per-game bonus. The young Gabriel couldn't make up his mind. Ralph Sazio suggested that the player sign two blank contracts with no figures typed in. When Gabriel made up his mind, he could phone the office, tell them the appropriate figures and they would be typed in. Gabriel and Sazio shook hands and parted. In July as the season began, Gabriel went back to Sazio's office feeling uneasy about having two blank contracts with his signature in the Tiger-Cats' possession. The contracts were torn up. He did not sign a contract for the 1972 season, in effect playing out his option at 90% of his 1971 contract. With the end of the 1972 season, negotiations continued not only for the 1973 season but for the 1972 season as well. Gabriel described part of the negotiation:

> After the Grey Cup game of that year, Sazio mailed me my share of the proceeds and stuck in a little note asking me to see him early in the new year to again discuss contract. I called and we had lunch at a restaurant near his office ... "Well, what do *you* think you're worth?" finally, I threw out the only figure I had thought about: $16,000. "Sixteen thousand dollars!" Ralph almost bellowed the words. "Sixteen thousand! Do you realize you're asking almost one hundred per cent more than you were making last year?" By this time, every head in the restaurant had turned in our direction. I was intimidated—and the thought crossed my mind maybe that was Ralph's point when he raised his voice.

In 1972, Gabriel's option year, he was paid $7,560. When he did sign with the Tiger-Cats, April 2, 1973, a retroactive contract for 1972 was signed for $14,000. It meant an additional $6,500 plus bonuses of $2,000 for making the EFC and All Canadian All Star teams, something the Tiger-Cats were not obligated to pay. For 1973, the basic contract was $16,000; for 1974, $18,000. He also had the possibility of earning another $5,000 in bonuses: $2,000 as the EFC Schenley Award nominee as the Best Canadian, $2,000 for selection to the All Canadian All Stars, and $1,000 for selection to the EFC All Stars.

The CFL Players' Association raised the issue of the increased schedule in early 1974. The league and the association were to look at individual claims placing players into three categories: those who signed prior to February, 1973, those who signed after, and those who were playing out their options in 1974—would they receive 90% of the 14 games or 16? In the meantime, an angry group of 10 Hamilton players, including Gabriel, took matters into their own hands. They hired a lawyer and initiated court action. Tiger-Cat quarterback, Chuck Ealey, had some foresight. When he signed his contract in 1972, he added "fourteen in number" to the clause "all scheduled games." Still, he supported his team-mates. A "hotter than a two buck pistol" Ralph Sazio took the players' suit as a personal affront. Chuck Ealey was later traded to Winnipeg for Don Jonas.

Meanwhile, the league and its Players' Association could arrive at no compromise and the beginning of the 1974 year was approaching. Throughout the CFL, veterans from each team submitted their intention to retire. According to the contract between the league and the association, anyone retiring prior to June 15 could rescind his retirement and play that same season. The players held their own training camps. Only rookies attended the clubs' workouts, but in Hamilton militant veterans set up a picket line to prevent the first-year players from attending the official workouts. Eventually, the pressure tactic worked. Faced with the loss of the season because of the short amount of time, the league and the association signed a new three-year contract. The issue of payment for the two extra games was to be submitted to binding arbitration according to the three categories previously mentioned.

Gabriel volunteered his particular circumstances as a test case. The case, which was not heard until March, 1975, centred on two recollections: Gabriel said that at no time during salary negotiations did Sazio mention that the Eastern Conference was moving to a 16-game schedule rather than the 14; Sazio's written statement said that he surely must have told Gabriel. Five weeks later, the judge ruled in favour of the Tiger-Cats and Sazio. According to Gabriel, however, "in 1976, Ralph was quoted in a *Quest* magazine article saying he had *not* told Tony Gabriel of the increase in the number of games because Gabriel would have asked for more money."

On the field, Gabriel was in the forefront of a transformation taking place. His position of tight end was undergoing a change. Teams used a tight end as much for his blocking abilities as for his pass catching. Occasionally, the ends shuffled laterally along the line of scrimmage to get a freer release from the line of scrimmage where a defensive end or linebacker was trying to hinder them. The tactic loosened up the defence and, in the process, lessened the need for a blocking type of end and de-emphasized the running game. The result was the birth of the "slot-back," a player who was positioned in a spot some five yards away from the tackle. He would line up there rather than "motion" to it prior to the snap of the ball. Players such as Tony Gabriel, Peter Dalla Riva of Montreal, and later Nick Arakgi and Rocky DiPietro were being phased out of the tight end position as the league evolved to a slot-back style of play.

The 1974 All Star game drew 15,102, almost ten thousand less than the game in Hamilton in 1973. Played in Ottawa, the hometown Rough Riders defeated the All Stars by a 25–22 score. Ottawa, however, was unable to repeat as champions under new coach George Brancato. He had replaced Jack Gotta who moved to the new WFL. The second-place Rough Riders defeated Hamilton in the Eastern semifinal by a 21–19 score and lost 14–4 to Montreal in the final. In the West, second-place Saskatchewan defeated third-place British Columbia 24–14 before losing to Edmonton in the Western championship game by a 31–27 score.

In Toronto there was the unusual occurrence of a team owner firing a coach "on the spot." In the eighth game of the season, the Argos were playing at home and losing 14–0 to the Alouettes. In the fourth quarter, the Argos moved the ball to the Montreal five-yard line. Two passes by quarterback Mike Rae were incomplete. Argonaut coach John Rauch sent in sparsely used half-back Ernie Carnegie with a play, a half-back option pass with Carnegie to do the throwing. The pass was intercepted. The Argos lost and at the end of the game, Bill Hodgson, the Argo owner, went immediately to the team's dressing room where he fired John Rauch. Interim coach Joe Moss finished the year and was replaced one week after the season ended with quarterbacking legend Russ Jackson.

The CFL also handed out its players awards for the year. Tom Wilkinson of Edmonton was selected over Johnny Rodgers of Montreal as the Most Outstanding Player; Sam Cvijanovich of Toronto was named the Outstanding Rookie over Winnipeg's Tom Scott; the Most Outstanding Canadian was awarded to Tony Gabriel who was selected over Rudy Linterman of Calgary; the most Outstanding Defensive Player went to Calgary's John Helton over Ottawa's Wayne Smith; the top Defensive Lineman Award went to Montreal's Ed George over B.C.'s Curtis Webster.

In the 1974 Grey Cup Game, played at Empire Stadium, 34,450 spectators saw the Marv Levy coached Montreal Alouettes defeat the Ray Jauch coached Edmonton Eskimos by a score of 20–7. Don Sweet kicked four field goals for the victorious eastern team. The game, played in poor weather, was a sell-out yet generated some $50,000 less than the previous year; Empire Stadium had a smaller capacity than the CNE, the site of the

1973 game. The gross gate was down by 424,436; Canadian television revenue was up by $20,000, American TV generated $24,750 less. Even with 2,000 fewer seats at Empire Stadium, the net gate revenue was up by $42,149 after park rental and taxes; there was no seat tax in B.C. Film revenue was also down by $32,000 from the 1973 game.[130] It had been a difficult time for the Alouettes. Their owner, Sam Berger, had sided with Bassett; their park, the Autostade, had only ten to eleven thousand seats between the goal lines; the park had been described as having poor lighting, not enough exits, and impossible to police. In the midst of all this, there was a hostile press calling for an NFL franchise.[131] Berger had notified the league that he wanted to sell his franchise.

It had been a tumultuous year!

1975 to 1976

Chapter Four

THE AFTERMATH OF 1974 with its players' strike, government intervention, the expansion controversy, the Montreal situation, and the designated import rule with its effect on the Canadian quarterback, continued to play a role in 1975. In Hamilton, Ralph Sazio began to revamp the Tiger-Cats. Jerry Williams was replaced by Bob Shaw. The "Terrible Ten" players who had challenged Sazio in the courts, were dispersed throughout the league. Among them, Gerry Kuzyk and Tony Gabriel were traded to Ottawa; Al Brenner, Chuck Ealey and Bruce Smith went to Winnipeg; Larry Brame was off to British Columbia; and George Wells and Bob Richardson were shipped to Saskatchewan.[1]

Meanwhile, the president of the Players' Association, George Reed, seeking league approval, sent a letter "dated February 14, 1975, that the 1975 All-Star game be played in Edmonton on either June 23rd or June 24th."[2] Edmonton was the city that had lost the Grey Cup Game to Montreal and by rights, that is, by the agreement of June 28th, 1974, signed by the players and the CFL, the game belonged in the winning Grey Cup team's city. After all, the rationale behind the competition was that the winning Grey Cup squad would compete with the league's All Star players. Reed was basing his request on the 1971 experience where, despite good promotion, interest in the game lagged, attendance was low, and the association took a loss. As well, the 1974 game in Ottawa resulted in a loss. "The Association [had] still not settled all of its accounts."[3]

Sazio, as the incoming league president, making him even more of a dominant figure, objected. He wanted to keep to the terms of the contract with the Players' Association as part of the settlement package which ended the strike. Not only that, he expressed the opinion that it would be an insult to the fans of Montreal to move the game. Did the association want the

Montreal team to travel to Edmonton to play the game? he wondered. As far as Edmonton was concerned, Norm Kimball was not too enthused with the idea. They had pre-season home games on two successive weeks; a third one would be a strain. He, too, was opposed to going against the established format but he left the door open by saying that Edmonton would go along with the league's decision. Reed's request was denied. The Players' Association was "granted approval to stage the 1975 All Star game in Montreal in accordance with the established All Star game format forming part of the agreement of June 28, 1974 on a mutually acceptable date which must not be later than Wednesday, June 25."[4] Sam Berger, owner of the Alouettes, was originally opposed to the All Star game being played in Montreal, "not wishing to be burdened with an extra game,"[5] but relented and was "now prepared to act as host for the game."[6]

Plans for the game were put into motion. Thirty-six players were to be allowed on each team; Ray Jauch was to coach the All Stars, Marv Levy the Alouettes. The Quebec Society for Crippled Children was to be the main charity beneficiary. Players were to be introduced to the public at a downtown shopping mall, followed by visits to a children's hospital. A golf tournament and a dinner followed by the third annual Players' Association Awards were also announced.

The game did not take place; it was cancelled. Less than one week before its June 24th playing date, only two thousand tickets had been sold, even though many were being offered at three dollars. There was the fear that the association would lose as much as $40,000 were they to play it, and their pension fund couldn't afford that. It appeared that the players had done all they could. They had not wanted to play in Montreal in the first place but the league left them no alternative, they said. George Dixon, the great Montreal running back of the sixties, had been selected as the game's chairman. Neither CBC nor CTV was interested in televising the contest.

Emotionally, the association members still wanted to play the game but business practicalities won out. The reaction was bitter in some quarters; fingers were pointed. Having Montreal as the site was called a "dumb move to begin with."[7] Ottawa's Frank Clair, speaking as a general manager, responded: "How can you win? If we had taken the game out of Montreal, they would have been screaming their heads off ... We'd have been criticized for taking the game out of Montreal when they are trying to build interest down there."[8] And there was condemnation for Montrealers who, it was said, preferred to spend three dollars, the reduced price of the game, "at the tavern with a couple of tall frosties and scholarly exchange with the boys on world affairs. They didn't even support the Second World War." The game that didn't go on would be known as "Le Grand Plouf (the big flop), a warning bell, a great flashing sign that football is dead, dead, dead."[9]

Others put on a braver front. Sam Berger, who insisted that he did not want the game in the first place, stated that football in Montreal was not dead, that season ticket sales were up to 10,000 from the 6,000–6,400 sold in 1974. He claimed that he could see a change in attitude among Montreal people that "yes, maybe it's time to go back to football." Berger was convinced that credibility had been re-established, the corner had been turned. His hopes were to reach an attendance of 22,00–25,000, his "break-even point."[10] George Reed, while disappointed, was not embittered. The association simply could not afford another loss such as the $24,000 in 1974. He blamed the cancellation "on the normal fight here for the entertainment dollar."[11] The St Jean Baptiste Day, a provincial holiday, the Expos' afternoon baseball game, Blue Bonnets' Raceway, and the Montreal Quebecois lacrosse game were all competitive attractions. After the fallout settled, the Players' Association proposed a new format. The Western All Stars would play the Eastern All Stars in Edmonton, May 29, 1976. The CFL accepted the proposal.[12]

The aftermath of the government intervention of 1974 and its implication continued to rear its head in a variety of ways. When the CAFA requested an increase in the CFL grant from $50,000 to $90,000 so as to implement a proposed seven-year master plan, the commissioner recalled that the previous Minister of Health and Welfare, John Munro, "had stated publicly that any participation by the government would be contingent upon the league not decreasing its own participation."[13] His suggestion was to arrange a meeting with Lalonde. The feeling was that while the CFL had no such discretionary funds, nonetheless, the proposal was well thought out and called for an intelligent response with a view to arriving at alternatives. Norm Kimball, in addressing that position, said that he saw the CAFA operation as one which developed "not only the players but officials and fans."[14]

Meanwhile, expansion was still a priority, with the league deciding "to try and search out, be proactive rather than reactive." Incoming league president, Ralph Sazio, commissioner Jake Gaudaur, Lew Hayman, and a Western conference representative were to form an expansion committee "to consider all aspects of expansion to such cities as Halifax, Sudbury and Windsor, including the estimate of a franchise fee and the economic impact on the league in each case."[15] The CFL move to London, rebuffed by Bob Harris, who with 10 other Canadians purchased the Portland Storm of the WFL, was reconsidered. CFL officials met with Ralph Duffus of London with a view to establishing a franchise in that southwestern Ontario city.

Gaudaur's meeting with Duffus confirmed that the primary reasons inhibiting London from entering the CFL now were the "upfront money cost of acquiring a franchise and the financing of an adequate stadium."[16] Duffus, who was not prepared to name the "prominent persons from the London area" who were to be the principal backers, was pushing for a franchise fee close to one million dollars. In return, he would be willing to waive, for a two-year period, participation in the league's gate equalization plan. Since there was no desire on the part of the London team to commence operations prior to 1977, it "would mean that the present clubs would not be required to share revenues before 1979 at the earliest."[17] The league and the London group seemed to be going in circles, however. The CFL wanted to have a stadium or plans for one confirmed prior to the expansion being committed; the London group said that a stadium was contingent upon the franchise being awarded.[18]

If the league was perceived to be moribund in some areas, it was thriving in others. Hap Shouldice, chief of officials described the 1975 meeting of the CFL Rules Committee in Washington as "the most progressive rules meeting we've ever had."[19] Of 36 proposals made by various league members, 16 were approved. Perhaps the major change was in the area of punt returns. For the first time, the CFL was going to allow unlimited blocking by every player on all punts and missed field goals. All contact was required to be above the waist. The five-yard restraining area would remain in effect, as would the right of the kicker and anyone onside to recover the ball. A proposal by Edmonton to allow a "fair catch" did not receive a seconder.[20] It was also decided that a team being scored upon by a single point would scrimmage the ball on the 35-yard line rather than the 25-yard line. The resultant better field position would help the scored-upon team, something which must have been on others' minds. It was also proposed that a team behind by at least seven points be given the option of kicking off or receiving after a touchdown was scored, but there was no seconder to this motion either.

The CFL also adopted the two-point conversion in 1975 in spite of the fact that a convert could then become equal to one-third of a touchdown.[21] In effect, two changes were necessary. The ball was to be spotted on the five-yard rather than the ten-yard line. From there, a team would have the option of kicking a placement through the uprights for a single point or advancing the ball over the goal-line by run or pass for two. The league also refined a rule which had been passed in 1974, prior to the season, but rescinded in mid-season, August 19. The rule in question had called for a time stop with each change of possession. It would start again with the snap of the ball rather than the official's whistle. Some 15 minutes had been added to the length of the game "creating problems affecting radio and television schedules, travel arrangements for the visiting teams and miscellaneous matters for the spectators."[22] In 1975 it was instituted only for the last three minutes of each half. It was also decided that following a field goal the team scored upon was to have three options. It could kick off or scrimmage from its own 35-yard line or have the scoring team do the kicking off from its 35-yard line. The last option was the new one to be included for the 1975 season. Yet another rule change attempted to remove unnecessary roughness from the game by awarding an automatic first down to the offended team in addition to a 15-yard penalty. Previously, only the latter had been the case but the situation could arise where a team could be granted the fifteen yards and still not have enough yardage for the first down; the offending team would have been granted a freer licence to commit an act of unnecessary roughness. This rule change sought to close that loophole.

At meetings such as these there was the constant dynamic of developing the game as an expression of the Canadian experience and at the same time of being aware of developments in the United States both at the college and NFL levels. Many of the general managers were of American origin, as were almost all the coaches. Yet some of the GMs had been in Canada for a long time, and they were just as apt to ensure that rules would be adopted for the right reasons rather than simply because they corresponded with NFL practices. A case in point was the matter of 11-man football. The concept had surfaced at various times in the past and it did so again in Washington at the Rules Committee meeting on January 7, 1975. There, John Barrow, the general manager of the Argonauts, proposed that a team have 11 rather than 12 players. Six would be on the line of scrimmage, rather than seven, and there would be four eligible receivers. He was supported by Ralph Sazio who felt that with one less player on the line, the game would be more wide open and a greater spectacle for the fans. Winnipeg's general manager, Earl Lunsford, was having none of it. Lunsford, who was a former American, as were Barrow and Sazio, said that coaches would simply revert to a U.S. style of play with the net result that two non-imports would lose their status as starting players.[23] It was not implemented.

Try as they might to remove judgement from situations, there were still some areas where officials had to use discretion. The CFL did not want to move to the CIAU rule that stopped play when a player's knee touched the ground. Yet, it wanted to protect the ball carrier. It stated that the officials would have the leeway of declaring the ball dead "when a player is down and in possession of the ball, indicating that he has no intention of getting up."[24] The officials were also being told to enforce the rule prohibiting a quarterback from deliberately drawing a team offside. It was aimed at Edmonton's Tom Wilkinson, yet officials were at a loss to describe how the rule was being broken when the opposition went offside, and invariably complained the offense caused them to do so.

The CFL decided to continue one experiment and not begin another. One idea, which received only scant attention, was that of metric football. With the country moving to the metric system, some felt that the time was ripe to incorporate it into the CFL. The 110-yard field translated almost exactly into 100 metres. Some even were suggesting that four downs could be used to make the 10 metres. In the end, however, partly because of tradition and partly because the clubs did not own the parks, the change was not pursued. The other initiative did continue. For the second successive year, the CIAU was awarded a $4,000 fee to provide information on its graduating players. Each school was to submit a list of its appropriate players complete with relevant physical data, height, weight, 40-yard speed, and the like. The money was a nominal sum and a means of putting all clubs on an equal footing regarding information about prospective players. Some clubs, such as Edmonton with Frank Morris and Toronto with Jim Copeland and Greg Barton, chose to rely on their own information in addition to the CIAU data.

In Ottawa there was an uproar surrounding another quarterback's arrival in that city. Bill Robinson was a Toronto native who had played his university football at St Mary's University in Halifax where he led that school to a Vanier Cup title in 1973. After being drafted by Ottawa and attending their training camp in 1974, he was released and decided to enrol at the University of Western Ontario to complete his degree. He quarterbacked them to a Vanier Cup victory, his second consecutive one. He was also named to the All Canadian team as a quarterback. Ottawa took advantage of a league rule which allowed them to declare the formerly drafted Robinson as their "property" and Robinson returned to the Rough Riders once again to compete for the quarterback position.

The situation looked made to order. The Riders were searching for a quarterback. Rick Cassata had played out his option. He had been publicly maligned by owner David Loeb during the 1974 Grey Cup week. Loeb was reported to have said that if Cassata returned to Ottawa in 1975, he would not be interested in going to any games, nor could he blame people who wouldn't pay to come and see the Riders with Cassata as quarterback.[25] Loeb's harsh public dismissal was considered to be unfair and insensitive to a player who had done his best and just the previous year had led the team to the Grey Cup. However, Lansdowne Park was being expanded by some

8,000 seats. They had to be filled. The park rent had increased, ticket prices were being raised; the club needed some new box-office appeal.

The quarterback hunt was on. Two All American players were signed: Tom Clements from Notre Dame and Condredge Holloway from the University of Tennessee. Each had good credentials. Clements had led Notre Dame to victory over Alabama in the Sugar Bowl; Holloway was a star performer in the Hula Bowl. Each had the attributes suited to the Canadian game. They were mobile, could pass, were leaders, and had recognized quarterbacking skills. Both had been overlooked by the NFL draft. By that league's standard, they were undersized. NFL teams were always looking for the "classic" drop back quarterback who was a minimum 6'3" tall. Holloway, generously listed at 5'11", was selected by the New England Patriots in the twelfth round as a defensive back; Clements, shorter still, was not drafted. Veteran quarterback Jerry Keeling was still with the Rough Riders but Ottawa would keep him for the training camp and later trade him to the Tiger-Cats prior to those two teams meeting for the first time in 1975. Cassata did not figure in the Ottawa plans.

When Holloway was flown to Ottawa in March of 1975, Frank Clair, George Brancato, and Tom Dimitroff met the young man at the airport. Over the next two days, he was shown the city, wined and dined, and introduced to David Loeb. When he left Ottawa, he had an offer of a signing bonus of $15,000 and a three-year no-cut contract at $125,000. As a further inducement, Frank Clair, as chairman of the City's Tulip Festival, invited Holloway's mother to sit with him on the lead float in the parade. "She loved Ottawa. She loved Frank Clair. She loved tulips. Clair told her she could come to Canada anytime and place to see Condredge play and the Rough Riders would foot the bills. Condredge's mother flew home and told her son he should sign with Ottawa."[26]

It was more of the same with Tom Clements; however, since Loeb was out of town when Clements arrived, the two did not meet. Clements, too, was offered a generous contract: $12,500 for signing and a three-year guaranteed contract for $105,000. Clair flew to Pittsburgh to sign Clements on May 28 and then went on to Knoxville, Tennessee, to sign Holloway on the 29th. The subsequent press release described them as the two finest quarterbacks produced in the United States in 1974. Both were brought to Ottawa for a media conference in June.

And Bill Robinson? The All Canadian quarterback who had led two different universities to national titles in successive years, had mixed emotions when he found out that he was put on the Ottawa "protected list" for the 1975 season—mixed emotions because he wanted to play professional football in his own country. He was pleased with the opportunity but was guarded because of the treatment he had received from the Rough Riders during the training camp of 1974. He had been drafted in that year by Ottawa, taken in the third round although they had never seen him play; since quarterbacks were usually good athletes, he might be able to play defensive back. All Robinson wanted, he said, was a chance to play quarterback. Ottawa had promised that he would. During training camp, Robinson was upset, and told his St Mary's University coach, Al Keith, that he wasn't being given a chance to show his talent. He was all but forgotten by the coaches and did not play in the first three exhibition games. During the fourth and final one, against Winnipeg, he was put in for two plays. On the day before the final roster was set, he was given a plane ticket home. The office secretary informed him of his fate; the coaches had not spoken to him. He was shattered, disillusioned, "non-important." It was George Reed, president of the CFL Players' Association, who threw some light on the situation:

> A Canadian quarterback doesn't have a chance to win a job on merit in the Canadian Football League and there [are] two reasons. One is the Designated Import rule; the other is prejudice toward Canadian players, especially quarterbacks, by the coaches who, except for Jackson, are all American and the [general] managers who are almost all Americans. Canadians just aren't supposed to have it, so they seldom get the chance to prove differently. I've seen the prejudice time and again. But the Designated Import rule is the worst thing. It's dumb and crazy, and anyone who tells you it doesn't discriminate against Canadian quarterbacks is dumb and crazy. If you're a Canadian quarterback out of college, you might as well go home. They say this is the *Canadian* Football League but it makes you wonder.[27]

And so, in 1975, Bill Robinson found himself still belonging to Ottawa. The club's approach to the All Canadian was in stark contrast to its treatment of the All Americans. A contract for $13,000 was mailed to Robinson. There was no guarantee, no signing bonus, no negotiation. Still, it was a contract; the door to a professional football career was ajar. It was signed and returned. Robinson was not invited to the media conference announcing the new quarterback candidates.

The difference in treatment continued. At training camp, Robinson was virtually ignored. It was almost as if the club had too much invested in the two first-year Americans. It didn't want to risk having Robinson upstage the Americans, not among the team, not among the fans. His skill, however, did not escape his team-mates' eyes. Tony Gabriel, newly traded to Ottawa from Hamilton, said: "He's definitely pro status and in my opinion, the best passer in camp." During the intra-squad game, Robinson completed 10 of 13 passes and caught the public's attention. He looked forward to the upcoming pre-season games, four of them. In the first one, the coaches played him towards the end of the game which they lost 21–20 to Edmonton. He played credibly, completing 3 of 6 passes, one for a 48-yard gain to Gabriel. Clements rated Robinson: "He's real good, throws a super pass. Better than me. He's got everything as far as I can see." During the next three exhibition games, Robinson's playing time was almost nil. In the four games, his total was eight minutes. Jerry Keeling declared: "He's just as good as the other two. All he needs is a decent chance to show it." George Reed was blunt and to the point:

> Robinson is the best Canadian College Quarterback I've seen since I came up here to play, but it doesn't matter—Ottawa has invested heavily in the Americans and they pretty well have to play them. Another problem: Ottawa probably knows the kid is good. If he shows up well, the fans are going to want to see him play. But with the DI rule, it hurts Ottawa to use a Canadian quarterback no matter how good he is. So don't use him. That way the fans don't see him.

What the fans did see, they liked. Robinson developed a following. Fans called Open Line shows, wrote letters to the editor. The media attacked the Ottawa club for not giving the Canadian quarterback an equal opportunity. The ghost of Russ Jackson was alive and well.

The lack of equal treatment wasn't restricted to the playing field. When training camp was over, Clements and Holloway moved into accommodations owned by David Loeb. Normal rent was $750 per month; it was reduced to $300. Robinson moved to a student residence at Carleton University for $5 per night. The writing was on the wall. Ottawa simply had too great an investment, locked in with the guaranteed contracts to Holloway and Clements. Robinson was "non-important" in more than one way but because of his following and the uproar surrounding the situation, the club had to manoeuvre. He was placed on the 21-day injury list; the club would have some breathing space. His injury was "tonsillitis"—in spite of the fact that he had no tonsils! The club told Robinson that he would have to work on defensive back skills and be part of special teams. Robinson was devastated:

> I'd heard about the Rule while I was at University but you don't think much of it. You always think that maybe you'll be the one to beat it, you know, that you'll be so good that they'll have to use you regardless or change the rule to accommodate you … I'm a

quarterback, I've always been one. I've played the Canadian game and the Americans coming up haven't. Why can't I be a quarterback in this league?

When Robinson returned to the roster, he played spot roles defensively, covered on kickoffs and special teams. The public clamour for him had dissipated. He was cut, stayed close to Ottawa and worked with the Canadian Amateur Football Association, and eventually moved back to Halifax. It was a disbelieving Bill Robinson who expressed sadly, "I never thought being a Canadian would be a bad thing." As far as the public was concerned, it was the designated import rule in action. Little did they know that it would be the first of many such cases to come.

The quarterbacking situation and its developments were not lost on some other clubs. At various CFL meetings, the questions of increasing rosters, doing away with the designated import rule, or creating a special category for Canadian quarterbacks all came up. Most of the initiative came from the west where community-based teams held sway. Edmonton proposed that the roster be increased to 34 by adding two non-import players. Winnipeg wanted an increase too, but by only one non-import.[28] Kimball's rationale was that by virtue of kicking specialists, who were usually non-imports, teams were under roster constraints. "As a result," he said, "it is often necessary to use import players in a secondary position which could be adequately filled by a non-import player."[29] Costs for the move were estimated to be $18–$25 thousand and because of the changes in the punt return rule and the anticipated increase in injuries as a result, it seemed that the change would be approved. When it came to a vote, however, it was defeated by a 6–3 vote.[30]

At a later meeting in May, Calgary proposed that the restrictions against the designated import be removed. Hamilton's Sazio spoke against the proposal, saying that prior to the rule, teams kept a defensive back as their reserve quarterback. With an injury to the regular quarterback, the defensive back, bruised shoulders and all, substituted. Play inevitably deteriorated. He was opposed to any changes because the present rule assured that a team "keeps a first string quarterback in reserve, ready to play without weakening the team elsewhere."[31] Edmonton's Kimball concurred, saying that Tom Wilkinson "might long since have retired from active competition in the League" were it not for the rule. Calgary's proposal was defeated 7–2. Winnipeg's proposal to increase the rosters to 33 was similarly defeated by a 6–3 vote. Higher costs, some $200,000 to the league for increased salaries, travel, and pension contributions, were factors.[32]

By the November meeting, the after-effects of the Robinson case were still with the CFL. Some questioned its commitment to the "Canadian" in its title. Ottawa sources let it be known that while the proposal, "developed to give Canadian quarterbacks a door into the League,"[33] was defeated by the 7–2 vote, the Rough Riders voted in favour. Those opposed were asking where nine Canadian quarterbacks could be found; those in favour were responding that as long as the rule remained as it was, it was guaranteed that they would not be found! Young athletes were looking at the quarterback position in developmental leagues as a dead end; they were staying away from the position.

> Just maybe, though, if the League would legislate to provide room for quarterbacks, there would be some in a few years to start filling the clubs. It's a paradox how we all jump up and bay at the Canadian sunset every time our nationalism is threatened by the "evil furriners" when there's talk of expanding to the United States or new Leagues in the U.S. expanding to Canada. Then, out comes the flag.[34]

At the 1975 Grey Cup week meetings, Ottawa moved to increase rosters to 33, the extra player "designated as a non-import quarterback subject to all the restrictions of an import quarterback."[35] Ottawa's Frank Clair was upfront about his move. He said that the club had received "considerable pressure from the local media" because of the presence of Bill Robinson. He defended the club's action by saying because of its commitments to develop two other first-year players, Condredge Holloway and Tom Clements, it simply could not give Robinson any playing time. Jake Gaudaur offered his opinion that "it would be unwise to require a club to use a non-import quarterback and it could be unfair to the player himself if he was forced to play quarterback but no other position."[36]

David Loeb approached the CFL's Executive Committee with Ottawa's proposal. For purposes of the designated import rule, the quarterbacking position would include punting, place kicking, holding the ball on convert, and field goal attempts. Discussion was stymied when Ralph Sazio, in his capacity as president of the CFL, "recalled that at a previous meeting, it had been agreed that roster matters would not be discussed at Grey Cup time."[37] Loeb agreed; the motion was withdrawn, to be reintroduced at a later meeting.

In the East, it appeared that the Ottawa Rough Riders with their two first-year quarterbacks would be Grey Cup-bound. They finished in first place, sporting a 10–5–1 record. They ended the regular season with a convincing 46–6 victory over their chief rivals, the Alouettes. Hamilton was the third-place finisher and were no match for Montreal, losing by a 35–12 score in the Eastern semifinal. In a rematch of the last game of the schedule, Montreal upset Ottawa 20–10 in a hard fought game. One of the touchdowns was scored on a 95-yard punt return by Johnny Rodgers whose "showboating" technique of crossing the goal-line while running backwards was adding to the controversy surrounding his "ordinary superstar" status. Marv Levy called it a "meat and potatoes type of game." Two of the Ottawa players, Wayne Smith, a non-import, and Al Marcellin, an import, levelled charges of racism against the Ottawa coaching staff. They both wanted to be traded out West.[38] There were also rumours of racial strife among the Alouettes. A *Maclean's* magazine article had reported that there was a "racist atmosphere in the Montreal Camp."[39] It suggested that Sonny Wade, a white quarterback from the southern United States, was ignoring Johnny Rodgers as a receiver, while Jimmy Jones, a black import and the Alouettes' other quarterback, did not throw to Peter Dalla Riva, preferring to pass to Rodgers. The Alouettes' coach Marv Levy, Jewish and opposed to racism in any form, denied the charge, calling the article racist.

In the West, Edmonton, with a 12–4 record, was the first-place team and earned the bye. It had really been a two-team race. Winnipeg, Calgary, and B.C. all had six wins but the Blue Bombers with two ties finished in third-place. Second-place Saskatchewan, with a 10–5–1 record, defeated Winnipeg 42–24 for the right to meet Edmonton in the final. The West was won with a heartbreaker for Saskatchewan and a triumph for Edmonton, and particularly for Bruce Lemmerman. With Saskatchewan ahead 18–8, Lemmerman had replaced Tom Wilkinson and led Edmonton to a second-half rally and a 30–18 win.

The Grey Cup Game of 1975 promised to be an exciting affair. After all, these were two high-powered, high-scoring teams. Edmonton counted 432 points and Montreal 353 during the season. The Alouettes had allowed only 345 while the Eskimos gave up 370. It was their second consecutive meeting in the final. There were visions of the classic series of three meetings in the fifties—offensive, entertaining football.

The Edmonton camp reported that Lemmerman was having circulation problems in his throwing hand. A blockage in his upper arm was preventing an ample blood supply from reaching three fingers.[40] The Alouettes were unpredictable; there were fears that they would leave their hotel accommodations for new ones, as they had done in Vancouver in 1974. Calgary was the host city for the first time. It was doing its best to put on a spectacular week and game, promising to have a "Cup blowout to end all blowouts."[41] It was not without its detractors though. It was the city's Centenary and some football fans weren't impressed with the Grey Cup week program, wondering what the city was promoting. Curling bonspiels and International Women's Year were prominent, the latter responsible for "throwing open some previously all male functions to wives and girl friends ... Schenley people are so terrified of making a public relations faux pas that they took International Women's Year into account and invited the ladies this year."[42]

It was another form of controversy generated at the Schenley Awards. When Calgary's Willie Burden was selected as the Most Outstanding Player over Johnny Rodgers, the Alouette "claimed he was a victim of politics and maintained a magazine article describing his off-season activities cost him votes."[43] Other Award winners were: Charlie Turner of Edmonton as Outstanding Lineman, Jim Foley of Ottawa as Outstanding Canadian, Tom Clements of Ottawa as Rookie of the Year, and Jim Corrigal of Toronto as Best Defensive Player.

In the game itself, Edmonton prevailed to win, but only barely. It was the first Grey Cup Game in 38 years without a touchdown being scored. Edmonton's Dave Cutler kicked three field goals; Montreal's Don Sweet accounted for two field goals and two single points. The Alouettes seemed poised to win the game with less than a minute to play. Sweet was attempting a field goal from Edmonton's 19 yard-line; the score was 9–7 in Edmonton's favour.

It was a bitterly cold day, and the whole play was mistimed. A frigid Jimmy Jones, the Montreal holder, mishandled the ball and placement. Sweet's timing was thrown off. The ball went wide for a single point. Edmonton ran out the clock and preserved the 9–8 victory.

Ticket prices for the game were $20 for seats between the goal-lines, $15 for those along the end zone, and $12 for those directly behind the goalposts. The gate generated $580,943. In spite of the game which was marred by the cold weather and in which no touchdowns were scored, one wag suggested that "the storied legends of the Grey Cup games, the Mud Bowl, the Fog Bowl, would record this game as the Year of the Streak in memory of the obviously well endowed blond who showed the turnout of 32,332 all she had in an unscheduled ten minute bare-breasted romp around the field during the pre-game ceremonies."[44] There was also a mild protest of another sort. Some B.C. Lions fans took the opportunity to get some of their gripes off their chests. They unfurled a banner which protested the mid-season firings of Jackie Parker and Eagle Keys and their replacement with Bobby Ackles and Cal Murphy. It proclaimed: B.C. took a dive in '75 but the Lions will roar in '84.[45]

There were freezing temperatures in Edmonton when the Eskimos returned home but nobody seemed to mind. A huge crowd braved the cold to welcome their champs. A parade, the players travelling in open cars, moved from the Legislative Building to City Hall, about a one-and-a-half-mile trip. It was a jubilant throng, made even more so by students who had been given the day off. Free bus service was provided to the downtown area. People threw snowballs, and climbed evergreens and statues in order to gain a better view; police linked arms in an attempt to hold back eager fans who wanted to get close to touch Coach Ray Jauch, General Manager Norm Kimball, and the players, especially Dave Cutler, the top Canadian and winner of the Dick Suderman Award. Meanwhile, in Montreal, some 300 turned out at Dorval Airport to welcome home the Alouettes.[46]

It was becoming evident that Johnny Rodgers, Montreal's "ordinary superstar," was having an effect on the field as well as in the boardrooms of the CFL. League policy, as enunciated in 1974, was that "the submission of a contract by a CFL club which did not conform to the By-Laws of the League could not be registered ... it would be necessary for the club to go back to the player to get a new contract which would conform."[47] The CFL's policy on this issue was a carbon copy of the NFL policy and there was the possibility the CFL might face a law-suit like in the NFL, where Joe Kapp was suing because that league would not register his non-standard contract with New England. There was also the possibility that the player would demand more money or similar improved considerations if negotiations were reopened. The Alouettes had submitted Rodgers' contract, which did not conform to CFL by-laws, to the league office. Jake Gaudaur refused to register it. The Alouettes and Rodgers sat down again. Negotiations were long, concluding only one day before the beginning of the season. Legal costs were high. Football in Montreal was fragile. The club and the league were under some pressure since Rodgers would only play with a signed contract. Had he not been allowed to play, there would have been a law suit and "media and fan reaction would have had a critical impact not only on the Montreal club but on the entire league."[48] By July 16, 1975, the negotiations had proceeded to the point where Rodgers was willing to accept the Standard Players' Contract but with a twist—"it was to be executed by the player's company and not by he [*sic*] as an individual."[49]

It was a different approach. Gaudaur had "always taken the position that a contract by a company was not registerable."[50] A compromise was set in motion, based on the league's legal advice that "if the player would sign an addendum to the Standard Contract whereby he personally guaranteed his compliance with all the by-laws, and rules and regulations of the League,"[51] the contract would be registered. It was the way the NHL, where there were approximately 80 such contracts, had solved the same problem. There was certainty that the practice would spread throughout the CFL since the change to be made to the league by-laws would be relayed to the Players' Association. Indeed, two other clubs were requesting the wording which would be used in the "intervention." The league would then have two Standard Players' Contracts; one for individuals, the other relating to "a personal services corporation." The word "company" was to be used in this latter case wherever "player" appeared in the contract.[52]

On the field, the gregarious Rodgers was having an equally prominent effect. Ever since the rule change allowing for blocking on punt returns, a new offensive weapon had been placed in the teams' arsenals. Montreal had been the first to capitalize on it. In the CFL, a team might punt the ball up to 15 times a game; the punt return was now an offensive threat.

Prior to the change, teams used non-imports who had reliable catching skills, wide receivers usually, as punt returners. The import was too valuable, too important to be subjected to the onslaught of 12 exuberant, uninhibited tacklers. He might also revert to his past and signal a "fair catch" in the heat of the game. The message to the non-import was simple: catch the ball, protect it, head upfield. With the rule change, what had previously been a "play it safe" defensive approach, had evolved into an exciting play which could bring the crowd to its feet. It was an absorbing offensive threat; no other play, save for the forward pass, was used more than the punt return in any given game.

Defensive teams were presented with two options: they could attempt to block the punt and leave the returner to his own wits, much as before, or they could design a return with an offensive thrust to it. Montreal's Marv Levy, with players such as Rodgers and Dickie Harris, chose the latter. The rule change and the offensive style developed gave "returners a chance not only to survive but to prosper."[53]

And prosper they did at the expense of the coverage teams, and Montreal's team prospered more than others. If the coaches couldn't stop them on the field, perhaps the boardroom could. At the rules meeting in Edmonton,[54] a wide range of rules related to the kicking game was proposed. Hamilton even suggested that NFL rules regarding the kicking game be adopted in their entirety—"like importing the black plague,"[55] suggested one wag. The coaches were opposed since it would mean too many changes in the rules. Montreal wanted no restrictions at all on punt returns, similar to the CAFA Junior regulation. Not only that, Montreal's general manager Bob Geary called for more severe penalties for any infractions in the punting game. They had an important commodity to protect and if Rodgers were injured and couldn't play, not only would they lose their star performer and gate attraction, they would be out his $100,000 contract, which was guaranteed, plus the salary they had to pay to his replacement! Geary proposed that any second and subsequent violation of the "no yards zone" be doubled to 20 yards.

His rationale was obvious to all. Rodgers was a threat to return every punt for a touchdown, certainly a long gain. As a tactic to minimize his runbacks, teams encroached upon the five-yard restraining area allowed to the punter and took the ten-yard penalty, gladly. Meanwhile, the threat of longer yardage was eliminated, but equally obvious to the Alouettes was the fact that a vulnerable Rodgers was in danger of being injured because of the unexpected contact. The league reacted: officials were told to strictly enforce the rule prohibiting encroachment. As well, they were told to add an additional 15 yards unnecessary roughness penalty "if the off-side player was well within the five yard zone and contacted the receiver in an unnecessarily rough manner." If the illegal contact were deemed to be deliberate, the officials were told to increase the penalty to 25 yards and disqualify the offending player.

None of the other teams was prepared to second Montreal's motion. Calgary proposed that the "no yards" penalty "be 15 yards, the same as it was in 1965 when it became 10 but when the average return then was less than five yards." It was turned down with no seconder. The overriding concern was that of "infringement and cheap shots." Montreal proposed a fair catch, but there was no seconder. They then advanced the motion that "the punt return team be given the option of having the no yards penalty applied from the point of the last scrimmage with the same down repeated." Again, no seconder.

Montreal was attempting to nullify the strategy used by opponents. Another tactic the punting team used was to kick the ball out of bounds as far downfield as possible. At any time, it made sense as a strategy—playing Montreal, it made even more sense. The Alouettes didn't like it. They proposed that a team should be penalized for it. Clubs countered that the kicking team should not be penalized for "shanking" the ball. They were already being hurt by the ball going out of bounds relatively close to the line of scrimmage and didn't want the official's judgement to come into play and be doubly penalized.

Some rule changes were also aimed at the other dominant team in the league, the Edmonton Eskimos. Saskatchewan proposed that the value of a field goal be two points; it was presently too high in relation to a touchdown. Edmonton's Dave Cutler and Montreal's Don Sweet were the league's two premier field goal kickers. Their teams had met in the 1975 Grey Cup Game. If the field goal had been worth two points then the score would have ended up 8–8 and overtime would have been required. Edmonton's Norm Kimball replied that perhaps the value of the touchdown should be increased but he couldn't see why excellence should be penalized.

Edmonton's quarterback, Tom Wilkinson, continued to attract attention too. "Someone, likely some club victimized by Edmonton's Tom Wilkinson, would like to see a rule in there which would require the quarterback to remain motionless for one second prior to the snap of the ball."[56] Both Montreal and British Columbia had proposed the resolution. While there was some sympathy from all teams because of the general tendency to be drawn offside by the Edmonton quarterback's method of delivering his cadence, there was also the realization that such a rule would invalidate a team's "hurry up" offence, that is, the offense would be unable to move on a quick count or first sound. With only three downs, the offence needed all the leeway it could garner, not less. Edmonton was quick to point out that the rules already gave the referee the power to penalize the quarterback for intentionally drawing the opponents offside. Besides, Norm Kimball, Edmonton's general manager, said, "quarterbacks look around when they are barking, their heads bob as they shout signals, some heads more than others, like Wilkie's."[57]

Four changes were made in the rules: a ball kicked out of bounds on a kick-off was to be penalized five-yards rather than 10; a blocked kick which went out of bounds in the end zone was to be considered a safety touch, rather than a single point; an interception in the defending team's area from the 10-yard line into the goal area would be scrimmaged on the 10-yard line; a player set up outside the offensive tackle on offence would not be allowed to be in motion towards the ball prior to the snap, nor block below the waist.

Despite the bickering around rules and the impending appeals of Tony Gabriel's and Al Brenner's court cases, the CFL was in a state of relative stability. The action of the two high-profile players was the result of the Eastern Conference decision to play a 16-game schedule. Each had signed a contract under the assumption that the length of the season was 14 games. The courts had ruled in the league's favour but both players were appealing. The Players' Association proposed to abandon its appeal on their behalf "if the league would waive its right of recovery costs."[58] The CFL, having already budgeted and paid for its costs, and anxious to avoid any more negative publicity, agreed unanimously. Besides, it had already won something of a victory. The association requested that those cases, plus 11 others which they identified, be brought up before a proposed new Arbitration Committee. The former one was made up of the CFL commissioner, the CFL Players' Relations head, and the president of the Players' Association. The new format called for the player to appeal directly to the commissioner "who would investigate as he sees fit and then render a decision in favour of the Club or the player."[59]

It was an endorsement of trust that Jake Gaudaur had with the players. Regardless, the league decided to stay with the collective agreement of June 28, 1974. But in so insisting, it opened up another case of negative publicity. The agreement defined the minimum salary to be $11,000 for a two-year veteran. Place-kicker Ian Sunter of the Tiger-Cats was said to be earning less than that amount. The association grieved his case. When Sunter kicked the winning field goal for Hamilton in the 1972 Grey Cup Game, it was rumoured that he was earning less than $5,000 per season. He signed a two-year contract in 1973 at a salary of $7,000. He continued to earn that amount in 1974 when the East expanded to 16 games; he was unable to come to terms with Hamilton for a new contract for the 1975 season and therefore played out his option at 90% of his $7,000 contract. As a two-year veteran, the collective agreement said he should have been paid a minimum of $11,000. The Arbitration Committee of Norm Kimball as league representative from the Players' Relations Committee, George Reed as the CFL Players' Association president and Jake Gaudaur as CFL commissioner, met on September 17, 1975. Ian Sunter was represented by Players' Association counsellors, Ed Molstad and Gerry Sternberg. Hamilton's position was outlined in a letter to the Arbitration Committee. It stated that Sunter had been offered a new contract, higher than the minimum salary: "The player has the option of signing such a new contract which would be retroactive to the beginning of the 1975 season or to continue on the 1974 contract at 90% of his salary."[60] The committee deferred a decision until October 27 in order to give the two parties a chance to work out their problem in a mutually acceptable way. They could not. When the Arbitration Committee convened October 30, they ruled that if a contract could be signed covering the 1975 season, before June 1, 1976, compensation was to be no less than $11,000. If not, the player would be a free agent, the 90% option clause would relate to the $7,000 earned in the 1974 season.[61] Sunter chose not to sign a new contract. The star of the 1972 Grey Cup Game, the leading Eastern Conference scorer in 1974 and the third-place finisher in scoring in the East in 1975, was declared a free agent in 1976, not to play again in the CFL.

Jake Gaudaur, probably at the high point in his career as commissioner of the CFL, had been able to balance, successfully, the tensions between privately owned and community clubs and deal in an even-handed way with owners and players. He was unanimously endorsed when the CFL offered him a five-year renewal of his contract from January 1, 1976, to December 31, 1980.[62] Television revenues were at an all-time high. The 1974 season and Grey Cup rights were sold to CBC for $1,400,300, "an increase of $203,300 paid by the CBC for the 1973 rights."[63] In 1975, Gaudaur had received notification from the CTV that they would not be submitting a bid. Gaudaur called for a meeting with CTV and, in anticipation of that meeting, visited with John Bassett, former owner of the Argonauts and owner of CFTO-TV in Toronto. He wanted to understand the CTV position better. Bassett spoke of some affiliates who were not keen to carry the CFL because of their small markets and the restrictive beer advertising policies. As well, the Montreal affiliate CFCF was lukewarm. In the past, Bassett said, he had been "able and willing" to exact pressure on the network but "since he no longer had a vested interest in Canadian football, his company [Glen Warren Productions], would no longer be a bidder."[64]

When Gaudaur met with CTV officials, they confirmed that their network would not bid on the CFL games for 1975 and could not see their position changing in the short term. Gaudaur was concerned that CBC would discover that it was the only bidder and might submit a tender lower than 1974's. In a meeting with CBC, called ostensibly to discuss the pre-empting of a CFL game because of the first game of the World Series, Gaudaur "took advantage of the opportunity to ascertain whether or not, [CBC Vice President Don McPherson] knew that CTV would not be bidding. There was no indication that he did."[65] Gaudaur also let it be known, "as an aside," that the league might be "amenable to a bid of more than one year," a possibility the CBC found attractive. In November of 1974, CBC was the only one to submit a bid; it was a one-year bid totalling $1,430,250. The CBC also offered to discuss a longer contract if they were selected as the successful party. By November 21, 1974, the dollar figures were settled. CBC was awarded the television rights for three years. The fee was set at $1,430,250 for 1975, $1,501,762 for 1976 and $1,576,851 for 1977, a total of $4,508,863 for the term of the contract.

Indeed, the league was relatively prosperous. Salaries for 1975 were $6,420,200; the average import earned $26,500, the average non-import earned $18,600, with the average of all salaries being $22,300. The figures included bonuses paid to veterans but not those to first-year players or for play-offs performance.[66] They also disregarded pre-season pay or allowances of any kind. The winning members of the Grey Cup team in 1976 were to receive $6,000, an increase of $500 over 1975. The losers would receive $3,000.

League meetings were usually punctuated with discussions about the need to add more Canadians, more Americans imports, or the doing away with the designated import role, an ongoing source of concern for the league.

Much of the discussion was related to the increasing quality of the Canadian non-import content in the CFL as typified by the annual draft of 1976. There was both quantity and quality. For the first time, all 10 rounds were utilized. Eighty-eight players were chosen by the nine teams. Saskatchewan declined to select in the last two rounds; the team was well known for its abundance of solid Canadian talent. In the two rounds prior to the draft, the territorial exemption selections, 13 of the 18 taken were from Canadian universities. This compared to the first such draft in 1973 when only 5 of the 18 protected were from Canadian schools. As well, after the territorial picks, the next nine players chosen by the CFL teams in the first round of the open draft were all from Canadian schools.[67]

The British Columbia Lions chose a quarterback, Lui Passaglia from Simon Fraser University, a player who was to make his mark in the CFL, not as a quarterback, but rather as a prolific place kicker. Canadian colleges were being called upon to supply ever-increasing numbers to the CFL and they were responding. Of the 153 non-imports on the CFL rosters in 1975, 104 had come from the Canadian college draft, 68 of those from the previous three years.[68]

There were other noteworthy events in the league. Saskatchewan Roughrider, George Reed, announced his retirement from play in 1976. The 36-year old full back had a remarkable record. During his 13-year career, all with the prairie team, he carried the ball 3,243 times, gained 16,614 yards, scored 137 touchdowns, 134 along the ground, was selected to the All Canadian team seven times and had eleven 1,000-plus-yards-gained seasons. In his last season, he showed no signs of slowing down; he gained 1,454 yards on 323 carries for a 4.5 average. His overall career rushing average was 4.97 yards per carry.[69] Reed continued to serve as president of the CFL Players' Association.

There were other departures from the CFL, not all voluntary. In Hamilton, the Tiger-Cats were off to a disastrous start under new coach George Dickson. General manager Bob Shaw replaced him after only two games. In Toronto, football was continuing its surge in interest. The newly redesigned CNE Stadium was bursting with fans, 50,212 to see Ottawa, August 11, and 49,724 one week later against Hamilton. The largest crowd prior to 1976 had been in the neighbourhood of 35,000. The Argonauts in 1976 had sold 40,000 season tickets. They were a curious mix. Owner Bill Hodgson had replaced John Barrow after the 1975 season with J. I. Albrecht, who had been fired by Montreal. Albrecht was to be made manager of Football Operations. Also hired was Argo favourite, Dick Shatto, initially as director of Marketing and Public Relations, later as managing director. Russ Jackson was entering his second year as head coach. There were great expectations based on his outstanding playing career. When he replaced Joe Moss, the interim head coach of the Argonauts, Toronto fans were ecstatic. He "was the indisputable, radiant, archetypal All Canadian Boy grown to manhood … had been for more than a decade, the single greatest consistently dominant player in Canadian football."[70] Surely, he would be the one to lead the Argos out of the wilderness to the Grey Cup!

Thrown into the amalgam of people who couldn't seem to get along with each other's approach was Anthony Davis. The import running back from Southern California, had excelled in University and in the WFL:

> [Anthony Davis] received a $120,000 signing bonus and a five year contract that would pay him $65,000 his first year with a gradual increase to $100,000 in his last. Bonus clauses would provide a potential $30,000 a year extra … Davis was to become yet another costly flop. A major reason was that friction developed between Jackson and Davis. Under the new setup, Jackson did not have the authority to rebuke his player. Jackson expected Davis to be another O.J. Simpson, a leader who would shine on and off the field. Davis was far from that.[71]

The inability of Jackson and Davis to get along was one of the reasons cited by Argonaut owner Bill Hodgson in the firing of Jackson at the end of the 1976 season. Hodgson had hoped that Anthony Davis would be another Johnny Rodgers, sort of an "extraordinary superstar." Indeed, when his signing was announced by the Argos, "a beaming Bill Hodgson said: 'I've made just one request of A.D. I've asked him when he scores his first touchdown against Montreal to turn around and cross the goal line backwards.'"[72]

Johnny Rodgers, too, had fallen from favour with his coach Marv Levy in Montreal. In the Eastern final game against Hamilton, the Alouettes had been listless, played with little emotion and seemed to go through the motions as they lost 23–0 to the Tiger-Cats. After the game, it was revealed that Rodgers had missed an important team meeting the evening prior to the game. His actions were described as "incredibly thoughtless selfishness."

> Rodgers will pay a fine for playing hookey as he has done before when he has missed workouts or arrived late but the punishment is meaningless to him … nothing more than a mildly irritating effect of doing what he pleases while the ranks and file of his team mates, fellows who can't afford $1,000 for an evening of fun (in Hamilton?) are required to obey the rules … Levy has made a serious mistake in allowing Rodgers to flout club rules. Either that or Club

owner, Sam Berger has erred in allowing an individual athlete to become more important than the team he plays on and the men he works for so that he can't be controlled. The cost of the blunder has been immense—the disintegration of an excellent Club.[73]

In the West, Edmonton defeated Winnipeg 14–12 in the semifinal game. Dave Cutler kicked the winning field goal with less than three minutes remaining. It was a 52 yarder. In the Western final, Saskatchewan defeated Edmonton 23–13, while in the East, Ottawa staved off a second-half comeback bid by Hamilton to gain a 17–15 decision.

The 1976 Grey Cup Game was played at Toronto's Exhibition Stadium and attracted a record attendance of 53,467: "Ticket sales will account for one million dollars with television rights bringing in another $257,000 and radio rights, sales of programs and other film rights adding another $50,000."[74]

The game itself was a thriller. The Saskatchewan Roughriders were listed as seven-point favourites over their Eastern Rough Rider counterparts. Indeed, the Western team was leading by 20–16 with less than 30 seconds to play. Then Tom Clements and Tony Gabriel teamed up to score on a dramatic touchdown pass. The convert by Gerry Organ meant that Ottawa, by virtue of a 23–20 victory, had won the Grey Cup. The play was a vindication of sorts for both the quarterback and the receiver. Just a week earlier, in Hamilton, the identical play to the opposite side had been called and Clements' perfect pass to Gabriel was dropped by the distracted receiver. Fortunately, for Ottawa and Gabriel, the 17 points which the Rough Riders had built up to that point was enough to stave off the Tiger-Cats' charge; Gabriel would have another chance.

In the Grey Cup Game, Ottawa was in the huddle as the clock was ticking down. With 44 seconds remaining and Ottawa on Saskatchewan's 35-yard line, Clements called a running play to Art Green. It gained less than a yard as the Roughrider defence stiffened. On second down, a pass to Gabriel took the ball to the Saskatchewan 20-yard line. The Ottawa huddle took form quickly before the official's whistle signalled the resumption of time. Coach George Brancato sent in a play from the sidelines. Clements ignored it. He was in the middle of calling his own play, the mirror of the one dropped in Hamilton by Gabriel. This time there was no mistake. There were 20 seconds on the clock when the huddle broke. Clements made a fake to his full back running right; Gabriel broke from the line and moved upfield, cut in from his wide position, and angled back out towards the corner of the end zone for the go-ahead touchdown. For the second consecutive Grey Cup Game in which Saskatchewan played, Gabriel had been their nemesis, first in 1972 and now again in 1976. Gabriel was selected the winner of the Dick Suderman Award as the Canadian Player of the Game along with two free tickets to anywhere flown by Canadian Pacific Airlines. Clements was chosen the Player of the Game.

Prior to the game, Gabriel had previously been awarded the Schenley for Outstanding Canadian over British Columbia's Bill Baker. Baker was also nominated for the Defensive Player of the Year and won that award over Granny Liggins of the Argos. Montreal's Dan Yochum was selected as Offensive Player of the Year over B.C. Lion Al Wilson. Quarterback John Sciarra of the Lions was the Rookie of the Year with Neil Lumsden of the Argonauts as the runner-up. Ron Lancaster, the veteran quarterback of the Roughriders, won the Schenley for Most Valuable Player over running back Jimmy Edwards of Hamilton.

The exciting finish of the 1976 Grey Cup Game, the huge record crowd in attendance, and the attendant afterglow kept football as a topic of public conversation well into the post-season. Behind closed doors, however, there were concerns. In Toronto where Russ Jackson had been fired by the owner of the Argos just two years into his five-year contract, the news was released that his contract would be honoured at "$75,000 annually plus fringe benefits."[75] Bill Hodgson was now in partnership with Carling O'Keefe, the brewery, as owners of the Argos. When he had purchased the Argos from John Bassett in 1974 for $3.3 million, he did so with the help of Vancouver businessman, Sam Belzberg. Each owned 50%. During 1976, Hodgson bought out his partner for $2.3 million. He sold a 40% stake to Carling O'Keefe for that same $2.3 million.[76] Meanwhile, the Argos were playing to capacity houses, had a solid season ticket base of close to 40,000, and had a stadium seating more than 50,000. To make it all work, it needed stability and harmony among the coaches, front office, and playing personnel.

Montreal gave the impression that it was turning around its lack of acceptance at home. Always a competitive team, it had benefitted and suffered because of the Rodgers' effect, but having moved into the Olympic Stadium after the Games, rather than into the Autostade, had a rejuvenating effect. Attendance was up and optimism prevailed.

1977 to 1978

Chapter Five

IN 1977, CFL COMMISSIONER JAKE GAUDAUR could confidently say that the league was solid financially. It had grossed $12,941,957 in 1976, an increase of more than $1,800,000 over 1975's $10,106,105.[1] Part of the success, Gaudaur said, was due to the stability afforded by good relations between the Players' Association and the league. Part of it was due, as well, to the increased attendances, particularly in Toronto and Montreal where crowds had increased dramatically. British Columbia, the league's third-largest market, was experiencing problems and had replaced Montreal as a league worry. The Alouettes had moved from being a recipient of the league's equalization pool to being a contributor. Over 2.5 million fans had been drawn to the CFL games, the Alouettes drawing an astonishing average of 61,000 for its four home games at the newly opened Olympic Stadium.[2] A new stadium with a capacity of over 50,000 was in the works for Edmonton which was hosting the Commonwealth Games in 1978, while B.C., according to Gaudaur, needed only a "contender to bring the people back."[3] And, most importantly, there were stable and good relations with the players.

A Montreal newspaper report, citing unnamed sources,[4] reported that the Alouettes had a 1976 player payroll of $1,069,500, the highest in the league, while Hamilton at the lowest end of the CFL was at $658,000 or $20,600, on average, per player. In between, were: Toronto, $824,500; Edmonton, $797,000; Winnipeg, $769,000; Saskatchewan, $764,500; British Columbia, $764,000; Calgary, $740,500; and Ottawa, $726,500. The Alouettes also had the highest paid player in Johnny Rodgers. He earned a basic salary of $124,000 and with bonuses, $165,000. They also had the two highest paid linemen in the league, tackle Dan Yochum at $68,000 and defensive end Junior Ah You at $59,000. Dickie Harris, a defensive back with the Alouettes, earned $65,000. "The highest paid native Canadian and the only homebrew among the 18 players earning at least $40,000 a year, was defensive end Bill Baker of the B.C. Lions." The highest paid quarterback in 1976, according to the source, was Saskatchewan's Ron Lancaster at $60,000. The Argos' Chuck Ealey was second at $53,000. The other Argo quarterback, Mathew Reed, had earned $50,000 with Ralph "Dieter" Brock of Winnipeg at $48,000, five hundred dollars more than Montreal's Sonny Wade at $47,500.[5]

Good and stable relations with the players were necessary and the league took a large step towards that with the signing of a new Collective Bargaining Agreement. It was a comprehensive agreement to be in effect from June of 1977 to December 31, 1979. It was signed by George Reed for the Players' Association, Norm Kimball for the CFL Players' Relations Committee, and Jake Gaudaur as commissioner of the CFL. The agreement was a 49-page typewritten legal document (plus appendices), covering three years, governing a host of matters relating to the league and its relationship with the players. Among its governance, practice times were established. Whereas all other teams would not begin practice prior to 4:00 P.M., Toronto would not practise before 1:00 P.M., and Montreal only after 2:30 P.M. On weekends, holidays, or road trips, the clubs could schedule practices, and/ or meetings "at such times as they desire." In addition, no veteran player was required "to attend a training camp where there is more than one organized practice a day for more than two weeks during any single season." The agreement also specified pay for exhibition games ($175, for 1977 and 1978; $200 for 1979) and the per diem for training camps.

Clubs were to collect dues by deducting $20 per game up to a maximum of $300 to be turned over to the Players' Association. As for the All Star game to be held in Toronto in 1977, the CFL authorized Kimball's committee to donate $25,000 to the Players' Association pension fund. In the final negotiation, the $25,000 were to be recovered from the profits of the game, in effect a $25,000 saving for the CFL. The collective agreement also called for the All Star game to become a cooperative venture. Clubs were to provide subscriber lists, "publicity and promotional vehicles," All Star ticket applications, and the like. The game was fixed for the last week in May or the first in June, the specific date to be set by the CFL Players' Association by January 15 of the current year. The 1977 game was scheduled for Toronto; it would be played in the West in 1978, "alternating between the Conferences and not to be played at the same site throughout the terms of this contract." Members of the winning team were to receive $200 and losing players $100. The coaching staffs were to receive $1,500. All Star players were to be covered by insurance taken out specifically by the association.

Both the players' salary and the clubs' expenses for medical or hospital costs were to be covered.

The term of the standard players contract was to be in effect until March 31 of the year following the football season contracted. Players were to receive 95% of their contract divided by the number of games per season (16) within 48 hours of each game. The 5% remaining was to be held back until after the final game played by the team. The player could be suspended, disciplined, or his contract terminated if he failed to live up to his contractual obligations. However,

> should the Player at any time be intemperate, immoral, indifferent or conduct himself in such manner, whether on or off the field, as in the opinion of the Club endangers or prejudices the interests of the Club or if the Player failed to attain or maintain first class physical condition, except because of injury, the club could discipline the player in such manner as the Club shall deem fit and proper.

The discipline was not to include suspension; the club could however, terminate the contract.

A club could still renew its option on a player's services by writing to the player prior to March 31. The option year was still 90% of the salary figure stipulated in the contract. A veteran player injured during the exhibition season would be paid for all games during the season and play-offs of that current year. If the team's doctor were to declare him physically fit and able to resume play, the player could refuse and within 96 hours notify the club that he was being examined by a physician of his choice. If the two doctors were in disagreement, they or the CFL commissioner would recommend a third "disinterested physician" whose report would be conclusive and binding upon the player and the club. If the "disinterested physician" agreed with the club, the player would be responsible for the costs; if with the player, the club would pay the fee. Non-veterans would have the same options if the injury took place during the season.

Play-off and Grey Cup bonuses were also revised. Each player on the teams receiving a bye to the Western and Eastern Conference finals was to receive $1,000, the same as each member of the losing semifinalists. The winner of the semifinals received $1,200 per player, the same amount as the loser of the finals. The winner of the finals received $1,400 for each player. The losing Grey Cup players were allotted $3,000 each; the winning players, $6,000 each.

The Players' Association was making sure that it wasn't about to get caught in the same bind as it did in 1974 when the Eastern Conference moved to a 16-game schedule. For 1977 and 1978, the Collective Bargaining Agreement bound the league to 16 scheduled games, no more than four exhibition games, and the same play-off format which was in vogue for 1976. If changes were envisaged for 1979, the last year of the agreement, the league and its Players' Relations Committee were to "make available to the CFLPA all information to be taken into consideration in making the decision and shall invite the response of the CFLPA ..." Should the league wish to change from the 1976 practice, it would have to decide "on or before the first day of December, A.D. 1977, by written notice" to the Players' Association. To ensure that some of the problems which arose in 1974 would not recur if the league did increase its number of games in 1979, the Players' Association would negotiate those contracts affected by the change with the league's PRC. It would be a collective renegotiation to include all the contracts of those players who requested the CFLPA to do so within 30 days of the announcement to increase the schedule.

In other areas, the Collective Bargaining Agreement stipulated that there must be a minimum of 96 hours (four days) between games, and that $14,000 be the minimum pay for a veteran and $11,000 the minimum for an incoming player. All bonuses, pre-season subsistence allowances, and payments for pre- and post-season games were excluded from those amounts. With the Ian Sunter case clearly in mind, the agreement stated that the club was obligated to pay those figures "regardless as to when the said player's contract of renewal of an option of a contract was signed or came into effect."

It was also agreed that an audited statement for the Grey Cup Game would be done by the CFL and sent to the clubs within 60 days following its playing. The statement was to set out "gross income, direct expenses, and net proceeds of the Grey Cup and play-off games." The reason lay in a clause which provided half the net proceeds of the Grey Cup and play-off games to the participating players (less their minimum compensation). The clause was probably included because of similar ones governing baseball and football in the USA. It was a far-sighted clause for the players. The Grey Cup crowd of 1977 was such that players received more than the "minimum compensation."

The CFL Players' Association pension fund also benefitted from the agreement. Each club was to deposit $500 per player, matching the player's $500 contribution, for each of the three years of the agreement. Other matters agreed to stipulated that the club was to forward an offer in writing to a player entering his option year prior to May 1. The contract was to be "for a specified consideration for the said option year." There was also a reward of sorts for a veteran who was released. Any player cut after six seasons or more during any one of the three years of the contract, was to receive 50% of what he had contracted for the remainder of the schedule still to be played after his release.

Yet, while there was a measure of stability with the signing of the Collective Bargaining Agreement, elsewhere there was ferment. With the league finances in relatively good shape and the Rough Riders having won the Grey Cup in 1976, David Loeb decided to sell the team prior to the 1977 season. The buyer was Allan Waters, owner of the radio stations CHUM in Toronto and CFRA in Ottawa, the broadcaster of the Rough Rider games.

During a telephone conference call among the CFL Executive Committee[6] just three days prior to the April 15 deadline for the sale, Bill Hodgson, as president of the league, asked if the normal 20-day period for a notice of motion could be waived. All but Hamilton's Michael DeGroote agreed; he "had been away and had not sufficient time to digest the material."[7] April 19 was selected as the date for a new call, the assumption being that Waters would agree to the extension. When the meeting reconvened and the notice of motion was successfully waived, it approved the sale from David Loeb on behalf of Tremblay Realty, Donald O. McLean, and John G. Dunlap of the Ottawa Football Club Limited to Radio Station CFRA Limited. That station plus "CHUM Limited, Allan Waters Limited and Allan Waters personally, took over Tremblay Realty's 17 common shares and 1,070 preferred shares, Donald O. McLean's 2 common shares and John G. Dunlap's one common share."[8] The price was a reported $1.1 million.[9] New owner Allan Waters as president and Terry Kielty as vice-president and chief administrator saw football as "important for the country ... as an ingredient for unity." From a business point of view, the Riders were seen as providing a "decent vehicle for promotion of CFRA."[10]

Both Johnny Rodgers and Anthony Davis were waived out of the league, their respective teams not being able to cope with their idiosyncrasies. Marv Levy continued to coach in Montreal, but in Toronto, Russ Jackson was replaced by Leo Cahill. The newly resurrected Argo coach had actually agreed to coach the B.C. Lions after meetings with General Manager Bobby Ackles. The Lions had fired Cal Murphy after the '76 season; it appeared that the two Leos—both Cahill, and the Lions—would be a perfect fit. Bill Hodgson, however, wanted Cahill for the Argos. Once the opportunity presented itself, Cahill asked Ackles to be released from his commitment. In the meantime, Edmonton's Ray Jauch moved from the coaching ranks to become general manager. He, in turn, hired former Saskatchewan receiver Hugh "Gluey Huey" Campbell as his new coach. A disgruntled Vic Rapp, an assistant coach with the Eskimos, disappointed that he did not receive the

Edmonton head coaching position which he said that Jauch had promised to him, moved to Vancouver where he became the new B.C. Lions head coach. John Payne had left Saskatchewan where he was replaced with Jim Eddy. In Calgary, Jack Gotta became the Stampeders' new head coach, returning to the CFL after a stint in the WFL. Gotta had left Ottawa over a salary dispute. After Ottawa's Grey Cup victory of 1973, he had two years remaining on his contract. Gotta pursued an extension plus an increase of $5,000 over the three years "just a small indication of appreciation by the party of the first part."[11] When it was refused, a miffed Gotta "gave Parliament Hill a snappy salute and flew away to Birmingham."[12] It cost him "$10,000 and a couple of thousand dollars in legal expenses."[13] In Hamilton, Bob Shaw, who replaced George Dickson after "Dickson had gone on radio before his last game against B.C. Lions [and] announced to the world that he was in charge of the worst team the CFL has ever seen,"[14] was named CFL Coach of the Year for 1976. George Brancato and Bud Riley were still in charge of Ottawa and Winnipeg, respectively.

The two-man non-import reserve list established by the league in 1976 was short-lived. It was abolished in 1977, replaced by an increase in the roster to 33 by adding one non-import.[15] There were other major refinements in rule changes. The CFL decided to allow unlimited blocking downfield after a completed pass. Previously, only the eligible receivers were allowed to do so. For all intents and purposes, the rule made it easier on officials; the only time linemen would be involved in blocking downfield would be on short passes or when a receiver changed directions and crossed back into an area where his linemen were. A penalty of 15 or 25 yards, depending on the severity of the hit, could be assessed on top of the normal 15-yard penalty if the punt returner was contacted prior to his touching of the ball. A five-yard penalty could also be assessed for "facemasking" when it was deemed to be "incidental."

If a short kick-off was touched or recovered by a player from the kicking team prior to the ball travelling 10 yards, the receiving team was given the choice of the ball at that point where it was illegally touched or receiving another kick-off. Similarly, the penalty on kick-offs for either team's being offside was reduced to five yards from ten.

There was also an attempt to bring uniformity to the rules of the game among the various constituencies, that is, the CFL and the CAFA. A meeting between Hap Shouldice and his amateur league counterpart, Jack Guerney, isolated 59 differences in playing rules between the two. Guerney agreed to recommend that the CAFA adopt 33 of the CFL's versions; Shouldice would propose 18 of the CAFA's. It was also agreed by each "that

8 of the rules remain different because of other considerations such as physical size, degree of skills and training backgrounds."[16]

Still, old ways died slowly. When Shouldice proposed that each CFL team be allowed one time out per half, "it was declared defeated for want of a motion."[17] The league also opposed a motion that when the ball was fumbled from the field of play into the opponent's goal area where it was recovered by the opposition, no points were to be given. Previously, it had been worth a point but beginning in 1977 the ball would be scrimmaged from the 10-yard line by the recovering team. Mathew Reed, a quarterback with the Argos, is recorded as the last player to have so scored a single, in 1972.

The decision of the CFL to reconcile its rules with those of the CAFA and particularly those of the CIAU was not taken in isolation. Intercollegiate football through its draft was the main supplier of talent for the CFL and the universities were attracting a public following of their own; the 1974 Vanier Cup game between the University of Toronto and the University of Western Ontario had attracted over 28,000 spectators to CNE Stadium in Toronto. The CIAU had been a critic of the CFL saying its policies in general and the designated import regulation in particular were harmful to the development of Canadian non-import talent. The criticism had been such that Gaudaur met with CIAU representatives and made his discussion known through a league memo, dated February 8, 1977. The requests and suggestions were brought before the CFL general managers at their March 21st meeting. The CIAU wished to abolish the territorial exemptions portion of the College Draft saying that it was "detracting from the importance of the main draft meeting." The league declined. That portion of the draft, it said, "doubled the publicity impact of the College Draft." The fact that the territorial choices were most likely to make the clubs "emphasized the importance of the feature." The CIAU requested that greater publicity be given to the signing of territorial or draft choices, making sure that the player's home town and university were especially targeted. The CFL saw this as a definite possibility but needed assistance and cooperation from the schools in "providing, in advance, pictures of the players most likely to be drafted." The CIAU requested the CFL's help in publicizing university games. The CFL commissioner contacted the CBC who agreed that it could be done if the quality of the material provided measured up. "It was suggested that CIAU officials meet with the proper persons at CBC to discuss the details." The CFL also agreed to include the weekly CIAU statistics in its weekly issue from the league office "provided that the CIAU could have the information in the league office in time for publication early Monday morning."

There were more concerns voiced at the meeting. Since a player who was on a CFL roster for a single game lost a year of eligibility at the college level, the CFL was being asked "to take this into account before deciding to activate a drafted player for one game." The concern was also expressed that CFL developmental camps for high school players "contravened NCAA regulations in the United States." The Canadian universities were concerned that the evaluation camps were thinly disguised attempts to send the best Canadian talent to the United States for their football skills. The threat of exposing these camps as contrary to NCAA rules would end that practice. The CIAU also wanted a time limit on the CFL's placing names on their negotiation list. Too many times, a player who thought he was a free agent and able to make his own arrangements with any club in the league found out that he was still a team's property by virtue of his name being on that club's "neg list."[18]

CFL reaction to all of this was mixed. Perhaps the CIAU should "review its own rules about the number of games in which a player could participate before being declared ineligible to return to CIAU football." The clubs also wanted to see the wording of the NCAA regulations referred to and they would be willing to examine a time limit for the negotiation list.

There was a general agreement among the CFL clubs that the calibre of players coming to the league from the CIAU, through the draft, "had improved substantially during the past few years ... because of higher calibre coaching." With all of that, however, there was still some ambivalence. Not all were convinced. When discussions were initiated about a proposal from a New York based organization, Sport Spectaculars Ltd., to solicit a $500 contribution from each CFL club towards the filming of the CAN-Am Bowl in Tampa, a game between Canadian and American All Star collegians, Hamilton's Bob Shaw's reaction was to ask "whether the Canadian team might be embarrassed if too strong a U.S. team is picked." On the other hand, Winnipeg's Earl Lunsford "felt more concern about exposing the better Canadian College players to NFL scouts."[19] It was left up to each individual club to "send a representative to the game and/or request a film of it."[20]

Meanwhile, tragedy struck the B.C. Lions. Two-year veteran Allan Gallaher, a 26-year-old import offensive lineman, died after suffering a heart attack in the early morning hours of May 12 near his home in Clovis, New Mexico.[21] That loss plus the coaching of Vic Rapp and his staff spurred the Lions to their best record, ten wins and six losses, since their Grey Cup win of 1964, to finish in second place in the West. Winnipeg, under Bud Riley, finished in third place while the Edmonton Eskimos, with new coach Hugh Campbell, were the first-place finishers and received the bye into the Western final. The B.C. Lions squeaked by Winnipeg 33–32. The play-off loss by the Bombers cost Bud Riley his job. In the Western final, the Edmonton Eskimos jumped into an early lead and defeated the Lions by a resounding 38–1 score. They would represent the West in the 1977 Grey Cup Game to be held in Montreal's Olympic Stadium.

In the East, the Argos, with Leo Cahill back at the helm, attracted an average attendance of 46,881 while compiling a 6–10 record for a third-place finish. Montreal as first-place finisher received the bye while Ottawa ended the season in second. A seemingly innocuous incentive had its effect on Ottawa. Management had introduced specialty team bonuses—silver dollars were given to all members of a specialty unit which reached a specific laid-out goal. "For example, everyone on a kick-off team gets two silver dollars if the kick-off team tackles the opponent behind their 25 yard line."[22] The defending Grey Cup champions had gained momentum during the season, even playing before the Queen in a game where they defeated Hamilton 36–28. Ottawa's Gerry Organ and Hamilton's Terry Evanshen, both born in England, were introduced to the Queen prior to the contest.[23] The Toronto Argonauts of Leo Cahill ("the Sleeping Giants of the Canadian Football League, he had named them at a hastily called press conference at the Hotel Toronto on a night when a lightning storm had forced a delay of an exhibition game with Ottawa"[24]), had ended up in third place. In their semifinal with Ottawa, it appeared as if they might provide the upset. With 43 seconds left and Ottawa ahead by less than a touchdown, 21–16, Toronto was in position to score on the four-yard line. There were no time outs allowed in the CFL at the time; Cahill wanted to discuss the situation with his quarterback. He ordered full back Neil Lumsden "to fake an injury to stop the clock."[25] There were two downs remaining to make the necessary yardage for the touchdown. Cahill sent in a play. Ealey dropped back to pass. Ottawa defensive end Mike Fanucci eluded his block, hit Ealey, and caused a fumble. Ottawa recovered the ball and preserved the win; the Argonaut season was finished. Ottawa moved on to the Eastern final with Montreal. They had lost four previous outings with the Alouettes and, before an appreciative throng of 55,000 fans, the Montrealers once again prevailed by a 21–18 score. It was as close as the score indicated. The home town supporters had collectively held its breath as Ottawa's Gerry Organ attempted and missed a tying 52-yard field goal on the last play of the game.

In the prelude to the 1977 Grey Cup Game, the Schenley Awards were distributed. Jimmy Edwards, a running back with Hamilton, was selected over quarterback Jerry Tagge of B.C. as the Most Outstanding Player; Leon Bright of B.C. was chosen over Ottawa's Mike Murphy as the Most Outstanding Rookie; and Tony Gabriel was presented with the Most Outstanding Canadian over Gord Patterson of Winnipeg. It was Gabriel's third win in four years. Dan Kepley, middle linebacker with the Eskimos, was the Most Outstanding Defensive Player, chosen over Montreal's Glen Weir, while B.C.'s Al Wilson was Most Outstanding Offensive Lineman ahead of Toronto's Mike Wilson.

Tickets for the Grey Cup Game in Montreal ranged from $12 to $24. It attracted the largest crowd in the history of the game, 68,318, recording the highest gate receipts to that time, $1,401,930. It was the second time that the league had surpassed the $1 million mark. The contest itself was unable to live up to the pre-game hype. Edmonton had the highest scoring team in the CFL. Its defence, particularly its front line, backed by Schenley Award winner Dan Kepley, was known as "Alberta Crude." Montreal was deemed to be only a minor obstacle in the Eskimos' path to the Grey Cup.

Montreal and the weather refused to cooperate. The game was played on a frozen field of artificial turf, an "ice floe"[26] Dan Kepley had called it. The Alouettes defeated the Eskimos 41–6, "the most one sided game since Queen's put it to the Regina hands 54–0 back in 1923. Alberta Crude was suddenly Alberta Crud."[27] Montreal's Don Sweet kicked six field goals, a new record. His 23 points made him the All Time Leading Scorer with 42 points. Sonny Wade, Montreal's quarterback, was chosen "the player of the game," the third time in his four appearances in Grey Cup games.

In what was an interesting "footnote" to the game, it was reported that the unfinished condition of the stadium played a role in the Alouettes' win. After their pre-game warm-up, the Alouettes complained about the poor traction they had on the icy field. Defensive back Tony Proudfoot, spotting an electrician's staple gun, shot some into the soles of his shoes. The other Montreal players, noticing Proudfoot's traction, followed suit. It was an illegal act. "The Eskimos complained to the officials but Hap Shouldice, the CFL director of Officials and others checked through the shoes and found nothing wrong."[28]

The huge crowd meant that the winning team would be awarded more than the minimum which the Collective Bargaining Agreement had called for. Each member of the Alouettes received $8,400 and each Eskimo received $4,200, plus an additional sum later of $31.53 and $15.77 respectively, when the Quebec government rebated a portion of the tax which should not have been collected.

Mistrust in the boardroom was a perennial concern of the league. Rumours had surfaced that during the expansion controversy of 1974 John Bassett had been attempting to entice the other three privately owned Eastern teams to leave the CFL and form a division of the WFL where they could earn their money and keep it rather than share it with clubs that the market-place wouldn't support. Money was certainly at the root of current problems between Hamilton and Toronto. Tiger-Cat owner Michael DeGroote accused the Argos of looking after themselves first rather than the CFL. The theory was that if the CFL folded, Bill Hodgson could always go to the NFL. The Argos were accused of ignoring a league-wide "properties agreement which had provided for each Club to relinquish its promotional rights to the League." The Argonauts countered that they would be happy to do so with national rights but that "each club should do its own promotional work in its own area." DeGroote also charged that the Argonauts were interested in negotiating their own television contract. General manager of the Argos, Dick Shatto, could only deny it, saying: "It's a hell of a thought. Maybe we should try it."[29]

The problem seemed to be related to the huge market that Toronto was able to access, the expansive stadium it had, and the money it was generating. At the league's February, 1978, meetings they decided to form another committee. The Argos' Bill Hodgson, the Eskimos' Norm Kimball, the Alouettes' David Berger, and the Blue Bombers' Ron Smith would "investigate all facets of the operations of all Clubs with the view of working together to assure the survival of one League, the CFL."[30] The aim was to develop a comprehensive revenue-sharing plan "to allow smaller teams to remain solvent in the face of competition from clubs in larger centres such as Montreal and Toronto."[31]

> The last time the League grew frightened about one team having a huge stadium and a population to fill it, the cry was identical: "They will throw the salaries sky high," the others moaned. "They'll buy the Grey Cup. We will never be able to compete." That was 23 years ago. The team was the B.C. Lions. The huge park, Empire Stadium. The League survived better than they ever did. There's a lesson there somewhere.[32]

When the sale of the Hamilton Tiger-Cats appeared on the agenda of the CFL's February meetings, there was evidence that publicity around the sale had already caused the Western clubs to have all of their antennae raised. Any sale of an Eastern team was subject to the most intense scrutiny of the principals. The new owner would have to have the league's best interests in mind. It was only when Saskatchewan's Bruce Cowie was assured that there was no connection between "the matter of Revenue Sharing and the Transfer of Ownership of the Hamilton Club that the Roughriders were prepared to accept the order of the agenda so that the transfer item would be the next item to be considered."[33]

By the time the application for sale made it to the CFL meetings, it had already generated huge amounts of publicity. The reason? The prospective new owner of the Tiger-Cats was the notorious Toronto Maple Leafs' boss, Harold Ballard. The publicity-prone Ballard had previously attempted to place a new CFL franchise in Toronto, something which the then Argonauts owner John Bassett had shot down. Ballard was persistent. In late January, 1978, Tiger-Cat owner Michael DeGroote announced that he had accepted Ballard's offer to buy the Tiger-Cats.[34] Almost immediately, there was a reaction. Member of Parliament John Munro, in his capacity as the elected member from Hamilton East, said that the sale was "not in the interests of Hamilton Tiger-Cats or of Canadian Football."[35] Ballard's decision to pay the $1.3 million for the club continued to elicit comments. Argo owner, Bill Hodgson, quipped: "You'd have to be a village idiot to expect to make money with the CFL franchise."[36] There was no indication to whom he was referring. Certainly, the Leafs were a financial success if not a competitive one. Would Ballard take the same approach with the Tiger-Cats that he did with the Leafs? After all, it was pointed out, television provided only approximately $300,000 to the CFL clubs; while the gate equalization subsidization could add some dollars to the struggling Hamilton coffers, it meant that profits would have to be shared.

It was Ballard himself who was the largest stumbling block to the sale. His irreverent comments were so plentiful and self-serving that the Toronto *Sun* had editorialized that it would not mention Ballard's name again. A short time later, it was convinced that Ballard's offer to buy the Tiger-Cats was genuine, not a publicity stunt. "The *Sun* had to eat its words."[37] As for Ballard, he fed the flames. He bought the club, he said, because "he has nothing to do in the summer when the NHL isn't in operation."[38] He spoke out against the league's policy of protecting Canadians, preferring unlimited importation. He railed against the gate equalization policy. In Winnipeg, his comments set off the predicted reaction. The Blue Bombers' Earle Hiebert, who was also the president of the Western Conference, declared that he would vote against Ballard's proposed purchase of the Tiger-Cats. Approval of seven of the nine clubs was needed. "Too many people are involved who have worked long and hard to make this thing work to have someone from Toronto let it go down the tube,"[39] said Hiebert.

There was opposition in Hamilton too. John Munro and Hamilton's Mayor, Jack Macdonald, called a press conference to announce that a group including Chester Waxman, John Agro, and Joyce Mongeon would match Ballard's offer. Munro held out a carrot that the federal government might also assist with funds to renovate Ivor Wynne Stadium. Further details of the consortium included the information that 60% of the CFL club would be owned by the aforementioned trio, the other 40% by the Vancouver-based Northwest Sports Enterprises Limited, a subsidiary of Western Broadcasting Co. Limited, which was 30% owned by the Toronto *Star*.[40]

Ballard's response was at his controversial best. Calling the new bid a "political thing," he said that the former legal counsel for the CFLPA, John Agro, "used to fleece the owners when he represented the players; now he wants to be an owner. He'll throw the players to the wolves." As for metal dealer, Chester Waxman, Ballard said, "the other guy should stick to selling his scrap" and "this Mongeon should stick to playing Mah Jong." He minced no words with the League: "The CFL Executives have no excuses to refuse me. If they do, they can ———."[41]

By the time the proposed transfer came before the league, Jake Gaudaur had already done much of the preparatory work. His recommendation was that "he had no hesitation in recommending the approval of the application to transfer the ownership of the Hamilton Club to Maple Leaf Gardens Limited."[42] He took special pains to assure clubs that Ballard agreed to have the league "approve any future transfer of the Club by Maple Leaf Gardens Ltd. and to cause the Hamilton Club, Maple Leaf Gardens Ltd., Harold Ballard Limited and Harold Ballard personally, to abide by the constitution, by-laws and rules of the League."[43] Having said that, Gaudaur called for "each club to express its views upon the application before calling for a vote."[44]

Winnipeg was first. Acknowledging that he had never met Ballard, Ross Smith said that he was basing his opinion on "what he had read and heard." Ballard "appeared to be controversial, unpredictable, undisciplined, lacking in credibility, without respect for authority and without any sense of remorse over certain highly publicized misdeeds in his past." Furthermore, he pointed out the possible conflict of interest between football and hockey, "which would work to the detriment of the Hamilton Club." If all of these perceptions were true, Winnipeg was opposed.

Montreal's Sam Berger was in favour. Ballard had paid his debts to society for any past misdeeds. "Since that time, he has proven himself to be a successful operator, is a man of considerable resources, is prepared to invest his money in the Hamilton franchise which badly needs his support."

The ping-pong discussion continued. Saskatchewan's Bruce Cowie shared "some of Winnipeg's concerns." He described the CFL as "a fragile association of public and private ownership entities working together with a common purpose." Ballard had shown himself inclined to "operate as he pleases in the NHL." There was some question in Bruce Lowie's mind that

Ballard could "comply with the more rigid standards of the CFL." Saskatchewan was opposed.

Hamilton's Ralph Sazio expressed no such doubts. The Hamilton directors "have expressed great confidence in Mr. Ballard and are pleased that a person of his calibre wants to buy the Club." He was in favour. So too was Ottawa. "Why," asked Allan Waters, "is there any hesitation? The Hamilton Club is a private firm. The owner is in business to make a profit. He wants to sell the Club at a price which Mr. Ballard wants to pay. The Commissioner approves."

The Edmonton Eskimos had some misgivings about Ballard. They were opposed and would like to hear more about the alternate group wanting to buy the club. The Lions' Jack Farley was somewhat more conciliatory. Recognizing that his fellow Westerners were concerned over Ballard's tendency to shoot from the hip before looking for the target, for the reasons already stated by Ballard's supporters, he was prepared to support the application even though "one disturbing fact is the power of veto Mr. Ballard has in some NHL matters." Gaudaur spoke to that concern. He had contacted the NHL commissioner Clarence Campbell, who said that Ballard had only been an obstructionist when it was within his rights to do so. Ballard's veto applied only to club property rights "under a different definition than that which prevails in football." In addition, Mr. Campbell informed the commissioner that "Mr. Ballard had never broken a rule which had been voted in under prescribed voting requirements of the NHL."

The Prairie bloc was firm. Calgary's Frank Finn concluded that "it would not be in the best interests of either the League or the Calgary Club to approve the application." It remained for the Argos' Bill Hodgson to express "his disappointment at the position taken by the four prairie clubs." He declared that if the application were turned down, it would have a damaging effect on the league. The Eastern clubs were privately owned; they depended upon strong ownership. The transfer of the Hamilton ownership was "a matter of critical importance to the eastern members, as the owners have substantial personal investments involved which are being threatened by the deterioration of the Hamilton situation." Declaring that the Eastern clubs, and Toronto in particular, had most to lose and offering the opinion that "Mr. Ballard runs a high class operation at Maple Leaf Gardens and is well respected by members of the media," he urged the four dissenting clubs to reconsider over lunch. Commissioner Gaudaur had the final say before he adjourned for the noon hour. He encouraged the clubs to do what was best for the league and not be swayed by media reports, pro or con, nor by the views of the Hamilton fans.

When the session reconvened after lunch, the clubs were polled once again. The Westerners had not changed their position. The core of their opposition was the public persona of Harold Ballard. His comments about the WHA entered the picture. His urging of the NHL to defer from absorbing the rival league made him a villain in the West. Once again, the Easterners rallied to his defence. Hodgson maintained that the requirements being imposed on Ballard were much more stringent than those imposed when he or Allan Waters entered the league. He suggested that Ballard be brought in for a face-to-face meeting with all concerned.

Ralph Sazio recalled that when Michael DeGroote first put the club up for sale, various Hamilton groups were approached with no success. Meetings were held with Mayor Jack Macdonald; a feasibility study was done with a view to returning the club to community ownership. Independent auditors were allowed access to the financial statements. But Sazio concluded, "no specific proposal was received until Mr. Ballard made his formal offer to Mr. DeGroote on December 16."[45]

Gaudaur commented that Mayor Jack Macdonald wanted to keep the franchise in Hamilton hands; that, in time, provincial and/or federal funds would surface. The new group's bid from Hamilton could not be acted upon until DeGroote withdrew the acceptance of the Ballard offer.

It remained for Saskatchewan's Bruce Cowie to speak and to put his fears into perspective. With the smallest stadium in the league, Saskatchewan had the most to gain or to lose. He had no concern with Hodgson or Waters. They had shown themselves to be "reliable partners in the League."[46] The Western clubs wanted some sort of "guarantee that Mr. Ballard would agree to conform to the constitution."[47] Hodgson, Berger, and Gaudaur spoke once again in favour of Ballard; Edmonton's Matt Baldwin asked for another adjournment to allow the Western clubs to caucus.

Returning from the brief recess, the Calgary club asked that the "room be cleared of all persons other than the nine voting delegates, the Commissioner and the Secretary."[48] The Westerners had some further questions. Ralph Sazio was asked: "How would Mr. Ballard vote on the matters of revenue sharing and player costs which are on the agenda?" Sazio reported that he had briefed Ballard on the "delicate balance of the League's financial structure and the need for gate equalization." He cited Ballard's refusal to pay exorbitant salaries to hockey players describing him as "a tough business man who will try to hold the line on player costs, but is realistic enough to pay what has to be paid."[49]

The Western opposition was softening, but had further questions. "Would the EFC members do everything in their power to make sure that Mr. Ballard understands why the League has to operate the way that it does and what would be expected of him as a League partner?" Hodgson assured the Western teams that "to the extent that he could give such a guarantee ... [the clubs] will try to control Mr. Ballard as best they may." When it was asked, hypothetically, how the EFC would react to the application of the other Hamilton group, Berger "replied that he knows some of the individuals mentioned and he doubted that the transfer would meet EFC approval."[50]

The time seemed appropriate for a resolution. Gaudaur summarized. He shared some of the West's concerns but the meeting agreed "that a primary concern should be: What is best for the Hamilton Club?"[51] It remained for the president of the session, Bill Hodgson, to speak. He declared that "all member clubs of the Eastern Conference are dedicated to the One League concept, want the League to grow and prosper and continue to be a symbol of unity in Canada. He then called for a motion."[52]

The application for sale of the Tiger-Cats to Ballard passed unanimously. Harold Ballard was "invited to join the meeting to be welcomed by his new League partners."[53]

The fate of football in Montreal was never far from sight in any CFL meeting at any time, and 1978 was no exception. Sam Berger, who was inducted into the CFL Hall of Fame as a Builder in 1993, was constantly trying to maintain and increase the momentum which had been built up since the Alouettes had moved into the Olympic Stadium. It had always been perceived that the key to success in Montreal was to encourage identification with, and the following of, French Canadians. The record crowd of over 69,000 at the 1977 Grey Cup Game was an encouraging sign, something to be built on. Montreal had won the game convincingly and during the season had set a CFL single-season record for attendance in drawing 476,201 spectators. True, they had lost their head coach Marv Levy to the NFL's Kansas City Chiefs; they had replaced him with Joe Scannella and hopes for football were still high.

Once again, Montreal pursued the increased use of French in the league. Berger asked whether the 1978 Grey Cup Game, to be held in Toronto, could be a bilingual presentation, French as well as English in the "game program, public address announcements, game tickets, media accreditation and press releases by the League."[54] He noted that fans from Montreal complained of the lack of French during the last Grey Cup Game held in Toronto in 1976. In addition, he suggested that the Football Hall of Fame in Hamilton should have more French content. The matter was looked upon as critical for the Montreal club. After all, ever since the Olympic Games of 1976, followed by the election of the Parti Québécois, there had been a resurgence of strong nationalism in Quebec. The success of football in Montreal and of the CFL hinged upon acceptance and closer identification with the "French fact." This, plus the continuing pressure to bring the NFL to Montreal were two factors which had to be addressed constantly for football and the CFL to succeed in Montreal.

Gaudaur's reaction was to submit that "only the League's Records' Manual was not bilingual, and that was being studied. The League office operated bilingually; it had a bilingual secretary, there were French language letterheads, correspondence, rule books and bilingual replay statistics."[55] When Gaudaur noted that he had "some reservations about the degree of bilingualism necessary for a game outside Montreal," Ralph Sazio asked "why the Commissioner showed reluctance in making the game totally bilingual regardless of the site." Gaudaur replied that he still had the image within him of the Toronto public booing bilingual announcements during the Canada/Russia hockey series. He did not want to see that adverse reaction occur during a Grey Cup Game. He conceded that "in all other respects the game should be bilingual."[56]

With the country in one of its seemingly endless debates on "national unity," it was a sensitive issue. Edmonton's Baldwin felt that while Montreal's feelings were justified, "he could see where an undesirable situation could develop if the bilingual aspect is overplayed outside of Quebec."[57] Toronto's Bill Hodgson felt that "bilingual PA announcements in Toronto could very well provoke a negative response and result in our achieving the opposite to what the League would hope to achieve." Ottawa's Terry Kielty suggested that the new score-board at CNE Stadium might serve the purpose and "could be used to advantage." While Berger's concerns were not totally satisfied, he, nonetheless, "thanked the members for their favourable responses to his concerns."[58]

Despite the previous year's successful resolution of the Collective Bargaining Agreement and improved relations with the CIAU, there was still friction in both areas. The question of practice time surfaced once again during 1978. Calgary's Jack Gotta noted that his club faced a problem with practices as the season progressed. The short winter days were more of a problem in the northern climes of Canada than in the southern. He preferred to practise in the daylight. All of his players with the exception of one, a kicking specialist, were willing and able to practise prior to 4:00 P.M. Other employment was not a problem, but because of the collective agreement with the Players' Association, the clubs were unable to begin practice any earlier. The association complained that both Calgary and Toronto had begun practices earlier than agreed to. When the clubs maintained that all players agreed to the change, the association countered "that such players when asked would most likely agree; to disagree would jeopardize their employment on the Club."[59] The league decided to request that the current agreement be amended in order to enable clubs to conduct practices anytime after 2:30 P.M.[60] Early in the 1977 season, Ottawa was struggling and increased the length of its practices. They were abnormally long. Not only that, at least one meeting was called for 11:00 A.M., contrary to the collective agreement. Ottawa player representative, Tony Gabriel, complained to the Ottawa defensive coach, Bob O'Billovich. "Later on, the coaches jokingly blamed me for the late practices because I had complained about the meetings during the day," said Gabriel.[61] The situation continued to worsen. The Argos and new coach Forrest Gregg ran afoul of the Players' Association in 1978. There was talk that a strike could occur because of Gregg's practice policies. He had the Argos reporting at 10:00 A.M. for much of the season.[62] While the rest of the CFL was restricted to practices after 4:00 P.M., the Alouettes and Argos were allowed to begin practice after 2:30 and 1:00 respectively because they shared parks with major league baseball teams. Gregg stated that "his players had voted to come in early but at least one member of the Argonauts said that the Coach had delivered an ultimatum to the players."[63] The CFLPA president, George Reed, was unimpressed with Gregg's explanation. In another case that same year, non-import guard Bart Evans retired. The five-year CFL veteran had been traded from Winnipeg to Toronto but decided to remain in Winnipeg where he worked in a bank as a financial analyst. "He said he couldn't handle both careers in Toronto since the Argonauts have afternoon practices. He would need a substantial raise to make the move to Toronto and with a future of only two or three years, he decided to give up football and concentrate on his job with the Winnipeg bank."[64]

University of Alberta football coach, Jim Donlevy, met with the CFL's Norm Kimball to discuss issues of concern. Again, the universities wanted to do away with the territorial exemptions for each club, saying that they "demeaned the college draft itself."[65] The league, through Kimball, countered that only four of the 18 exempted in 1978 were from American schools. "The fact that 14 Canadian college players were chosen in this manner was a compliment to the CIAU."[66] The Canadian universities had objected to the term All Canadian being used to describe the CFL All Stars; that term, they felt, should be reserved for genuine Canadians selected from the university teams. The league agreed to ask Pat Marsden as president of the Football Reporters of Canada to investigate the use of a more appropriate designation. Evaluation camps and requests from individual clubs about university personnel were also criticized, the latter because the requested information seemed to be a duplication of what was on CIAU evaluation forms provided to the league currently. Again, the league's designated import rule was criticized as being detrimental to the non-import, particularly the quarterback. The league countered that, were the designated import removed, all 15 imports would play, resulting in a net loss of one starting non-import (Canadian) position.

The profile of the designated import rule was raised considerably during the 1978 season with the case of Jamie Bone. The quarterback from Halifax had led his team, the University of Western Ontario Mustangs, to the Vanier Cup championship in 1976 and 1977. He was taken by Winnipeg in the College Draft in 1977 but he returned to school. Winnipeg traded his rights to the Hamilton Tiger-Cats prior to the 1978 season. Bone hired lawyer Alan Eagleson as his agent. The Tiger-Cats offered a $14,000 contract; it appeared to have been offered on a "take it or leave it" basis. Negotiations proved fruitless. Nonetheless, a meeting was arranged between General Manager Bob Shaw, Eagleson, and Bone at Brock University, site of the Tiger-Cats' training camp. Upon arriving at the May 30 meeting, Eagleson and Bone were surprised to notice that training camp was in progress. No one had notified Bone when practices were to begin.[67]

When the three sat down to negotiate, it was clear that Shaw was holding firm. He was prepared, he said, to offer to trade Bone but, with training camps in progress throughout the league and rosters set, it would be difficult.[68] Shaw appeared indifferent as to whether or not Bone accepted the contract offer. Nonetheless, he did sign and attended all practices up to the team's first pre-season game of June 14.

It became obvious that the other two quarterbacks, Jimmy Jones and Tom Schuman, were being given the bulk of the practice time by Head Coach Tom Dimitroff. Bone was discouraged. He complained to Shaw that he was not being given a chance to demonstrate his talent. The Tiger-Cat manager replied: "Well, it takes a hell of a lot of guts for a coach to play a Canadian quarterback."[69] Bone did not have a play book. When he approached Dimitroff, he was reported to have said: "We don't have any."[70]

Bone, frustrated at not being allowed any practice time and released after a brief appearance in a Tiger-Cat uniform, was discouraged. His university coach, Darwin Semotiuk, decided to lodge a complaint with the Ontario Human Rights Commission on Bone's behalf. He claimed that Jamie Bone was discriminated against in his pursuit of the quarterback position because he was a Canadian. A formal hearing was held before Judge John McCamus over five days: June 26, July 10, 11, 12, 17, 1979. Lawyer John Sopinka acted on behalf of the Commission and Jamie Bone.

Hamilton coach Tom Dimitroff insisted that the designated import rule played no part in his decision. He maintained that Jimmy Jones and Tom Schuman had the advantage because of their talent and experience. Under Sopinka's incisive probing, however, Dimitroff admitted that he believed that U.S. players were superior to Canadians "because they are better trained at high school and college levels." Further prodding by Sopinka elicited the response that Dimitroff had made up his mind before training camp that Bone would not be his quarterback. Bone's lone hope "had lain in a possible change in the rules that would have allowed teams to keep an extra non-import as a designated quarterback."[71]

Dimitroff's testimony appeared to verify what many had been saying: a non-import, Canadian, would not be given an equal chance to play quarterback in the CFL; American coaches were more likely to trust in the system of the American colleges, the one that they knew best, and had preconceived notions about non-import talent, particularly at the quarterback position. Ironically, Dimitroff had been the offensive coach at Ottawa when Bill Robinson was trying to earn a berth with the Rough Riders. Judge McCamus's ruling wasn't dwelling on coincidences, though. He "reached the conclusion that a contravention of the code occurred, according to the facts of the case."[72] He ordered that the Tiger-Cats "comply with the provision of the Human Rights Code and compensate the complainant for injuries caused as a result of the contravention of the code."[73] McCamus ordered the Cats to pay Jamie Bone compensation of $10,000—$7,000 for "the loss of fair opportunity" to make the 1978 team roster and $3,000 "for injuries to feelings and loss of reputation." In addition the club was ordered to offer Bone "as soon as reasonably practicable," a five day trial with the club. There were other directives in the judgement, including a contract for the 1980 season. Bone was vindicated. He chose not to pursue a try-out with the Tiger-Cats and the CFL; instead he accepted an offer from the Dallas Cowboys of the NFL, where he was given full opportunity to be a part of "America's team."

Meanwhile, Tom Scott had played out his option with the Winnipeg Blue Bombers, thus becoming a "free agent." When the top receiver signed with Edmonton, it became obvious that he was "free" in name only. The Eskimos awarded Winnipeg the rights to their outstanding prospect Joe Poplawski, their first pick in the territorial exemption draft of 1978. Poplawski's talent as a wide receiver at the University of Alberta was well known to Winnipeg's new head coach, Ray Jauch, who had replaced Bud Riley. An earlier 1977 proposal, which would have seen money change hands as compensation when a "free agent" was signed by another club, had been turned down. Saskatchewan's Ken Preston summed up the feeling: "What does money matter? It's the players that matter. Money doesn't go out and win games."[74]

In the continuation of the East-West All Star game, the West prevailed in 1978. The game was played at Calgary's McMahon Stadium and attracted an attendance of close to 21,000. The 12-point margin in the 24–12 victory was mainly provided by Edmonton Eskimo Dave Cutler. He kicked two field goals, two singles and two extra points. The game might have been considered a success on the field, but off the field, there was a monetary loss, a deficit of $9,000. In addition, there was a "$25,000 law suit pending over the cancellation of the television broadcast."[75]

After only five games into the season, Tom Dimitroff was released by the Hamilton Tiger-Cats. He was replaced by John Payne. The Cats had lost three of their first five games, including the home opener with the Argonauts. Dimitroff later moved to Toronto where he became the defensive coordinator under interim coach Bud Riley. The Argonauts had fired Leo Cahill, again. The Argonauts, in spite of their prize catch, Terry Metcalfe, had tumbled from a 3–1 to a 3–6 record. Cahill, in his two terms as head coach, 1966–1972 and 1977–1978, had won more games than any other Argo coach and had also lost more with a record of 59–59–1.

In Edmonton, the Eskimos were fashioning a formidable team but not without complications. Their offensive coordinator, Joe Faragalli, had suffered a heart attack in August. Later, during the same season, Line Coach Cal Murphy, who held a similar position with the Grey Cup champion Alouettes in 1977, suffered the same fate and was forced to miss two months of the season while recovering. "Now," said Head Coach Hugh Campbell, tongue firmly planted in his cheek, "I suppose that everybody who has a heart attack is going to want time off."[76]

Despite their problems, the Eskimos finished the season in first place and awaited the play-off between second-place Calgary and third-placed Winnipeg. B.C. finished in fourth place, ahead of last-place finisher Saskatchewan, in what turned out to be quarterback Ron Lancaster's last year as a player. In 19 years in the CFL as a quarterback, Lancaster had fashioned an enviable career with his two teams, Ottawa and Saskatchewan. He set records in the number of passes thrown, 6,233, passes completed, 3,384, yards gained, 50,535, touchdowns thrown, 333. His completion rate over the nineteen consecutive seasons played, yet another CFL record, was a remarkable 54.5%. He moved immediately into the coaching fraternity, replacing Saskatchewan coach Jim Eddy for the 1979 season. Calgary defeated Winnipeg 38–4 and ventured north to play the Eskimos in their new Commonwealth

Stadium; the Eskimos repeated as Western champions by defeating the Stampeders 26–13.

In the East, Toronto finished in fourth and last spot, Ottawa in first with an 11–5 record. In the semifinal, played in Montreal, the Alouettes defeated the Tiger-Cats 35–20. In the Eastern final, Montreal travelled to Ottawa where the Alouettes were victorious, overcoming the favoured Riders, 21–16. After the game, the Toronto *Star* asked: "If football is war, is Sweet a traitor?"[77] It was all because Don Sweet, the Alouette place kicker, offered off-season assistance to Ottawa's J.T. Hay who had missed four field goals in the Eastern final.

In anticipation of the second consecutive meeting in the national final between Montreal and Edmonton, the league held its meetings and Schenley Award presentations. Most notable, the CFL voted against the sale of the Toronto Argonauts franchise to Douglas Bassett, son of former owner, John Bassett. The application was vetoed by a 5–4 vote, said to have been orchestrated by Harold Ballard, whose "motives for torpedoing the sale is not only his self confessed hatred of John Bassett but also a desire to own the CFL club himself." Owner Bill Hodgson "said Ballard recently sought to manipulate a deal with Argo minority shareholders, Carling O'Keefe Breweries."[78]

At the Schenley Awards ceremonies, Tony Gabriel became only the second player to win both the Most Outstanding and Canadian Player awards. Runner-up to the Canadian Player award, Joe Poplawski, who was also selected the Most Outstanding Rookie, suggested that the Canadian Player award should "be renamed the Tony Gabriel Award and be done with it;"[79]. The Ottawa receiver had won it four of the last five years. Other award winners were Edmonton's Dave Fennell as Most Outstanding Defensive Player and Jim Coode of Ottawa as Most Outstanding Offensive Lineman. The week also saw the return of many outstanding CFL favourites such as Hal Patterson, Jackie Parker, George Reed, and Ron Lancaster.

In the return match between the Eskimos and the Alouettes, the Westerners prevailed, once again thanks to the foot of Dave Cutler. The score was 20–13 and Cutler accounted for 14 points—four field goals, a single point from a missed field goal, and an extra point. His performance, which overshadowed Don Sweet's seven points, was foreshadowed by Montreal coach Joe Scanella's "sniping at the use of the shoelace"[80] Cutler used when he kicked field goals. In the game itself, Edmonton's "Alberta Crude" defence contained Montreal running back David Green; defensive tackle Dave Fennell was overpowering against all who attempted to block him; a roughing penalty by Montreal's defensive back, Vernon Perry, allowed the Eskimos to move from their own end when the Alouettes seemed to be gaining the momentum; Perry atoned somewhat by intercepting a long pass for the touchdown-bound Waddell Smith. The finest individual perform-ance, most observers felt, was turned in by Edmonton's middle linebacker, Dan Kepley, who seemed to be all over the field.

1979 to 1980

Chapter Six

WHEN THE TORONTO ARGONAUTS OWNER, Bill Hodgson was rebuffed in his attempt to sell the Argos to the Bassett group, some club owners were incensed, particularly Sam Berger of the Montreal Alouettes. Berger found it "outrageous that the Hamilton Club had expressed its opposition and stated that there should not be any room for animosity in a business such as this."[1] Hodgson recalled that he "had decided to step out of the picture"[2] for health reasons, and had written to the league's club presidents to that effect. The resulting publicity generated a number of telephone calls, "one of which was from John W. Bassett, who asked that his sons be given the first opportunity to purchase the Club. This, Hodgson agreed to do."[3] After all, Hodgson had reacted similarly when Bassett was selling in 1974 and subsequently, had bought the club. "Even though he did not know Mr. Bassett, the deal was settled in ten minutes with everything above board" and he felt that he had "a moral obligation to give the Bassetts first chance."[4] Hodgson's personal preference was that the club be sold to Agincourt Football Enterprises Ltd. "which is the same corporate body that previously operated the Toronto Argonaut Football Club Limited ... wholly owned subsidiary of Baton Broadcasting Inc ... controlled by the Telegram Corp. company owned by seven trusts, the beneficiaries of which are members of the Eaton and Bassett families."[5] In his opinion, the league would be better served by "having such high calibre individuals as the Eatons and the Bassetts operating the Toronto Club."[6] Berger was adamant that "whatever objection may exist against John W. Bassett, should not be held against the younger Bassetts and Eaton."[7]

Nonetheless, the sale was denied, defeated by a 5–4 vote. Other offers were, of necessity, entertained by Hodgson. One which seemed to be particularly attractive was from a group of 10, headed by insurance executive and former president of the Argonaut Playback Club, Ron Barbaro. This group offered $3.5 million, two hundred thousand more than the Bassetts, for Hodgson's 60%.[8] When Hodgson consulted his minority partners, Carling O'Keefe Breweries Ltd., the latter soon discovered that although they would be the largest stockholding party, the Barbaro group would be responsible for the direction of the club. Carling O'Keefe decided to buy the Argos.

Carling O'Keefe matched the $3.5 million. That, plus the $2.3 million it had paid in 1976 to become a minority shareholder, represented a total investment of $5.8 million. Owning the Argonauts would allow Carling O'Keefe to rebuild the team as they saw fit, and, like their ownership of the Quebec Nordiques, it would allow them to use the football club as a tool to market their beer products. Carling O'Keefe's ownership of the Argonauts would also provide an interesting aspect to the Toronto sporting scene. The Blue Jays were owned by Labatt's and would share CNE Stadium with the Argos, who by virtue of their being first on the scene had priority as far as dates were concerned.

The CFL was hesitant. They preferred that owners not be public companies. There was the "potential that the control of the parent company would fall into the hands of a person not acceptable to the League as a Club operator."[9] It meant that the league would need guarantees that it would have the final say in approving new ownership. The owners would have to agree to be bound by the league's constitution. There were other fears as well. Carling O'Keefe was a subsidiary of a foreign group, Rothmans of Pall Mall, controlled from South Africa. Could the CFL still claim to be Canadian owned and controlled?

A series of letters from the numbered company 338507 Ontario Limited were sent to Jake Gaudaur. They stipulated that 338507 Ontario Limited would engage only in business related to the operation of the Argonaut Football Club; that it would not transfer, sell, or assign any interest nor any assets, either as a whole or substantially as a whole, of the Argonauts, "without the prior approval of the Canadian Football League obtained in accordance with the constitution of the Canadian Football League." [10]

Corroborating letters from Carling O'Keefe Breweries of Canada Limited, Carling O'Keefe Limited, and 338507 Ontario Limited were also sent. As well, 338507 Ontario Limited verified that should it sell its interest, the CFL would have the right to accept the change or "require 338507 Ontario Limited to dispose of the Toronto Argonaut Football Club upon reasonable terms within a reasonable period of time to a buyer acceptable to the CFL."[11]

There was only one more obstacle before the CFL could confirm the sale. The Federal Investment Review Agency (FIRA) had to approve it. Liberal party organizer and former CFL commissioner, Keith Davey, arranged for John Barnett, vice-president of the brewery, to meet with Jack Horner, Minister of Industry, Trade and Commerce and responsible for FIRA. Barnett was assured that the sale would not be rejected by FIRA.[12] That being said, the CFL approved the sale. Carling O'Keefe Breweries of Canada Limited, through 338507 Ontario Limited, was the new owner of the Toronto Argonaut Football Club.

The first action of the new owner was to select long-time Argonaut executive Lew Hayman as president. Hayman, in turn, hired Forrest Gregg, a former player with the Green Bay Packers and coach with the Cleveland Browns, both of the NFL. Hayman followed with a new general manager, Tommy Hudspeth. In response to rumours that Dick Shatto was being fired, Hayman said that the popular former player would "continue to pursue the areas of marketing and licensing as they pertain to the Argonauts."[13] Shatto had three years remaining on his contract with the Argos.

Bill Hodgson was still thinking of the CFL. The recent owner of the Argonauts wrote to Gaudaur to enquire about placing a new franchise in Halifax. His letter said that meetings had been held with "different authorities." The main obstacle was the lack of a stadium seating 30,000 but the proposed ownership group of himself, an institution and a local industrialist, were endeavouring to create a team tentatively called the "Maritimers" representing the three Maritime provinces.[14] It turned out to be an exercise in frustration for Gaudaur and the league. On three separate occasions, Gaudaur "had confirmed appointments with [Minister of State Fitness and Amateur Sport] Mrs. Campagnolo but the Minister had found it necessary to cancel each one."[15] In the end, "no such application was ever filed and after a number of telephone conversations, the Commissioner received a copy of a letter from Hodgson to Premier John Buchanan of Nova Scotia advising he was abandoning the project."[16]

The Argonauts were somewhat of an anomaly. Perhaps it was because they were located in Canada's biggest market, perhaps because of the newly expanded and refurbished CNE Stadium, perhaps because of their marketing practices; certainly it was not because of its record. From 1974 through 1979, there was no season when the team won more than it lost. Overall, their record was 33 wins, 60 losses, and 3 ties. Yet, during that time, attendance figures rose steadily. Had there been more seats between the goal-lines in the 53,000 plus capacity stadium, the Argonauts could have increased their attendance even more than the 46,861 average peak that it reached. It was the "end zone seats" which were a truer reflection of football fans' interest in the Argonauts. These seats, especially constructed because of the Blue Jays, were for the most part vacant because of their poor sight-lines. One had to be a fervent follower of the Argos to purchase a seat in that section.

The bulk of the Argonaut appeal came from the corporate sector. In 1979, 39,000 seats were "held by subscription ticket holders. Eighty per cent of these tickets or 31,000 are held by the corporate client."[17] Corporations were anxious to be involved with the Argonauts. The Bank of Nova Scotia and A&P both "made a commitment to buy 250,000 tickets over the next 5 years." In the A&P case, any customer who purchased $5.00 worth of goods could buy a $4.50 ticket for 99 cents. The Argos also reciprocated with program ads and had players appear at company functions. Other corporate sponsors were: Simpsons Sears with their Junior Argonaut Club, Akai, who sponsored the Argo Rookie of the Year Award, Travelways, and Ross Wemp Chev-Olds.[18] Of course, there were other sources of revenue for the Argonauts such as rights from concessions, logos, radio, and television, but most importantly, they were still the team that people, especially the corporate sector, identified with during the summer and fall seasons.

Elsewhere in preparation for the 1979 season, Calgary was adding to McMahon Stadium, Winnipeg Stadium was being given a complete facelift, and Taylor Field in Regina was outfitted with artificial turf, a new dressing room, and office facilities. In Edmonton, the newly constructed Commonwealth Stadium was a huge success, combining with the winning Eskimos to attract a record season crowd for the West of 340,239.

In Montreal, despite the winning record and the "Big O," the Alouettes were under seige, again. Mayor Jean Drapeau was openly pursuing the NFL for a franchise and the French media were not only actively supportive but they "were vehemently opposed to the Alouettes."[19] Drapeau had even offered to send the Alouettes to Quebec City, once an NFL team had located in Montreal. It was perhaps a facetious gesture but, nonetheless, the Alouettes were feeling unwanted in their own city. Sam Berger concurred with a recent statement by John McHale, president of the Expos, who found that they were forced to pay higher salaries to attract players to Montreal with its political climate and higher cost of living. When Drapeau returned from a visit to the Super Bowl, where he was continuing his efforts to sell Montreal as an expansion site to the NFL, Berger complained, "the French press gave all its attention to the NFL and disregarded the presence of an outstanding U.S. college quarterback in town to talk with the Alouettes."[20]

With the huge crowds being attracted to the larger stadiums in Montreal, Toronto, and Edmonton, it was only natural that gate equalization and revenue sharing be discussed. The total amount that a team could contribute had been $75,000 since 1968. Some clubs felt that it was time to increase that figure. Not Montreal. It was adamantly opposed. At the February 15th meeting, the club decided that it "could not entertain any change in revenue sharing formulas at this time."[21] David Berger, Sam Berger's son, insisted that the team was still "$2,000,000 in debt, had suffered an operating loss in 1978 and is involved in a life and death struggle in Montreal."[22] When Argonaut president Lew Hayman attempted a self-deprecating remark to lighten up the meeting with an aside that "higher salaries did not necessarily mean a better team, as the Toronto team has learned to its regret,"[23] the elder Berger, Sam, stated ominously that "football is in serious trouble in Montreal with the closing of high schools and exodus of large companies."[24] He wondered aloud why the matter of revenue sharing was even on the agenda since all these problems were so well known that "everything that has been said today, has been said at a previous meeting."[25] Clearly, he was sending a message that he was not prepared to give up any more of his hard-earned revenue.

The Argonauts' Lew Hayman did not consider salary ceilings to be a practical solution to be pursued. He offered that they paid "a good one third of revenue towards salaries in 1979."[26] Total revenue was said to be $4.45 million with 90% generated through gate receipts.[27] Player salaries were 30% of gross revenue.[28] Taxation policies also assisted the club's financial position; it was allowed to depreciate 50% of a player's salary over a 10-year period.[29] As a result, the league took another look at gate equalization that fall. The league decided to double the maximum contribution a team could be called upon to make, to $150,000.[30] Montreal's Sam Berger had a decision to make.

When the CFL Rules Committee met in January at Edmonton, it heard some disturbing news. Hugh Campbell, speaking for the coaches, reported on his having called a meeting of all CFL coaches at the American Football Coaches Association Convention (AFCA) in San Francisco, January 9, to hear their input and suggestions for any refinements or changes in the rules. He was "disappointed that only three head coaches and one assistant showed up. There were two other coaches in the hotel but they didn't come and two other clubs didn't send their representatives."[31]

Jake Gaudaur was concerned. Coaches' input was considered important to the Rules Committee; at the same time it was a courtesy extended to the coaches. "Unless the representative of the coaches could come to the meeting with a true consensus of all coaches, he saw no point in having the coaches represented."[32] It was left to Calgary coach Jack Gotta, who also doubled as general manager, to poll the coaches: "Should a Club require a head coach to attend the dinner at the AFCA Convention or Coach of the Year dinner in Edmonton?"[33] The CFL's Executive Committee acted on the information to legislate both. The club's head coach was "to attend the League function at the ACFA and to attend the meeting of head coaches prior to the Annual Meeting of the Rules Committee convened for the purpose of developing a consensus on current rule change proposals for the information of the Rules Committee."[34]

As popular as the CFL appeared to be, there were still mixed signals being sent. The Players' Association decided to cancel its All Star game for 1979. Yet its awards dinner was successful in raising almost $11,000 in 1978, and matching that again with its May 2 dinner at the Calgary Inn in 1979. On May 3, the public was invited to play 18 holes of golf with invited CFL and NFL players. In spite of temperatures of 2° C, 90 participants paid $100 to play with the celebrities.[35] The association also announced plans to reconvene its All Star game in Japan.

With the increasing competition for the entertainment dollar, there was a never ending attempt to keep football before the public. In addition to attending events such as the All Star dinner and golf tournament in Calgary, teams reconvened during the off season for basketball where "success was measured by good exercise, good fun and goodwill."[36] Edmonton, Ottawa, and Toronto focused on basketball; Hamilton was so busy in the off-season that "many of the home town players are thinking that the city should change its name to Hamil-thon. They've been involved in Bowl-a-thons, swim-a-thons, run-a-thons, etc., raising money for many organizations. It's been a lot of fun and if you really want to get in shape quick ... try broomball."[37] In Montreal, the Alouettes played 24 hockey games over the winter before more than 40,000 spectators, "raising in excess of $50,000 for charity, local minor sports programs, etc."[38]

In Saskatchewan, seven days in June were set aside by Premier Alan Blakeney as "Ron Lancaster Week." A dinner, attended by 900 people, was included in a four-hour testimonial to the retiring player and new coach of the Roughriders. Speeches, telegrams, a packaged highlight film of the "little general's" career, the retiring of his sweater #23, a presentation of a van, a portrait from the Province and news from Mayor Baker that a Regina street was to be named after him, were all part of the evening, which also saw former teammate George Reed make a personal presentation as well as one from the Players' Association. The turf company that was installing the artificial material in Taylor Field also announced that they would "ring Lancaster's home swimming pool with Super Turf."[39] When the Roughriders played the Alouettes in an exhibition game at Taylor Field, there were more gifts: a silver tray engraved with all of Lancaster's records, a set of golf clubs from his players, a trip to Disney World in Florida for his family, and a fur stole for wife, Bev.[40] "It was a week quite unlike any other week in Lancaster's life. But then, when you consider what he did for football in Saskatchewan and in Canada it was indeed a worthy celebration, even if he will never be repaid for his contributions and years of brilliant play."[41]

Ron Lancaster's coaching début was not up to par with his playing career. The Roughriders suffered through a 2–14 record to finish in last place. Some thought that the biggest problem Lancaster the coach had was that he did not have Lancaster the quarterback playing for him. Attendance fell off in the newly expanded Taylor Field, this in spite of the province-wide TV blackout for all home games.

In Edmonton, however, the Eskimos, under Norm Kimball, were becoming the model for others to emulate. They were adaptable. When Carl Crennel, a linebacker with Montreal, became available because of the Alouettes' having signed Tom Cousineau, the Eskimos wasted little time in picking him up. They already had the best linebacker in the country, Dan Kepley, playing in the middle of their 4–3 alignment. Theirs was a traditional defence; it had gained notoriety as "Alberta Crude" with four strong powerful defensive linemen and three mobile reactive linebackers. When Crennel became available in October, the Eskimos evolved to a 3–4 defence, taking advantage of both Crennel and Kepley in the inside linebacking positions.

The adjustment was the right one for many reasons, one of them based on Edmonton's success. Passing teams traditionally had employed a straight drop-back passer. Edmonton was one of the first teams to employ a "sprint" type of passing offence featuring a quick release after three steps to either side of the line. The defence was spread out by the formation; backs were used as receivers; linemen had to obstruct the defence but not necessarily block them for any extended period of time. It was an ideal opportunity for Canadian offensive linemen, too, since the new pass blocking rules were just coming into effect. Tight ends were being replaced with slot-backs; there was less emphasis on the running game. Non-imports were being moved into offensive line and backfield positions. The reorganization of the "front seven" into four linebackers and three down linemen meant that it was easier to take away the short passing game. Edmonton's defensive backs were also among the best in the league, having the capability to play either zone or man-to-man coverages, allowing the linebackers and linemen to work to-gether to control the run and short passing game.

Norm Kimball was also proving to be a shrewd negotiator with his players, secure enough to use all the means available to him. When Edmonton's top receiver Waddell Smith was negotiating with Norm Kimball prior to the 1979 season, the two were far apart. Smith wanted to play out his option; Kimball's stated club policy was to have no players on the team who were playing out their option. Neither would budge. Kimball sent Smith to Hamilton. During the exhibition season it became obvious to coach Hugh Campbell that Edmonton lacked speed among its receiving corps. Campbell contacted Kimball to seek the opportunity to get back and sign Smith. Kimball concurred. Campbell contacted Hamilton coach John Payne for permission to speak with Smith, offering defensive back Leroy Paul and a first round draft choice for the opportunity. Campbell wanted only four days in which to pursue Smith: "If we didn't sign him in four days, he would revert back to them."[42] Payne met with Smith and was convinced that the speedster would not sign with Edmonton; he agreed to the deal. Campbell swung into action. In three days, Smith signed a three-year contract with a clause allowing him to renegotiate at the end of the 1979 season. Kimball knew enough to allow Campbell to conduct all the negotiations with Smith who went on to have an outstanding year. He was Edmonton's and the West's nomination for the Schenley as the Most Outstanding Player of 1979.

Edmonton reached the national final again by defeating Calgary 19–7. The Stampeders had earlier overcome the B.C. Lions by a 37-2 score.

Montreal ended up with an 11–4–1 record and a first-place finish in the East. In the play-offs, Ottawa squeaked by Hamilton 29–26 before losing to first-place finisher Montreal 17-6. Montreal fans were still clearly disgruntled with quarterback Joe Barnes. The Alouettes' offence was described as "punchless" in spite of the East's leading rusher, David Green. Only 35,000 spectators attended the Eastern final at Olympic Stadium. Barnes, who completed 10 of 25 passes for 99 yards and one interception, was the subject of much discussion. Appearing on CJAD's "Open Line" radio show after the game, he repeated the list of charges against him: "I know they call me unimaginative, conservative; I don't throw the ball enough; I don't throw it well enough; we have a stereotyped offense."[43] It was a recital of every quarterback's lament.

The meeting between Ottawa and Montreal was the sixth of the season between the two teams, a fact many referred to in describing the game as "boring." It probably played a reinforcing role in the decision the League made at its Grey Cup meetings to approve a full interlocking schedule starting with the 1981 season.[44] The other ascendant figure in the league, Edmonton's Norm Kimball, was a central figure in attempting to convince the CFL to move to a full interlocking schedule where each team would play the others twice in a home-and-home arrangement. Hamilton's Ralph Sazio had mixed emotions about the concept. While some teams fretted about playing an arch rival five or six times, Sazio had no such compunctions with his team's adversaries, the Argonauts of Toronto. He would rather play them than many of the Western teams who simply did not draw well in Hamilton. He seconded Kimball's motion for an interlocking schedule at the November 23, 1979, meeting. He was later to argue in February of 1980 that the 1981 "experience be reviewed at the 1981 Grey Cup meeting. If results are favourable, the decision could be made to go ahead in 1983. The others weren't buying. The decision to move to a full interlocking schedule in 1981 was re-affirmed."[45]

At the 1979 Schenley Awards presentation, David Green, Montreal's running back was selected as the Outstanding Player over Edmonton's Waddell Smith. Green had rushed for nine100-yard games, four consecutively, in amassing 1,678 yards rushing on 287 carries and 11 touchdowns. Edmonton's Brian Kelly, known as "Howdie Doody" to his team-mates, was chosen as the Most Outstanding Rookie over Ottawa's Martin Cox; Dave Fennell, the Most Outstanding Canadian over Hamilton's Leif Petterson; Ben Zambiasi of the Tiger-Cats, the Most Outstanding Defensive Player over John Helton of Winnipeg; and Edmonton's Mike Wilson, the Most Outstanding Offensive Lineman over Montreal's Ron Watrin.

Edmonton fans came to Montreal dreading a repeat of the severe weather conditions of 1977, but they came with enthusiasm. Dorval Airport was "a sea of yellow and green badges, rosettes and ribbons ... [and a] banner saying 'L'Esprit d'Edmonton'."[46]

With the game in Montreal, the source so often described by Jake Gaudaur as the league's number one problem, the commissioner took the opportunity to do some selling of the importance of the game:

> If there ever was a Canadian institution worth preserving, it is the CFL. It is the only pro sport in Canada that has achieved national stature. It is the only event, the Grey Cup Game, in Canada which must be covered on three television networks, the CBC, Radio Canada and the CTV as well as both CBC radio networks and overseas to our armed forces. What other event brings tens of thousands of people from all parts of the country together in a spirit of friendly competition? You just have to look at the friendly betting rivalry between Premiers Lougheed and Levesque which has devel-

oped in the past three years ... We have to understand that we live next door to the greatest nation in the world. We will probably always be in a cultural shadow but I believe in football, we have been able to have our cake and eat it. The talented Americans we brought in raised the game into the big time but it gave the Peter Dalla Rivas and the Gord Judges and Glen Weirs the chances to develop to the point where they can hold their own against the best in the world.[47]

Perhaps because of the 1977 field conditions and the subsequent stories about the Alouettes shooting staples into their shoes, there seemed to be a fair amount of coverage related to equipment. Not only were the 20 balls ordered for the game especially stamped with "Grey Cup 1977 Montreal," but they were also tested by the officials for the proper air pressure and with callipers over the long and short axis of each ball.[48] The Montreal equipment people kept size 12 snowmobile boots close by the players' bench as a means of keeping kicker Don Sweet's feet warm. Both benches were to have propane heaters blowing hot air; hand warmers and a cream to prevent frostbite were also available.[49] The late-season setting meant extra equipment expenses. Toques, thermal underwear, and gloves, usually the handball or racquetball variety, became part of the practice and/or game dress. Football lore has always ascribed winning qualities to the quality of shoes. Certainly, the 1969 Ottawa Rough Riders' victory over the Argonauts in the second game of the two-game total-point series Eastern final and the 1977 Grey Cup Game were part of the mythology. For the 1979 contest, the Alouettes were leaving nothing to chance. Their footwear included broomball-style shoes, 33 pairs of them, in the event of snow; in case of rain they had canvas shoes "with black rubber soles with the 100 little teeth marks on the bottom for traction. If the field freezes, its the grass shoes with 1/2 inch steel cleats. Shoes are so important. They're just like tires."[50]

There was also the need to have replacement sweaters and pants available in the event of wet conditions and the need to change to drier, lighter clothes. Play-off and Grey Cup attire also included pouches sewn on the players' sweaters and used as hand warmers. Some teams were hesitant to provide their offensive backs and receivers with these since they might assist the defence in tackling the ball carrier.

In the 1979 Grey Cup Game, 65,113 fans filled Olympic Stadium to see the rematch of the Alouettes and Eskimos. While the number was 3,205 lower than the 1977 record, the 1979 game generated the highest gate revenue to that point—$1,402,733. To some, it was again the reincarnation of the classic series of the fifties when Edmonton and Montreal teams met in 1954, '55, and '56. This was the rubber match in the three-game series of the seventies. It lived up to its hype: "The overwhelming majority of the 65,113 fans who jammed the Olympic Stadium on this most benign of November 25 afternoons, went away caring not if the home team had won or lost but delighted with the way both teams played the game."[51] The game was a crowd pleaser. Tim Burke wrote: "It seems just when the disgruntled public is about to drive the final nail into Canadian football, Commissioner Jake Gaudaur invokes some divinity to stay the wintry tempest for re-affirmation of the wondrous advantages of big fields, 3 downs and men in motion and other identifying features we cling to with such stubbornness."[52]

The game was a "contest of complete football, offence and defence, by the best two teams in the country playing at their fiercest."[53] It ended with a 17-9 victory by Edmonton. There was excitement right to the end. Montreal's Keith Baker apparently tied the game, with a successful extra point, on a 90-yard punt return for a touchdown with one minute and twenty seconds remaining. The play was called back because of a clipping infraction attributed to Montreal's Gerry Dattilio. The Alouettes who were the league's second most penalized team were assessed 145 yards on 16 infractions; Edmonton, the least penalized, had four penalties and 25 yards.

Unlike the fifties, when the Edmonton–Montreal contests were high-scoring affairs, those of the seventies were defensive struggles. In their three most recent Grey Cup meetings, Montreal had scored four touchdowns, Edmonton three. The remainder of the points were generated by the kickers: Don Sweet scored 39 of Montreal's 63 points while Dave Cutler scored 25 of Edmonton's 43. Edmonton won two of the three games played; they had won all three of the fifties' series.

Roster decisions and the designated import rule were always at the surface of discussions in the CFL. Rosters were either too small (not enough Canadians, not enough Americans, etc.) or should be abolished or retained. There was no question that the discussions with the Players' Association to renegotiate the Collective Bargaining Agreement were paramount in the CFL's eyes. Both Ralph Sazio and Norm Kimball, wary of the ramifications such moves could have on negotiations, "argued that any decision on roster matters should be delayed until current negotiations with the Players' Association have been concluded."[54]

The CFL and its Players' Association announced a new collective agreement at a press conference, May 18, 1980. It covered three seasons, 1980, '81, and '82, expiring December 31, 1982. The contract sought to smooth over those areas which had been an irritant to relations between the two groups. It addressed the issues of playing out one's option, becoming a "free agent," and compensation. Technically, a player was a "free agent" after playing out his option; realistically, that was not the case. Players might wish to play out their option in order to be free to sign with another team in the CFL or NFL. Upon returning to Canada following an unsuccessful bid with the NFL team, a player found himself still bound to the club he last played for in the CFL. If he wished to move to another CFL team, some form of compensation was sent to the last club played for, as was the case with Tom Scott and Joe Poplawski. The matter was looked into by Players' Association General Counsellor John Agro. He concluded that "the use of the expression 'play out his option' is quite incorrect. The option is that of the Club … It is only when the Club wants the Player that the right of option arises." With respect to the player who played out his option, tried out with an NFL team, was cut, and returned to the CFL, "lo and behold, who do you belong to—the club who last held your contract" in spite of the fact, Agro said, that the club didn't pay a "five cent piece to have the right … you gave that 'parent' club 10% of your compensation to gain your freedom." Further, concluded Agro, "other teams in Canada would not touch you because they don't know what the Commissioner will insist be paid to your 'parent' club … So not only does your 'parent' club save 10% of your compensation, but also gains a player in your place instead. Standard Players Contract? or Indenture? Anyone for option year?"[55]

The option year figured prominently with Ottawa's quarterback Tom Clements. When the Rough Riders couldn't sign him and with rumours that he really wanted to go to the NFL, they traded his rights to Saskatchewan in exchange for Steve Dennis and Bob O'Doherty and a 1980 draft choice. Saskatchewan, too, was unable to sign Clements, who was rumoured to be heading to Kansas City to join Marv Levy and the Chiefs of the NFL. Not wanting a quarterback for only one season and particularly one who had injured his shoulder in the first exhibition game of the season as Clements had done, they traded him to the Hamilton Tiger-Cats who were in need of a veteran quarterback while rookies Dave Marler and Ed Smith developed.

The problem was once again highlighted when Calgary quarterback John Hufnagel, a veteran of five years with the Stampeders, played out his option and headed to Saskatchewan's Roughriders, immediately setting off discussions about compensation the Roughriders would have to send for the "free agent." The new collective agreement left the existing policy in place for the 1980 season; that is, "when a player plays out his option and signs with another CFL Club and the two Clubs cannot work out a mutually acceptable agreement on compensation, the Commissioner has the right to determine compensation."[56] For the 1981 season, compensation was to be awarded only if the club had offered a minimum 15% pay increase to induce the player to sign a new contract. For the 1982 season, compensation would only be given if the player was with his club for three years or less.[57] CFL negotiator Jake Dunlap of Ottawa stated that the league decided to opt for the "free agency" agreement "after concluding that restricting player movement posed a legal question on restraint of trade. On top of that, the players were reasonable in their money demands."[58] While the question of compensation was to be eliminated for the 1983 season, allowing any player to move freely within the league after playing out his option, there was one minor loose strand: "The only sticky point is that the current agreement expires December 31, 1982 and the clause allowing total freedom for free agents will have to be renewed at that time."[59]

The players' "reasonable salary demands" included the following: first-year players who received a salary of $11,000 in 1979 were to receive a minimum of $16,000 for 1980 and '81, rising to $18,000 in '82; second- and third-year players who were at $14,000 minimum in '79 were to receive $19,000 in their second year, and $22,000 with two years of experience—in 1982, these minimums were to rise to $22,000 and $24,000.

With respect to training camps, the new agreement called for $325 per week in 1980 (up by $60), $340 in 1981, and $355 in 1982. Grey Cup bonuses were increased to from $6,000 to $8,000 for the winning team and from $3,000 to $4,000 for the losing club. Players playing out their option would receive 100% of their salary rather than the traditional 90%.[60]

While the CFL was winning over its players, it was continuing to alienate the Canadian universities. The president of the Canadian Universities Football Coaches Association, Cam Innes, was recommending "that as of June 1, we sever all contacts with the Canadian Football League."[61] Traditionally, the CFL had played its Grey Cup Game on the last weekend of November. The universities, wanting a time when the glare of publicity would be more available to them, moved into the second last weekend for their College Bowl. In 1980, the CFL decided to play the Grey Cup Game on the same weekend as the already scheduled university final. College Bowl officials were furious at yet another apparent slight. Reluctantly, they moved their final to the following weekend.[62]

As much of an irritant as that was, it was the plight of the Canadian quarterback and the Jamie Bone affair that would not go away. Montreal was making news with its quarterbacks: Sonny Wade had retired; Joe Barnes was the heir apparent. The Alouettes also had Gerry Dattilio, a Montrealer who had played football at the University of Northern Colorado in the United States. Dattilio, who was protected by Montreal in the 1975 draft, was getting a chance to play and making a name for himself. In an exhibition game against Saskatchewan, he was sent in with Montreal on its own one-yard line. He responded, promptly. With passing and timely running, he moved the team to midfield where he threw a 50-yard pass to Bob Gaddis, who was tackled at the one-yard line of Saskatchewan. From there, David Green scored. The previous week, against Ottawa, Dattilio had combined with Gaddis for two touchdown passes. It appeared that Montreal's coach, Joe Scannella, had intended to use Joe Barnes as his quarterback. His plan was to use Dattilio in his all-round utility role during the season and throw him into games at the quarterback position to rest Barnes and to give Dattilio some playing time. It appeared that he hadn't counted on the huge impression that Dattilio was leaving with Montreal fans and his team-mates.

He wanted to deploy his imports in the traditional way, the designated import being a quarterback, probably Ron Calcagni, with Joe Barnes being the starter and Dattilio on special teams and anywhere but quarterback. Dattilio's quarterbacking skills, plus Barnes' slow start—he had completed only three of 11 passes with one interception in the first half against Saskatchewan—were causing a lot of questions to be asked in Montreal and throughout the CFL public. The pressure was getting to Scannella. When the Alouettes beat the Argos in an exhibition game, Barnes once again had a sub-par performance. The quarterbacking issue had become so prominent that "after the game, head coach Joe Scannella kept a tight lid on the issue and refused to field questions following the contest concerning Barnes' performance."[63] The Montreal media had a story; they were "discovering" Dattilio as a newsmaker. Features were written about him. Articles about his love of "soaps," especially "All My Children," were highlighted, as was the information that Dattilio would be asked to testify in the Jamie Bone case before the Ontario Human Rights Commission.

Montreal was also making news in another area. High-profile American collegian Tom Cousineau had signed with the Alouettes for the 1979 season. Cousineau, a linebacker, was the first draft choice of the Buffalo Bills of the NFL, but he did not want to play there. His option was to boycott the NFL for two years, after which he could return to that league and play with another team. Cousineau's signing with the Alouettes prompted them to drop linebacker Carl Crennel, who was promptly picked up by the Edmonton Eskimos where he became an integral part of their defence. Scannella also decided to go with his original thrust: Joe Barnes would be his quarterback, Ron Calcagni the designated import. Gerry Dattilio was relegated to special teams, removed from the quarterbacking position.

When the University of Toronto's quarterback, Joe Hawco, was drafted in the first round by Montreal, it was noted that he was being selected because of his speed and all around athletic ability. The point was made that "before one hits Hawco with the fact that the designated import rule prevents Canadians from occupying the quarterback position in the CFL, please rest assured that he is aware of that tragic fact." [64]

The college coaches were also incensed over the fact that Scott Mallender, the University of Windsor quarterback who was selected as the Hec Crighton Trophy winner as the Outstanding University Player in the Country for the 1979 season, was signed by the Argonauts, then released even before the beginning of training camp. The Argos had originally signed Mallender for one year with a bonus of $1,000. His release was blamed on a review of the Argos' roster, which was described as "overloaded," heading into training camp.[65] Mallender was later signed by Ottawa. Their coach, George Brancato, "announced that he didn't do it just to get the CFL off the hook. 'I think we need three quarterbacks on a team. A third quarterback can help us out especially if he can play another position like Dattilio of the Alouettes who doubles as a wide receiver and is the mainstay of the Als' special teams.'"[66]

There was fallout from the Ontario Human Rights Commission decision regarding the Jamie Bone case. A conference telephone call linking all CFL clubs with commissioner Jake Gaudaur and Secretary Treasurer Greg Fulton was held on August 30, 1979, to decide upon a course of action in the wake of the judgement. The Hamilton Tiger-Cats, specifically, were given until August 31 to decide whether to appeal the Commission's findings. The CFL decided to become involved because while the "designated import rule was not referred to in the language of the complaint ... it was obvious from the testimony of the player and his public remarks that the designated import quarterback rule was the real object of the player's complaint."[67] On the assumptions that the league would retain the rule and had the right to make it, the decision was important to the league, notwithstanding the fact that the Ontario Human Rights Commission had no authority over the Canadian Football League.

Gaudaur expressed his opinion, supported by league counsel, that:

(a) the decision confirms that a Club should be required to keep a Canadian quarterback only if he is deemed more capable than an American competing for the same position and; (b) the decision concludes that the designated quarterback rule does not in itself offer a rational basis for preferring the American or import quarterback to a Canadian candidate at the quarterback position.[68]

Gaudaur stated further that the league rules had been upheld and should the case proceed to the Canadian Human Rights Commission, "the language in the decision may be helpful in defending the League's position."[69] As for Hamilton's $10,000 cash outlay, Gaudaur cited that there were precedents where member clubs shared in costs which impacted on the league and this, in his opinion, was one such time: "If the League values a decision which clearly upholds the DI quarterback rule and which states that a Canadian quarterback, to be kept over an import, must be judged more capable, one-ninth of $10,000 to each Club to achieve it was not expensive."[70] He recommended that if the five-day trial were extended and Hamilton did not appeal, the CFL clubs should share equally in the $10,000 assessment.

The reasons for not appealing the decision were laid out. Neither league nor club counsel was optimistic that the appeal would be successful. Any new trial would provide a new surge of anti-league publicity as had the original one. Furthermore, there was the possibility that the favourable league ruling about the designated import could be reversed. Most of those who spoke at the conference call were in support of CFL commissioner Jake Gaudaur, but there were some other comments. Robert Berger of Montreal wondered whether the failure to launch an appeal might be perceived by the public or players as "buckling under," thus encouraging them to do more of the same thing. The commissioner replied that it was a possibility but "the only precedent he could rely on would be one in which the Club coach could be judged to have discriminated against because of nationality."[71]

Lew Hayman wondered whether an import might be encouraged to complain that he was an object of discrimination because he was an American. The Commissioner replied that Mr. McCamus had concluded "that the language by which the League defines the non-import and import is an illusion to mask that what the League really meant was that a non-import was a Canadian and an import was an American." Gaudaur concluded that since the Americans played from time to time "as non-imports because they qualified," the league could defend itself.

There was some opposition to having the other clubs share in the cost assessed against Hamilton. Earl Lunsford of Winnipeg reiterated that the judgement was against Hamilton and its head coach. Frank Finn of Calgary asked "whether or not the league, by sharing the fine, was, in effect, acknowledging that it was involved in the complaint."[72] Ross Smith, another Winnipeg delegate, thinking about the damaging publicity to the CFL which had been generated during the hearing, asked whether there was any benefit to the league in the ruling. Further, he wondered whether the sharing of the financial assessment "in a situation where the decision dealt essentially with the conduct of one person on a Club could set an undesirable precedent acting as a disincentive to Club personnel to conduct themselves in a proper manner."[73]

Jake Dunlap of Ottawa, himself a lawyer, agreed with all the arguments presented by Gaudaur. He concurred with his recommendation. In fact, he moved that "the compensation in the amount of $10,000 ordered to be paid by the Hamilton Club be shared equally by all members of the League."[74] Unanimous consent was required and received.

In any case, the league had been given a tremendous amount of negative publicity about the case. It refused to go away. The CFL had become increasingly wary of the whole question of their treatment of Canadian quarterbacks. The Jamie Bone decision had sensitized the public into believing that the designated import regulation was discriminatory, regardless of what the league's legal opinion was. When Ralph Sazio decided to introduce a motion setting club rosters at 34, "of whom two shall be designated as quarterbacks, with no fewer than 19 non-imports,"[75] the motion was passed by a 7-2 vote; Calgary and Montreal voted against it. Gaudaur, however, stated that in his opinion, the change had to be "defensible in terms of being a decision that would improve the Canadian player's chances of making the team or it would simply be interpreted as window dressing and a concession to political pressure."[76] Gaudaur, once again, commented about the difficulty of getting critics of the designated import rule to "understand or accept the fact that there is a built-in incentive for a club to use a non-import quarterback."[77] He continued:

> The particular resolution appears to be motivated by a desire to eliminate the criticism by changing the rule but [Gaudaur] expressed misgivings about changing a rule which the league can support because of its incentive to use a non-import quarterback for another rule which might be indefensible because it would be impossible to show how the rule change would make it easier to make it.[78]

Having been convinced that the designated import rule was "not discriminatory and to change it would be tantamount to an admission of guilt,"[79] Gaudaur convinced the meeting to refer the Hamilton motion back to the Commissioner for his consideration.[80]

Ever since Harold Ballard had purchased the Tiger-Cats, there had been fear that the team would deteriorate to the same level as Ballard's other interest, the Maple Leafs. The city had responded well to the new owner. The buses and trolleys of its transit system, the Hamilton Street Railway, shed its traditional colours of red and cream in favour of yellow with stripes of black, white, and blue, all colours of Ballard's sports teams. The Hamilton public was supportive as well. Attendance at most games hovered around the 24,000 mark.

League officials appeared to be sure of Ballard. He applied to the CFL to merge the football club with the parent company, Maple Leaf Gardens Limited. "The net effect was the Hamilton Tiger-Cat Football Club Limited will disappear as a Club with entity and would become a department of the amalgamated Company."[81] The problem was that the league constitution stipulated that the primary purpose of membership was to be the operation of a professional football club. Over some mild objections, the merger was approved and, legally, the Hamilton Tiger-Cat Football Club Limited was absorbed into Maple Leaf Gardens Limited.

Ralph Sazio operated without a contract on the understanding that should he or Ballard wish to sever the relationship, either of them only had to walk away. He returned to managing with a passion; his goal was to return the club to its glory days as Grey Cup contenders. Trades were concluded with Winnipeg. Sazio sent Larry Butler there for kicker Bernie Ruoff, the league's leading scorer, and he picked up linebacker Carl Crennel and receiver Marco Cyncar from Edmonton, sending them Neil Lumsden prior to the beginning of the season. Hamilton's other non-import fullback, Jim Reid, was sent to Ottawa along with linebacker Bill Banks in return for Ray Honey. The purse strings were even loosened up in an attempt to retain Tom Clements who, after playing out his option, joined Marv Levy and the Kansas City Chiefs. It was reported that Hamilton had offered him $1.25 million over five years.[82]

The CFL was still endeavouring to increase its crowds and revenues. The agreement with the CBC, due to expire at the end of the 1980 season, called for $2.1 million.[83] At least one owner, Sam Berger, was upset with the apparent lack of competition between CBC and CTV. The public network CBC preferred to telecast Sunday and Tuesday games; CTV, Wednesday and Saturday. To Berger's protest that slightly more than $200,000 per club was not enough, Johnny Esaw, in charge of CTV Sports, declared that "neither CBC nor ourselves have ever sold all the time available ... I doubt there is much more money in the market place."[84] United States television rights were considered to be negligible too. For the 1980 season, Total Communications Systems Inc. had picked up its option for $115,000 (U.S.).[85]

Sam Berger's son Robert was also concerned about radio rights, that local radio stations could not do a play-by-play of the Grey Cup Game. Gaudaur replied that it was difficult to convince the CBC that, as a condition of acquiring the rights, it would be required to provide a free signal of the game to the six stations in the east and 17 in the west which carried the Clubs' regular league and play-off games and were the CBC's competitors, for the most part.[86] The starting times of games were becoming important in an attempt to attract more of the public to the stands and the television sets. Saskatchewan announced that it was starting its afternoon games at 1:30 instead of 2:00 PM, "giving out of town supporters more time to drive home after the matches."[87] The league was also able to make a concerted effort for the 1981 season to have all Friday evening games start no later than 9:00 PM for the eastern markets; the exception would be in B.C. where a 10:00 PM eastern time start would be sought. The move was directly tied to trying to increase the audience in the prime television markets, something which always lay open the possibility of the charge that the West was again being manipulated for the benefits of the East.

Politics were always close to the surface but not necessarily of the East/ West variety. The Grey Cup Game had been alternating between Montreal and Toronto since 1977. It was being played in Toronto in 1980; Montreal had bid for it in 1981. In the meantime, however, there was the referendum being held in Quebec, May 20, 1980. It would determine whether Quebec would remain in Canada or become independent. "A wire service story out of Winnipeg implied that if Quebec voted 'yes' May 20, the CFL might refuse to hold the game at Olympic Stadium in '81."[88] Gaudaur was quick to deny the report. The referendum issue would not be a determining factor. In fact, the CFL would make its decision on May 15, five days before the referendum. He saw no reason why the rotation between Montreal and Toronto would not continue. It would be his "strong recommendation to the Executive Committee that the game should be played in Montreal."[89] Indeed, the meeting of May 15, 1980, approved Montreal as the site of the 1981 Grey Cup Game.

Once again, changes in league personnel were the order of the day. The Argonauts were again looking for a coach. Forrest Gregg was off to the Cincinnati Bengals of the NFL; he was replaced by his assistant Willy Woods. Jim Corrigal became the Argos' playing line coach. In Calgary, Jack Gotta decided to concentrate on managing; he was succeeded by his assistant Ardell Wiegandt. In Regina, Jim Spavital was appointed as the general manager; he would seek to translate "Rider Pride" into increased ticket sales. The Winnipeg Blue Bombers continued trading players in what was appearing as an attempt by Head Coach Ray Jauch to move out players who were loyal to the old regime. Duncan McKinley, John Melanowski, and Leon Lyskiewicz were all sent to Toronto in return for Nick Bastaja, Mark Bragagnolo, and a third-round draft choice.

In the East, balance was the word to describe the parity which had occurred. Hamilton, with an 8–7-1 record, finished in first place with 17 points; Montreal at 8–8 was in second with 16 points; Ottawa, with its 7-9 record, had 14 points and third place, Toronto, although improved to a 6–10 record, once again finished in last place and was out of the play-offs with its 12 points. In the West, Edmonton was clearly the class of the conference, with its 13–3 record and 26 points, Winnipeg at 10–6 and 20 points was a strong second; Calgary at 9–7 and 18 points finished in third, one point ahead of British Columbia, with its 8–7–1 record and 17 points; Saskatchewan continued its dismal performance with two wins and 14 losses and four points. In the play-offs, Winnipeg defeated Calgary 32–14 in the Western semifinal before falling to Edmonton, 34–24. Meanwhile, Montreal, after edging Ottawa 25–21, succumbed to Hamilton by a 24–13 count.

The Sunday, November 23, Grey Cup Game in Toronto between the Hamilton Tiger-Cats and Edmonton Eskimos was preceded by a week of meetings and events. They included a Miss Grey Cup Press Reception, the Metro Toronto Grey Cup Kick-off Luncheon, Acceleration '80 Fashion Show and Singles Dance at the CN Tower, Monte Carlo Nights, The Grey Cup Dinner, Grey Cup Breakfasts, The Grey Cup Parade, Las Vegas Nights, the Miss Grey Cup Pageant and Dance, and of course, the game itself. The 1980 Schenley Awards were also presented: Mike Wilson of Edmonton received recognition as the Most Outstanding Offensive Lineman, Gerry Dattilio as the Most Outstanding Canadian, Dieter Brock as the Most Outstanding Player, William Miller as the Rookie of the Year, and Edmonton's Dan Kepley as the Most Outstanding Defensive Player. For Dattilio, it was recognition of the way he "stepped in and helped turn around the fortunes" of the Montreal Alouettes after Joe Barnes was traded to Saskatchewan. It was "his first real shot as a starting quarterback."[90]

Meanwhile, Harold Ballard, the ebullient owner of the Tiger-Cats, was revelling in the publicity being generated by the media crush, all anxious for a story. They weren't disappointed. Ballard said that he had his players measured for Grey Cup rings, and had brought the Tiger-Cats to Maple Leaf Gardens to watch the Leafs and Los Angeles Kings, be introduced to the crowd, and hear the reaction of the crowd as messages of derision aimed at the Argos flashed on the electronic scoreboard. The Hamilton Float in the Grey Cup parade carried four "hairy legged undergraduates recruited by Ballard from the University of Toronto. They wore blue tights, construction boots, padded brassieres, wigs and lipstick. Each had a bright yellow sweatshirt bearing the words 'Moonshine Girls.'"[91] It was part of Ballard's jab at the Argos and their "Sunshine Girls." The Toronto newspaper had threatened to sue Ballard when he remarked that "they closed all the body shops on Yonge Street so they'd have no trouble getting cheerleaders for the Argos."[92] Sharing the platform with the "Moonshine Girls" was a 25-foot tiger, a dummy dressed in Argonaut uniform firmly held in its mouth, the tiger's tail wrapped around another replica of an Argo.[93] Harold and his sidekick, King Clancy, dressed in yellow and black, rode in a golf cart, while the crowd was being encouraged to shout out the traditional Hamilton cheer of "Oskie Wee Wee."

Perhaps it was Harold Ballard's bravado rubbing off; perhaps it was simply a matter of some Tiger-Cats attempting to "psych" themselves before the game. In any event, it appeared that Hamilton was doing much of the pre-game talking. Some of their players had been critical of the Eskimos after a 53–18 beating during the season, saying that Edmonton "had rubbed their noses in it."[94] Running back Obie Graves of Hamilton had been quoted as saying he was ready for a 200 yard game against the vaunted Eskimo defence. That, and of course Ballard's quote about measuring his team for the Grey Cup rings, received much prominence in the Edmonton dressing room before the game. At least one reporter, the *Edmonton Journal*'s Ray Turchansky, wasn't being fooled. He predicted an Edmonton victory by 40 points.[95]

Hamilton, a traditionally intimidating football team, couldn't intimidate the Eskimos. Early in the game, receiver Tom Scott was knocked to the ground even though he was far removed from the ball. The linebacker "shook a finger in his face, sort of warning him that he'd better keep his head up because he was in for that all day. Scotty went out for one play, came back and caught twelve passes for 174 yards and three touchdowns. Obviously, they scared the hell out of him."[96] The game ended with an Edmonton win by a 38-point margin, 48–10. It could have been higher. With four seconds remaining and Dave Cutler lined up for a field goal, the ball on Hamilton's 35-yard line, fans poured onto the field, and referee Don Barker called the game. Ballard's team lost; not only that, Argo Sunshine Girl Susan Spencer was selected as Miss Grey Cup!

If the game was a demonstration of the superiority of the Eskimos, the half-time show was a celebration of Canadianism. A giant Canadian flag was carried out to the field. Tommy Ambrose serenaded and led a spontaneous sing-along of Canadian songs. "The sheer eye misting pride that we all take in this country, whether we cheer for Hamilton or Edmonton, reached a crescendo as folk singer Roger Wittaker belted out his big hit 'Canada Is', a song written for him by Canada's Erik Roberson."[97] The show was a salute to multiculturalism. Fourteen hundred performers representing various ethnic groups were featured: ballet dancers from Quebec, rhythmic gymnasts from Ontario, the Dofasco Male Chorus from Hamilton, and Ukrainian and Portuguese dancers. "Perhaps the feeling of the afternoon is best captured by what happened in the VIP section of the stands where Ontario Premier

Bill Davis and his Alberta counterpart sat together although miles apart in political and economic philosophy, applauded and cheered together as only Canadians can. It was fifteen minutes those in attendance will never forget."[98]

Not all were so imbued with such patriotism and generosity. Harold Ballard was looking for scapegoats. He was unhappy with John Payne, the Hamilton coach. He had wanted to fire him in mid-season but was talked out of it by Ralph Sazio. Ballard railed against Canadian talent saying that the game had provided him with an education in football:

> I now know there's no difference between the East and the West because we all get our supply of good players from the U.S. In fact, as soon as we get that damn rule changed so we don't have to play Canadians, we will be a hell of a lot better off. We shouldn't be penalized having to play guys just because they are Canadians. People pay a lot of money to see these games and they deserve to see the best. How would you like to see 10 Canadians on the Blue Jays? If a Canadian is good enough to play, all right, but the trouble is you get one who's anywhere near capability and he wants an arm and a leg to play.[99]

Ballard did not attend the City of Hamilton's banquet for the Tiger-Cats. "'We didn't win so I'm not going. Besides, I had a previous engagement,' he explained."[100]

While the 1980 Grey Cup Game, with its attendance of 54,661 and its receipts of $1,244,797, faded into the background, the CFL continued to generate news and interest as 1980 came to a close. In Saskatchewan, an era was at an end. Ron Lancaster, wishing a longer contract, reluctantly agreed to a one-year deal, changed his mind, quit, and requested his job back all within two weeks. General manager, Jim Spavital, declined his offer to return. Lancaster's days as a Saskatchewan Roughrider were finished; he was replaced by Edmonton assistant Joe Faragalli. As the year closed, the CFL announced a breakthrough in its television contract. It signed a record agreement with Carling O'Keefe Breweries, a three-year television deal covering the 1981, '82, and '83 seasons for $15.6 million.

1981 to 1982

Chapter Seven

THE REORGANIZATION OF THE CFL went far beyond the complete interlocking schedule of the 1981 season. To the fans, it may have appeared that a different visiting team for each game was the extent of the changes which had taken place. Indeed, some liked the idea that new faces were being introduced; others lamented the demise of traditional rivalries. To the clubs the changes were much deeper and they all seemed to be made with a view to changing the tarnished image of the CFL.

Different clubs had attempted in the past to produce "Marketing Reports" directed to the CFL. The Montreal Alouettes and Edmonton Eskimos were the chief initiators. On November 21, 1980, an Ad Hoc Committee on Marketing had made its report to the CFL Executive Committee. The ad hoc group which included Jake Gaudaur, Terry Kielty of Ottawa, and Norm Kimball of Edmonton had been struck in response to yet another "Marketing Report prepared by independent consultants retained by the league."[1] Its recommendations were accepted almost in their entirety; it sought to put the league on a business-like footing. The Eastern and Western Conferences were disbanded as formal business entities although, for purposes of playing, the East and West Divisions were kept. The CFL's Executive Committee was replaced with the Board of Governors while the General Managers' Committee was supplanted by the Management Council. Actually, the ad hoc groups had recommended that the office of commissioner be abolished, to be replaced by president but that was too much. There was resistance. The title "commissioner" had a much stronger connotation in the eyes of the public. It was more readily accepted than president. In the end, "commissioner" was retained.

As simple as those moves appeared, there were great implications, particularly in the revenue sphere. In the area of voting procedures, all constitutional and financial matters could be "effected by the affirmative vote of no less than seven–ninths (7/9) … all other matters by a vote of no less than two–thirds (2/3) of the members voting."[2] The message was clear: the clubs were in the enterprise together and there had to be a climate of trust because of their mutual interests. No longer was it appropriate that a single club have the right to exercise veto power. The report continued to say that "the existence of single veto power may at one time have been a necessary safeguard. Now it is seen as a symbol of suspicion and mistrust, and a negative, stultifying and needless barrier to league progress."[3] In fact, the ad hoc committee was recommending that in other matters a simple majority would prevail.

The whole purpose of the exercise was to develop a one-league approach in all matters. To that end, the committee proposed that a statement of purpose be adopted:

> The CFL is dedicated to producing the highest quality, distinctively Canadian football product possible, consistent with its available financial and other resources. While building upon and reflecting the traditions of the past, the CFL will be progressive in the outlook and address the realities of the present. The CFL recognizes that it has a collective responsibility to the public, players, officials and franchise holders and will manage its affairs in a professional manner so as to:
> - maintain the highest integrity in all matters;
> - present an exciting product on a continuing basis;
> - strive continually for both excellence of play and competitive balance throughout the league;
> - provide for the safety and well-being of players and officials; and
> - provide financial returns appropriate to the need for continuing stability of the franchise.[4]

The statement of purpose was necessary in order to have all clubs in agreement and heading in the same direction. There were very real implications for the new arrangements. They were outlined in opinions advanced by the law firm of McCarthy and McCarthy in a letter to Jake Gaudaur.[5] Abandoning the Eastern and Western Conferences meant that instead of having two equal partners, the CFL was to consist of "nine autonomous and equal member clubs divided into an Eastern and Western Division." Because the new divisions were for competition purposes only, the veto power of individual clubs was reduced since the conferences and their veto power were eliminated. The second area of change was in the matter of revenue. While the two conferences were in existence, each shared equally in the revenue from the Grey Cup Game. However, the East split its revenue among four member clubs, the West among five. Not only that, the conferences might have regulations which called for shares of the revenues based on a club's finish in its standings. Under the new arrangement, "the nine member teams will each have equal status ... all league revenues will be shared equally." The net result was that the winning clubs would get less money than they would have traditionally, the losing clubs more.

To "wind up" the Eastern and Western Conferences legally, it was necessary to effect "amendments to the CFL constitution, by-law regulations and the Standard Players Contract." Assets of the two conferences were to be distributed evenly among members: "trophies, plaques, pennants, awards or other memorabilia" were to be delivered to the CFL which was to become the custodian and presenter of them.

The CFL was given the right to negotiate all television rights from preseason to the Grey Cup Game, all revenues to be shared equally by the nine member clubs. In order for a television signal to be shown in a member city where a game was being played at the same time as the televised game, only the consent of the home club was necessary since its ticket sales would suffer most. Clubs still had autonomy and "their property interest in radio broadcasting, game films and game programs ... and industrial property ... the legal umbrella which embraces patents, trademarks, copyrights and industrial design ... the responsibility and the authority for grants to minor football."

With reference to the players' standard contract, the CFL did some fancy footwork. Paragraph 16 called for the termination of the contract "and the remuneration to be paid to the player" as per "paragraph 11 herein." Lawyers recommended that paragraph 16 be eliminated. However, there were problems: many players had already signed a contract with paragraph 16 as part of it; the collective agreement with the Players' Association was current until after the 1982 season.

The league was in a quandary. The collective agreement stipulated that "there can be amendments to the Rules and Regulations ... only by agreement in writing signed by all parties." It was vital that paragraph 16 be eliminated. "If it is not, it would be open to any player who is dissatisfied with his contract to state that it is now terminated because of the suspension of the Conference in which he plays and he is now a free agent."[6]

At the same time, there were players who were not members of the Players' Association. The league decided to follow the advice of legal counsel George Finlayson that "the Players' Association is the agent for the player whether he is a member or not."[7] In spite of the fact that the association was "not certified as the bargaining agent for the players under any provincial or federal legislation,"[8] agreements made with it were considered to be binding on all including those players who were not members.

Several parts of the Players Contract supported George Finlayson's legal opinion. In Section 4(a) the player agreed to participate in the Pension Plan and authorized the club to deduct and contribute appropriate sums for that purpose; Section 4(b) authorized dues of $40 per game to be paid monthly by the club to the association; Section 7 acknowledged that the player agreed to be bound by the "all the rules and regulations in existence at the time of entering"[9] the contract and that the Canadian Football League Players' Association was the "the authorized agent of the Player."[10]

Summarizing his opinion, Finlayson submitted that "once the player agrees in a Standard Players Contract that he will be bound by any changes in the Constitution, By-laws and Regulations of the league, then he is bound by changes in the Standard Players Contract which were negotiated and agreed upon by his acknowledged agent, the Canadian Football League Players' Association."[11]

Without a great deal of fanfare, the Eastern and Western Conferences, each meeting separately, decided to "collect all awards, trophies, replicas of awards, pennants and other memorabilia owned by the said Conference and to deliver the same without compensation to the Canadian Football League for its sole control and ownership ... [to] disperse of the remainder of its property and to distribute its net assets equally among its members ... the said Conference ... [to be] the same is thereby dissolved effective 12:01 EDT on Friday, the 20th day of February, 1981."[12] The new administrative organization was praised by at least one reporter. Jim Coleman predicted that because of the "brand new image, a sensible full interlocking schedule and a vast preponderance of games on weekends only ... 1981 will be the most successful season in the history of Canadian football ... the beginning of Canadian football's most prosperous era."[13]

There was certainly more attention paid to another change within the CFL. Sam Berger, the gate equalization decision weighing heavily on his mind, decided to sell the Montreal Alouettes to Vancouver entrepreneur Nelson Skalbania. It was Berger who had been insistent that the CFL stay with the title of "commissioner" and not replace it with "president." His feeling was that "it had attained a certain amount of stature through tradition." Lew Hayman had supported him saying that the public perception was impor- tant. "Commissioner" had a greater impact of authority. The name had a "connotation unique in professional sport."[14] Berger had made a significant contribution to the league, first as owner of Ottawa, then of Montreal. On March 6, 1981, he accepted an offer from Skalbania to purchase 100% of the

Alouettes. There were some fears expressed within the league. Gaudaur preferred local ownership. Berger countered with the information that local money didn't match Skalbania's. A later offer from a Montreal group was similarly turned down by Berger who "would not in the future, accept the offer. He was confident that Skalbania would be good for the league in that he would revitalize the Montreal franchise, and would involve some local ownership in the Club."[15]

There was no doubt that the Alouettes were in need of revitalization. Season ticket sales had dropped from 18,000 in 1980 to 11,000 for the 1982 season.[16] Attendance had fallen off drastically from the heady days coinciding with the availability of the Olympic Stadium in 1976; and there were still the persistent rumours of an NFL franchise in Montreal. The question to be answered, however, was whether Nelson Skalbania was the right person to own the Montreal club. There were stories about his financial problems relative to an Edmonton shopping centre, and a class action suit brought against him as a result of the collapse of the Indianapolis hockey team. He had already been turned down in his application to bring an NBA franchise to Vancouver[17] in spite of the fact that he proposed to pay more than the $12 million paid for its team and offered to forego any national television revenue. There were fears that Skalbania would take the Montreal club out of the league and apply for an NFL franchise.

Gaudaur replied to all concerns, noting that the new owners would have to agree to conditions similar to those which bound Harold Ballard in 1978. As far as moving Montreal from the CFL to the NFL, Gaudaur insisted that wasn't about to happen "even though," as Berger mentioned, "the attitude of federal officials in Ottawa is not as protective towards the league as it was previously."[18] Gaudaur insisted he was "in regular contact with NFL Commissioner Pete Roselle and has excellent rapport with the NFL office."[19] Besides, if Skalbania were inclined to move the team to the NFL, it would be an expensive proposition. "Article 3.06 of the Constitution provides that a Club withdrawing from the league would have to surrender its player contracts and stadium lease and pay a $1,000,000 fee to the league."[20]

The Calgary representative, Howard Paillefer, still had to be convinced. His move to table the motion to sell the Alouettes was withdrawn only after an endorsement of Nelson Skalbania by Sam Berger. The motion was passed unanimously; Nelson Skalbania become the new owner of the Montreal Alouettes.

Bob Geary remained the general manager of the Alouettes and Joe Scannella the coach but there was some question as to who was making the decisions about personnel. When a story circulated in February 1981 that the Alouettes would be trading their premier running back David Green to

Hamilton in return for the rights to sign Los Angeles quarterback Vince Ferragamo, who was on Hamilton's negotiation list, Bob Geary quickly denied it. There were two aspects to the story. Green was reported to have earned $33,000 in 1979 and $60,000 for the 1980 season.[21] He was anxious to increase his earnings beyond what the Alouettes were willing to pay. The two parties devised a plan. Green signed two contracts, one for $300,000, another dated February 2 for $75,000. The Alouettes simply did not believe that Green could command $300,000 from any team. They signed him to that sum and put him on waivers. Green said:

> The Alouettes had no intention that I would play for them for $300,000 but they were willing to let me see whether I could make a deal for the amount for myself. If I wasn't able to do that, they would file the $75,000 contract and I would have to play for that amount.[22]

Geary explained later that Green had wanted to play in the NFL. The Alouettes were willing to accommodate his wish to earn that amount if he could get it. The $300,000 contract was meant to frighten off other CFL clubs. Having been successful with that ploy, it was agreed that the $75,000 contract would be filed with the CFL after February 2 if Green was unable to sign with an NFL team. "Geary said it was Robert Berger's [vice-president of the Alouettes] decision."[23] The Alouette general manager was already on record as saying that he was not interested in the NFL quarterback Ferragamo: "I want a mobile quarterback who can roll out. He can't."[24]

Both Bob Geary and Ralph Sazio denied the possibility of the swap; each had similar reasons. Geary thought it necessary "to get our payroll in line, not out of whack." Sazio said that he checked out the CFL office to find out the figures on Green's contract. "At that price I am not interested," he said. "Remember running back is not one of our priorities." Sazio said that he remembered "the great team in Hamilton and there never was a vast difference in what guys were earning."[25]

In spite of the protestations, David Green was sent to Hamilton; Vince Ferragamo became an Alouette for a reported contract calling for $400,000. The new Montreal quarterback was considered to be a coup for the Alouettes. After all, he had a high profile throughout football as a result of his play with the Los Angeles Rams, leading them to a near victory over the Pittsburgh Steelers in the Super Bowl. He had classic All American good looks, was aiming towards a career in medicine, and was generally considered to be the dominant NFL quarterback of the future. The Alouettes under the ownership of Skalbania didn't stop there. James Scott, a proven receiver in the NFL with the Chicago Bears, and Billy "White Shoes" Johnson from the Houston Oilers, were signed to give Ferragamo high profile targets for his aerials. The fourth major acquisition was David Overstreet, the first draft choice of Miami Dolphins. He was a superb running back in spite of a tendency to fumble. The Alouette front office churned out the publicity. Montreal was on everybody's list as a favourite for the Grey Cup. To some it was reminiscent of the Argos under Harry Sonshine, when in 1954, they raided NFL teams in an effort to win the Cup.

The signing of Ferragamo struck a sensitive chord in another area, that of the designated import regulation. Montreal's Gerry Dattilio, having demonstrated that he was a quality quarterback, seemed to be getting squeezed out. Once again, the issue of the Canadian quarterback was resurrected. When the CFL and CIAU representatives met in January 1981 to discuss relations between the two groups, the matter surfaced again, although "it was agreed that such discussions would be kept private to avoid media speculation."[26] The CIAU said that it "was not seeking an increase in the non-import roster or requirements to use non-imports in any specified position. All it wanted was the right of a non-import to compete for a position on a fair basis."[27] At the general managers' meeting, Ralph Sazio "asked whether the CIAU would be satisfied if the club would designate two players as quarterbacks regardless of classification before considering the import-non-import ratio."[28] It was generally agreed that such a move would be a positive step.[29] The CFL was in need of such publicly perceived "positive steps." Once again, the CFL incurred the wrath of CIAU supporters by scheduling the Grey Cup Game in the weekend normally reserved for the Vanier Cup College Bowl Game.

One of Sam Berger's last comments as an Alouette representative at the CFL meetings referred to the league's designated import rule. He "questioned whether the league would be subjecting itself to public criticism through not changing the designated import legislation."[30] CFL officials were convinced that the designated import rule did not discriminate against Canadians; they had the language of the Jamie Bone case to prove it. The public was adamant in its belief that the rule did discriminate. It perceived the Jamie Bone case differently. Gaudaur was not anxious to change the language "until such time as a Canadian Human Rights Commission ruled on the Bone complaint."[31]

The Canadian Human Rights Commissioner, Gordon Fairweather, did report,[32] somewhat ambiguously compared to the provincial body. He stated that "the Commission carefully considered the designated import rule in the wider context of the import rules and concluded that it is always in a team's interest to select the most talented quarterback regardless of his

national origin."[33] As to whether the CFL's quota on imports was discriminatory, Fairweather concluded that:

> the import rules are designed to protect job opportunities for players
> trained in Canada who are disadvantaged in comparison to players,
> regardless of their national origin, who have had superior training
> and experience in the United States. The rules have the effect of
> allowing Canadian-trained players to acquire professional experience
> and develop playing skills, so as to be able to compete on an equal
> footing with American-trained players.[34]

If the CFL was hoping that the ruling would be the last word on the
designated import rule, it was wrong. Typical of the public's reaction were
the comments of Trent Frayne of the Toronto *Sun*:

> What goes on here? What sort of sweetheart arrangement is it that
> the CFL can't lose even when the decision may just reverse their
> field halfway to the goal line. Fairweather wants it both ways. On
> O'Leary's point that Americans are discriminated against, his argu-
> ment is not that the best player should get the job but that the
> Canadians must be protected because they lack the superior training
> and experience of Americans. Then Fairweather does a complete
> about face on the Bone contention. He doesn't think a Canadian
> quarterback should be protected. He claims it is always in a team's
> best interest to select the most talented quarterback.[35]

The sensitivity of the issue was perhaps highlighted by the case of Dan
Feraday, a quarterback from the University of Toronto. When the 1980
season concluded, Feraday, in spite of a successful university career, was not
drafted by the CFL. He had more CIAU eligibility remaining but one of his
goals was "to have a tryout with a CFL team."[36]

In 1981, the Argonauts and their coach, Willie Wood, placed Feraday on
their negotiation list. His plan was "to bring him to training camp and
groom him for one year ... a good public relations idea as well as good for
the city of Toronto."[37] Feraday had been scouted by the Argos. It was done
on the University of Toronto campus in secret. Willie Wood met with
Feraday after the evaluation session. He wanted none of this "leaked" to the
press. If it was, "then the Toronto Club would deny it had talked with
him."[38] Furthermore, if Feraday hired an agent to represent him, he was
told, he would lose his opportunity. Feraday wanted to play; he agreed.

At the training camp, the Argos had four other quarterbacks. Feraday
performed in the drills but not in the scrimmages. There he stood and

watched. At the Argonaut intra-squad game, Feraday did play and performed well. Wood promised him a chance to play in the pre-season.[39]

By this time, Feraday had decided to return to university. He was still hopeful of leading his team, the Blues, to the national title. Despite the fact that he had had limited practice with the Argos and the possibility of injury was always there, his hopes for a career in the CFL were such that he accepted the chance to play in the pre-season. He performed well, creating a problem for the Argos. How could they cut a non-import who had played well? The Argos solved the problem by asking Feraday to retire. That way he would remain Argonaut property and could stay with the team through the summer. He practised with the Argos and charted opposition defences until he returned to school in the fall. Feraday didn't lead the University of Toronto Blues to the national title. However, his play was so superb that he was awarded the 1981 Hec Crighton Trophy for the most outstanding university football player in Canada. Because of his high profile, he was constantly sought out by the press who were anxious to write about the designated import rule, the CFL, and Canadian quarterbacks. Feraday disciplined himself to refrain from responding to "the press in a negative manner towards the Argos, because that would blackball him and his chances of playing would become non-existent."[40]

As disciplined as Feraday was, he was convinced that an occurrence which was announced partway through the summer of '81 sealed his fate. Ralph Sazio left the Tiger-Cats to become the president of the Toronto Argonauts. It was Feraday's perception that Sazio did not like the idea of having a Canadian quarterback because of his experiences in Hamilton. Feraday was even more determined to make the team in '82 and resolved to say nothing publicly about his experience.

Ralph Sazio had been part of the Tiger-Cat scene since he was recruited by Carl Voyles for the 1950 season. He had been a player, assistant coach, head coach, general manager, president and part owner of the Hamilton club during his 31 years. There was perhaps no bigger rivalry in the CFL than that between Hamilton and Toronto. It was obvious that Carling O'Keefe Breweries, owner of the Argonauts, had instructed President Lew Hayman to hire the best football person available. He chose Sazio.

The reaction was predictable. Harold Ballard accused the Argonauts of tampering, Sazio of being unethical in breaking his contract. As for the latter, Sazio disagreed. He had no contract with Ballard. The two had not even a handshake. Each was able to walk away from the deal whenever he wanted to. With respect to the tampering allegation, the league concurred and imposed a wrist-slapping fine of $2,000.[41] The Tiger-Cats were not impressed. They sought $25,000 and a player.[42] Joe Zuger, Sazio's replacement, felt that the $2,000 fine, the maximum allowed under Article 11.7 of the CFL constitution, "did not serve as a sufficient deterrent to the club seeking the services of a person with another club who was of the calibre of Mr. Sazio."[43] Jake Gaudaur agreed to look into the matter and bring in a recommendation which would be retroactive to November 20, 1981.

At the Rules Committee meeting of January, there were continued attempts to become more American in the league rules. Some of the rejected proposals, apparently made by Montreal, included playing 11-man football, removing the one-yard restraining area between the lines of scrimmage, eliminating the single point on an unsuccessful field goal attempt which went through the goal area, and allowing four downs to make 10 yards rather than three.[44] Some rules were changed. When an errant field goal hit the goalpost in flight, the ball would be awarded to the non-kicking team at the line of scrimmage or the 35-yard line, whichever was further from the goal-line. Previously, the ball was declared "dead" and scrimmaged by the defending team at its own 10-yard line. The league also was to allow downfield blocking on a screen pass, that is, one caught behind the line of scrimmage. "Spearing," the use of the helmet in contacting an opponent in on unnecessarily rough manner, was assessed as a major penalty. The league still had a hold-over rule from football's early days: "If during a dribbled ball, an offside player touches the ball, possession shall be awarded to the opponent at the point the ball was touched."[45] And it was still concerned with its visual image. The Rules Committee declared that "a player must wear an undershirt of the same colour as the main parts of his jersey."[46] The CFL also decided that beginning in 1981, any CFL veteran, that is, one who had played in five games, who left the CFL to try for a spot with an NFL team, was free to sign with whomever he chose on his return to the CFL. Previously he was bound to return to the team on which he last played.[47]

Players and coaches continued to make the news in the off-season. It was obvious that non-import talent was continuing to improve. Of the 80 players selected in the 1980 draft and protected list, 64 signed with CFL clubs; at the end of the season 26 were still on the active rosters.[48] Ray Jauch was selected as Coach of the Year for his efforts in Winnipeg. He had previously won the Annis Stukus Award in 1970, his first year as a head coach with Edmonton. In Saskatchewan, while the transition from Ron Lancaster to Joe Faragalli proceeded smoothly after the confusion surrounding Lancaster's change of heart, there was a flurry surrounding the Roughriders' assistant coach Bud Riley. After signing a contract with Saskatchewan, he did similarly with Hamilton. Gaudaur was called in to arbitrate; however, prior to his having to make a decision, the two clubs settled. Riley would stay with Hamilton; the Roughriders would get the Tiger-Cats' first choice in the 1981 draft.

The Tiger-Cats were in the middle of another controversy. During the off-season they had replaced John Payne with Arizona State coach Frank Kush. Known as a task master, Kush was being sued by one of his former players, Kevin Routledge. It was alleged by an Arizona assistant coach that "Kush told his aides at Arizona State to lie and perjure themselves to help him beat a $2.2 million lawsuit. 'We were given instructions by Frank that we should all stick together even if it meant lying and perjuring ourselves or we would all get fired,' former Kush assistant Bob Owens said."[49]

Kush had the reputation as a tough and demanding coach. Football practices were likened to a Marine "boot camp." It appeared to be paying off. The Tiger-Cats finished in first place in the East with a record of 11–4–1. They were clearly the class of the division. Ottawa, Montreal, and Toronto seemed to be competing with each other to see who could lose the most games. Ottawa ended in second place with a 5–11 record, Montreal in third at 3–13. The Argos won just two games while losing 14 to finish in last place. Ralph Sazio scurried about after his arrival on the scene in an attempt to gain the last play-off place. Recognizing that Argo coach Willie Wood had some limitations in understanding the concept of offence in Canadian football, Sazio sought to inquire about the availability of at least one Canadian university coach to act as an unofficial coaching assistant to Wood. With that option not being a possibility, the Argos stumbled to their 10th consecutive loss. Wood was fired; General Manager Tom Hudspeth replaced him. The Argos lost their next game, to B.C., by a 45–14 score but ended up winning two of their next five in their run for a final play-off spot.

It was the Alouettes that they were challenging, both in futility and the play-offs. Montreal had become the talk of the league; Vince Ferragamo, their high-profile, high-price, quarterback, "White Shoes" Johnson, James Scott, David Overstreet, *et al.* had not responded to expectations. When the Alouettes were at 1–8, after their eighth loss, Joe Scannella was fired, replaced with defensive specialist Jim Eddy. He attempted to simplify the offense for Ferragamo in order to take some of the pressure off the quarterback who was being pilloried in the media and the stands. The first game with the simplified approach was a continuation of the same. The Alouettes were soundly beaten by Edmonton 62–11. Their next game against Calgary was a 20–3 loss. The struggling Ferragamo was replaced in the fourth quarter by Gerry Dattilio. When the two teams, the Argos and Alouettes, met on October 17 at CNE Stadium, a crowd of 31,008 saw the Argos pull out a squeaker and were left to wonder whether the "Argo bounce" had returned.

The Alouettes were ahead 14–13. The Argos had the ball just inside the Montreal 50-yard line with fourteen seconds remaining. Condredge Holloway dropped back and threw a wobbly pass towards the sideline on the right. A cluster of Alouettes in the area moved to intercept the ball, but knocked it back into the waiting hands of Martin Cox who raced into the end zone for the winning touchdown. The Argo masquerade as a team bound for the play-offs was uncovered on Halloween when the Tiger-Cats defeated them in their last game of the season. Meanwhile the Alouettes won their last game to move into the play-offs with a 3–13 year.

In the Eastern semifinal, Montreal's woes continued. They lost 20–16 to Ottawa in a game described as "hardly a ringing endorsement for re-employment as head coach of the CFL team with a three million dollar player budget that just experienced its worst ever 3–13 season and will lose upwards of two million dollars."[50]

Alouette fans were deserting the team in droves. Montreal fan Andy Nulman provided lyrics for "a catchy country beat" by Ian Cooney. The song detailed a "litany of curses the team faced during the season … 14 losses, three paltry wins, staff shake-ups and fan desertion."[51]

Vince, The Prince Ferragamo
had all the hero assets,
good looks and endless charms.
Too bad most of his passes
met opposition arms.
You'd figure these new players
would make Als-watching fun.
The only thing that thrilled us so
was the bang of the game end gun.
Jim Eddy then replaced him,
promised changes at all cost,
The only real change in the next game was
the score by which they lost.
The fans they started faithful.
They roared like grizzly bears.
Before long they were showing up
Disguised as empty chairs.[52]

In the Eastern final, Hamilton was heavily favoured. Playing at home in Ivor Wynne Stadium and having finished in first place by a wide margin, they assumed that they would represent their division in the 1981 Grey Cup Game in Montreal. Ottawa was a two-touchdown underdog in the game but "came away with a 17–13 victory before 28,104 disgusted Hamilton fans and had the distinction of having the worst record, 5 and 11, of any Grey Cup finalist."[53] Red Fisher, columnist with the Montreal *Gazette* wrote:

> Try this one. Ottawa will represent the East in next Sunday's Grey Cup Final. Come on now, have I ever lied to you before? In this wondrous Canadian Football League season of non-accomplishment, anything can happen. A rookie named Vince Ferragamo was brought in all the way from Los Angeles at $450,000 per season and finishes the season as a cab driver; another word for it is taxi squad. An owner named Nelson Skalbania opened his wallet so wide for people, for Vince F., White Brogans Johnson, James Scott and David Overstreet; well all that's necessary to mention is that cash flowed and flowed to the point where it's flawed. With the Tiger-Cats leading 13–7, a rumour named Pat Stoqua, hauled in a pass at the Ottawa 30 yard line, eluded one defender and raced the rest of the way for the 102 yard touchdown.[54]

In the West, Edmonton once again was the class of the league, winning 14 while losing one and tying one. Winnipeg was a strong second with 11 wins, while B.C. finished with 10 for third place. Saskatchewan in fourth place finished with a 9–7 record; Calgary was last at 6–10. A strong defence helped B.C. to defeat Winnipeg by a 15–11 score in the semifinal. Dieter Brock was sacked four times as B.C. neutralized the Blue Bombers' long passing threat. In the Western final, the Lions continued their strong play, forcing Edmonton to rely on a fourth quarter rally to win 22–16.

It was Edmonton's fifth successive appearance in the Grey Cup Game, their eighth in the last nine. Their last meeting with Ottawa was in 1973. The Rough Riders won that game 22–18 but Edmonton was the prohibitive favourite in 1981. The West was playing better football. Of the 40 interlocking games, the West had won 30, lost 9, and tied 1. Fans were more appreciative of the calibre in the West too. Edmonton, Winnipeg, and Saskatchewan all broke attendance records; crowds were also up in Vancouver. The league as a whole needed the attendance increases, occurring in the West, but in the East, only Hamilton showed any increase in attendance. Montreal and Toronto, the two biggest markets, won only five games between the two of them "and suffered big losses at the gate for the second straight year ... The CFL registered an overall draw of 2,122,870, a modest increase of 5,720 fans."[55]

The Alouettes' problems seemed to be spilling over to the 1981 Grey Cup Game and its Montreal site:

When the Alouettes can't even sell Grey Cup tickets, you know football is in trouble in Montreal. They averaged only 27,754 a game, only half the tickets needed to break even. Now they've only sold 16,000 of the 22,000 tickets they've been allocated by the Canadian Football League. The Alouettes have to pay for the tickets in advance. The CFL is adamant on that score. Half the money 30 days before the Grey Cup game, the other half 10 days before the game. The final payment, approximately $225,000 is due today and Bill Putnam, vice-president of the Alouettes is playing catch-up trying to get that money.[56]

The Montreal fall-out continued. The CBC program "Fifth Estate" televised a documentary on the CFL and the Alouette situation, hosted by former Ottawa centre Bob McKeown. Earl Lunsford, the general manager of Winnipeg, contended that Nelson Skalbania was the "worst thing that ever happened to Canadian football."[57] There was criticism that the CFL had accepted Skalbania's offer of $2.4 million over that of a group led by a former owner of the Montreal Canadiens, Bill Molson. As for Skalbania, he said that he would be willing to sell the Alouettes "if as big a sucker as himself could be found."[58]

The CFL suddenly found itself the subject of scrutiny. The full interlocking schedule was being blamed for some of the problems. It had regularly pointed out, for all to see, the growing disparity between the East and West. Some wondered aloud whether with a balanced schedule, it was necessary to have an East-West Grey Cup final; why not just the two top teams, they argued. "So instead of whooping it up during the week that once was known as Canada's 'grand national drunk' the people who run the CFL must soberly plough through what Jake Dunlap calls one of the deep valleys into which the league frequently finds itself nowadays."[59]

The deepest "valley" seemed to be in Montreal. In Quebec, with a party committed to separation in power, many English speaking people were leaving. Among the French population, baseball was king of the summer and autumn, aided by aggressive marketing. Dunlap lamented: "I'm beginning to wonder if there are enough English fans to support football in Montreal anymore. Everybody's leaving. And these Expos, they're killing us. Rough Riders too! Hundreds of buses coming down on those fall weekends."[60]

Even Gaudaur was beginning to come in for some public criticism. Columnist Michael Farber wrote:

It's time the CFL had a shake up. It needs a "best interest of the league" clause in its constitution and a benevolent despot who will exercise his football version of martial law as he sees fit. Gaudaur, who has been in the league for 42 years as a player, owner and commissioner may be unwilling or unable to provide the stern hand the league needs at a time when credibility is challenged. The CFL is a microcosm of the country, a fractious mosaic, a diffused organization operating on consensus. Nobody is sure if this eminently reasonable approach is working for Canada right now. Certainly it isn't working for the league.[61]

As for the two teams meeting in the Grey Cup Game, they were a study in contrasts. One had a winning record, the other a losing one. Edmonton's attendance during the season was a new high; Ottawa's support had fallen off—so much so that management threatened to move the franchise if support didn't improve. To this, former coach Jack Gotta cracked: "Where's he going to move it, Kemptville, Ontario, the moral equivalent of Regaud, Quebec?"[62] Edmonton was listed as a 22-point favourite by game time. George Brancato put on a straight face when responding to the question of how it felt to be such an underdog: "The same way it felt the previous 22 weeks."[63]

Indeed, the Eskimos were considered such prohibitive favourites and their organization such a model that their approach was closely followed. Some traced their resurgence as the dominant team in the CFL to a move made by Hugh Campbell prior to the 1980 Grey Cup Game against Hamilton. Their top offensive lineman, Mike Wilson, was injured, unable to play. A decision was made to go with an all non-import line. The resultant success in the Grey Cup Game caused the same deployment of personnel to be used in the 1981 season. Bill Stevenson, Hec Pothier, Eric Upton, Ted Milian, and Leo Blanchard gave "quarterback Warren Moon excellent protection most of the season. It has developed the ability to stop most of the stunting. It's quite an advantage when you can handle those things without having to keep the running backs in to block because you have more people downfield to catch the ball. The opposition has to honour that so it opens up more holes and improves the whole offense."[64]

The 52,478 in attendance and a national television audience were expecting a blow-out. They were stunned when a charged-up Rough Rider team left the field at the end of the first half leading by a 20–1 score. Indeed, it took a last second field goal by Dave Cutler to clinch the Edmonton 26–23 victory. To some, the miraculous come-back was due to Edmonton's having

a thirteenth man on the field, even though the officials or the Riders couldn't see him. He was stiffening an Edmonton defence that had been porous for the first 30 minutes. He gave Warren Moon the

pause to regroup and dominate the last half. He certainly had a
mystic way in guiding Cutler's aging legs, steadying Tom Wilkinson's
hold and promising a sure snap from centre Bob Howes just as sure
as he was glaring daggers over the shoulder of every Eskimo when
they came out of the chute down 20–1 following their half-time
intermission. The 1981 season was dedicated by the Eskimos to
their former teammate Don Warrington. Not just this game but
every down, every game, even though it might have escaped them
for the first 30 minutes. He was a journeyman defensive back who
died in a car accident before the season started but his lifestyle
earned him the name "giver." "Giver your best every damn down"
was the crutch every Eskimo leaned on this season. Each and every
one of them wore Number 21 on their sleeves in honour of their
fallen comrade.[65]

In 1982, the Canadian Football League lost a franchise and gained a
franchise: the Montreal Alouettes flew the coop; the Montreal Concordes
landed. It was a long and tortuous development. In some ways, the seeds for
the Alouettes' demise were sown by the nature of the CFL operation: a team
pursues a "superstar"; it has success on the field; financial stability is in hand;
more and bigger-name U.S. talent is sought after; disharmony and loss of fan
support occur; money is lost; the franchise is forced into bankruptcy. Some
said that the club's demise had had its beginning once Nelson Skalbania
bought the Alouettes from San Berger. Certainly, the Alouettes had been
convulsing for some time. Operations had been in limbo since the end of the
1981 season. Skalbania was attempting to sell the club. As a result, there was
"an understandable reluctance to appoint key personnel or commence
projects in which the proposed new owner would have no say."[66]

In a "Report to the Governors of the Canadian Football League concerning the operation of the Montreal Alouette Football Club," dated
February 3, 1982, Jake Gaudaur detailed the developments relating to the
Alouettes to that point. The first inclination that there were financial problems in Montreal appeared when a Montreal newspaper article alleged that
the Alouettes were in default of players' payments, so much so that "such
players might be unwilling to participate in future games."[67] Alouette officials, when contacted by Gaudaur, stated that the problem related to
deferred payments. The "Club had not paid an estimated $135,000 into
Confederation Life which had been held back from players' salaries with
which to purchase annuities at the end of the 1981 taxation year."[68]

Although Gaudaur was assured that payment would be forthcoming
soon, on October 14 the Players' Association called to let him know that

none had been made. Gaudaur determined that player payrolls were being met otherwise; there appeared to be less chance of a strike for the October 18 game. On the 21st, one week later, Gaudaur was told by the Players' Association lawyer that the September deferred payments were still unpaid. Alouette officials were "surprised" that the players had complained since they had indicated, Gaudaur was told, that they would agree that the Club could "pay the interest on the September payments until the date the funds were paid in."[69]

On the next day, October 22, the Alouettes received $375,000 in cash and used $217,000 to bring the club up to date. The threat of a players' strike in Montreal appeared to be quelled.[70]

Other cracks began to appear. Media reports surfaced to the effect that the Alouettes Club "was in default of rental to Olympic Stadium."[71] Again Gaudaur contacted Alouette representative Bill Putnam. The Alouettes had failed to obtain a performance bond worth $300,000 necessary under the lease agreement. The Alouettes "had only now become aware that such a bond was necessary."[72] They would look after it immediately. On the basis of their balance sheet, however, the bond could not be arranged; the stadium "wanted $300,000 cash to be put in escrow to guarantee the club's financial obligations under the agreement."[73] The stadium confirmed "that it had to threaten to take action to get the rental paid."[74] It appeared to be the only way to ensure that the rent would remain current.

When Gaudaur contacted Putnam in January, the "bond situation" was still unresolved. The Olympic Stadium offered to wait until February 28, 1982. In the meantime, it declared that if the team were sold, the new owners would have to resolve the issue before any new lease was signed.[75] The Olympic Stadium continued to work actively to secure the bond or funds. Sam Berger was called upon to post the bond. When Gaudaur was informed, he wrote to the president of the Olympic Installation Board, Mr. Saulnier on the same day, January 12, "to confirm in writing his verbal advice to me that there would be no action prior to February 28."[76] By early February, Skalbania had offered to put up $150,000 in cash and was hoping to meet with Saulnier to settle the problem.

It was obvious that Skalbania and the Alouettes had become "cash-short." On September 21, 1981, the Players' Association advised the league that the Alouettes players' dues had not been received. Despite three assurances that "the cheque's in the mail," payment had still not been made. Gaudaur met with Alouette President René Forté in Montreal to explain that such trust fund payments "should be given priority along with payroll … [and] asked if the Club would authorize the deduction of this amount from its share of the television rights fee that was payable on October 1."[77]

As a result, a cheque dated October 5 was sent by the Alouettes to the league office, covering the August "hold-back." The September portion was sent in on October 26; the Ottawa money was "deducted from the Club's November share of television and given to the Players' Association on November 6 at a meeting in Toronto."[78]

There were also shortfalls with the Players' Pension Plan. The collective agreement called for $500 to be deducted from any player on the team roster for seven games and to be sent in to the league office by September 15. It had still not arrived by October 1 despite Alouette assurances that the money had been forwarded. Again, on November 5, the Alouettes decided to dip into the November television payment. They deducted $38,500 to pay for the players' and matching club contributions to the pension plan.[79] In effect, the Alouettes had used more than $20,000 of the players' money, that is, funds that they had contributed, for other purposes.[80]

The income tax authorities were also pressing for their funds. Instead of paying taxes in the prescribed instalments, the Alouettes were funnelling the money into other areas. Nelson Skalbania advised Gaudaur that he was not aware that he still owed 1981 taxes, including tax hold-backs.[81] It was determined that the Alouettes still owed $200,000 to the Quebec tax authority, so said Alouette official Bill Putnam. Gaudaur "was to be advised later that the sum owed to the Quebec tax authority was double the figure given."[82] In addition, $100,000 was owed to the federal government and "50,000 to the City of Montreal for seat tax."[83] A schedule of payment was worked out. Gaudaur's fear was that "if the schedule is not met, the potential would exist for the authority to take action … [there is] concern that the Province of Quebec owns and manages Olympic Stadium."[84]

The league was also being pressured even more directly by Alouette money woes. Montreal was the site, and the Alouettes the host club, for the 1981 Grey Cup Game. Gaudaur had always felt that the league would be perceived according to how the public reacted to the Grey Cup festivities and game. The Alouettes were sent $557,000 worth of Grey Cup tickets in September. league regulations called for 50% of the sum to be paid to its offices by October 21. The cheque was sent, but it was only as a result of "daily dialogue on the matter"[85] that the $278,000 was cleared on October 30. The remaining 50% was due November 16. There were insufficient funds to cover the cheque issued. Another was brought in and given to the commissioner at the CFL Board of Governors' Meeting. It was certified immediately. The CFL at least had some leverage in financial matters with the Alouettes. It used it when the Montreal club was late in its monthly assessment payments of $8,000 in 1981 and $7,000 in 1982. They were "never forwarded to the league voluntarily."[86] Gaudaur was authorized in each case to hold back an equivalent amount "from television and play-off revenue which was payable from time to time to the Club by the league Office."[87]

The Alouettes also owed money to hotels for accommodation, for air travel, to companies such as Spaldings and Blacks for footballs and films. The situation could adversely affect the 1982 season preparations; "To a considerable degree, the Club, as of February 1, was on a C.O.D. basis."[88]

Personnel appointments were also uncertain. Vice-President Bill Putnam had resigned on February 3. Bob Geary was confirmed as general manager on January 11, but by January 21, the Alouettes were still unable to hire a football coach. At meetings that day in Edmonton, Geary was to have met with Nelson Skalbania. The meeting did not take place. The name of Harry Ornest surfaced as a potential investor in the Alouettes. Skalbania, Ornest, and Geary were to pour over some 50 applications for the head coaching position. Gaudaur described the club's present management as "uncertain at best, at worst, non-existent."[89] He continued:

> In a situation where fan apathy had developed to the point it had, by the end of the 1981 season and where the necessity of regenerating fan interest was so important particularly as it related to season ticket sales, a lack of positive action or action that was perceived publicly to be positive, in the matter of confirming the appointment of key management and coaching personnel has understandably provoked on-going negative media reaction.[90]

Commissioner Jake Gaudaur's impulse was to serve notice on January 8 that unless assurance was given "on or before January 15 that the Alouette Club was not in a suspended state,"[91] he would take the first step in revoking a franchise. Skalbania made some movement. Geary was rehired and meetings were scheduled to redress all the concerns from 1981. At the same time, as the serving of notice was not effected, Bill Putnam's and René Forté's relationships with the club were severed. Skalbania was looking for an investor. Pat Bowlen, an Edmonton businessman, declined an opportunity to invest. Harry Ornest similarly declined. He did however agree to "act as a management consultant particularly with regard to the control of costs at the club."[92] One of Ornest's cost-cutting features, which was "learned inadvertently" by Gaudaur, was that the "Club's 1982 marketing plan had been shelved by Mr. Ornest and that in its place the Club was asked to approach service clubs to ask them to sell tickets on commission."[93]

The situation appeared grim. Skalbania operated from Vancouver; Ornest was in Los Angeles. Bob Geary was in Montreal with little authority. Ornest said that three different budgets had been presented while attempting to finalize one. Meanwhile, "Geary was given a firm budget guideline for player salaries."[94]

When Pat Bowlen declined to become involved and Harry Ornest was unwilling to inject any new money into Alouette operations, Skalbania came up with a high-profile apparent solution. George Allen, former coach of the Washington Redskins of the NFL and an acknowledged football expert, was offered the opportunity to become a part and eventual owner of the team. Since Allen was an American citizen, the whole deal was to be subject to approval of both the CFL and the federal government's Foreign Investment Review Agency (FIRA). The plan was for Allen to become the president and chief operating officer of the Alouettes. He would move to Montreal and begin employment with the Alouettes immediately. In return for his involvement with the club, Allen was to receive 20% ownership and an option to purchase another 31% interest before March 31, 1982, for $1,400,000. "Originally the option date had been shown as December 31, 1982 but the parties agreed to advance the date to March 31, 1982."[95] When George Allen, along with his son Bruce, joined Skalbania with the rest of the CFL executives, he confirmed that he would give up his television contract with CBS and his chairmanship of the President's Council on Physical Fitness in the United States, in order to have his own club.

Gaudaur was careful to assure Allen that "this discussion was not a form of inquisition."[96] He wanted to make sure that Allen was fully cognisant of the situation. Allen assured him that he was, that Skalbania would be responsible for settling present debts while he would take over a club "free of encumbrances."[97] His interpretation of the agreement was as outlined by Skalbania previously. Allen stated that he would have to put $500,000 down if he took up the option to purchase 31% on December 31, 1982, and that there was a further option to buy the remaining 49% prior to December 1983. Allen also agreed to advance the first option date to March 31, 1982.[98] Gaudaur stated that the 20% transfer would first have to be approved by the league and if it was, then it would be held in escrow until the March 31 option date. If he wished to exercise the option, that too would have to be approved by the league.[99] When the three Alouette officials left the meeting, the league executives continued meeting to develop their strategy. The bottom line was that the league was being asked to agree to the proposal for a six-week period. In the Alouettes' favour was the knowledge that the club was having discussions with the various levels of government to resolve the tax issue; that the Alouettes were current in their obligations with the league; that all players' contracts had been honoured.[100] The CFL advised Nelson Skalbania and George Allen that it had reacted positively to their proposal.

While all of this was progressing, there were less favourable comments being made outside board meetings. When information had been leaked that the league had given Skalbania a deadline for resolving the Montreal situation, Skalbania had said, "Well, they can go to hell. If they can find some other idiot to take over the franchise, they can have it."[101] Earlier reports, too, had squelched rumours that Pat Bowlen had until February 28 to purchase 51%. "Bowlen's lone interest was, in fact, and still is, to recoup a one million plus cash investment used for the original purchase."[102] Larry Woods likened Nelson Skalbania's approach to the way the "RAF repaired the Ruhr."[103]

Skalbania was not adverse to fighting back: "What did I do, rob someone? Murder this man? Did I hit anybody? Am I the villain for going broke writing cheques to keep football in Montreal? Why is everybody giving me hell for blowing my brains out?"[104]

When it became obvious that Skalbania was not going to be free of all encumbrances by March 31, Allen was successful in moving his option date back to the original December 31. He later withdrew from the situation entirely. The news continued to be all bad for the Alouettes and Nelson Skalbania. Newspaper reports circulated that the Alouettes were down to one football and it was a free sample, at that.[105] In court, Skalbania was being sued by a Memphis businessman who said that he was owed money. Sam Berger was also suing to regain control of the Alouettes once again because he had not been paid $280,000 from the original sale. Berger was claiming the "Club's trademarks, player contracts and outstanding television revenues from last season."[106]

Developments were fast and furious. The public, either with a sense of humour or affection for the Alouettes, swamped the Montreal team's office with footballs; the CFL decision to revoke Nelson Skalbania's ownership was put into motion; the other eight franchises anted up a total of "$500,000 for operation costs which will then be recovered once the team is sold."[107]

Meanwhile, the Quebec Superior Court denied Sam Berger's writ of seizure of the Alouettes. At the CFL semi-annual meetings, Harry Ornest, Skalbania's designate to the Board of Governors meetings of the CFL, was a no-show.[108]

On Thursday, May 13, 1982, the Alouette franchise was dead; a new Montreal team, the Concordes, joined the CFL. Nelson Skalbania, "through lawyers in Hong Kong, served notice that he was withdrawing his membership."[109] The league was anxious that it not be identified with any of Skalbania's or the Alouettes' debt. In revoking the franchise, it left the financial woes with the owner. It simply awarded new membership to the Concordes, hoping to leave the Alouettes' debtors to deal with Skalbania.

The procedure of awarding membership to a new franchise usually took three years but, in this case, the unanimous consent allowed it to be speeded up. Hot on the heels of the announcement was the formation of a new group of Montrealers ready to take over the new CFL franchise. Charles Bronfman, head of Seagrams and chairman of the Expos, was heading up the new ownership. Sam Etcheverry was president and chief operating officer. Directors included: Sidney Maislin, owner of a large Quebec trucking fleet, and prominent Montreal businessmen Lorne Webster and Hugh Hallward— all directors of the Expos.[110] At the same time, the CFL posted a bond for $280,000 should Sam Berger win his case against the previous owner. It was done in order to allow the team to be sold without any previous debts impinging upon the agreement.

The name "Concordes" and logo were introduced at the new team's opening press conference. According to Bronfman, the new name "was derived from the city of Montreal's motto 'Concordia Salus,' latin for 'Salvation from harmony.' It also conformed to the team's wish for a name spelled and pronounced the same in English and French."[111]

If any further verification was needed that a concerted effort to attract French-speaking fans was underway, the press conference provided it. The Concordes announced that they had signed Montrealer Luc Tousignant, a quarterback, who had attended Fairmont State University in West Virginia. He had been drafted in the eighth-round draft by the Buffalo Bills, the first Canadian quarterback to be drafted by the NFL. His outstanding career was highlighted by his having broken five all-conference records. In his final year, he had a 54.5 passing percentage, and threw for 2,216 yards and 29 touchdowns. The Concordes were ready to move him into a prominent role. Last year's quarterback Vince Ferragamo would not be back; Gerry Dattilio had been traded to Calgary for Ken Johnson who was considered to be only a short-term solution for the new year.[112] Luc Tousignant was "the quarterback of the future."[113] It would be up to Coach Joe Galat to develop him to the point where the Concordes would once again challenge for the Grey Cup. Galat had been hired by George Allen during his tenure. The Alouette coaching job had been labelled by Allen as "The Greatest Challenge in North America."[114]

Although the Montreal story and its unfolding had dominated football news for the better part of a year, there were other developments as well, some familiar. The Players' Association announced that George Allen, former Alouette executive officer, would be their guest speaker for the annual association dinner. A new football league, the United States Football League (USFL) was announced in the United States on May 11, 1982.[115] The CFL was still having its problem with the CIAU. Its main concern was still the designated import rule; the CIAU wanted it eliminated and said so. The CFL dug in its heels. Earl Lunsford moved and Jake Dunlap seconded "that the CIAU be informed through the Liaison Committee the designated import rule is no longer an item for discussion."[116] It was carried unanimously. The universities were also experiencing other problems, some of which were laid at the feet of the CFL.

The conflict between the playing dates of the Grey Cup and the College Bowl games was still an irritant. The universities preferred that their game be played in the third week of November and the Grey Cup Game the following weekend. The CFL had recently taken to moving the Grey Cup Game to the third weekend, as was the case with the 1981 game. The CFL agreed to move its showcase game back to the last weekend in November for 1982 and 1983, but it clearly wasn't happy with this. Norm Kimball advised that Edmonton would prefer "that the 1984 Grey Cup game be played on the earliest possible date." Ralph Sazio's motion to that effect, seconded by Bob Geary, was passed unanimously. The date fixed for the 1984 game was November 18.[117] The CFL maintained that it had the interests of university football at heart but when those interests conflicted with its business objectives, the latter came first. The CFL had also restricted its officials from working CIAU games since CFL rules were not used there. The university league was concerned about its resultant quality of officiating. It wished to meet with the CFL "to discuss areas of variance."[118] For a combination of reasons, finance being among them, some universities were having second thoughts about football. In the past five years, three had dropped the program. Simon Fraser University, a non-CIAU school which played with American schools and which had always been a valuable source of talent for the CFL, announced that it would "terminate its football program for budgetary reasons."[119] Simon Fraser was in need of $320,000 over a four-year period. The CFL had been approached and each club was asked to make a donation. There were concerns that teams couldn't give to one university and ignore others. Earl Lunsford mentioned that he had already been approached by the University of Manitoba for financial support. Would the University of British Columbia want funding too if Simon Fraser were assisted? Norm Kimball floated the possibility of the league's setting up "a one million dollar trust fund, the annual interest from which would be used to finance a troubled university."[120] It was generally agreed that if the university programs were to collapse, the league would be damaged "since the valuable source of both player talent and fan support would be lost."[121] There was also an allusion to the number of Canadians playing mainly at the high school level, which also was undergoing financial constraints. Gaudaur estimated that "some two hundred thousand young Canadians are involved in football up to the college level who were a primary source of fan support for the league, which, if lost, could make it more difficult for the league to survive."[122] With respect to the Simon Fraser problem, it was left up to each club to decide on its own. The B.C. Lions gave $25,000. Simon Fraser's athletic director, Lorne Davies, was upset that other CFL clubs did not respond in like fashion "particularly the Toronto Argonauts, since Argos annually refer Toronto's best high school players to Simon Fraser University."[123]

The reaction to the designated import rule would not go away. It was fuelled once again by the Argonauts and Dan Feraday. After his 1981 try-out for and subsequent "retirement" from the Argos, Feraday had returned to the University of Toronto team as quarterback where he won the Hec Crighton Trophy as the country's most outstanding university player. In addition, Feraday had been drafted in the 12th round by the Cincinnati Bengals of the NFL. Bengals coach Forrest Gregg, formerly coach of the Argos, had been impressed with the University of Toronto quarterback while in Toronto, had scouted him for the NFL, and made Feraday the second Canadian quarterback to be drafted that year. Luc Tousignant, as mentioned earlier, had been selected in the eighth round by Buffalo. The draft selection appeared to put a crimp in the Argos' plans. Condredge Holloway was returning, Joe Barnes was picked up from Saskatchewan, and Mike Williams was a third Argo quarterback. The Argonauts had also invited John Fourcade to work out with them, having given him a media build-up while he waited for the NFL draft. He was not selected. It was left for the fans to conclude that the non-import Feraday had been given the NFL stamp of approval; the other, Fourcade, had not. The rights to Fourcade were traded to the B.C. Lions. The Argos brought in former Atlanta Falcon quarterback June Jones as their fifth candidate and one who was familiar with assistant coach "Mouse" Davis' "Run and Shoot" offense. This offensive approach helped hasten the demise of the tight end position. Its emphasis was on three-step drops by the quarterback, reading on the run by receivers, as well as the pivot, quick, and free release by all players eligible to receive passes. Tight ends, those immediately adjacent to the tackles, would have to fight through a defensive player in order to run a pass pattern. The solution appeared to be to split the end some distance from the tackle, thus ensuring a freer release. Since the possibility of a running attack was lessened by the new alignment, the use of the slot-back became more prevalent.

It was Jones who encouraged Feraday once he was apprised of the designated import rule. He told Feraday that "with his arm he could go anywhere that he wanted to play in the States,"[124] and that this was where

Feraday had to go, to the States. As far as the media was concerned, Feraday was released by the Argos. "What actually occurred was that Cincinnati paid the remainder of his contract so they could obtain his rights."[125] It was a heady experience for the youngster. He had left a last-place CFL team which didn't want him and arrived in the camp of a Super Bowl finalist where he "received the royal treatment."[126] Despite a good training camp, the Bengals seemed interested in keeping the chemistry of last year's team alive in their attempt to return to the Super Bowl. Feraday was among the last cuts. He was offered an opportunity to stay, unofficially, but "Feraday did not like this idea; 'he wanted everything above table.'"[127]

Feraday continued his odyssey. Edmonton had come to Cincinnati's camp to evaluate him. They invited him to join the Eskimos. In September, he arrived in Edmonton where Warren Moon was firmly ensconced as quarterback, where Hugh Campbell was saying publicly that 1982 would be his last year and, in addition, where "the Eskimos reneged on a couple of promises which were made to Feraday's agent."[128] He was released. Saskatchewan called. Unbeknownst to Feraday, Forrest Gregg had attempted to "hide" the Canadian with Joe Faragalli and the Roughriders on the condition that Cincinnati could reclaim him if any of their quarterbacks were injured. He joined Saskatchewan in October. It was a brief stay. Because of what Feraday termed "bad advice," he left Saskatchewan, a decision he later called "his biggest mistake." He went to the new USFL, "the first quarterback to sign with the 'Michigan Panthers' in November of 1982 … [with] a good signing bonus."[129] Released in February of 1983, he signed the following day, once again, with Cincinnati. However, the merry-go-round continued. Since Feraday had been drafted earlier, signed, and released by the Bengals, according to league rules he had to clear a 10-day period of "procedural waivers."[130] He was claimed by the Kansas City Chiefs, Detroit Lions, and New York Giants. He went to Kansas City in May, but was released after a heated exchange with their general manager. Feraday was furious because travelling to Kansas City had stopped him from joining Cincinnati, a team that wanted him.[131] He went to Detroit but "threw ten passes in six weeks" and was released. He returned to become a quarterback coach with the University of Toronto. In February of 1984, Forrest Gregg came calling again, this time as coach of the Green Bay Packers. Ferraday was invited to their evaluation camp, was assessed by the coaching staff, signed to a contract, and reported to training camp. In the meantime the Packers drafted a Wisconsin native, Randy Wright, and signed him with a sizeable $150,000 bonus. Feraday was eventually released and returned to Toronto where he joined the police department in 1985.

Ralph Sazio was busy in his first full season as president of the Toronto Argonauts. He was determined to put his stamp on the club. All were surprised by his signing of Ottawa's defensive coach Bob O'Billovich as the new Argo head coach for the 1982 season. Another former Ottawa coach, Frank Clair, had also been appointed as a "special scout" for the Argos. When players or their agents complained publicly about pay cuts and/or the low salaries Sazio was offering, Sazio replied, "negotiating like that should be done privately, not through the newspapers."[132]

Meanwhile, in Saskatchewan, Joe Faragalli, who replaced Ron Lancaster and was winner of the 1981 Annis Stukus Award as the CFL's Coach of the Year, was not adverse to using his heart attack as a coaching tactic. It was common knowledge that he and Cal Murphy had suffered heart attacks while coaching in Edmonton. Faragalli recalled a game the past season, when Saskatchewan was playing B.C. It was raining. The game was important for Saskatchewan's play-off hopes. He emphasized that because of the sloppy conditions there was a good possibility the game would be decided by a mistake. Care was to be taken to "cover up the ball." "Stew Fraser fumbled the ball twice on punt returns so when he came off the field I said to him: 'Give me your hands.' And he did. And I put them inside my coat on my heart and said: 'Stew, you're going to give me a heart attack. You fumble the ball once more and you'll kill me right here on the sidelines.' Stew didn't drop the ball again."[133]

The league continued to make subtle refinements to its rules for the 1982 season. Officials were now able to whistle play dead when a defensive player moved across the line of scrimmage prior to the snap. The ball was to be brought out to the 20-yard line after an interception in the end zone. Previously, it was scrimmaged on the 10-yard line. On a safety touch, there were now three options available to the scoring team. Previously, the ball was automatically kicked off by the team scored upon at its 35-yard line. As of 1982, the scoring team could kick off from its own 35-yard line; could scrimmage from its own 35-yard line, or could have the scored-upon team kick off from its 35-yard line. A safety touch was expanded to include any ball fumbled and "propelled by a team into an end zone and [where it] bounces out of bounds."[134] The penalty for contact being made above the waist on any kick return was reduced from 15 to 10 yards. The league also sought to give more opportunity for plays during the last three minutes of each half. As of 1982, time-in would start with the snap of the ball rather than with the referee's whistle.[135] The league also showed some flexibility in its roster numbers. At times during the pre-season the number of players dressed related directly to travel expenses. The CFL decided that in games involving rivals within close geographic distance to each other, leeway would be allowed from the normal 45 players per club. Montreal and Ottawa could dress 50 for their games, Toronto and Hamilton the same for theirs, while Edmonton was given permission "to dress all its players on its training camp roster for its game at British Columbia on June 10."[136]

In addition to all of the controversy surrounding the Alouettes/ Concordes, the designated import rule, and relations with the CIAU, there was a huge turnover in coaching staff. (Only Saskatchewan, Winnipeg, and British Columbia remained constant. In the East, there were wholesale changes in Hamilton, Toronto, and Montreal. In fact, among the 21 assistant coaching positions in the East, only one, Don Sutherin at Ottawa, was a hold-over.)[137] Football still appeared to be popular throughout the country. The outstanding Grey Cup Game of 1981 attracted 6.2 million television viewers, "some two million more than watched the Super Bowl."[138] As an aside, "the only show on Canadian television which topped the Grey Cup ratings was the movie *Superman*."[139] Indeed, even in the United States, much to the delight of the CFL executives, ESPN "concluded a new agreement under which the league will receive a rights fee in the amount of $550,000 U.S. for each of the 1982 and '83 seasons."[140]

Expansion appeared to be a distinct possibility. A CFL team, to be called the Atlantic Schooners, had "been approved in principle for the Halifax area ... [to] a group headed by J. I. Albrecht and John Donaval of Mississauga, a trucking executive with extensive holdings in the Maritimes."[141] The major concern of the group was its ability to erect a stadium with 30,000 seats. The expansion fee had been publicized at $1.5 million.[142] The announcement, a bold attempt by the CFL to assure all that everything was under control, was publicized the same weekend of the demise of the Alouettes and the birth of the Concordes. Commissioner Jake Gaudaur was in Montreal while the announcement was made out of the Toronto office. There was hope that the CFL would truly be a coast-to-coast league with five teams in the East and five in the West. Tentative plans called for the Atlantic Schooners to select four players, two imports and two non-imports, from each club in January of 1984 in anticipation of play that year.[143]

Meanwhile, Jake Gaudaur continued to work on damage control. The league had been hurt by the publicity across Canada and the United States that one of its teams, the Montreal Alouettes, was unable to meet its payroll. He stressed, somewhat inaccurately, that "the league has been in existence as a sport leading to a Canadian championship since 1892."[144] The league was durable, and although it could be "an exercise in economic frustration to own a team,"[145] the saving grace, said Gaudaur, was that the CFL had "attracted into the sport, persons who are primarily concerned with keeping the sport alive and viable as opposed to people motivated by making a fast buck."[146]

Far from being upset at the media attention focused on the league problems, specifically the Montreal situation, Gaudaur was "encouraged."

> If no one was asking about it at Grey Cup time or at the annual meeting, I would have wondered if it does matter to anyone. It obviously did matter and it mattered to me that so many were concerned. The other thing that was very comforting was to have the indication from so many people in Montreal that under any circumstances the sport must be continued there. That's all the way from the Head of the Chamber of Commerce to the fans, to the groups of persons indicating an intent in operating the team from day one. My clear preference was to put that club in the hands of Quebeckers and everything I was doing was directed towards the end result of seeing the Club operate there this year. I did not feel we should leave the franchise dormant for a year.[147]

In a move clearly aimed at streamlining operations according to the needs of television while attempting to maintain the integrity of the game, the CFL issued its broadcasting guidelines for each game. They replaced the "highly conspicuous flag waving routines"[148] where an official would stand at the side of the field in order to get the referee's attention to either stop or start play because of a commercial time-out. Commercials were now to be inserted "during the natural delay which occurs following the scoring play, a change of possession or delay because of a player injured."[149] Six commercials were to be inserted in each quarter. If all six had been aired prior to the three-minute warning, permission for another commercial would have to be obtained from the league, whose preference was a public service announcement.[150]

The CFL broadcasting guidelines included the following:

1. A sixty second time-out shall be taken with three minutes to go in each half;
2. A sixty second time-out may be taken by each club in the last 3 minutes of each half;
3. A ninety second time-out shall be taken between the first and second and third and fourth quarters;
4. On three occasions in each quarter, a ninety second time-out may be taken but only following the scoring play or change of possession, during the delay of a game because of a player injury requiring the presence of a trainer on the field;

5. If six of the allowable time-outs referred to in item 4 have already been taken when the three minute warning is given, the television broadcaster shall not be permitted to air a commercial message during this time without the consent of the league, it being the intent that the league shall be permitted to require a non-commercial;

6. The kick off shall occur three minutes after the advertised start time for the game.[151]

The new arrangement was passed 8–0, with one abstention. Perhaps thinking that there might be a conflict of interest since the chief television sponsor was Carling O'Keefe, owner of the Argos, Ralph Sazio chose to abstain.[152] Meanwhile, the Argos were in resurgence. Led by their "run and shoot" offence directed by Condredge Holloway and Joe Barnes and featuring Cedric Minter and Terry Greer, they were fast becoming the toast of the town. Toronto fans were enthusiastic in their support. More than 52,000 were in attendance for a Toronto-Hamilton game at CNE Stadium, the Tiger-Cats winning 30–25. The Argos ended up with a 9–7 record and first place, while the Tiger-Cats who had good success against the Argos during the regular season finished in second place with an 8–7–1 record. Ottawa captured the final play-off spot with a 5–11 record. The Montreal Concordes' success proved no better than that of the Alouettes of the previous year. Quarterback Ken Johnson, whom the Alouettes had received for Gerry D'Attilio in 1981, injured his shoulder in training camp with the Concordes. He returned in time for Montreal's second game, against Toronto, a 16–13 loss, but in the next game, against Ottawa, a 55–5 loss, he was replaced by freshman quarterback Luc Tousignant. Johnson was eventually traded to Toronto; the Concordes gave Tousignant a baptism by fire and ended up in last place with a 2–14 record.

In the play-offs, there was a surprising upset. In Hamilton, Ottawa out-played and out-scored the Tiger-Cats to win by a 30–20 score. They were led by the rushing of Skip Walker who gained more than 250 yards, a play-off record. Toronto fans were ecstatic by the turn of events. The Argos had not fared well with the Tiger-Cats during the season. In that Eastern final game, the weather alternated between mist, sunshine, rain, and fog. An excited and expectant crowd watched the Argos cruise to a 29–0 half-time lead, on the way to a 44–7 victory. The Argos were back in the Grey Cup Game for the first time since 1971.

In the West, Saskatchewan and B.C. finished out of the play-offs with 6–9–1 and 9–7 records respectively. Calgary edged into third place by one point with its 9–6–1 performance. In the semifinal game between second-place Winnipeg and third-place Calgary, the Blue Bombers won 24–3 over the Stampeders. First place in the West had been decided by a formula. Both Edmonton and Winnipeg finished with 11–5 records but the Eskimos were awarded first place on the basis of having scored more points than Winnipeg in their games with each other.

The Western final was as tightly played between the two teams as was their season. Edmonton prevailed, winning 24–21. The difference in the scores was a touchdown run by Edmonton's Jim Germany scored halfway through the fourth quarter. Just prior to that, a Winnipeg interception of an Edmonton pass was nullified by a late penalty call against John Helton.[153]

The Argos would be the fourth Eastern team in four years that Edmonton would face in the Grey Cup Game. There were some who were concerned that the Eskimos kept appearing in the game; it was their sixth consecutive appearance and they were looking for their fifth straight win. Even the chairman of the CFL's Board of Governors, Gord Staseson of Regina, was quoted as saying: "The Grey Cup's half made with the Argonauts in there. Now if we can get something different from out here for the good of Canada, it would be great."[154]

Not all agreed with Staseson that the Argos were a welcome participant in the game. Harold Ballard appeared in photographs holding an Edmonton Eskimo banner. He was "still sore at the Argonauts for nabbing Ralph Sazio from his Ti-Cats and will advertise his wrath by cheering on the Eskimos."[155] Jake Gaudaur, a former Tiger-Cat player and executive, wasn't concerned. "When he was a player," he said, "he could always tell how competitive the Argos were that year by how much the people in Hamilton hated them. It's part of that old 'Hog Town' syndrome that's been around for 75 years. When 'Hog Town' does well, everyone likes to beat them and everyone wants to see them beaten. As a result, they were a very good draw on the road this year."[156]

At the week's festivities in Toronto, there was the anticipation that the event would generate more than $12 million for the city's businesses.[157] The Westin Hotel ordered in five times "the amount of booze it usually does … 10,000 pounds of ice to go along with it."[158] A Toronto novelty company had 5,000 illegally made Argonaut buttons confiscated. Since the exclusive rights were owned by Irwin Toy Limited, H.A.S. Novelty Company was charged with forgery.[159] At the 1982 Schenley Awards presentations, there were none of the criticisms of the CFL which surfaced during the 1981 ceremonies in Montreal. Condredge Holloway was chosen the Most Outstanding Player over Edmonton's Tom Scott, and Rocky DiPietro, a slot-back of tight-end size with Hamilton was selected as the Outstanding Canadian over Winnipeg's Rick House. Rookie of the Year was awarded to

Chris Issac, quarterback with Ottawa, over B.C.'s Mervyn Fernandez. The Most Outstanding Offensive Lineman award went to Ottawa guard Rudy Phillips ahead of Calgary's Lloyd Fairbanks. The Most Outstanding Defensive Player was Edmonton's James "Quick" Parker who was chosen ahead of Toronto's Zac Henderson.

In the game itself, the Eskimos won 32–16. Some attributed this to the weather; it rained in the second half, conditions which appeared to affect the Argos most. Others (Toronto fans, of course) said that the game was anticlimactic—the play-off game with Ottawa was the real high. There had been all sorts of conjecture about whether the Argos could win their first Grey Cup since 1952. It was almost 30 years to the day. Some wondered whether the announcement that Hugh Campbell would leave Edmonton at the end of the game to join Los Angeles in the newly announced spring league, the USFL, would hinder or help the Eskimos. When all was said and done, however, 1952 remained the last year that the Argos had won the Grey Cup, and the Edmonton Eskimos were victorious in an unprecedented five consecutive Grey Cup Games!

In the aftermath, two points of controversy emerged. During the singing of the national anthem, a version of "O Canada" was sung by St Michael's Boys Choir. The official government version had added "a couple of verses ... changed others. Half way through, the fans started cheering and whistling. They thought the song was over. Most of the crowd was singing the original version."[160] In the stands there were 54,741 fans in attendance and according to some, it was bedlam, especially in the concessions area. During the driving rain that fell, people poured out from the stands into the crowd of people who were using the concessions or facilities. According to one eye witness it was terror:

> While on my way to get a hot dog, I spotted three fist fights, two guys throwing up and one little boy who was knocked into a wall by a drunken fan. I left to get the hot dog at half-time but didn't make it to my seat, less than one hundred feet from the vendor's booth, until 3 minutes into the last quarter. At one point, the crush was so bad, all 230 pounds of me was lifted and carried about six feet. While many joked about the situation, it was terrifying to some people. One man thrashed about in a panic while they tried to locate his small daughter. He found her a few minutes later, jammed into a crowd and crying. Drunks, fortified by the booze they brought with them, sloshed the beer they bought from the vendors, other fans crammed together in the stadium's walkways. There appeared almost no crowd control on the second level where I was stuck and missed the third quarter of the game. One Winnipeg fan ended up

missing the second half because he couldn't get back to the his seat from the vendor's booth. 'The stadium just isn't equipped to handle those kinds of crowds,' he said angrily.[161]

1983 to 1984

Chapter Eight

MUCH OF THE FOOTBALL NEWS OF 1983 emanated from the far West where Canada's first functioning dome stadium was built in time for the 1983 football season. B.C. Place was the home of "Crazy George," the Lions' "cheerleader," and the site of the "wave" formed by spectators standing and sitting in sections simulating movement around the seating perimeter of the dome. And B.C. Place was not for sensitive ears. The noise reverberated to a deafening point. Visiting teams especially had difficulty in hearing the quarterback's signal; hand movements became a means of communicating with wide receivers.

B.C. Place was an amazing structure: "The world's largest air supported dome in terms of area, because of the size required to host Canadian football."[1] Ten acres were covered by the building, a maximum width of 623 feet, a maximum length of 760 feet, a maximum height of 200 feet. The roof, made of Teflon-bonded fibreglass, covered 40,000 square yards. Its 46-ton weight was "supported by air pressure inside that is six points per square foot above outside atmospheric pressure."[2] The total cost of the facility was $126 million. The stadium officially opened June 19, 1983, with an exhibition game played four days later, B.C. defeating Calgary 41–19. The first regular-season CFL game there was with the B.C. Lions and Saskatchewan, the Lions winning 44–28. Mervyn Fernandez scored after only 57 seconds of play with a 30-yard pass from Roy Dewalt.

Previous to the opening of B.C. Place, the largest crowd to witness a single B.C. Lions game was in 1965 when 36,704 saw the Lions and Stampeders play in Empire Stadium. In 1964 when the Lions won the Grey Cup a record season attendance of 260,039 had been attracted. B.C. Place erased all of that. A season total of 448,857 watched the Lions in '83. B.C.'s first pre-season game attracted 53,472. A regular-season record of 56,852 spectators watched B.C. and Winnipeg on August 12, 1983; even more, a capacity crowd of 59,409, saw the same two teams in the Western final of 1983.[3]

The B.C. Lions were the envy of every team in the CFL in 1983. Not only did they have what some considered to be the most outstanding stadium in North America in which to play, but their training facilities were similarly outstanding. The club opened its own private office and practice complex in nearby Surrey, B.C. Ticket offices, dressing rooms, storage area, weight training equipment, laundry facilities, a sauna, whirlpool, and shower, along with athletic therapy areas, were all part of the new headquarters; all of this was on the ground floor. Four meeting rooms for simultaneous sessions were also available. The practice field was immediately outside, "only a matter of stepping out the back door."[4] Administrative offices were located on the upper floor of the two-storey building.

B.C. Place was not only affecting the league attendance-wise, but it was also responsible for removing a one-hundred-year tradition in Canadian football. There had always been end zones of 25 yards in depth. Throughout the history of the league, adjustments had been made in individual parks if they couldn't meet the specifications. For example, before the Alouettes moved to Molson Stadium at McGill University, they played at Delormier Downs which could only support 10-yard end zones. Corners were rounded and fenced in some parks, such as at Taylor Field in the sixties. In other cases, the chalk lines were extended from the field onto the surrounding track in order to get the full 25 yards past the goal-line. When the matter of B.C. Place and its 20-yard end zones came up during a pre-season meeting of the CFL Management Council, Calgary's Jack Gotta proposed that other stadiums be made to conform. His motion was defeated 5–4. Edmonton's Norm Kimball suggested that the proposal was a Rules Committee matter. He would consider submitting a proposal for the 1984 season.[5] It did not, in fact, receive approval until January of 1986 in time for that year's season but the reason for the change was directly attributable to the building of B.C. Place in 1983.

There were other standardizations as well. Television and video equipment was making its presence felt in the league. The Football Reporters of Canada requested that television monitors be placed in the main print area of the press boxes. The league was pleased to concur since, as Norm Kimball advised, "very little cost is involved because the equipment is usually supplied either by a sponsor or by the television network."[6] They also asked that each radio broadcast booth be equipped with a signal light that could be activated by the game timekeeper to indicate when time was called for a commercial. While both of these suggestions were incorporated for the upcoming season, there was some delay over another recommendation. The installation of 20-second clocks was suggested but a decision was deferred until the May general manager's meeting. In 1982, Ottawa, Saskatchewan, and Montreal had the clocks in their stadiums. B.C. Place would have them in 1983. The other five were at various stages in the decision-making process; Winnipeg's new general manager Paul Robson thought the lack of uniformity among teams in the matter to be very "unprofessional."[7]

The designated import rule continued to be discussed in the CFL boardrooms but for another reason other than the typical one. During the 1982 season, a team had put its designated import quarterback into a blocking back position on a third down punt. It was a classic case of coaches being able to stretch the rules. The argument was made that the snap could still be made to the quarterback even though he was not in the traditional under-the-centre position. Norm Kimball "argued that it was never intended that a designated quarterback could line up at another position; however, he could see permitting a direct snap to another player while another quarterback is operating in his normal position."[8] While there was much discussion about the situation at the January meeting, a final decision was made at the Management Council meeting of February 15. There, it was decided that "the provision would be interpreted to mean that the player would be deemed to be playing at quarterback if at the instant the ball is snapped he is in a position to receive the ball directly from the centre, whether or not he actually receives the ball."[9]

The topic of imports and non-imports was always a focus of discussion at CFL meetings. The 1983 meetings were no exception. By 1983, all the so-called "grandfather clauses" which were enacted in order to avoid making legislation retroactive in 1965, were no longer necessary. "All the players who had been protected by these transitional provisions were no longer active in the league." The grandfather clauses were therefore eliminated. A non-import could now "be a player who was physically resident in Canada for an aggregate period of seventeen years prior to his attaining the age of 21 years."[10]

If Harold Ballard had his way, the whole notion of non-imports would be swept away. Ballard stated: "I'm a Canadian but I believe we have to do something to improve our product. Sure you can look at it from the Canadian point of view but you've also got to look at it as a business and I'm not going to sell any more seats the way it stands now"[11] For whatever reason, Ballard did not communicate his preference to Tiger-Cat general manager, Joe Zuger. The latter voted against Montreal's proposal that the number of imports be increased from 15 to 18, the designated restrictions to apply to the 18th import, that rosters be increased to 38, and that the number of non-imports be 20. Only Montreal, its vote cast by Sam Etcheverry, voted in favour while arguing that the money spent on the (to-be-abolished) four man taxi squad would fund the increased roster and improve the calibre of play.

There were other instances where individual clubs chose to act autonomously as opposed to taking a league approach. Property rights, logos, trade marks, team names and the like could not be vested in the league in Canada until the current rights in Toronto and Montreal expired. A plan was approved to merchandise them in the U.S. through a firm called West Nally Inc. of New York. The period would not go beyond December 31, 1984. In return, the league was to receive a guarantee of 60% of the profits or a minimum of $15,000.[12]

From time to time, the media requested information from the league offices about players' options and which players' contracts were due to expire. Jake Gaudaur, noting that "the NFL issues press releases on the subject," asked for guidance on the matter. The clubs preferred to handle it individually.[13] They took a similar approach with a scouting combine. There was such a league operation, but the Ottawa, Toronto, Hamilton, and Calgary clubs did not belong; Calgary's Jack Gotta spoke for the four when he stated that his club "feels it could do a better job on its own."[14] With such an individualistic approach among league members, it was only natural that there were continuous strains on the CFL as it sought to speak and act with one voice.

Expansion of the CFL to the Maritime region was also anticipated. The name of the new team was to be the Schooners, a reference to the famous schooner, the Bluenose, which adorned the Canadian 10 cent coin. It was also the name of a popular beer; so there was prestige and the possiblity of a corporate sponsorship tie-in as well. The league gave the Schooners a May 1983 deadline "to prove beyond a doubt they will be able to field a team for the 1984 season."[15] The Schooners' general-manager-in-waiting, J. I. Albrecht, who had held similar positions with the Alouettes and Argonauts, sought to soothe any fears: "Sure there are skeptics and cynics but if you had to depend on skeptics and cynics nothing would get done. I've just come back after spending 11 days in Halifax/Dartmouth and everything down there is favourable. We've got seasons ticket orders coming out of our ears."[16]

Albrecht's optimism didn't deter the league from deciding that the Schooners would not be part of the 1984 schedule. Its May meeting identified three major shortcomings with the Maritime expansion franchise: the lack of "a clear financing picture of the proposed $6.5 million stadium; a failure to clearly spell out the breakdown of shareholders in the Maritime

Professional Football Club Ltd.; the absence of required statements of undertaking from their principal owner, R. B. Cameron."[17] Perhaps even more critically, however, "the group didn't bring along the required $900,000 of the $1.5 million franchise fee."[18] The Schooners were given until June 17 to "get their ship out of dry dock and be up to specifications," otherwise they would "be sent to the bottom for good."[19] And they were! Expansion to the Maritimes came close but was ruled out when the June 17 deadline arrived and passed without the league being assured that a viable franchise was possible under the arrangements of the time.

The league also announced its 1983 Grey Cup Game prices. All seats at B.C. Place would be $30 "regardless of location."[20] Eighty-five per cent of all the tickets were allocated to the West for the game which was certain to attract record revenue for the league and its clubs. The 1982 play-offs and Grey Cup Game yielded $514,714 and $624,761 respectively for a total of $1,139,475.[21]

The business of football was brought home with Edmonton's end-of-year statement of finances. Grey Cup champions for five consecutive years, the Eskimos offered some sober insights into their operations. They drew a record 616,000 spectators to their 11 home games, generated $5,136,000 in gate receipts and suffered a $230,000 operating loss. Winnipeg, too, was raising its ticket prices.

The CFL still had a system of revenue sharing which had been agreed to at the November 20, 1981, meeting and would be effective through 1983. "The contribution by each club would be 20% of the amount by which its gross gate exceeded the league average. This contribution cannot exceed 5% of the club's gross gate for the season.[22] The Clubs had to make a decision whether to increase each club's maximum contribution to $225,000 or "$150,000 times the annual compounded consumer price index factors for 1981, 1982, and 1983 ... whichever is greater,"[23] or whether "to extend the existing provisions beyond the 1983 season."[24] Among the factors to be considered was the knowledge that when the changes were introduced in 1980, the figures were based on the fact that six of the nine clubs either made a profit or broke even, whereas "in 1982, it is understood that at least seven of the nine clubs suffered significant operating losses."[25] Some attempt was made to pinpoint players' salaries as the culprit. The players salaries and bonus costs had risen to 55% from 47% of the average revenue for all clubs.[26]

The league also showed its tendency to be pragmatic. When there was a complaint that teams were not adhering to the 15 minute half-time intermission period, they were more likely to take 20 minutes, the Rules Committee acted to change the intermission time to 20 minutes and placed the onus on the clubs to have their teams on the field ready for the kick-off "at exactly 20 minutes after the conclusion of the first half."[27] There were to be no exceptions, but the league softened its hardline stance somewhat by adding the rider, "the guilty team will be subject to penalty, possibly."[28]

Time was important, especially if the CFL wished to improve and maximize its exposure and revenue from the media, particularly television. A subtle balancing act was necessary. Starting times which were ideal for television were not necessarily good for the live gate. As well, East-West tensions might surface at the best of times, but especially when it appeared that decisions were being made to cater to the Eastern markets. Schedules were set in 1983 only after refinement were made as a result of meetings with Carling O'Keefe representative Mrs. Shirley Slade, CTV's Oliver Babirad, and CBC's Bill Sheehan.[29] The three had spoken with each other prior to the meeting and had analyzed the schedule with a view to station availabilities and maximum viewership. Each club was dealt with individually.

Winnipeg was asked whether it would schedule its games of August 13 and September 24 at 8:30 P.M. and its Sunday, October 23, contest at 3:00 P.M. in order "to minimize the overlap with other games on those dates and thus permit all games to be televised." Toronto was asked to reschedule a 7:00 P.M. game on September 24 to 1:30 P.M. Sazio refused but "he would agree to lift the secondary blackout of the Winnipeg game coming into Toronto at 8:30 EDT." Hamilton liked to have its night games start at 7:30. They were requested to move to a 7:00 P.M. start and play the Saturday October 1 and 15 games in the afternoon instead of the evening. Joe Zuger replied that a 7:00 P.M. start was acceptable but afternoon games on October 1 and 15 were not. Ottawa's dates and times were acceptable, as were Montreal's. British Columbia was asked to start its games, "particularly against eastern opponents," at 7:30 P.M. General Manager Bob Ackles agreed to do so if all of its games were moved to 7:30 but he stated that a city ordinance prevented an earlier start. Saskatchewan's starting times of 1:30 P.M and 7:00 P.M. were acceptable except for Sunday, October 30. On that date, Standard Time resumed in all areas. The Carling O'Keefe representative requested a 2:30 P.M. start in order "to permit the telecast of two games on that date." Saskatchewan, which drew its audience from a wide geographical area, had its doubts that it could accommodate but General Manager John Herrera promised to look into the matter and advise. Edmonton's Norm Kimball turned down a request by CTV's Oliver Babirad for a 7:00 P.M. start, as opposed to 7:30 P.M., because "the city transit systems provide 600 buses for home games and a 7:00 P.M. start would be too close to the evening rush hour to permit bus service at that earlier time."

He supported his contention by advising that an earlier start "had been tried on a previous occasion and was found to be unsatisfactory."[30]

When Calgary's Jack Gotta requested a later starting time on Sunday, July 31, because of a conflict with the World Student Games, the 7:30 P.M. start was ruled out because of previous television time commitments.

CTV had "some interest in Sunday evening games in July and August, but not thereafter." Five clubs felt that Sunday summer games merited consideration. They were Winnipeg, Calgary, Ottawa, Hamilton, and Edmonton. The whole process was then repeated with reference to the lifting of blackouts, allowing games to be telecast into areas where games were being played that same day. It was an exercise in balancing individual club interests with league requirements, accepting as an article of faith that a sacrifice for the common good would result in increased revenues in the long run even though attendance might fall.

The cooperation paid off. The league was rewarded with the highest television contract in its history. Carling O'Keefe Breweries paid a record $33 million to televise the CFL games in 1984, '85, and '86. There were probably some very good reasons for the deal. Carling O'Keefe owned the Argonauts who competed with the Toronto Blue Jays for the entertainment dollar. At the same time, the baseball team was owned by Labatt's. The two breweries were fighting for a larger share of the southern Ontario market. Carling O'Keefe also had ownership interests with the Quebec Nordiques. Their biggest rivals were the Montreal Canadiens who were owned by Molson's. Even with Carling O'Keefe's sponsorship, however, it was not assumed that the other clubs would automatically stop what promotional affiliations they had with rival beer companies. The *B.C. Lions 1984 Fact Book*, under the heading "Lions and Labatt's," paid special tribute to their relationship with the Carling O'Keefe rival, "whose support and assistance of the B.C. Lions over the past years has been invaluable. Their contribution to B.C. Lions football, and the overall development of the sport in our province cannot be measured, but certainly the people at Labatt's are one of the finest friends the club could have."[31] Labatt's even sponsored a Canadian Superstars competition comprising 10 events, with each competitor having to compete in seven events including the final obstacle course. Canadian athletes from a wide variety of sports competed. These included: skiiers Ken Read and Todd Brooker; swimmer Alex Baumann; hurdler Mark McKoy; ski jumper Horst Bulau; basketball player Leo Rautins; hockey players Darryl Sittler, Rick Vaive and Lanny McDonald; and football players Rocky DiPietro, Paul Bennett, and Nick Hebeler. Rocky DiPietro, the Tiger-Cat slot back won the "$10,000 first prize plus $100 for each point earned for a total of $14,100. He quipped: 'This makes up almost all my salary for last year.'"[32]

The Concordes replaced Montreal legend Sam Etcheverry for the 1983 season. In a dispute over who was running the team, the chairman of the Imasco's board of directors, L. Edmond Ricard (also president and chief operating officer) made it known that if the Concordes wanted to continue to have Imasco money involved, Etcheverry would have to go. Ricard won his showdown; Etcheverry was replaced with Joe Galat who added the general manager position to his coaching duties. Bob Geary was director of football operations. There was a feeling in the CFL and particularly in the West that the run to the 1983 Grey Cup was wide open for the first time in years. Hugh Campbell had left Edmonton to join the Los Angeles Express of the USFL. After some delay he was replaced by Peter Kettela, more noted as a film "breakdown" coach with the Green Bay Packers of the NFL. There was a flurry of activity as teams sought to recruit the Eskimo coaching staff. Joe Faragalli had already moved to Saskatchewan where the Roughriders were invigorated. Don Mathews who had served as defensive coordinator with the Eskimos and who had been part of the previous six Grey Cup appearing teams, was appointed head coach of the Lions in January of 1983. Cal Murphy, Edmonton's line coach and a coaching member of the winning Grey Cup team for the past six consecutive years, became head coach of the Blue Bombers in Winnipeg, replacing Ray Jauch, who was moving to the USFL. It was part of a general reorganization for the Bombers. Earl Lunsford was replaced in the general manager's position by former player Paul Robson and quarterback Dieter Brock, who had complained about there being nothing to do in Winnipeg but go the zoo, was traded to Hamilton, which sent its top quarterback, Tom Clements, west.

Quarterbacks were still a major draw with most teams and there was a wealth of experience and talent at that position in the CFL in 1983. Roy Dewalt and Joe Pao Pao were in B.C.; a young veteran Warren Moon and a first-year Matt Dunigan were in Edmonton; in Calgary, Bernard Quarles and Gerry Dattilio split the assignment; John Hufnagel, along with Homer Jordan, was in Saskatchewan until he was sent to Winnipeg to replace an injured Tom Clements. In the East, Dieter Brock was with the Tiger-Cats; Ottawa had Chris Issac and Dave Marler; Montreal had Vince Evans; the Argonauts were led by the veterans Condredge Holloway and Joe Barnes.

During the 1983 season, it soon became obvious that the Edmonton Eskimo dynasty was at an end. Hugh Campbell's successor Pete Kettela lasted less than half a season as head coach and was replaced by Eskimo legend Jackie Parker. Edmonton still managed an 8–8 record for a third place finish but was defeated in the Western semifinal by a 49–22 score by Winnipeg led by former Edmonton line coach Cal Murphy. The B.C. Lions, first-place finishers and led by former Edmonton defensive coordinator Don

Mathews, defeated the Blue Bombers 39–21, to represent the West in the 1983 Grey Cup Game to be played in the familiar surroundings of B.C. Place. Saskatchewan and Calgary finished out of the play-offs, the former with only a 5–11 record and Calgary just barely with an 8–8 record. The Stampeders finished with an identical record to the Eskimos at 8–8, but third place was awarded to the northern Albertans on the basis of the tie-breaking formula. The Stampeders were becoming a CFL trouble spot. Their total attendance had been falling steadily in the eighties. Almost 40,000 fewer fans attended their games in 1983 than in 1982; average attendance had fallen from more than 30,000 to just over 25,000 in the same year.

In the East, Montreal and Hamilton had the same 5–10–1 record but the Tiger-Cats were awarded third place and a play-off spot. Bud Riley's team, quarterbacked by Dieter Brock, surprised the second-place Ottawa Rough Riders by defeating them 33–31 at Lansdowne Park. The Eastern final was a classic Toronto-Hamilton match-up, the Argos prevailing by a 41–36 score and qualifying for the Grey Cup Game.

Grey Cup week in Canada has always been a mixture of pageantry, fun, business, and the game. The first Grey Cup Game to be played in Vancouver since 1974 was no exception. With "Crazy George" leading the way, B.C. Place was described as "a frenzy cauldron of fan mania"[33] during the Lions' defeat of Winnipeg. Preparations received maximum media exposure. The city seemed just as anxious to show off its jewel of a facility as the league was to hype its Grey Cup. The game was called the "most popular show in Canadian television … the 1982 game drew a record audience of 7.8 million viewers on the combined CBC, CTV and CBC French networks … with CBC attracting 3.8 million or 47% of all viewers in Canada at that time."[34] The CBC was planning to use 17 cameras, 10 more than were used in a regular season game. Eleven were to be used for the game itself: eight in the stands or on scaffolds, one at each team's bench, and another in the broadcast booth. For off-field action, two were to be in the dressing rooms, two with host John Wells in the B.C. Place studio, one roaming through the crowd "looking for celebrities and the final camera [was] suspended from B.C. Place roof."[35]

John Wells was son of "Cactus Jack" Wells the former Winnipeg broadcaster who also covered Grey Cup Games for the CBC. One couldn't help make the comparisons with the growth of the game from that era. The first Grey Cup Game to be televised was the 1952 Toronto–Edmonton contest. The Canadian Rugby Union (CRU) sold the television rights to the Toronto CBC station for $7,500. The announcers for that first game were Norm Marshall, the voice of the Tiger-Cats, and Larry O'Brien, a sportscaster from Montreal. They were paid $250 each.[36] It was 1957, during the Hamilton–Winnipeg contest, that the first network telecast occurred. "The television rights for that game brought $75,000."[37]

The Schenley Awards had been a tradition in Canada from their inception in 1953 when Billy Vessels was selected the Outstanding Player in Canada, the only award presented. Twenty years later, in 1983, another Edmonton player, quarterback Warren Moon, was chosen over Toronto's Terry Greer as the Most Outstanding Player; the Rookie Award was given to Johnny Shepherd, running back with Hamilton, chosen over Willard Reaves of Winnipeg; Paul Bennett of Winnipeg was selected as the Most Outstanding Canadian, and the Concordes' Denny Ferdinand as the runner-up; Rudy Phillips of Ottawa was the recipient of the Most Outstanding Offensive Lineman Award over John Bonk, the Winnipeg centre; Greg Marshall of Ottawa was picked ahead of Calgary's Danny Bass as the Most Outstanding Defensive Player.

But it was the stadium, B.C. Place, that necessitated almost as much preparation for the opposition as did the Lions. The noise was the major topic of concern among opponents. It was deafening when "Crazy George" whipped up the fans into a screaming frenzy. Toronto's Ralph Sazio suggested that the orchestrated outbursts at strategic times, that is, when the opposing quarterback was calling signals, was "unsportsmanlike, a remark greeted with a few gentle scoffs on this side of the Rockies."[38] Winnipeg centre John Bonk, who had trouble hearing the quarterback's voice during the noise even from his close proximity, likened the crowd to "a thirteenth and fourteenth man out there."[39]

Hamilton's Dieter Brock, who also quarterbacked Winnipeg during its exhibition game in B.C. Place and had played there twice, concurred: "The building is very tough to play in. The noise doesn't trowel [*sic*] out; it just sort of bounces around. You have troubles with the signals and you have trouble with concentration. And then there is the human wave, one of Crazy George's specialities. While no player would admit having a lapse of concentration during a big game, it's hard not to notice when all those people are jumping up and down in their seats."[40]

But the B.C. Lions had much more than a noisy stadium on its side. Lui Passaglia was the leading scorer in the CFL with 191 points; Mervyn Fernandez was one of the premier pass receivers with 78 receptions for 1,284 yards.; Roy Dewalt had matured as a quarterback completing 62.2% of his 442 pass attempts for 22 touchdowns. Defensively, Larry Crawford led the league with 12 interceptions in addition to his outstanding punt returns. The defensive line was anchored by Mack Moore, a Western All Star in 1983.

It was the Argonauts' second consecutive appearance in the Grey Cup Game. They had become a dominant team in the league, just what Carling O'Keefe hoped for when they signed Ralph Sazio away from Hamilton. Some still considered the Argonaut president to be the most astute football man in the country. There were those who criticized his choice of Bob O'Billovich as the Argonaut head coach in 1982, suggesting he was a no-name. But the Argonauts under O'Billovich made it to the 1983 Grey Cup Game, their first in a decade, and the Argonaut coach was selected as winner of the Annis Stukus Trophy as the CFL's Coach of the Year. This was to be his second consecutive appearance in the national final.

The two seemed to work well as a team: Sazio wanted some hands-on involvement and O'Billovich knew who the boss was. When "Mouse" Davis wanted more money and more authority, neither Sazio nor O'Billovich was willing to grant it. They agreed to part company, but the Argonaut output still increased in 1983. Sazio also made some astute player moves. The Argos claimed slot back Emmanuel Tolbert on waivers from Saskatchewan, and linebacker William Mitchell on waivers from Ottawa at the end of the 1982 season. Carl Brazley, who had played out his option with Ottawa and was later cut by the Buffalo Bills, was pursued and signed by the Argos. Another defensive back, Leroy Paul, had originally signed with Sazio in Hamilton where after three seasons he played out his option. Toronto signed him after Paul and Hamilton could not agree on a contract. When Saskatchewan's Ken McEachern was dissatisfied with contract negotiations with the Roughriders, Sazio acquired the talented defensive back for a draft choice. Like Brazley, Mitchell, and Tolbert, McEachern was selected to the Eastern All Star team for 1983. To cap it all off, the outstanding CFL punter Hank Ilesic, was brought to Toronto in 1983. Unable to resolve a contract dispute with the Eskimos, the young kicker (who originally joined the Eskimos as a 17-year-old grade 12 student in 1977) brought consistently good punting and field goal kicking to the 1983 Argo team.

The Argonauts had other weapons as well. Quarterback Condredge Holloway and Joe Barnes, a receiving corps led by Terry Greer and an inspired defence led the Argos to an 18–17 victory over the B.C. Lions. After trailing 17–7 at half-time, the Argonauts' defence stiffened; the offence scored the 11 points necessary to win. It was the first Argonaut Grey Cup victory since 1952; the Lions had last won in 1964. "One drought is over, the other continues" reported the Vancouver Sun.[41] The Argonauts returned to Toronto where "police estimated 40,000 boisterous fans lined the downtown core exorcising 31 years of pent up frustrations." O'Billovich put in his bid for an improved facility: "Last year at this time the city made a promise we were going to get a domed stadium if we promised to go for the Grey Cup. Now it's up to them to keep their part of the bargain."[42]

There was excitement in Toronto and throughout the league with the Grey Cup Game. Played indoors for the first time, the game attracted a sell-out of 59,345. Every ticket in B.C. Place was priced at $30. It was the first $2 million gate in CFL history, the receipts being $2,068,385. The league was happy because Toronto appeared to have turned the corner; its franchise was one of the cornerstones of league prosperity.

Along with the Argos' resurrection, there was the resuscitation of the All Star game. A group from Hamilton, which included Tiger-Cat linebacker John Priestner, sought to capitalize on the newly found fervour in Vancouver and the indoor facility at B.C. Place. It signed a five-year agreement with the Players' Association for the revival of the game and negotiated a television contract with Carling O'Keefe. The game was played Saturday, December 3, less than one week after the Grey Cup. Fewer than 10,000 fans were in the stands, although "organizers claimed there were 10,500 tickets sold."[43] The CFL Players' Association was to have benefitted by receiving $25,000 or 15% of the gate for its pension fund. All of the selected players appeared, encouraged also by the knowledge that there was insurance coverage guaranteeing them $50,000 should an injury occur. "Several players, notably Edmonton quarterback, Warren Moon and defensive back David Shaw purchased additional insurance."[44] "The West defeated the East 25–15 in a game totally lacking in drama or excitement."[45]

There was news of significance in other areas. Jake Gaudaur announced in February that he would not seek another term as CFL commissioner.[46] Although his term extended to 1985, Gaudaur chose to step down one year earlier and serve the last year of his contract as a consultant to the new commissioner. Doug Mitchell replaced Jake Gaudaur as of June 1, 1984, although the latter continued to serve as an "executive consultant" for the last year of his original contract. He would leave his association with the league December 31, 1985. Mitchell's appointment was a surprise. His name had never been mentioned as a possibility. Others touted for the job had been former Argonaut player Mike Wadsworth, Saskatchewan Roughrider President Dick Rendek, Ottawa great Ron Stewart, and Ontario Premier Bill Davis.[47] Mitchell's credentials were solid. He was a lawyer, had attended the University of Colorado on a hockey scholarship before transferring to UBC. On graduation he signed with the Lions playing as a centre and middle linebacker in 1960 before being traded to Hamilton in 1961 where he was released. He returned to his native Calgary where he articled and set up a law practice and immersed himself in the Calgary sport scene. He had wide interests. He was a member of the Hockey Canada Advisory Board, served as legal counsel to the Calgary Flames, had a string of standard bred racing horses, played a key role in Calgary's attainment of the 1988 Winter Games, was a co-chairman of the Willy DeWitt Trust Fund, and was a colour commentator for Stampeder games on CFCN radio. Lois Mitchell, his wife, headed up All-Pro Contracts Limited, the firm which had concession and souvenir rights at McMahon Stadium.[48]

The new commissioner did not come cheaply. His yearly salary was "$175,000 with annual cost of living increases at the annual Consumer Price Index rate, which increments would be payable into a pension or deferred income plan."[49] His contract was for a three-year term with a review after two years and an option "to terminate or to renew for a further two years."[50] Mitchell was to have an expense account to cover those expenses "incurred in carrying out his duties and responsibilities as Commissioner," an automobile, memberships at an athletic club and business club, and moving expenses to a maximum of $35,000.[51] The CFL would have preferred to make the announcement closer to the end of January to allow the new head to familiarize himself, through Gaudaur, for a greater period of the pre-season but the announcement was delayed until March 8. Mitchell was committed to being in Sarajevo for the Winter Olympics in order to gain first-hand knowledge and experience for the 1988 Calgary games. The league took a "key man" insurance policy in the amount of $250,000 on the commissioner designate, the CFL being the beneficiary.[52]

When Doug Mitchell took over as commissioner of the CFL, June 1, 1984, it was obvious that while his preference was to be forward looking and expansionary, the reality of the CFL required him to address familiar concerns. The new commissioner had met with the mayor of London informally "to discuss what it would take for the southern Ontario city to acquire a franchise."[53] Mitchell also floated the idea of "neutral site" games in London and Halifax. The idea was "to test those particular markets as potential franchise areas"[54] by playing pre-season games involving Eastern clubs, mainly Hamilton and Ottawa, who would simply shift their home game. The current agreement with the players called for a maximum of 20 games, four exhibition games plus a 16-game schedule. Any exhibition games in the neutral sites would have to be from the 20. Immediately, the obstacles were thrown up: the "game would not likely be self-supporting unless there were subsidies from government levels and there are stadium commitments with concessions to be considered."[55]

Television continued to be a factor in a variety of ways in 1984. What with the large contract the league had signed with Carling O'Keefe and the networks, there was always the question of how the medium was going to be effected. The year would be a busy one for television, many demands being put on its capabilities. The Olympics, a royal visit, and a papal mass in Toronto were all occurring during the football season; all would add to the log jam of programming. Concern was expressed that some games during 1983 required more than three hours to complete. Television networks, not only in Canada, but also ESPN in the United States, had other commitments after the third hour. Thus, when a proposal was made to increase the amount of time a team had to put the ball into play from 20 to 25 seconds, it received little support. It was defeated by a 2–7 vote.[56] The league could ill afford to be legislating regulations which would add valuable seconds and minutes. It had to find other ways. The half-time intermission which only the previous year had been increased, was cut back to 15 minutes "with the team subject to a yardage penalty if it fails to be ready for the second half kick-off and with the home team subject to a fine if it fails to have the team field cleared in time for the second half kick-off."[57]

The starting time of the Grey Cup Game was also a question. In 1983, the game was played in Vancouver and began at 3:00 P.M. PST allowing the game to be shown in the East in prime television time. The 1984 game, to be played in Edmonton, could not be played that late since the weather would turn colder as the sun went down. It was the first time Edmonton was to host the game; city and team officials were anxious to see that the most favourable arrangements were made. Some critics were publicly chastising the league for playing the Grey Cup Game outdoors in northern Alberta when the indoor B.C. Place was available. Norm Kimball preferred a 12:30 or 1:00 P.M. MST start; the TV people "indicated a preference for 1:30."[58] Jake Gaudaur sought to speak to the television networks about a 1:00 P.M. compromise.

Television blackouts were also a concern. On the one hand, televising a game could affect the sale of tickets. People would stay home to watch the game on television rather than buy a ticket. On the other hand, television revenue was important too. The more people who watched a game on television, the better the case for a larger television contract could be made. The CFL was still concerned with "pirating" of signals by taverns, hotels, and restaurants who were able to bring in a distant telecast by means of their satellite dishes. In some ways, this too was a "no win" situation. Carling O'Keefe was not opposed since there was increased viewership and beer sales would increase particularly in those target areas. The league had given Gaudaur the authorization "to use his best judgement whether or not to instruct the CBC to install scrambling equipment as a means of protecting the League's primary blackout."[59] Gaudaur asked to CBC "to proceed with the installation of the necessary scrambling equipment."[60] The CBC agreed on the condition "that when it commences the distribution of scrambled signals in Canada the League would take such steps as are necessary to preclude the exhibition of unauthorized signals in Canada which are available as a result of the distribution of them in the U.S.A. by satellite."[61]

As always, the league was concerned about the image it presented to the public. Ever since the mid-seventies with the U.S. expansion controversy, government intervention, the Jamie Bone affair and the failed expansion into other areas of Canada, the league had taken a beating in the media. Prior to Gaudaur's stepping aside as commissioner, club general managers were instructed to hold seminars for their coaches and employees with "the purpose of improving the image of the League."[62] A meeting was also arranged with broadcast crews from CBC and CTV and the CFL general managers. The meeting which took place at the Westin Hotel in Toronto discussed a variety of issues. In what was described as a "constructive" move, the "League officials requested the announcers to stop referring to the small crowds at some CFL games. For another, the League would like to ban sideline interviews and keep cameras away from the players' bench."[63] The league had previously sought to tighten up its rules in an effort to stem criticism resulting from an incident during the 1983 season. Montreal Concordes' defensive back Phil Jones, a former Argo, was "traded" back to the Argonauts "for a brief period ... but didn't know it. He never left Montreal. For that matter, he didn't even miss a Concordes' meeting or practice. The trade to the Argos was a convenient vehicle that allowed the Concordes to dress another player in place of Jones who was injured but not seriously enough to be placed on the injury list. Jones was 'traded back' to the Concordes a couple of days later."[64] It resulted in a by-law change at the Management Council meetings "that will prevent such phoney trades in the future. A team, now, cannot trade a player back to his former team within two days of acquiring him."[65]

It was the Concordes' coach and general manager Joe Galat who had been critical of the league's approach to the new USFL. Amid news that CFL players who were still under contract were practising with USFL teams, Galat stated: "I think we waited too long ... We let in the Trojan Horse last year by allowing Ray Jauch and Hugh Campbell to sign with one league while coaching in another. That was ridiculous. We're not competing with the NFL; we're competing with their minor league. It won't be long before we're signing USFL cuts."[66] Yet another former coach, Jack Gotta, announced his intention to work as a guest coach at a USFL camp. He was careful to say that he would volunteer his services and work for free, not wanting to jeopardize his contract which called for him to earn "$100,000 this year not to coach in Calgary."[67]

The USFL was a spring league. Its games were held at a time when there was no other football being offered to the public. The idea was also to restrict team budgets until attendance increased and a television contract was gained. For that reason, coaches from the CFL were desirable, since they had worked under those constraints. As for the two "name" coaches attracted to the fledgling league, Ray Jauch was fired after his team, the Washington Federals, was defeated 53–14 by the Jacksonville Bulls early in his second season. Jauch's team had a 4–14 record in 1983, his first year.[68] Meanwhile, Hugh Campbell had moved from the Los Angeles Express to coach the Houston Oilers of the NFL in 1984. The Oilers had also signed Edmonton quarterback Warren Moon who had played out his option in '83. The Express team had surprised many when it announced that it had signed quarterback Steve Young to a four year contract for a reported $40 million with $34.5 million in deferred payments over 43 years.[69]

Once again, the issue of the designated import emerged and assumed some prominence. This time it revolved around University of Calgary Dinosaurs' quarterback Greg Vavra. He had led his team to a come-from-behind win over Queen's in the 1983 Vanier Cup Game and was selected as the winner of the Hec Crighton Trophy as the Most Outstanding Collegian in Canada. He had been selected by Calgary as their territorial exemption in the 1983 draft. His rights were picked up by Edmonton who released him. Vavra returned to school, led his team to the title, won his award, and waited to hear of his fate. At the eleventh hour, the Stampeders signed him. If they had left it any later, his rights would have reverted to the Eskimos. Born and raised in Calgary, Vavra was clear about his goals: "I prefer to play in Canada. I'm a Canadian and, naturally, ambitions I've set for myself exist in Canada, not the United States."[70] Again, the publicity surrounding the issue surfaced: "It is generally said that the designated import rule is to blame. In fact, it means that Vavra would have to replace an import to see any playing time and coaches say a Canadian quarterback must be better than an import to make a team."[71]

There was some conjecture that "the bad publicity [Jamie] Bone caused the CFL"[72] was a cause of the hesitation teams had to sign a Canadian quarterback. Calgary, in fact, found itself with two non-import quarterbacks, Greg Vavra and Gerry Dattilio. It would stick with hometown Vavra and send Dattilio back to his city of Montreal.

The league also decided to do away with the Canadian territorial protection concept. Beginning with the draft of 1985, there were to be no more protected players. Commissioner Doug Mitchell explained: "The League unanimously agreed to do away with the protected player concept. There will be a legitimate non-import Canadian Football League full scale draft. The protected concept allowed the first place team to protect a player of equal calibre to that of the last place team. The League felt that if its draft was to be effective and proper, the last place team should get the first pick."[73]

Just as in Gaudaur's tenure, the Montreal situation kept surfacing. Some said that Montreal had already suffered its third strike. Joe Galat recalled: "The first one was Black Saturday. That was the day when the Alouettes cut all those veterans, Dan Yochum, Don Sweet, Gord Judges, Larry Uteck, in 1980 in order to save money. Strike two was Skalbania and having a team with Vince Ferragamo, James Scott, Billy Johnson, which finished 2 and 14. The third strike was George Allen leaving. By then I had to stay and pick up the pieces."[74] There were plenty of pieces to pick up. Prior to Bronfman's purchase of the club, money from trust accounts for deferred salaries, taxes, and other payroll deductions were taken for unauthorized uses. When the Alouettes withdrew from the league on May 13, 1982, it had already received its share of the 1982 television rights; none was available for the Concordes "which provided the actual service for which the payment was received."[75] It resulted in a change to the CFL by-laws. A new article, 507, of the Constitution was passed unanimously by the CFL: "any and all revenue received by the League as an advance payment ... signed by the League on behalf of the member clubs, shall be placed in a trust bank account for distribution, including interest therein, to the member clubs within seven days after the first game of the regular season's schedule of the year to which such advanced payments apply."[76] There were other "horror stories." The Concordes, on taking over the Montreal franchise, were informed that George Allen had not paid a two-month hotel bill and that he had not returned the footballs from a free agent camp he conducted in California. The Concordes had their phone disconnected for failing to pay their own bill.

On the field, there were two leftovers from the Nelson Skalbania days, Keith Gary and David Overstreet. "They were two of the big money players ... They didn't really want to play and we wanted to get rid of them but their contracts were guaranteed. One day the word came down from Bronfman to pay them off and cut them. When that happened, I knew we were going to make it," stated Galat.[77] But the Concordes were not out of the woods yet. Sam Etcheverry was let go. Season ticket sales for 1983 were at 6,000. The club's ills were diagnosed as due to quarterback problems. Gerry Dattilio was brought back. Two prominent American collegians, Turner Gill and Steve Smith, were signed; season ticket sales reached the 12,000 mark.

But the Concordes were still pressing for more. Pre-season games were a problem in Montreal, said the Concordes' Edmond Ricard. He proposed moving to a schedule of two exhibition games and 18 regular-season games and urged the CFL's Players' Relations Committee to explore the possibility with the Players' Association. While the interlocking schedule would continue, he proposed that the two extra games be played with teams in the same division. Ricard also expressed a familiar refrain: Since the four players on the reserve list were being paid why shouldn't they be allowed to dress? He proposed that the rosters be increased therefore to 38, with 19 imports and 19 non-imports. Ricard was aware that by increasing the roster size and dressing 19 Americans, it would "admittedly ... reduce the number of non-import players in the starting positions." He was convinced, however, that "it would not diminish the unique Canadian aspects of the game." It was the larger playing field, the more exciting playing rules which made the game Canadian, not the players on the field.[78] Ricard elaborated on his reasons for suggesting the changes. The Concordes seemed to be on the upswing. They finished the 1984 season with a 6–9–1 record, the same as Hamilton, but were relegated to third place on the basis of points between the two teams. In a city where comparisons with the Expos and Canadiens were inevitable, the Concordes were criticized by the media for charging full price for two pre-season games which the coaches publicly describe as secondary games. In mentioning that the reserve list had served its purpose, Ricard stated that it had become yet another source of criticism in Montreal with "comparison being made to a baseball team which permits all players on the roster to dress for a game."[79]

On November 6, 1984, the day after the Eastern semifinal, a reception was held at the Harbour Castle Hotel to honour Jake Gaudaur. The former commissioner, who had been inducted into the Hall of Fame as a Builder on April 10, 1984, was the object of "a meeting of people gathered to congratulate Jake Gaudaur one more time on all the marvellous things he had done during the 16 years as Commissioner of the CFL."[80]

Gaudaur had always insisted that the way the Grey Cup Game was accepted by the public was the best indicator of the vitality of the league. The 1983 game in Vancouver provided the league with its first $2 million gross gate receipts and "television coverage on CBC, CTV and Radio-Canada" resulted in the "largest viewing audience in television history for a Canadian sports program as 8,118,000 people watched Toronto edge B.C. 18–17."[81] During the 1984 season, however, CFL attendance was down by about 200,000 for the regular season and by some 17,000 for the play-offs. The latter figure was 156,126. While it was lower than 1983's 173,842, it was still the league's third highest play-off game total excluding the Grey Cup Game.

In Calgary, where local talent Greg Vavra had done much of the quarterbacking, the Stampeders attracted 22,332 spectators on the average, despite finishing in last place in the West. The Montreal Concordes who finished in third place in the East and played Dattilio only as a back-up to Turner Gill averaged 17,345 spectators. The lowest average crowd for the season was in Hamilton with only 14,738 fans.[82] The Argonauts' average attendance of 32,760 was the club's lowest in 15 years. Both Hamilton and Toronto experimented with early starting times of 5:00 p.m. for their Sunday games in July and August. The experiment was less than successful. The B.C. Lions who finished with a sell-out of 59,429 for their last home game against Winnipeg led the league with an average attendance of 41,859 fans per game. The Eskimos were second at 40,977, the Argonauts third.[83] When some mentioned that the 1984 game would attract a TV audience of 20,000,000, with American viewers, there were the inevitable second guessers. They wondered why the 1984 Grey Cup Game should be risked being played in northern Alberta when there was a beautiful indoor stadium in Vancouver.

> That can be a mixed blessing actually. They're apt to witness on the telecast, a blizzard in the Alberta capital. Cold temperatures? The highest temperature in Edmonton noted lately was a record low for November 18 which happens to be the date upon which the eastern and western champions are scheduled to square off. In other words, it could be a burlesque instead of Canadian football at its finest. Now that the CFL has at its disposal a beautiful covered stadium in Vancouver, it's summer all the time. The field is perfect and 60,000 spectators can get along without overcoats, goloshes, scarves, mittens and earmuffs. Equally as important, the participating athletes are afforded an opportunity to put all their skills on display. The contest is fair to everyone.[84]

In the East, Ottawa finished in last place with a 4–12 record. As a result, George Brancato was fired from the head coaching position he had held for 11 years. Montreal and Hamilton finished with 6–9–1 records, the latter having been awarded second place on the basis of its two victories over the Concordes in the regular season. In the semifinal, Hamilton continued its mastery over Montreal, scoring a 17–11 victory at Ivor Wynne Stadium before "20,736 soggy onlookers."[85]

The Toronto Argonauts had finished in first place in the East. Some were calling for them to repeat as Grey Cup champions. In the week prior to the Eastern final between Hamilton and Toronto, indeed even as the Montreal-Hamilton game was winding down, "it didn't take long for the old rivalry to bob to the surface. A-R-G-O-O-O-S, came a bellow from a group of brave, if not necessarily wise, Argo followers."[86] Others noted that while the Argos finished with a 9–6–1 record, over the last eight games they were only 3–4–1. While the Tiger-Cats were a poor second to the Argos, during the regular season the games between the two teams had been close. The Argos had won one game by eight points and lost one by five points. Indeed the Tiger-Cats were playing so poorly at one time that owner Harold Ballard referred to them as "overpaid bums." His comment was pointed to by some as being the reason why the Tiger-Cats were "apparently reborn."[87] The Tiger-Cats defeated the Argonauts in overtime by a 14–13 score to represent the East in the national final.

In the West where Calgary and Saskatchewan both finished out of the play-offs again, the Edmonton Eskimos finished in third place. Their hopes to play at home in the 1984 Grey Cup Game were dashed when second-place Winnipeg defeated them handily 55–20. Once again the noise of B.C. Place became an issue. The Lions had defeated the Blue Bombers by a 20–3 score in the last week of the season and home fans were looking for a repeat. It was not to be. The Bombers flew past the Lions by a 31–14 score to become the West's representative.

Ever since 1921 when the first East-West rivalry took place on the Grey Cup field, there had been the opportunity for the country's normal geographical tensions to surface. The 1984 game allowed for even more comparisons to be made. A Hamilton–Winnipeg Grey Cup Game had guaranteed one of the most hard fought and unpredictable championships for the league for over 50 years. It was in 1935 that Winnipeg defeated the, then named, Hamilton Tigers in what was the first victory for the West. In 1953, Hamilton won the Grey Cup Game over Winnipeg when a controversial tackle by Lou Kusserow on Tom Casey in the end zone prevented the tying touchdown pass from being caught. In the next six meetings between the two clubs, from 1957 to 1965, the unpredictable contests included an ejection of Tiger-Cat defensive back Ralph Goldston, an incursion by a fan who tripped Tiger-Cat Ray "Bibbles" Bawel on his way to a touchdown, the first overtime Grey Cup Game, the "Fog Bowl" when the game was played over two days, and the so-called "Wind Bowl" when high winds led Winnipeg to concede three safety touches, the margin of the Tiger-Cat victory. The 1965 game had been Winnipeg's last appearance in the Grey Cup Game. Their coach Bud Grant had long departed to the NFL. Winnipeg was resting its hopes on Cal Murphy, the Canadian coach who had been part of Grey Cup victories as an assistant in Montreal and Edmonton. Hamilton's legendary coaches, Jim Trimble and Ralph Sazio, had also departed from the scene. Al Bruno had taken over the Tiger-Cat coaching. He appeared to be spending much time defending his team's right to be in the game. The Edmonton *Journal* commented that a Hamilton win would be a "smear" on the CFL[88] because it would be the "first time a CFL team with a losing regular season record would win the Grey Cup in 73 years."[89] Al Bruno, a former player with the Argonauts in 1952 and more recently a coach at Harvard University and the Tiger-Cats' director of Player Personnel, was incensed:

> Why don't they build the League up instead of downgrading the League when they talk about a team being a smear on the CFL. Every club is losing money because of attendance. The NFL are making money because they back their game up. If we start to wise up and back our game up and protect our game, we'd be a hell of a lot better off![90]

An intense rivalry had also continued to grow since the mid-season trade of 1983 when the two teams exchanged quarterbacks. Tom Clements came to Winnipeg; Dieter Brock was sent to Hamilton. Brock had upset Winnipeggers because he wanted to leave the Manitoba capital to pursue a career in the United States. As part of the Grey Cup high jinks, he had "been taking verbal abuse all week. There are 'Brock Buster' t-shirts, 'Brock Buster' placards, 'Brock Buster' songs. The 'Booze Brothers', a bunch of smart alecks from Vancouver, marched in the parade dragging a dummy with a noose around its head and a number 5 Hamilton sweater on its back. One guy beat it with a whip while Winnipeg fans cheered."[91]

And then there was Harold Ballard, the owner of the Tiger-Cats. As an incentive for his "overpaid bums" he promised them a diamond ring should they defeat the Argos in the Eastern final. He constantly referred to them as the "censored Argos." During the game he wore a jacket, blue and white on one side for the Leafs and yellow and black on the other for the Tiger-Cats, "and a double brimmed baseball cap with the Leaf Emblem on one side and the tiger on the reverse. Boy George would have attracted less attention."[92]

Edmonton was agog with "Grey Cup Fever." Events were well attended. Canadian astronaut Marc Garneau led the Grey Cup parade. The Schenley Awards were distributed: Willard Reaves of Winnipeg was chosen over Hamilton's Rufus Crawford as the Most Outstanding Player; the Most Outstanding Rookie was Montreal's Dwaine Wilson, selected over Edmonton's Stewart Hill; another Concordes' player Nick Arakgi was the Most Outstanding Canadian, with Winnipeg's Joe Poplawski the runner-up; B.C.'s James Parker was the winner over Montreal's Harry Skipper as the Most Outstanding Defensive Player, while Winnipeg centre John Bonk was chosen Most Outstanding Offensive Lineman over Toronto's Dan Ferrone.

In the game itself, Winnipeg spotted Hamilton a 17–3 second-quarter lead but roared back to win 47–17. A crowd of 60,081, a record for Commonwealth Stadium, watched the game, nicknamed the "Tundra Bowl" by one newspaper.[93] The temperature at game time was -11°C and ended with a reading of -17°C. Winnipeg equipment man Len Amey gave the Toronto Blue Jays credit for the victory. He noted that "the Winnipeg receivers and defensive backs had little problem with the slippery field conditions because they used a baseball shoe recommended by the Blue Jays. Many of the Bombers used a plastic based shoe with a baseball cleat on the outside and smaller spikes on the interior of the sole which helped cut through the thin layer of ice on the frozen turf of Commonwealth Stadium."[94]

As 1984 came to a close the CFL continued to make news. Earl Lunsford returned to the CFL as general manager at Calgary. Jack Gotta was hired as the general manager and head coach at Saskatchewan. George Brancato was brought in as Gotta's assistant. The CFL also announced its plans to move its offices from 11 King Street East to 1200 Bay Street in Toronto where the entire 12th floor would be taken over. The structure was to be renamed The Canadian Football League Building with the "league's logo prominently displayed at the top of the building."[95]

1985 to 1986

Chapter Nine

IF EVER A LEAGUE was immersed in introspection, it was the CFL in 1985—and with good reason. A whole host of problems had surfaced, problems that threatened the very survival of professional football in Canada. When the CFL met in Edmonton in January of 1985, Commissioner Doug Mitchell wasted little time in driving home the point. The league's television contract with Carling O'Keefe would expire after the 1986 season; it was important that the CFL have a good year in 1985 since the TV ratings of 1985 would "have a significant impact on the success of negotiations for a new television agreement starting in the 1986 season."[1] After distributing the A.C. Neilson Company ratings for the 1984 season, Mitchell "pointed out that if the league was trying to negotiate a new agreement now, it would be difficult in terms of a bargaining position based on the 1984 Neilson ratings."[2]

Television ratings were an important consideration since the league's contract was due to be renegotiated in the next year. The upcoming TV difficulties were highlighted when ESPN of the United Stated decided not to renew its option for CFL telecast rights in 1985. The B.C. Lions wanted to investigate the possibility of lifting the television blackout when there was a sell-out for the Lions' home games. B.C. had a unique problem in that the entire province was blacked out during the Lions' home games. Discussion of the possibility was only agreed to on the understanding that it be deliberated without the public's knowledge. Even Carling O'Keefe, owners of the Argonauts, "were somewhat disturbed by a statement in a report from the Commissioner which criticized the company for sponsoring television broadcasts of United States Football League games."[3] They let it be known that the arrangements had been made before Carling O'Keefe was awarded the rights to sponsor CFL telecasts. Similarly, they weren't too thrilled with the numerous side deals teams had throughout the league with competitors Molson's and Labatt's.

The in-fighting continued. When the CFL interested The Sports Network (TSN) "in a weekly program of Hits and Highlights of the Week, Carling O'Keefe asked the league not to go with them because of the competitive aspect, ie., TSN being owned by Labatt's." The commissioner acceded to their request although he repeated: "I am at a loss to understand how in the same breath, they give money to the USFL, our competition, for TV rights."[4]

The commissioner identified declining attendance as "the most critical problem facing the league today."[5] The public's perception that the league was "hanging on" would adversely affect television and marketing revenues. The shortfall was blamed on "competitions from other entertainment and sport attractions, the economy and the perception that the league is less than it should be."[6] This assessment triggered more observations. Norm Kimball noted that "suggestions for improvements are more often greeted with reluctance than enthusiasm."[7] Nonetheless, he offered that the league should extend the schedule and improve media relations and marketing. Winnipeg's Paul Robson suggested changing the television broadcast crews "so the visiting team commentators are heard in the club's home area as is the case with radio broadcasts." In support, Kimball voiced his concern over "negative reporters," a charge which Mitchell levelled at the clubs themselves whose officials and coaches were "downgrading pre-season games, repeatedly emphasizing the players who are playing out options and consistently finding fault with non-import players."[8]

Kimball was convinced that "the decline in attendance is directly related to the decline in quality of play."[9] In his opinion, players were not performing with the intensity for which they were paid. "Coaches had to work harder to get more out of the players and the clubs had to work harder to sell tickets, promote the league and the game."[10] He continued his theme: "Daily practice should start at 10:00 AM and the full working day dedicated to football. The onus should be placed on players to produce at all times. The club should insist that the coaches have an organized work plan which strives to develop players to their full potential. If they do not have such a work plan they should be replaced."[11]

Earl Lunsford, now the general manager in Calgary, saw another area for improvement. With most teams using non-imports on the offensive line, the defence was loaded with imports. Since there were "not enough qualified non-import linemen to make all clubs competitive, he suggested some legislation be introduced to place a limit on the number of import players on defence at any one time."[12]

As always, comparison with the NFL was inevitable. Some members of the media were critical of CFL play as compared with that of the NFL. Edmond Ricard, the chairman of the league's Board of Governors felt so too; his solution was that "consideration should be given to increasing the import quota."[13] Once again, the shaper of perceptions, television, came in for scrutiny. NFL telecasts were superior to those of the CFL "because its TV commentators stress only the positive aspects of the game." As well, only the best game of the week was telecast, it was suggested. There were complaints that the CFL's TV commentators were "ill prepared for the game and did not perform in a professional manner." The commentators were said to "often by-pass the pre-game press conferences," thus not having the "preparation and dedication" of the NFL commentators.

What was clear was that the league was struggling with its declining acceptance among the public. It gave the appearance of flailing in its attempt to identify factors contributing to the decline. Ralph Sazio wanted "The league to take an aggressive position in a number of issues which apparently are harmful to the league's image as perceived by the media and fans."[14] He advocated: "elimination of the designated quarterback; elimination of the single point after a missed field goal; limitation of the number of imports on defence; application of pressure on coaching staffs to have players ready for a game; requirement of players to devote full time to football and not regard it as a hobby."[15]

In its concern over falling attendance, the league had commissioned the Longwoods Research Group to study the problem. Their market survey had been conducted during the latter part of the 1984 season. The first phase, dealing with schedule-related matters, was presented at the CFL's November 1984 meetings. The report identified 12 factors that affected game attendance. They were: (1) identification with team and players; (2) involvement with sports and football; (3) quality of officiating; (4) excitement of the game; (5) involvement with the crowd; (6) television commentators; (7) stadium facilities; (8) ticket prices and outlets; (9) attitude towards the playing rules; (10) the league structure; (11) the schedule; and (12) the overall image of the league.[16]

In addition, the report suggested that "there was evidence of goodwill towards the league and genuine interest in its continuing survival."[17] The CFL was encouraged "to take a more aggressive approach, as a league and individual clubs, to advertising [and] public relations with improvements in marketing."[18]

In an interesting aside, Ralph Sazio, referring to the "identification with players" point in this report, "noted that as soon as a player reaches superstar status his price tag increases to the point that he leaves the league."[19] The solution according to Commissioner Doug Mitchell was that "identification should be concentrated on Canadian players." It's interesting to speculate as to why he suggested such a course of action. Were Canadian players the real superstars? Because they were Canadians, would they not achieve the status "to leave the league"? Were they the team members who stayed in the community and contributed to it after the season?

Scott Taylor of the *Winnipeg Free Press* listed his own ten reasons for staying away:

1. Canadian football is boring.
2. The balanced schedule hasn't worked.
3. The price of tickets, $17.00 a pop in Winnipeg.
4. Player defections. The big stars have gone to the NFL making the CFL look like a minor league operation.
5. The size of the roster.
6. Lousy concessions. Warm beer and a cold hot dog on a summer evening.
7. Weekend games. For years football fans have refused to drive back from the lake to watch a game.
8. Great TV delays. Going to a CFL game is becoming a day's outing.
9. Player identification. People can't name anyone including General Manager Joe _____ of the Ottawa Rough Riders.
10. Marketing. The CFL just doesn't market itself.[20]

Taylor was writing after the Grey Cup champion Blue Bombers had played two home games in which they drew 3,279 fewer spectators than at the same point the previous year.[21] He didn't stop there. The next day he listed ten more reasons why attendance was in decline.

11. Drunken, obnoxious fans.
12. Cheerleaders. Some football purist said yesterday he was tired of "the bimbos. They play their loud jungle music and dance around like hookers. I don't pay 17 bucks to watch that."
13. Earl Lunsford. Trade Lunsford bumper stickers are lying around. In '83 the Winnipeg Football Club dumped Lunsford as General Manager and it hasn't made a difference in attendance.
14. Lousy refereeing.
15. The home team always wins.
16. Too many games on TV.
17. Negative media coverage.
18. Minor league football. Earl Lunsford once said: "It really isn't what you are but how you are perceived what is important."

19. I can watch it in the bar, satellite dishes being the problem.
20. Other things to do. This is the most frightening reason of all facing professional football in Canada. For instance, to attend a Blue Bombers game will cost a husband and wife with one child upwards of $100 for an entire evening out. There indeed may be better things to do with $100.[22]

It was a critical situation for the CFL. Revenue from attendance was falling; revenue from television could not be far behind unless the trend reversed. Ratings had declined especially during the second half of the 1985 season, compounded by blackout conditions in its largest markets of southern Ontario and British Columbia.

The consensus was that the league was fortunate to have signed its television contract with Carling O'Keefe when it did. Brewery profits had been high; there were huge sums available for promotions. Molson's was anxious to get some summer identification to compete with Labatt's and the Blue Jays and with Carling O'Keefe and the Argos. With the then resurgence of the Argonauts, there was a feeling that football interest would peak once again. The bidding for the television contract for CFL games had been artificially boosted. "The CFL won a $33 million three-year contract, twice the previous high but also as one senior executive said yesterday, twice what they are really worth."[23] It was obvious that changes had occurred: "The Jays continue to improve, Argos [have] plunged competitively, Tiger-Cats stumble early when interest is being generated for a new season, marketing of both teams is atrocious, attendance is at post-1960 lows in both cities and the Eastern Conference has remained mediocre over all."[24]

And change had also occurred on the sponsor and advertising side. Expansion of a schedule to 18 games would add production costs if any of the extra contests were to be shown on television. Brewery profits were in decline, and after years of using a standard bottle size, each company began designing its own. Marketing of beer now included different sizes and shapes of bottles, cans, anything to accentuate the difference between one brand and another. The consensus was "the CFL clearly has to come up with something to make its product attractive to at least two breweries or get out and sell some other corporate giant on the advantages of a rights bid. A non-competitive situation would be a disaster."[25]

No one knew this better than the CFL. A planning and marketing committee was appointed. Its mission was "to set short- and long-term goals for the league and in particular to set a plan of action to turn around the current trend of attendance decline."[26] Meetings were held with the media in different league cities. Interim findings were that the "hard core" of season ticket supporters, while loyal, were not enough to support the franchise, Edmonton perhaps being the exception. The task was to "get the old fans back and bring out new ones ... to create a desire to want to see something new or different."[27] A number of recommendations were made:

1. *Financial Viability.* Financial success was dependent upon putting people in the seats not only from a "gate" point of view but from television as well. No television rightsholder wants to hold the rights to an event playing before half empty stadiums or is perceived to be declining in interest.[28] The report recommended promotions to increase fan support by "1,000 fans per game each year for each team over a five-year period." There was to be an opening-night concentration across the league on the assumption that "first impressions are lasting." One pre-season game would include a "bonus" of one ticket for a regular season game, the cost to be picked up by a sponsor. Opening night promotions could include "junior" fans and "senior" citizens being charged half price, the difference again being picked up by a corporate sponsor.

Two other promotional strategies were proposed along the lines of baseball-style give-aways. Calendars and radios were suggested, a calendar because it was seen as a bonus to be "taken home and hung up in an obvious place and not only highlights the schedule of home games and TV games but also contains many other promotional coupons for use of the purchase of CFL products."[29] The radio was perceived to be costly whereas "in actual fact it is a very inexpensive item."[30] Again, it was suggested that with all of these approaches combined, the cost to the league would be very minimal because a sponsor would be picking up the majority of the cost for the promotional item, the fan would be occupying an otherwise unused seat, a new fan or new old fan would be introduced to the game and increased overall attendance would create the perception that the league was on the way back up.[31]

2. *Player Identity.* According to the study, fans perceived players as "no stars" because those who were "stars" left to play in the United States. Not only that, there was the perception shaped by the media in some cities "that changes are made for the sake of saving a team a few thousand dollars by dropping a veteran in favour of a rookie."[32] Indeed, the league office had become so sensitive to this criticism that when a major sponsor wanted to use a player from each team on a poster, the CFL offices "felt it necessary to confirm with the General Manager of each team that the player used will be with the team for the duration of the year."[33] The suggested solution was to "ensure that each team does have as many players as possible under long-term contracts for the next five year period."[34] It was also proposed that higher visibility be given to the CFL's draft by ranking the top 20 players

available, again to enhance identification. The whole concept was based on the proven formula used by rock promoters. They showed that "no one buys tickets to a rock concert just to hear Lionel Ritchie music. They go to see Lionel Ritchie, someone they identify with."[35]

3. *Schedule*: The study further suggested that the full interlocking schedule should be reviewed because of some "considerable conjecture of whether this format has been as successful as originally anticipated."[36] Such a review, it said, should not be perceived as "accepting the failure if a move off such a schedule were to be made but only an attempt to increase attendance."[37]

4. *Rule Changes*: There were some blunt suggestions regarding rule changes. With respect to the designated import rule, the message was simple and direct: "Nothing we could do would have more positive impact on the image of the league than eliminating the rule."[38] It was suggested that "no one understands why we put it into effect nor does anyone care. No rule has given the league more static and negative reaction than this rule ... the media allege that it works to the detriment of the Canadian college quarterback despite Vavra and Dattilio."[39]

There was no doubt that the media were playing an increasingly important role or, perhaps more correctly, that there was more recognition of the value it had to the league. The CFL hired *Toronto Sun* reporter John Iaboni as Director of Media and Public Relations, replacing Information Officer Larry Robertson. If commissioner Doug Mitchell's notion that the CFL's image problem was more one of perception than substance was correct, the hiring of Iaboni was a move to change that perception. He had some raw material available from the interim report of the planning and marketing committee to provide a beginning.

The report suggested that each team have its own marketing person in order to make the league's scheme successful. Teams were also encouraged not to engage in "self-destruct public relations." The report was very critical of a coach who was quoted as saying about the Montreal situation: "You have to get yourself motivated when you walk in there because there is no one in there to get your adrenalin flowing. It's like playing in a cave."[40] In an effort to have the clubs control their players' and coaches' comments, the report recommended that "the league office will fine the team for conduct unbecoming a professional football operation."[41]

The report also cited public awareness as a problem. The secrecy of the negotiation list was deplored. It was not the way to get more publicity for what was the CFL's answer to "an import draft."[42] The CFL was encouraged to "make the negotiation list public, let the media review the lists, find out who the people are, follow the chase to sign the player so that when the player is signed the public and the media both know who the player is. If the player isn't signed, who cares, the team has received free coverage and the fans have been following the development."[43]

Clearly the league was feeling the pinch of reduced coverage in many media outlets, particularly because of increased coverage of the Blue Jays, American League baseball teams, Expos, and National League stories. Since much scouting and recruiting was done via free-agent camps, the report suggested that the media be invited "to attend the camps even if a team pays the expenses. Even though it is a nuisance to have media around, let them get familiar with the players being signed from these camps. Maybe they will do a human interest story that will introduce a new player to the public back home."[44]

The final item discussed in the interim report was the matter of TV quality control. TV was considered to be the "greatest marketing tool [if] utilized in the proper manner. If not it becomes the greatest marketing deterrent."[45]

The importance of the media, in general, was underlined by Iaboni in his "Media Report" presented to the league September 16, 1985. The veteran reporter made a tour of all CFL cities with a view "to observe the home site in game action." Iaboni spoke with each media/public relations director in the league, his or her assistants, senior members of the Football Reporters of Canada, and drew upon his own personal experience to detail a comprehensive league approach to attack the perception image problem. He found that many clubs had no one person responsible solely for media matters. Toronto, Hamilton, Winnipeg, and Calgary combined "marketing and other club related matters." While there was an assistant who dealt with the media, the latter took "a dim view of the structure because sometimes a request he (or she) has cannot be met until the information officer clears the demand or becomes better informed with the situation in question by talking to his immediate supervisor." In Toronto, Winnipeg, and Calgary, the media information people were around the press box on game day but "the media perception of each is that none is qualified to deal with some of the requests they may make. And in Hamilton, the club's information officer is not available because he is at field level as T.C., the club's mascot." Iaboni reported that when the media perceived the league or a club to be "unfeeling" towards their needs, "the term 'bush' surfaces anytime a problem arises." His recommendation was that each club have a person responsible for marketing separate from another person for media/public relations.

Iaboni proposed a code of ethics for reporters and that each team appoint a media/public relations person who could develop a good relationship with the reporters covering the game. He looked at "the entire procedure from pre-game meal to post-game working facilities." Pampering of the media was the norm, he said, at professional sporting events. The media "include the food rating as something else to talk about regarding that club." As an example, he mentioned that all clubs aside from Hamilton and Winnipeg provided pre-game meals for media and hot dogs at half-time. Winnipeg served hot dogs at the beginning of the game; Hamilton at half-time. He commented: "Well, you won't believe the number of times media people refer to the serving of 'only' hot dogs at half-time in Hamilton."

Press-box allocations were also important. Visiting media were to be placed in the front row "because to make a visitor feel inferior leads to complaints of poor working conditions." Necessary equipment to be included were telephones, electrical outlets, pre-game notes including "records, streaks, birthdays, on this date in club history, etc. for the home and visiting sides plus the league's This Week in the CFL and official statistical package."

Again, Iaboni stressed perception. There had to be a unity in the approach. When a press kit states: "the total [QB] sacks in these stats will differ from the CFL Official [stats] because of interpretation of rules on QB sacks," Iaboni asked, "if our CFL stats are 'Official' then how can we have a different interpretation?" He drew a parallel with baseball: "Does one go with the official scorer or does one at the club level interpret things his own way?" Such an approach "leads one to wonder about the professionalism of the entire league," he said.

Clearly, Iaboni was attempting to educate the clubs' media people to the pragmatic aspects of the CFL operations. He spoke of one of the league's initiatives, "This Week in the CFL," a telecast which sought to highlight the top stories of the week. Club media directors were asked to "send any information to our office and we would gladly incorporate such. No one has responded, leaving the entire compilation of material for the four games each week, covering 8 teams and in excess of 40 players each week"[46] up to the CFL office. Iaboni wasn't complaining about the workload, but rather about the lack of communication with the clubs which might prevent the league from promoting "special nights or highlight player milestones, club milestones, anything that may escape our research."[47]

He also recommended the use of a microphone and sound hook-up in the press box, not to repeat the obvious as in Winnipeg where a report of the public address announcer's words were piped into the press area, but to make "key tidbits such as 'Willard Reeves needs 3 more yards rushing to record his 15th 100 yard rushing game' or 'his next point will make Trevor Kennerd the first Blue Bomber to score 1,000 in his career', etc."[48] The reality of the situation, Iaboni said, was that with morning newspapers and on-the-spot radio reports, there was a need for quick reports on injuries especially to front line players. Details which might not be known until a coach's post-game discussion, should be made known to the media at the time the injury occurred. It might only be necessary to say that a player left the game "with an injury to the left leg and we will up-date you once we get further details."[49] Later editions and reports could elaborate. The microphone could also be used in conjunction with a club's record manual to comment on records as they happen, none being too small to be overlooked. The idea was to deluge the media with "statistical information, records, etc. to create more identity for clubs and players, stimulate interest among the fans."[50]

As a practitioner for 16 years, Iaboni was well aware of the mutual interdependence of the CFL and the media. The latter needed information; they were not that well versed in football per se but had to appear as being so. The league needed to get its message out. Iaboni concluded: "We have a great game with a wonderful tradition and a bright future so the worst thing we can do is to keep all of this a secret when the media is starving for CFL news. The level of reports on the CFL, be it on radio, on TV or in newspapers, depends on how well we accomplish the task of feeding the news required to assist the media."[51]

The CFL immediately upgraded its record manual for 1985. The 1984 version, entitled "Official Record Manual" (containing records dating back to the 1960s), had cost $30,000 to publish 5,000 copies "of which $20,000 was recovered in sales and grants making the net cost to the league $10,000."[52] The expanded version, "Canadian Football League Facts Figures and Records," would be available beginning in 1985. Twenty-thousand copies were to be printed at a cost of $75,000. If no copies were sold, the cost to the league was to be $20,000. At the time of the announcement some $55,000 in advertising revenue had been committed. If all were sold, "the league could realize a profit of $100,000."[53] The release was to be kicked off with a news conference in Toronto, with complimentary copies available for members of the Football Reporters of Canada, and three hundred complimentary copies for each club. The books would be on sale at bookstores, and clubs could also sell them from their offices at a lower price.[54] In addition, *Maclean's* was planning a 16-page supplement for its June 24th, 1985, issue. Editorial content of which was to be under Iaboni's control.[55]

Media accessibility to teams was also considered important. When the Concordes "proposed that the members of the media be prohibited from entering the team dressing room for post-game interviews and that the home club be required to provide another room adjacent to the dressing room for post-game interviews,"[56] there was little support. Joe Galat complained that most visiting-team rooms were small and that players were complaining about dressing in cramped quarters and "becoming resentful of media questions when trying to dress."[57]

At that time there was a 15-minute delay after the game before the dressing-room doors were opened to the media. In many cases, players lingered on the field, either being delayed by post-game television and radio interviews or what one team official called "the College reunion atmosphere where players of opposing teams meet at midfield after the game to renew acquaintances."[58] Deeming such meetings "unprofessional," the league took action. "At the conclusion of the game, the members of both competing teams shall be required to leave the playing field and proceed directly to their respective dressing rooms."[59]

While the 15-minute period after the game was considered the maximum time that the media would wait, anything more was deemed to be "counter productive" by the CFL commissioner. A change was made prior to the 1985 season. Noting the increasing number of female reporters across the league, the commissioner "pointed out the possibility of charges of discrimination and human rights violations if such a reporter was denied access to the dressing rooms."[60] The CFL decided to extend the waiting period to 20 minutes, ostensibly to allow the players more time to shower and dress, and "agreed that women reporters would be permitted equal access to the dressing rooms at all times."[61]

In some ways, there appeared to be some resistance to changes initiated and proposed by new commissioner Doug Mitchell. When he first became commissioner of the CFL, he sought to introduce innovations which he thought would be beneficial to the game. He was against a single point being awarded after a missed field goal, but the board voted 8–1 in favour of keeping the single point. He also wanted overtime, despite the opposition of the TV networks, increased rosters and new divisions[62] Mitchell had proposed that the league change its two divisions to three. His object was to "eliminate the possibility of a club qualifying for the play-offs in one division with a lesser record than another club which fails to qualify in another division." Mitchell still wanted to guarantee that there would be an East-West Grey Cup Game. His proposal called for an East, Central, and West Division as follows:

East	Central	West
Montreal	Toronto	Calgary
Ottawa	Winnipeg	Edmonton
Hamilton	Saskatchewan	British Columbia

His plan called for the last-place team in each division to be eliminated; the two remaining "in the Central Division would revert to their former divisions for play-off purposes." This plan, too, failed to be accepted, but Mitchell said that he wasn't disheartened. When he was selected as commissioner, he had a moustache. He shaved it off just before the CFL's May, 1985, meetings. "He explained: 'It's symbolic; I hope to show I'm flexible enough to accept change.'"[63]

The NFL wished to play an exhibition game in Toronto in August. Commissioner Mitchell objected and spoke to the federal Minister of Sport Otto Jelinek, seeking to "support his position." The August 24 game was cancelled.[64] It was an important consideration. What with the success of the Blue Jays and the possibility that they would appear in the 1985 World Series, the CFL was finding itself under attack. It had already decided to adjust its schedule in the event of a Blue Jays victory as American League Champions. The October 20 Argo game was to be moved to Friday October 18; the October 27 contest to Friday October 25. If the Blue Jays were not in the World Series, the former schedule would prevail.[65] Former Argo owner John Bassett was in the forefront of an NFL movement: "My views won't be popular with the CFL but then they never were. I could only speak for Toronto but my view is that Toronto is a world class city and the time is long past when the CFL will satisfy Toronto fans." Bassett's view was based on the success of the Blue Jays. Toronto's baseball fans had responded well to the team. They looked forward to seeing "big league" cities such as New York and Chicago and "the legendary teams in baseball." Toronto fans, he said, now wanted to see "the legendary teams of football, the Dallas Cowboys and the Washington Redskins." Bassett gave his forecast: "I think there will always be a CFL but it will be a secondary league with more and more Canadians playing in it. Such a league, operated at lower costs might allow a city like Halifax to have a team. Toronto could even have a second team, one in the NFL and one in the CFL."[66]

There were other problems. While B.C.'s attendance had risen because of the Lions' on-field performance and B.C. Place—they had made a profit of $354,106 in 1983 and $321,172 in 1984 —they also had a long-term debt of $825,670 due in 1985.[67] The real trouble spots, though, were in Calgary and Montreal. The Stampeders had a debt of $783,000 in 1984 making their accumulated total amount owing $1.5 million since 1982.[68] Their 1984 attendance fell by 7%, an average of 3,500 people per game. Club officials feared a loss of in excess of $1 million in 1985. Costs of operations which were in excess of $6 million for 1985 were being kept alive by a whole host of schemes. Corporate donations contributed $300,000; the sale of 20,000 shares of Stampeders' stock at $10 each provided $200,000; a Red And White Dinner Club earned $90,000. There was a $1 million line of credit from the Bank of Commerce secured by $500,000 collateral.[69] During the first three games of 1985 only 45,000 fans came, and fewer than 13,000 came to a game which the Stampeders lost to the Concordes. Head Coach Steve Buratto was replaced by elder statesman Bud Riley. The 59-year-old was with his fourth CFL team as a head coach, having held similar posts with varying tenures at Winnipeg, Toronto, and Hamilton. Turmoil would not be an inappropriate word to describe the situation which had evolved in Calgary. In the space of little more than one year, three head coaches were in charge; two general managers were in place; and a coup of sorts was implemented when shares sold to the public were mobilized and a new board of directors emerged. Trades were plentiful, one wag suggesting that "program sales are at an all-time high as no one can tell who's playing without one."[70] The upshot was that Calgary drew 14,100 fans on the average for their home games in 1985. The break-even point was 24,000.[71]

By October, it was obvious that league attendance had fallen, franchises were in trouble, and television ratings had declined especially during the second half of the season. The CFL Board of Governors held a special meeting in Halifax, October 7, 1985. "The Chairman explained that the meeting had been called in a non-league city in order that the Governors could engage in a frank discussion on matters of great importance to the league." While Maritime hopes had been raised that perhaps expansion to the east was still alive, the real reason for the meeting was that "there have been disturbing reports about clubs in financial trouble, attendance has been disappointing in most areas and the league's public image has suffered through media perception that the league is less than what it really is."[72]

Montreal seemed to be a microcosm of the league's problems. On the surface, it appeared to have turned the corner during the 1985 season. A positive spin was put on developments. In a report to the league in May of 1985 news was given that Montreal's campaign was "largely successful," that community involvement was high, large corporations had "come forward to offer assistance and the season ticket base has been doubled."[73] The franchise future was said to look "more promising than it has in several years." While three of its original partners had withdrawn, there were indications that others would be admitted. Charles Bronfman and the Imasco group continued to have controlling interest. Season tickets had rebounded: 12,144 in 1985 compared to 5,000 in 1984.

Joe Galat of the Montreal Concordes had another problem. His club had conducted a "free agent camp" in the United States "at a considerable expense and had permitted observers from other clubs to be in attendance."[74] The Concordes identified one player as being an outstanding prospect. When the session was finished "the Montreal club called the league office to place the player's name on its negotiation list only to learn that an observer from another club who had been watching the same practice had already called the league office to place the player's name on the other club's list."[75]

Agreement was given to the Concordes' request that season ticket holders be given the opportunity to purchase the same seats for the Grey Cup Game with a deadline of April 30 instead of April 1. The league agreed, with the understanding that "said information and said extension not become public information."[76] Such concessions were necessary because by now it was apparent to the league that Montreal was indeed a troubled franchise, its magnitude deflected by the highly publicized events in Calgary. In a confidential report to the Board of Governors, Edmond Ricard of the Concordes brought the rest of the league up to date with events in Montreal. He said that when Charles Bronfman and his partners joined the league in 1982 "with a three-year commitment to save football in Montreal" they did so "to rescue it from what appeared to be an unfavourable situation."[77] But the situation was much more serious than first thought. It was compounded by the fact that the Concordes "had no identity in the Montreal market and was living in the shadow of past glories of the Alouettes."[78] The French media was critical of the name Concordes; any attempt to resurrect the name Alouettes was tied up in legal complications. Ricard announced that since 1982, the experiment had cost the partners $13 million. Even 1985 with its encouraging beginning and improved attendance brought "a negative impact on its home gate receipts" due in part to five straight losses in September and October.[79] The subsequent loss of $3 million for the 1985 season[80] forced the Concordes' management to take a second look at their commitment. Ricard referred

> to the partners as dedicated, responsible people but reluctant owners of a football team. Mr. Bronfman is committed to baseball while Imasco is involved for advertising purposes. There is no intention to embarrass the league but the partners would like to turn the club over to other parties. He emphasized the importance of keeping football alive in Montreal but he acknowledges that the team's field performance has not made it attractive for a purchaser.[81]

Ricard proposed a deal to the league. The partners could either "pay the $3,000,000 penalty provided by Article 3.06 of the Constitution and turn the franchise over to the league to find new owners" or continue to operate the club for one, possibly two years under the following arrangement: that the league would "waive the $3,000,000 penalty in lieu of notice, with no further notice required"; that the entire first year loss would be borne by the partners; that a commitment for a second year would be given "only if it can be projected that as a result of tax concessions or other government assistance, the combined after tax loss after two years will not be greater than $1,500,000."[82] During this two-year time period, Ricard stated, he and the partners would endeavour to attract other investors with a view to their "eventually taking over."[83]

All felt the urgency to keep football in Montreal. The CFL commissioner reported "that he had met with senior officials of the Department of Finance to discuss the possibility of tax concessions similar to those available to petroleum exploration and other high risk taxpayers. Such concessions would be an advantage to the private entrepreneur clubs and be attractive to potential investors."[84] When costs of the Montreal operation were questioned, Ricard stated that he welcomed a review by the commissioner to see if costs could be reduced. He pointed out that Montreal had a unique situation. Taxes and rental costs were higher, and media service was provided in two languages. In addition, wives of players could not find employment if they were not fluent in French; as a result, players' contracts were higher. In view of all of this, Montreal decided that it would not proceed with a motion to increase the import quota to 19 players.[85] When all was said and done the CFL decided to accept the Montreal offer to carry on for one or two years under the conditions described.[86]

The East showed a remarkable amount of balance. Parity had arrived. The Argonauts missed the play-offs with a 6–10 record but first-place Hamilton was at 8–8, the same as Montreal. Ottawa earned third place with a 7–9 record. In the play-offs, the Concordes defeated their arch rival Rough Riders by a 30–10 score. The Concordes had made a change with two games to go in the season. Joe Galat continued as general manager but relinquished his head coaching duties to Gary Durchik. A three game win streak was halted when the Tiger-Cats defeated the Concordes by a 50–26 score. In the West British Columbia and Winnipeg were the class of the division, the Lions ending up in first place with a 12–3–1 record, the Blue Bombers at 11–4–1. Edmonton was again in third place at 9–7, while Saskatchewan at 5–11 and Calgary with a 3–13 record were once again out of the play-offs. Winnipeg defeated Edmonton in a close game by a 22–15 score, only to fall to B.C. 42–22.

With the Grey Cup Game being played in Montreal on Sunday, November 24, it was an interesting week leading up to the game. The CFL was not being well received in the city; Grey Cup hoopla seemed a bit strained. Play-off fever didn't seem to be there. The Concordes had drawn only 11,372 fans to their play-off game with Ottawa.[87] Even out West, in the Winnipeg-Edmonton play-off game it seemed at times like the Blue Bombers were trying to give the game away. The score was close only because Winnipeg fumbled six times and was intercepted twice.[88] Attendances at Hamilton and Vancouver were good—24, 423 at Ivor Wynne Stadium, the largest of the season, and 59,478 at B.C. Place. But the Grey Cup Game, the league's showcase, and Montreal didn't seem to blend together.

There were attempts to generate excitement. In the Schenley Awards, British Columbia's Mervyn Fernandez was selected over Hamilton quarterback Ken Hobart as Most Outstanding Player; another B.C. stalwart Michael Gray was chosen Most Outstanding Rookie over Ottawa's starting guard Nick Benjamin (the first pick in the CFL's first completely open non-import draft); Hamilton's Paul Bennett was Most Outstanding Canadian Player, and Winnipeg's Joe Poplawski was runner-up; Bennett was second to Winnipeg's Tyrone Jones as Most Outstanding Defensive Player; another Winnipeg player, Nick Bastaja,was Most Outstanding Offensive Lineman, and Dan Ferrone of Toronto was runner-up.

Discussion at league meetings addressed items such as four-down football and a proposed 18-game schedule with 2 exhibition games for 1986. The four downs were dismissed, with Mitchell stating: "We have a unique game and I don't want to make it another USFL."[89] The 18-game schedule would have to be approved by the Players' Association which would naturally want to be paid more money for the two extra league games. "Mitchell said he feels it is illogical for teams to voluntarily compensate players for two extra league games ... It would be a poor business decision for running business is not a voluntary payment centre."[90] Mitchell, a lawyer by training, argued that the total number of games, pre-season and scheduled, would still be 20. Players were obliged to play 20 no matter how they were split between exhibition and regularly scheduled games.[91]

Although an official count of 56,723 people attended the Grey Cup Game, generating receipts of $2,041,230, it was obvious that all was not well in Montreal. Some called it "the last tango for the Canadian Football League in Montreal ... The usual dancing in the streets seems subdued ... one of the quietest Grey Cup festivals in years, despite the fact that thousands of football fans have been arriving from across the country."[92] In the game itself, the Lions prevailed over the Tiger-Cats 37–24. Lui Passaglia scored 19 points and was chosen as Best Canadian in the game. He also provided a key play. With B.C. one point behind and third down and nine on their own 38-yard line with only two minutes to go to half-time, Passaglia lined up to punt. Hamilton's Mitchell Price broke through and appeared ready to block it. Passaglia sidestepped him and picked up a first down at the 51-yard line from where B.C. quarterback Roy DeWalt connected with a 59-yard touch-down pass to Ned Armour, after which the game never appeared to be in doubt.

As part of its quest to restore goodwill and a sense of its roots and role in the community at large, the league made a number of initiatives. Among these was the naming of Bill Davis as chairman of the Board of Governors. The former Ontario premier had been serving as the president of the CFL Football Foundation, having been asked to do so by Doug Mitchell in 1985. The Foundation had been an initiative of the commissioner who had hoped to assist minor football. Davis would assume his new position in 1987.

After years of festering, the CFL decided in 1986 to do away with the designated import rule and treat the quarterback position as a category separate from "players." Ever since its inception in 1970, the rule had been pilloried by the press and public alike for its effect on discouraging non-imports at the quarterback position. The regulation came about when Edmonton's Norm Kimball "proposed that quarterbacks be placed in a separate roster category from imports and non-imports."[93] The designated import legislation arose from that. In 1986, it was Winnipeg's Paul Robson who proposed that a "club be permitted to dress for a game a maximum of 36 players of whom not more than 16 may be imports of whom three may be designated as quarterbacks."[94] Robson's rationale was that each club was presently carrying a third quarterback on its reserve list and such a change would allow a team to give him playing time. There was always a need to develop quarterbacks. Discussion resulted in some modifications to the proposal. Some were concerned with the increase in rosters; others with whether one of the three quarterbacks could partake of other roles and duties. After the motion was approved with a total roster of 35, the league issued a directive.[95] Team rosters were fixed at 35—32 players including not more than 13 imports and a "maximum of three players who shall be permitted [to] alternate for each other during the game at the quarterback position exclusively." The quarterbacking position was defined to include "holding the ball for a kicker on a convert or field goal attempt." There were other conditions: the player named as a quarterback could not enter the game at any other offensive or defensive positon, nor could he be on the field for a kick-off or when the opposition was scrimmaging the ball. The quarterback could not replace any player, other than another quarterback.

While each club was allowed 35 players, fewer could dress. If 35 were dressed, three quarterbacks could be so categorized but only one could be in the game at any one time. If 34 were dressed, two would be named as quarterbacks with the same restrictions. If 33 were dressed, one would be a quarterback with the same restrictions. If the club chose for whatever reason to dress 32, there were to "be no restrictions on the quarterback position."

Violations would be subject to a fine and be considered "valid grounds for protest." A later clarification allowed "a quarterback to be a kicker but [did] not permit a kicker to be identified as a quarterback."[96] The league was clearly hoping that by developing a quarterback category consisting of players who could be import or non-import, it could recoup some of the Canadian public's confidence that it wanted to tear down any perceived roadblocks for non-import quarterbacks. The only non-import quarterback in the CFL at the end of the 1985 season was Greg Vavra of Calgary. After a season of reduced playing time, he was picked up by the B.C. Lions with whom he played two games in 1986.

For the first time in its history, the CFL college draft was to be telecast live from the Toronto Convention Centre by TSN. Since a number of players had attracted NFL attention, there was a fear "that a club might be faced with a dilemma of possibly wasting a choice or missing a chance on a star player."[97]

The fear was that Canadian players such as Reuben Mayes, Marcus Koch, and Michael Schad, all first-round draft prospects, would choose to play in the NFL. The league struck a committee of three "to review the list of candidates and select a maximum of 12 to be invited to the draft meeting at league expense."[98] In the end the CFL put on its best face when the three, in spite of being first-round choices in the CFL, cast their lot with the NFL's New Orleans, Washington, and Los Angeles teams respectively.

One ongoing area of concern was in the matter of players' relations. From time to time there were grievances and differences in interpretation of the collective agreement between the league and its players. Ralph Sazio noted that the players "were invariably represented by Ed Molstad who is fully familiar with the procedures and understands the thought processes of various arbiters."[99]

Sazio was referring to the former Edmonton Eskimo defensive lineman who had been legal counsel for the Players' Association since the early 1970s. Not only that, Molstad had also played with the Eskimos and negotiated his own contract with Norm Kimball. Those factors and his continuity were perceived to give the association an advantage. On the management side, Sazio stated, "the club is usually represented by an outside lawyer who has to be thoroughly briefed on the machinations of football disputes. Then, quite possibly, the club is placed at an immediate disadvantage."[100] Sazio recommended that the league appoint one person to represent it in these negotiations. His suggestion was Richard Rendek "a practising lawyer in Regina and a member of the league's Player Relations Committee."[101] The league concurred. Richard Rendek accepted the position of counsellor-at-large for the league.

The CFL was able to effect its 18-game schedule as part of the new collective agreement signed with the players in 1986 and it was able to do so at no extra cost. In effect, revenue from two extra games was a bonus for each club. The players had hoped for an increase in pay since they were moving from a 16- to 18-game schedule but the CFL argued "that the players were paid on a per season basis, an annual payment basis ... a player's contract never stated how many games you play in." The new contract was to specify 18 league games.[102]

The agreement announced in Vancouver on April 28, 1986, called for training camps to be shortened from six to five weeks. Players with two years' experience were to receive $500 ($100 more than in 1985) with three-year veterans to be paid $600 per week. There were also new salary minimums: first-year players were to receive $26,000 for 1986 and '87 and $28,000 in '88. In the preceding contract veterans of one year received $26,000 and rookies $22,000. The contract also called for two-year veterans to have a minimum of $32,000 for '86 and '87 and $36,000 in '88. The minimum annual compensation for a three-year veteran was to be $38,000 in '86 and '87 and $40,000 in '88. There was also some protection for veterans of six years or more. These players would receive full payment of their contract if released after September 1; five-year players would be similarly treated after September 15.; October 1st would remain the cut-off date for all other players.[103]

Grey Cup compensation was also increased: winners were to receive a minimum $11,000, and players on the losing team a minimum of $6,000. Divisional semifinalists were to receive $1,800, finalists $2,200. Players on the first-place teams were to receive $1,200. The contract also dealt with the issue of practice times. Clubs could start at 1:30 PM "subject to the agreement of a majority of veteran players."[104]

While Greg Vavra faded from the scene, his former team, the Stampeders, was the focus of public attention for much of 1986. Their financial woes were the subject of much debate. There was concern as to whether the franchise would survive. It was unable to pay its assessments to the CFL during December of 1985 and January of 1986. The league agreed to waive them so as not to hinder the search for new operators who would not want to take over past debts.[105] Mixed signals seemed to be emanating from Calgary. In the midst of a campaign to keep the Stampeders in the foothills city, Calgary City Council was asked to subsidize the football team's rent of

$500,000 for McMahon Stadium. The proposal to do so for a three-year period was turned down by a 7–6 vote.[106] The club was distraught. An earlier plan to provide a group led by businessman Doug Hunter with a loan of $2 million and a $4 million line of credit "prompted hundreds of letters and phone calls from people opposed to taxpayers' money being used to prop up the sports team."[107] Some $6 million dollars were needed over the next five years. The Alberta government was offering a $1 million loan guarantee; the club, after first considering a $6 million loan and a break on the rent, had begun a fund-raising campaign with the purpose of raising $4 million. After five days it "had raised only $202,000 in donations and $61,000 in pledges."[108]

Mayor Ralph Klein "who spear-headed the efforts to grab the rent subsidy, said the Council left him sick and disappointed."[109] Linebacker Bernie Morrison, an eight-year CFL veteran, was especially bitter: "I'm thinking just how gutless the City Council is. I put eight years in the city on and off the field and it's not the type of place I want to raise my family in."[110]

The Calgary team was officially listed as community owned, as were all the Western teams. Some felt there was private money involved, a reason given by dissenting politicians and the public as to why public money should not be spent. Surely, these critics said, the league had an emergency fund with which to deal with such concerns. By mid-February, the Stampeders seemed to be assured of enough of their resources that they announced they would operate for 1986. A group of businessmen agreed to form an interim Board of Directors. Personal contributions from members of Calgary's business community of $10,000 to $20,000 would give a much-needed injection of money. A season ticket campaign with a target of 25,000 was initiated for the new community-owned operation. The provincial government agreed to give a loan guarantee of $1 million "if the city offers some financial assistance also."[111] The local media got involved to the extent that the public was bombarded with the message. Eventually 20,413 season tickets were sold in the month, the result of "an all-out sales blitz which resembled a charity drive ... to preserve a tradition. The blitz included everything from charity style dinners to a strip-a-thon organized by exotic dancers."[112]

There were strong indications that the public's attitude towards the CFL was continuing to change; that the competition for the entertainment dollar was intensifying; that perhaps new approaches to the marketing of the league were needed. The years of criticism directed at the league seemed to be peaking:

> It's become fashionable to fire darts at Commissioner Doug Mitchell's rag-tag band of recent years, mostly because it offers such a large inviting target. The league takes so many polls, becomes defensive

about so many contradictory policies, and lives so far beyond its means, it sounds like our government. If the Stamps had folded, it didn't take a rocket scientist to figure out the whole league would be in trouble. A future with no professional football in six CFL cities, an NFL franchise in the domed or soon-to-be domed playpens of Vancouver, Montreal and Toronto was not difficult to picture ... The Calgary crisis may finally have convinced the Governors it's time to bring in the old bus for a check-up.[113]

The feeding frenzy continued. Another reporter with the *Toronto Sun* reported that the league did have an emergency fund. It quoted "confidential sources" that the money was "spent on new office space and salaries for enlarged staff." The *Sun* continued: "The fund has disappeared and no one seems to know much about where the money, as much as $753,000 in June 1984, was spent."[114] Commissioner Doug Mitchell denied the story. There was no emergency fund, he said, the money had been "used to bail out the Montreal franchise in 1982 when the Alouettes became the Concordes."[115] The general managers canvassed were unaware as to whether the fund still existed. Bob Ackles of B.C. said he knew it once existed, but Winnipeg's Paul Robson described the *Sun* story as "ludicrous" while Joe Galat of Montreal seemed to come down on both sides: "The CFL has a new high profile office you know but I really don't know if that's where the money went."[116] A beleaguered Doug Mitchell angrily denied the story and "reportedly retained the services of a lawyer to investigate whether the story carried by the *Sun* was libellous."[117]

The play-off format came under fire. Some blamed the Western woes on the fact that some of their teams had better records than clubs which qualified for play-offs in the East. The fact that three of four teams in the East qualified for play-offs while three of five did in the West, meant that the two Western teams could be eliminated from contention early resulting from a drop in attendance and "substantial cash flow reductions." In a report prepared for the league, Commissioner Doug Mitchell met the problem head on but his solution antagonized traditionalists. He recommended that the top finisher in each division be given a bye. The next four top finishers in the CFL regardless of division were to be given "wild card" berths. The net effect would be that the two surviving teams would compete for the Grey Cup Game, which would not necessarily be an East-West match-up.

It was radical, perhaps too radical for some. Scenarios such as a Saskatchewan versus Calgary game in "a yawning Montreal or ... Ottawa versus Hamilton in an equally indifferent Vancouver,"[118] were debated. Milt Dunnell, an observer of the Canadian football scene for years, continued:

the true afficionado with team ribbons flying from the lapel and a concoction of rum and coke in the side pocket is able to disregard such trivia as having a league with the same club name as Rough Riders and Roughriders as long as the Tiger-Cats get the traditional win over Argonauts and the Saskatchewan stubblebenders score occasionally over the Winnipeg Blue Bombers. At least that's the way it has always been. But there is evidence that the love fest could be cooling. Two teams had a death rattle in their throats at the end of the past season. Grey Cup tickets are no longer something you have to obtain in the last will and testament of a rich relative. There has been an alarming dip in Grey Cup television ratings.[119]

Dunnell's comments about the ratings were confirmed in Mitchell's report to the league. He called the drop "frightening." In 1983, the total rating was 8,118,000; in 1984, 6,897,000; and in 1985, 5,283,000.[120]

Former CFL commissioner Jake Gaudaur entered the fray. He too was wary that a Grey Cup Game could be played without the traditional East-West rivalry: "the East-West confrontation is essential to the Grey Cup. If we ever get around to a situation where it's east versus east or west versus west, the Grey Cup game will lose its identity. Under a wild card play-off format, that's exactly what could happen."[121]

In the end, a compromise was effected. The league accepted a Winnipeg proposal. The play-off structure would remain as it was in 1985 unless the fourth-place team in one division had a better record than the third-place finisher in the other. In that event, the two top teams in the one division would play a two-game total-point series to determine a winner; the other four teams would play off against each other, 1 versus 4 and 2 versus 3, to determine the division champion. The two division winners would meet for the Grey Cup; East versus West would be preserved.

An increasing number of complaints had been received from players about the league's official ball, the Spalding J5V. The major complaints had to do with the size. The balls didn't seem to hold their shape and often new ones were of different sizes. By the end of the year, complaints had increased to the point where the commissioner was left to decide whether to pursue an American machine-made ball from Wilson or Rawlings or stay with the Canadian hand-made Spalding product. It was an important consideration. After all, the vast majority of quarterbacks in the CFL were still American; they were used to throwing the machine-made balls which were manufactured at lower tolerances and held their shape. Indeed, the imports' proficiency at throwing was what made them attractive to the CFL coaches.

There was some thought that they were being handicapped by using the "oversized" J5V Spalding ball.

By 1986, the football was made to conform to the NFL size. The CFL had always allowed the manufacturer to work within the size tolerance of the American ball but, while the NFL insisted on the lower end of the tolerances the CFL had accepted the higher. Since many of the quarterbacks had difficulty throwing the "fatter" CFL ball, the league decided to insist on the lower tolerance limit since all of its quarterbacks were more comfortable with it.

The league invited and "received proposals from Spalding, Rawlings and Wilson to provide official footballs for the league."[122] Perhaps because Spalding balls were the only ones made in Canada—the material used was from the same source as the other two—Spalding was given a chance "to match or improve on the Wilson offer ... the most attractive of the three."[123] The result was a new three-year contract with Spalding which called for the manufacturer to supply each club with 125 J5V balls per year at no charge. A further 175 balls per year were to be available at special prices of $41.00, $43.00, and $46.25 over the life of the agreement. Twenty-four Grey Cup balls were to be supplied to the league each year at no charge.

As a further means of sweetening the deal, Spalding was to give to each club, at no charge, "96 dozen golf balls or 80 autographed footballs or a combination of the two."[124] Spalding also paid a royalty fee of $12,500, $15,000, and $17,500 in the three years respectively. The league also gave Spalding something more tangible in addition to "official football of the CFL" status. It was to receive a full-page ad in the league's Official Record Manual plus a full-page ad in each club's program. For its part, the CFL would ask that the ball conform to NFL dimensions and that the CFL "have input into the quality control" with the officiating director inspecting the first production "to ensure that the standards are being met."[125] Commissioner Doug Mitchell estimated that the total package would "save the clubs collectively nearly two hundred thousand dollars over the three years."[126]

A similar type of arrangement was entered into with Ravensknit, the Canadian subsidiary of Champion Products of the USA. In the three-year agreement, each club in the CFL would be provided, in the first year and at no cost, 120 pairs of game pants, 200 jerseys, and 200 name plates, all conforming to club standards. In return, the league would not allow any authorized uniformed person in the bench area wearing any headgear or other article of clothing with a commercial identification "unless approved by the league."[127]The arrangements were good for each party: the suppliers' products were given "official" status; the league received sponsorship and free products in return.

In an effort to provide leadership and to be seen doing so, Commissioner Mitchell left for an 11-day trip, having been invited by the European Football League to visit Italy, England, and the Netherlands. The CFL became a founding partner of the International Football Federation. Visions of an expanded federation where the CFL could play a "big time" role were contemplated. There were 375 teams playing in eight countries of Europe, the largest group in England with 80 teams. The league received a request from the Italian Football League to allow two coaches and eight players "to come to Canada at their own expense and spend a week or ten days at a club training camp in the role of observers."[128] While the European calibre of play was not up to CFL standards, as far as the CFL was concerned there was the "great potential for television exposure and the playing of pre-season games."[129] A group from France had previously attended the Montreal training camp in 1984. By the end of the 1986 season, a group from England, London Gridiron Football U.K. Ltd., actually made a preliminary presentation to the league to inquire about a franchise.[130]

Based on the information that "market research and general assumptions are consistent and that the East-West concept of Grey Cup must continue," expansion was still a major concern.[131] As a result, the consensus was expansion should occur in the East in order "to equalize the play-off structure."[132] CFL market research showed that 73% of fans felt the league should expand; the Maritimes and London, Ontario seemed to be the most viable areas. A five-year target time was recommended to be pursued.

The league decided to play an exhibition game between Winnipeg and Montreal in the Maritimes at Saint John, New Brunswick. There was a dual purpose: to increase the viability of the league beyond the franchise areas; to demonstrate to the federal government the league's interest in the Maritimes by testing the interest for a potential franchise there.[133] There had been hints about federal government support for a stadium. Interest in the game was such that two breweries, Labatt's and Moosehead, wanted to be involved but exclusively.[134] The players were not to be paid for participating in the game.[135] The money generated by the Montreal and Winnipeg game was to be divided up: the CFL Players' Pension Fund would receive the first $50,000; $25,000 was to be designated for league expenses; and the rest was to be split between Saint John and the Football Foundation. The game, won by Winnipeg 35–10, attracted 11,463 spectators in the stadium normally holding 8,000. It was described by Mitchell as an "outstanding success."[136]

The game also served as the reintroduction of the Montreal Alouettes. The team officially known as the Montreal Football Club and Company Limited dispensed with the Concordes name, and reintroduced the name Alouettes and announced a new part owner. Norm Kimball of the Edmonton Eskimos joined the team in March as part owner and chief operating officer. It was in keeping with the plan that Charles Bronfman and Imasco would phase themselves out. The hope was that Kimball, long recognized by many as one of the most astute general managers in the CFL, could turn around the Montreal situation. But returning with the original name was a problem. The Superior Court "ruled in favour of five former Montreal players in a suit against the league."[137] The players had been part of the Alouettes when owned by Sam Berger and later Nelson Scalbania. When the latter turned the team over to the CFL, the five were left off the 65-player roster. The court ruled that "when the league acquired the title to the contracts of the 65 players on the Montreal active roster, it also accepted 'all liabilities under the player contracts.'"[138] The judge ruled that "when the league later assigned the contracts to the new Montreal club (Concordes) there was a specific exclusion of contracts with other players who were not presently active but who may be entitled to compensation for services previously rendered."[139] The five players and their judgements rendered by Mr. Justice Denis Derocher were: Junior Ah You, $118,587; Ron Singleton, $15,002; Richard Harris, $17,465; Sonny Wade, $18,514, and Dan Yochum, $15,000. The league's Montreal solicitor Alan Hilton recommended an appeal but the news was yet another opportunity for critics to sound off against the CFL.

Among the CFL rules approved for the 1985 season, the league sanctioned a proposal for regular season overtime. There had been the possibility of overtime in play-off games, two 10-minute halves with a kick-off between them. In 1985, the league decided to change the format to two 5-minute halves with a 90-second intermission and a kick-off to start each half. Each tied game during the regular season would see the two 5-minute halves in an attempt to resolve the tie. If at the end of the overtime, the teams were still tied, the game would end that way. The play-offs would continue with "a further 10 minute overtime session until a winner is declared."[140] Not all were happy with the decision. The Players' Association declared its opposition since the decision bypassed the collective agreement. As well, the television networks were not enthralled. They preferred a definite starting and finishing time for their telecasts. It made it easier to attract sponsors and also to schedule programming. Overtime could require a decision either to cancel a program which followed the football gome or not to carry the overtime. It meant the possibility of complaints from one constituency or another and the possibility of increased costs without reimbursement. The concept was introduced into league play for the first time in 1986. Two games needed overtime, neither one producing a winner. Saskatchewan and

Hamilton tied in Regina at 21 on September 14 while in Ottawa on November 1, Edmonton and Ottawa played to a 16–16 draw.

The year also put into practice the new play-off rule change. Montreal as the third-place team in the East had a 4–14 record while in the West, Winnipeg and Calgary ended in third and fourth places with identical 11–7 records. It meant that under the new formula, first-place Toronto and second-place Hamilton with 10–8 and 9–8–1 records respectively would play a two-game, total points to count series to determine the Eastern representative in the Grey Cup Game. In the West, Edmonton, as first-place finisher at 13–4, would play Calgary while second-place B.C., at 12–6, would meet Winnipeg in semifinal sudden death action. Doug Mitchell's original proposal would have seen the same six teams involved but since all four Western clubs had better records than the two Eastern clubs, it was conceivable that the Grey Cup Game might not have had an Eastern representative in B.C. Place Stadium.

In the first play-off weekend, all went according to form. The Argonauts took a 14 point lead over Hamilton winning in the Tiger-Cats' lair 31–17. Don Mathews, winner of the 1985 Annis Stukus Trophy, and his B.C. Lions defeated Winnipeg 21–14; Edmonton beat Calgary 27–18. During the second play-off weekend, Edmonton rolled over B.C. by a 41–5 score. In Toronto, Hamilton mounted one of its traditional play-off comebacks and won by a 42–25 score to win the round.

To some extent the debate about the league intruded on what should have been a joyful week for the CFL. In the Schenley Awards presentations, James Murphy of Winnipeg won the Outstanding Player award and the $5,000 that went with it. Calgary's Harold Hallman was chosen as the Most Outstanding Rookie worth $2,500. The top Canadian was Winnipeg's Joe Poplawski, who had been runner-up the previous two years. His award was worth $3,500. The Most Outstanding Defensive Player award, accompanied by $3,500, went to B.C.'s James "Quick" Parker. Saskatchewan's Roger Aldag won the Offensive Lineman Award and $3,500. It was the first time since 1974 that a division swept all the awards and further testimony to the feeling that the West was best and the East still played "dumb football."

Some 59,621 spectators made their way into B.C. Place Stadium for the 1986 Grey Cup Game. Expectations among most of them were that the Eskimos coached by Jackie Parker were prohibitive favourites over Al Bruno's Tiger-Cats. When it was all over, the Tiger-Cats were Grey Cup champions. Led by itinerant place kicker Paul Osbaldiston and quarterback Mike Kerrigan, who had replaced Ken Hobart, the Eastern representative won a decisive 39–15 victory. It was a glorious culmination to a checkerboard year for Osbaldiston. He started with B.C., moved to Winnipeg, and found a home in Hamilton. He kicked six field goals to tie a CFL Grey Cup record. In Hamilton, there was a huge outpouring of emotion. Fans took to the streets after the game to celebrate, some too exuberantly. At least one car was turned over, buses were rocked, phone booths ripped out of their moorings, and fires set. Police arrested 13.[141] The majority of the fans who entered the downtown area were noisy but well-behaved. Police closed off the area around Gore Park to let fans dance in the streets, chant "We're number one" and Oskie Wee Wee the night away. "One fan tried to snatch the steel football from the statue outside the CFL Hall of Fame and gave up when the big metal titan wouldn't budge. A two kilometre stretch of King Street from Wellington to Bay, which was closed from 8:30 P.M. to 11:30 P.M., was wall-to-wall people."[142]

For owner Harold Ballard it was "one of the nicest things that's ever happened to me in life. I've waited a long time and there's been a lot of grief and misery and now I want the Stanley Cup. We'll get that too, you'll see."[143] On Tuesday, December 2, an estimated 10,000 gathered along the slushy streets to celebrate the Tiger-Cats at City Hall. The noon-hour crowd saw Harold Ballard present the city with the Grey Cup flag, the first one since 1972. A civic reception was followed by a private party for the players, many of whom would leave afterwards for their homes.

To some "the Grey Cup game is like one of those scratch and win lottery tickets. When you erase the layers of show biz parades, breakfasts, luncheons, dinners, speeches, beauty pageants and obligatory bets between Mayors, you are left with a message that begins 'sorry.'"[144] The lament was based on the fact that for the fifth time in seven years, the West was a heavy favourite; that according to the interlocking schedule, it was the best against the sixth. "It isn't even a good excuse of a grand national drunk any more,"[145] whined one reporter.

The introspection and darts hurled at the Eastern teams continued to question how the CFL could survive. After all, where Edmonton once drew crowds of 50,000 for any game, only 24,000 and 32,000 attended the play-off contests. The Argonauts and Rough Riders were for sale, the latter without a price tag, the owners ready "to donate them to a responsible group with the good of the community at heart."[146] Could the Alouettes survive with their small crowds? Who would pick up the bills in Hamilton after 83-year-old Harold Ballard died? With all this turmoil within the league, the Hamilton-Toronto final game was riveted with emotion. As one reporter put it, "Anyone who didn't like the Argos, Tiger-Cats thriller has got no ear for music."[147] The CFL

suffers in comparison with the NFL and with major league baseball which has cut into allegiances in Ontario and Quebec for Toronto and Montreal fans. Playing Ottawa and Hamilton isn't nearly as socially stimulating as playing New York and Chicago. In Toronto, eyes turn longingly towards Buffalo where quarterback Jim Kelly has instilled fresh hopes. Across the country, NFL office pools keep stats not to find out who won but who beat the point spread.[148]

To many the Grey Cup Game results had seemed a foregone conclusion. After all, it was the best place team in the country versus the sixth best. As if to underline that conviction, an Angus Reid poll was released. The survey showed that "only 40% of Canadians feel the survival of the CFL is very or quite important. The survey also shows that only 28% of Canadian adults bothered to keep track of the CFL this year but 49% plan to watch the Grey Cup game ... 70% said they would be against any form of government funding to keep the league alive."[149] As if to underline the severity of the results, a spokesman for the polling firm was quoted as saying: "When I look at these stats, I figure the league is living on borrowed time."[150] As if to underscore that sentiment, an announcement was made in Ottawa on the same day that if "area businessmen could show the financial stability to maintain it," president of the Rough Riders, Terry Kielty, would recommend "the franchise be transferred to the community group as a gift from owner Allan Waters."[151] The club had been bought in 1977 for $1.5 million and "had lost an estimated $5 million"[152] since then.

1987 to 1988

Chapter Ten

IT WAS THE 75TH PLAYING of the Grey Cup Game. A commemorative stamp was issued by Canada Post in what should have been a year of constant celebration for the CFL. But in 1987 the very existence of the league was continually called into question. Crisis followed crisis as clubs scrambled to come to grips with new realities; the public pressing for more information, the league reluctant to make too much public.

The first new awakening was the expiry of the CFL's television contract. The three-year $33 million bonanza worth more than $1 million per year to each club expired after the 1986 season. When negotiations began on a new contract, the scope of the reality became more evident. Rights holder Carling O'keefe was given 30 days to submit a proposal. After two delays and extensions, it finally "offered a two year proposal at $4,700,000 per year."[1] The league informed Carling O'Keefe that the bid was not acceptable and pursued other avenues. It turned to CBC, CTV, Labatt's, and Molson's for bids. In October of '86 Molson's decided against purchasing the rights but did offer to be an advertiser. Labatt's was interested only if "there was a total lift of television blackouts in the Toronto area." CBC and CTV responded with $3,300,000 and $3,100,000 respectively for 1987.[2] All parties seemed aware that the league was in a poor bargaining position. The networks and Carling O'Keefe were offering to telecast only 54 of the 81 games but still wanted the "exclusive rights to the other 27." [3] The networks were asked for "certain promotional rights which they refused to consider."[4]

With the blackouts particularly in the southern Ontario area perceived to be the stumbling block, the league sought to remove it. They requested new "tenders" on the basis that there would be some relief from blackouts. The league was clearly in a quandary. Figures showed that lifting a blackout in Calgary would increase the potential television audience by 4% but lifting it in the Toronto/Hamilton area "could amount to a potential average increase of at least 24%."[5] The finding, presented in the league's report on TV blackouts and start times, was significant. The same report catalogued the fall in numbers of viewers suffered by the CFL: 1983, 952,600; 1984, 736,800; 1985, 837,000; 1986, 735,000.[6]

Lifting blackouts and catering to the Ontario TV market would eventually have their effects. There was the Canadian tendency to "cottage" during the summer. The league had long refrained from playing weekend games during the summer for this reason. Television, on the other hand, was attracted to weekend games. After all, even at the cottage people could watch the game on their TV sets. Some even felt that there were too many games in the summer, not a traditional time to play football. It was a double-edged sword for the CFL. It wanted high viewer numbers for its television sales but not necessarily at the expense of fewer "bums in the seats."

Television was both a saviour and an irritant. There was no question that the league needed it as a source of revenue to sustain it in the style to which it had become accustomed. Yet the developing policy of lifting blackouts and catering to the large markets was annoying westerners who saw 5:00 PM and 6:00 PM starts to their games as just more evidence of the West catering to the East. And the Argonauts didn't seem to be benefitting from it either. Its operating costs for the 1988 season were expected to be $2 million with "radio revenue lower by $100,000 because of the cancellation by CFRB of the existing contract."[7] The radio station's contract with the club giving it exclusive rights to Argo broadcasts was ineffective because of the league's attempt to generate more sponsorship money by lifting blackout restrictions.

While the league was lifting its blackouts in the Toronto/Hamilton area on an experimental basis to attract more revenue from television advertisers, satellite dishes continued to pose a threat in the smaller league centres. In Winnipeg with the bars lobbying to stay open Sunday afternoons, their "pirating" of the game's signals "would seriously impair the team's home gate."[8] It was an old problem but there had been changes in government. Prior to 1984, there had been an interventionist approach; latterly the approach was one of allowing "market forces" to work. The CFL Commissioner recalled that "the former Liberal government had laid several charges of satellite piracy against bars which were stealing signals. When the government changed in 1984, all such charges were dropped."[9] Cal Murphy, general manager of the Blue Bombers, "advised that a former Winnipeg player, Steve Patrick, is a member of the CRTC and has promised his cooperation if the league acts quickly."[10]

Identifying a problem and finding a solution, however, are two different matters. Everybody seemed certain that lifting the blackout, particularly in the Toronto/Hamilton area, was the key. The Argonauts again seemed to be central. They also were the stumbling block. Their owners were Carling O'Keefe, who were vying with Molson's and Labatt's for the beer market. Would they be willing to assent to the lifting of the blackout, should a rival win the TV rights? The Argonauts also had a written agreement with CNE Stadium whereby the club would have to pay additional rent should the blackout be lifted. The club had also signed a contract with radio station CFRB giving them exclusive control over the broadcasting of Toronto games.

When the league offered to make some concessions, Carling O'Keefe replied that it could not improve on its offer. Labatt's withdrew from discussions on January 20, 1987.[11] The networks were clearly in the driver's seat. The league decided to "break the schedule into packages and sell them independently, hopefully to encourage competitive bidding from the networks." [12] They didn't bite. On a package of 21 games CTV offered $1,500,000 and wanted the blackout lifted for all Friday night games; CBC's offer was $1,100,000 for 22 games. Both said the games were too hard to sell. When the league sought to purchase air time to produce its own games, the networks refused.[13]

In the end, with few options remaining, the league decided to develop its own production, utilizing a variety of independent television stations. CFL Productions, a league subsidiary, was to be responsible for 42 games, selecting the play-by-play announcers as well as selling the advertising. Global Television, CHCH in Hamilton, and independent stations serving the whole league were attracted and formed the CFL Productions' on-air marketing arm, the Canadian Football Network (CFN). CBC "eventually offered to participate if it could produce its own games and use its air crews. The league agreed to this but retained the right of independent appraisal of CBC's on-air performances."[14] The league's network was to show the Friday night games, as well as late Sunday ones after Labour Day; CBC had Saturday and Sunday games. The remaining games, mostly on Thursday nights and not carried by the league or CBC, "would be assigned to TSN for $20,000 per game."[15]

The league realized that developing its own production was "a mammoth undertaking with great risk involved," but it also knew that there was "a potential to realize nearly $12,000,000 in revenue which could be enhanced by lifting the blackouts in each of Toronto and Hamilton and a commitment to lift a blackout anywhere if a stadium has achieved 90% sellout 48 hours prior to game time."[16] It was Toronto's Ralph Sazio who injected some financial reality into the situation. He noted that in order to reach 1986 levels of revenue from television, the $4,000,000 rights fee added to the hoped for $12,000,000 from advertising would be reduced by the anticipated $5,000,000 cost to the league in producing the games. The alternative expressed by Norm Kimball was to accept the television networks' offers "in the total amount of $4,700,000 ... but to receive only $500,000 [each]."[17] Kimball summarized: "The league position was either to accept the networks' offer and be at their mercy with limited prospects for the future or to accept the challenge of becoming master of its own destiny where its future depends largely on its own efforts. Without a formal resolution, it was unanimously agreed to proceed on this latter basis."[18]

The CFN had only one goal—to resurrect the value of the television rights by a three-pronged approach: (1) demonstrate that the capability existed in Canada to produce NFL calibre programming; (2) re-establish the premium value to advertiser participation in CFL telecasts; (3) demonstrate that properly produced and marketed programming will generate substantially increased revenue.[19]

What the league considered to be the beginning to a list of responses to the financial problems began in October of 1986 with the submission of a report by Paul Robson and Leo Cahill who had returned to Toronto as their general manager in 1985. Titled "Report on Roster Considerations for 1987," it had its genesis in a discussion about club rosters. It centred around the continually recurring question of import and non-import players. There was a conviction as expressed by Earl Lunsford of Calgary that the product on the field was damaged because of the use of "inadequate personnel in key positions ... a club will generally use non-import players in the leftover positions where they may not be best suited to play." His solution was to increase the number of imports to 16 which, combined with the quarterback position meant only seven non-import starting spots rather than the current 10. Hugh Campbell questioned the wisdom of the proposal. Would this lessen the incentive for aspiring Canadian players? Would it jeopardize the league's relationship with the CAFA and CIAU? And, more realistically, would it result in the same sort of media criticism which the designated import rule had generated? Campbell mentioned "that there is more stability in a club roster among its non-imports, while the regular turnover of import talent is a subject of complaint."[20]

Other general managers had different views. Ottawa reported that high schools were dropping football programs because of insurance costs. Toronto reported similarly, citing equipment, coaching, and insurance as expenses. Leo Cahill also expressed a reality which had been developing for some time: "The better quality non-imports are in a highly favourable bargaining position ... they have reached salary parity with imports."[21]

Hamilton's Joe Zuger continued along that line. Present non-imports were "somewhat complacent" because of the lack of competition for their jobs. "The large turnover in import personnel is due to greater competition for positions," he said.[22] Earl Lunsford agreed: "When Calgary recently added an import offensive lineman, the play of the non-imports suddenly improved."[23] Zuger expressed the opinion that "an increase in the number of imports would not necessarily increase overall salary costs. Some imports will play for less than what some non-imports are receiving." Speaking from many years in the league as a player and general manager, Lunsford "pointed out that he ... has gained the impression that fans do not really care where the players came from. The game itself is exciting and could be more so with improved talent."[24]

Cahill's and Robson's report, based on information shared at CFL meetings September 28 and October 4, 1986, was thorough and clear. It highlighted some concerns. Some non-imports, specifically offensive linemen, were being demanding and being paid "salaries far in excess of their ability to perform and the reluctance of coaches to play import players at line positions has enabled non-import linemen to demand higher salaries ... Compounding the entire problem is an abundance of import players willing to sign contracts at salaries well within the league's ability to pay."[25] The report however stressed the wider context. Television revenues were uncertain; gate revenue had fallen; prices of tickets even for strong franchises had increased in order to generate needed operating revenue. "In plain and simple language," the report stated, "we have been operating beyond our means for some time ... We require $1.2 million in television revenue annually just to exist."[26] Western teams were having problems with fundraising because of the perception that monies were going to salaries "rather than building a reserve fund for the long term stability of the franchise."[27] Privately owned teams were being forced to "depend on the enthusiasm of their ownership to continue to absorb losses."[28] Clearly, in Robson's and Cahill's minds the league had "reached the 'Catch 22' point, where to field a competitive team, we face bankruptcy or to live within our means and be non-competitive."[29]

Figures were provided to show the concerns graphically. Players' salaries as a percentage of gross gate revenue had increased dramatically. In 1981 they stood at 58.4%. By 1985, they represented almost 75%. In the same period, salaries had increased by 50%—$14,688,700 in 1981 and $21,280,000 in 1985. In the same time period the average import had moved from a salary of $52,600 to $72,259 while the average non-import was at $34,300 in 1981 and $53,189 in 1985. The report laid out three strategies for dealing with the problem: (1) determine a roster size and ratio which is viable economically and competitively; (2) accept a formula which will distribute talent to non-competitive teams; and (3) effect salary cost controls.[30]

While club and league revenues were shrinking, the CFL also instituted a stabilization fund. Effective January 1, 1987, each club was to remit a lump sum payment of $52,000 each year until $260,000 had been contributed. Concurrently, $4,000 was to be sent to the league office monthly until a further $200,000 had been collected. The total amount of $4,500,000 (500,000 x 9 clubs) was to be used in the event a club withdrew from the league constitution. "The chief concern was that community-owned and operated [teams] were not in a position to pay such a sum in the event they become insolvent."[31] The idea was that the stabilization fund could "be used as an interior source of financing for the league to operate a franchise until a new franchise owner(s) could be put into place."[32] It would also contribute to the league since the fund's annual earnings were to be "paid to the league and become part of the league's operating funds which at the end of 1986, was $2,524000."[33] At the same time, it was made clear that it was "*not* a source of financing for a member club which may be encountering financial difficulties ... Unanimous approval of members voting at a duly constituted meeting of the Board of Governors"[34] was required.

Curiously enough, however, it wasn't the community-owned clubs that were suffering the most. League gate equalization figures for the year ending December 31, 1986, showed that the four Eastern clubs, all privately owned, had withdrawn funds from the league's gate equalization fund. Montreal received $281,342; Hamilton $208,851; Ottawa $171,676; and Toronto, $82,230. Only Saskatchewan in the West received funds in the amount of $67,281. The two largest contributors were Edmonton at $221,547 and B.C. at $362,612. Each put in the limit which was determined by taking a maximum of 20% of the difference between the club's gross gate revenue minus the league average.

Clearly the league needed to regroup. In what was called "a clandestine meeting in San Diego,"[35] the CFL met to lay the foundations for the new approach. A "Roster Control" report that was undertaken to examine the clubs' decreased revenue situation, prepared by Norm Kimball and Paul Robson, made a number of proposals.[36] Each club was to "target its gross gate revenue at a minimum of $3.6 million." In addition, a maximum of $2.8 million was to be set aside for salaries, including players on the reserve, injured and non-active lists. As part of the means of equalizing talent and lowering salary costs, an equalization draft was proposed. If such a draft did not work, clubs would have to make decisions whether "to renegotiate or terminate through the waiver process." In any event, "Kimball cautioned that this discussion should be treated in a confidential manner … [there was] no reason for this information to become public … [It was] strictly an internal matter of cost control." Further, he stated: "There could be damaging consequences in media reaction, fan perception, and player morale if this subject reaches the public forum."

There were some dissenters. Saskatchewan's newly appointed general manager, Bill Baker, complained that he had inherited a number of "long-term bonus commitments to high priced players." He doubted that he could meet the $2.8 million salary target and suggested he should not be penalized as a result. As for Edmonton's Hugh Campbell, he had a variation of Yogi Berra's connundrum: "If people don't want to come to the game, how are you going to stop them?" In other words, Campbell asked—perhaps with one eye on the 1986 figures that showed losses in Montreal ($1,145,250), Ottawa ($1,985,573), Toronto ($2,670,954), Hamilton ($1,700,714), and Saskatchewan ($2,785,495)—"How can a club be forced to attain the gate revenue target of $3.6 million?"[37]

Injuries could have an undesirable and unanticipated effect on the salary structure; all clubs knew that. The league decided that while all teams would be bound by the salary cap of $2.8 million, clubs whose injury costs were over the allowable $200,000 limit would not be penalized. If a club did otherwise exceed the cap, 20% (originally proposed as 33%) would be required to be contributed to the stabilization fund.[38] Another area of concern was the player who was in his option year. The collective agreement called for such players to receive 105% of their contracts in their option year. Larry Shaw of Calgary asked how "the salary limit will respond if a veteran player elects to play out his option with a mandatory 5% increase in his salary. Mr. Kimball replied that the solution to that problem is not to permit a player to play out his option if it is not possible to negotiate with the player, the club should release him."[39]

The league's response was to limit each club, commencing in 1988, to $3,000,000 in expenditures "to cover all competitive aspects including salaries and allowances for players, coaches, personnel directors, scouts and trainers and the cost of training camps and tryouts." Each club would be restricted to one head coach, four assistants, and one personnel director. A sliding scale of penalties was put into effect:

(a) 20% on the first $100,000 in excess of $3,000,000.
(b) 40% on the second $100,000 excess.
(c) 80% on the third $100,000 excess.
(d) 100% on any amount greater than $300,000 in excess plus loss of draft choices at the discretion of the Commissioner.[40]

When the equalization draft was discussed, there was a fear that too much knowledge by the players and public would harm the league. Doug Mitchell asked directly: "Can a draft of sorts now be held without it becoming public information that a certain player was available for the draft and another was not, and only this player and not that player?"[41] The result was an indication of some of the methods of conveying misinformation. Paul Robson said, "It could be done discretely with subsequent announcements about being traded." Joe Faragalli's view was, "the head coach should be able to control his staff ... [There is] no reason why a player should know whether he was or was not made available for the draft." And Joe Galat thought that "the waiver process [should] be used by each club to expose to the market those players whose costs now exceed their value."

Almost immediately, the report was leaked and the league was again putting out fires. Some blamed Leo Cahill for the information which "appeared in an Ottawa paper of January 9th which prompted adverse reactions from the Players' Association, the media and general public."[42] At the Management Council meeting in Edmonton, January 21, 1987 "on a point of order" Cahill stated emphatically that he was not in any way responsible for a lapse in security following the meeting of January 7th.[43] The league was still sensitive to stinging criticism it received, again from an Ottawa source, for meeting "in the United States when the value of the Canadian dollar was low as well."[44]

The owners denied that there was to be any such draft. George Reed, president of the Players' Association, said the owners had told him: "there will be no equalization draft and no 24-man protective list in the CFL," and he was taking them at their word.[45]

Clearly, however, it was the adverse publicity surrounding decisions which bothered the league. Mitchell's plan was "to turn the adverse publicity around to make it a positive message. The clubs are acting collectively to improve the league's product and to help the non play-off clubs to be more competitive without damage to the quality of the clubs already in a competitive position."[46]

What the league termed its Competitive Balance Plan took place during the week of February 15, 1987. The three teams with the worst records—Montreal, Ottawa, and Saskatchewan—were able to select four players each from the non-protected list from each of the remaining six teams. No team could lose more than two players. The "secret equalization draft" was "intended to be strictly hush-hush."[47] The Hamilton Tiger-Cats were reported to have been "howling because they had two players pilfered."[48] Eastern All Star centre Marv Allemang was chosen by Ottawa and running back Walter Bender by Saskatchewan. The fact that the word "pilfered" was used illustrates that some of the clubs were attempting to deflect the criticism of the secret draft from themselves to elsewhere. Saskatchewan probably benefitted most from the plan in terms of quality, picking up quarterback John Hufnagel from Winnipeg. The CFL plan to have clubs lower their salary costs continued in other areas. The Argos announced that centre Willie Thomas, reportedly earning $85,000, would have to take a pay cut or be released.[49] Thomas signed later with the Alouettes as a free agent. Winnipeg's running back Willard Reeves was asked "to take a hefty pay cut in his $160,000 a year contract, which he had signed with Paul Robson."[50] The league's Outstanding Player of 1986, the Blue Bombers' James Murphy, was reported to be having difficulty negotiating a raise from his $90,000 salary.[51]

Players were not receiving much money because there wasn't much to be had. The reality of the lost television revenue was felt throughout the league. While an optimistic Doug Mitchell informed clubs to budget for television revenue of $400,000, a shortfall of $800,000 from the previous year, Saskatchewan's Bill Baker estimated that his club was "starting the season $1.5 million worse off than last year."[52] Edmonton and Calgary were counting on a "$450,000 rent abatement." In addition, "the two clubs approached the Alberta Gaming Commission for the rights to jointly stage a lottery with $100 tickets offering opportunities to win new houses, new cars and vacations,"[53] something Saskatchewan did in 1986 to earn close to one million dollars. The cost cutting moved into the organizations. Edmonton froze the salaries of "all employees including secretaries, coaches, players and support staff with three or more years tenure with the team."[54] B.C. did similarly, with General Manager Joe Galat and Head Coach Don Mathews taking salary freezes. While most teams invited some 90 players to training camp, Winnipeg sought to lower expenses by bringing in only 70 as a further cost-cutting scheme. The day before training camp began, the Blue Bombers released seven-year veteran lineman Mark Moors who was also the Players' Association Rep. The somewhat bitter Moors "had some advice for younger players. I wouldn't recommend Players' Association involvement to anyone who wants a nice secure career in the CFL."[55]

Province-wide lotteries, $1 million lines of credit, government assistance, choosing less expensive hotels, and seeking cheaper fares from airlines were all becoming standard practices for CFL teams in 1987.

Compounding all of the league's problems was the Montreal Alouette franchise. They "reduced ticket prices by $2.00 in an attempt to lure more fans into cavernous Olympic Stadium."[56] The club also divested itself of the hefty pacts of quarterback Brian Ransom ($100,000) and offensive lineman

Glen Keeble ($75,000) while negotiating salary cuts with defensive end Doug Scott and tight end Nick Arakgi. The latter was returning to action after suffering two broken vertebrae in his neck early in the 1986 season.

Both Charles Bronfman and Imasco Limited had informed the CFL that they wished to withdraw from ownership. They would continue their involvement until an additional $3,000,000 was lost. "The loss in 1986 was close to $4,000,000 making their cumulative losses since 1982 close to $20,000,000."[57] Norm Kimball, who had joined the club in March of 1986, suggested that it "was not in their best interests to withdraw quickly but that they should first explore other alternatives."[58]

A poll confirmed that if the team's performance improved, fan interest would "increase from 3% to 41%. The major challenge was to appeal to the Francophone community which is 73% of Montreal, and change its perception of the club as an Anglophone operation which reluctantly condones the Francophone."[59]

Kimball proposed to Bronfman and Imasco, "in return for their undertaking to assume responsibility for all liabilities of the club to date plus the posting of a $2,000,000 line of credit,"[60] he would assume control of the Alouettes and seek other investors. The league, on its side, was to guarantee that the 1987 season would be completed and that it would be responsible for costs beyond "the $2,000,000 line of credit if further partners could not be found."[61] This last point was not well received by the CFL; it chose to strike a committee of Ottawa's Dave Gavsie and Toronto's Ralph Sazio to meet with Kimball "to develop the details of an accommodation package that will be acceptable to all parties."[62]

By April, 1987, Kimball was able to announce to the league that he had attracted Edmonton businessman Jim Hole as a partner with the Alouettes.[63] By June, however, it became obvious to all that the franchise was in deep trouble. Only 4,000 season tickets had been sold; "a substantial number of cancellations particularly in block purchases from the business community"[64] were made. Norm Kimball had "reached the conclusion albeit reluctantly, that Montreal was no longer a viable market for a football franchise."[65]

A special meeting of the Board of Governors was called on June 23, 1987 at the Airport Marriott Hotel in Mississauga, Ontario. The CFL was presented with five alternatives. The CFL could continue to operate the Alouettes in the hopes that improvement would occur. It could use the league's new stabilization fund to provide financial support. It could have a three-game trial period to buy some time to revise the 1987 schedule. The team could be moved to another city (London was mentioned) but no large stadium was available and time was too short. The operation could be terminated immediately, the schedule reconstructed, Montreal's home games eliminated, and its away games taken by teams in the bye position for the most part.

In the end, the league chose the latter option. A formal resolution was passed. The Alouette ownership was to be responsible for all debts incurred to that date; the league would pick up the salaries of the players on the roster for one game. All contracts of the players were to be terminated after that and the waiver process would disperse them throughout the league.[66] To the chagrin of Winnipeggers and the confusion of others, Winnipeg was moved to the Eastern Division.

There were other decisions as well. Bill Baker flew to Calgary to meet with George Reed to inform him personally of the Alouettes' demise. Norm Kimball was given a vote of thanks "for his contributions to the league as a club executive for 22 seasons, and in particular his most recent efforts to direct the Montreal club into a viable franchise operation."[67] Kimball's two committee roles were filled by Winnipeg's Ken Matchett on the Television Committee and Saskatchewan's Bill Baker on the Player Relations Committee.

One month later, although the Alouettes and Norm Kimball had faded from the public's mind to a great extent, they were still uppermost in discussions at CFL meetings. Grey Cup ticket prices, which had previously been set at $45, were readjusted to $60 along the sideline and $50 in the east end zone of B.C. Place. At a previous meeting, the league had awarded the 1990 Grey Cup Game to Montreal but had not publicized it. It was moved to Vancouver. Similarly, a meeting scheduled in September for Montreal was transferred to Mississauga. There were second thoughts from some about the league's hasty rush to rescue Norm Kimball. B.C. felt that the league was "entitled to more specific information about the disposition of the final payment by the major partners in the amount of two million dollars."[68] Ottawa stated that they weren't looking for a detailed and itemized report on disbursements; nonetheless, Dave Gavsie said he "would feel more comfortable if he could see a letter from Mr. Kimball to the Commissioner confirming that neither he nor Mr. Jim Hole had received any personal benefit from the two million dollar payment by the major partners."[69] There was also a fear that the league, in agreeing to pay for the one-game salaries, opened itself to possible suit for monies due to creditors by the Alouettes.

Just when it appeared that the league had its television concerns under control, the Montreal demise presented even more problems. The CBC dropped two games from its telecast schedule and renegotiated its financial commitments. The league's CFN was also forced to drop two games of the revised schedule while TSN was forced to drop seven in reducing its telecasts to 12 games. CTV had been a lukewarm participant and had even intervened against the CFN when it applied to the CRTC for a licence. The most dramatic effect, of course, was with CBC's Radio Canada whose two major sponsors, Carling O'Keefe and Petro-Canada, cancelled their contracts with the French language station. The league pumped some funds into the operation because "it was deemed important that the league continue to enjoy French language exposure not only in Quebec,"[70] but wherever the league's message was lacking.

There also was some backtracking on advertising contracts. They had to be revised. Where alternative dates were not acceptable, the league issued credits. Carling O'Keefe was given $160,000 in credits.[71] The "net effect of Montreal folding [was] estimated at between three-quarters to a million dollars."[72] There was also the loss of potential advertisers. "Those who were considering a CFL buy preferred to invest discretionary television budgets in other properties [i.e.] Blue Jays, Canada Cup, Olympics."[73]

In mid-season, the CFL teams were asked to assess their season's financial state and their prospects for 1988. B.C. had budgeted for revenue of $9.2 million and a profit of $140,000. After the first four home games, attendance had declined by 40,000 "reducing projected revenue by $1.1 million and a resulting operating loss of $660,000." Part of the blame was attributed to Saturday night games starting at 5:00 P.M. for 8:00 P.M. prime-time viewing in the East. With its season ticket base of 27,000, B.C. was projecting total expenses of $7.7 million and salary reduction of $300,000 for 1988.[74]

In Edmonton, the Eskimos had budgeted for a loss of $500,000 on football operations. In spite of the adverse league publicity which had "damaged the game's image in Edmonton,"[75] the club was not in financial trouble. It had a base of 28,000 season tickets, a player budget of $2.8 million, and an overall expense budget of $7 million.[76]

Calgary was having cash flow problems. A loss of $1 million was indicated based on the average attendance of 21,000 and 19,000 season tickets. The original budget had been based on a break-even attendance of 27,000.

In Regina, the effects of "increased ticket sales, rent concessions, forgiveness of 1986 rent and a lottery"[77] had trimmed the projected loss from $1 million reported at the meeting May 11, 1987 to $100,000. It had a season ticket base of 17,000, expected revenue of $5.2 million from all sources, and expenses of $5.3 million. Its total gate revenue forecast was $3.5 million.

Winnipeg was anticipating gate revenue of $4.3 million plus other sources amounting to $625,000. Total expenses, including "roster costs of $2.9 million," was forecast at $5.6 million. The loss of $740,000 in football operations would be offset by "off field producing revenues of $530,000.

The net loss for 1987 was estimated at $200,000 bringing the club's total deficit to $400,000."[78] Winnipeg had 19,000 season ticket subscribers and was planning to raise prices in 1988.

In Hamilton, the costs of the operation were $7 million and included players' salaries of $2.9 million. Hamilton had a base of 8,000 season tickets; the 1987 loss was predicted to be the same as it was in 1986, $2.7 million. Hamilton's general manager, Joe Zuger described the club owner, Maple Leaf Gardens Limited, as "very positive and helpful." Indeed, in spite of his ongoing losses, Harold Ballard "sprung for about $100,000 to have rings made for his Grey Cup Champion Tiger-Cats."[79]

In Toronto, where Carling O'Keefe had been taken over by another company, the Argonauts expected to lose $1.5 million as a result of $4.8 million revenue and expenses of over $6 million. Player costs were $2.6 million and, according to Ralph Sazio, exceeded net gate receipts. The Argonauts had 18,527 season tickets and its "walk in crowd [had] been below expectations."[80] Ottawa was anticipating total revenues of $4 million and total costs of $5.8 million which included $2.8 million players' salary costs. Off-field revenues were expected to reduce the loss to $500,000 for 1987.

Almost all were in agreement that the on-field product of the game was excellent. It was in the area of marketing and public perception where improvement was needed. The media had "downgraded the league unjustly. Somehow it had to be convinced that a quality product is being provided and is definitely worth another look."[81] Doug Mitchell confirmed what some had been saying all along, that the games were exciting and TV ratings on the increase. Indeed, one report suggested that CFL telecasts "have never been better particularly those produced by the CFN. They're not home grown cheer leaders. Analyst Neil Lumsden is the best thing that's happened to CFL telecasts in years. Knuckles Irving and Dave Hodge can't make the games any better but they certainly made them sound better. Together, they've made the CFL action so entertaining, some viewers may be tempted to rush out and buy tickets."[82]

The league had taken a calculated risk in operating its own television productions. Some said it had no real option: advertiser confidence had been low because of the Montreal collapse and "other organizational difficulties"; the breweries had no competitive incentive to bid on the rights; previous to the league's takeover of production "the calibre of CFL television programming had been steadily declining" with the networks unable or unwilling to correct the situation or, indeed, acknowledge it; the decline in viewership was blamed on the games and the league, with the networks unwilling to shoulder any of the blame. The bottom line was that advertising revenue had declined dramatically.[83]

Attendance at the ball parks was down throughout the league, close to 300,000 less in 1987 than in 1986.[84]

With the plethora of problems ready to surface at any time, the league decided it needed an Executive Committee "to form accessory plans and with authority to act on behalf of the Board of Governors when necessary."[85] The committee members were Commissioner Doug Mitchell, Ken Matchett of Winnipeg, Ralph Sazio of Toronto, and Chuck Walker of B.C. Perhaps the time had come to eliminate the cap on what wealthier clubs could contribute to the gate equalization plan, or perhaps it was time to do away with the equalization plan altogether and replace it with some sort of gate sharing practice as was the case in the NFL. Later, the committee recommended that the gate equalization plan be replaced with "gate sharing arrangements … [and] visiting teams would receive 40% of the gate. The home club would receive 60% minus appropriate taxes. The money accrued by visiting clubs would be pooled and divided eight ways at season's end."[86] As forward looking as it appeared to be, the plan was turned down at the Board of Governors' level.

There had been some rumblings from various sources about the import/non-import quota, usually ending with the suggestion that the quota be abolished. Mitchell was adamant: "There's no movement afoot to change the existing Canadian-American ratio … We've operated as the Canadian Football League and are very committed to Canadians. I'd have to be dragged across the parking lot, kicking and screaming if we ever reduced the number of Canadians."[87] It was not entirely evident that the commissioner had the complete respect of his members. A request that notice of motion be waived for a telephone conference meeting on October 30, 1986 "to deal with the Commissioner's contract" had been defeated by a 6–3 vote. Not until November 26 was the contract discussed and then it was renewed until May 1989 but with a 40% pay cut to a reported $165,000.[88] To what extent the cut was voluntary is unknown but there was a feeling that the commissioner's power was being eroded. He had suspended Saskatchewan's James Curry for a hit on Argonaut quarterback John Congemi. The one-game suspension was not being served since Curry, with the backing of the Players' Association, had appealed. "'If I told you I like the process, I'd be less than candid. We're working towards putting the Commissioner's authority back into these matters,' he said bluntly."[89]

In early January, the affairs of the CFL attracted a wider interest because of the ownership situation. Allan Waters had offered to turn the Ottawa club over to the community for the token fee of $1. On January 2, 1987, Paul

Robson resigned as general manager of the Blue Bombers to take a similar position with the Rough Riders. He signed a three-year contract. In Winnipeg, the successful Cal Murphy, winner of his second Coach of the Year award in 1984, moved from coaching into the general manager's position. His replacement as coach was the youthful Mike Riley, son of the former Winnipeg coach Bud Riley. In Ottawa, the new owners were identified as "The Ottawa Rough Rider Limited Partnership and a general partner 685367 Ontario Limited."[90] They would begin operations with a clean financial slate.

As the 1987 season was coming to a close, Ottawa, the city where the 1988 Grey Cup Game was to be held, was in danger of folding its franchise after the 1987 season. Some of the limited partners of the community-operated club were reluctant to make further contributions to its operation. A further $450,000 was needed. The outlook was "not promising."[91] Ottawa Mayor Jim Durrell, invited to assure the league that the Grey Cup plans were well under way, offered some unsolicited advice to the CFL. He stated that the league's overall image was at fault. "What is needed," he continued, "is for the league to address the problem by making changes to improve its image … expansion to the U.S.A., modification in playing rules, revision of the import quota, and elimination of the television blackout."[92] The mayor said that the media criticism across the country was "a well orchestrated campaign to destroy the league … The public perception of Canadian football is that it is inferior to the American game in its presentation and entertainment value."

Some major reforms were announced for the 1988 season. It was to begin one month later than in 1987, July 20 being the target date with training camps opening around June 15. The league would still play an 18-game schedule but squeeze them into 16 weeks, the "double headers" being played prior to Labour Day on the understanding that a club would not have to play within three days of its previous game.[93]

In the East, Winnipeg finished with a 12–6 record, Toronto at 11–7, Hamilton at 7–11, and Ottawa won three and lost 15 to end up in last place. In the Western Division, B.C. was at 12–6, Edmonton at 11–7, and Calgary in third place with a 10–8 record. Saskatchewan at 5–12–1 missed the play-offs. Toronto defeated Hamilton in the Eastern semifinal by a score of 29–13 and in Winnipeg defeated the home team by a 19–3 score. Toronto's opponent in the 1987 Grey Cup Game was to be Edmonton. The Eskimos had defeated arch-rival Calgary 30–16 and first-place finisher B.C. 31–7.

Criticisms of the CFL and its Canadian quota system came under renewed attack. Just one week prior to the Grey Cup Game, Harold Ballard launched a salvo:

> The salvation of the Canadian Football League lies in ditching the sport for the version played south of the border. We should play on their field and have four downs and break down the resident rule: Everyone seems to like American football so who are we to sit and buck it? ... It's a shame to deny thousands of boys in the United States a chance to play in Canada and if we can get some of those hillbillies out West to think that way, we'll be alright.[94]

This sounded like a typical Ballard grab for the headlines, enough of a grab that John Robertson, a reporter with the *Star*, rushed to challenge Ballard. Pointing out quality Argo players who happened to be Canadians, Robertson asked: "How long can we perpetrate the myth that Canadians can't sell tickets if we keep letting these guys go out there and play so great?" Challenging Ballard's belief that the CFL should go to unlimited imports, Robertson wrote:[95]

> That would not only get rid of those Canadians but would also destroy the native belief that CFL football is a different game and a more exciting game. If we used only Americans who can't make the NFL, they could turn out to be as marketable as the now defunct World Football League or the equally defunct U.S. Football League. Oh yes, one more thing Harold, when you do your Tepperman number for the benefit of the gullible Canadian media, make sure you alienate the Western owners. We've all been getting too chummy lately. Disunity is where it's at. Go for it Harold. We desperately need a CFL downer this week, anything to take the fans' attention from Sunday's Grey Cup game. It could be a classic.

In the lead-up to the game, the week's festivities in Vancouver included the presentation of the CFL's outstanding player awards. Winnipeg players won the majority of them: quarterback Tom Clements as the Most Outstanding Player; defensive back Scott Flagel as the Most Outstanding Canadian; and Chris Walby as the Most Outstanding Offensive Lineman. Other awards were presented to Toronto's Gill Fenerty as Rookie of the Year and B.C.'s Gregg Stumon as Most Outstanding Defensive Player of the Year.

In the 75th playing of the Grey Cup Game, 59,478 spectators and a nation-wide audience watched John Robertson's prediction come true. It was a "classic" contest, settled by Gerry Kauric's 49-yard field goal with only 45 seconds remaining. The Edmonton Eskimos, coached by Joe Faragalli, defeated the Argonauts 38–36 to claim the Grey Cup which had been rebuilt at a cost of $15,000. It now contained the name of every player who had been on a winning Grey Cup team.

There were game highlights which would keep fans talking for a long time: Henry "Gizmo" Williams ran a missed field goal back 115 yards for Edmonton's first touchdown; Danny Barrett, on a quarterback draw, sprinted 25 yards into the end zone to give the Argos a 36–35 lead with less than three minutes to play; Edmonton quarterback Damon Allen gave a strong performance as he took over from Matt Dunigan with his team trailing 24–10 and led them on two 80–yard drives; Milson Jones's "clutch carries down the stretch enabled the Eskimos to keep their … drive alive."[96] Some reporters saw the game as a chance to counter the prevailing negative publicity about the CFL and the Canadians in it. Milt Dunnell, paraphrasing Mark Twain, wrote: "The reports of Canadian Professional Football's demise are greatly exaggerated."[97] Others pointed out that "Edmonton started only 11 imports among the 24 and played nine Canadians on offense in the greatest game in CFL history … some corpse, eh?"[98]

Once again the league decided to hold a draft to aid the two last-place teams in each division. Whereas in 1987 it was called the Competitive Balance Plan, in 1988 it was more appropriately named the Equalization Draft. The rules for the draft, held in March, were streamlined. Only Ottawa and Saskatchewan, the two last-place teams in their divisions, were eligible to choose up to three players from the other six teams. Ottawa was to have first selection. Edmonton, Toronto, B.C., and Winnipeg were allowed to protect 26 players, Hamilton and Calgary, 27. With the selecting team responsible for the existing contractual obligations, no team could lose more than one player from its roster.

It was contracts and money which attracted most of the headlines. Once again the CFL was attempting to stay below a $3 million expense cap. Throughout the league, higher-paid players were waived, traded, or re-signed to a lower contract. Edmonton's Matt Dunigan was sent to British Columbia, Roy DeWalt, signed as a free agent by Winnipeg in June, was traded to Ottawa in October. Tom Clements, it was rumoured, was asked "to take a whopping $100,000 cut in his $280,000 contract."[99] Clements chose to retire, forcing the Blue Bombers to go with two first-year quarterbacks, Sean Salisbury and Lee Saltz. Slot-back John Pankratz was able to receive money he felt B.C. owed him ($12,500) only after he threatened a law suit. Lui Passaglia was placed on waivers by the Lions in order to renegotiate his contract. Passaglia was later re-signed, but that was not the case with defensive lineman Rick Klassen "who was to make $125,000 this year and has been asked to take a 40% pay cut."[100] Klassen, who was later signed to a contract by Saskatchewan, had flippantly announced that "he'd do it if General Manager Joe Galat revealed how much he made and then took a similar cut."[101]

The league seemed anxious to leak information that all were doing their part. Managers and coaches were not immune. Argonaut coach Bob O'Billovich, who was awarded the Annis Stukus Trophy as CFL Coach of the Year for 1987 and the $5,000 that went with it, was seeking a three-year contract renewal "or at least a two-year deal with a raise in the second year. For all his worth, the Argos wanted him to sign a new contract for two years without a contract increase in either season. He settled for a one-year deal with the same pay level."[102] Winning Grey Cup coach, Joe Faragalli, "took a reported 20% cut in pay when signing a long term contract."[103] Among the general managers, Joe Galat revealed that he had "agreed to a substantial cut in pay," as had Winnipeg's Cal Murphy and Head Coach Mike Riley. In Ottawa, General Manager Paul Robson took a "$40,000 cut from his reported $110,000 contract."[104]

The CFL seemed to be convulsing. The widespread reports about its woes spawned all sorts of "solutions." Some wanted to go back to a 16- or 14-game schedule. Some wanted to start practices later to allow players to have a career outside football and encourage them to settle in the community and thereby develop more identification with it. Some solutions called for expansion into the United States, four-downs and 10-metres football, removal of the yard between the opposing lines, and moving the goalposts to the end of the goal area to make for more difficult points after touchdowns. Some even wanted to remove the extra point attempt altogether, substituting the running or passing of the ball for the after-touchdown score. And of course there were still those who advocated the removal of awarding a point for a missed field goal attempt. The league seemed to be more interested in fine tuning its rules than tampering with them. Winnipeg even proposed playing an exhibition game in Ottawa on June 29 and experimenting with four downs and the elimination of the one-yard restraining zone on the line of scrimmage;[105] the proposal was defeated 3–2 with two abstentions.

Rule changes approved by the league included the elimination of blocking below the waist on interception and fumble returns, the shortening of half-time from 15 to 14 minutes, and the speeding up of kick-off procedures following a touchdown or field goal.[106] There was a change in rosters for the 1988 season, as well. The league decided to allow each team to dress 36 players, 20 of whom were non-imports, 14 imports, and 2 quarterbacks. In 1986, it had been 35 players (13 imports, 19 non-imports, 3 quarterbacks) There had been a downward adjustment in 1987 to 34 players (13 imports,

19 non-imports, 2 quarterbacks). The designated import returned with a bit of a twist. He was to be a "special team" player and originally able "to enter the game at another position only upon the understanding that another import player is required to leave the game for that play."[107] At a later meeting "special team" players were defined to include those related to the kicking game rather than a "short yardage" unit. The same meeting clarified that the "designated special teams player," if he had replaced an import of another position, "could remain in the game provided there was no increase in the number of imports on the field."[108]

The league was also attempting to restrict those who wanted to play out their option. Any such player who signed a contract with another league could not return to the CFL in the same year. If he did so in some other season, his status as a veteran was to be forfeited.[109]

The NFL wished to play an exhibition game in Toronto. Promoters scheduled it. The CFL objected and it was cancelled. A similar game was scheduled for Montreal which now was a non-CFL city. When Doug Mitchell complained to NFL Commissioner Pete Rozelle, he was told that "the clubs arranged their own pre-season game." The CFL decided, "to inform the Federal Government of the league's displeasure."[110] The NFL's promoters in Toronto were persistent. They asked the CFL to withdraw its objections, specifically the Argonauts' control over which football teams could play at CNE Stadium. They cited a statement from Hugh Campbell saying he had "no objections" to such a game being played. Campbell for his part declared to the league that his statement had been taken out of context and "emphasized that he is and always has been totally opposed to such a game and urged that the league do everything to prevent it."[111] The promoters attempted to appeal to the CFL's need for cash from a game which would probably attract over 50,000 spectators. They offered to play an "NFL-CFL double header." The league wasn't buying. They voted to continue "to oppose the playing of an NFL game in Canada."[112]

In spite of its consolidation approach the league was attracting interest from afar. Expansion outside the country was becoming an option. There was a proposal from a group in London, England, seeking to hold a pre- or post-season game. In addition, it wanted to discuss televising games throughout Europe "and eventually to have a franchise in the league."[113] An American, Russell Moon of Norcross, Georgia, had also sent a certified cheque for $25,000 while "making application for new membership based in the Province of Quebec."[114] A third application was received from Sentry National Sports Production Limited. The firm invited the CFL "to hold a pre-season game in Los Angeles in July, 1988. Sentry would fund and promote the game and pay the expenses of the teams involved and in return, would expect to receive exclusive rights for expansion into the USA for a period of three years. It would guarantee at least two new teams during that time."[115] The feeling was that Sentry, in part, was attracted by the league's efforts to control its costs but that the proposal raised more questions than it answered. Did the league want to play a pre-season game in NFL territory when it was objecting to that league's proposed exhibition games in Montreal and Toronto? Did the league want to expand into the U.S.A.? If it did, should the league give that right "exclusively to other persons"?[116]

The league was constantly seeking to address the concern about its image in an effort to upgrade it. Player cards were one way of addressing the situation. They had been part of the CFL since the fifties but had fallen out of favour in the seventies. The entrance of baseball onto the Canadian scene had revealed the huge latent interest in sport cards. The Players' Association was "dealing with the producer of player cards who was creating a collection series such as done in hockey, baseball and the National Football League."[117] If the league chose to get involved, it would cost "less than two thousand dollars a club," the remaining 50% to be borne by the players. O Pee Chee bubble gum was making a similar proposal which Cal Murphy would present at a later meeting.

In a more specific way, however, the league addressed the "image" problem by hiring a public relations firm from Toronto. Fraser Kelly Corpworld Inc. comprised of Fraser Kelly, "well known as a former journalist in the print, radio and television media," Bill Wilkerson, who had a "background in government industry and banking," and Larry Stout, "a former CBC news commentator."[118] Kelly and Wilkerson had approached the CFL commissioner and "offered to help develop a coherent communications strategy which combines the flexibility and imagination of each franchise with the collective clout of the league as a whole and at the same time being aware of fiscal responsibility."[119]

It was exactly the message that the league wanted to hear when the trio appeared at a January Management Council meeting. The "great interest in the league across Canada" had to be "translated into attendance." Tradition was an asset. Cities could be twinned, East with West, to develop new rivalries. There needed to be a coordination of "the kinds of messages being sent out by working with the league Office to accentuate the positive so that the same message is treated the same way in each city."[120] The firm foresaw "sessions with head coaches or media directors as well as general managers ... at a cost of $800 per club per month for three months or a grand total of $21,600."[121] The proposal was unanimously endorsed by the Management Council.[122]

At the close of 1987, Edmonton, the self-styled "city of champions" because of its hockey and football successes, continued to be the model for a CFL operation. Its season ticket base in 1987 was 27,000, still a far cry from its high of 52,000 in 1982, but the highest in the league and the envy of the other clubs. It was for that reason primarily that the league and the Players' Association decided, once again, to resurrect the All Star Game with yet again a different format. The Grey Cup champion Eskimos met the league All Stars on June 23 at Commonwealth Stadium. A record turnout of 27,573 saw the All-Stars prevail by a 15–4 score. The All Stars' quarterbacking duties were shared by former Eskimo now B.C. Lion Matt Dunigan along with erstwhile B.C. player Roy DeWalt, now a member of the Winnipeg Blue Bombers.

In 1988, money woes continued to be the dominant news about the CFL prior to the opening of training camps. It was obvious that "the clubs missed the opportunity to build up reserve funds during the halcyon days of high television revenue."[123] Not only that, according to Doug Mitchell "a good rule of thumb for a club is to keep its player salary cost at less than 50% of its overall revenue."[124] That was not happening. As a result, the clubs' financial reports read like a litany of woes prior to the opening of training camps. Almost every club was counting on a high "walk-in" count to augment their season ticket sales. Ottawa had sold 12,700 and was hoping for another 1,000. If it averaged 21,000 for each home game, it would still incur a loss of $1,200,000. Even with an attendance of 25,000 and a break in taxes and rent the loss would still be in the neighbourhood of $100,000. Toronto had sold only 9,571 season tickets but it was "in a more fortunate position with its generous ownership." Leo Cahill, in a subtle reference to President Ralph Sazio's approach, declared that Argos would not have "any problem in meeting the expense cap since costs are strictly controlled." Hamilton's season tickets were at 6,900 with a hoped for goal of 8,600. A new stadium rental plan was being pursued in order to reduce costs. Winnipeg's report was encouraging: 18,000 season tickets were sold, and over 20,000 were anticipated. Expenses were high, making the $3 million expense target doubtful. In Saskatchewan, there was a "large deficit." Response to the ticket campaign was disappointing with only 12,000 sold. While average attendance in 1987 was 23,699, severe drought conditions prevailed in the south where the club's main support was. The City of Regina had agreed to replace the turf at Taylor Field and the club was opening a CFL merchandise shop at the stadium. In Calgary where the glow of the Winter Olympics was still in the air, the club was hoping to "capture the local enthusiasm." Fifteen thousand seats had been sold toward the club's target of 22,000 and a profit of $100,000. There was an accumulated debt of $1,600,000 which still had to be paid. In B.C., the club had a "substantial debt on its Surrey training facility, high rental at B.C. Place Stadium and the legacy of bad publicity arising from its financial position and its relations with players DeWalt, Pankratz and Passaglia." It had sold 12,000 season tickets and paid $300,000 to the club's creditors.[125]

At a subsequent meeting in September, the clubs agreed that they should give a monthly outlook update to each other in order "to provide an early warning system to isolate trouble spots in the league."[126] The reports revealed some of the areas which affected the teams' profit and loss. There were debts to service. Saskatchewan, for example, began the season with a deficit of $1,000,000, "financed by three bank lines of credit in the aggregate of $800,000 and a stabilization fund loan of $200,000."[127] One of the major unknowns was the number of injuries a team would suffer. Contracts would continue to be paid and replacements would be brought in. An uncontrollable rise in expenses was the result, chiefly because of the nature of the game. It was therefore in the best financial interests of the league to legislate as much safety, through the rules and equipment, as possible. Examples of equipment were multi-cleated shoes and knee braces; examples of rules were the prohibition of blocking below the waist on returns and interceptions and the banning of "spearing" or making primary contact with the helmet.

On the field, Orville Lee, a young rookie running sensation from Simon Fraser, burst onto the scene but not even he was able to propel Ottawa past another dismal season. Lee was the league's Outstanding Rookie for 1988 but the Rough Riders finished with a 2–16 record, costing Head Coach Fred Glick and General Manager Paul Robson their jobs. Hamilton at 9–9 with Al Bruno back at the helm, returning after suffering a heart attack in 1987, finished in third place in the East. Winnipeg with an identical 9–9 finish was awarded second place and hosted the Eastern semifinals defeating the Tiger-Cats by a 35–28 score. Hamilton's Grover Covington was selected as the CFL's Most Outstanding Defensive Player for 1988. Toronto Argonauts, at 14–4 were the class of the Eastern Division during the season, but Winnipeg prevailed in the final, defeating the Argos 27–11 in Toronto. The Argonauts not only lost the chance to appear in the 1988 Grey Cup Game but they also lost General Manager Leo Cahill, who was relieved of his duties, again.

In the West, the Stampeders, under Normie Kwong as general manager and Lary Khuharich's first full year as head coach, finished with a 6–12 record and in last place. The Western semifinal was played between B.C. Lions, third-place finishers under Head Coach Larry Donovan, 10–8 in his first full season, and Saskatchewan which finished second with an 11–7 record under General Manager Bill Baker and Coach John Gregory. B.C. won a surprisingly easy 42–18 victory led by Matt Dunigan and David Williams, selected as the Outstanding Player in the CFL for 1988. Saskatchewan's Roger Aldag was chosen the Most Outstanding Offensive Lineman and receiver Ray Elgaard as the Most Outstanding Canadian. B.C. travelled to Edmonton to play the first-place finishers, also with an 11–7 record. Again, the Lions provided the upset, defeating Edmonton by a 37–19 score and winning the right to travel to Ottawa to contest the 1988 Grey Cup.

It was the smallest crowd for a Grey Cup Game since 1975, but that was because of design rather than poor fortune. The league had decided where possible to move the game around to various cities in the league, the chief stipulation being seating capacity of over 50,000. There were all sorts of dire predictions about the foolhardiness of playing the game outdoors on November 27 when the domed B.C. Place was available. None of the fears about frozen turf or blizzards or freezing weather materialized. A capacity crowd of 50,604 at Lansdowne Park watched in 57°F (14°C) temperature. The field was dry, the wind somewhat gusty, and the sky overcast. While the stadium capacity accounted for a difference in attendance of close to 9,000 from the previous year, it was obvious that a decline in attendance at all levels of the CFL was in progress. It was down for the season games, the regular season and play-offs, by a total of more than 170,000 spectators from 1988 figures.

The 76th Grey Cup Game made headlines for a number of reasons. It was the fifth Grey Cup Game to be played in Ottawa, the first since 1967 when national unity, the Grey Cup, and the CFL were all enmeshed in Confederation year. As mentioned previously, the weather in Ottawa at the end of November was a constant source of speculation. It was also the first time that two teams from the geographical west of the country met. Commentators were having a field day with the fact that the traditional East-West confrontation translated into Winnipeg versus British Columbia. But it was the money woes of the league and B.C. which were the subject of scrutiny by commentators. There were rumours that the B.C. club couldn't pay its hotel bills earlier during their season's visit to Ottawa. "During Grey Cup week, the players checking into their Ottawa hotel were asked for their personal credit cards"[128] as a precaution. The team itself was expected to lose $2 million on the season and "had to get a line of credit for that much from the B.C. government."[129] Only last minute fundraising by private business allowed the Lions' cheerleaders to attend. Larry Donovan referred to his club as "a crisis a day organization and if we don't have our crisis, we've not had a day."[130]

The old complaint was made about the CFL's "revolving door syndrome being a curse to the league." There was the constant turnover of players and the resultant lack of fan recognition —barriers to the league in its attempt "to lure back the big crowds."[131] B.C., it was pointed out, had used "eleven different combinations on the offensive line; its "offensive triumvirate," Matt Dunigan, Anthony Cherry and Dave Williams were in their first year with the Lions. The Bombers had made changes seemingly out "of desperation." Top quarterback Tom Clements retired, running back Willard Reeves went to the NFL, receiver Jeff Boyd was traded to the Argonauts. Gone also were linebacker Tyrone Jones, corner back Roy Bennett and defensive back Scott Flagel. Even so, the youthful Winnipeg coach Mike Riley rejected the suggestion that it had been a rebuilding year.[32]

There were two key plays in the 1988 Grey Cup Game won by the East (Winnipeg) by a 22–21 score. One occurred in the third quarter. B.C. was ahead by four points and chose to gamble on its own 20-yard line. It was third down and a "long yard" to go. The Winnipeg team stopped Dunigan's quarterback sneak and Trevor Kennerd kicked a field goal to bring the Bombers to within one point of B.C. The second key play occurred when Dunigan spotted a receiver in the end zone and threw for what he thought was going to be the winning touchdown. Instead, as Dunigan recalled later, a Winnipeg player who had been blocked out of the play, Mike Gray, had the ball hit his hand, deflect off Winnipeg safety Barry Thompson, and back into the arms of Gray who by this time was lying flat on his back.[133]

For Gray, the hero of the moment, it was a curious turn of events which brought him to that point. The import from Baltimore and the University of Oregon had signed with B.C. in November 1984, was left unprotected by the Lions, and was taken by Ottawa in the Equalization Draft of 1987 in February. He was released by Ottawa in June of '87 and signed by Winnipeg as a free agent later that month. Trevor Kennerd provided the winning margin by kicking a field goal with less than three minutes to play, his 14th point of the game. The Blue Bombers also won all of the individual awards presented. Wide receiver James Murphy was chosen as the Offensive Star of the game; punter Bob Cameron received the Dick Suderman Trophy as the Canadian Star, and defensive tackle Michael Gray was the Defensive Star.

Minutes after the Blue Bombers won, a wild street party started in Winnipeg and downtown traffic ground to a halt. Hundreds of fans in cars and on foot streamed into the streets honking horns and screaming their joy. About 130 city bars, hotels, and restaurants held Grey Cup parties. Sidewalks quickly became littered with discarded beer bottles and cans.[134] CFL football could still attract an enthusiastic throng!

1989 to 1990

Chapter Eleven

THE 12TH OF DECEMBER OF 1988 was a significant date for the CFL: the Toronto Argonauts were sold and the CFL replaced its commissioner.

The Argonauts had been owned by Carling O'Keefe Limited which had been part of Rothman Enterprise Limited until sold to an Australian company where it came under the control of IXL Canada Inc.[1] The new owners were seeking to sell the team during the 1988 season; by December, the company wished to retain only a 5% share in the club. The remaining 95% was sold to Harry Ornest and his family who owned, "OFE Inc., a Missouri corporation,"[2] thus winding up the Argonaut Football club Inc. and forming the Toronto Football club "as a limited partnership with OFE Inc. as the general partner and Carling O'Keefe's interest held as a limited partner."[3]

OFE Inc. formerly owned the St. Louis Blues of the NHL and had been inactive since selling that franchise. Ornest was from Edmonton and lived in California while retaining his Canadian citizenship. His plans were to live in Toronto for nine months of the year.[4]

Carling O'Keefe's decision to sell the Argonauts "resulted from a new corporate policy of not being directly involved in the operation of sports franchises."[5] Under the new arrangement as a minority shareholder, it would "retain the marketing rights of the Toronto Football club for a period of 21 years and would also retain the rights to operate a football team in the SkyDome on the happening of certain events."[6] Both were of concern to the CFL. The exclusive rights to market the Argonauts could be in conflict with a league marketing plan while the new SkyDome, due to open in 1989, was being touted as "world class" and, as such, some were calling for world class, (that is for NFL) football for it. While media coverage indicated a $5 million sale,[7] the only reference to money in the league minutes was number three of five undertakings Ornest had to give the CFL—he was to provide

"$1,500,000 working capital to the Toronto club for at least one year."[8] According to some, Ornest was really interested in bringing in an NFL team; the purchase of the Argos and their exclusive lease with SkyDome would allow him to do that. "Terms of the Argonaut lease with the Dome allows the owner of the club 18 months under the same lease to bring in another football team if the Argos ceased to play in the CFL, or the Eastern Division of the league folds or the CFL folds."[9]

The league was adamant that corporate ownership was not one of its priorities. Carling O'Keefe was a culprit as far as the CFL was concerned. The "ambitions of corporate ownership" were considered to be "sometimes at odds with the ambitions of the league."[10] CFL officials were concerned that Carling O'Keefe was involved with a "Toronto group that is pursuing an NFL franchise."[11] The rumours appeared to have been well-founded. Ralph Sazio, president of the Argos, was rumoured to be a member of the group. He denied it, but former Argos general manager Leo Cahill, who blamed Sazio for his release from that positon, threw some oil on the fire. He "implicated Sazio in the affair by revealing a letter from a high powered Washington law firm that provided hints on obtaining an NFL franchise. Cahill said that he had obtained the letter from Sazio."[12] A further source of irritation to the league occurred when one of Carling O'Keefe's officers "was photographed wearing an NFL jacket."[13] The brewery was taking the positon that it was not promoting an NFL franchise; that it was concerned "about public reaction and was attempting to undo the harm which may have been caused."[14] "Ornest added that negotiations are proceeding behind the scenes to resolve the matter."[15]

When Carling O'Keefe President John Barnett was reported to have said that his firm had not been paid TV money owing to it from the 1988 season as owner of the Argonauts, the by now sensitive CFL sprang to defend its fiscal integrity.

> Shown Barnett's statement, [CFL President Bill] Baker said it was true but that Carling O'Keefe negotiated away the money as part of the new television deal. Carling signed a two year $15 million television and promotional deal with the CFL last month. 'There's no confusion' said Baker, 'as part of our negotiations we kept Carling's T.V. money, which was Toronto's money last year.'[16]

The same meeting of the CFL also dealt with the replacement of Doug Mitchell as commissioner. Toronto representative Ralph Sazio asked to have the Argonaut sale moved up on the agenda so that prospective owner Ornest "would have some input into the question of league leadership."[17] Mitchell's tenure as commissioner was tempestuous and fraught with problems. He was decidedly pro-Canadian in his approach and at times seemed to be the recipient of much bad publicity aimed his way particularly from Eastern clubs. During his tenure, the Alouettes had folded, and the league had lost its huge television contract and, initiated the CFN which, while an artistic success, was not bringing in the necessary revenue. His initiative in moving the CFL offices to a higher-profile location and the corresponding increase in league expenses was a source of speculation by the media. Indeed, even after he had stepped aside as commissioner there was conjecture about an approach by Mitchell made in 1986 to the federal government. Mitchell had submitted a brief "on his own initiative to federal Finance Minister Michael Wilson in November, 1986, asking for a $10 million grant, a $20 million interest free loan, another $9 million grant to match team contributions to the stabilization fund and tax concessions for club owners that suffered losses."[18]

Former commissioner Jake Gaudaur was critical of Mitchell's approach saying: "In recent years that league has suffered from a perception that it is not major league. If that had happened, it would have been perceived as a Canadian charity."[19] He also criticized his successor by saying that "two large financial mistakes were made": the turning down of "between 9.4 million and 12 million over two years in a new television contract"—instead, Mitchell created the CFN which "brought in only $5 million over two years"; and the turning down of the Alouettes' offer of $3 million to fold the team. Instead the CFL kept the team alive only to see it succumb prior to the 1987 season. Gaudaur continued to be critical of Mitchell, terming his assertion to Ottawa in August 1987 "about a lack of advertising support ... 'incredible.'"[20]

When Mitchell was appointed commissioner, it was widely reported that "the Argos and the Ti-Cats were advocating [former Argo and lawyer] Mike Wadsworth. The Ottawa Rough Riders supported them and maybe that was the problem. The western clubs sensed another eastern plot was taking shape. They unified behind Mitchell, the Calgarian, and the Montreal Alouettes joined them to produce a 6–3 margin."[21] In Calgary, Mitchell had turned down the presidency of the Winter Olympics for 1988. "The CFL offer was simply a diversion that found him in a moment of weakness."[22] Mitchell's whole tenure seemed to be "a never-ending exercise in crisis management" as he "agreed to try to keep the CFL from being a sporting obituary."[23]

In a radical move, the CFL decided to eliminate the position of commissioner much as had been discussed in the seventies. Mitchell was replaced by a two-man team. Roy McMurtry, a former Ontario attorney general in Bill Davis's Cabinet, combined some of Davis's and Mitchell's duties as chairman and chief executive officer. Bill Baker of Saskatchewan was appointed president and chief operating officer. Both appointments were effective Sunday, January 1, 1989. The move was controversial.

The appointment of the twin positions was not without question. James Hogan of B.C. was concerned that the Board of Governors, who were making the decision, had to vote for both or none rather than deal separately with each one. There was also some discomfort "with the fact that one of the appointments would be a part-time positon."[24] That was McMurtry's. He was taking over from Bill Davis, the former Ontario premier who had been appointed first chairman of the league's Football Foundation in October of 1985. Effective 1987, he was named chairman of the board of governors, the league taking the position that it wanted someone of stature in that position who was independent from the clubs. His position too was part-time, bearing a stipend of "not more than $12,000." The league continued with McMurtry's appointment, it being "clearly understood by the Board that the senior positon of the two would be Chairman and Chief Executive Officer ... [who would assume the] duties of commissioner until the duties were formally divided."[25] It was not all unanimous: Ralph Sazio, Joe Zuger, and Winnipeg's Ross Brown "without intending any disrespect for the two individuals named ... opposed the principle of currently appointing two people ... [and] would prefer that the Board appoint one party and give him the authority to hire the second person."[26]

Bill Baker, whose nickname while he was playing with Saskatchewan and B.C. was "the undertaker," had excelled as a player for eleven years. He left a position as vice-president of IPSCO to become general manager of the Roughriders after the 1986 season. Some credited him with the resurgence of that franchise; others, particularly in Calgary, were upset with him. The Stampeders charged that while they were trying to abide by the salary cap, Baker's team was not. Calgary "traded veterans Richie Hall and Vince Goldsmith to Saskatchewan for next to nothing in order to get down to the limit. Both turned in sound seasons for the Roughriders as did defensive tackle Rick Klassen who was pried loose in the salary dispute with B.C. Lions."[27] Under Baker's leadership Saskatchewan was reported to "have overspent the cap by $400,000."[28] However, the bottom line was that with "bingos, tele-thons and other fund raisers appealing to a community spirit, the work paid off this season as Saskatchewan made a small $29,000 profit, thanks to a hefty increase in attendance as fans packed Taylor Field to at last see a winning team."[29]

The political benefits of Roy McMurtry's appointment as chairman and CEO became apparent prior to the 1989 season. One of the concerns of the league had always been the player's lack of identification with the community. Players did not stay after the season and one of the major reasons was that they were not allowed to pursue a career if they did not have landed immigrant status. McMurtry had asked that each club "report directly to him with specific problems concerning immigration and work permits for players, coaches and their families ... [so as to allow him] to intercede with the proper government authority."[30] The invitation was repeated once again at the Management Council meeting two weeks later. By June, McMurtry was able to advise the league's Board of Governors that "he had met with senior officials of the Department of Immigration and Employment, including the Minister, and has been informed that effective immediately, all U.S.A. resident players, coaches and their wives will be entitled to obtain employment authorization and work permits without going through the regular validation procedure and which will be effective during the terms of the players' and coaches' contracts."[31]

It was a double-barrelled bit of good news for the club. Not only would it enable players to develop better community relations but, as was noted by Dr. Ross Brown of Winnipeg, it "would make such persons eligible for provincial Medicare after three months."[32] Chairman McMurtry asked the clubs to temper their enthusiasm. He "cautioned that any public announcement on this matter should come from the Ministry."[33]

McMurtry was also busy lobbying for the CFL on other matters. He had met with Jean Charest, the Minister of State for Sport, to discuss the formation of the new World league of American Football and the possible inclusion of a team in Montreal. His lobbying in this matter proved unsuccessful. The NFL had staged an exhibition game in the summer of 1990 in Montreal. A report to the CFL declared it to be "neither an artistic nor financial success with the attendance below expectations."[34]

Each club was urged to lobby the Ministers in their respective areas but political workhorse McMurtry "reminded the members that Government officials are under constant pressure to provide assistance for various causes, so it is often difficult to obtain a commitment on a specific issue in such politically sensitive situations."[35] The league was also being hit with the loss of revenue because of the imposition of the new Goods and Services Tax (GST). Across the league the total impact was expected to be "$2.5 million in one season ... [and] no exemption will be permitted."[36] It was noted that horse racing was granted an exemption because it was "deemed to be an agricultural activity."[37]

In Hamilton, Harold Ballard served notice through Maple Leaf Gardens Limited that he was intending "to withdraw from the league as of January 31, 1992,"[38] a notice which was in keeping with the CFL constitution and "the requirements of the Ontario Securities Commission to disclose any significant events concerning a public company."[39]

Ballard was not planning to operate the club in 1989; it was necessary to find a buyer if the league were to continue to operate in Hamilton. Ballard had "lost an estimated $3.3 million last season and a reported $20 million in the last 11 years."[40] His battle with the City of Hamilton over Ivor Wynne Stadium was like a soap opera. The City wanted $300,000 it said was owing in stadium rental. Ballard refused to pay it. "On the morning of the Grey Cup, November 27, 1988, Ballard had a truck cart away all the team's equipment from Ivor Wynne Stadium."[41]

When all the smoke and dust settled, the Tiger-Cats were sold to David Braley, a Hamilton businessman, hand-picked by Mayor Bob Morrow. Even then, the saga continued. Braley's deal with Ballard called for him to take over the club debt-free, effective March 1, 1989. Any accrued revenues and debts to that point would be looked after by Maple Leaf Gardens Limited.[42] The City of Hamilton, led by Bob Morrow, made "a number of undertakings to assist the club in its re-organization."[43] Braley was "prepared to commit up to $1,500,000 in excess of club revenues … through a wholly owned company 815562 Ontario Limited"[44] and attract other investors from the community. On the City's part, a first effort to consummate the deal was declared illegal by the acting City solicitor. There was objection to the agreement which would see Braley pay only $1 a year rent whereas Ballard was charged $300,000 which was still less than the $500,000 actual cost, according to Morrow.[45] In the end Braley was "to pay $100,000 a year rent plus $25,000 for play-off games. But the City is to pay the team $300,000 a year for the promotional use of the Ti-Cats' logo and trademark and 10 new stadium billboards worth up to $125,000. Beyond that the City would shell out up to $67,500 for security and $6,700 for clean-up costs previously paid by Ballard."[46]

On March 29, 1989, in a poll taken for the Hamilton *Spectator* by Decima Research, 456 interviews were conducted to discover the feelings of the fans. Summarized, it found that: 90% were aware of the sale; 49.5% called themselves football fans; 66% felt that the city should make concessions and support the team financially; more women then men were in favour of the support; 65% of all felt that the demise of the team would hurt the city (85% of the fans and 46% of the non supporters). Thirty-five per cent of Hamiltonians said that they attended a Tiger-Cat game in 1988; 10% attended more than five games. The survey also found that 29% attended a Blue Jays' game, 19% attended a Maple Leafs' game and 5% saw the Buffalo Bills in action.

On questions surveying attitudes about the CFL, the following statements elicited the indicated responses. "Hamilton Tiger-Cat games aren't as entertaining as they used to be"—38% agreed; 31% disagreed; 31% didn't know. "The CFL is not as popular as it used to be"—67% agreed; 17% disagreed; 16% didn't know. "People are more interested in other professional sports such as baseball and hockey"—56% agreed; 25% disagreed; 14% didn't know (the other 5% unaccounted for). "People don't know very much about last year's team"—58% agreed; 22% disagreed; and 20 % didn't know.[47]

While Harold Ballard might have been looked upon as a maverick and loose cannon by the public and media, he was held in high esteem by his players and by the CFL. He had always paid his bills. The league passed a motion thanking him for being "unfailing in his personal commitment and financial support of the club" from 1974 to 1988 inclusive.[48]

Meanwhile in Ottawa, the Rough Riders were undergoing a similar trauma. After two unsuccessful seasons as a community-owned club, Paul Robson was replaced as general manager by Jo-Anne Polack, the first woman to hold that position with a CFL club. Head Coach Fred Glick was let go; Steve Goldman was the new field man in charge. The club had cost $2.5 million during its last two years of operation and was on course to lose a further $1.1 million in 1989.[49] The Rough Riders were asking the league to extend the time by which the club had to pay its debt to the CFL. The amount was $750,000 made up of a loan of $500,000 plus stabilization fund loans of $400,000 less Ottawa's share of the 1988 TV revenue amounting to $333,000 and other smaller loans.[50] In addition, the team was asking the city "to return to the club, revenues generated from football games ... profits from stadium rentals, concession income and parking revenues."[51] That included: rent owed from '87 and '88 seasons of $161,337, parking revenue of $50,000 (estimate) for '89, food concession revenues of $72,000 (estimate), beer revenues of $117,300 ('89 estimate), private box revenue of $43,250 ('89 estimate) and the city write-off costs for operating the park for games of $170,000 for a total of $614,687.[52] The team was also seeking a grant from the Regional Municipality of Ottawa-Carleton "for $500,000 in recognition of the club's economic contribution to the area."[53] A fourth creditor was the Province. The club was asking the Ontario government to forgive an outstanding debt of $260,000 "the team owed in amusement tax, which was levied on all tickets of more than $4."[54] City Council agreed in a 9–7 vote on August 2, 1989, to the Rough Riders' request. Regional government also acceded. The CFL froze the debt owed to it by Ottawa and released the club's share of television revenues for the months of June, July, and August so as to inject some much-needed working capital into the club. Only the provincial government refused to overlook the amusement taxes the team owed.

Controversy swirled within the Ottawa region. One alderman, Lynn Smith, who voted against city assistance, declared: "the message I got from residents of my ward is that 99% don't want to further subsidize the Rough Riders and the league."[55] Jo-Anne Polack was blunt: "It's no secret the CFL cannot absorb the negative repercussions of another team folding."[56] Mayor Jim Durrell was delighted: "Obviously we think the football club performs a valuable function in our city. We want to be a strong, well balanced, healthy city and the football club … is one of those ingredients."[57]

Calgary too was having serious "cash flow" problems. It needed an immediate two payments of $150,000 each from the league for the last two weeks in July to make up for "a delay in the receipts of moneys from promotions."[58] There was an understanding that the club would "repay the league forthwith upon receipt of other revenues."[59] By mid-July, league President Bill Baker observed that "it would appear that at the end of the 1989 season, the member clubs collectively will be in debt to the extent of $17.5 million with no plans in place to retire the debts in 1990."[60]

Foremost among the debtor clubs were the B.C. Lions. The community-owned operation was looking for a buyer. Prior to the beginning of the 1989 season, it had "a deficit of $8.8 million and could reach $10 million by the end of the season."[61] It owed $3 million to the league, much of it from the stabilization fund. After five possible buyers withdrew from purchasing the Lions, largely because of the debt, the club underwent a form of bankruptcy; the "heavy debts were absorbed by the Province."

Bill Baker's approach to the B.C. Lions' huge debt was simple: "Creditors will have to take some big swallows and accept write downs on debt or the CFL will fold, leaving creditors with nothing."[62] His style was there for all to see: "We're going to white knuckle it to get things done. I'm not going to be involved in an organization that keeps dragging on like this. So hang on. We're either going to land this SOB or else we're going to crash it. We're not going to keep flying around and wait until we run out of gas."[63]

Mining promoter Murray Pezim "bought the B.C. Lions as a favour to Premier William Vander Zalm."[64] Pezim, an 80% owner of the club along with six minority owners who "kicked in $100,000 towards the purchase price of $1.7 million,"[65] was given an extended deadline "to November 15 … to file a letter of credit in the amount of $2,000,000 to guarantee the operation of the B.C. club in the 1990 season together with a conditional letter of withdrawal."[66]

Injuries were causing problems for clubs. Expenses resulting from injuries would fluctuate. A rash of injuries and subsequent signing of replacements could wreak havoc with a club's budget. According to the collective agreement, injured players were not to be released; their contract remained in effect until they were healthy enough to play. Only then could a club release the player on the basis that he was not good enough to make the team. That was the theory. In practice, said the Players' Association, it was "amazing how often the same scenario's [sic] repeat themselves from each club. The names may change, but the events continue to repeat themselves, i.e. releasing players while they are injured."[67]

Typical of the situation was the case presented as "grievance #9" to the Players' Association membership.[68] A player was injured during training camp, placed on the injury list temporarily, and given his release approximately five weeks after the injury. The next day, August 4, 1988, the player, as was his right under the agreement, "served written notice on the club and submitted to an examination by a neutral physician." Once his report was received, August 31, 1988, the club was advised that the player would make himself available for a "further examination by a neurologist." A subsequent examination occurred in October followed by a report from the neurologist in mid-November, and by January the association served a "Notice to Arbitrate" to the club. By this time, January 13, the club had responded in a letter "indicating that they acknowledged their responsibility but were not in a position" to pay the player. On March 29, 1989, the association sent a formal letter to the arbitrator "requesting that he render his decision in favour of the player." That decision was made on June 14, 1989, in favour of the player, almost one full year after the original injury. The player was awarded his full contract "in the sum of $41,667.67 plus interest in the sum of $6,875.00." The club was also to make the "contribution to the pension plan, deduct dues from the player's monies and remit them to the CFLPA ... costs to the CFLPA in the sum of $1,250.00." The arbitrator gave the club terms of payment: by June 23, 1989, $18,541.67; by July 23, August 23 and September 23, $10,000 each. When the club failed to make the August and September payments, the CFLPA sent a formal demand on October 10, 1989. "On November 2nd, 1989 the balance of the payments and costs were received from the CFL."[69]

Largely due to continuity and the long-term experience of George Reed, president of the CFLPA, and Ed Molstad, legal counsel, the association was gaining strength. As former players, both were aware of the league's operations. Molstad, who had an outstanding career with the University of Alberta and the Edmonton Eskimos, had been legal counsel since the seventies succeeding John Argo who was still active in a capacity as senior advisor. He represented the players' interests in legal matters and brought continuity to the interpretation of the contract. More and more the league was being forced to recognize that the CFL was a partnership rather than a fiefdom run by owners. When CFL Commissioner Doug Mitchell had suspended James Curry of Winnipeg for his hit on John Congemi, the Argonaut quarterback, and fined him $2,000 despite there not having been a penalty on the play, the Players' Association sprang into action. The player had received written notice but the CFLPA had not, contrary to what the collective agreement called for. The association grieved; its view was upheld and "the matter was settled on the basis that the player was repaid the sum of $2,000.00."[70]

When the league passed a stipulation that players who played out their option and sought to try out with another league's team would not be able to return to the CFL in the same year of their failed NFL try-out, the Players' Association once again challenged. The association had only become aware of the regulation by virtue of a press release dated March 29, 1988. On the same day it served notice that the proposed league policy was "contrary to the terms and conditions of the Collective Agreement."[71] The league disputed this contention. Rather than back down, the association pursued the matter with a test case. An interim injunction was granted for the Province of Alberta in favour of the association on August 10. With the publicity surrounding the case, the federal government got involved because of the Competition Act. Subsequent meetings with the CFL caused them to rescind the regulation, pay $5,000 and $3,000 to the association for costs.[72]

The Players' Association continued to flex its muscles. During the next year, the league directed its member clubs to refrain from holding back a portion of players' salaries. Some clubs held back as much as 25% of a player's pay cheque, paying it all back, less income tax, at the end of the season. It was a handy source of cash flow for the various clubs during the season. Some clubs depended on that source to keep them going. Cal Murphy "estimated that withholding would provide additional cash flow of $28,000 per week while it would cost $11,000 in interest to borrow the equivalent amount from the bank." The Players' Association would only allow a hold-back if the other clubs or the league would guarantee that it would be paid in case of a club's inability to do so. The league refused. Any hold-backs in the clubs' possession were to be given to the players "forthwith."[73]

The collective agreement between the CFL and its Players' Association was due to expire June 14. The league's position was overseen in its negotiations by Hugh Campbell, Edmonton's General Manager. In his summary to the league he "reported that the Players' Association negotiating team is fully aware that the clubs cannot afford to increase monetary benefits at this time" so the discussions were concentrating on non-monetary issues.[74]

In money matters, the CFL and the players decided to bury the concept of the All Star game. In its stead, each club was to pay a grant of $1,200 to the CFLPA and "require its head coach to participate in the Association Awards Dinner." Other compensation deals were struck: Pre-season payments would be $200, $225, and $300 for one-year veterans, with an extra $100 added to each category for each of the next two years. Play-off byes were worth $1,800 in 1989 and $2,000 in '90 and '91. Finals were worth $2,400 for each year, while Grey Cup winners received $12,000 and losers $6,000, the players not to "participate in any further income from the Grey Cup Game in 1989 and 1990 but will in 1991."[75]

The league also received a report prepared by Angus Reid Associates. The polling organization conducted a survey of 1,506 adult Canadians in 1988 of whom three quarters were classified as sports fans and two thirds of those or 753 representing 50% of the adult Canadian population comprised the "CFL audience." The findings were interesting: major changes to the rules were not supported, neither were four down football, eliminating the point on a missed field goal, nor "reducing import restrictions would enhance the appeal of the CFL."[76] Perhaps it was with this survey in mind that the CFL rules committee proposed only minor changes to the game. Bill Baker, attending his tenth rules meeting, his first as the league's chief operating officer, stated: "Everybody in the room wanted to play Canadian football rather than something else."[77]

In the East, the Winnipeg Blue Bombers and Toronto Argonauts, each with a 7–11 record, met in Toronto's SkyDome with the Blue Bombers victorious by a 30–7 score in the play-off game. Probably, the Argos' loss was the main reason for the decision to fire Bob O'Billovich as Argo head coach. In the division final, Winnipeg was edged out by first-place finisher Hamilton by a 14–10 score, putting the revitalized Tiger-Cats into the Grey Cup Game once again. Ralph Sazio retired from the Argos, attending his last meeting February 23 in Hamilton where his career started in 1950. The League gave a vote of thanks to Sazio who was described as an "influential force on the league's governing body since February 1968 and previously had distinguished himself as a player and coach since the 1950 season."[78] Sazio's replacement with the Argos was Mike McCarthy whom the club hired from Hamilton in November of 1989.

In the West, the Edmonton Eskimos, led by the outstanding quarterbacking of Tracy Ham, finished in first place with an impressive 16–

2 record. Third-place Saskatchewan (9–9) defeated the Stampeders in Calgary 33–26. The Roughriders continued their march by humbling the mighty Eskimos in Edmonton by a 32–21 margin to represent the West.

The Roughriders always seemed to be "getting by," were always looking to "next year," always appeared to be perilously close to folding, as had Hamilton lately. Both teams were a "long standing cultural obsession"[79] in their respective communities, their only professional sports franchise. There was a strong bond, historically, between the citizens and their football team. "The fortunes of both franchises have fluctuated, at times fan support has wavered. But there is too much baggage, too much personal history tied up in their lore for a sport-watching citizen of either place to completely let them go."[80]

While Hamilton had won more than its share of Grey Cups, Saskatchewan, since its first appearance in 1923, had only won once, in 1966. Nineteen eighty-nine was only the second time since 1977 that the team had even made the play-offs. Its Western Division win against Edmonton brought 1,000 delirious fans to the airport to welcome home the team. "Rider Pride" was alive and well not only in Regina but in all of Saskatchewan. Ever since 1948 they had been a provincial team forging links to a province wide community through dinners, bingos, memberships and with as many Saskatchewan natives among their non-import contingent as possible. Fans drove from miles around to Regina to watch their team play, streamers and pompoms of green and white waving.

Amongst the fanfare, however, the Schenley Distillery Company had decided that it no longer would sponsor the CFL's Outstanding Player Awards. Ever since the first presentation was made to Billy Vessels in 1953, the Schenley Awards had been synonymous with outstanding achievement in the CFL. By 1989, however, the firm decided that the "considerable moneys" spent each year "did not increase sales and therefore could no longer be justified."[81]

Yet another tradition was being questioned. The Miss Grey Cup competition was coming under closer scrutiny. Jo-Anne Polak, the Ottawa Rough Rider's general manager, and Morrey Rae Hutnick, the CFL's director of marketing, both of whom were in their first year with the league, questioned the contest. President Bill Baker asked "whether there would be any objections from the clubs if the Miss Grey Cup pageant were discontinued."[82] Dr. Ross Brown of Winnipeg seemed to speak for the majority when he stated that such a decision should be made by the league rather than the local Grey Cup Organizing Committee. Handwritten notes in the margin of Winnipeg's minutes expressed the thought that "Jo-Anne and Morrey Rae aren't running the league yet."[83]

Nonetheless, there was some concern in Toronto that the days for such beauty contests were long past, that people in that city would not support such a concept. As late as October, "Miss Hutnick advised that it was not planned to hold the Grey Cup Pageant as had been done in previous years."[84] It was not a universally accepted position. A compromise was put into effect after much behind-the-scenes discussion. "Each club could send its Grey Cup Ambassador who would make appearances at various functions without any contest between them ... [and] one of the ladies should be named Miss Grey Cup since the league has not made any decision to discontinue the event."[85]

Both the Saskatchewan and Hamilton teams had held their pep rallies prior to the 1989 Grey Cup Game but Saskatchewan was making the greater impression. The team had been shut out of the week's awards doled out by the CFL. Edmonton and Hamilton representatives won those. Tracy Ham, Rod Connop, and Danny Bass received the Outstanding Player, Offensive Lineman, and Defensive Player awards respectively. Hamilton's Rocky Di Pietro and Stephen Jordan garnered the Canadian and Rookie Awards. After all, they were the two top teams in the country, according to the season's standings. Saskatchewan almost seemed like an aberration. Ms Saskatchewan, Pheona Wright, "won" the Ms Grey Cup Pageant. Wright was described as "a woman of the nineties, a Fine Arts student, raised on a hog farm who worked summers for the Department of Highways driving oil trucks and spreading gravel."[86]

Toronto's SkyDome, the site of the Grey Cup Game, provided a stark contrast to the upcoming game. "I'd hate to try to sell it [the game] if it weren't for the 'Dome"[87] said Peter Labbett, Chairman of the Festival Committee. The up-to-date technical marvel with its retractable roof ensured that the "game is a far greater draw because it will be played under perfect conditions ... spectators won't have to bundle up. They can dress for a dinner out, drive to the dome and then enjoy the game in comfort."[88] Ticket prices were scaled at $100 for Skyboxes, $70 for between the goal-lines, $60 for most end zone seats, and $50 for the worst seats, those from which the Jumbotron viewing screen could not be seen. Some would also be able to see the game from Windows, the restaurant overlooking the field, an item which had not escaped the attention of the Argos or the league who were negotiating for a fee per person from Windows, the restaurant, of up to $60 for the Grey Cup Game. It all seemed so efficient, so "taking care of business." To some, Toronto seemed unaware of the game. "All this national festival east versus west stuff is just too hokey for the urban sophisticate to fathom ... the hub of western civilization remained unaltered by a football game between the teams of two hick towns."[89]

Prior to the Grey Cup Game, expatriates and those in Toronto for the game gathered at Maple Leaf Gardens for a pep rally. Harold Ballard had made the arena available at their request for $15,000, considerably less than he would normally charge. It was a three-hour display of enthusiasm. There was the Pride of the Lions Marching Band waving green toques and playing stirring music. Also present were Premier Grant Devine, Gainer the Gopher, Toronto Maple Leafs' Wendel Clark, and the Flame, Sandy Monteith, who jetted a stream of fire from his appropriately coloured helmet. The most popular welcome was saved for two Saskatchewan legends, Ron Lancaster and George Reed, imports who stayed. There was a party atmosphere: youths in long, green underwear, grandmotherly types with bouquets of white and green balloons, cheerleaders, a mock arrest and booing of someone dressed up as a Hamilton fan. Once again, the West was demonstrating how to turn the Grey Cup Game into a national celebration.

The game was climactic in every sense. It "was the Canadian Football league at its finest—a dizzying series of offensive strikes sprinkled with bone-rattling defence that brought the most remarkable franchise in professional sport its first Grey Cup in 23 years."[90]

A record SkyDome attendance of 54,088 fans saw Dave Ridgeway kick the winning 35-yard field goal on the second last play of the game edging the equally magnificent Tiger-Cats 43–40. It was described as "Blue Collar Football" by Hamilton's coach Al Bruno, and "the best Grey Cup Game ever" by many others. It was a tonic for all. "In a province still battered by poor harvests and a weak agricultural economy, the success of the Roughriders has been the biggest news in every region of Saskatchewan in the past week."[91] Typical of the reactions was the report: "For the third successive year, the CFL produced a stunning Grey Cup game. The financially troubled league is consistently written off, yet has produced three wonderful endings to three of its darkest seasons."[92]

The game produced 15 Grey Cup records including most points scored in a game, some electrifying moments, a magnificent catch by Tony Champion to pull the Tiger-Cats into the lead with 44 seconds to go, superb quarterbacking by Saskatchewan's Kent Austin who was selected as the game's Most Valuable Player, and of course Dave Ridgeway's winning field goal with time running out. He was selected the winner of the Dick Suderman Trophy as the Outstanding Canadian in the game. Meanwhile, back in Regina:

> Within an hour of the game's conclusion, traffic on Regina's main arteries had ground to a standstill as Roughrider fans whooped and waved banners and flags from the backs of their pick-up trucks. Albert Street, the city's main north-south thoroughfare, was shut

down for several kilometres by ecstatic fans who soon abandoned their vehicles and wandered through the streets. The drivers of huge semi-trailers joined in the celebration blowing their foghorns.[93]

When the Roughriders returned home, 18,000 fans went to Taylor Field in -10°C weather to welcome the club. "They drank free hot chocolate, waved green, white and red signs saying 'I love the 'Riders' and sent up cheer after cheer for the Roughriders and everyone associated with the club from the coaches to the ball boys and the office staff."[94]

It was a sober outgoing president, Tom Shepherd, and first-year general manager and former player, Al Ford, who addressed those in attendance of the club's annual meeting less than three weeks later. "Winning the Grey Cup cost the Saskatchewan Roughriders more than a quarter of a million dollars and pushed the team's debt to an almost unmanageable $1.6 million."[95] Ford said that the club would have made a "profit of $85,000 a season but lost $195,000 because of the cost of the three play-off games."[96] The club's "post-season expenses were $280,000,"[97] he said.

The league itself generated $3,944,430 from the 1989 game, compared to $2,211,115 in 1988. Its expenses were higher too ($2,016,598 in '89 compared to $1,574,789 in '88) but its net income was tripled ($1,927,831 against $637,326). Combined with net income from play-off games of $57,053 ($46,985 in '88) the league distributed the money according to finish.

Distribution of Grey Cup and Play-off game Net Income[98]

	1989		1988	
	Percent	Amount	Percent	Amount
Saskatchewan	15.0	$297,732	12.0	$82,117
Hamilton	14.0	277,884	12.0	82,117
Winnipeg	12.5	248,111	15.0	102,647
Edmonton	12.5	248,111	12.5	85,539
Calgary	12.0	238,186	11.0	75,274
Toronto	12.0	238,186	12.5	85,539
B.C.	11.0	218,337	14.0	95,804
Ottawa	11.0	218,337	11.0	75,274
Totals:	100.0	$1,984,884	100.0	$684,311

Public perception and economic reality were two serious concerns facing the CFL as it entered the nineties. According to Ron Lancaster, former outstanding quarterback with Saskatchewan and currently a commentator with the CBC, perception was the "league's main problem ... we are not perceived as a first class operation." The league had gone "downhill" in that area; it had to work "like heck to get that perception back." The point was driven home to Lancaster during a post-Grey Cup luncheon. When Tiger-Cat receiver Tony Champion, playing with a severe rib injury, made an outstanding twisting catch in the end zone to tie the game at 40 points apiece. The superlative play was described to Lancaster as a "Superbowl catch," not "a great catch ... [they] compared it to an NFL feat." That perception, "that the CFL is somehow second class even when the league puts on one of its greatest shows, that bothers Lancaster. The league needs someone at the top that people know. The person has to have a deep concern for the league, be willing to commit himself for the long term and have credibility with football people."[99] Just as much of a concern to Lancaster was the view that the league was living "too much in the past." In a reference to the public having lost identification with the present-day CFL, he was of the opinion that "the fans know who played in the past. They know about Jackie Parker's famous touchdown run in '54, but they don't know about today's stars."[100] It became obvious as the year progressed that the CFL's two-man leadership team was in trouble. The league seemed to understand how the twin commissioners it appointed in January of 1989 were supposed to function but did anyone else? You could never tell exactly who was in charge at any given moment, possibly because no one really was. Sometimes Bill Baker, the president and chief operating officer appeared to be the boss but then statements from Roy McMurtry, the chairman and chief executive officer, sounded equally authoritative. Were these fellows interchangeable, overlapping, or redundant to the same degree? Who could tell? Another worse possibility arose. In the confusion the fans might cease to care. Two heads are better than one, the old saying goes, but that didn't apply to the CFL. The set-up had only one virtue, a highly dubious one: when things went wrong, blame would be harder to lay.[101]

By the first week in October, Bill Baker had resigned effective December 31, 1989. Family and personal concerns were cited as reasons as well as the frustrations presented by the twin arrangement. Baker was said to have had a "pass rushers mentality," with a clear goal of reaching the quarterback, "cognizant that a single hesitant stride is a step towards failure."[102] He was said to have maintained his "lineman's mindset," his term as CFL president characterized by "setting objectives and chasing them down ... [He] believes in meeting confrontation head on, forcing issues and figuratively speaking, butting heads."[103]

The CFL formed a search committee of three men to find a successor. It was chaired by Roy McMurtry and included Tiger-Cat owner David Braley and Eskimo President Bill Gardiner. Ralph Sazio for one was calling for a return to a single commissioner.[104] The experiment was over. The public seemed to be confused by the titles president, chief operating officer, chairman, and chief executive officer—either that, or they were confused by the numerous stories during 1989 which hinted at friction between the two men in charge of CFL operations. In any event, the resignation of Bill Baker paved the way for the return of the title "commissioner" and the discontinuation of "president" and "chief operating officer."[105]

In the end, it appeared that financial reality won out over public perception. The CFL announced that its new commissioner was Donald "the name is Crump not Trump" Crump,[106] a chartered accountant who in his position with Maple Leaf Gardens and the Tiger-Cats, both Harold Ballard operations, had "a great deal of experience in how to tie down loose cannons."[107]

Crump's background as a chartered accountant with Peat, Marwick, Muthed and Company, Revenue Canada, Famous Players Canada, Canadian Tire Corp. Ltd., and Bushnell Television, in addition to his work as treasurer of Maple Leaf Gardens and the alternate governor of the CFL's Tiger-Cats, was greeted with mixed enthusiasm by league personnel. There were those who suggested that "Crump's strong financial background [was what] the CFL needed these days. We have to get our financial situation in shape so we can function in an efficient manner within our fiscal restraints."[108]

Not all were convinced. The president of the Edmonton Eskimos, Bill Gardiner, and Calgary's general manager, Norm Kwong, "questioned whether the CFL needs Crump's financial brains at this time. Someone more personable and able to sell tickets might have been a better choice."[109] At times the CFL appeared to be fractured; clubs seemed to carry on their competitive stance off the field. So much so that Crump was photographed bringing a five metre-long bull whip into his office.[110]

If there was one issue that typified the growing sniping among the clubs, it was the area of "free agency." It surfaced between British Columbia and Winnipeg. Lary Khuharich left Calgary after the 1989 season and became B.C.'s Head Coach and Director of Football Personnel. Noted for his volatile personality, he had first raised the ire of Winnipeg's Cal Murphy in 1988 when he signed free agent Scott Flagel, a six year Bomber veteran. Now, in 1990, Khuharich was saying that "he thought some of the Stampeders 'will matriculate to the B.C. Lions.'"[111] Murphy had his staff telephone newspapers in Vancouver "looking for stories in which Khuharich talked about the possibility of some Stampeders following him to B.C."[112] In 1989, there were three free agents who changed teams. Notable among them was

Damon Allen who signed with Ottawa "two days after his contract expired ... provoked angry cries from the Eskimos of tampering."[113]

While it was always professed publicly that there were no "under the table" deals between clubs to ensure compensation for free agents, it soon became obvious that some clubs were operating with such an understanding. Edmonton's Joe Faragalli threatened a bidding war: "Obviously we've got more money to spend than most people and players want to come here. But is that any good for the league? We've got to have some sanity here. I think either there has to be some compensation when free agents are signed, which is our personal philosophy with the Eskimos, or maybe we should just not have it in our league."[114]

Despite expressing concerns about their very real financial difficulties, the clubs appeared to be unable to live within their means. Every club had exceeded the $3,000,000 "competitive expenditures" limit for the 1988 season.[115] For example, Winnipeg's Mike Riley, the CFL Coach of the Year, stunned the Blue Bombers and their supporters when he announced he was leaving to take an assistant coaching job in the U.S. with Stanford University.[116] The announcement seemed to serve its purpose: he was signed to a contract to coach the Blue Bombers for the 1989 season.

Some wondered just how serious the financial problem was; others saw action by Calgary and Ottawa as being a sign that they were interested in fielding the best teams that they could, regardless of financial worries. When the Toronto Argonauts left their top offensive lineman, Dan Ferrone, unprotected during the league's equalization draft, they believed he would be unclaimed. After all, they reasoned, Ferrone was 30 years old, was earning in the range of $85,000 as the Argos' "highest paid Canadian," and with the combination of his age and salary "he might slip by."[117] The Calgary Stampeders, financially strapped or not, acted otherwise. They claimed the respected lineman with no hesitation, much to the chagrin of the Argos. In Edmonton where heir apparent Damon Allen played out his option, the Eskimos were shocked when the Ottawa Rough Riders signed the "free agent" to a contract for the 1989 season. They were stunned for three reasons. Allen was being counted on as the long-term quarterback since Matt Dunigan had been traded to B.C. for the 1988 season. There had been in the past a gentleman's agreement that players playing out their option would not be pursued by member CFL teams. Perhaps the overall cause of chagrin in Edmonton was that the Rough Riders, whose financial problems were well-publicized and who were in a sense being supported by the very solvent Eskimos, would spend the money for a high salary when Edmonton was not prepared to do so. In the end, however, new coach Steve Goldman, who had been the offensive coordinator with Edmonton and knew Allen well, would prevail. The move propelled Tracy Ham into Edmonton's starting quarterback position.

The Eskimos were able to exact a high price from B.C. Lions for the 1988 trade of Dunigan. At the time of the deal the Eskimos granted receiver Jim Sandusky and "future considerations." The "future" arrived in January of 1989. Sent to the Eskimos to complete the deal were linebackers Gregg Stumon and Jeff Braswell, running back Reggie Taylor, defensive back André Francis, and B.C.'s first-round draft choice who turned out to be linebacker Leroy Blugh. According to Edmonton's coach Joe Faragalli: "The B.C. Lions got the huge diamond; Edmonton Eskimos get the six rubies."[118] B.C.'s general manager Joe Galat described the deal as an attempt to "not let them have any of our untouchables and we bought them off basically with more players."[119] His reference was to the original terms of the deal. B.C. was to "protect two players on their roster; Edmonton would select one of the unprotected players. B.C. would protect another player and the Esks would choose again."[120] The revised deal not only protected B.C.'s "untouchables," but it also helped the club to trim its already high players' budget.

The whole matter festered and became a consideration in the league's fourth equalization draft. The last-place teams in each division, Ottawa in the East with a 4–14 record and B.C. in the West with a 7–11 performance, were to be recipients of the draft. Some general managers balked at allowing B.C. to take part. Toronto and Winnipeg both had the same record in the East. Whereas B.C. finished fourth in the West, the Argos and Blue Bombers made the play-offs in the East. Winnipeg's Cal Murphy, perhaps still incensed that B.C.'s Lary Khuharich had suggested that "maybe Cal needs to get a dictionary to look up the term 'matriculation,'"[121] explained: "If we're going to let B.C. take people, why shouldn't we? We had the same record."[122]

The B.C. Lions did not endear themselves to their league partners when they announced that they had signed free agents Chris Major and Larry Willis from Calgary's roster and followed later with Ray Alexander. But the biggest collective shock was registered in what was described as "one of the most memorable press conferences held in Ottawa,"[123] the Ottawa Rough Riders announced the signing of five free agents and the acquisition of two players by trades. The "free agents" were: Glenn Kulka, Toronto; David Williams and Anthony Cherry, B.C.; John Mandarich, Edmonton; and Bryon Illerbrun, Saskatchewan. Those traded to the Riders were Terry Baker from Saskatchewan and Rob Smith from B.C. Later, the team that some had dubbed the "Rough Raiders," acquired their sixth free agent: Gregg Stumon from the Eskimos.

Reactions were "swift and for the most part, bitter."[124] The Riders "took money out of our pockets and now they're buying our players,"[125] said Joe Faragalli. He was referring to the fact that the league agreed to freeze Ottawa's $750,000 debt to 1993. Faragalli, among others, agitated "to force the Riders to pay back that sum immediately."[126] Calgary's Normie Kwong was "deeply disappointed." The Stampeders were also deep in debt. He criticized the Rough Riders for their "total disregard for their seven partners … others besides them have to win too."[127] The Toronto Argonauts' general manager Mike McCarthy was concerned "that the Riders' actions would disrupt the league's salary scale and financial position."[128] Joe Zuger in Hamilton commented that it was "wrong to have other teams doing their work for them … an admission that the Riders don't have the ability to go out and find players within the financial structure."[129] The Argos cancelled a proposed planned scrimmage with Ottawa in Kingston on June 23, the profits of which were to go to amateur football in Kingston. Ottawa reacted to charges that the team was ignoring the salary structure and cap. Jo-Anne Polack countered that her team was $140,000 under the $3,000,000 salary cap in 1989 and "besides, how we spend the $3,000,000 is up to us."[130]

There was open questioning as to how a team like Ottawa, so mired in debt, could sign David Williams from B.C. for a reported $125,000 compared to the average for wide receivers of $54,000; John Mandarich and Glenn Kulka were said to have signed for $100,000 and $80,000, the average for defensive linemen being $56,000 in 1989. Offensive lineman Bryon Illerbrun was to receive $80,000, compared to the average of $53,000. Anthony Cherry had turned down $55,000 from B.C. and joined the Rough Riders for $75,000.

Perhaps seeing the writing on the wall, Ottawa announced that they would not participate in the equalization draft. In the meantime, the Argos, Stampeders, Bombers, and Eskimos announced they would not contribute any players to it. B.C. was undaunted; they wanted the draft to continue. CFL Commissioner Donald Crump put the best face on the situation: "I can understand the other teams' being annoyed. But if as a result of these moves, the league becomes more exciting and Ottawa ends up with a winning team and contributes to the gate equalization plan, then maybe something good will come out of all of this."[131]

Later that day the CFL commissioner announced the cancellation of the CFL equalization draft, trying in the process to put a positive spin on the whole matter. "The exciting events of the past several days seem to demonstrate that there is a definite effort being made by the teams to create parity among the member clubs of the CFL! Because of that, it seems unnecessary to hold the draft so it's hereby cancelled."[132]

It was, indeed, hard to tell that teams were cash-starved, judging from the way quarterbacks were being wooed to come to the CFL. Saskatchewan courted and won over Notre Dame quarterback Tony Rice. The B.C. Lions had both West Virginia's Major Harris and Boston's New England Patriot Doug Flutie on its negotiation list. The mixed messages being sent to the public about finances continued. The Stampeders announced a $1.4 million loss for the 1989 season, almost double their $764,000 loss in 1988. With a total deficit of $4.2 million, it was anticipated that in excess of $400,000 would be needed just to pay the interest on the debt in 1990. It meant that even if the Stampeders drew 11,000 more fans in 1990, it would be no further ahead financially.[133] Ottawa was reportedly asking the CFL to "turn a blind eye" to the $750,000 it owed to the league, much as was done with the B.C. Lions' $800,000 debt when Murray Pezim bought the club.[134] The Edmonton Eskimos, the league's most stable franchise, reported that it had a profit of $13,000 for the 1989 season, "the second year in a row the Eskimos have made a profit, a feat that unfortunately has not been matched by any other CFL club."[135]

Cancelled though the equalization draft was, the "raiding war" on free agents continued. The Edmonton Eskimos signed Keith Gooch as a free agent from B.C. In signing Gooch they made no mention of reimbursement, whereas when they signed Hamilton free agent Mike Walker, Hugh Campbell proposed to compensate the Tiger-Cats saying that "he believes in compensation for signing a free agent because it tends to keep a team competitive."[136] Even Winnipeg ventured into the fray by signing free agent receiver Eric Streater from the B.C. Lions. He was the 12th player to switch teams under free agency. Calgary was once again struck when the Argonauts reclaimed Dan Ferrone. The popular lineman had been taken by Calgary in the 1989 equalization draft and had played out his option. Calgary's Normie Kwong pressed Toronto for compensation, something which Mike McCarthy seemed to lean towards. The whole situation prompted Ed Molstad of the Players' Association to issue a statement against collusion. He aimed straight at Hugh Campbell, describing his "admission that he'll compensate Hamilton as an overt breach of the Collective Agreement and that the Association will act on it if Campbell doesn't back off."[137] Reports were that the commissioner, Donald Crump, "shrugged it off as a normal course of business."[138]

It did appear that money was a problem in the league. If not, why all the players declaring themselves "free agents"? Some left to find greener pastures over the border to the United States; Gill Fenerty, Tony Champion, Gerald Alphin, and Romel Andrews were among the 10 who did so. Yet there were others, some 12 in all, who were unsigned by their clubs because the clubs said they couldn't afford them. Yet they were coveted and given contracts with other CFL clubs.

Even a "blockbuster" trade involving Toronto and B.C. added to the controversy and at the same time seemed to be considered part of the solution. The Argos sent quarterback Rick Johnson, linebackers Willie Pless and Tony Visco, slot-back Emmanuel Tolbert, defensive back Todd Wiseman, and defensive tackle Jerald Baylis to B.C. in return for disgruntled quarterback Matt Dunigan. A further trade saw the Argos receive James "Quick" Parker and a 1991 fifth-draft choice from B.C. in return for the rights to quarterback Major Harris, the highly touted player from West Virginia.

In May, Matt Dunigan was traded; in March the quarterback's agent announced that B.C. did not honour a verbal commitment to reimburse Dunigan for bonuses and appearances. "The lapsed payments were critical in Dunigan's demand for a trade after two seasons with the Lions."[139] Therefore, said the agent, B.C. lawyer Peter Perrick, Dunigan was declaring himself a free agent. When the quarterback left the Lions, he was under contract for $205,000. It was said that his goal was to sign a contract with Toronto for $300,000, topping the previously highest CFL contract of Tom Clements, quarterback with Winnipeg in 1987. The Argos had offered, and were turned down, a $240,000 contract before Dunigan signed with the club. General Manager Mike McCarthy would only confirm that the agreement was for "more than $1 and less that $1 million."[140]

League relations appeared to be even more strained when Argonaut owner Harry Ornest criticized publicly the league's decision to play the 1991 Grey Cup Game in Winnipeg. At the heart of the issue was money. The Grey Cup Game and television revenues were considered primary assets in generating profits. Weather in the west during late November play-off games had reached folkloric proportions. Visions of blizzards, gales, frozen fields, and numbing temperatures were conjured up. The NFL, it was said, would never allow its Super Bowl to be played in an open arena in the north, not even in Chicago and New York, if ideal playing conditions couldn't be guaranteed. Indeed, Western teams in the CFL (most would argue that Winnipeg was in the west even though the Blue Bombers played in the Eastern Division) had generally been in favour of finishing the season earlier. They wanted to avoid the type of late November weather often striking the west "so that a play-off game can be played under the kind of conditions that allow the athletes to put on their best show."[141]

Critics of the CFL's decision to award Winnipeg the 1991 Grey Cup Game were more in favour of alternating the game between domed stadiums in Toronto and B.C. "The concept of moving the league's showcase game around the country is a noble one ... [but] it isn't likely to be a profitable one. And without profit, there will be no league and noble motives won't matter."[142] An incensed Cal Murphy took dead aim at Harry Ornest, asking that the question be put on the league's agenda in order "to squelch speculation"[143] that Winnipeg was about to lose the game. Murphy, citing recent Grey Cup Games in Edmonton and Calgary, complained that Winnipeg was "being singled out unfairly. It's a [Toronto Argonaut owner] Harry Ornest issue." Ornest's rebuttal was blunt: "What I'm trying to do is insure that Cal has a football job for a long time even if he doesn't realize it. With some of the recent neanderthal thinking by guys who haven't got a dime invested in the league, one would think that we were as successful as the National Football league and I'm including Cal Murphy."[144] Winnipeg was confirmed as host of the '91 game. The league "agreed to establish a 'business plan' that would cover all future Grey Cups."[145]

When the CFL agreed to a new television contract with Carling O'Keefe Breweries, the two-year agreement was to begin in 1990 and called for $12 million plus "promotional support" of an additional $3 million. Within those figures, the league had to address two Toronto concerns because of the change in its blackout policy. The CFL was experimenting with the lifting of the blackout in its large southern Ontario market. In the process, however, it meant that the contracts the Argos had were being bent, if not broken. Radio station CFRB, the "exclusive voice of the Argos," cancelled its contract. The Argos made a hurried agreement with CJCL but the decision cost the Argos $100,000 in lost revenue for the 1988 season. In addition, the Exhibition Stadium Corporation was also suing "for a share of the revenue received for lifting the blackout ... approximately $180,000."[146] The television revenues were to cover those expenses.

The CFL announced that for the first time since 1984, its games would be shown on American television. There was to be little financial return to the league since the American rights holder Molson Brewery sold the package to Sports Channel America. The latter also carried NHL games and would telecast 23 live CFL games including the Grey Cup from Vancouver. League officials were happy. More than 10 million cable households were served in the U.S. in the country's top five markets—New York, Chicago, New England, Philadelphia, and San Francisco.[147] Commissioner Donald Crump tied the two circumstances together: "With the league back on TV in the United States, having players of this calibre [Harris, Flutie and Rice] playing in the CFL will entice even more good players to come up here. I think signing all three would be a big deal."[148] Echoing that line was Winnipeg's Cal Murphy: "When players aren't able to see the games on TV, Canada is a real foreign country to players."[149] Short term gain was not a consideration as far as Crump was concerned: "I think by showing there is interest in the United States it will help us attract investors for next year."[150]

At the CFL's Rules Committee meetings in Edmonton, where only minor changes were made, the major news was that Saskatchewan's John Gregory was selected winner of the Annis Stukus Trophy for coach of the year. In return for Saskatchewan's first Grey Cup win since 1966, Gregory was rewarded by General Manager Alan Ford even before the regular season ended. His contract was extended "through the 1990 season with the proviso that they would discuss a further extension" prior to the start of the schedule.[151] Gregory showed up at the Awards Dinner wearing "a set of suspenders only a coach could love. Little men in striped shirts ran up either side, their eyes covered by their hands."[152] He also presented his Hamilton counterpart Al Bruno "with a referee doll, complete with arms, legs and a head that could be pulled off."[153]

It was a reference to Bruno's "'heat of the moment' shots at the officiating"[154] in the 1989 Grey Cup Game. Gregory had expressed the thought that "hopefully we'll never be in the ditch again. It's nice to be on the highway rather than in the ditch."[155] It was also a recognition that "no matter how good a coach you are, you might be only a missed call, a missed block or a missed player away from the unemployment line. In the here today, gone tomorrow world of coaching you get your kicks when you can."[156]

The reality of that statement hit home, East and West, midway through the 1990 season. In Hamilton, popular Al Bruno, the longest-serving head coach in the CFL, was released. He had begun the season in some controversy when owner David Braley offered him a one-year contract with "a 5% pay cut from his estimated $100,000 salary."[157] Bruno accepted, grudgingly, only after the owner's "assurance that his assistants got a raise."[158] By late September, Bruno was replaced by David Beckman, director of player personnel. The Tiger-Cats had lost five games in a row. Forgotten was Bruno's accomplishments of four Grey Cup appearances and a 1986 win over Edmonton and his "knack for inspiring his charges to great heights in post-season play."[159]

In British Columbia, what seemed to be at first glance a promising relationship was becoming a "circus." When owner Murray Pezim, the self-styled "world's greatest promoter," bought the Lions, one of his first acts was to hire former star quarterback Joe Kapp, the Lions' quarterback from the sixties, to return as club president and general manager. Pezim was quick to seek to influence the CFL. He advocated expansion into the United States saying without it the league was going "nowhere ... You'll just get duller and duller. You can't keep giving them [fans] what you've been giving them."[160] In turn, former Calgary coach Lary Khuharich was signed on as head coach. The team was constantly in the news, not all of it connoting stability. Free agent losses and gains were recorded, each one having a domino effect. Matt Dunigan's trade set off a search for quarterback replacements and the eventual signing of Major Harris and Doug Flutie. Harris's agent accused Joe Kapp of lacking integrity.[161] He charged the Lions president with preparing a "lower priced contract" than one discussed and agreed to the previous evening in negotiations. Kapp replied that figures "discussed the night before were only proposals, not an actual offer."[162] Harris eventually signed after coach Lary Khuharich was sent to Pittsburgh to talk with the quarterback. The former West Virginia standout became disenchanted, however, as Doug Flutie and Joe Pao Pao became the Lions' choices to play.

B.C. was attempting to forge new ties with the community, to heighten its visibility in the province. Joe Kapp began a Team-Up program "designed to integrate the club and its players into the community through a series of tie-ins with service, charity, community groups and corporate sponsors."[163] Premier Bill Vander Zalm agreed to be the team's honorary head coach, "a signing that gives a whole new meaning to the term political football,"[164] suggested one wag. It was part of Kapp's community bonding, to show "support from our leader, making a statement to the public that the Lions are important."[165]

Murray Pezim was seen on Vancouver's Howe Street, complete with the B.C. Lions cheerleaders, trying to convince his stock market friends to buy season tickets and proving that he was "the world's greatest promoter."[166] Promotion was the name of the game. The Lions were back in the public eye. Former NFL player Mark Gastineau was brought in to generate more publicity, sell season tickets and encourage speculation that he might suit up to play defensive end for the Lions. He actually did suit up and played in the Lions' first game, a 38–38 overtime thriller with Calgary. Gastineau blocked a field goal attempt, after which B.C. scored a touchdown. However, he did not live up to the pre-season hype surrounding him and did not finish the season.

At times it was like a three-ring circus, the spotlight shifting from Khuharich to Kapp to "the Pez." Then the beam faded as it moved from one to the other, finally resting on "the Pez." Defensive coordinator and linebacker coach Charlie West was first to go. He "quit because he couldn't get along with Khuharich"[167] even though the two had known each other and had worked on the same coaching staff with Kapp at the University of California in 1982–83. Former Lions' player Jim Young, who had been an assistant coach in 1989 and was described as a "marketing gopher for Kapp and Khuharich,"[168] replaced him. Next to leave was Larry Dauterive who was in charge of quarterbacks, receivers, and running backs. He originally came to the Lions with the hope of working with his former college quarterback Matt Dunigan. His replacement was Jim Young who was given the additional duties of receiving and running back coach. Meanwhile, as the Lions moved into their season, it became obvious that there were trouble spots. Major Harris played little; Doug Flutie sporadically. The most impressive quarterbacks were the young Rick Foggie and a rejuvenated Joe Pao Pao. B.C.'s attendance going into September was averaging around 34,000 but the club had won only two games, by one and two points. When the Lions played a home-and-home series with Toronto the first week in September the light shifted. In a game which set a CFL record for points scored, the Argos defeated the Lions 68–43 in Toronto. In the return match before more than 36,000 at B.C. Place the Argos completed their rout by posting a 49–19 win. It was the end for Khuharich and Kapp. Young became interim head coach and general manager, then acting head Coach and vice president of business operations. Murray Pezim hired Bob O'Billovich to take over as head coach, declaring that "the circus is over."[169] Not quite. Kapp lingered in the spotlight calling Pezim "an idiot"[170] and Jim Young "a hood ornament."[171] "I've been to Hollywood," said Kapp, "and I'll tell you there's nothing that compares with this zoo."[172] O'Billovich was not able to take over the new position until after a game with Edmonton. Young's appointment caused one reporter to comment that "there are two options here. Either Young is a football genius or he's one of Murray Pezim's favourite people."[173] When B.C. player Doug "Tank" Landry, a former Argo who had played for O'Billovich before being traded to Calgary, announced first he wouldn't play for O'Billovich and then said he would, it was left for "the Pez" to declare the circus over. Some were doubtful: "At least that's what we think he said. It was hard to hear over the noise of the calliope."[174]

Aside from the turmoil in British Columbia, the Lions had a league-wide impact in at least two other areas. On the playing field a style of play reminiscent of the late sixties and early seventies was making a comeback. Canadian football has always placed a premium on the mobile quarterback. Offensive systems incorporated straight drop-back passes but in order to add another dimension, the roll-out pass was integrated into the scheme. That style of play was one in which the quarterback moved his pocket of protection and rolled out wide from the centre with depth before moving towards the line of scrimmage. Defensive personnel would not know whether the quarterback was intending to run or pass. The quarterback, for his part, did either one depending on the play of the defensive person's reaction. Eventually, defensive teams saw the manoeuvre so often that they developed pre-determined reactions to it.

Offensive teams went back to the black-board and developed what some coaches called a "dash" style of play. Russ Jackson in the sixties used it very effectively. The quarterback in this style dropped back in a normal way; the defence went into its drop-back passing mode. After a five- or seven-step drop by the quarterback, he would "dash" to one side or another. In effect, it might look as if it were a "broken play," the quarterback being flushed out of the protective pocket. But it was a designed tactic, a move to effect a roll-out style after first indicating a drop back pass. The Lions' Doug Flutie and Joe Pao Pao were masters of the deceptive art, each one presenting a unique problem. Edmonton's coach Joe Faragalli rated the two: "Each guy presents a different thing. Flutie scares you with his running ability. Joe has that quick release. He hits the seams."[175]

The Lions' play had a subtle effect, the fact that it had four good quarterbacks helped to make a league-wide change. Much publicity had been generated with the courting and signing of quarterbacks Tony Rice, Doug Flutie, and Major Harris. The Lions also had the veteran Joe Pao Pao, having released Rickie Foggie who was picked up by Toronto. In Saskatchewan, Kent Austin and Jeff Bentrim were veteran quarterbacks. Tom Burgess had been dealt to the Blue Bombers in July. The result was that once the league settled into its season, players who were used to attract fans to the park, the "quarterbacks of the future," were not able to dress and gain any game experience. The league decided to expand its rosters to 37, allowing three quarterbacks to be dressed for each game.[176]

Some took it as another lost opportunity to develop a Canadian quarterback: "Ludicrous, absolutely ludicrous" was the way Larry Uteck, a former CFL player and head coach of St Mary's Huskies, describe it. "Everybody in their right mind knows that no player is developed overnight. Yet here, when the CFL has an opportunity that would enable Canadians to develop at the quarterback position, they blow it."[177] Uteck stated further that what the public really wanted to see was "local talent playing the game."[178]

The Argos' general manager Mike McCarthy responded: "I'm supposed to pay a Canadian kid, let him travel with the team, and then just let him stand on the sidelines holding a football. Come on, get real. If the kid's good enough to play, he'll play. They could be Martians … Chinese … Irish … even Canadians but we've got to go with the best players available."[179] McCarthy was more concerned about the salary cap of $3 million. The Argos were the only team with two quarterbacks on their playing roster;

Matt Dunigan was injured. McCarthy had voted against the three quarter-back proposal and criticized the "little guys," the Winnipegs and Saskatchewans who were "the first guys to bitch about the salary caps ... they can have a bingo to get their money back. We can't."[180]

Controversy continued to swirl around the CFL in a variety of areas. Calgary's coach Wally Buono questioned the ethics of the Argos' coach Don Mathews and his "shoot the lights out" approach. In a game against Hamilton, the Argos set up for a field goal. Lance Chomyc, their place-kicker, ran towards the bench while calling out for his tee. The ball was snapped, Chomyc turned up-field and caught a pass which resulted in a first down and, later, a touchdown. Buono was not impressed: "Although it was a great play, it raises the question of what's ethically right. That's why they got rid of the old sleeper play. You couldn't tell if the guy was leaving the field or not."[181]

In a move to effect savings, the CFL was also planning to change its address. It had been at 1200 Bay Street in Toronto since April 1, 1985, where it leased 8,000 square feet of floor space. During 1989, the cost-conscious league sublet some 60% of its floor space to an advertising agency and was planning to shrink even more. The resulting space was too cramped. The CFL moved to the top floor of a five-storey building at 110 Eglington Ave. West where it had use of 7,300 square feet of space.[182]

As the 1990 season progressed, it became obvious that the CFL was, once again, in trouble. Finances and perception had combined to portray an image of a "minor league." Attendance in two of the league's traditionally strong cities, Toronto and Hamilton, were "down substantially. Torontonians have begun to whisper that the CFL isn't good enough for their 'world class' city and yearn for an NFL team, the prospect of which threatens the viability of a better Canadian product."[183]

It was a sensitive matter. Meanwhile, an NBC news report had NFL Commissioner Paul Taglibue "pushing for an expansion franchise in Toronto." It went on to say: "The Commissioner has been humming a tune that sounds a lot like O Canada."[184] Concurrently it was reported that even though Molson's had "invested more than $10 million in the CFL "in television and marketing rights, it was a trifle strange that former CFL Commissioner, Jake Gaudaur is on its payroll, aiding in the pursuit of an NFL franchise for Toronto."[185] Gaudaur who was inducted into Canada's Sports' Hall of Fame was nonplussed. He had reactivated his management consulting firm. "More importantly, when I walked out of the Commissioner's office for the last time, driving home I took a look back on those forty-four years and felt sort of good about my life's work and decided that I owed the sport nothing and it owed me nothing. I still feel that way today and if that bothers anyone, that's their problem."[186]

Donald Crump was assured that in spite of the NFL's exhibition game in Montreal and the movement of the World League of American Football (WLAF) into Montreal, the new spring league would honour CFL contracts and its own salary structure would be lower than the CFL's minimum scale. The commissioner also met with NFL head Paul Taglibue on September 26. He was assured that the NFL had no plans to expand into Canada for at least 10 years.[187] Much of the uncertainty in the CFL relative to the NFL was due to the failure of the Argos to negotiate an exclusivity lease with SkyDome officials. The CFL wanted a lease which precluded NFL exhibition games; SkyDome officials were unwilling. The league passed a motion that the proposed lease "with the Argonaut Football club includes an undertaking that the Corporation will not permit the stadium to be used for professional football by any club that is not a participating franchise holder in the Canadian Football league or any successor league."[188] That was coupled with the good news that, from 1989, the Argos had earned a profit of $1,000,000 with a season ticket base of 27,600.[189]

One solution advanced was to "sell the Canadian game as boutique football ... to appeal to the true football aficianado."[190] It was proposed that the CFL: (1) eliminate mid-season importing of players; (2) reduce the numbers of imports at all positions to encourage the use of Canadian quarterbacks; (3) concentrate CFL games on a single day (Saturday) with one feature game on Friday evening; (4) eliminate the blackout rule; (5) actively promote the game's distinctive features.

Alison Gordon, writing in the *Toronto Star*,[191] had her own interpretation of what was happening. When asked by a reporter why Canadians were "so mad keen for baseball," her "flippant response" was that it was "because it is American ... part of our famous national inferiority complex that we find more legitimacy in things that are hits south of the border than we do in our home grown accomplishments." She pinpointed the time when Torontonians went overboard for the Blue Jays. It was in 1985 when "our guys beat the Yankees at their own game" winning the divisional pennant, the American league East. "The Blue Jays were at last, in the minds of those who love the phrase, 'world class.'"

Relating how a "world class temple" was built for the "world class team," Gordon wrote that "way in the back of those tiny minds was the hope that one day we would have a world class football team to play there too." She continued: "The Argonauts, of course, are not world class. The CFL is not world class. Everybody know that the only world class football is played in the NFL ... The tiny minds who lust after an NFL franchise for the

SkyDome just wish the CFL would hurry up and die so they can get on with their scheming." Gordon was also aware that the NFL was searching for new markets, part of what she called "sports imperialism." Exhibition games were being played in diverse areas such as England, Japan, and Berlin as well as Canada, wherever the American way was advancing or as she put it: "When democracy comes can NFL football be far behind?" She concluded:

> I would like to believe that Canadians are too smart to throw over their own, much more exciting, brand of football and embrace the phoney glitz and glamour of the American game, but on recent evidence, I can't ... This city wouldn't be the same without the Argos. And the country wouldn't be the same without the Blue Bombers or the Tiger-Cats or the Eskimos or the Rough Riders and the Roughriders. What wonderful names, quirky and anachronistic. The football they play is quirky, too. That's what makes it unique. That's what makes it Canadian. And that's what makes it worth protecting. Uniquely Canadian institutions are becoming endangered species these days ... I plan to fight them with the only weapon I've got. I'm strolling down to the SkyDome and buying a ticket to watch the Boys of Autumn play.

Even Commissioner Donald Crump seemed to be caught up in the "world class" syndrome. He had made the decision to increase the price of the best tickets for the Grey Cup Game to $100, twenty dollars more than they were in 1989 at the SkyDome. He based his decision upon the awareness that they wanted to obtain a certain level of revenue with the number of seats at B.C. Place. When some complained that the seats were overpriced, Crump commented that: "This is a world class city and this is a classy event. A hundred dollars for an event like this is not a world class price."[192]

In fact, Crump was more and more at centre stage as the CFL year wound down. He suspended Ottawa's leading tackler, Bruce Holmes, for one game, for twice taking "viscious swipes at Rickie Foggie's head as the quarterback stepped out of bounds." Holmes had been warned earlier in the season "when he hit a prone John Congemi, knocking the Argo pivot out of the game."[193] Crump defended his decision saying, "someone has to protect the quarterbacks," but Ottawa players weren't so sure of his motivation. Kicker Dean Dorsey typified their prevailing mood: "We have to beat Toronto, the Commissioner and everybody else. They've been screwing us since we signed the free agents."[194] The third-place Rough Riders lost on all counts. The Argos won the play-off game 34–25, only to lose the Eastern Division final to Winnipeg by a 20–17 score. In the West the second-place

Eskimos defeated Saskatchewan 43–27 and then the first-place Stampeders by a 43–23 score.

It was the indifference of Vancouver and the host of empty seats at B.C. Place for the Grey Cup Game that gave the impression of a league again in disarray. "There were 13,000 unsold seats at B.C. Place and about twice that many remained empty."[195] Thousands of tickets were given away to youngsters who later overran the field so as to make the size of the crowd respectable. The CFL had always maintained that the league and the Grey Cup were important nation-building forces, but on the other hand,

> at an event that is advertised as a unifying force in this country, the national anthem was roundly booed when part of it was sung in French. Think about that one for a while. This is what this sporting extravaganza has sunk to — some institution, eh?[196]

In the game itself, Winnipeg, described as "an old-fashioned Canadian team," defeated the Edmonton Eskimos by a score of 50–11 score—scoring a record 28 points in the third quarter. "The outcome was a rebuke to changing styles in the CFL."[197] For Edmonton, it was an ignominious end to a controversial season. It had started the season at 9–3 and then stories of dissension and racism surfaced. There were rumours of rifts between white and black players and between different groups of black players. Late in the season, Edmonton Coach Joe Faragalli tried to put it all in context to illustrate the situation: "It's like this. When you win, it's daylight and when you lose it's dark and when it's dark the cockroaches come out. But now that we are winning again the cockroaches have disappeared."[198] "With some difficulty," it was reported, "[Hugh] Campbell and coach Joe Faragalli finally did get the lid back on ... For clues about what really went on, watch to see who's replaced before training camp next summer."[199]

For Winnipeg, it was their second Grey Cup victory in three years. Much of the credit was given to a strong defence and the play of quarterback Tom Burgess, playing on his second consecutive Grey Cup team. Winnipeg's defense was anchored by Greg Battle, the linebacker who was selected as the league's Most Outstanding Defensive Player. Other award winners were Toronto's Mike "Pinball" Clemons as Most Outstanding Player, Reggie Barnes of Ottawa as the Rookie of the Year, Saskatchewan's slot-back Ray Elgaard as Most Outstanding Canadian, and tackle Jim Mills of B.C. the Most Outstanding Offensive Lineman.

If the 1990 season was a success on the field, it was not so at the till. The league decided at its February 1991 meetings to stop club contributions to the league's stabilization fund and to keep club assessments at 1989 levels of

$22,500 per month. The CFL itself was maintaining a deficit of $958,023[200] as it entered 1990. At the end of the year it had grown to $1,013,056. The league had advanced loans of $1,000,000 to Ottawa, $600,000 to Calgary, and $300,000 to B.C. from the stabilization fund which at the end of 1990 stood at $2,103,405. As for the Grey Cup Game, the revenue generated was $2,883,219, more than one million less than 1989's $3,947,625. When expenses were considered, the net income was $707,409 in 1990 compared with $1,928,844 in 1989. Net income from play-off games were higher, however, in 1990, $258,920 as opposed to $61,346 in 1989. The result was that clubs received much less in 1990 than they did in 1989. Hamilton, for example, which finished last in the East, received 11% or $106,296 of the play-off and Grey Cup Games in 1990. In 1989 as a Grey Cup finalist it received 14% or $278,627.

Gate equalization was still in effect too. There were five contributors: Toronto, $179,139; Winnipeg, $59,685; Saskatchewan, $88,850; Edmonton, $147,211; and B.C., $84,474. Three teams withdrew funds: Calgary, $111,988; Ottawa, $154,269; and Hamilton $293,102. At the end of the 1990 season one was still left with the impression that financial reality had caught up with the fans' perception. The CFL was in trouble.

1991 to 1992

Chapter Twelve

BY FAR THE MOST PUBLICITY ever generated by a sale of a CFL team occurred when Harry Ornest sold the Toronto Argonauts on February 25, 1991, to a triumvirate—"Three Amigos"—of Bruce McNall, John Candy, and Wayne Gretzky for a reported $5.5 million. A press conference called to announce the sale attracted a "media turnout, the likes of which haven't flocked to an Argo gathering since Green Bay Packers' great Forrest Gregg came north to coach the Boatmen in 1979."[1] It was front-page news. The "rich one," the "funny one," and the "great one" were seen to be the means of "reviving interest in the Argos and the struggling CFL."[2]

When the Argos were bought "there was a condition that the league constitution would be amended to give each club its own television rights and in approving the transfer ... the Board of Governors had accepted this condition."[3] The same reasoning was used for property rights, another area traditionally administered by the league rather than the teams. The Argos agreed that while "national merchandising rights should be assigned to the league ... a club should have some control over local rights ... the league would be entitled to match a local offer otherwise it would remain club property."[4]

The area of gate equalization was also disputed by the Argonauts; a concept of "gate sharing" was worked out. Each club would submit an audited statement showing its gross gate and net gate receipts on a per-game and season basis. The league commissioner was then to figure out the 90% to be retained by the home club and the 10% for the visitors and distribute that information. Within ten days of receiving the information, each club was to submit to the league payment of the difference between the amount due to it as a visiting club and what it owed visiting clubs from its home games, up to a maximum of $125,000. The total amount was referred to as the

"Gate Sharing Pool."[5] A formula was then used to distribute the pool: "A numerator equal to the amount of that club's net entitlement and a denominator equal to the total net entitlements of all clubs whose visiting club entitlement exceeded their home club obligations."[6] A team's "gross gate" was the total proceeds from ticket sales while its "net gate" was the gross gate less GST, Retail Sales Tax, per capita seat tax of stadium authority to a maximum of 50% of tickets sold, and any legal or statutory sum directed by the jurisdiction in which the game was played. As a concession to the Argonauts, there was "an allowance for rental of the playing facility for each home game not to exceed 10% of the gross gate after the deductions above."[7]

Media interest gained even more momentum when the Argos announced the signing of Raghib "Rocket" Ismail to a four-year contract which could "pay him $26.2 million for 1991–94. Of that, $18.2 million is guaranteed."[8] The former Notre Dame star spurned offers from the NFL and immediately set off publicity drums throughout North America. Hugh Campbell of the Eskimos was ecstatic: "It's a wonderful thing. [McNall] signed the guy less than 48 hours ago and already the CFL is on the map like it's never been before. Who wouldn't be excited. You'd have to be made of stone not to be. When have we ever had this kind of attention?"[9]

If there was any criticism of the deal it was that the spirit of the salary cap was violated. Ismail was to receive a guarantee of $4.5 million for the year; the salary cap was pegged at $3 million per team! The Argo solution was to pay Ismail a salary of $100,000 from the club, the rest as a personal services agreement with owner Bruce McNall.

The first CFL meeting attended by John Candy and Susan Waks, the McNall group's chief financial officer and vice-president for sports and entertainment, was held June 5, 1991, coincidently the one being chaired by Phil Kershaw of Saskatchewan; Roy McMurtry had resigned as chairman in order to become Associate Chief Justice of the Supreme Court of Ontario, General Division.[10] Susan Waks suggested that the league allow Toronto to host the '92 and '93 Grey Cup Games "as part of the new marketing strategy of the Toronto club."[11] It was passed in two separate resolutions. Only Edmonton voted against the '93 proposal since it already had a group working to host the game there. Again there was no news of applications or transfers of franchises. When the matter of expansion came up, Hamilton's David Braley spoke of Windsor, and Candy acknowledged Montreal and inquired about the possibility of Halifax. After some discussion Candy asked a question which in retrospect has become a guiding principle for the CFL. He asked "whether the league would consider U.S. cities close to the Canadian border which are not potential NFL franchise areas but would be large enough to support a team."[12] After discussion about a request from a Portland, Oregon, group to have an exhibition game played there and a similar request from Fargo, North Dakota, where a domed stadium was being built, it was agreed "that an Expansion Committee would be created under the Chairmanship of Mr. Candy with Mr. Braley and two representatives from the Management Council who could be named later."[13]

By September, John Candy reported that "he had met with individuals in Portland, Oregon, and Detroit, Michigan, and was informed that both cities were prepared to join the league in 1992."[14] At the next meeting, Candy reported that three different groups wanted a franchise in Portland and that there was some interest in Washington, D.C. But there were also some logistics to work out, such as, playing rules, field dimensions, the import quota, expansion draft, franchise areas, territorial rights, scheduling, revenue sharing, officiating, salary caps, currency for payment, broadcast regulations, property rights and player relations, to name a few.[15] It was suggested that "a strategic expansion plan would be developed."[16]

By the end of October, the ardour had cooled somewhat, perhaps because of all of the details to be worked out. "It was agreed to recommend to the Board of Governors that expansion not be considered until the 1993 season at the earliest."[17]

Candy also reported that he had been contacted by the Glieberman family of Detroit, Michigan about the Ottawa team, which at the time was still being operated by the CFL, placing "a considerable burden on the league resources."[18] The Gliebermans proposed to take over the team for the remainder of the '91 season and continue in '92 "and subsequent years. The long range plan of the Glieberman family is to operate a team in Detroit and it would like the first opportunity in that area. At that time the Ottawa club would be transferred to a new owner."[19] The same meeting unanimously passed a resolution moved by Susan Waks and seconded by Murray Pezim: "That the league accept applications for expansion to the new franchise areas effective if necessary in 1992."[20]

In his search for new U.S. owners, Candy had inadvertantly solved a huge and growing problem for the league. The Ottawa Rough Riders club gave notice that it could not continue to operate. Its Board of Directors resigned *en masse* on Wednesday July 24, 1991, forcing the CFL to hold an emergency meeting at the Airport Marriott Hotel in Toronto on the 26th.

Ottawa had a history of financial losses in recent years. When Allan Waters sold the club in 1987, it was estimated that he had lost $13 million over his 10-year tenure as owner.[21] He sold the club for $1 to a limited partnership of 27 businessmen who injected $1.5 million to cover team losses in '87 and '88. They added an additional $450,000 for 1987 expenses.[22] The team's performance on the field matched its financial picture. Its 1988 record was the worst of any team in CFL history at 2–16.

Bail-outs were provided from a variety of sources. The City of Ottawa allowed the club revenue from concessions, parking, and rent to the tune of $600,000. The regional government provided an additional $500,000 relief for 1989. The CFL did its part too. As of December 31, 1990, the league had provided $1,000,000 from its stabilization fund.[23] At the same time, however, the CFL made arrangements to recover its short-term loan. Ottawa's 1990 Grey Cup, gate and travel equalization payments along with 1991 season tickets receipts were assigned to the CFL.[24]

Just three games into its 1991 schedule, with its record 0–3, the Rough Riders team had reached the crisis point. The league was told that "all of the directors and officers of the general partner had resigned and none of the limited partners was willing to advance any further funds necessary to operate the Ottawa Football Club. Consequently the club is effectively not carrying on business at the present time with no one in command and with no one prepared to advance necessary funds."[25]

The CFL moved to fill the hole. Citing Article 3.08 of the league constitution, Ottawa's membership in the Canadian Football League was "deemed to be automatically terminated due to the fact that the Ottawa Football Club has disbanded its business organization and/or ceased to carry on its business."[26] In the next breath, the league granted a new franchise for a transitional period until a new owner was found. Numbered corporation 943399 Ontario Limited was created, a franchise in the CFL awarded to it "effective July 26, 1911 [sic]."[27] Commissioner Donald Crump went to Ottawa to oversee the transition. Jo-Anne Polack continued to direct the day-to-day operations of the club reporting "directly to CFL controller Paul Mihalek and legal counsel John Tory."[28] She had been told "not to comment on the change of ownership because of sensitivity between the limited partnership and its creditors."[29] As far as the CFL was concerned, the Riders' debt to it had been wiped out but not all were pleased about the transaction. "Terminating the Ottawa Rough Riders," it was reported, "and then moving to establish a new corporate entity, under the same name, seems to be the franchise equivalent of putting the house in your mother's name."[30]

A procession of prospective buyers were mentioned as the schedule unfolded. Toronto businessman Jim Manis and former New York Islander Denis Potvin were said to be interested, as was a partnership of Ron Cassidy, owner of Handyco Canada Ltd. of Vancouver, and rock and roll entertainer Bobby Curtola. Former players Larry Fairholm and Skip Eamon, both of whom were mentioned as possible Montreal franchise revivers, were also courted.

At the end of September, 1991, the CFL was still operating the franchise. Its controller noted that "the net cost could be as much as $3.1 million without taking into account any possible revenues from concessions, television and the Grey Cup."[31]

More and more, it appeared that the league was looking to the McNall group for leadership. Susan Waks was suggested by Saskatchewan's Phil Kershaw as someone who could help sell the Rough Riders because of her knowledge of "a number of prospects in Los Angeles."[32] While the league was preparing a plan to operate as a seven-team league, there w"as also a report from the chairman of the Expansion Committee, John Candy, citing Portland and Detroit as possible members in 1992—"If possible existing teams could be transferred to those cities."[33]

Not until October 18 was the Ottawa club sold, the buyers Bernie and Lonie Glieberman, father and son, from Detroit, Michigan. There was controversy before the sale and after. The league was criticized for not insisting that debts prior to the club's takeover be cleared up.[34]

Three instances of poor resolution of outstanding debts were cited. Willie Gillus, now the Argonauts' backup quarterback, was still attempting to get the Rough Riders to pay a $2,000 medical expense from 1989 when he was a member of the Ottawa team. Ottawa's former offensive line coach Bob Weber, who was owed "more than $100,000 from the Riders' previous owners" sued the CFL and won his case in October. Head Coach Steve Goldman, fired by CFL Commissioner Donald Crump on August 3, was issued one pay cheque. He was "giving the league 10 days to pay him what's left of his $120,000 contract otherwise he'll pursue court action."[35] Goldman was replaced with Joe Faragalli who led the Riders to a 7–7 record after taking over. He too was a subject of controversy. When the Gliebermans formally took over the club, their arrangement with the league was that it "would take over the existing stadium lease, player contracts, office premises and staff and would assume all obligations thereafter."[36] The CFL gave further protection to the Gliebermans declaring "they would be indemnified from charges incurred and applicable before the transfer date, in particular, salary claims by former coaches and players."[37] There was protection guaranteed should the former owners attempt to seize the equipment. The Rough Riders would also "become entitled to any share of the league revenues accruing to the Ottawa franchise after the transfer date."[38] Ownership of the Ottawa Football Club was transferred from 943399 Ontario Limited "to Ottawa Rough Riders Inc., a Michigan corporation owned by the Glieberman family of Detroit."[39]

At the end of the season the Gliebermans hired Dan Rambo as the team's new vice-president and general manager of Football Operations. Rambo promptly announced that he would "conduct a thorough search before hiring a coach."[40] Joe Faragalli, convinced that the had been told by the Glieberman family that he would be the coach, resigned in a huff: "I do not work for people I have no respect for. So there's no way they could get me back there under any condition."[41]

Another instance of the McNall group's influence was the sale of the Calgary Stampeders to friend Larry Ryckman. It represented another of the growing influences of the new owners of the Argonauts. Throughout the eighties the club had been on the verge of collapse only to be rescued by the City or the Province as a community-owned and -operated project. By the end of July 1991 the club was in jeopardy again. It had a loan for $1.5 million from the Canadian Imperial Bank of Commerce (CIBC), another for $2 million from the Alberta Treasury Branch. Both were guaranteed by the Province. The club's creditors were questioning the health of the league. Cash flow was being severely strained early in the season when only two of its first six games were at home.[42] On the same day that the league terminated and resurrected the Rough Riders, "they also handed the Calgary Stampeders $270,000 worth of pogey, in effect. Another day at the office for Crump and the CFL, that most Mom and Pop of football leagues,"[43] wrote one disgruntled Ottawa reporter.

In a telephone conference call September 23, 1991, the Stampeders were sold to Larry Ryckman after club personnel advised CFL officials "that the only alternative to a sale to Ryckman would appear to be the collapse of the franchise." Approval in principle was given until formal approval was conveyed at the October 2nd Board of Governors meeting. Ryckman agreed to pay $1,500,000 to satisfy existing creditors with an immediate injection of $400,000 and to assume the $3,500,000 loan from Alberta. One condition was that the league forgive a debt of approximately "$450,000 arising from past advances."[44] A current advance of $150,000 was to be "repaid at the rate of $50,000 at the end of the years 1992, 1993 and 1994."[45] The new owner assured the CFL of three undertakings: that the Calgary club would notify the CFL of any change in ownership, that the club would have the necessary working capital to carry on its league operations and that it would not support or promote "directly or indirectly an NFL franchise in Southern Alberta." The undertakings were binding only while "the CFL is in operation and the Calgary club is using the McMahon Stadium for professional football."[46]

Television revenues had always been the pot of gold at the end of the rainbow as far as the CFL was concerned. It was to be the engine which could power the CFL to financial respectability. Prior to the 1991 season there was the expectation that each club would realize $1 million or more from that medium. The CFL, still without a television contract for the '91 season turned to the McNall group even "before the signing of Ismail."[47] The Los Angeles-based McNall group stated that "one of our goals was to become involved with the entire CFL not just the Argonauts, and to lend our expertise where we could, including marketing and the new television contracts ... an area where the league has had problems with the last few years and one where we had considerable success."[48] Once again, in addition to the negotiations with Canadian networks, the CFL started looking south for television revenue to rescue it from its "sea of red ink." When the television contract was announced, it was without a major rights holder. CBC was to telecast 25 regular season games and had exclusive rights to play-offs and the Grey Cup Game. TSN was to show 28 regular season games. CTV was shut out, as was the league's Canadian Football Network which was too expensive for the CFL to operate. The league also decided to lift Argonaut blackouts in an effort to appeal to sponsors in the largest market, all in the hope of earning $1 to $1.25 million for each club.[49]

At best, however, there was a certain amount of wishful thinking. CBC was paying $1.7 million to the league and was providing technical facilities costing $4 million. All advertising revenue generated would be the CFL's property. TSN was paying the league $800,000. Molson's, even though it was not assuming its role as rights holder, was still substantially involved. It would buy $800,000 of advertising for the CBC games and $250,000 for TSN games. In addition, should the Nielsen ratings reach a predetermined level, it would pay CBC a bonus of $150,000. For the lifting of each blackout of the Toronto games, the Argonauts would receive $200,000. The lifting of the blackout games in Hamilton would result in the purchase of 500 home-game tickets by Molson's. As well, Molson's would contribute $100,000 to each of the eight CFL clubs. The cash gift would be supplemented by $30,000 in services for each CFL member. Each club would receive $1 million only if the CBC production costs were included. The big winners in the deal were the Argos who could receive a maximum of $1.8 million extra should all the home games be televised and the blackouts lifted.

Indeed, it was later demonstrated that the CBC was playing hardball with the CFL. In 1992 the league owed the network $3,000,000 for 1991 production costs.[50] John Tory, who was appointed the league's chairman of the Board of Governors in February 1992, offered to "phone CBC to request deferral of payment until the end of January."[51] In the meantime, he suggested a payment of $200,000 be made "as an act of good faith." The CBC gave its answer that it wasn't interested in faith; it wanted good works. CBC wanted its money by March 10, 1992. It also stated "it will not make a proposal for the 1992 season until the 1991 matter is settled."[52] The CFL had no alternative. It authorized "a payment of $675,000 forthwith and a payment of $75,000 prior to February 4, 1992 and the balance of $1,600,000 prior to March 10, 1992."[53]

Television negotiations, always an important consideration for the CFL, were also another area of influence by the McNall group. In effect, they brought a businesslike approach to a league which was more used to operating with greater informality. Clearly the McNall group was not pleased with the television contract negotiated for 1991. In order to finalize the deal with its largest rights holder, CBC, "it was necessary to agree to blackout lifts of CBC games played in Toronto and Hamilton."[54] The CBC had been "adamant on this condition."[55] While the McNall group agreed that the league had little choice in the matter, it did object to a blanket payment to Hamilton "for lifting the primary blackout for four home games. McNall added that the amount should be determined by the extent of the monetary damage to the home gate receipts which can be directly attributed to having lifted the blackout."[56]

Hamilton owner David Braley replied that the announcement of the lifting of the blackout for the Toronto area resulted in an immediate "900 season tickets cancellations from long-time subscribers" and a halt to new subscriptions. The loss of fans was estimated at 4,000 to 8,000 per game.[57] Braley was ready to withhold his approval for the lifting of the blackout, should Hamilton not be compensated, and unanimity was required.[58]

Subsequently the matter surfaced once again. Susan Waks was "disturbed that payments had already been made to the Hamilton club for its agreement to lift the blackout on four of its home games."[59] Her understanding of the television agreement was that such compensation should be at the end of the season "based on provable damage to the home club."[60]

Commissioner Donald Crump "advised that the absence of a major rights holder had a damanging effect on the league's television revenues in 1991."[61] The league was forced to hire an "outside agency" to sell advertising for its televised games. Commissions and CBC charges were such that there was a "net for each club in the estimated amount of $285,000."[62] Not only that, "the nature of the advertising business is such that the revenue is received long after the event."[63] The outcome of all of this was that Susan Waks "advised that the Toronto club would like to have income contracts and expense commitments approved by the clubs beforehand,"[64] another implied criticism of Crump. After some discussion the league passed a unanimous resolution that "a contractual commitment or expenditure by the league in excess of $25,000 shall require the prior approval of Mr. John Tory on behalf of the Board of Governors."[65]

Because of the extraordinary number of televised Argonaut games, the publicity generated by the McNall group, the signing of Raghib Ismail and the tough businesslike approach taken at the league level regarding funds and blackouts, there was a certain amount of nervousness in Hamilton. There, the Tiger-Cats were undergoing financial strain. Fans were staying away; the season tickets base was being eroded. The Hamilton-Toronto rivalry seemed to be spilling over from the field. Hamilton Mayor Bob Morrow was "told by reliable sources that the Argonauts are trying to drive the Tiger-Cats out of Hamilton ... and absorb the entire Canadian football market in southern Ontario."[66]

Of course, the Argonauts denied it. But the Hamilton officals might have thought so just because of the overwhelming amount of publicity generated by the Toronto team: the arrival of McNall, Gretzky, and Candy on the scene, the signing of Ismail, and the marketing surrounding him (the Argos season tickets campaign kicked off with a half-page ad with the simple message on a plain background "Put a Rocket in Your Pocket"). Television seemed to be hooking its coverage to the Argonauts: the CBC was telecasting seven of their ten home and four away games; TSN was carrying five Toronto games.

True to the people's impression that the California trio would bring glitz and glamour to the league, the Argonauts showcased Mariel Hemingway and the Blues Brothers at the 1991 opening league game. *Sports Illustrated, The New York Times,* and a host of American media were featuring the upstart Canadian Football League which had attracted Ismail and Flutie and the deep pockets of Bruce McNall. Suddenly, the game was being noticed once again by Canadians. Some didn't see the whole scenario as unusual:

> Nineteen ninety-one may go down as the year the Americans discovered Canadian football. While at home the papers and the airwaves are full of stories about financial woes of the teams, it's left up to American publications and TV networks to come up with upbeat news about our game ... Grasping for American approval—isn't that the Canadian way?[67]

Indeed, there seemed to be a thirst for American approval. It was hoped, of course, that this would pay off in much-needed revenue from television. When McNall representative Roy Mlakar announced "that Prime Ticket wished to carry the game live to its 254 million viewers in the U.S.A.,"[68] no financial consideration had been mentioned. League officials in discussing the proposal "agreed that while the exposure itself was a benefit to the league, there should be some more tangible receipt such as a contribution to the cost of the AFCA [American Football Coaches Association] reception in Dallas on January 7, 1992."[69] It was obvious that league officials were anxious to defer immediate revenue in the hope of the long sought after major American television contract.

Rightly or wrongly, the league was committed to continuing to widen of the door to the United States. As a result, rule changes for the 1991 season were minimal, confirmation that the game was exciting and would be accepted in the U.S. on its distinct merits and needed only tinkering.

There were changes in the coaching ranks. In Toronto, Don Mathews left the team mid-way through his two-year contract, citing "philosophical differences" with the Argos' general manager Mike McCarthy.[70] Mathews had come to Toronto with a promise to bring a "shoot the lights out" approach to football. He delivered. In spite of injuries to all of his quarterbacks (Matt Dunigan, John Congemi, and Rickie Foggie) during the course of the season, the Argos set a CFL record by scoring 689 points. Mathews moved to Orlando, Florida, where he was announced as the head coach for that city's WLAF team, surfacing later as a mid-season appointment as Saskatchewan's head coach. Mathews was replaced in Toronto by assistant Adam Rita.

There was an even greater surprise in Winnipeg. The CFL was losing its Coach of the Year. Again, the newly created WLAF was the culprit; Mike Riley signed to become the new head coach of the San Antonio Riders on January 18, 1991, just five days before he was announced as the Canadian Football League Coach of the Year for 1990. If seemed as it was "*déjà vu* all over again." After 1988, Riley was selected the Coach of the Year and took a job as an assistant at Stanford University where he was to be offensive coordinator. Two weeks later he returned to Winnipeg to coach the Blue Bombers. This time, however, Riley was determined to see his decision through. It was an "opportunity to build something that's not there. A chance to start from the ground floor."[71] Riley's decision was aided by a reported salary of $100,000–$125,000 (U.S.)—more than the $90,000 he earned with Winnipeg—plus a new car, a share of the San Antonio club, and membership in a country club.[72] Winnipeg responded by signing former NFL coach Darryl Rogers to replace Riley for the '91 season.

A third major change in coaching took place in Edmonton. On February 4, 1991, the Eskimos announced that they were replacing Joe Faragalli with Ron Lancaster. There had been rumours that former quarterback Tom Wilkinson had been offered the task, "accepted it and then turned it down after further thought."[73] For Lancaster, the quarterback turned sportscaster, it was a second chance at coaching, his first one in Saskatchewan having been a disappointment.

In league play, both Hamilton and Saskatchewan ended up in last place in their respective divisions. Hamilton, with a 3–15 record, replaced its coach David Beckman with fired Saskatchewan coach John Gregory who was in turn supplanted in mid-season by Don Mathews. At the other end of the standings, the Argonauts and Eskimos finished in first place at 13–5 and 12–6 respectively to earn byes. In the East, Winnipeg hosted the Rough Riders and subdued them by a 26–8 score; in the West, the visiting British Columbia Lions were edged by the Calgary Stampeders by a 43–41 score. In the finals, Toronto handled Winnipeg easily 42–3, while Calgary, rapidly gaining a reputation as the "Cardiac Kids," defeated Edmonton by a 38–36 score, highlighted by a 20-point fourth quarter comeback.

Winnipeg, the site of the 1991 Grey Cup Game, was a welcome relief after the disastrous 1990 Grey Cup Game in Vancouver. It was obvious to all that the city was aware of the game, that it was important to the community, and that it would attract over 50,000 paid spectators as opposed to the 26,827 who bought tickets for the 1990 game.[74]

Weather and the comparisons with the covered stadiums of Vancouver and Toronto were the topic of conversation. Any report about the game was sure to include references to "bone-chilling … sub-zero temperatures and brisk winds."[75] The Stampeders' middle linebacker Alondra Johnson was quoted as having said that his "working for six months in an ice cream packing plant in Los Angeles"[76] helped him to prepare for the Winnipeg weather. Just two days before the game, one estimate of the game day temperature was "the mercury slumping somewhere between -8 celsius and death from exposure … the artificial turf will be frozen and the ball will be like a rock."[77]

There were two camps forming. On the one hand, Calgary coach Wally Buono was in favour of the Grey Cup site moving around the league. "The CFL is steeped in tradition because of climate,"[78] he said. "You're doing a disservice to the smaller cities of Canada if you don't allow them to host it."[79] Some disagreed, however, saying that an era was coming to an end. The 79th Grey Cup Game was to "bring to a close a chapter in national sports history."[80] Some passed it off as just another case of Hog Towners thinking the world started and stopped at Toronto when Stephen Brunt of The Globe and Mail mentioned that

> the Grey Cup will be played at SkyDome for the next two years. It
> will likely never again be played outdoors or in a smaller city. Like

the Super Bowl, it will become primarily a television-driven exercise, a 'culmination event' (as the WWF calls Wrestlemania), an excuse to squeeze the maximum exposure and maximum dollars out of a single football game.[81]

Winnipeggers seemed to be oblivious to the developing dictum that "the CFL can evolve or die."[82] Indeed they seemed to revel in the developing mystique about "Winterpeg." Among the many souvenirs offered to the public was a teddy bear "named Shivers, appropriately."[83]

At the awards ceremonies held on Thursday evening before the Sunday game, the West won four of the five categories, B.C. Lions players winning three of those four. Doug Flutie was selected Most Outstanding Player over Winnipeg's Robert Mimbs. B.C.'s tackle Jim Mills won his second consecutive Most Outstanding Offensive Lineman award; Chris Walby of the Blue Bombers was runner-up. The third B.C. winner was running back Jon Volpe selected as Rookie of the Year ahead of the Argonauts' high profile Raghib Ismail. Edmonton's fullback Blake Marshall won the Most Outstanding Canadian award; Lance Chomyc of the Argonauts was runner-up. Winnipeg's Greg Battle was the only Eastern player selected, winning the Most Outstanding Defensive Player award over Calgary's defensive end Will Johnson.

When Volpe won over Ismail, it prompted one reporter to write that "deeds won out over dollars,"[84] a not-so-subtle reference to the huge contract being paid to the "Rocket." There was no question that Volpe was a deserving choice. He had rushed for 1,395 yards on 239 carries and scored 20 touchdowns, a record for a rookie. The "Rocket" had his defenders and detractors. He scored 13 touchdowns and had 2,959 all-purpose yards mainly from pass receptions and returning kicks. Throughout the league he was an attraction the public wanted to see. There were "several incidents with crowds on the road that resembled scenes out of Beatlemania."[85] At home, the Argonaut ticket revenue was "up 40 per cent, advertising and sponsorship up 144 per cent and concessions up 92 per cent."[86] Evidence of how the Argonauts and the CFL benefitted from his status as a "marquee player" can be gained from the Eastern final. Season tickets holders were not forced to buy tickets for the game and because of that "the club had no real idea of how many people would show up."[87] In addition, the TV blackout was being lifted; no headline entertainment was being provided; only the Argonauts and Blue Bombers and the game were being offered. Fifty thousand spectators packed the 'Dome to cheer the Argonauts to win entrance to the Grey Cup Game in a one-sided game.

But not all were pleased with the "Rocket." Earlier in the season, Calgary linebacker Dan Wicklum hit Ismail with what some called a "late hit" while others saw it as a normal defensive tackle. It caused the "Rocket" to be "woozy." Tempers flared. Commentators fretted about run-of-the-mill players acting as "hit men," robbing the league of excitement and drawing power. The CFL commissioner reacted by sending a missive from his office to all teams "about the value of the marquee players to the CFL's health in general. Translation: lay off the high priced talent."[88] Argonaut partner Wayne Gretzky was also critical about the Calgary player's hit. To show that there were no sacred cows, Wicklum responded, "calling Gretzky's comments 'ignorant and ill-informed.'"[89] Calgary receiver Demetrius "Pee Wee" Smith, who caught the last-minute pass to propel the Stampeders past the Eskimos in the Western final, was also critical of the Argonauts in general ("Toronto's spoiled. They don't want to come outside and play.") and the "Rocket" in particular ("So he's a marquee player and can't be tackled hard? Every time he's hit hard, it seems there's a flag. But he's got a uniform on, just like me.").[90]

The Toronto club seemed eager to protect their young 21-year-old who at times did not show up for engagements. During the early morning "Meet the Players Breakfast" on Friday of Grey Cup week Ismail was absent. It was the second incident in a week. He was a half-hour late for the Eastern final workout at SkyDome, saying that he had gone to the Exhibition grounds where the Argos normally practised. On this occassion, "a publicity bonanza for the game ... to thank everyone who contributed to the club's success and hopefully impress some buyers of the television time next year,"[91] the Argos were embarrassed. It was a mandatory event; the Argos sent word to him. Ismail "did honour them with his presence briefly and then took off."[92] Publicly, the Argo players seemed less concerned with the Rocket's absence. Said quarterback Rickie Foggie: "He sleeps more than anyone I know. He also runs faster than anyone I know."[93]

Foggie might have been right. In the Grey Cup Game it was a dash by Ismail, 87 yards on a kick-off return, that provided the spark and deflated Calgary. It made up for two earlier plays by Ismail. In the first half he fumbled after a 67-yard punt return. In the second half, his objectionable conduct penalty early in the fourth quarter contributed to Calgary scoring a touchdown which put them only one point behind, 22–21. A Toronto recovery of a Calgary fumble on the subsequent kick-off culminated with a touchdown pass to Paul Masotti from Matt Dunigan to clinch the game 36–21. The game was also a testimony to Matt Dunigan who directed the Argonaut attack in spite of a broken collar-bone, the pain and feeling deadened by novocaine. A crowd of 51,985 fans sat in temperatures of -17°C and winds from the north-west blowing at 13 km/h. It generated receipts of $3,246,180. It was the first Grey Cup Game ever played in

Manitoba. The CBC's live Grey Cup broadcast was "the top rated Canadian produced TV show of the year—it drew an average audience of 3.531 million."[94] It was a continuation of the good news that the league had received about the Western championship game between Calgary and Edmonton. The A. C. Nielsen ratings for that game showed "an average minute audience of 1.4 million, an increase of 30 per cent from last year's game."[95]

In Toronto, where a parade was held to honour the Argonauts, there were innumerable comparisons with the Blue Jays whose fans were prepared for a world series berth but were disappointed when the team lost three home games in a row. The season-long improvement of the Argonauts, their growing acceptance by the public was reflected in the chants of "Rock-et," "Rock-et" and "Broooce" paying recognition to Ismail and McNall. It gave credence to the idea that "when owner Bruce McNall signed Ismail, he was paying for an idea, the veneer of the big time, the kind of American celebrity validation that seems so important in the southern Ontario Market."[96]

The revival of the Argonauts, the successful Grey Cup Game, the excitement created by the play of the injured Mike "Pinball" Clemons and Matt Dunigan who served as the delivery system for the "Rocket" created a sense of optimism about the CFL for the first time in years. Stephen Brunt wrote:

> The challenge now is to bottle that excitement, to sell it, to keep the league on an even, disaster-free, keel this winter, to present a united front, get some games on television in the U.S. and press on for expansion. That's a helluva task. But look at where things are today, then look at where they were a year ago. The worst is over.[97]

On the surface, it appeared as if the new WLAF would be a thorn in the side of the CFL. Underneath, however, there was really no threat at all. As a spring league, the WLAF had a low salary structure; it honoured CFL contracts, allowing a player to play in its league in the spring, gather experience, and move on to the CFL in the fall. In addition, the WLAF franchise in Montreal—the Montreal Machine—served to keep football alive in that city and provide a barometer of acceptance for the CFL.[98] Ever since the Alouettes left Montreal, the league had been searching for ways to re-enter the Montreal market.

When the WLAF folded after their 1992 season, it left the Quebec market of more than 6 million unserved, with football interest revived in Montreal. There was interest but no application as yet for league membership. Expansion of the CFL into the United States was obviously becoming a cornerstone for the league's success and was in keeping with the new

Argonaut owners' vision. But there were two camps, the one wanting expansion to occur in the Canadian markets first, the other seeking the United States fields. Murray Pezim was in favour of the latter: "The only basic problem you have with expansion is Canadian content and that's a big hurdle to overcome."[99] Perhaps he was thinking of the new agreement which had to be negotiated with the players prior to the '92 season. The CFL governors decided to test the market in Portland, Oregon, scheduling an exhibition game there in June between the Lions and Argos, two teams which had good players who would be recognized by the American public, Doug Flutie and the "Rocket" Ismail.

In the end, it was the McNall formula and its acceptance that spelled the end for Commissioner Donald Crump. Despite improvements in ratings, television revenues for the '91 season would result in approximately only $200,000 per team. Even then, that figure was considered to be more the result of McNall's entrance on the negotiating scene than Crump's efforts. The league was hoping to have its '92 schedule finalized before the end of the current year in order to capitalize on the high ratings. There was a consensus however that Crump would not be in charge, that he would "jump or be pushed"[100] from his lofty perch.

Crump did not seem to fit in with the image the CFL was attempting to promote. The new owner of the Calgary Stampeders, Larry Ryckman, was described as having "nice hair, nice suit, talks smart and talks business with the right amount of new-age missionary zeal";[101] In contrast, Donald Crump appeared to be uncomfortable in his role. There were problems in public relations: "It seems all I do is answer questions that there aren't any answers to. I don't know."[102] His answers at times were considered by some to be irrelevant. When asked to "explain the tough season the league had just weathered" Crump answered, "When we started the year there was the recession and we were in a war and three teams were in trouble."[103] Reporters were puzzled as to what the Gulf War had to do with the CFL, one wondering, tongue in cheek but nonetheless indicative of some of the feelings toward Crump: "Did he think former Montreal tight end Nick Aragki was Nick Iraqui?"[104]

Crump seemed to be a reluctant passenger. He didn't enhance his credibility any when at a media conference during Grey Cup week, he referred to the possibility of expanding to Portland but placed it in Washington rather than Oregon.[105] But it was the television contract and the entrance of McNall into the CFL which sealed his fate. From that point on he had "been on the outside looking in as the Californians began to recast Canadian football in their own image."[106]

On December 11, 1991, Donald Crump announced his intention to step down as commissioner once a successor was found. "I think my general feeling was that every time I had to go to a board meeting, it was like walking across a mine field. I guess I just don't want to put my foot on another mine,"[107] said a beleaguered commissioner. The committee to find a successor consisted of Phil Kershaw of Saskatchewan, Hugh Campbell of Edmonton, Toronto's Susan Waks, and Ottawa's Bernie Glieberman.

The CFL had succeeded in restoring the title of "commissioner" to its titular head in 1991, but ever since it had struggled with the type of commissioner it wanted in office. Donald Crump had an astute financial background, was able to ride shotgun for that "Maverick Mule" Harold Ballard both with the Toronto Maple Leafs and Hamilton Tiger-Cats, but there was also the growing realization that the commissioner was first and foremost working for the clubs and doing their bidding. In the end, Crump was done in by his inability to perform as the league's Board of Governors, the owners, wished him to perform.

Television revenue was one of the major areas of concern. Whereas clubs had targeted revenues of $600,000 to more than $1 million each, there was only $240,752 for each club at the end of the '91 season.[108] Crump "insisted that several of the governors did not understand the difficulty he had in attracting potential advertisers. 'Some people thought that there was a hole in the ground full of money. And I guess they blamed me for not finding that hole,' said Crump."[109] Some thought that the CFL was still living in the past, in those heady days when it had the large television contract with rights sponsor Carling O'Keefe. The more than $1 million per club from one source provided by that contract was a large slice of the revenues each club had to generate. Cash flow had been pretty well guaranteed; front offices had more time to spend on other areas. All of that was in the past, said Crump: "it's not just a matter of getting someone to sign on the dotted line and getting the money from them up front. It doesn't happen that way anymore."[110]

Crump also refused to look upon expansion to the United States as the road to greater revenues through American television contracts, something which brought him solidly in conflict with the Los Angeles group which owned the Argonauts. He compared American interest in Canadian football to Canadians' interest in Australian-rules football. He downplayed the effect that adding one or two American teams would have on American television saying, "the only viable medium is the CBC. And they have fixed costs, so they aren't going to budge on their financial demands. So it's up to the CFL to go out and sell advertising."[111]

In some ways Crump suffered from the same image problems as the CFL. Some thought that "he could have been sent to California for a buff and polish ... [it was] a matter of style as much as anything else that made a change necessary especially in the new veneer conscious CFL of Bruce McNall and his pals where there are no dweebs allowed."[112]

Susan Waks thought Crump was "more of an individual player"[113] in an area where a team approach was needed. As a member of the league's Executive Committee which was charged with spearheading the search for the new commissioner, she felt he should be "a strong business person and communicator."[114] Phil Kershaw, president of the Saskatchewan club and also a member of the CFL Executive Committee, thought that "the Grey Cup and the television contract are the two most important areas under the Commissioner's jurisdiction. Ultimately, he's judged on his performance in those two areas."[115] There was a perception problem, said Kershaw. Crump "was over-blamed and under-credited for the things he did during his two years as Commissioner. But the perception problem almost became a problem in itself."[116]

When Donald Crump resigned on December 11, 1991, he offered to stay on as long as the league wanted him to, up until the new commissioner was named if necessary. The league declined. "The members of the Executive Committee felt that December 31, 1991, was most appropriate in all of the circumstances."[117] The Board of Governors' meeting, held via a telephone conference call, was considered so confidential that even long-time league Secretary Greg Fulton along with Controller Paul Mihalek, were asked to leave the line. John Tory kept the minutes relating to the discussion about the commissioner.[118]

The same meeting also decided to use a "head hunter" firm, Heidrick and Struggles Canada Inc., to assist with the selection of the new commissioner. Contact had been made between the company, a Toronto-based "executive search firm with experience in the sports industry,"[119] and a member of the Executive Committee, Hugh Campbell, in a letter to Campbell dated December 18, 1991.[120]

Heidrick and Struggles made its report at the Board of Governors meeting in Edmonton on January 29, 1992, once again in camera with only governors and alternates in attendance. It was reported that as many as 30 and as few as 15 applied, or were considered for the position. Among the most notable names mentioned were Tony Gabriel, Leif Petterson, John Michaluk, and Larry Fairholm (all former players and now successful businessmen), former Ottawa mayor James Durrell, insurance executive Ron Barbaro, former B.C. Lions general manager Bobby Ackles, and Senator Norm Atkins.

After the report by Heidrick and Struggles representative Bruce Ward, the CFL decided to expand the selection committee to include one member from each club "not represented on the Executive Committee, plus league Counsel"[121] in order to interview candidates, make a selection, and announce the choice of commissioner at the league's annual meeting in Hamilton, February 27, 1992.

That choice, announced at 7:00 P.M. in Hamilton's Football Hall of Fame, there among the love and tradition of the game in Canada, was Larry Smith. "When we interviewed him, we said, 'Stop right there—we knew he was our man," said Ottawa Rough Riders owner Bernie Glieberman, a member of the CFL's search committee.[122] Smith had impressive credentials. He had been a first draft choice of the Alouettes as a running back and tight end, played in 140 consecutive games, appeared in five Grey Cup Games and won two. He retired after the 1980 season. As impressive as that was, he maintained that he was "not coming in to be a jock. I'm a business man. I was a jock 20 years ago."[123] His business credentials were equally impressive. A graduate of Bishop's Economics and Business program in 1972 and McGill's Civil Law program in 1976, he was president and head of the frozen bakery products division of Ogilivie Mills Ltd., a division of John Labatt Ltd.

Reaction was almost totally positive; many comparisons were made between the old and the new. Noting that the announcement was made in the Hall of Fame at 7:00 P.M., "too late to make the dinner hour television newscasts," the inevitable comparison was made:

> Lots of history, lots of nods to the ancients, and a stupid organizational botch: that's the CFL Past in a nutshell. And the CFL Future? Well from the current confusion, amidst the fallout from last year's McNall Revolution, emerges a guy who talks like a business school textbook.[124]

Calgary owner, Larry Ryckman was also pleased, saying that Smith was "a contemporary man, someone who is disciplined, confident and one who can handle any distractions. I'm not criticizing Donald but perception ultimately becomes reality. Larry is the perfect individual at the best time. He has been given total authority by the governors."[125] Brian Cooper of the Argonauts was equally supportive: "We've always maintained that we need a person who has ties to Bay Street. Sport is a business and there's no disputing Larry's business sense."[126]

At his first press conference, Larry Smith left an immediate positive impression. His quick quips caused one wag to report that "for once the critics were laughing with a Canadian Football League Commissioner instead of at him."[127] He answered a variety of questions dealing with problem areas in the league. He stressed the importance of financial viability, gaining partnerships with the corporate sector, and aggressive marketing. Regarding league expansion, Montreal was high on the list but expansion to the United States was a distinct possibility since "as a business you have to go where you can grow."[128] Other priorities were stabilizing the Hamilton Tiger-Cat franchise and the unique blend of privately and community owned clubs that comprised the CFL. Television came up, of course, and the new commissioner was in favour of continuing to lift the blackout as the Argonauts had insisted: "The Argos proved last year that lifting blackouts works. You have to deal with each market separately. Obviously a good TV deal is essential."[129]

The CFL was a league with serious financial problems both from a collective and individual club perspective. It owed money to the CBC. Operation of the Ottawa club prior to the Glieberman sale from July 26 to October 19 "cost approximately $2.1 million."[130] The stabilization fund was gone, its money used mainly "to recover the funds expended by the league in the operation of 943399 Ontario Limited to maintain the Ottawa franchise"[131] before it was sold. At the end of 1991, the CFL's deficit as a league was $1,954,724, having grown from $1,162,673 at the beginning of the year.[132] The league had attempted to eliminate the deficit by increasing club assessments from $14,500 per month in 1989 to $36,935 in 1991. It was too large an increase for clubs to handle. At the June 5, 1991, meeting in Regina, the assessment was cut back "to the 1990 rate of $22,500 per month plus GST."[133]

Television which was always seen as the potential "cash cow" to save the league was generating revenue but the league's costs in manufacturing that revenue were high. The Canadian television rights fee was $1,603,000; that of the U.S., was $113,260. The league earned a bonus of $123,000 because of good ratings. Advertising revenue was $6,470,992 but it cost $1,539,821 to generate that amount. Other costs were administration ($4,478), blackout compensation ($500,000), consulting ($8,200) and telecast charges ($4,323,913). The total remaining from television was $1,933,840, or $241,730 per club.[134] Fortunately the net revenue from the 1991 Grey Cup Game in Winnipeg was high, $1,748,732 compared to $707,409 in 1990. But net income from play-off games in 1991 was only $4,942, down from $253,873 in '90.[135]

It was in the midst of this financial upheaval that Larry Smith gave his first major presentation to the league's Board of Governors.[136] Aided by a visual display, he stressed the need to attract revenues from "gate receipts, television and marketing ventures"[137] in addition to having a good on-field product. He wanted to reorganize the league office "to make it more responsive to the clubs, the media, the business community and the players." His vision for the league in 1996 was to have: nine profitable Canadian franchises with solid, committed ownership; three profitable U.S. franchises; four to six major national sponsors, five to six major regional sponsors and five to ten minor national sponsors; a successful licensing business with a 15% market share generating revenues in excess of $3,000,000; a self-supporting league office regarded as an innovative, dynamic organization with strong management and player relations; and a success story integrated into the community with a new generation of supporters.[138]

While the commissioner was commended for his long-range view, it was the short-term view which was the immediate concern of most. Edmonton, saying that the deficit could not be swept under the rug, wanted that addressed before any other proposals were considered. Toronto, represented by Rosanne Rocchi, "complained that the figures in the presentation [were] misleading." She was particularly concerned that the "potential liability of the league with regard to its operation of the Ottawa club has been under-stated, which could impact on the distribution of revenues to other clubs."[139] Saskatchewan's Phil Kershaw "asked whether it would be feasible to seek out a source of bridge financing to ensure that the clubs and the league survive the season."[140] Nothing was too insignificant to come under the scrutiny of the board members in their effort to search for ways to cut costs. Hamilton's Braley, noting that the league's budget for officiating was $768,400, asked how much of that was attributable to the use of a seventh official on the field. It was "approximately $72,000."[141] Even the office space costs, which were higher in 1992 because of a "rent-free period during the early months of 1991," were considered high by Rocchi who pointed out that office space was available in downtown Toronto at $8 per square foot.[142]

In the words of Calgary owner Larry Ryckman who was described as the "personification of the new guard" of the CFL owners, "There's really been a change of the tides here."[143] The new appointment was at a critical point in the life of the CFL.

> Changing tides, a watershed, the end of the beginning of the beginning of the end: the fate of Canadian professional football whatever it turns out to be, will certainly be decided during Larry Smith's five year term in office. The traditionalists might as well get used to the jargon, get used to the new style and hope like hell there's genius somewhere.[144]

In some ways the idea that the McNall group was a boon to the league was wearing thin. They seemed to have caught the feeling that individual clubs were to look out for themselves first rather than having a league perspective. When the McNall group bought the Argonauts from Harry Ornest, there were "certain understandings reached" which included the "awarding of the 1992 and 1993 Grey Cup games to Toronto, the exclusive marketing rights in the Toronto area, the granting of local television rights to the Toronto club and exemption from gate equalization."[145] For its part, the Toronto club, as a tradeoff, "would make available to the league and the other clubs its marketing expertise and the public relations services of its high profile personnel."[146]

Apparently the "understandings" were not written down. Clubs balked at incorporating them into the league regulations. Ottawa's Bernie Glieberman said he was "disturbed by what he has learned since his purchase of the Ottawa club."[147] The league struck a committee comprising Gary Campbell of Edmonton, Larry Ryckman of Calgary, and John Tory, league chairman, "to meet with a group from the Toronto club to clarify what was agreed to by both the league and the new owners" of the Argonauts.[148] The Argonauts had also exerted considerable pressure for resolution of the issue. It presented the league with an invoice for $422,000 related to travelling expenses for public relations performed by its high-profile leadership on behalf of the league. The cost to each club would be in excess of $50,000.[149] At the same meeting, the Toronto club reported that John Candy had asked to be relieved as the chair of the Expansion Committee "because of his heavy professional commitments."[150] Apparently Candy still wished to stay on the committee,[151] but the league replaced him both on the committee and as chair with Calgary's Larry Ryckman. It also offered the Argonauts a "settlement of the outstanding public relations account with payments of $125,000 per year for two years which amounts to $15,000 per club."[152]

The Argonauts had other complaints. Its rental of the SkyDome was $70,000 per game. Not only that, the lease arrangement "provided that the landlord must be compensated in the event of a blackout lift."[153] Such compensation had been "waived in 1991 because of the ongoing negotiations."[154] The SkyDome and Bruce McNall were at odds over the collection of receipts from the restaurants overlooking the field during Argo games: the Argos wanted revenue but the restaurants were unwilling to pay it. When McNall was buying the team "he was told that he would be allowed to sell advertising but ... found out the SkyDome's exclusivity with some advertisers means he can't sell to the competition."[155] McNall wasn't complaining about the exclusivity. Rather, he was upset about not being told about it when he was negotiating to buy the Argonauts saying he "would have asked to have it made up in other areas such as lower rent or more of a percentage of concessions."[156]

McNall was also venting his frustrations with the lack of progress he was making with the league on items that he thought were agreed to when he purchased the team. "The attitude seems to be ... 'don't worry, they've got deep pockets.'"[157] He was critical of the other CFL owners who spoke of "revenue sharing" but not "cost sharing." "No one," he said, "offered to pay a share of Ismail's $18 million salary, although everyone argued his presence helped rejuvenate the CFL last season."[158] Not only the CFL, but also the Argonauts whose average attendance rose by "more than 14,000 per game."[159] McNall was more critical of his fellow league members than of new commissioner Smith who "has a lot of people yapping at his heels."[160] But it was obvious that McNall was "disheartened to the point where he talked about the possibility of releasing marquee wide receiver Raghib (Rocket) Ismail to the NFL's Los Angeles Raiders and even selling the team."[161]

In the end, the league compromised. The television arrangement in effect in 1992 was to continue through the 1994 season as "a transitional provision."[162] Beginning in 1995, the league would select five home games from each club's schedule and have the right to include those in the national television package "with the proceeds to be distributed equally."[163] The TV rights to each club's remaining home games would be its own responsibility and it would retain all broadcast revenue from these games.[164] In the future any constitutional amendments regarding the television arrangements would have to be approved by six of the eight clubs.[165] The new arrangement passed by a 6–1 vote at the June 29 meeting (Calgary was not represented at the meeting), with the stipulation that the decision would be reviewed at the annual general meeting in 1993.[166] Only the Hamilton club voted against the motion.

Hamilton was clearly not pleased with the developments. Its crowds were falling off. Owner David Braley had lost some $5.2 million since he became owner of the franchise. He had the most to lose by the changes in the new "gate sharing" formula. Under the previous formula, his club received $410,398 in 1991 whereas under the new "gate sharing" formula it would have been $250,603, and only $202,603 if television blackout arrangements were also factored in.[167]

Braley was actively trying to sell the Hamilton club. He was having problems with the municipality which was refusing to continue with a payment of $300,000 per year for advertising and trade-mark rights at Ivor Wynne Stadium, although it had offered to cut the rent from $100,000 to $50,000.[168] When Braley threatened to move, the City issued a termination notice. The club would be forced to vacate Ivor Wynne Stadium by July 7 although permission was given to play the opening game on July 9 against

Winnipeg.[169] Braley was frustrated. He needed cash flow; the league was slow in coming forth with money it owed from the 1991 season. He also resented the fact that the league had supported Ottawa and Calgary out of CFL revenue and thus created some confusion as to "the question of unlimited liability: Is it $1.5 million? Or is it $3 million"?[170] For newly acquired quarterback Damon Allen, it was *déjà vu*, "the Ottawa Rough Riders of '91 without the fans."[171] The situation stabilized itself somewhat with the announcement that the club was to become a "not for profit" community-based club headed up by lawyer Roger Yachetti and former player and banker John Michaluk. The announcement was greeted with temporary relief all around. It was "no longer third and long [but] the win isn't secured either."[172]

As serious as Hamilton's situation was, the B.C. Lions' was even more precarious. The Hamilton change cost the league no money. That was not the case with the B.C. Lions and their flamboyant owner Murray Pezim.

The 1990 Lions of Murray Pezim, with Doug Flutie at quarterback, led the CFL with an average attendance of 40,000. B.C. supporters had forgotten about the circus atmosphere of the early Pezim years; Coach Bob O'Billovich seemed to have brought some stability to the organization. But unquestionably the greatest attraction for all was the play of quarterback Doug Flutie. Under his leadership, the Lions had an 11–7 record; he threw a record number of 730 attempts, completing 466 for 6,619 yards and 38 touchdowns. He was selected as the CFL's Most Outstanding Player for the '91 season. Flutie was also in his option year in '91 earning a reported $350,000,[173] set to become a "free agent" on February 15, 1992.

Discussion between Flutie's agent Bob Woolf and Murray Pezim became rancorous. Flutie threatened to go back to the NFL; Pezim called it a ploy. "I'm not prepared to go any further; I can't go any further," said Pezim. "Bob Woolf won't listen. We can't afford any more. I've said this before and I'll say it again. Doug Flutie works for me. I don't work for him. And I don't intend to work for him."[174]

Pezim said that he had offered Flutie a three year contract of $600,000, $600,000, and $700,000; Woolf was seeking $600,000, $800,000, and $1,000,000 in U.S. funds.[175] Negotiations broke down completely. Flutie announced that he would not return to B.C. to play football. Enter Calgary and owner Larry Ryckman. The Stampeders announced at a press conference on March 23, 1992, that they had signed free agent Flutie. In what was described as a "creative deal," Flutie could earn $5 million in a four-year contract, bonuses included, with partial ownership which the quarterback said "was a major, major part of my decision."[176]

While Ryckman was gushing over his new quarterback, "Doug is the Wayne Gretzky of football, that's what he is"[177] and "the greatest of the great, the best player in the history of Canadian football,"[178] and Calgary fans and the media trumpeted the team's new acquisition, B.C. fans, the Lions, O'Billovich, and Pezim were more than mildly upset. Pezim demanded that the Stampeders trade him Danny Barrett as compensation. He described the Calgary owner as "that chicken Ryckman"[179] when he refused.

In the wider context of the league, comparisons between two franchises were made. In Hamilton where David Braley was selling the club, a proposed consortium of local business people bowed out, able to raise only one million of the $3 million price tag for local ownership. Meanwhile in Calgary, Flutie had signed for $1 million per season. "The Calgary situation ... [is] a perfect example of what Bruce McNall and his progressive pals want the league to become. The Stamps sign a 'marquee player'; interest in the franchise is sure to peak; the veneer of big time, deep pocketed ownership is maintained," commented Stephen Brunt.[180]

Danny Barrett was traded to the B.C. Lions in return for offensive tackle Rocco Romano and first-year centre Jamie Crysdale. "The deal also included a cash payment estimated at $250,000 and the right to play an exhibition game in Portland, Oregon, against the Toronto Argonauts."[181] Pezim, a stock promoter, paid the $250,000 to Ryckman with shares of a Jamaican gold property, the value of which dropped from $1.27 to 24 cents.[182] Ryckman was furious, threatening not to bring the Stampeders to Vancouver for a July 23 game. Media in both cities ridiculed the whole exercise. Pezim countered by saying he would "hand out rubber fowl so the fans can pelt Chicken Ryckman."[183] Even the Calgary media were upset, one reporter calling the whole scenario "a circus run by clowns" and chastising the Stampeders' owner Ryckman whose "remarks ruined the credibility of his cause, not to mention the credibility of those of us who want to treat the CFL as a professional league."[184]

By mid-August of 1992, the Lions were 0–7. In 1991, they averaged 40,000 spectators per game, whereas in 1992, 26,000 was the largest crowd they drew. Pezim announced that the team was for sale, that he wouldn't "put another dime" into the club.[185] When no takers were available at the $1 price and assumption of team debt, the league decided to act. In a conference call meeting on August 26, the league rescinded Pezim's franchise owned by Prime Sports and awarded a new one to Vancouver Football Operations Limited.[186] Once again, the CFL was forced to use its funds to operate a club. It was estimated that $180,000 per week would be the cost. The B.C. Pavillion Corporation offered to contribute $100,000 per week up to six weeks; Canada Safeway was set to contribute $25,000 per week.[187]

Realizing that "the temporary operation of the B.C. club would impact on the total distribution of revenues at year end,"[188] the time limit for the league's involvement was set at 30 days. During that time, it was decided that the commissioner and two members of the Board of Governors members would be a management committee; that private and/or government funds would be sought to relieve the league's financial burden; that all suppliers and associates, for example, the CFLPA, were to be approached to secure "substantial cost reduction or revised financial arrangements"; that the maximum amount of funds advanced for the operation at any one time be $200,000.[189]

The Players' Association was to be contacted since Prime Sports had not remitted contribution to the CFL Players' Pension Plan.[190]

As arranged, another conference call was held seven days later to review the situation. One hundred thousand dollars of the estimated $1,600,000 needed to operate the B.C. club was spent in the first week. Canada Post joined Safeway and the B.C. Pavillion Corp. in offering "cash contributions." It appeared "that no matter who becomes the new owner, the league may have to be responsible for up to $1,000,000 in charges."[191] The league decided to continue the bailout "until September 19, by which time it must have transferred the franchise to a new owner or terminate the operation."[192]

When the CFL Board of Governors met at the Delta River Inn in Richmond, B.C. on September 16, 1992, it was with the idea that "the meeting had originally been called to ratify the sale of the B.C. club to the Pattison Group as the new owner."[193] The deal fell through, "the main reason ... a concern about the financial viability of the league more so than the recent history of the B.C. franchise."[194] The proposed "sale" had called for financial arrangements whereby the Pattison Group, the B.C. Pavilion Corporation (PAVCO), and the league would be one-third partners for the balance of the 1992 season.[195] In return for its involvement, PAVCO was expecting the 1994 Grey Cup game to be played in B.C. to help it recover its costs, tougher cost control measures by the league, a lower salary cap, and reduced administration costs.[196] Indeed, the clubs passed a resolution that on all monies owed to them by the league as of September 15, an interest rate of prime plus one percent be added.[197] On September 23, the CFL met again, by means of a telephone conference call, and under similar terms as would have been the case for Pattison, named Bill Comrie as the "new member." Comrie, the owner of The Brick furniture chain, a former director of the Edmonton Eskimos and co-owner of the San Diego Gulls, was the new partner with the league and PAVCO for the 1992 season, and was to be sole owner for 1993.[198] Throughout the league, there appeared to be a collective sigh of relief. A commentator reported: "And so ends The Crisis That Could Have Killed The Canadian Football League, Chapter XXVII."[199]

If the salary demands of Doug Flutie and his subsequent signing by Calgary were contributing factors to the B.C. turmoil, the move of Matt Dunigan from Toronto to Winnipeg played a similar role in Toronto. Dunigan played out his option in 1991 and quarterbacked the Argonauts to a Grey Cup victory while playing with a separated shoulder. The Argonauts, contending that Dunigan was injury prone wanted to structure a contract based on the number of games played by the quarterback. Dunigan refused, arguing that the Argonauts' system called for minimum protection on passes with a maximum number of receivers being released in the pattern. When running back Mike Clemons at 5'6" and 180 lbs. was kept in to block, he was responsible for a defensive lineman who might weigh upwards of 250 lbs. The overall effect, said Dunigan was that the quarterbacks in the Argonaut system were underprotected and more likely to be hit and therefore injured. Dunigan who was offered a reported $250,000 with the Argos, had missed 20 of 36 games since joining them in 1990. Prior to that he missed only 11 of 120 regular-season games in Edmonton and B.C.[200]

Dunigan was seeking a guaranteed salary per year; owner McNall would not authorize more than $450,000 unguaranteed for the year. In the end, Dunigan signed with the Blue Bombers. His contract called for a guarantee of $500,000 for each of two years with an option for a third season at $500,000. Winnipeg also "took out an insurance policy—for a premium of $100,000—that will indemnify them for the full $1,000,000" if Dunigan suffered a career-ending injury.[201] The move was not without great pressure on the club. Winnipeg's general manager and head coach, Cal Murphy contacted a bank "to arrange a loan in order to meet Dunigan's demands."[202] The bank refused his request citing the $1.1 million deficit and the $800,000 in playing contracts for the year.[203] Murphy approached Winnipeg Enterprises Corp., the operators of the Winnipeg Stadium and Arena. They agreed to the loan with the stipulation that "Murphy had to promise ... to raise ticket prices by $2 across the board for 1993."[204]

The moves had predictable results in Calgary and Winnipeg, the two cities which were to meet in the 1992 Grey Cup Game, and in B.C. and Toronto. The latter two teams ended up in last place in their respective divisions.

In Ottawa, the Rough Riders created ongoing controversy with the signing, at the Gliebermans' insistence, of former NFL stalwart Dexter Manley. Prior to that, they decided to change the team's logo. Normally there would be a year's notice required to do so since all CFL teams might be left with obsolete merchandise in their stores. The requirement was waived since there were "possible legal consequences of using the old logo which the previous bankrupt owner might claim as its property."[205] The new logo, a flaming "R," generated some controversy but not nearly as much as the "football toting beaver with a skull and crossbones across its jersey." It was just another in the seemingly endless number of pratfalls performed by the Ottawa club with its "new ownership, new management, no quarterback and salary problems."[206]

Indeed, it was later revealed that the team had been able to circumvent the salary cap going back to 1990. That year, the team signed "a gaggle of high priced free agents." It was an attempt to get the fan interest back but, said Jo-Anne Polack, "Now how are we going to get away with it."[207] Polack wasn't aware that the salary cap wasn't going to be enforced when she first joined the Rough Riders. Having signed the "free agents," however, the club expected that it would be monitored. It set up an elaborate scheme to escape detection. A moving company issued cheques to players to "help disguise a player's bonuses."[208] The moving company issued the player a T4 slip for Income Tax purposes and "would then invoice the team 'for services,' Polack said. The same thing was done with an Ad agency and a printing company."[209] Polack stated that the practice was done "in case an auditor came in and started to go through the payrolls; that they couldn't trace it—from the league's purposes." She also mentioned that the practice was stopped "because after 1990 we realized no one was going to check anyway, so why bother."[210] Polack also said that only about three quarters of players' contract addendums that contained bonus clauses were filed with the league office. The rest were be held back. All of this was designed to give the impression that the Rough Riders were within the league's "competitive expenditures" ceiling. She also said that "the Riders filed all the contract addendums they had been holding back in the weeks before the team's board resigned en masse in July of '91. The concern was that the players get paid their due."[211]

The year was also one in which the league's collective agreement with the Players' Association came up for negotiation. It promised to be a tough negotiation for the league since it was strapped for cash. It decided that "a specialist in labour law" would be hired to help it prepare for the negotiation.[212] At a subsequent meeting, Warren K. Winkler, QC, of the Toronto law firm of Winkler, Filion, and Wakely, specialist in labour legislation, was introduced and hired on a retainer basis "to assist the Player Relations Committee as its chief negotiator and spokesman."[213] Winkler was also to submit a "bi-weekly confidential report to the league by telephone conference on the progress of negotiations."[214] The Player Relations Committee consisted of Commissioner Larry Smith, Hugh Campbell, Alan Ford, and

Mike McCarthy. It was evident however that Winkler, Campbell, and Smith were most involved. Winkler, in his report to the league after successful conclusion of the agreement, reported that as "a person outside the league," he had observed a change in attitude on the part of the Players' Association representatives "from one of extreme antagonism and distrust to the other extreme of understanding the league's problems and the desire to co-operate in solving them."[215] Winkler concluded that the reason for this was "the high level of credibility which the Commissioner and Mr. Campbell presented on behalf of the league."[216]

Not all felt the same way. Indeed, Mike McCarthy complained at the league's meeting for the collective agreement ratification vote that he "had not been consulted during the negotiations on key financial issues which affected the Toronto club, such as disclosure of financial statements and the release dates for veteran players."[217] The league had in fact been successful in having the association's financial demands withdrawn. Pre-season compensation was raised to $325, $425, and $525 per week for first-, second- and third-year veterans.[218] Pensions were also improved. Players were to contribute $1,250, $1,350, and $1,500 in 1992, 1993, and 1994 while the clubs would add $1,050, $1,150, and $1,300. In addition, $200 per player would be contributed from the Grey Cup receipts to the Players' Pension Plan. The league also agreed to double its life insurance premium to provide $60,000 coverage per player and to allow a meal and travel per diem of $55, except if the club provided a pre-game meal in which case the per diem was to be $40. No meal/travel allowance was to be paid if on the return trip after an away game, the team departed prior to noon local time and did not have a meeting or practice that day.

The agreement also called for the Players'Association to aid the league in its move towards the salary cap or as it was formally called, the Competitive Expenditure Cap; for the president of the Players' Association to be an ex-officio member of the league's Expansion Committee; and "for each club to provide two pairs of shoes to each player."[219] This latter stipulation generated a great deal of discussion and "considerable objection" by the member clubs. In the end, the association and the league compromised: the association withdrew its "two pairs of shoes" demand; the league agreed to limit its right of recall of waivers to "two occasions during a year."[220]

Much of the criticism regarding the CFL seemed to be emanating from Toronto where the initial enthusiasm for the Argonauts, their owners, and the Rocket had subsided dramatically. The Argos had a dismal season; they suffered under the red glare of the Rocket's diminished performance on and off the field. In the aftermath of the success of the Blue Jays and their World Series triumph, the ultimate validation for a city wanting to be known as "world class," the Argonauts, their owners, and the CFL suffered in the comparison. It was "fashionable to ridicule the ownership of the Toronto Argonauts ... their crime is that they saved the CFL and therefore hindered Toronto's chances of getting an NFL franchise."[221] Outside of Toronto the league was flourishing, particularly in the west where "to many of its inhabitants, the CFL is an important aspect of life ... [McNall, Candy and Gretzky] don't deserve abuse for that. They deserve the Order of Canada."[222]

There was also some consternation within the league. The Argonauts, as part of the McNall group's purchase, would host the 1992 and 1993 Grey Cup Games. These games were expected to be a source of revenue for the club and the league. After all, the 1991 game in Winnipeg had shown a profit of $1,748,732 for the league.[223] It was reported that Winnipeg, in addition to its CFL share of $218,592, also reaped $800,000 from its hosting of the game. The league's Grey Cup budget was "based on the agreement with the Toronto club guaranteeing a gross gate after taxes of $3,700,000."[224] Together with other incidental Grey Cup related revenues, it was anticipated that $3.9 million would be generated which with expenses of $1.9 million would leave a profit of $2 million for distribution among the teams.[225]

Not all were enthusiastic about the Toronto plans for the 1992 national celebration. Two long-standing institutions, the Grey Cup Parade and the Miss Grey Cup Pageant, were abolished. There were objections from the other clubs but the Argonauts' executive vice-president Brian Cooper prevailed: "When times change, we have to change as well ... [the pageant] is just no longer politically correct and beyond that, it's just something I personally wouldn't want to do."[226] The Grey Cup Parade, which dated back to the 1948 arrival of the Calgary Stampeders and their chuck-wagons, was cancelled because it would have been held 2 weeks after the Santa Claus Parade. It was felt that people would "not come back two weeks later [after the Santa Claus Parade] when its colder, and do the same thing."[227] Grey Cup tickets were priced at $85, $115, and $125 for the game, to be played November 29 in the 'Dome. The Argonauts also decided to surround the Grey Cup Game with a variety of appropriate events. The club put $500,000 into "Fanbowl," an interactive theme park. Running from November 26 to 29, the Fanbowl included such items as a 30-yard field goal kick, a 40-yard dash against a row of lights timed to simulate the speed of Rocket Ismail, and a quarterback challenge: throwing a football to a "sensor driven target in a game simulation." In addition, there were exhibits of a football factory, a film with some of the Grey Cup's great moments, the opportunity to sit in a CBC director's chair to direct camera angles, plus some 5,000 square feet for exhibitors to merchandise their wares. Social events included an indoor tailgate party on game day, a black tie gala featuring Celine Dion who would also feature in the half-time show, a casino at the Convention Centre, mass parties at the St Lawrence Market with Michelle Wright and Prairie Oyster, a "power breakfast" hosted by the Junior Board of Trade on November 25, in addition to traditional "flapjack" breakfasts hosted by Calgary and Edmonton on November 26 and 27. The Argonauts were optimistically looking forward to a full house of 52,000 and a gate revenue of $5 million.[228]

Meanwhile, as some predicted, Winnipeg and Calgary, the teams with the high-profile quarterbacks, prepared to meet in the 80th playing of the Grey Cup Game. Calgary had finished in first place with a 13–5 record, having defeated Edmonton 23–22 in a close Western final. Edmonton itself had barely squeaked by Saskatchewan, edging them 22–20. Winnipeg ended up tied for first place with Hamilton in the Eastern division but was awarded first place on the basis of having outscored Hamilton in the four games they played with each other. The Tiger-Cats staged a great come-from-behind victory in a snowstorm at Hamilton to defeat Ottawa 29–28 but were no match the following week for the Blue Bombers who earned a decisive 59–11 victory. It had been a traumatic year for the Blue Bombers who had seen their coach and general manager undergo a heart transplant operation early in the season, and return as an observer in time for the Grey Cup Game. Assistant Urban Bowman took over as the interim head coach.

Murphy received a standing ovation from the assembly at the Bassett Theatre at the Metro Convention Centre when he presented the Most Outstanding Player award to Calgary's Doug Flutie for the second consecutive year. He defeated the Eastern representative Angelo Snipes of Ottawa. Western division players won three of the league's five awards. Ray Elgaard of Saskatchewan was chosen the Outstanding Canadian over Hamilton's Ken Evraire; Edmonton's Willie Pless was chosen over Ottawa's Angelo Snipes as the Most Outstanding Defensive Player; Winnipeg's running back Michael Richardson was chosen as the Most Outstanding Rookie over Calgary tackle Bruce Covernton; Ottawa's tackle Rob Smith won the Most Outstanding Offensive Lineman award over Saskatchewan's Vic Stevenson.

In the end, Calgary won the Grey Cup 24–10 on the strength of Doug Flutie's pin-point precise passing. Chosen the game's Most Valuable Player, Flutie's 480 passing yards were only 28 yards short of the Grey Cup record set by Montreal's Sam Etcheverry in 1955. Flutie completed 33 of 49 passes including touchdown passes to Allen Pitts and Dave Sapunjis who was selected as the Outstanding Canadian in the game.

While there was celebration in Calgary, there was consternation throughout the CFL. The official attendance at the 1992 Grey Cup Game was announced as 45,863. Only three days prior to the game, the Argonauts' Brian Cooper "reported that 38,000 tickets had been sold for the Grey Cup Game."[229] The CFL's 1993 Record Manual, for the first time, did not to list the previous years' Grey Cup Receipts. There was disappointment. Various reasons were advanced: the absence of an Ontario team in the final, the Argos' poor season, "fallout from the euphoria over the Blue Jays," general economic conditions, overpriced tickets, poor distribution methods.[230]

When Commissioner Larry Smith reported at a year-end meeting that there was a "shortfall in Grey Cup revenue," he was asked by the Edmonton representative "how there could be a shortfall on Grey Cup revenue if the gross gate was guaranteed by the Toronto club."[231] It was Brian Cooper who responded that "the guarantee was conditional upon a sellout, which did not happen. The Commissioner stated that the Toronto club lived up to its commitments."[232]

When the Argonauts' attempt to sell the rights for the 1993 Grey Cup Game to Calgary was questioned, prior approval by the Board of Governors of the CFL not having been given or sought after, league Chairman John Tory replied that there were "extenuating circumstances" revolving around the 1992 and 1993 games. He might also have mentioned 1994 and the awarding of the game to Vancouver. "Otherwise," he agreed "the Game is the property of the league and the site must always be determined by the Board."[233]

The 80th Grey Cup Game should have been a happy occasion for the CFL. Yet there was a strange pall which had fallen over the league, much of it due to the uncertainty over the announced expansion plans.

1993 to 1994

Chapter Thirteen

THROUGH ALL THE TURMOIL OF 1992, the league took concrete steps towards a very new future for itself; they culminated in an announcement at the end of the year to expand into the United States. It was only with the sale of the Toronto Argonauts from Harry Ornest to Bruce McNall, John Candy, and Wayne Gretzky, that expansion into the United States was proactively sought. It was no secret. "The long range plans of the Toronto ownership included expansion into the U.S. when it acquired the club."[1] Indeed John Candy became chairman of the Expansion Committee of the league; he took his position seriously, making contacts extensively throughout the United States. The league had parameters: it would only seek out those cities which would never gain an NFL franchise and which preferably were in proximity to the Canadian border.

The first target was Portland, Oregon. Interest had been demonstrated there. The league decided to showcase itself with an exhibition game between the Argonauts and the Stampeders. Both had marquee players who would be familiar to the fans, Raghib Ismail with Toronto and Doug Flutie with Calgary. As the June 25 game in Portland neared, Commissioner Larry Smith and the members of the Expansion Committee were to meet with the potential franchise applicants. With all of the attendant publicity, Bernie Glieberman expressed the opinion that, in Ottawa, he "sensed an attitude that the league is becoming Americanized with reference to two American owners and the talk of expansion into Portland."[2]

Such talk was something that the league wanted to avoid. It wanted the U.S. market, its fans, and its revenues but not at the expense of alienating the Canadian public. The U.S. was the dessert; Canada, the meat and potatoes. Glieberman felt that "such attitudes could be partly offset by stories of a revival in Montreal."[3] Along the same theme Calgary's Larry Ryckman, also

332

chairman of the Expansion Committee, was reported to have "received overtures for a team in Halifax."[4]

At the first meeting after the Portland game, won by Calgary 20–1, Larry Smith reported to the CFL's Board of Governors. He was pleased with the result of the game in Portland, which drew 16,000 fans: the sponsors of the event had indicated their interest in having a franchise, media response was favourable, and he stated that, "he expects a formal application to be filed in support of an expansion franchise" soon.[5] Indeed the possibility of expansion into the U.S. was more probable at this point than at any other time, so much so that Smith asked for directions as to "how the league would react to such an application."[6] The question of non-import players was discussed. Smith had "received an opinion from CIAU officials that a U.S. player in Division II would be comparable to a CIAU player and suggested that might become the equivalent non-import status for a Portland player."[7] It was the first real discussion of the practicalities of expansion. Interestingly enough, it was Ottawa's Glieberman who defended the status quo regarding the league's import/non-import ratio, suggesting that "the league should stick to its present eligibility rules unless it is forced to change by U.S. government action."[8] Winnipeg's Cal Murphy wasn't enthralled with the proposal either. He argued that if Portland were able to classify Division II players as non-imports, so too should other CFL clubs.[9] The matter was referred to a committee, to be formed by the Management Council, for review and a report.

With the British Columbia Lions' ownership problem dominating much of July, August, and September in 1992, expansion became a less urgent topic, but at the CFL meetings in October in Hamilton, the commissioner's strategy was outlined to the league in a presentation which would serve as the dry-run for one to the media on November 12. There were questions by the owners: Would there be a reaction from the NFL? Would they retaliate by moving into major Canadian cities? Would expansion clubs make a firm commitment to the CFL and not use their acceptance as a stepping stone to somewhere else? Had surveys been done to determine the acceptability among Americans of Canadian rules? Should the league play its games earlier to avoid conflict with the NFL and U.S. college football? What would be the position of the federal government? Would the league's existing level of support be maintained or diminished? To these latter questions, it was league Chairman John Tory who "replied that expansion would be regarded as an export of Canadian culture and would likely be encouraged."[10]

The league decided to form two working committees to assist the commissioner. Hugh Campbell, Mike McCarthy, Wally Buono, and Greg Fulton were to "study the logistics of expansion including *inter alia*, expansion draft, negotiation lists, territorial rights, college draft, import status, scheduling, officiating and other operational matters."[11] The other committee was formed to screen expansion candidates and consisted of Bernie Glieberman, Bill Comrie, and Bruce Robinson.[12]

The same meeting saw the report of Hugh Campbell's committee, which had been formed at the June 29 meeting. Its purpose was to review "the status of the non-import category in the event of expansion outside Canada."[13] The consensus was that current CFL players were of higher calibre in ability than those of the World League; that "experienced non-import players are capable of playing in an expanded league" but the feeling was that new non-import recruits "may find it difficult." As a result, the committee made its major recommendation: that the present total number of non-imports on the eight teams (8 x 20) be, in the expanded league, spread over "a greater number of teams, with a plan to phase out the non-import category in two or three years."[14] It was a major step. There had been restrictions upon the number of imports in Canadian football since 1936. It had been brought into effect after Winnipeg won the Grey Cup Game of 1935 with nine Americans in its 28-man line-up. Governing body officials brought these restrictions into effect because they wanted the game to be an expression of Canadian talent, thinking that Canadian genius would be blunted by importation without restrictions. To that end, an American would only be eligible to play in the Grey Cup Game if he had been in the country for one year. In fact, the 1936 Grey Cup Game was not played between the East and West because the Regina Roughriders' American players had not been residents of Canada for the one-year period.

Interestingly enough, it was the Saskatchewan and Hamilton clubs, two organizations with a history of local talent, who inquired about the recommendation. Saskatchewan's Phil Kershaw noted the political nature of such a decision: various levels of government had supported the league; "any action to diminish participation by Canadian players could be controversial."[15] He was in favour of forcing U.S. teams to use local talent. Hamilton's John Michaluk feared a reaction from CIAU and high school leagues "if they feel their players are being deprived of an opportunity to play in the league."[16] Roger Yachetti suggested that the league offer "some greater financial incentive to universities and junior leagues to produce players."[17]

In response, the commissioner noted that the 1936 import regulation, "a protectionist rule for Canadian players," had served its purpose. The expansion of the league into the U.S. "would provide an even greater incentive to produce players of a higher standard."[18] Campbell suggested that the Canadian rules on a "Canadian field to the extent possible" would provide the alternative, a different game from the NFL. It was left for

Chairman John Tory to respond. He also had ties to the Conservative party in power. He responded to the "political controversy" comment. "When Canada entered a Free Trade Agreement with the U.S. in 1988, the national congenital inferiority complex became manifest with ominous predictions of loss of sovereignty, cloning of industries and being swallowed up by the American giant. Although these did not come true, the same reaction might be expected when expansion is announced."[19]

After announcing that he "would discuss the proposals with the Players' Association in order to defuse possible public reactions from this source,"[20] a motion was framed to help defuse some of the governors' reactions. "It was moved by Bernie Glieberman and seconded by Hugh Campbell that approval in principle be given to the proposal to phase out the non-import status as the league expands outside of Canada provided that the league continue to support minor football in Canada." It was carried by a 7–1 vote, with Phil Kershaw asking "that his dissenting vote be recorded."[21]

On November 12, 1992, Commissioner Larry Smith met the media at the SkyDome to discuss the expansion of the Canadian Football League. The media were there *en masse*; TV cameras whirred; reporters were busy scribbling notes; the "Fan Radio" broadcasted the press conference live. It had been years since the CFL had attracted such attention.

With the help of his visual aids, Smith made the presentation in favour of the league's expansion plans. From among potential sites in Portland, Montreal, Halifax, Sacramento, San Antonio, Orlando, San Jose, St Petersberg, Las Vegas, Birmingham, and Hawaii, the CFL had isolated "four hot buttons": Portland, Montreal, Sacramento, and San Antonio. These were "the most serious" possibilities. Indeed Smith had instructed Greg Fulton to prepare schedules for 10 and 12 teams for 1993. Smith explained that the recent demise of the WLAF provided a "window of opportunity" for the CFL to move into areas not served, nor likely to be served by the NFL, with a "differentiated product."

Expansion had not occurred in the CFL since 1954 with the entrance of the B.C. Lions. In the meantime, the league had lost the Alouettes. It had two choices: remain stagnant with the status quo or expand into new markets. As what Smith called "the oldest professional league in North America," (it was able to trace its roots back to 1892 without difficulty), the CFL was attractive to American investors because of its competitive expenditures cap and could be "run as a business." Not only that it, was providing a model whereby the break-even point was 25,000 to 27,000 fans; the league was driven by gross gate receipts and local sponsorship. Television was not the financial necessity for its franchises although it was expressed that ultimately it would generate high revenues.

Smith emphasized that the NFL was fully aware of the league's plans, that there was no intent to compete with the acknowledged number one league in the United States. Rather, the CFL was pursuing the "Wal-mart" strategy of going into smaller markets and being a "major player" there. Football interest was portrayed as being such that the public would embrace the distinctive "differentiated" Canadian game. He maintained that "if it's not done right we're not going to do it for '93." Describing the league as a "low cost producer with a high quality product," Smith detailed the five criteria by which prospective applicants would be judged: quality of ownership, that is, financial worth; experienced sport management personnel; local expertise (since it was driven by gross gate and local sponsorship); stadium capabilities of 30,000 to 50,000; sharing the league's virsion of growth.

Smith also listed the benefits of expansion for the CFL: the value of the base franchises would increase; the economic benefits to a community with a CFL franchise in Canada had been shown to be in the range of $25 to $30 million; jobs would be created as the fan base expanded.

There must have been a certain amount of confidence on the part of Smith about the "four hot buttons." He discussed the ownership groups involved. Portland's bid was spearheaded by Paul Allen, the owner of the NBA Trail Blazers. He was finalizing negotiations with the city of Portland for a planned $205 million entertainment facility to house his basketball team. Once that was finalized, it was anticipated that Portland would turn its attention to the CFL franchise. Smith, a former Alouette, had had conversations with both the Olympic Installations Board and Roger Dore, owner of the Montreal Machine of the WLAF. It was obvious that Smith wanted Montreal back in the league and that he recognized that involvement by the francophone community was essential—his presentation was bilingual. A Montreal franchise could not be "run as a large social club for a small part of the community," he said.[22] Sacramento's ownership group was headed by Fred Anderson, owner of a large Pacific Coast Construction company. San Antonio's Larry Benson, described by some as being wealthier than any of the present CFL owners, was doubly valuable as a prospective owner since the new state-of-the-art facility, the 65,000-seat Alamodome, was due to open in '93 and could accommodate a Canadian-sized field.

During his press conference, Smith also brought up the issue of Canadians, or non-imports, playing in the expanded CFL. Noting that it was the "$64 question," he said that the league had struck a committee to look at it, that immigration lawyers were being consulted, and while no decision had been made, a "philosophical position" had been taken "to support Canadian University football." He made it clear however that the prevailing free market economic mentality would govern. The "1936 protectionist rule" had "served its time."

> I'll be honest with you. When I played, I thought I played because I was a good football player not just because I was a Canadian. And when I knocked the crap out of somebody who was bigger than I was, I didn't care where he came from as long as we were going to win the game. I can't see how people like Mike Soles or Blake Marshall wouldn't play on any team in any league, anywhere ..."[23]

As might be expected, the CFL announcement elicited a variety of media responses. *The Globe and Mail* in a generally supportive editorial called it the "CFL's Hail Mary pass."[24] Its readers had already been primed for the news. One of its columnists, Marty York, had already written of the expansion two days before the conference, highlighting the major points which would be made and commenting on the import/non-import ratio. Citing league Secretary Greg Fulton "who considers himself a nationalist ... not hot and bothered about the imminent changes," York reported that "Canadians today seem more global minded, particularly the younger generation. I'm sure that it has a lot to do with television. Look at baseball. People didn't seem to be complaining that there were no Canadians on the Blue Jay roster ... [T]he bottom line is that most Canadians covet the best talent possible, regardless of origin. Hey, nationalism is great, but it doesn't pay the bills."[25]

York's cohort, Stephen Brunt, scooped all other reporters. One day before the press conference, in what Larry Smith described as deserving "the award for investigative journalism," Brunt listed the four main possibilities for CFL expansion, Montreal, Portland, Sacramento, and San Antonio, and detailed their owners, stadiums, history, and intangibles. He even organized the proposed 12-team CFL into "the new look: Eastern: Toronto, Hamilton, Montreal and Ottawa; Central: Winnipeg, Edmonton, Saskatchewan and San Antonio; Western: Calgary, B.C., Sacramento and Portland."[26]Another *Globe and Mail* reporter, James Christie, speculated that the Canadian Football League, "as it is known and loved, will move towards extinction today."[27]

In the *Toronto Star*, Jim Proudfoot wrote that the '92 Grey Cup Game signalled the "end of an era for the CFL."[28] While there would certainly be others in the future, "as an expression of something uniquely Canadian, the game's institutions are dead—or certainly will be if things work out as planned."[29] Proudfoot acknowledged that Larry Smith felt that it was the Canadian rules which gave the game its distinct feature, would make it marketable in the United States, and thus the Canadian game would never change. Proudfoot continued:

What if it turns out just a little tinkering here and there could enhance that marketability? Why would the CFL, having bitten the expansion bullet hesitate to go one step further? And what if the Texans, Californians and Oregonians decide they absolutely detest this strange looking sport? Will the CFL pick up its marbles and go home, or try to adjust? You know the answer, eh?[30]

A sceptical Alison Gordon wrote of the CFL's "Wal-Mart approach" of competing only in non-NFL markets:

I wish it didn't sound so much like settling for less. I mean, do people who can afford Nieman Marcus shop in Wal-Mart by choice? Of course not. They shop there because they haven't much choice and they take no particular pleasure in it. Is that the image Smith is building for the CFL?[31]

She also commented on Smith's assertion about the rules of the game being the distinctive Canadian feature:

And that's non-negotiable? I wonder. What if, a few years down the road, more American cities want to get in on this good deal, this exciting Canadian Football League that's such a success. Except that, gee, it's tough to revamp the stadium, and we're not talking a *really* big deal, just lop off a few yards here, another few yards off there. Is that asking too much?
And gosh, its kind of hard to get anything going with just the three downs. It's not like *real* football, know what I mean?[32]

On the 1992 Grey Cup weekend, the *Ottawa Citizen* published an article by former Rough Rider great Ron Stewart. In "Bye Bye Canadian Football,"[33] Stewart acknowledged the financial woes of the CFL, and that the decision to expand into the U.S. had been made—"any discussion on the merits of the decision at this point is no more than an exercise."[34] After advancing his opinion that an ever-declining number of Canadians would invariably be part of the proposed "open market" CFL, Stewart proposed that

When the CFL goes south, all that tradition, all that history, all that East-West glue will subside into the realm of old memories. Sad and unnecessary. I believe that someday, the Canadian Football League will rise again. It has been too big and too important in our country, to disappear forever. Until then, let's return the Grey Cup to Rideau Hall and retire it with the honour its place in our history deserves.[35]

The depth of feeling of Canadians was evident in letters to the editor.[36] Not only were they saying that the Canadian Football League was important, but they also wanted to ensure that there would be continued opportunities for Canadians in the expanded version.

In Winnipeg, acting General Manager Lyle Bauer expressed a view which was to be heard often: "From a strictly business point of view, it makes sense. But it would mean taking away a lot of the emotion and the tradition for the sake of business. I don't think you can do that with the Canadian Football League."[37] It was reported in Winnipeg, which some liked to refer to as "the land of the dinosaurs,"[38] that "perhaps one in a hundred calls [to the Blue Bombers offices] is in favour of teams in the United States. The local radio seers and most of the press is dead set against it."[39]

Winnipeg's Cal Murphy, recently allowed to leave London's University Hospital where he had undergone his heart transplant operation in order to attend Grey Cup week festivities in Toronto, also opposed expansion to the United States "not based on patriotic fervour ... strictly a matter of dollars and cents."[40] After noting that the NFL injected $30 million into the WLAF which also had a television contract and the league still failed, he asked, "What makes us think we can go in and be the Grand Poobah?"[41] He mentioned that travel from Winnipeg to San Antonio and Sacramento would cost $40,000 a trip. Three days would be necessary since it would be impossible to get red-eye flights back to Winnipeg. San Antonio, he said, was the site of the Houston Oilers' training camp in session "for six of the first eight weeks of our season." Mentioning that Houston would probably play a couple of exhibition games there as well and, after September 1st, San Antonio would have high school football Friday nights, college football on Saturday afternoons, and the NFL on Sundays, Murphy asked: "When are we going to play our games?" Canadian teams, he said, were not good draws in the United States, illustrating his sentiment with examples of the Edmonton Oilers even with Wayne Gretzky, the Blue Jays, and the Expos. San Antonio, Sacramento, Orlando, and St Petersberg were too close to NFL cities, he reasoned. More could be done to sell the game in Canada, he argued, and "until all Canadian avenues have been explored, a move to the U.S. should not be contemplated."[42]

Murphy reacted with a huff to the $3,000,000 franchise fee from expansion teams and the "suggestion that the new teams would be able to pay that amount off over five or six years," each team realizing "$125,000 to $130,000 a year." "You could make that in a bake sale," he retorted.[43] Murphy said he "might" listen to talk of expansion if the $3,000,000 fee was paid up front to the league which in turn would operate its office from the interest and use the principal to bail out any team that ran into a financial crisis similar to Ottawa in '91 and the B.C. Lions in '92.[44]

Expansion and the side issues generated from it continued to evoke strong sentiments in the days following the Smith press conference. CIAU coaches, feted only six days later by the CFL at its annual luncheon recognizing the winner of the Frank Tindall Trophy as the CIAU Coach of the Year, were overwhelmingly opposed to the removal of the "quota system." They instructed the CIAU executive vice-president Mark Lowry "to lobby on behalf of maintaining the quota."[45]

A number of reactions from a variety of sectors issued forth. Liberal MP Lloyd Axworthy of Winnipeg announced that he would introduce a private member's Bill to prevent expansion of the CFL into the U.S. While the tactic was successful almost 20 years earlier with a Liberal party in power, there was no chance that it would be so well received with the Conservative government of the day.

Former university quarterback Jamie Bone, described as exemplifying that "even the best players in Canada have trouble finding jobs in the Canadian Football League, especially at the quarterback position," commented: "it's a sad day if they can't include Canadian content."[46] He might have been thinking of St Mary University's outstanding quarterback Chris Flynn who was unsuccessful in his attempts to make the Ottawa Rough Riders and later the Toronto Argonauts.

Two Toronto residents of the same street, St Clements Avenue, each playing a large role with the Stampeders, were opposed to the CFL plan. Dave Sapunjis and Andy McVey could agree with expansion but not with elimination of the quotas. When Dave Sapunjis won his second consecutive Dick Suderman award for the best Canadian in the 1992 Grey Cup Game, it was speculated that the award was "probably on the endangered species list."[47] Sapunjis called for the league to continue with community-based players: "I know there's kids in Calgary that look up to me because I'm playing in the league. And I know there's a lot of people in North Toronto that follow the CFL because I'm playing in it."[48]

McVey was more blunt: "It hurts me to hear Larry Smith say the CFL no longer needs that Canadian rule. If it hadn't been for that Canadian quota, Larry Smith would not have played nine seasons with the Montreal Alouettes after he came out of Bishop's University. He wouldn't be Commissioner of the Canadian Football League today if he hadn't spent those years with the Alouettes."[49]

Hamilton's non-import receiver Nick Mazzoli speculated that while he thought that he could play in the new non-quota league, "you'd see a steep reduction [of Canadian players] I don't think there'd be many Canadian offensive linemen and guys like Ray Elgaard, Jeff Fairholm, Dave Sapunjis and I would be fighting for jobs. And without Canadians the CFL would be a very antisocial thing—It's not going to be a fan's game."[50] Former player Peter Dalla Riva echoed those sentiments later when it was announced that he would be inducted into the Hall of Fame: "Being a Canadian, that rule got the door open for me. It gave me the chance to try. If they decide to change things and some Canadian kids don't ever get the chance to try, that's sad."[51]

Years later, during preparations for the 1994 Grey Cup Game. B.C. tackle Vic Stevenson addressed the same issue: "A good coach will see the raw talent but why keep the guy around for two years when you can bring in a kid from an American school who'll be a lot closer to being ready? Coaches get paid to win today. They might not be around in two years."[52] Calgary linebacker Matt Finlay was even more candid, "American coaches are prejudiced. They don't want to play Canadians."[5] Mary Ormsby of the *Toronto Star* reinforced the point:

So don't curse the Baltimore All Americans for ruining a cherished moment of Canadiana today. Canadians have managed to do that all on their own ... The CFL, long before Larry Smith bounded aboard as Commissioner, compromised its Canadian identity. This is a league, after all, that gives U.S. quarterbacks the benefit of the doubt even when they clearly don't understand the Canadian game ... Meanwhile, such Canadian pivots as Dan Feraday, Jamie Bone, Chris Flynn and countless others didn't even get a second glance and still don't. The CFL's moribund quota system did not protect their dashed dreams—nor will it protect those of Laurier hero Bill Kubas—because their breeding is suspect. This is also the league that stereotypes the precious homegrown talent it is supposed to nurture and display.

The unwritten rule is that Canadian players anchor the offensive line, kick, punt, fetch coffee, fill in at linebacker, give happy face interviews to grumpy reporters on off days, log a few downs at receiver, block for the star running back, squeegee the training table, run errands, attend union meetings, wash the coach's car and answer phones. Glamour positions are reserved for Americans.[54]

In Calgary, a Winnipeg fan at a sports bar "trying to smile away the abuse he took from the Stampeders faithful" said, "We have to keep this game Canadian. You don't get this excitement in the States."[55] There was also some humour injected. At the 1992 Grey Cup Game, a sign announced "CFL Expansion 1994: Gander Guppies," while another proclaimed "My Canada includes Portland."[56]

It appeared that talk of expansion of the CFL into the American market might be a case of "if you can't beat them, join them." For others, the concept of expansion which was just beginning to surface in November as a viable option was the only way: "You can keep the CFL the way it is and have a truly Canadian failure or you can expand into the United States, see the game regain some of its stability and then find ways to re-establish a greater Canadian presence."[57]

A sociological study by Reginald Bibby of the University of Lethbridge offered insight into the attitudes of Canadian youth towards Canadian football. Despite the fact that Bibby's study offered as one of its conclusions that "Canadian youth are choosing American [*sic*] in virtually every area of life [because] of the unprecedented presence of U.S. media"[58] and that survey participants ranked Michael Jordan, "Beverly Hills 90210," Guns and Roses, Julia Roberts, Stephen King, Dan Rather, and George Bush at the top in their various categories, Bibby also noted that there was only one category, "one Canadian institution that has managed to keep up with the American competition—the Canadian Football League."[59] Of the 4,000 teens surveyed nationally, 26% said they followed the NFL closely while 22% indicated they followed the CFL. His national adult survey of '90–'91 indicated that of those 18 years and older, 16% followed the CFL and 11% the NFL.

To Bibby, it was "something of a cultural miracle"[60] that the CFL figured at all in the survey, given the strikes against it. Firstly, the CFL was "surviving the American television onslaught" of NFL telecasts on American networks, such as CBS, NBC, ABC, ESPN, and TNT, received in Canadian homes. Secondly, "as if the NFL needed help, two of our indigenous channels, Global and TSN, supplement the five American networks in piping NFL games into Canadian homes,"[61] and NFL scores, injuries, comments, pre-game hype, and post-game discussions were taking up time and space in local sportscasts and sports pages. According to Bibby, "these first two factors alone should virtually bury the CFL."[62] And thirdly, Canada's "strangely sadistic" media "annually go out of their way to contribute to the perception that the league is fragile and probably near death."[63] He acknowledged that there were "objective problems"—some unstable franchises and a lack of promotion—but nonetheless sports reporters "rather than contributing to calm, have—in John Candy's words—been like sharks smelling blood."[64] Bibby concluded:

If the CFL ever fails, let's be clear about something: its failure will in large part reflect the failure not merely of the league but of the Canadian media to neutralize the impact that their American media counterparts are having on this century-old sports institution of ours. The CFL might be Canada's ugly duckling; but a remarkable duckling it is in an age when most things distinctively Canadian have gone the way of the U.S. cooking pot. Who knows what the CFL could look like if ethnocentric Americans could be persuaded to give it a closer look and masochistic Canadians stopped trying to put its head on the chopping block.[65]

When the CFL met in Calgary January 12, 1993, it was a foregone conclusion that it would expand into San Antonio and Sacramento. While the announcement was made in Calgary, the details were left for a press conference called the next day, January 13, in Toronto. Only the Winnipeg Blue Bombers voted against the plan. Describing the club as "pro expansion in Canada," the Blue Bombers' president Bruce Robinson declared "we're a Canadian game. We're proud of our Canadian players and our Canadian heritage. We felt we had to take a stand and make our point."[66]

As much as anything else, however, the Winnipeg club's objection was based on its perception of the revenue accruing from the expansion fees. With the league keeping half of the monies to dissolve its deficit problems, there would only be $75,000 for each club which "wouldn't be enough to offset travel costs."[67] Winnipeg said the clubs were to put up $600,000 a year for two years and the balance of the $3,000,000 was to be paid from profits.[68] Winnipeg's cost of expansion, predominantly in travel, was estimated to be $200,000.[69] When the press conference was held in Toronto, Robinson declined to attend, much to the chagrin of Calgary media who pressed for details after the announcement of league expansion to San Antonio and Sacramento was made there. Some dubbed the Blue Bombers' management personnel "dinosaurs," but they claimed they had the "facts to back up their arguments."[70] Bill Comrie and Phil Kershaw, two other representatives who were wavering about the decision to expand into the U.S., in the end voted "yes." Kershaw said: "We see this as an experiment ... we need a little bit of sizzle back in the CFL."[71]

The American flag accompanied the Canadian flag as the CFL made its historic announcement. The media conference in Toronto was telecast live by TSN from Ontario Place. Players' Association representatives, while voicing apprehension about the player quotas problem which had not yet been addressed, were enthusiastic. Dan Ferrone of the Argonauts described the announcement as "absolutely fantastic ... this will make the league better." George Reed said it would "bring some stability and growth to the league and get away from the death watch." Annis Stukus, the coach of the last expansion team in 1954, the B.C. Lions, said he knew it was coming and hoped the league watched the budgets. "I just hope Hamilton isn't dead," he said. Queen's University Coach Doug Hargreaves guessed that "there will be fewer jobs for Canadian players ... However the move to expand to the U.S. was strictly a business decision."[72]

Politicians were less enthusiastic. This move meant "the end of the CFL as we know it" said Liberal sports critic Bob Kilger, the MP from Cornwall. The NDP sports authority John Brewen of Victoria gave a blunt response: "I can't imagine very many issues in which I would have no comment but this is it. I've joined that great group of Canadians who probably don't care one bit."

In San Antonio, a press conference was held at the 65,000-seat Alamodome, the playing home of the new San Antonio Texans. Hard hats were issued to all, not as was suggested by one reporter, because of "the weaker mentality that has long prevailed among the league governors," but because the stadium was still under construction.[73] There were sceptics who said this was just another of the many football teams and leagues who had passed through. Former Winnipeg head coach Mike Riley resurfaced as the new San Antonio coach. Referring to the city's "bundle of teams," he spoke prophetically of the ever-present "death watch for these football teams." Civic officials and the "movers and shakers above Riley [were] considerably more optimistic."[74] But there were also warning sounds: unpaid bills from owner Larry Benson's WLAF team contributed to the perception that he "doesn't seem to be revered locally ... [he was] advised to keep a low profile."[75]

Perhaps the indicator as to what could transpire should have been taken from a local businessman and one of Benson's partners, Paul Sides, who ventured that "it's like being married. You make that commitment, but I don't know if it always lasts."[76] And it didn't last. The whirlwind romance courtship and marriage was over in two weeks. The Coach of the Year dinner in Edmonton should have been a joyous occasion celebrating the two-week honeymoon and the announcement of Wally Buono as the recipient of the Annis Stukus Trophy. No members of the Texas based team were at the meetings in Edmonton and Larry Smith announced that the San Antonio franchise had been put on hold until 1994.[77] A blockbuster 16-player trade between Edmonton and Toronto—the largest trade in CFL history—defused some of the fallout, but there was still speculation as to what had happened: Team officials were said to have needed 25,000 season tickets as a base to operate in the Alamodome and it was obvious that it wasn't going to happen. The San Antonio *Express News* suggested that the situation deteriorated when the team's "Board of Directors was re-figured giving Benson less say in the team's daily operations."[78] There were some who said that Larry Benson's brother Tom, owner of the New Orleans Saints, influenced the pull-out. Both Larry Benson and Fred Anderson had received $2 million each in a settlement with the NFL over the WLAF, the money to be used in financing the CFL franchise fee. Benson had left "a lot of unpaid bills." He was not available for comment, "having gone away on a little vacation to try and regroup himself."[79]

When Benson did surface to make a comment, he blamed "the Alamodome's management commitments to events in 1993" for his withdrawal. Stadium officials were upset; they had spent "nearly $250,000 (U.S.) preparing the Alamodome for CFL play." The general manager of the city-owned facility was irate and denied Benson's charge: "I'm very very disappointed if that's his view. We stuck our necks out for him. We supported him every step of the way."[80]

Amid all the furore, a Gallup poll taken prior to the San Antonio decision showed that Canadians were still divided on expansion to the United States. Nationally, 33% disapproved, 31% were in favour, the rest were undecided. Sentiment against the expansion was higher in the Prairies where 43% were opposed and 36% in favour, with 22% undecided. At the same time, nationally, 65% were in favour of the CFL returning to Montreal; 56% of Quebeckers were also for the CFL returning to the former league city.

While all of this might have caused Winnipeg's Cal Murphy to say "I told you so," he didn't, publicly. One reporter commented: "getting in and out of the Canadian Football League is easier than getting in and out of matrimony—and a lot cheaper."[81] Concerned that Benson had paid no money for his franchise, Murphy did however announce that the Blue Bombers would no longer send assessment cheques to the league.[82]

It was a disappointing turn of events for the CFL and for Larry Smith. His "four hot buttons" were reduced to one. Former Montreal Machine owner, Roger Dore, had given up on reviving football in Montreal and, on March 3, 1993, the Portland group formally announced that it too would not pursue a franchise in the CFL, saying that "building a new arena for basketball is more important."[83] Only the Sacramento Gold Miners answered the call to form the CFL's first new franchise since 1954 and the first American one ever. The league announced that a "hold" would be put on U.S. expansion for 1993. Since the San Antonio decision, inquiries from Nick Mileti (Ohio) and Sal Biondo (Florida) were pursued but by February

At the CFL meetings in Toronto, in November after the 1992 Grey Cup Game, the league had made it known that it wanted to phase out what it called "the Canadian quota." Larry Smith had informed the Players' Association "that 160 non-import positions would be guaranteed over the next two years regardless of the number of teams."[85] The Winnipeg, Saskatchewan, and Hamilton clubs all chose to address the non-import question as part of their remarks on expansion. Winnipeg expressed "genuine concern about the status of the Canadian player whose role may be considerably lessened in direct competition with more readily available and better trained American players."[86] Saskatchewan noted that its club relied heavily upon non-import talent and took its commitment to develop football in the province seriously. Saskatchewan was concerned how various levels of government support would be "affected ... if it can be perceived as a denial or diminution of opportunities for Canadian players."[87] Hamilton wanted "the present import ratio maintained and to enhance the supply lines of Canadian talent, the league should increase its support at the amateur levels."[88]

The Argonauts' general manager Mike McCarthy was opposed to a proposal to exempt American teams from the import quota: "By mid season, when the Americans begin to learn our rules, we'll get our butts kicked. With all those Americans, we'll definitely be at a disadvantage."[89] One of his players, guard Dan Ferrone, did not share McCarthy's view. Ferrone was also an executive with the Players' Association which was holding firm to its collective agreement. "There are a lot of guys in this league who believe there is a misconception when it comes to the ability of Canadians" he said.[90] Ferrone repeated what had been advanced by others: as long as the salary cap was in place and adhered to, the type of American currently attracted to the CFL would continue to be attracted and Canadians had demonstrated their ability to compete with them. Ferrone laid out the CFLPA position: "As players, we are totally for expansion, provided the ratio isn't altered."[91]

Regardless of what was being said, economics were dictating the league's stance. The CFL salary cap for 1993 was to be $2.5 million; previously it was $3 million. It included players' salaries, coaches' salaries, those on the injury list, practice rosters, signing bonuses, performance bonuses, any extra training camp salary costs, vehicle expense, and anything defined as salary or salary benefits under the Canadian Income Tax Act.[92] Not only that, salaries of marquee players presently in the league were to be "grandfathered"; the new salary cap for marquee players was placed at $250,000. "Rocket Ismail, Doug Flutie and/or other marquee players over the $250,000 amount" were to be exempted for 1993.[93] Salaries in 1993 would have to be trimmed. Unlimited imports were the solution, especially with the demise of the WLAF and the huge market of football players in the United States who would play for less than what CFL teams had to pay for their talent currently. A comparison using salary, exchange, and taxes illustrated the problem:

	American on an American team	American on a Canadian team
Salary	$85,000	$85,000
Income Tax	$23,800 (28%)	$32,300 (38%)
Net CDN:		$52,700
Net U.S.:	$61,200	$38,471 (78%)

As far as the players were concerned, "the answer is clearly defined in the collective bargaining agreement."[94] Twenty non-imports were required by each team even among expansion teams "except where such a restriction would be unlawful."[95] The contract ran through the 1994 season and the Players'Association wasn't budging from its position in vowing to protect the Canadian players. Dan Ferrone, the Association's second vice-president, said "if we don't, it will be an insult to those who fought for it."[96]

Smith had always maintained that "your top Canadians are going to play even if the league is on the moon. It's the fringe players, the ones on the practice roster, the ones who aren't on the active roster" who would be affected.[97] Some weren't impressed. Jim Proudfoot, calling Canadian players an "endangered species," wrote:

> please drop that sanctimonious claptrap about Canadians remaining competitive under any circumstances. CFL coaches wouldn't trouble themselves with Canadian players at all if they weren't compelled to dress some for each game. They're a colossal pain in the neck. Always have been. Recruiting Americans is easier and cheaper and they come fully prepared.[98]

In an effort to speed up the process of Sacramento becoming ready for the '93 season, the league tentatively approved its expansion draft of Canadian talent. There would still be 160 non-imports required among the nine teams. Eighteen would be required for each Canadian team and 16 for the new Sacramento club. As far as the American team was concerned, it would select eight non-imports from a pool provided after each club protected five players. A second round of eight selections was to be made after the Canadian clubs protected one non-import after the first round.[99] The draft never did take place.

Negotiations continued with the Players' Association about the number of Canadians on each team. The CFL proposed that the non-import requirement be reduced to zero after a five-year period, decreasing the number from 160 by 40 each year. At the end of five years, it was proposed that competition be open, that market forces determine who would play. The Players' Association balked; it wanted the existing contract to apply for two years as per the agreement, after which negotiations could occur. On February 11, 1993, Larry Smith suspended talks with the players. The existing contract would be honoured until it expired after the 1994 season; after that the league would push for no non-import restrictions.

Players were critical of Smith: "I hope Larry Smith understands he'll be recognized as the commissioner who killed the Canadian in the CFL,"[100] said the Argos' Dan Ferrone. Winnipeg's Players' Association representative Chris Walby lamented that the game was becoming "too much like a business. There's no concern for the guys who make the league."[101] The players were upset that the talks were suspended without warning, that the league was attempting to make a unilateral decision. Walby continued: "Larry has got to realize he's the commissioner not the judge. There's a guy who forgot where he came from. This is a black day."[102]

From the perspective of the league, it appeared to be strictly a business decision. Clubs had already decided to drop the salary cap to $2.5 million from the $3 million of '92. There was also the "ultimate life saving goal of Smith and the American owners to bring the salary cap down to a mere $1.5 million."[103] It could be done by removing the non-imports and their salaries from the equation and concentrating on the huge talent pool in the United States where the supply would dictate lower salaries for players. The WLAF, for example, "set up a salary structure based on position. Quarterbacks earned $25,000 a season; running backs, receivers and linebackers earned $20,000 a season; linemen, blocking backs, specialty team players, kickers and defensive backs earned $15,000 a year."[104] Under such a threat, it was in the best interests of the CFL's imports to support the Players' Association's attempt to maintain the non-import regulations.

Reactions were swift. Media lined up on either side. In Winnipeg, veteran columnist Hal Sigurdson tied the league's decision to the larger political issue: "the blueprint was sitting there in Ottawa all along. You save the league the way we're saving the country. Turn it into a minor league U.S. branch plant."[105] He blamed "the transient professionals, the coaches and general managers ... predominantly American" for turning the CFL "into the bag lady of professional sport."[106] He labelled Smith's assertion that "import restrictions were first established in 1936 to protect Canadian jobs" as "codswallop." He explained that nobody had a "job" playing football in 1936. "They played for team jackets."

The real reason, he said, for the import rule passed by the Canadian Rugby Union (CRU) in 1936 was to "accelerate the development of Canadian football" but at the same time "to prevent some egomaniac with deep pockets from importing a winner." Sigurdson supported his view by citing long-time Winnipeg observer Vince Leah "who was there ... the original intent was to gradually phase out imports as the level of Canadian football improved."[107] Sigurdson maintained that

> the number of imports gradually increased, not for the betterment of Canadian football but because some American coach thought it might save his job. The fact a Canadian Commissioner is not being lynched for taking a decision that will ultimately remove all import restrictions tells you how far the league has strayed from its original concept. It also tells you it is dead. It may continue to twitch for another few seasons, but rigor mortis is already setting in.[108]

On February 26, 1993, Smith made the announcement that Sacramento would be allowed to play with whichever players it wished. The league's regulations concerning imports and non-imports would not apply to the American team. As well, the draft on non-import talent would not be held. The Players' Association president George Reed was fuming because Smith made the information public "without first consulting his association."[109] Smith said that "he had spoken to Reed about what he was going to announce."[110]

When the Sacramento Gold Miners were ready to play their first exhibition game, it was eagerly anticipated for a number of reasons. It was against Winnipeg, the team which was so opposed to expansion into the United States. The Blue Bombers, however, recognized a business opportunity when they saw one. That game was promoted as "U.S. vs Us" and "Us vs Them." It was a great chance to draw a good crowd when expenses were at their lowest because it was an exhibition game. On the wider front, there was the potential for all sides to say "I told you so!" There were those who felt that Sacramento with its unlimited imports would prove too much for the non-import laden Blue Bombers.

The game attracted a good-sized crowd of 23,191. Sacramento won 21–15 but nobody really had the chance to crow. Quarterback Matt Dunigan was ejected from the game, less than three minutes into it; he took exception to the play of Sacramento's Randy Thornton and Basil Proctor, ripping Thorton's helmet off his head, throwing it downfield.[111] Winnipeg finished the game with untried rookie Keithen McCant. The Bombers came under criticism from the public and media. "Words like 'pitiful' and 'pansies' were echoing from the West side stadium crowd" and the fans who paid up to $24 a ticket "were not referring to the U.S. guys who had been together for a mere nine days."[112] The team was criticized for playing the "Star Spangled Banner" after "O Canada" since it was "standard operating procedure to play [the American National Anthem] first."[113] Dunigan, was criticized for being thrown out after two minutes and 11 seconds: "the million dollar man ... four-for-four for 55 yards before he lost his cool."[114]

When the Gold Miners moved into Ottawa to open the '93 CFL regular season, they had a perfect record in the exhibition season, having defeated B.C. 38–20. Sacramento was less than excited about its early schedule, meeting first Ottawa and then Hamilton in less than 72 hours. Again the game was a matter for conjecture. It was billed as the "first international" CFL game. Russ Jackson, the former Ottawa standout, ventured an opinion that the ground rules would change. "The name of the game in football is injuries. And when a Canadian gets hurt he's difficult to replace. But the Gold Miners have an entire country of not-ready-for-the-NFL players from which to choose."[115] Ottawa owners, Bernie and Lonie Glieberman, decided that the local TV blackout would be lifted for the TSN telecast saying, "This is a historic game and we think everyone should be able to see it."[116] Twenty-four thousand showed up to watch the Rough Riders win the game 32–23. When the Sacramento team returned home after losing its first two games in the CFL, it was to play the Calgary Stampeders and Doug Flutie. There was a crowd of 20,082 in attendance; Calgary won 38–36 and there was a host of positives responses. The game received superb publicity in the Sacramento *Bee*, one columnist calling the game "an improved version of an old game that was a crashing bore,"[117] another writing that "it works, the CFL has built a better mouse trap."[118] Larry Ryckman, Calgary owner and head of the CFL's Expansion Committee, perhaps thinking of the prospective owners invited to the game to witness CFL football first hand, was delighted: "I think we could sell three franchises off that one game alone."[119]

The fact remained however that Sacramento was 0–3 after its first three games. By mid-August, Sacramento had one victory and was on the verge of its second against Hamilton but was still in last place in the Western Division.

It was reported that the move to four rather than three teams in the play-offs was made "in order to provide the expansion Gold Miners with a better shot at generating interest in their market."[120] It was necessary because apparently the gilt was tarnishing for Sacramento. Owner Fred Anderson estimated he would lose $3.5 million in 1993.[121] The average attendance figure of 15,000 was inflated; the club was giving away about 2,000 tickets per game. For the Edmonton game, season ticket holders were given two free tickets. Anderson lamented that "tax write-offs don't make up for the kind of losses I'm taking. This is a very hard hit, take my word for it."[122] He said that Sacramento needed at least 25,000 fans per game to break even. Several reasons for the team's lack of success were offered. The NFL and college football, especially San Francisco 49ers and Stanford University, were attracting most of the interest. The team was in last place; CFL players were not well-known. Even David Archer's abilities as a quarterback were being questioned: "he's not a good CFL quarterback. He just stands there and gets sacked while other CFL quarterbacks roll out of the pocket."[123] Anderson was critical of the lack of assistance from the CFL: they offer "almost nothing in the way of marketing support ... they don't have even one person here [in the U.S.]."[124]

It was evident that CFL franchises were struggling throughout the league. In Hamilton, attendance had fallen off. Financial resources were low. Long-time general manager and former player, Joe Zuger, resigned in early January. The club had traded its "marquee player," quarterback Damon Allen, to Edmonton and pinned its hopes on second-year quarterback Don McPherson. When he was unable to generate victories the team turned to non-import quarterback Bob Torrance who started two games, the first non-import to do so in the CFL since Greg Vavra in 1987. Purchase inquiries for Hamilton were received from Americans Sal Biondo of Washington, Paul Snyder of Buffalo, and Nick Mileti from Cleveland. The club was forced to approach the CFL for advances in income. When the CFL was requested to assist in a bail out, it refused. Memories of the expensive costs of the B.C. and Ottawa franchises were still fresh in everyone's mind. Calgary's Larry Ryckman contributed $100,000 to assist the Tiger-Cats in meeting their payroll.[125]

While Ryckman's money was appreciated, some of his later comments were not. He suggested that there was a possibility that the Tiger-Cats might move to Halifax "if Hamiltonians were not more supportive."[126] An unsigned circular was distributed during the Tiger-Cats' Labour Day game with the Argos suggesting that "Ryckman's involvement in the Tiger-Cats was insulting and unnecessary and that he should be received with scepticism."[127] Hamilton's chairman Roger Yachetti in interviews with the CBC and *The Globe and Mail* also challenged Ryckman, calling for him to be more discreet in his comments: "I don't see why he would say this. Perhaps it's wishful thinking by Mr. Ryckman but I haven't heard anything about the Ticats going to Halifax."[128] Ryckman countered that "when Roger goes on TV and says everything is okay in Hamilton *that's* wishful thinking, in my opinion."[129]

When the CFL's Board of Governors met in Ottawa on September 14, 1993, the Hamilton situation had deteriorated to the point that the Tiger-Cats requested $1 million in aid from the league. The league refused, but in the end it was the new franchise of Las Vegas and Nick Mileti which came to the rescue. In return for early payment of his franchise fee, the league gave

Mileti a discount fee of $500,000. His payment of $1.5 million U.S. gave the Tiger-Cats their share of $150,000, enough to see them through.

In mid-October, the hemorrhaging was stopped. Toronto financier David MacDonald, put in touch with Hamilton by Larry Ryckman, surfaced with a plan to inject $1.5 million in 1993 and a further $1.5 million (less commissions and royalties) in early 1994. It guaranteed that payments on the club's debt of close to two million dollars over the past two seasons would be made and that the Tiger-Cats would remain in Hamilton at least through 1994.

In Toronto, there was turmoil of another kind. The Argonauts seemed to be in the business of "divesting." The club sent eight of its players to Edmonton to join former Argonaut coach Adam Rita and Rocket Ismail was dispatched to the Los Angeles Raiders. It gave up its rights to the 1993 Grey Cup Game, selling it to Larry Ryckman and the Calgary Stampeders. It gave up its "exclusivity clause" to football in the SkyDome to allow the first pre-season NFL game in Canada since 1961 to be played there in August, matching the Cleveland Browns against the New England Patriots. Cleveland's record was 7–9 in 1992 and New England's was 2–14, prompting Dan Barreiro of the Minneapolis St Paul *Star Tribune* to give them the "Give It Up And Join The CFL Award."[130] The game was sponsored by Molson's and was advertised as "the football event of the year in Toronto." Cleveland defeated New England 12–9 before a "turnstile count" of 33,021 fans.[131]

The Argonauts also replaced Brian Cooper, the club's executive vice-president. The announcement was made in an "Argo release datelined Los Angeles rather than Toronto."[132] Chris Flynn, who was seeking to gain a spot as a back-up quarterback was also released, his football days as an aspiring CFL quarterback now over. The Argos had also lost their first draft choice in the university draft plus $50,000 for having gone over the league's salary cap of $3,000,000 in 1992.[133]

By mid-season, with the Argos sporting a 1–9 record, further changes were made. Ron Barbaro, former president of the Argonaut Playback club and a successful insurance executive, was named the president and chief executive officer of the Argonauts. His moves to resurrect the floundering franchise were swift. The man who was proclaimed for having saved the Toronto Zoo and the Santa Claus Parade moved to replace General Manager Mike McCarthy, reassigned Head Coach Dennis Meyer to defensive coordinator, fired offensive coordinator "Mouse" Davis, and hired former Argonaut and B.C. Lion coach Bob O'Billovich—all within 48 hours of his appointment. He gave some indication of his approach when during the team's first game in the 'Dome against Winnipeg, September 19, when he had the play-by-play televised on the Jumbotron so that fans could enjoy and see the game as they would if they were at home. It was the first time it had been done. Apparently Barbaro had not inquired about the club's right to do so: "It's easier to say I'm sorry rather than to request permission," he philosophized.[134]

In a further effort to attract past season ticket holders, the Argonauts offered two free tickets to all 1992 subscribers who hadn't renewed for '93, for the October 31 game with Saskatchewan. The team's average attendance of 20,000 in 1990 rose to 36,304 in the Grey Cup year of '91, fell to 32,053 in '92, and was averaging 25,334 in '93.[135] Over the same period as the attendance fall-off, the team was losing and missed the CFL play-offs with a 3–15 record. No sooner had the team lost its last game of the season to Winnipeg 12–10, than the rumours started. A guest of Barbaro at the Saskatchewan game was newspaper magnate Ken Thompson. Was he being courted as "part of the group Barbaro is trying to put together to take the Argos off Bruce McNall's hands?"[136] McNall denied a story that he was trying to sell the Argos but it was in couched terms: "As long as the people of Toronto indicate they want the Argos, he's 'here to play,'" the *Toronto Star* reported.[137]

McNall's partner, Wayne Gretzky, was convinced that the time had come to sell. "The fact is, people in Toronto don't want the CFL ... I've told McNall, I think it's time [to sell] ... As far as I'm concerned, time's up."[138]

In Ottawa 1993 was a "soap opera season."[139] It had its start early in the year. The Rough Riders announced the signing of John Ritchie as their chief executive officer on the recommendation of Brian Cooper of the Argos.[140] Ritchie had formerly been with Alpine Canada and had no football experience. It was an attempt to address the business aspects of operating a football team with a businessman, rather than an ex-player.[141] When General Manager Dan Rambo "balked at reporting to Ritchie," he was fired June 2nd. His position was not filled. Ron Smeltzer was given the title of Director of Football Operations reporting to Ritchie in addition to his duties as head coach. While there was some uproar, it was minor; Rambo had made few friends among the media.

On August 16, with the Riders at 1–6, owner Bernie Glieberman annnounced that J. I. Albrecht would be hired as a "consultant to the President/Chairman" and that Dexter Manley would be brought back as quickly as possible to start at defensive end.[142] The announcement about the arrival of Manley was said by Irv Daymond, Ottawa's centre, to have "taken the Riders down to the level of Professional wrestling ... Not only is Lonie

[Glieberman] insulting the players in this dressing room, he's insulting the football fans of Ottawa who want honest to goodness football, not cheap marketing crap."[143] Don Campbell wrote that for the club's announcement "there was no possible better backdrop than that provided by the ongoing preparations for the opening of the Super Ex Midway."[144] Linebacker Gregg Stuman asked, "Why do we take pay cuts when [the Gliebermans] have that kind of money to throw around? It's a slap in the face to every player in this room. He's not going to help."[145]

When the Rough Riders defeated the Argonauts on August 26, their one point victory, without Dexter Manley, propelled them into third place and gave the coaches a stay of execution but the guessing game of when the firings of the coaches would take place continued. Ottawa's Gliebermans seemed to have replacements at hand. George Brancato, Ottawa's last coach when the team won the Grey Cup was hired to work with the defence. John Salavantis, former offensive coordinator with the Tiger-Cats, assumed the same role with the Rough Riders.

When Bernie Glieberman gave the directive that Manley had to dress and start against Toronto on September 25, two assistant coaches, Jim Daley and Mike Roach, quit in protest. Fights among players became common-place. Angelo Snipes and Danny Chronopoulos on the field; Ken Walcott and Michael Allen in the parking lot; Andrew Stewart and Glenn Kulka in the locker room. When Dexter Manley was suspended and fined by Glieberman for calling Coach Ron Smeltzer a "liar," it was described as "just another day at the nuthouse that goes by the name Ottawa Rough Riders."[146] The Gliebermans responded by suspending Manley "for conduct unbecoming a professional athlete."[147] They had previously ordered Smeltzer to start Manley for the October 30 game against Winnipeg in spite of the head coach making "it clear he was not only opposed to playing Manley but didn't even want him in camp."[148] In Manley's first game against the Argos, he left after 16 plays with a hyperextended elbow and slight tear in his knee. His teammates disputed the injuries, irritated further that Manley was being paid handsomely for not being able to play while they had taken pay cuts in order to contribute to the team.

Owners said the players were jealous, players responded by calling the situation "the Season from Hell."[149] Still, the Rough Riders had a chance to salvage their season. Going into the last game of the season, tied for third with the Argos with a 3–14 record, they had only to see the Argos lose or the Riders win their final game against Hamilton. They won 27–26, oddly enough aided by a hit on quarterback Todd Dillon by Manley late in the fourth quarter. Dillon fumbled, Ottawa recovered, and went on to score the winning touchdown. It was Manley's "first statistics in the CFL—a tackle and fumble recovery"[150] and enough to prompt him to speak of his "disfigured helmet" and how he would have three sacks and cause the quarterback to lose the ball at least twice as a result,[151] in the play-off game rematch. Manley also "revealed" that he was fined for saying that the "Riders had offered a pre-game reward to the player who could knock Dillon out of the game, as Manley did."[152]

In the Eastern semifinal, the Tiger-Cats, led again by Todd Dillon, ended the "Riders' Nightmare Season" defeating them by a 21–10 score. Manley was still on everyone's mind. "For the record, Manley had no sacks yesterday. No fumble recoveries. No tackles. No nothing."[153] On November 15, Albrecht, Brancato and Salavantis were told that they were no longer needed. Lonie Glieberman said that he intended to bring Manley back in '94. On November 22, "one hundred and three days after owner Bernie Glieberman first threatened to fire Ron Smeltzer, the axe finally fell."[154] Smeltzer was informed over breakfast by John Ritchie who then went to Lansdowne Park to fire assistants Harry Justvig, Jim Clark, and Dick Maloney. Only secondary coach Larry Hogue, whose contract had expired November 30 was invited to apply when a new head coach, the Riders' ninth in ten years, would be selected. The "soap opera season" had come to an end.

The play-offs continued as Hamilton moved to Winnipeg for the Eastern final, eager to make amends for having lost the play-off game of '92 to Winnipeg by a 59–11 score in a game which saw the Tiger-Cats' bench pelted by snowballs from some Winnipeg fans.

The Blue Bombers had had their share of adversity during the season. Cal Murphy, after his return from heart transplant surgery, broke a hip and arm in a fall early in the season. He coached practices from a golf cart and from a press box perch for games. Then the Bombers lost quarterback Matt Dunigan with a torn Achilles tendon during the team's 33–26 victory over Sacramento. Quarterback Sam Garza, also the son-in-law of Murphy, only had two games to hone his quarterbacking skills before meeting Hamilton. And as successful as the club was on the field it was having financial woes. It was into its $1.2 million line of credit from the Winnipeg Enterprises Corp., the club's landlord, had a second line of credit with the corporation, and an outstanding loan of $500,000 from the Royal Bank, the Province having approved a loan of $1 million in September.[155] Nonetheless, the Bombers beat Hamilton in the Eastern final, for a second time, by a 20–19 score.

The CFL had decided in March to change its play-off format in the West. It moved from three teams, the traditional first-place team receiving a bye while second- and third-placed teams played-off, to four teams in the play-offs, first versus fourth and second versus third, the winners to meet for the Western Division championship. As a sweetener, the league announced that the second- and third- place teams would still receive $1,800 per player, the fourth-place team $1,300, and the first-place team $2,500.[156] The change, however, had to be approved by the Players' Association. By the time the matter was ready to be voted on, training camps had ended and such matters were not to be negotiated during the season according to the contract. By August, the announcement was made once again. Calgary players whose team was solidly ensconced in first place were upset. The Calgary public initiated a boycott of the play-off game. Eventually the league agreed to a vote by the Players' Association for their determination and only by the first week in November was the change ratified.

In the West, the expanded play-offs took place. The Saskatchewan-Edmonton game between the second- and third-place teams was expected to be a close one. When the game was over, however, the Eskimos, behind a confident Damon Allen, defeated the Western 'riders by a 51–13 score. A crowd of 15,407 showed up for the game between Calgary and B.C. in which the Stampeders were victorious by a 17–9 score.

The Western final was, once again, "the battle of Alberta." Calgary, which according to sources had paid $350,000[157] to Bruce McNall's Argonauts to buy the rights to the game, was gearing up for its own Grey Cup party. It had promoted the B.C. Lion game as a film with the billing: "How the West will be won. Part I of a two week mini series. Starring Doug Flutie, the Ultimate Weapon as the Rifleman, Co-Starring the Wild Bunch—Alondra Johnson, Marvin Pape, Matt Finlay. Directed by Wally Buono. A Larry Ryckman Production. General Warning: Some scenes will not be suitable for the opposition."[158]

When Larry Ryckman bought the rights to the 1993 Grey Cup Game from Bruce McNall's Toronto Argonauts, he fully expected that his Calgary Stampeders would be playing. It was a gamble but a calculated one. Published reports had him paying $350,000 plus $24,500 GST to the Argos and a further $350,000 guarantee to the league.[159] It was not stated whether the latter was above the $3,000,000 guarantee the Argos had given when they were awarded the '92 and '93 games. Calgary City Council approved $390,000 worth of services while an additional $1.1 million was to be spent to bring McMahon Stadium capacity close to 50,000. All in all, it was estimated that some $13 million would be the total cost of all activities.[160]

Everything seemed to be proceeding smoothly and according to plan—until that fateful Sunday, November 21, when the Eskimos spoiled the Stampeders' plans, defeating them by a 29–15 count. Only 20,218 spectators showed up for the game which was played in -20°C temperatures, winds of 24 kph and blowing snow. Conditions were so hostile that the beginning of the third quarter was delayed an extra 15 minutes to clear the snow from the field. Flutie's hands were "frozen" to the point where he had no feeling in them and was forced to miss a play at the end of the game while trying to thaw them out. It was a disappointing end to the season for Calgarians who attended the game, some saying it was the coldest they had ever been to, enduring frostbite on their uncovered skin, staying "until the last second waiting for the Flutie miracle."[161]

Stunned Stampeder fans faced the reality that they would be hosting a Grey Cup celebration for their rivals from the north and Winnipeg. Calgary became "the city of the big hurt."[162] Grey Cup plans were in jeopardy. Some 20,000 seats had been sold prior to November 19, including those purchased by Safeway for its family huddle section "where admission is cheap."[163] An additional 30,000 were still to be sold and in one week. The emphasis was now on attracting Edmontonians. Two columns of classified ads offering Grey Cup tickets for sale appeared in the *Calgary Herald* as late as November 26.

After having been defeated by a Calgary team in the 1991 and 1992 Western finals, Edmonton and its self-proclaimed City of Champions descriptor, had become the butt of Calgary jokes. Not this year though! In spite of recent -30°C temperatures, only smiles were frozen on the faces of its citizens as a result of the Edmonton win. Monday morning at work saw Edmontonians "laughing and happy. It was like someone won the lottery."[164] The tables were turned and Edmonton loved it. News reports chortled that Calgarians were "still numb from the loss." An Edmonton newspaper asked its readers for their favourite Calgary jokes ("What's the difference between a loonie and Calgary quarterback Doug Flutie? You can get four good quarters from a loonie").[165]

At a reception and send-off at City Hall in Edmonton, the Edmonton euphoria, at Calgary's expense, continued. "What more could we ask for? Calgary's throwing a big party and it's just for us," said Mayor Jan Reimer. Her bet with Calgary Mayor Al Duerr was that Edmonton's City of Champions sign on the outskirts of town would be polished by her counterpart. Clearly, she was enjoying the moment: "I'd like to personally thank [the Eskimos players] for saving me from the embarrassment of riding in the Grey Cup parade wearing a Stampeders' sweater."[166]

Fears of the weather inflicting its wintry grip on Calgary's Grey Cup Game, particularly because of the 3:30 P.M. start, proved unfounded. Temperature at game time was 6°C, positively balmy in comparison with the previous week, but regardless of the warming breezes, there were still some disgruntled patrons who booed the playing of the American anthem prior to the game. It was played along with "O Canada" in recognition of Sacramento's membership in the league. In the press box, though, "not a single regular media person from Sacramento was among the approximately 300 accredited writers and broadcasters"[167] save only for Gold Miners' quarterback David Archer, who was hired as the colour commentator for the Telemedia radio broadcast of the game and also sent "a scene setting column to a newspaper and radio clips for three stations" back to Sacramento.[168] The Edmonton Eskimos, aided by seven uncharacteristic Winnipeg turnovers, won the Grey Cup contest by a 33–23 score. Damon Allen was selected the Most Valuable Player of the game.

In the pre-game awards, Doug Flutie was selected the Most Outstanding Player for the third consecutive year, a league record. He was chosen over Winnipeg's Matt Dunigan, who because of a severed achilles tendon, did not play in the Grey Cup Game. Flutie, whose 1993 league statistics included a record 6,092 passing yards and 44 touchdowns in 18 games, was a near unanimous selection. Fifty two votes were cast for him, one against, with one spoiled ballot.[169] Other award winners were: Most Outstanding Non-import, Dave Sapunjis; Most Outstanding Lineman, Chris Walby; Most Outstanding Defensive Player, Jearld Baylis; Rookie of the Year, Michael O'Shea. In another break from the past, the winners and runners up received no monetary prizes, instead being rewarded with "rings, trophies and prizes from the league and Grey Cup Festival organizers."[170] The league also made known its all time "dream team," voting for which was conducted by fans attending CFL games during the '93 season. On defence, the All Time CFL All Stars were: Joe Hollimon, Edmonton; Dickie Harris, Montreal; Garney Henley, Hamilton; Dick Thornton, Toronto; Jerry Keeling, Calgary; James Parker, Edmonton; Mike Widger, Montreal; Wayne Harris, Calgary; Herb Gray, Winnipeg; Bill Baker, Saskatchewan; John Helton, Calgary; John Barrow, Hamilton; on offence: Frank Rigney, Winnipeg; Roger Nelson, Edmonton; Roger Aldag, Saskatchewan; Tony Pajaczkowski, Calgary; Ted Urness, Saskatchewan; Ray Elgaard, Saskatchewan; Tony Gabriel, Ottawa; Hal Patterson, Hamilton; Brian Kelly, Edmonton; Leo Lewis, Winnipeg; George Reed, Saskatchewan; Ron Lancaster, Saskatchewan; Lui Passaglia, B.C.; Dave Cutler, Edmonton; Henry Williams, Winnipeg. Jackie Parker, Edmonton, who played halfback, wide receiver, placekicker and punter in his career was voted Most Outstanding Player; Bud Grant, Winnipeg, was the coach; and Norm Kimball, Edmonton, the general manager.

When Commissioner Larry Smith delivered his "State of the League" address followed by a question and answer session, some obviously pent-up emotions were vented. Among other items, Smith revealed that 1993 would probably be the last year guaranteeing an East-West final. With expansion into the United States proceeding, a North-South final, with seeded play-offs and wild cards, was more likely. Sacramento had requested a name change, substituting "North American" for "Canadian," reasoning that such a name change would make the league "more attractive to U.S. investors."[172]

In December, the CFL's newest team announced its name in Las Vegas, Nevada, with all the glitter and glitz that city could muster. The "First Lady of Magic," Melinda, was fired from a cannon carrying a blank banner and, when the smoke cleared, she was standing on the other side of the stage. She unfurled the banner to reveal the team's logo and name, the Posse. The team colours were light brown (sand), black, and white; the logo silhouetted black horses on a sand background with white lettering.[173] Having originally awarded the franchise to Cleveland businessman Nick Mileti on July 27, 1993, the CFL had finally arrived in Las Vegas, "The Entertainment Capital of the World."

There were detractors in Las Vegas, however. The *Record-Journal's* sports writer Stephen Nover reported that the NFL was the game of choice and college football drew about 8,000 per game. The Canadian-sized field would mean "pads on the walls" and end zones of 17 yards depth rather than 20.[174] The *Toronto Star*, after sympathizing with the CFL and its problems suggested that

> had the energy poured into the pursuit of franchises in third-rate American cities been put, instead, into resurrecting the Alouettes in Montreal, re-invigorating the Tiger-Cats in Hamilton and the Argos in Toronto, and creating a team in Halifax, maybe we could have kept a distinctive Canadian league.[175]

Smith, too, was getting his share of the criticism. One reader wrote "Commissioner Larry Smith, if he's remembered at all, will be a footnote in sports history as Canadian football's Brian Mulroney."[176]

Two more American teams were added in time for the 1994 CFL season. Each as a result of some form of rejection and in a city that the original CFL vision had not included, Baltimore and Shreveport. In its original approach to expansion into the United States, the CFL wanted to go into markets which were too small for NFL consideration, but still in major television markets as the search for a television contract was an ongoing CFL objective. Baltimore had been an NFL market, but after a long association and identity with that league, it had been unceremoniously dumped. Its team, the Colts, had left, some said, in the middle of the night, for Indianapolis, leaving a bitter community behind. The other American team was from Shreveport, Louisiana. The arrival of the league in Shreveport was tied directly to the Gliebermans who decided to take their "circus" from Ottawa and travel to Louisiana. Originally, the long-range plan of the Gliebermans was to operate a team in Detroit and it wanted the first opportunity in that area. If that occasion arose, the Ottawa club was to be transferred to a new owner.[177] As a result, when the Gliebermans purchased the Ottawa franchise in 1991, they had a written agreement that, at the end of the three years, they would be allowed to place a club wherever they chose, leaving the Ottawa franchise for new owners.

Unlike the Baltimore Colts, the NFL and Robert Irsay, however, the Gliebermans did not go quietly in the night. Already the butt of much criticism in Ottawa because of the 1993 season, they were the centre of increased controversy both inside and outside the city. From a league perspective, there were fears that the Ottawa franchise, a 118-year tradition in that city, would cease to exist. If the league were going to have a team in Shreveport, it preferred that it be an expansion franchise and therefore generate the $3 million fee. The Glieberman family was insistent about the move, stating, "the ideal situation would be for part of the [Ottawa] team to move ... to Shreveport as a new team and a buyer for the Ottawa team could be found to keep a franchise in Ottawa."[178]

Tempers began to heat up and flared into fisticuffs when Lonie Glieberman, along with his body guard Steve Wilson, and his girlfriend, found themselves in an argument with patrons at the Yucatan Liquor Stand on a Saturday night. "A patron of the bar slugged the 300 pound Wilson." According to the patron "Glieberman's popularity [has] plummeted with the crowd at the bar. Last year ... no one would harass him. But this year is a different story."[179]

The furore continued. The Gliebermans had only recently signed a ten-year lease to play in Frank Clair Stadium, while at the same time, they had investigated Louisville, Lexington, San Antonio, Columbus, Memphis, and Richmond as possible franchise sites before settling on Shreveport. It appeared as if they were ready to act without the "due process" insisted upon by the league.[180] Equipment manager Jim Rempel had been instructed by Bernie Glieberman "to pack up the equipment bags and prepare for a move."[181] Special consultant J.I. Albrecht had "already set up shop as the Gliebermans' front man for the possible new club, the Pirates."[182]

The new franchise and the sale of the Ottawa club were tied together. Since there would be one more team in the CFL, the $3 million price tag had to come from somewhere, either from the Gliebermans for the Shreveport franchise, the new owners of the Rough Riders, or a combination of both. In addition, there were Ottawa's debts, estimated at $1.2 million to $1.4

million, which had to be addressed. As a consequence of all of this, the CFL sought to develop more strict guidelines which would ensure that teams would not move to greener pastures. There was some speculation that the NHL by-law 36.5 would be used as a model, causing one scoffing reporter to state that "we already know how 'protected' our Canadian asset is going to be" if that were the case.[183]

All of this seemed to be a continuation of the carnival atmosphere which prevailed during the 1993 season. Former general manager, Jo-Anne Polack sought, and was granted, an injunction to prohibit the Gliebermans "from taking any Rider assets out of Ottawa."[184] The Gliebermans' lawyer countered that the $15,000 she was seeking was owed by previous owners and that if Polack wanted the money "let her sue the CFL."[185] The injunction was lifted as soon as the Gliebermans' lawyer appeared in court to contest it. The CFL was getting nervous. It had a schedule to draw up.

Ottawa City council entered the equation. It proposed that it spend $3 million to upgrade Frank Clair Stadium. It seemed to be the key to attracting former Ottawa Senator owner Bruce Firestone. Before that key could be turned, however, the city wanted a guarantee that it would be paid the $340,000 it said that the Gliebermans owed. By means of a convoluted arrangement, put together over a two-day period by David MacDonald (Toronto financier, Ottawa Senator and Hamilton Tiger-Cat investor, and CFL consultant) that included the Gliebermans, Firestone, the City of Ottawa, and Bretton Woods Entertainment, a deal was secured. Bernie and Lonie Glieberman gave the CFL $1.7 million for the right to field a team in Shreveport. A further "$1.85 million in deferred payments … from ticket surcharges and a share of Ottawa's take on future expansion fees"[186]made for what Smith labelled "a hybrid situation. It's an exit for Bernie Glieberman and an entry for Bruce Firestone."[187]

The completion of the deal set the wheels in motion to finalize a number of pending announcements. Firestone, while serving on the CFL's expansion and marketing committees, was to remain in the background. Phil Kershaw was to take over as the operational manager of the club, much as Paul Robson had done when he moved from Winnipeg to Ottawa, and Norm Kimball when he left Edmonton in an attempt to resuscitate Montreal. Kershaw, in turn, hired Adam Rita, as head coach, and Mike McCarthy, as a player personnel consultant. The following day, February 18, CFL Commissioner Larry Smith announced at a press conference in Shreveport the acceptance of the Gliebermans' Pirates as the twelfth team in the league, and the fourth American club for the 1994 season. The team, whose colours were purple, orange, silver and black, also took with it five members of the Rough Riders—linebacker Gregg Stumon, quarterback Terrence Jones, wide receiver Wayne Walker, cornerback Joe Mero, and defensive end Dexter Manley. J. I. Albrecht became the executive vice-president of Football Operations and it was apparent that his hand was active in the selection of other personnel. John Huard was appointed head coach; George Brancato was to be an assistant in charge of the offensive backfield and quarterbacks; Albrecht's son Dean, an agent who had Huard as one of his clients, was named the team's general manager and director of player development. The other assistant coaches were Steve Dennis, former defensive back with the Argonauts and Roughriders; Bob Surace, the offensive line coach who was from Huard's Maine Maritime Academy, as was Mark Hedgecock, an assistant listed as "'quality control coach' ... a post created by the NFL Dallas Cowboys a few decades ago ... considered one of the most important factors in professional football today."[188]

Controversy continued to follow the Gliebermans. John Huard was fired before the season began and replaced with former Argonaut coach Forrest Gregg. "Philosophical differences"[189] were cited by Lonie as the reason, but there had been complaints about training camp conditions and Huard's military style, which was "abrasive at the best of times."[190] Gregg was placed in full control of football operations, a situation which made the Albrechts' and all of their appointments' positions tenuous. They were later relieved of their duties. By September the purge was complete. George Brancato and Bernie Ruoff, in charge of special teams, were fired.[191]

The third American franchise had been awarded on February 17. Baltimore, Maryland, spurned by the NFL, proposed to the CFL and the league accepted. It was a calculated gamble. After all, this was an NFL market, albeit an abandoned one, but at the same time, one which would have preferred to carry on its NFL relationship. Was the CFL simply being espoused on the rebound? How would the Baltimore public respond to Canadian Football? Owner Jim Speros was betting heavily that the public would be overwhelmingly in favour of the team, which he would name the Colts. Others weren't so sure. They saw the NFL as an inferior game played by superior athletes; the CFL might have been a superior game but it was played by inferior athletes. A letter to the *Baltimore Sun* put it more pragmatically:

> There are three reasons why we should support Speros. The first is the number of 3–0 games the CFL had last season. The second is the CFL Colts have a chance to make the play-offs before the end of the next century. The third is that if we got behind the CFL Colts the NFL would be more likely to award us an expansion franchise the next time."[192]

There was no doubt that the former NFL team had left a long and storied legacy in Baltimore. Speros tried to evoke that by naming his new team the Colts. The NFL would have none of it. It sought and received a court injunction to prohibit the CFL team from using the name. It seemed to be one more reason for the fans to support the new team. Royal blue, white, black and silver were adopted as club colours; a horse head with a flowing mane, emulating stripes with stars interspersed, was the team's logo. Don Mathews, who had resigned from Saskatchewan, was selected as head coach. He sought to surround himself with people knowledgeable of the Canadian game: Steve Buratto became the offensive co-ordinator while Joe Barnes became the quarterback coach. One of Mathews' first moves was to sign former Argonaut quarterback Tracy Ham.

Marketing of the club revolved around the animosity toward the NFL, Robert Irsay, and to some extent, Indianapolis. A season ticket theme was the "Indy Challenge." In 1993, the NFL team had sold 36,112 tickets; the goal for the Baltimore club was to exceed that. Animosity towards the NFL increased when a court ruled that the club could not use the term "colts" in their name. Even "CFL Colts" was prohibited. The decision was made to call them the Baltimore "CFLers."

Meanwhile, in Las Vegas, the smoke and mirrors began to clear as the hype faded into the background. Owner Nick Mileti arranged for Las Vegas Major League Sports Inc. to be on the Boston Stock Exchange. The NASDAQ listing at eight dollars per unit was expected to generate $4.7 million in operating capital in addition to paying off the $2.5 million he borrowed to buy the club.[193] The innovative and successful approach caused other CFL clubs to look closely at duplicating the venture as a means of eliminating their debts. Las Vegas continued to be innovative by announcing that they would begin their training on a specially-built field in a parking lot behind the Riviera Hotel. Twelve hundred tons of sand topped with grass sod were to be used to build the 70 yards by 80 yards area complete with bleachers to seat 600 fans who were to receive free vouchers from the Casino in the Riviera.[194] A four-storey banner hanging from a parking garage in the background proclaimed it to be the "Field of ImPOSSEable Dreams"[195] Ron Meyer, a former NFL coach with Indianapolis and New England, was named the head coach with assistance from former Ottawa mentor Ron Smeltzer. Fans from around the league made arrangements to join excursions to Las Vegas to watch their teams and visit the self-proclaimed "entertainment capital of the world."

If it all seemed too good to be true, it was. By June 30, the club's quarterly report was showing a loss of $2.24 million.[196] Attendance was dwindling. Ticket prices were cut. Much of the problem, according to one local source, was that "the town is based on a major league perception. People bet on major league sports all the time and they perceive the CFL as minor league."[197] By the end of August, Mileti had resigned as chairman and chief executive officer. He was replaced by Los Angeles investment banker, Glenn Golenberg.[198] The controversy surrounding the Posse refused to fade. In a game with Shreveport, Las Vegas was ahead by 34–21, having scored with 16 seconds left on the clock. Gamblers had made Las Vegas 14-point favourites. A decision was made to attempt a two-point conversion. It failed but it was obvious that someone had bet that the Posse would cover the spread. One of the fears that CFL followers had when a decision was made to encourage CFL games to be listed by gamblers was becoming realized.

Financial concerns were such that when Hamilton and Las Vegas, two teams strapped for cash, met on September 25, Ron Meyer suggested that the game "should be called the Bankruptcy Bowl. Whoever wins the coin toss should keep it."[199] Things had gone downhill from the first home game, on July 16, when the Posse defeated Saskatchewan 30–22 in overtime. The temperature was 96°F at half time but more notable was the singing of the Canadian national anthem by Dennis K. C. Park. The words were wrong, the tune was more like O Tannenbaum and it was sung off key. And all before a national CBC television audience! The rendition set off an immediate reaction. The *Ottawa Citizen* invited its readers to "call Touchline at 721–1990 and on your touchtone phone, select code 7505 to hear this original rendition of O Canada."[200] Nick Mileti wrote an apology to PM Jean Chretien. Even the vice-president of the United States, Al Gore, remarked "I was certainly glad to see that the U.S. players reacted so strongly and better than the singer."[201] Park was immediately sought after by a variety of talk shows and television programs in Canada. The Hamilton Tiger-Cats, keen to seize an opportunity to sell more tickets, invited him to sing the national anthem once again, this time correctly, before one of their home games.

By the end of the season, it was obvious that the Posse had ridden into the sunset. After a combined total of 5,000 watched two home games, the final one was "moved to Edmonton and league officials perform[ed] euthanasia."[202]

In Sacramento, meanwhile, the Gold Miners, burdened by missing the play-offs for the second straight season, the small crowds it was drawing at Hornet field, and large financial losses, made plans to move to another locale in search of a new life, but it wasn't only the American teams that were struggling.

In Toronto, the triumvirate of Gretzky, Candy and McNall was conspicuous by its absence. By February, the club had an estimated $1.3 million in debts and according to SkyDome officials, owed $300,000 in rent.[203] It was a large comedown from the hectic media-fanned promotional days when the "Big League" veneer was bandied about. Interest was in decline and the Argo ownership had left a lonely Ron Barbaro to manage as best he could. It seemed as if all were in a holding pattern. Barbaro's approach, a complete switch from the early heady days, was announced at a buffet breakfast meeting for the media and sponsors. An attempt was made to attract youth and families to the games. Daycare, face-painting, pre-game parties, appeals to university football programs, tickets for high school students in the upper level, a revival of the Argo Playback club, a float shaped like the good ship Argonaut, "fresh-faced cheerleaders," and inexpensive tickets were all part of the attempt to recapture the public's interest. The club had gone from a high of 51,000 for the Eastern final game in 1991 to a low of 16,000 in 1993 for the game with Edmonton.

In the midst of all of this restructuring, Gretzky and McNall announced that they were selling their shares. John Candy proposed to put together a group to buy the club. The news continued to get worse before it got better. John Candy, at 43, suffered a heart attack on location in Mexico and died March 4, 1994. Aside from his great status as a film star, he was described as "the most supportive in the Argo organization ... the strength of the ownership in Toronto ... one of the positives of the CFL."[204] Gretzky, on a visit to Winnipeg, elaborated to *Winnipeg Free Press* columnist Scott Taylor:

When John Candy died, it was a devastating blow for a lot of reasons. Most importantly, he was a great friend but he was going to buy out Bruce and I and take over the Argos ... We don't believe the CFL has a future in places like Toronto and Vancouver. In Canada, the CFL is a league for community owned teams that don't pay rent and get government help. The business of the CFL doesn't work in places like Toronto and Vancouver. Those are major league cities that expect a major league product. The CFL, now that it has expanded to second tier markets in the United States, is perceived as minor league football.[205]

By early May, the Argos had been sold to TSN, a subsidiary of Labatt's. Paul Beeston, president of the Blue Jays, was named to head-up the football team. Some cynics suggested that Labatt's had bought the Argonauts in order to obtain the rights to an NFL franchise since "whoever owns the Argos also owns the rights to professional football in the SkyDome." Beeston was clearly irritated by the insinuation: "Do you think that we want to be associated with something that won't work?"[206] What was referred to as the "Blue Jays-ization of the Toronto Argonauts"[207] continued when Bob Nicholson, vice president of the baseball club, took a similar position with the Argos. In an effort to reconstruct ties with the past, the club returned to the traditional logo of "a football-shaped ship with oars sticking out the side and a sail."[208]It was stylized in an effort to make it more contemporary, riding on a rippling sea, all enclosed within a circle. Designed by the Stanford Agency, the logo "would adorn the team's letterhead and program but not the side of the helmets."[209] The letter A would remain on the helmets since a year's notice was needed because of merchandising contracts. Bob O'Billovich was retained as general manager and coach.

The four American teams had contributed approximately $14.3 million (CDN) in expansion fees: $3 million (US) from Sacramento, $2.5 million (US) each from Las Vegas and Baltimore and $2.8 million (CDN) from the combined sale of the Rough Riders and the creation of the Shreveport Pirates.[210] It was money that was sorely needed. The league was in debt to the tune of approximately $2.5 million and called upon the various clubs to eradicate it. In spite of the improved cash situation, clubs were still having financial problems as the season evolved. The Blue Bombers, for example, were beginning the year with a debt of $2.6 to $2.8 million. Included was "the existing deficit of $1.8 million, a payment towards the leagues debt of $450,000 and a projected loss of $800,000 for 1994."[211]

In Edmonton, the Grey Cup champion Eskimos released a financial statement showing a loss of $171,269 for 1993, some $36,000 less than the previous year. The B.C. Lions reported an operating loss on the 1993 season of $2.6 million. "The real loss, said Bill Comrie, after taking into account the receipt of expansion fees, was $2.19 million." [212] The B.C. owner was angry that his words were being challenged by a columnist in the *Province*. He sent out an open letter to the media in which he admitted that his team spent over $3,000,000 on coaches' and players' salaries. In addition, he said, the club spent $300,000 on equipment and training room supplies, more than $100,000 for General Manager Eric Tillman, $70,000 in wages and car expenses for Personnel Director Bill Quinter, $60,000 in salary and expenses for two secretaries, $135,000 in medical coverage, $60,000 for U.I.C. and C.P.P. and $55,000 for the players' pension fund. Travel costs were $430,000 plus $30,000 for ground transportation, $150,000 for hotels and $120,000 in per diems for players on away trips. Training camp expenses were an additional $350,000.[213]

Comrie was determined that the team would stay within the salary cap for 1994. When former player Mike Gray was "hired" as a defensive line coach, he was taken on with no salary. The only way that he could travel with the team on a road trip was if one of the normal travelling party, usually the manager or player personnel director, decided not to go.[214]

The CFL Players' Association, fearing that its members would be trapped by the public's perception that they, the players, were the cause of the clubs' financial woes, decided to make their salaries public. The vote of the association was 15–3 in favour. The three dissenting votes were by Winnipeg's Chris Walby, Edmonton's Randy Ambrosie and Saskatchewan's Dave Ridgeway. All were year-round residents of their communities, one of the reasons given for their reluctance. They were not convinced that neighbours reading in the paper of their salary would say "Darn, I didn't know that you played for so little." Another reason the association gave for the disclosure was the hope that "general managers could no longer mislead players and agents in contract negotiations."[215]

Speculation was rife that Larry Smith would be asked to resign. The hectic pace of old franchises with problems, new franchises, potential new sites for expansion, and settling disputes, plus the need for day-to-day, hands-on business decisions, all contributed to Smith seeking a lower profile. It was noted that "Smith had distanced himself from the media, becoming increasingly more difficult to reach. Club executives have long complained that keeping track of Smith's travels and finding him has been tricky." The suggestion was made that the initials CFL stood for more than the name of the league: "The new phrase: Can't Find Larry."[216] In time, the dust settled and the season began. Attention was more focused on league play and criticism temporarily subsided. There were still kinks to work out but Smith was named "Marketer of the Year" by the Toronto chapter of the American Marketing Association "for his success in reviving the CFL despite the many obstacles facing him both financially and in terms of fan appeal."[217] As if to recognize that Smith couldn't be everywhere at the same time, the league announced that it had hired Jeff Giles as its chief operating officer, a "newly created position [to] focus on the day-to-day business dealings" of the CFL.[218]

"Smith and the owners are apparently getting what they want; one wonders if they can handle it," pondered Doug Smith of the Canadian Press early in the new year.[219] The reporter's comment was triggered by a press release announcing a serious expansion bid from Orlando, Florida. He had tried to contact the league but Larry Smith "was at home recovering from a hernia operation … VP of Communications [was] in a car on a snow bound highway and the league's expansion czar, Larry Ryckman, [was] in western Canada." The fact was that "no one in authority was near the league's Toronto office and a news release replete with spelling and grammatical errors hammered that point home."[220] The reporter continued that with the league having expanded into the United States, with a game a week on ESPN2, the all sports U.S. cable network, with the publicity that the CFL craved emanating from the league approved betting in Las Vegas, it was necessary for the league to "shed its Mickey Mouse image."[221] It was an ironic choice of words.

A meeting of the CFL Board of Governors was rescheduled from Toronto to Orlando for 7:30 A.M., January 18. It was strongly suggested that a franchise would be awarded and a press conference for that purpose was scheduled for 11:30 A.M. It had all the appearances of a "sure thing." The CFL had "planned to charter a plane to fly the Canadian sports media south, at least until it found out that most of the organizations wouldn't accept the trip."[222] On the evening of February 17, the league sent out a news release, including satellite coordinates so that television stations in Canada and elsewhere could carry the announcement live. Larry Smith told a reporter that "the only thing that needed to be tidied up was a bit of 'paperwork'"[223] before Orlando was granted a franchise.

Not all agreed. Larry Guest, writing in the *Orlando Sentinel*, suggested: "Mayor Hood, Orlando, tell CFL to take hike."[224] There had been too many times in the past when "the reps of every gadget sports league convene monthly at our City Hall" to tell how their organization would put Orlando on the "big league map." Guest's advice was: "Anything short of the NFL should be given directions to Valdosta."[225]

The Governors' meeting dragged on for more than two hours; it was obvious that something was amiss. In a statement issued by the league, it was announced that the franchise for Orlando had been put on hold. The CFL was concerned with the lack of financing and a lease for the Citrus Bowl. Even so, some things didn't ring true. It appeared that while the league was prepared to accept 15-yard end zones, five less than the rules called for, city officials declared that the maximum end zone could only be 12 yards![226]

A scapegoat was sought. Rumours even circulated that the league was no longer enamoured of its commissioner who, reportedly, had asked to have his salary doubled from $250,000 to $500,000.[227] "Business consultant," Bill Hunter, "hired by Smith to preside over potential expansion"[228] was identified by others as the culprit. Fred Anderson, owner of the Sacramento team was particularly upset. His quarterback, David Archer, had travelled to Orlando to be part of the ceremonies. Orlando would have provided a boost to Sacramento's season ticket sales, as it would have in Las Vegas, where leaked news of the "expansion" to Orlando had become front page news.

"Mickey Mouse" was also the term used by Ottawa Rough Riders personnel director Mike McCarthy when he learned that the league had decided Ottawa would lose its first round draft pick. In order to present as few roadblocks as possible to the new owners of the Riders, Smith had told them that they "should not be held accountable for the previous Glieberman ownership's exceeding the salary cap."[229]

The reaction of the league's clubs was swift when an announcement was made that Ottawa would be treated as if it had been within the salary cap. "General Managers were unanimous in their outrage ... [and] asked the league's governors to address their concern."[230] It was revealed that four Canadian clubs were over the cap: Toronto, Edmonton, B.C., and Ottawa. The CFL put a positive spin on the situation. Rather than announcing that the four teams would not participate in the first round, it declared that Hamilton, Saskatchewan, Calgary and Winnipeg would be allowed to choose first in what was termed a bonus round. Only Canadian-based teams participated in the draft since American teams did not have any import/non-import restrictions. Hamilton's first pick was offensive lineman Val St Germain from McGill University.

There were changes from teams trying to trim their budgets by allowing free agents to leave and by trading. Compounding the situation was the fact that there were an additional three American teams bidding for players and all starting from the ground up. Baltimore, especially, made a concerted effort to stock their team with players having CFL experience. Tracy Ham left the Argos to join the CFLers as did Jearld Baylis from Saskatchewan and O.J. Brigance from B.C. and Mike Pringle from Sacramento. The Roughriders also lost Jeff Fairholm to the Argonauts. Winnipeg lost Michael Richardson to Ottawa, Elfrid Payton to Shreveport, and Greg Battle to Las Vegas. The Tiger-Cats lost Mike Jovanovich, an offensive lineman, to Toronto and receiver Nick Mazzoli to Ottawa. Complicating the issue was the relative value of Canadian and American currency. A contract for the same dollar figure would have a difference of 30% because of the higher value of the American currency. A case in point was Elfrid Payton. He had been selected as the Eastern Division Outstanding Defensive Player of 1993. Payton had a contract for $49,000 with bonuses capable of bringing in another $7,000.[231] Winnipeg had offered him a new contract for $52,000. His team mate Greg Battle had signed with the Las Vegas Posse for $85,000 (US). Payton negotiated a contract with Shreveport which included: "$75,000(US), bonuses worth $7500 in cash, and a percentage of all tickets sold for Shreveport home games ... the club also agreed to allow him the use of a luxury apartment ... year round."[232]

Quarterbacks continued to move around. When Tracy Ham left Toronto to join Baltimore, it was assumed that Reggie Slack would inherit the position. He was traded to Hamilton, who needed a quarterback when high-profile Timm Rosenbach didn't live up to the club's expectations. Don McPherson had moved on to Ottawa. Yet another "major" signing fell through, this one in Winnipeg where the Blue Bombers, perhaps anticipating that Matt Dunigan would not return from his achilles tendon operation or that they could not afford his contract, signed Todd Marinovich. The former NFL quarterback injured his knee the first day of training camp and left abruptly. The comings and goings caused Bruce Cheadle of the Canadian Press to dub it the Carousel Football League, especially after a three-team quarterback swap. Saskatchewan sent Kent Austin and offensive lineman Andrew Greene to Ottawa in return for quarterback Tom Burgess, defensive back Anthony Drawhorn, linebacker Ron Goetz, and defensive tackle Ron Yatkowski. When Yatkowski didn't pass the Saskatchewan physical, Ottawa took him back in return for first- and second-round picks in the 1995 draft.[233] Ottawa then traded Austin to B.C. in return for Adam Rita favourite, Danny Barrett, and defensive back Cory Dowder. A philosophical Barrett reacted: "You join the CFL and you get the tour of Canada."[234]

There were twelve teams in the CFL for 1994, six in each division. In the East were Winnipeg, Hamilton, Toronto, Ottawa, Baltimore and Shreveport; the West included Saskatchewan, Edmonton, Calgary, British Columbia, Sacramento and Las Vegas. A change was made in the play-off structure. Four teams from each division were to continue in post season play. There was still an East-West format provided for the Grey Cup Game and the possibility that two American based teams could be playing in it. Play-off money had been adjusted. Losing teams earned $1,900 and the winning club players received $2,400 each. In the Grey Cup Game, the winners were rewarded with $12,000 and the losers $6,000 each.

Several records were set during the '94 season. Lui Passaglia of the B.C. Lions, the all time leading scorer in professional football, was noted as the "CFL career leader in games played."[235] Ray Elgaard of the Saskatchewan Roughriders passed Rocky Di Pietro in most career receptions. Calgary's Allen Pitts and Baltimore's Mike Pringle set records in pass-receiving and rushing and Pitts caught passes for 2,036 yards and Pringle established a new CFL rushing total of 1,972 yards.

During a Winnipeg-Ottawa game—won by Winnipeg 46–1—there were charges of electronic eavesdropping. The game was broadcast on ESPN2. Producers had approached Cal Murphy, wanting to "wire him up" with a live microphone so viewers could be aware of plays that were being sent in from the bench. Murphy declined. Adam Rita, coach of the Rough

Riders agreed. Winnipeg's director of player personnel, Paul Jones, was watching the game in Tennessee. He overheard Rita calling a set of plays, and phoned the Bombers' assistant general manager Lyle Bauer in the Winnipeg Stadium press box. Bauer, in turn, relayed the information down to Murphy who signalled in appropriate defences.[236]

In Shreveport, the Pirates won their last three games to finish with a 3–15 record. Though relatively well supported by the public, the club was still seeking to have the taxpayer "guarantee a loan of up to $4.5 million … the Pirates (were expecting) to lose up to $2 million more than anticipated."[237] The franchise in Las Vegas was all but finished and would relocate because of the poor fan support. One report headlined that "Desert Flop takes to road: Posse to end its run in Edmonton."

A franchise was awarded for 1995 to Memphis, Tennessee, the owner being Fred Smith of Federal Express. Although the value of the next round of franchises had been set at $6 million (US), the reported price paid by Memphis was $1.8 million (US).[238] The CFL was most anxious to have Fred Smith in the league because of his "deep pockets" and because he had been mentioned as one of the parties behind the proposed North American League, which some wanted to begin as a rival to the NFL in the United States, pre-empting eligible American cities from being available for the CFL.

In the 1994 play-offs, Calgary defeated Saskatchewan 36–3 and B.C. won over Edmonton on a last minute field goal by Lui Passaglia, 24–23. The winning field goal was set up by Charles Gordon's interception of a Damon Allen pass thrown from the B.C. four-yard line. Gordon ran it back to the Eskimo 41-yard line and might have run it all the way for a touchdown. Linebacker Virgil Robertson was in a position to provide the last block that would enable Gordon to reach the end-zone, but Robertson went to get Damon Allen instead. "They had a little bet going," it was rumoured. "If somebody got a good hit on Damon there was a little money involved."[239]

In the Eastern Division, first-place Winnipeg defeated Ottawa 26–16 while Baltimore, the first American team to make the play-offs, scored a 34–15 win over the Argos. It was the first CFL play-off game played outside Canada and drew an attendance of 35,223 to Memorial Stadium.

In division finals, Baltimore surprised Winnipeg 14–12 in a game played in frigid temperatures made more so by a howling wind gusting up to 60 kph. In the West, Calgary fell short for the second consecutive year. The Stampeders lost to the Lions 37–36. B.C. scored a touchdown on the last play of the game; the four-yard line again providing the setting. Amid a swirling snowfall, Danny McManus threw a pass to Darren Flutie. It was the winning score and provided the match-up the league wanted, a Canadian team playing an American. There was the added bonus that the Lions would be playing before their home fans.

In Baltimore, more than 500 fans showed up at the airport to welcome back their "Colts For Life." The game with Winnipeg had been well received and during the final 15 minutes of the game, which was picked up by the local NBC affiliate, it drew a "34 per cent share ... an NFL rating in America"[240]. The CFLers' advancement to the Grey Cup was hailed by the *Baltimore Sun* as a "symbol of an era passed by."[241] Some in the Maryland city were concerned about the "fresh round of anti-American hysteria" surely to be whipped up, referring to banners in Winnipeg which read "no Grey Cup in U.S.A." and the flying of the American flag upside down.[242] Baltimore coach Don Mathews saw it all simply as "the home team trying to rattle his players."

The B.C. Lions were also basking in the adulation of their fans. They were favoured because of home field advantage. In successive weeks, they had come from behind to score dramatic victories. There was some concern whether the "cost" had been too high. Some perceived that they were at a distinct disadvantage, "Canadian riddled,"[243] as one reporter described them, tongue-in-cheek. They did have injuries at the quarterback position. Both Kent Austin and Danny McManus were hurt, Austin with a slight shoulder separation and McManus with a bruised thigh.

If, in Baltimore, the Grey Cup was "just another ball game ... [it had] turned into a referendum on nationalism in Canada."[244] There was some good-natured bantering taking place. *Vancouver Sun* reporter Pete McMartin commented: "This is not the first time a Baltimore team has met a Canadian team in a championship. They met once before. It was for the championship of North America in a series known as the War of 1812. The best Baltimore managed even with the home field advantage was a draw. Baltimore played a defensive game. We were on offence." The *Baltimore Sun*'s Ray Frager replied in kind: "A draw? Oh yeah Mr Big Shot historian Pete McMartin. You don't even know how to spell offense. And you had to steal from Baltimore to get a name for your newspaper."[245] The *Vancouver Sun* continued to play up the Canadian angle. It published a photo of Ian Sinclair, Donovan Wright, Glen Scrivener and Sean Foudie over the caption: On Guard For Thee.[246]

The debate continued. Baltimore's coach, Don Mathews, was described as being "freed from the traditional roster restrictions ... finally able to recruit exactly the right types of athletes to play defence in the pass-happy Canadian game."[247] In the midst of all the hoopla, the question of "Canadian" kept surfacing. American owners seemed to prefer either a new name for the league or at the very least, playing down the "Canadian" aspect in order to refer to it as the CFL. CBC play-by-play man Don Wittman and co-worker Scott Oake both noted that the Canadian players would be "playing to save their jobs."[248] The *Toronto Star* printed a cartoon showing a football player under the stars-and-striped letters CFL and hanging from the L was a sign: "No Canadians Need Apply."[249] Earlier, the *Star* had published a group of football players in an Iwo Jima-like pose, planting a flag on top of "Lord Grey's Cup."[250] Even the Prime Minister was brought into the debate. Asked by Canadian Press who would win the game, Chretien said that "he would be cheering for B.C. but the endorsement came only after the PM needed to ask who exactly would be playing for the 1994 Grey Cup."[251] When Gerald Wilcox of the Winnipeg Blue Bombers won the Outstanding Canadian Award, over Edmonton's Larry Wruck, he "took the opportunity of his acceptance speech to say to a national television audience: 'I hope this isn't the last time we see this award.'"[252] The *Toronto Star* gave Wilcox's comment a laurel in its "darts and laurels" feature while proclaiming: "Our feelings too as the league continues to Americanize itself."[253]

Other awards went to Doug Flutie, chosen over Baltimore's Mike Pringle as the Most Outstanding Player. It was Flutie's fourth consecutive selection, a first in the league. Another Baltimore player, Shar Pourdanesh, was chosen the Outstanding Offensive Lineman. Still another CFLer, linebacker Matt Goodwin, took the Rookie of the Year award over the Las Vegas kicker Carlos Huerta. Edmonton's Willie Pless, a linebacker, was chosen as the Most Outstanding Defensive Player. Baltimore's Mike Pringle won the first-ever Terry Evanshen Award, newly instituted to replace the Jeff Russel Trophy which was retired during the year by its board.

Although B.C. was listed as 3.5 to 4.5 point favourites, there were those who saw Baltimore as next to a sure thing. CBC analyst James Curry suggested that "Baltimore doesn't have any weaknesses at all, from their coaching staff on down. Even their special team guys are better than average players in the Canadian Football League."[254] Others spoke of "Baltimore's massive offensive line" and how the Lions' defensive line and linebacking corps were "vulnerable to Baltimore's rushing attack."[255] Curry's sentiments were echoed by Matt Dunigan who thought that it was "Baltimore's game to win or lose" because of their huge offensive line led by Shar Pourdanesh. It would allow Tracy Ham to "run around and create time for his receivers to get open. It'll be tough to get to Tracy." [256] The speed of Baltimore's defence, their running attack of Pringle and Drummond behind its "oversized offensive line"[257] going against the all-Canadian three man front of the B.C. team, was pointed out by many "objective" pundits as "keys."

Baltimore was concerned with other matters—crowd noise specifically. Don Mathews, as a former coach of the Lions, was well aware of how deafening an obstacle the crowd noise in B.C. Place could be. The CFLers took specific aim at the B.C. Place "fan-o-meter" which gave a reading on the level of crowd noise and encouraged the fans to increase it. Baltimore's operations director E. J. Narcisse pointed out that the contest was a league one as opposed to a home game for either side and as such "emphatically oppose[d] anything that would artificially stimulate the crowd."[258]

Before 55,097 highly-charged and entertained fans, the B.C. Lions defeated the Baltimore CFLers 26–23. The margin of victory was a last-play field goal by venerable Lui Passaglia, the first time in his 19-year career he had ever kicked a game-winning field goal in a play-off game. There were a number of turning points. In the third quarter, B.C. stalled at the Baltimore 27-yard line. Passaglia was called in, but instead of kicking the field goal, Darren Flutie, who was holding the ball for Passaglia, ran to his right to gain the first-down. Later, with B.C. on the Baltimore one-yard line, B.C. gambled on a third-down keeper by sore-legged quarterback Danny McManus. It was a big play by the quarterback who entered the game in relief of Kent Austin after Baltimore had jumped into a 14–3 lead.

The CBC later announced that its coverage of the Grey Cup Game peaked at 5.2 million for the half hour between 9:00 and 9:30[259] and "drew an audience of 3.9 million viewers," up from 2.6 million in '93, 3.2 million in '92, 3.5 million in '91, 2.3 million in '90 and 3 million in '89. In the United States, the live presentation drew 145,000 on ESPN2 while the taped version on ESPN was viewed in 377,000 homes.[260] The live audience was only 4,000 seats short of a sellout.

At the end of the game the field was overrun by spectators, requiring that the presentation of the Grey Cup be made under the stands rather than for all to see outdoors. It might have contributed to the confusion in the awards presentations. Passaglia was named by CBC as the game's Most Valuable Player; Millington was named the top Canadian.

Each was presented with his prize. Passaglia's was the key to a Dodge Ram truck; Millington's was a travel voucher worth $5,000. When the votes by the Football Reporters of Canada were counted, however, the five ballots showed that Baltimore's defensive back Karl Anthony was the winner of the Most Valuable Player and Passaglia the top Canadian. Anthony was not impressed, saying that the league could stick the award "where the sun doesn't shine."[261] Passaglia's team mates made the most of it later, presenting the kicker with a toy model truck. A group of six business men, perhaps practicing "ambush marketing," collaborated to present Passaglia with a

Chevy pick-up. They allowed him to trade it in later on for a Chevy Blazer which more adequately suited Lui and his family of a wife and four children.

The un-sung heroes of the game were undoubtedly the B.C. Canadian contingent—Ian Sinclair, Denny Chronopoulos, Rob Smith, Jamie Taras, and Vic Stevenson, the "all Canadian offensive line, was savage in its treatment of Baltimore's front seven."[262] Meanwhile, the three-man Canadian defensive line of Dave Chaytors, Andrew Stewart, and Doug Peterson, gave the Baltimore offence all it could handle, allowing its linebackers Newby, Robertson, Chatman, and Snipes to harass Ham throughout the game. Safety Tom Europe, a winner of the Harry Jerome award in 1993, was another who excelled with his defensive coverage and sure-handed tackling. Emotions among all, but especially the Canadian players, were high. After the game was over, lineman Denny Chronopoulos "was one of the first to grab a Canadian flag and start waving and dancing on the field after the victory."[263] In the stands, hundreds of fans, red maple leafs painted on their cheeks, roared with approval. Police, fearful of a repeat of the violence which marred the end of the Stanley Cup play-offs in June, were in the streets. But it was a good natured crowd. Some marched in the middle of Robson Street chanting "No Grey in the USA"; others were waving B.C. Lions standards or draped in Canadian flags.

A Passing Game

Epilogue

DESPITE THE SUCCESS OF THE GREY CUP, 1994 was not a stable year for the league. Changes during and after this year meant that it was a different group of owners and teams who prepared for the next year.

In Ottawa, where the team ownership, image, colours, and logo had changed, disenchantment was the mood throughout the previous season. Bruce Firestone had announced his intention to sell the team in 1994, and sold it was, to Chicago businessman Horn Chen, but only after long negotiations in 1995. Unsecured creditors from the earlier regime settled for 14 cents on the dollar, while a reported $1.25 million made its way to secured creditors, with the league gaining $350,000 of that amount.[1]

Hamilton also had ownership problems. John Michaluk had resigned effective September 15 as president and CEO of the Tiger-Cats. He had been under fire from a variety of sources for his method of guiding the club's off-field operation. Hamilton was a mix of community ownership and private investors, and just like Ottawa, there had been an accumulation of debt. Retiring it seemed to be the key to attracting new ownership. A deal with unsecured creditors owed $2.2 million was made there too. They were to get 20 cents on the dollar, receiving half immediately and the other half within six months. Secured creditors—the CFL was owed $1 million and the Hamilton Wentworth Regional Government $750,000—were to be paid in full.[2] The club was sold, with the deal finalized in April, 1995, to a group of investors headed by David Macdonald.[3]

Ultimatums were given to the fans of Hamilton, Ottawa and Calgary—support the teams or lose them. Targets for season ticket sales and corporate sponsorships were set and met: 12,000 tickets and $1 million, respectively, for Hamilton; 15,000 and $1 million for Ottawa; and 16,000 season tickets for Calgary. The Stampeders, who averaged 25,000 fans during the last season, had threatened to move to San Antonio during difficulties negotiating its lease with McMahon Stadium.

choice and yet, the club offered the league a tempting financial deal. Based on a projection of "$5.5 million from game and event revenue" and expenses of $3.5 million, the remaining $2 million profit would be shared by the CFL and Saskatchewan. "Cost overruns cutting into the $2 million profit would be shared by the two sides."[4] It was the province's 90th birthday and the theme of the game would be a call for previous Saskatchewan residents to "come back." As early as March, 1994, phones at the 'Riders offices were being answered with "Home of the 1995 Grey Cup."[5] Plans were for only 5,000 tickets to be available outside the Province.[6] Hamilton and Baltimore were selected as '96 and '97 Grey Cup hosts, respectively. Initially, it appeared as if Baltimore would host the '96 game but "tax questions and revenue sharing"[7] details were unclear. With the league "unable to decide between Hamilton and Baltimore for 1996 ... it went ahead and awarded the '96 and '97 games."[8] It was a major coup for both cities. Hamilton had been all but written off by many as a viable franchise while Baltimore, in its first year, was impressive in leading the league in attendance and was generating much enthusiasm for the CFL throughout the United States. Regardless, there was still that nagging worry as to what would happen if the NFL ever decided to return to Baltimore. Nonetheless, $500,000 in grants and loans was to be made available by Maryland's Department of Economic and Employment Development to assist the CFLers in their attempt to improve Memorial Stadium.[9]

Prior to the new season, efforts were also being made to relocate the Las Vegas and Sacramento teams. While the Gold Miners relocated in San Antonio to become the Texans, the Posse, after a frantic and protracted attempt to move to Jackson, Mississippi, folded. Their players were redistributed throughout the league in a dispersal draft on April 18, 1995. All the while two new American franchises were welcomed into the league: The Mad Dogs, of Memphis, Tennessee, and the Barracudas of Birmingham, Alabama.

The radical changes that the league underwent since it decided to expand to the United States has returned it to the same issues that were prevalent 20 years previous. Perhaps because of the expansion into the U.S., reporters had recently taken to calling the CFL commissioners' Grey Cup news conferences the "State of the League Address," a not so subtle reference to the American President's State of the Union Address. At the 1994 Grey Cup Game news conference, Smith brushed off rumours that he would be fired and instead he forecasted greater U.S. content and spoke of league plans for a shift from the East-West to a North-South rivalry in a Grey Cup Game which could be played permanently in December.[10] With the

collective bargaining agreement due to expire in June of 1995, it was
necessary to attempt to negotiate a new one for the 1995 season. The league
had already addressed the issue publicly by initially stating it wanted to
remove the quota altogether. Opponents of the proposal argued that, of the
four American teams, three had not even made the play-offs. Only Baltimore
had demonstrated some success but it was suggested that was more due to
the approach taken by the club to seek out players with CFL experience than
successful U.S. expansion. A proposed method of ensuring equality amongst
the Canadian and U.S. clubs was to place restrictions on where the American
teams would be allowed to pick their players; a method which might also
make for more local identification and acceptance. However, the league
retracted by saying that twenty spots on the Canadian teams' rosters for non-
imports were too many. While the number ten was mentioned as a possibility, Smith would only say that "our objective is not to eliminate the quota."
It is interesting to note that the CFLPA was formed over the issue of the
import ratio; thirty years later, the question was still one which had to be
resolved. The place for the Canadian player in the Canadian game had been
an issue from the days of the forward pass and later, during the controversies
over the designated import regulation. If the CFL did move towards an
eventual target of a ten Canadian player quota, it would mean that all starters
would be Americans. It would be unnecessary to develop Canadians to take
over first string positions.

The increasing influence of the American clubs was being felt in some
"cosmetic" areas, as well. For example, the very name of the league was
being questioned. American owners, specifically Jim Speros of Baltimore,
wanted the "Canadian" removed to de-emphasize the non-American aspect
of the league. The CFL was also contemplating a change in logo to
incorporate the new reality of its American clubs and had moved away from
the Canadian Spalding football to the American-made Wilson. Also at issue
was the talk of moving the Grey Cup Game to a later date in December to
take into consideration the American Thanksgiving holiday at the end of
November. Other concerns were the end zones, in danger of being shrunk
because many American parks could not accommodate the 20-yard goal
areas or 110-yard playing fields.

There were influences on more substantial aspects of the game too. After
years of stability in its rules, a recognition that the league was happy with its
distinct game, American owners were now continually suggesting changes
such as moving to four downs rather than three as a means of appealing
more to American fans. While the business aspect of expansion was recognized as desirable by most Canadians, there was concern that, like the NHL,
control of the game would shift to the United States by having more

such as moving to four downs rather than three as a means of appealing more to American fans. While the business aspect of expansion was recognized as desirable by most Canadians, there was concern that, like the NHL, control of the game would shift to the United States by having more American than Canadian teams, or a decline in Canadian players, or even the head office and the commissioner locating to the United States.

Expansion of the Canadian Football League, controversial when it was announced, will continue to be the critical issue around which the health of the league will revolve. Expansion might ultimately solve some of the league's problems but it might also create additional ones.

Historically, the CFL has always perceived and defined itself in terms of regions. The Grey Cup Game played on the natural and competive differences between the East and West. The season culminated with one side's representative team gaining the bragging rights for the nation. While everyone knew the American players had more of a contributing role than Canadians, the essential feature was that all the cities in the league were Canadian—civic, provincial and national pride were at stake.

With the South (American) and the North (Canadian) divisions, somewhere down the road the league will have to establish a more official presence in the United States—an aide to the commissioner, an office to expedite American matters—until eventually, as the United States division strengthens and gains more clout, the possibility exists for the head office and commissioner to give up its Canadian roots to become American.

One has to examine the motives of the American owners wanting to join the Canadian Football League. It is different in style, both on and off the field, from the American: it is an established league with a salary cap; spectator driven in terms of revenue with more opportunities for growth; and relatively inexpensive in terms of the cost of purchasing a professional franchises. In short, there is good opportunity for profit.

But all of these advantages can quickly turn into disadvantages: because the Canadian game is different, some Americans perceive it as not being "real football." The name "Canadian" verifies it in a land where "American" is a synonym for the best. There will be a tendency on the part of U.S. teams to Americanize the game, to make it more like "real football," and the demands of the larger Canadian field on American stadiums will contribute to that movement. The salary cap also has its disadvantage—at $2.5 million Canadian, with the weakness of the Canadian dollar, the American equivalent is so much lower. One would think that with the huge talent supply in the United States, the calibre of player would remain uneven among the clubs or leagues.

With all its disadvantages, the American owners still had good reasons for wanting CFL franchises: Some are in locations where they have been rebuffed by the NFL, leaving the feeling of abandonment, which, in turn, could be cultivated to sell tickets: A "we'll show them" attitude to promotion. There are other owners who would try to use the CFL as a way to get into the NFL via the back door, in the hope it will grow to compete with the NFL and later merge with the premier "real football" league. There is also a very real fear clubs will ignore the salary cap in an effort to attract high profile collegians or established NFL players in order to secure credibility with the U.S. public and the possibility of the South Division simply becoming an entity in itself by breaking away from the CFL to form its own league.

Maintaining the salary cap is critical to the Canadian aspect of the league. The CFL has already served notice that it wishes to do away with what it calls the "quota system" of Canadian players, wanting more access to the huge and inexpensive supply of talent in the American market. (It's interesting to note that normally quota systems are imposed upon products coming into the market as opposed to those already existing—it is akin to Canadian players being defined as non-imports.)

The league's Players' Association has stood firm. It has been demonstrated on the field that Canadian talent can play competitively with the Americans in the CFL. All recognize that the Canadian needs two years or so to gain experience and benefit from intensive practices to bring himself up to the level of the American collegians. The "quota system" allows that to occur. Without the "quota system," Canadian content would be minimal, since coaches would never have any reason for playing Canadians in starting positions. (As an aside, if the North–South divisions are to work, there might be more interest, all around, if a "quota system" of sorts was implemented in the United States. The same principle would see American teams restricted to a defined number of players from their cachement area, i.e., a state or a number of states.)

The whole area of "free agency" is another one which will continue to be a problem unless the salary cap is maintained. Ever since the "gentlemen's agreements" were eliminated, players have been free to move to another team after playing out their option. In some ways it has served to create interest as established players left or joined a club. If the salary cap is enforced, the net effect would not allow any one team to corner the best players available. Owners being who they are, however, could find a way to circumvent the cap and in doing so, unable to afford the new reality, would be forced to drop out of the league.

Television will also play a role in the future CFL, as it has in the past. In Canada, it appears necessary to attract more networks, especially CTV, into the bidding process. In the United States, there are a few more obstacles. It's more likely that the American teams will be the ones to attract a network simply on the basis of public identification. The shortness of the CFL season remains one impediment—in addition to being the American Thanksgiving weekend, the last week in November is traditionally the end of the college season. There is a void until the bowl games begin and networks are looking for programming to fill space. The CFL's Canadian teams, however, especially in the prairies, are unable to play later than the present schedule. (That is why the Grey Cup Game of 1995 in Regina was scheduled for the third week in November.) The pressure will be enormous on the United States teams to break away once their South division is established, or for the CFL to form a Spring-Fall league to lure the big television contracts from the American networks.

Franchises in Canada will continue to be important if the league wants to maintain the North-South division approach. Until television revenue increases, finances will have to be brought under control and community support for clubs will have to be increased. The "Canadian" aspect of the clubs, particularly in the North-South alignment will play a large role and expansion to Montreal and the Maritimes will be future considerations again.

It's interesting to speculate as to what will happen if American clubs, for reasons stated above, were to break away and start their own league. It would leave the North Division where it was prior to U.S. expansion. Perhaps the pass would be completed after a deflection. Would it be an indication of future trends if some of the higher profile owners were to move out of the CFL? Would some owners be tempted to sell their high-profile American players to United States teams who have the cash available? Would bridges have been burned beyond repair?

Would the Canadian Football League have set itself up, once again, to be a passing game?

Notes

Chapter One

[1] Leo Cahill, with Scott Young, *Goodbye Leo* (Toronto: McClelland and Stewart, 1973), p.92.

[2] CFL Commissioner's letter in his annual report, February 4, 1970.

[3] CFL Commissioner's report letter dated February 4, 1970. This is in spite of a doubtful receivable of $13,500 and it is at odds with the League's Record Manual (Facts, Figures & Records) of 1992 which lists the receipts as $402,196. According to Gaudaur's letter, the sum included all-time highs for television ($199,000), film ($35,000), radio ($20,5000), and programme ($20,5000).

[4] *The Globe and Mail*, December 1, 1969.

[5] Minutes, CFL Semi-annual Meeting, June 5, 1969.

[6] Eddie McCabe, *Profile of a Pro* (Toronto: Prentice Hall Ltd., 1969), 148.

[7] *The Globe and Mail*, July 3, 1969.

[8] *Regina Leader-Post*, November 28, 1969.

[9] Minutes, CFL Meetings, November 26, 1969.

[10] Jake Gaudaur, Grey Cup Report, February 4, 1970.

[11] *Ibid.*

[12] *Ibid.*

[13] *Ibid.*

[14] *Ibid.*

[15] *Ibid.*

[16] *Ibid.*

[17] Gaudaur, Letter, July 24, 1969.

[18] *Ibid.*

[19] Minutes, CFL Meetings, January 13, 1970.

[20] *Ibid.*

[21] Gaudaur, Letter to Atwell, July 24, 1969.

[22] Gaudaur, Letter, January 21, 1970.

[23] *The Globe and Mail*, February 13, 1970.

[24] *Ibid.*

[25] *Ibid.*

[26] *The Globe and Mail*, February 17, 1970.

[27] Minutes, CFL General Managers' Meeting, February 10, 1969.

[28] *The Globe and Mail*, February 15, 1969.

[29] Minutes, CFL General Managers' Meeting, February 10, 1969.

[30] Minutes, CFL Executive Committee Meeting, February 13, 1969.

[31] *The Globe and Mail*, February 14, 1970.

[32] Minutes, CFL Rules Committee Meeting, January 13, 1970.

[33] Minutes, CFL General Managers' Meeting, February 10, 1969.

[34] *Ibid.*

[35] *Ibid.*

[36] *Ibid.*

[37] Minutes, CFL Executive Committee Meeting, June 5, 1969.

[38] Minutes, CFL General Managers' Meeting November 26, 1969.

[39] *Ibid.*

[40] Minutes, CFL Meeting, February 12, 1970.

[41] *Ibid.*

[42] *Ibid.*

[43] The next few paragraphs borrow heavily from Frank Cosentino, *Canadian Football: The Grey Cup Years*, pp. 178–79.

[44] *Montreal Gazette*, February 22, 1965.

45 *Montreal Gazette,* February 19, 1965.

46 *Montreal Gazette,* February 22, 1965.

47 *Montreal Gazette,* February 22, 1965.

48 *Edmonton Journal,* February 7, 1965.

49 *The Globe and Mail,* August 14, 1968.

50 *The Globe and Mail,* February 13, 1970.

51 Minutes, CFL Rules Committee Meeting, January 7, 1969.

52 Minutes, CFL Meeting, February 10, 1969.

53 *Ibid.*

54 *Ibid.*

55 *Ibid.*

56 Minutes, CFL Executive Committee Meeting, February 13, 1969.

57 *Ibid.*

58 Minutes, CFL Executive Committee Meeting, May 28, 1970.

59 *Ibid.*

60 Minutes, CFL Meetings, June 3, 1969.

61 Minutes, CFL General Managers' Meeting, June 3, 1969.

62 *The Globe and Mail,* June 16, 1969.

63 *Ibid.*

64 *Hamilton Spectator,* July 8, 1969.

65 Minutes, CFL Executive Committee Meeting, July 2, 1970.

66 *The Globe and Mail,* July 14, 1970.

67 Minutes, CFL Meetings, February 12, 1970.

68 *Ibid.*

69 Robert Nielsen, *Garney Henley* (Hamilton: Potlatch Publishing, 1972), 76.

70 Minutes, CFL Executive Committee Meeting, May 28, 1970.

71 *Ibid.*

72 *The Globe and Mail,* November 28, 1970.

73 Minutes, CFL Executive Committee Meeting, July 2, 1970.

74 *The Globe and Mail,* November 25, 1970.

75 *Ibid.*

76 *Canadian* Magazine, November, 1970.

77 *The Globe and Mail,* December 24, 1970.

78 *Ibid.*

79 *The Globe and Mail,* November 21, 1970.

80 *Ibid.*

81 *London Free Press,* October 28, 1970.

Chapter Two

1 CFL Annual Report, 1971.

2 Minutes, CFL Meeting, February 11, 1971.

3 *Ibid.*

4 CFL Commissioner's Report, 1971.

5 *London Free Press,* July 13, 1971.

6 CFL Commissioner's Report, February 13, 1969.

7 *The Globe and Mail,* April 19, 1969.

8 *The Globe and Mail,* February 14, 1969.

9 Minutes, CFL Meeting, February 11, 1971.

10 *London Free Press,* February 1, 1971.

11 *Ibid.*

12 Minutes, CFL Meeting, June 1, 1971.

13 *The Globe and Mail,* November 23, 1971.

14 Cahill, *op.cit.,* p. 182.

15 Leo Cahill, *Goodbye Leo.* Toronto: McClelland and Stewart, 1973.

16 Cahill, *op.cit.,* p. 121.

17 *Ibid.,* p124.

18 *Ottawa Journal,* February 18, 1972.

19 CFL Commissioner's Report, February 13, 1969.

20 *Ibid.*

21 *Ibid.*

22 *Ibid.*

23 *Ibid.*

24 Minutes, CFL Rules Committee, January 11, 1972.

25 Minutes, CFL General Managers' Meeting, January 13, 1971.

26 Minutes, CFL Meeting, February 12, 1970.

27 *Ibid.*

28 Minutes, CFL Executive Committee Meeting, May 28, 1970.

29 *Ibid.*

30 *The Globe and Mail,* February 13, 1971.

31 Cahill, *op.cit.,* p. 149.

32 Cahill, *op.cit.,* p. 173.

33 Cahill, *op.cit.,* p. 173–74.

34 *The Globe and Mail,* September 1, 1971.

35 *The Globe and Mail,* February 8, 1972.

36 *Ibid.*

37 *Ibid.*

38 *The Globe and Mail,* February 11, 1972.

39 *Ibid.*

40 *London Free Press,* January 14, 1971.

41 *Ibid.*

42 Minutes, CFL Meeting, January 13, 1971.

43 Minutes, CFL Meeting, February 11, 1971.

44 *Ibid.*

45 *Ibid.*

46 Minutes, CFL General Managers' Meeting, June 3, 1971.

47 Minutes, CFL General Managers' Meeting, June 1, 1971.

48 *Ibid.*

49 *Ibid.*

50 Minutes, CFL General Managers' Meeting, February 11, 1971.

51 *Ibid.*

52 *Ibid.*

53 CFL Commissioner's Report, 1971.

54 *London Free Press,* February 11, 1972.

55 *The Globe and Mail,* June 5, 1971.

56 *Ottawa Journal,* February 17, 1972.

57 *Ibid.*

58 Leo Cahill's *Goodbye Leo* is the source of what follows relating to Joe Theismann's pursuit and signing.

59 *London Free Press,* August 1, 1972.

60 *The Globe and Mail,* March 14, 1972.

61 CFL Commissioner's Report, 1971.

62 *Ibid.*

63 *The Globe and Mail,* August 13, 1971.

64 Minutes, CFL Executive Committee Meeting, November 23, 1971.

65 Initially the word "disciplinary" appeared before "action" and after "such" but it was deleted before the agreement was signed. Minutes, CFL Executive Committee, November 23, 1971.

66 Jake Gaudaur, letter to the expansion committee, CFL minutes, February 13, 1972.

67 CFL Commissioner's Report, February 13, 1972.

68 *Ibid.,* January 1, 1971.

69 Minutes, CFL General Managers' Meeting, June 1, 1971.

70 *London Free Press,* February 5, 1971.

71 Minutes, CFL Meeting, February 11, 1971.

72 *London Free Press,* February 5, 1971.

73 *The Globe and Mail,* November 27, 1971.

74 *Ibid.*

75 *Ibid.*

76 Minutes, CFL Executive Committee Meeting, February 10, 1972.

77 *Ibid.*

78 *Ottawa Journal,* February 26, 1972.

79 Minutes, CFL Meeting, February 10, 1972.

80 *Ibid.*

81 *Ibid.*

82 *Ibid.*

83 *Ibid.*

84 *Ibid.*

85 *Ibid.*

86 Minutes, CFL Executive Committee Meeting, November 16, 1972.

87 *The Globe and Mail,* December 2, 1972.

88 Minutes, CFL Meeting, December 1, 1972.

89 *The Globe and Mail,* December 2, 1972.

90 *The Globe and Mail,* November 20, 1972.

91 *Ibid.*

92 *Ibid.*

93 Minutes, CFL Meeting, December 1, 1972.

94 *Toronto Star,* December 2, 1972.

95 Minutes, CFL Meeting December 1, 1972.

96 *Toronto Star,* December 2, 1972.

97 *The Globe and Mail,* December 6, 1972.

98 *Ibid.,* December 4, 1972.

99 *Ibid.,* November 25, 1972.

100 *Ibid,* November 16, 1972.

101 Tony Gabriel, *Double Trouble.* Toronto: Gage Publishing, 1978, p. 60.

102 Minutes, CFL Meeting, January 17, 1973.

103 *The Globe and Mail,* November 15, 1972.

104 *Ibid.,* November 22, 1972.

105 *Ibid.,* November 28, 1972.

106 *Ibid.,* December 4, 1972.

Chapter Three

1 *The Globe and Mail,* November 1, 1972.

2 *London Free Press,* November 28, 1972.

3 *Ibid.*

4 *Ibid.*

5 Minutes, CFL Meeting, January 17, 1973.

6 *Ibid.*

7 *Ibid.*

8 *Ibid.*

9 *Ibid.*

10 *Ibid.*

11 *Ibid.*

12 *Ibid.*

13 *Ibid.*

14 *The Globe and Mail,* February 9, 1973.

15 *The Globe and Mail,* February 10, 1973.

16 *Ibid.*

17 *Ibid.*

18 *Ibid.*

19 *Ibid.*
20 *Ibid.*
21 *Ibid.*
22 *The Globe and Mail,* February 9, 1973.
23 *Ottawa Journal,* June 21, 1973.
24 *The Globe and Mail,* October, 1972.
25 CFL Annual Report, 1973.
26 Minutes, CFL Meeting, November 20, 1973.
27 Minutes, CFL Meeting, May 1, 1973.
28 Minutes, CFL Meeting, November 20, 1973.
29 *The Globe and Mail,* June 20, 1973.
30 *Ottawa Journal,* June 16, 1973.
31 *Toronto Star,* December 6, 1972.
32 *The Globe and Mail,* June 20, 1973.
33 *Ottawa Journal,* June 23, 1973.
34 *Vancouver Sun,* November 24, 1973.
35 *Vancouver Sun,* November 20, 1973.
36 *Vancouver Sun,* November 21, 1973.
37 *Vancouver Sun,* November 26, 1973.
38 *Ibid.*
39 Minutes, CFL Meeting, February 21, 1974.
40 *Ibid.*
41 *Ibid.*
42 *Ibid.*
43 *Ibid.*
44 *Ibid.*
45 Minutes, CFL Meeting, November 23, 1973.
46 *Ibid.*
47 Minutes, CFL Annual Meeting, May 31, 1973.
48 Jack Batten, *Hockey Dynasty* (Toronto: Pagurian Press Ltd.), 186.
49 *Ibid.*
50 *Ibid.*
51 *The Globe and Mail,* February 22, 1974.
52 *Ibid.* March 7, 1974.
53 *Ibid.*
54 *Ibid.*
55 *Ibid.*
56 *Ibid.*
57 *Toronto Star,* March 12, 1974.
58 *The Globe and Mail,* February 22, 1974.
59 Cross Canada Check Up, CBC Radio, March 17, 1974.
60 *Ibid.*
61 Lalonde Speech to Kiwanis and Rotary clubs, Regina, February 21, 1974. p. 2.
62 *Ibid.,* p. 5.
63 *Ibid.,* p. 6.
64 *Ibid.*
65 *Ibid.*
66 *Ibid.,* p. 8.
67 *Ibid.,* p. 10.
68 *Ibid.,* p. 11.
69 *Ibid.,* p. 11.
70 *Ibid.,* p. 12.
71 *Ibid.,* p. 12.
72 Minutes, CFL Annual Meeting, February 21, 1974.
73 *Ibid.*
74 *Ibid.*
75 *Ibid.*
76 *Ibid.*
77 *Ibid.*
78 *Ibid.*
79 *Ibid.*
80 *Ibid.*
81 *Ibid.*
82 *The Globe and Mail,* February 22, 1974.
83 *The Globe and Mail,* February 27, 1974.
84 *Toronto Star,* February 28, 1974.
85 *Ibid.*
86 *Ibid.*
87 *Ibid.*
88 *Toronto Star,* February 28, 1974.
89 *Ibid.*
90 *Ibid.*
91 Letter from Rene Toupin, March 1, 1974.
92 *Ibid.*
93 *Ibid.*
94 *Ibid.*
95 *Ibid.*
96 *Ibid.*
97 *Ibid.*
98 *Ibid.*
99 *Ibid.*
100 *London Free Press,* March 13, 1974.
101 *Ibid.*
102 *Ibid.*
103 *Ibid.*
104 CFL Brief to MPs, April 10, 1974, p.2.
105 *Ibid.,* p. 8.
106 *Ibid.*
107 *Ibid.*
108 *Ibid.,* p. 11.
109 *Ibid.,* p. 12.
110 *Ibid.,* p. 13.
111 *Ibid.,* p. 14.
112 *Toronto Star,* April 2, 1974.
113 Lalonde's speech second reading Bill C-22, April 18,1974.
114 *Ibid.,* p. 19.
115 CFL press release, n.d., April, 1974.
116 *Ibid.*
117 *Ibid.*
118 Minutes, CFL Meeting, April 30, 1974.
119 *Ibid.*
120 *Ibid.*
121 *Ibid.*
122 Commissioner's report, February 8, in Minutes, CFL Meeting, Feb 18, 1975.

[123] Minutes, CFL Meeting, May 30, 1974.
[124] *Ibid.*
[125] *Ibid.*
[126] *Ibid.*
[127] *Toronto Star*, August 31, 1974.
[128] *Ibid.*
[129] Much of what follows in this section is taken from *Double Trouble* by Tony Gabriel, Toronto: Gage Publishing, 1978, p. 33, etc.
[130] Commissioner's Report, CFL Meeting, February 18, 1974.
[131] Minutes, CFL Meeting, May 19, 1974.

Chapter Four

[1] Tony Gabriel, *Double Trouble*. (Toronto: Gage Publishing,1978) p. 88.
[2] Minutes, CFL Meeting, February 18, 1975.
[3] *Ibid.*
[4] *Ibid.*
[5] Minutes, CFL Executive Committee Meeting, February 20, 1975.
[6] *Ibid.*
[7] *Ottawa Citizen*, June 22, 1975.
[8] *Ibid.*
[9] *Ibid.*
[10] *Ibid.*
[11] *Ibid.*, June 20, 1975.
[12] Minutes, CFL Meeting, November 22, 1975.
[13] Minutes, CFL Meeting, February 18, 1975.
[14] *Ibid.*
[15] *Ibid.*, February 20, 1975.
[16] *Ibid.*
[17] *Ibid.*
[18] Minutes, CFL Meeting, November 22, 1975.
[1919] *The Globe and Mail*, January 8, 1975.
[20] Minutes, CFL Meeting, January 7, 1975.
[21] *Ibid.*
[22] *Ibid.*
[23] *Ibid.*
[24] *The Globe and Mail*, January 8, 1975.
[25] *Ottawa Journal*, June 6, 1975.
[26] This next section—ending at Robinson's statement: "I never thought being a Canadian would be a bad thing"—leans heavily on an article by Earl McRae, "The Odds Against Bill Robinson," in the *Canadian Magazine*, nd, 1975.
[27] *Canadian Magazine*, October 4, 1975.
[28] Minutes, CFL Meeting, February 20, 1975.
[29] *Ibid.*
[30] *Ibid.*
[31] Minutes, CFL Meeting, May 20, 1975.
[32] *Ibid.*
[33] *Ottawa Citizen*, June 25, 1975.
[34] *Ibid.*
[35] Minutes, CFL Meeting, November 18, 1975.
[36] *Ibid.*
[37] *Ibid.*
[38] *Ottawa Journal*, November 17, 1975.
[39] *Ibid.*
[40] *Ottawa Journal*, November 19, 1975.
[41] *Ibid.*
[42] *Ibid.*, November 20, 1975.
[43] *Ibid.*, November 21, 1975.
[44] *Ibid.*, November 24, 1975.
[45] *Ibid.*, November 26, 1975.
[46] *Ibid.*, November 25, 1975.
[47] CFL Commissioner's Report, 1975.
[48] *Ibid.*
[49] *Ibid.*
[50] *Ibid.*
[51] *Ibid.*
[52] *Ibid.*
[53] *Ottawa Journal*, January 21, 1976.
[54] Minutes, CFL Meeting, January 20, 1976.
[55] *Ibid.*, January 21, 1976.
[56] *Ibid.*
[57] *Ibid.*
[58] Minutes, CFL Meeting, May 27, 1976.
[59] *Ibid.*, February 17, 1976.
[60] CFL arbitration hearings, September 17, 1975.
[61] *Ibid.*, October 30, 1975.
[62] Minutes, CFL Meeting, February 19, 1976.
[63] Commissioner's Annual Report, 1974.
[64] *Ibid.*
[65] *Ibid.*
[66] Minutes, CFL Meeting, February 19, 1976.
[67] *Toronto Star*, February 19, 1976.
[68] *Ibid.*
[69] *Vancouver Sun*, May 31, 1976.
[70] Jay Teitel, *Argo Bounce*. (Toronto: Lester and Orpen Dennys, 1983) p. 123.
[71] Goodman, *op. cit.*, p. 177.
[72] *Ibid.*, p. 129.
[73] *Toronto Star*, November 15, 1976.
[74] *Toronto Star*, November 27, 1976.
[75] *Toronto Star*, November 19, 1976.

76 Goodman, *op. cit.*, p. 190.

Chapter Five

1 *Toronto Star*, February 18, 1977.
2 *Ibid.*
3 *Ibid.*
4 *Toronto Star*, March 22, 1977.
5 *Ibid.*
6 Minutes, CFL Meeting, April 12, 1977.
7 Minutes, CFL Executive Committee Meeting, April 12, 1977.
8 Minutes, CFL Executive Committee Meeting, April 19, 1977.
9 *Ottawa Journal*, April 22, 1977.
10 *Ibid.*
11 *Toronto Star*, February 17, 1977.
12 *Ibid.*
13 *Ibid.*
14 *Vancouver Sun*, Jan 20, 1977.
15 *Vancouver Sun*, May 13, 1977.
16 Minutes, CFL Meeting, January 18, 1977.
17 *Ibid.*
18 Minutes, CFL Meeting, March 21, 1977.
19 Minutes, CFL Meeting, November 22, 1977.
20 *Ibid.*
21 *Ibid.*, May 13, 1977.
22 Gabriel, *op. cit.*, p. 11.
23 *Ibid.*, p. 118.
24 Teitel, *op. cit.*, p. 144.
25 *Ibid.*, p. 142.
26 Dan Kepley, *The Edmonton Eskimos* (Toronto: Metheun, 1983) p. 38.
27 *Ottawa Journal*, November 28, 1977.
28 *Ibid.*, November 29, 1977.
29 *Vancouver Sun*, May 11, 1977.
30 *Ibid.*, May 13, 1977.
31 *Ibid.*
32 *Ibid.*, May 11, 1977.
33 Minutes, CFL Meeting, February 15, 1978.
34 Calgary *Herald*, January 24, 1978.
35 Calgary *Herald*, January 25, 1978.
36 Calgary *Herald*, January 26, 1978.
37 *Ibid.*
38 *Ibid.*
39 Calgary *Herald*, January 28, 1978.
40 *Ibid.*
41 *Ibid.*
42 Minutes, CFL Meeting, February 14, 1978.
43 *Ibid.*
44 *Ibid.*
45 Minutes, CFL Meeting, February 16, 1978.
46 *Ibid.*
47 *Ibid.*
48 *Ibid.*
49 *Ibid.*
50 *Ibid.*
51 *Ibid.*
52 *Ibid.*
53 *Ibid.*
54 Minutes, CFL Meeting, February 14, 1978.
55 *Ibid.*
56 *Ibid.*
57 *Ibid.*
58 *Ibid.*
59 Minutes, CFL Meeting, April 18, 1978.
60 Minutes, CFL Meeting, May 16, 1978.
61 *Ibid.*, p. 108.
62 Calgary *Herald*, October 25, 1979.
63 *Ibid.*
64 *Montreal Gazette*, May 14, 1980.
65 *Ibid.*
66 *Ibid.*
67 Dunwoody, Derm, "Passing the Buck on Canadian Content", *MacLean's*, August 13, 1979, p. 38.
68 Bone, David James. *The Ontario Human Rights Code, R.S.O. 1970, Chapter 318—Inquiry.* Toronto, June 26, July 10, 11, 12, 17, 1979. p. 44.
69 Dunwoody, *op. cit.*, p. 38.
70 Bone, *op. cit.*, p. 47.
71 Dunwoody, *op. cit.* p. 38.
72 Bone, *op.cit.*, p.58.
73 *Ibid.*, p. 71.
74 *Ibid.*, May 11, 1977.
75 Minutes, CFL Meeting, January 25, 1979.
76 *Toronto Star*, November 23, 1978.
77 *Ibid.*
78 *Toronto Star*, November 25, 1978.
79 *Toronto Star*, November 24, 1978.
80 *Toronto Star*, November 25, 1978.

Chapter Six

1 Minutes, CFL Meeting, November 11, 1978.
2 *Ibid.*
3 *Ibid.*
4 *Ibid.*
5 *Ibid.*
6 *Ibid.*
7 *Ibid.*
8 Goodman, *op. cit.*, p. 190.
9 Minutes, CFL Meeting, November 24, 1978.
10 Letter from Carling O'Keefe to the CFL, January 3, 1979.
11 *Ibid.*, January 10, 1979.

[12] Goodman, *op. cit.*, p. 191.
[13] *Montreal Gazette*, February 27, 1979.
[14] Letter from W. Hodgson to Jake Gaudaur, February 8, 1979.
[15] Minutes, CFL Meeting, May 10, 1979.
[16] *Ibid.*
[17] *Ibid.*, p. 5.
[18] *Ibid.*, p. 30.
[19] *Ibid.*
[20] *Ibid.*
[21] Minutes, CFL Meeting, February 15, 1979.
[22] *Ibid.*
[23] *Ibid.*
[24] *Ibid.*
[25] *Ibid.*
[26] Melvyn Chin, David Cohen, Bill Hurley and James Pettigrew, Unpublished paper on Toronto Argonaut Football Club, MBA Policy, York University, 1979.
[27] *Ibid.*
[28] *Ibid.*
[29] *Ibid.*, p. 24.
[30] Minutes, CFL Meeting, November 24, 1979.
[31] Minutes, CFL Meeting, January 24, 1979.
[32] *Ibid.*
[33] *Ibid.*, January 25, 1979.
[34] Minutes, CFL Meeting, May 10, 1979.
[35] *CFLPA News*, June, 1979.
[36] *CFLPA News*, June, 1979, p. 3.
[37] *Ibid.*
[38] *Ibid.*
[39] *CFLPA News*, September, 1979, p. 1.
[40] *Ibid.*
[41] *Ibid.*
[42] *Montreal Gazette*, November 21, 1979.

[43] *Montreal Gazette*, November 21, 1979.
[44] *Ibid*, November 24, 1979.
[45] Minutes, CFL Meeting, February 21, 1980.
[46] *Ibid.*, November 22, 1979.
[47] *Montreal Gazette*, November 23, 1979.
[48] *Ibid.*, November 23, 1979.
[49] *Montreal Gazette*, November 23, 1979.
[50] *Ibid.*
[51] *Montreal Gazette*, November 26, 1979.
[52] *Ibid.*
[53] *Ibid.*
[54] *Ibid.*
[55] *CFLPA News*, August, 1979.
[56] *Toronto Star*, May 19, 1980.
[57] *Ibid.*
[58] *Ibid.*
[59] *Ibid.*
[60] *Toronto Star*, May 19, 1980.
[61] *Toronto Star*, April 24, 1980.
[62] *Toronto Star*, April 11, 1980.
[63] *Montreal Gazette*, June 26, 1980.
[64] *Toronto Sun*, February 21, 1982.
[65] *Montreal Gazette*, May 15, 1980.
[66] *Montreal Gazette*, May 15, 1980.
[67] Minutes, CFL Meeting, August 30, 1979.
[68] *Ibid.*
[69] *Ibid.*
[70] *Ibid.*
[71] *Ibid.*
[72] *Ibid.*
[73] *Ibid.*
[74] *Ibid.*

[75] Minutes, CFL Meeting, May 13, 1980.
[76] *Ibid.*
[77] *Ibid.*
[78] *Ibid.*
[79] *Ibid.*
[80] *Ibid.*
[81] Minutes, CFL Meeting, February 21, 1980.
[82] *Toronto Star*, April 22, 1980.
[83] *Montreal Gazette*, May 13, 1980.
[84] *Ibid.*
[85] Minutes, CFL Meeting, February 19, 1980.
[86] Minutes, CFL Meeting, February 21, 1980.
[87] *Toronto Sun*, February 14, 1980.
[88] *Montreal Gazette*, May 15, 1980.
[89] *Ibid.*
[90] *Toronto Sun*, November 21, 1980.
[91] Beddoes, *Pal Hal*, *op.cit.*, p. 253.
[92] *Ibid.*, p. 251.
[93] *Toronto Star*, November 23, 1980.
[94] Kepley, *op.cit.*, p. 146.
[95] *Ibid.*
[96] *Ibid.*
[97] *Toronto Sun*, November 24, 1980.
[98] *Ibid.*
[99] *Toronto Sun*, November 25, 1980.
[100] *Ibid.*

Chapter Seven

[1] Minutes, CFL Meeting, November 21, 1980.
[2] *Ibid.*
[3] *Ibid.*
[4] *Ibid.*
[5] Letter to J.Gaudaur, December 9, 1980.
[6] *Ibid.*

7 *Ibid.*
8 *Ibid.*
9 *Ibid.*
10 *Ibid.*
11 *Ibid.*
12 Minutes, CFL Meeting, February 18, 1981.
13 *Toronto Sun*, February 20, 1981.
14 Minutes, CFL Meeting, January 23, 1981.
15 *Ibid.*, March 30, 1981.
16 *Toronto Sun*, March 31, 1981.
17 *Calgary Herald*, January 24, 1981.
18 Minutes, CFL Meeting, February 19, 1981.
19 *Ibid.*
20 *Ibid.*
21 *Toronto Sun*, February 20, 1981.
22 *Ibid.*
23 *Ibid.*
24 *Ibid.*, February 18, 1981.
25 *Ibid.*
26 Minutes, CFL Meeting, January 22, 1981.
27 *Ibid.*
28 *Ibid.*
29 *Ibid.*
30 *Ibid.*, February 19, 1981.
31 *Ibid.*
32 Letter from CHRC, February 19, 1981.
33 *Toronto Sun*, March 31, 1981.
34 Letter from Gordon Fairweather, February 19, 1981.
35 *Toronto Sun*, March 3, 1981.
36 Ralph Sturino, *The Plight of the Canadian Quarterback* (Independent Study, York University, 1987), 10.
37 *Ibid.*
38 *Ibid.*, p. 11.
39 *Ibid.*
40 *Ibid.*, p. 12.
41 Minutes, CFL Meeting, November 18, 1981.
42 *Ibid.*
43 *Ibid.*
44 *Calgary Herald*, January 22, 1981.
45 *Official Playing Rules of the CFL*, 1980.
46 *Calgary Herald*, January 22, 1981.
47 *Toronto Sun*, February 20, 1981.
48 *Ibid.*, February 19, 1981.
49 *Ibid.*, February 11, 1981.
50 *Montreal Gazette*, November 11, 1981.
51 *Ibid.*
52 *Ibid.*
53 *Ibid.*, November 16, 1981.
54 *Ibid.*
55 *Ibid.*, November 11, 1981.
56 *Ibid.*, November 13, 1981.
57 *Ibid.*, November 19, 1981.
58 *Ibid.*
59 *Ibid.*, November 19, 1981.
60 *Ibid.*
61 *Ibid.*, November 21, 1981.
62 *Ibid.*, November 21, 1981.
63 *Ibid.*, November 19, 1981.
64 *Ibid.*, November 18, 1981.
65 *Ibid.*, November 23, 1981.
66 Letter to CFL officers from Jake Gaudaur, February 11, 1982.
67 *Ibid.*
68 *Ibid.*
69 *Ibid.*
70 *Ibid.*
71 *Ibid.*
72 *Ibid.*
73 *Ibid.*
74 *Ibid.*
75 *Ibid.*
76 *Ibid.*
77 *Ibid.*
78 *Ibid.*
79 *Ibid.*
80 *Ibid.*
81 *Ibid.*
82 *Ibid.*
83 *Ibid.*
84 *Ibid.*
85 *Ibid.*
86 *Ibid.*
87 *Ibid.*
88 *Ibid.*
89 *Ibid.*
90 *Ibid.*
91 *Ibid.*
92 *Ibid.*
93 *Ibid.*
94 *Ibid.*
95 *Ibid.*
96 *Ibid.*
97 *Ibid.*
98 *Ibid.*
99 *Ibid.*
100 *Ibid.*
101 *Calgary Herald*, January 13, 1982.
102 *Ibid.*, January 14, 1982.
103 *Ibid.*
104 *Toronto Sun*, February 21, 1982.
105 *Calgary Herald*, May 11, 1982.
106 *Ibid.*
107 *Ibid.*, May 12, 1982.
108 *Ibid.*, May 13, 1982.
109 *Ibid.*, May 15, 1982.
110 *Ibid.*
111 *Ibid.*, May 27, 1982.
112 John Palzet and Frank Kosecn.
113 *Toronto Sun*, May 27, 1982.
114 Concordes Media Guide Book '84, p. 12.
115 *Calgary Herald*, May 12, 1982.

[116] Minutes, CFL Meeting, February 16, 1982.
[117] *Ibid.*
[118] *Ibid.*
[119] *Ibid.*
[120] *Ibid.*
[121] *Ibid.*
[122] *Ibid.*
[123] *Toronto Sun*, February 25, 1982.
[124] Sturino, *op. cit.*, p. 14.
[125] *Ibid.*
[126] *Ibid.*
[127] *Ibid.*, p. 15.
[128] *Ibid.*
[129] *Ibid.*, p. 16.
[130] *Ibid.*
[131] *Ibid.*
[132] *Calgary Herald*, January 21, 1982.
[133] *Calgary Herald*, January 22, 1982.
[134] *Calgary Herald*, January 21, 1982.
[135] *Ibid.*
[136] Minutes, CFL Meeting, January 21, 1982.
[137] *Calgary Herald*, January 21, 1982.
[138] *Toronto Sun*, May 23, 1982.
[139] *Ibid.*
[140] Minutes, CFL Meeting, November 20, 1982.
[141] *Calgary Herald*, May 14, 1982.
[142] *Ibid.*
[143] *Toronto Sun*, November 25, 1982.
[144] *Toronto Sun*, May 27, 1982.
[145] *Ibid.*
[146] *Ibid.*
[147] *Toronto Sun*, May 27, 1982.
[148] Minutes, CFL Meeting, February 16, 1982.
[149] *Ibid.*
[150] *Ibid.*
[151] Minutes, CFL Meeting, February 16, 1982.
[152] *Ibid.*
[153] *Toronto Sun*, November 22, 1982.
[154] *Ibid.*
[155] *Toronto Sun*, November 24, 1982.
[156] *Ibid.*
[157] *Ibid.*
[158] *Ibid.*
[159] *Toronto Sun*, November 26, 1982.
[160] *Toronto Sun*, November 29, 1982.
[161] *Ibid.*

Chapter Eight

[1] *B.C. Lions 1984 Fact Book*, p. 59.
[2] *Ibid.*
[3] *Ibid.*, p. 60.
[4] *Ibid.*, p. 16.
[5] Minutes, CFL Meeting, May 3, 1983.
[6] Minutes, CFL Meeting, January 19, 1983.
[7] *Ibid.*, May 3, 1983.
[8] *Ibid.*
[9] *Ibid.*, February 15, 1983.
[10] *Ibid.*, May 3, 1983.
[11] *Toronto Sun*, February 16, 1983.
[12] *Ibid.*, February 15, 1983.
[13] *Ibid.*
[14] *Ibid.*
[15] *Ibid.*
[16] *Ibid.*
[17] *Vancouver Sun*, May 6, 1983.
[18] *Ibid.*
[19] *Ibid.*
[20] *Ibid.*
[21] CFL Memo, January 25, 1983.
[22] Minutes, CFL Meeting, February, 1983.
[23] *Ibid.*
[24] *Ibid.*
[25] *Ibid.*
[26] *Ibid.*
[27] *Ibid.*
[28] *Ibid.*
[29] *Ibid.*, January 20, 1983.
[30] *Ibid.*
[31] *B.C. Lions 1984 Fact Book*, p. 60.
[32] *Toronto Sun*, May 24, 1983.
[33] *Vancouver Sun*, November 21, 1983.
[34] *Ibid.*, November 22, 1983.
[35] *Ibid.*
[36.] *The Globe and Mail*, November 24, 1993.
[37] *Ibid.*
[38] *Vancouver Sun*, November 22, 1983.
[39] *Ibid.*
[40] *Ibid.*
[41] *Ibid.*, November 28, 1983.
[42] *Ibid.*, November 30, 1983.
[43] *Ibid.*, December 5, 1983.
[44] *Ibid.*
[45] *Ibid.*, December 5, 1983.
[46] *Toronto Sun*, February 18, 1983.
[47] *Toronto Star*, February 16, 1984.
[48] *Ibid.*, March 8, 1984.
[49] Minutes, CFL Meeting, March 6, 1984.
[50] *Ibid.*
[51] *Ibid.*
[52] *Ibid.*, May 2, 1984.
[53] *Ibid.*, May 4, 1984.
[54] Minutes, CFL Meeting, November 7, 1984.
[55] *Ibid.*, November 7, 1984.
[56] Minutes, CFL Meeting, January 18, 1984.
[57] *Ibid.*
[58] *Ibid.*, February 13, 1984.
[59] *Ibid.*, February 15, 1984.
[60] *Ibid.*
[61] *Ibid.*
[62] *Ibid.*
[63] *Calgary Herald*, May 4, 1984.

64 *Toronto Star*, February 14, 1984.
65 *Ibid.*
66 *Calgary Herald*, January 19, 1984.
67 *Ibid.*
68 *Toronto Star*, March 1, 1984.
69 *Ibid.*, March 7, 1984.
70 *Ibid.*, November 29, 1983.
71 *Ibid.*
72 *Ibid.*
73 *Ibid.*, November 15, 1984.
74 *Calgary Herald*, May 6, 1984.
75 Minutes, CFL Meeting, November 25, 1983.
76 *Ibid.*
77 *Calgary Herald*, May 6, 1984.
78 Minutes, CFL Meeting, May 2, 1984.
79 *Ibid.*, November 16, 1984.
80 *Toronto Star*, November 7, 1984.
81 *CFL Facts and Figures*, 1985, p. 9.
82 *Toronto Star*, November 4, 1984.
83 *Ibid.*, November 4, 1984.
84 *Ibid.*, November 7, 1984.
85 *Ibid.*, November 5, 1984.
86 *Ibid.*
87 *Ibid.*, November 8, 1984.
88 *Ibid.*, November 18, 1984.
89 *Ibid.*
90 *Ibid.*
91 *Ibid.*
92 *Ibid.*, November 12, 1984.
93 *Ibid.*, November 19, 1984.
94 *Ibid.*
95 Minutes, CFL Meeting, November 16, 1984.

Chapter Nine

1 Minutes, CFL Meeting, January 16, 1985.
2 *Ibid.*
3 *Ibid.*
4 *Ibid.*
5 *Ibid.*
6 *Ibid.*
7 *Ibid.*
8 *Ibid.*
9 *Ibid.*, September 24, 1985.
10 *Ibid.*
11 *Ibid.*
12 *Ibid.*
13 *Ibid.*, October 7, 1985.
14 *Ibid.*
15 *Ibid.*
16 *Ibid.*
17 *Ibid.*
18 *Ibid.*
19 *Ibid.*
20 *Winnipeg Free Press*, July 28, 1985.
21 *Ibid.*
22 *Ibid.*, July 29, 1985.
23 *Toronto Star*, November 5, 1985.
24 *Ibid.*
25 *Ibid.*
26 Minutes, CFL Meeting, July 23, 1985.
27 *Ibid.*
28 *Ibid.*
29 *Ibid.*
30 *Ibid.*
31 *Ibid.*
32 *Ibid.*
33 *Ibid.*
34 *Ibid.*
35 *Ibid.*
36 *Ibid.*
37 *Ibid.*
38 *Ibid.*
39 *Ibid.*
40 *Ibid.*, October 7, 1985.
41 *Ibid.*
42 *Ibid.*
43 *Ibid.*
44 *Ibid.*
45 *Ibid.*
46 *Ibid.*
47 *Ibid.*
48 *Ibid.*
49 *Ibid.*
50 *Ibid.*
51 *Ibid.*
52 *Ibid.*, May 7, 1985.
53 *Ibid.*
54 *Ibid.*
55 *Ibid.*
56 *Ibid.*, February 19, 1985.
57 *Ibid.*
58 *Ibid.*
59 *Ibid.*
60 *Ibid.*, April 18, 1985.
61 *Ibid.*
62 *Montreal Gazette*, May 9, 1985.
63 *Ibid.*
64 *Ibid.*, May 9, 1985.
65 *Ibid.*, September 24, 1985.
66 *Toronto Star*, November 17, 1985.
67 *Ibid.*, February 19, 1985.
68 *Ibid.*
69 *Winnipeg Free Press*, August 25, 1985.
70 *CFLPA News*, September 1985, p. 3.
71 Minutes, CFL Meeting, October 7, 1985.
72 *Ibid.*, October 7, 1985.
73 *Ibid.*, May 9, 1985.
74 *Ibid.*
75 *Ibid.*
76 *Ibid.*
77 *Ibid.*, November 22, 1985.
78 *Ibid.*
79 *Ibid.*
80 *Toronto Star*, November 23, 1985.
81 Minutes, CFL Meeting, November 22, 1985.
82 *Ibid.*
83 *Ibid.*
84 *Ibid.*
85 *Ibid.*
86 *Ibid.*

87 *Toronto Star*, November 11, 1985.
88 *Ibid.*
89 *Ibid.*, November 21, 1985.
90 *Ibid.*
91 *Ibid.*
92 *Ibid.*, November 24, 1985.
93 Minutes, CFL Meeting, February 11, 1986.
94 *Ibid.*
95 CFL Letter to General Managers, March 13, 1986.
96 Minutes, CFL Meeting, May 8, 1986.
97 *Ibid.*, January 22, 1986.
98 *Ibid.*
99 Minutes, CFL Meeting, February 19, 1985.
100 *Ibid.*
101 *Ibid.*
102 *Winnipeg Free Press*, April 29, 1986.
103 *Ibid.*
104 *Ibid.*
105 Minutes, CFL Meeting, May 8, 1986.
106 *Winnipeg Free Press*, January 21, 1986.
107 *Ibid.*
108 *Ibid.*
109 *Ibid.*
110 *Ibid.*
111 *Toronto Star*, February 13, 1986.
112 *Ibid.*
113 *Winnipeg Free Press*, January 25, 1986.
114 *Toronto Star*, January 22, 1986.
115 *Ibid.*
116 *Ibid.*
117 *Ibid.*, January 24, 1986.
118 *Ibid.*, February 17, 1986.
119 *Ibid.*
120 Minutes, CFL Meeting, May 27, 1986.

121 *Toronto Star*, February 17, 1986.
122 Minutes, CFL Meeting, January 22, 1986.
123 *Ibid.*
124 *Ibid.*
125 *Ibid.*
126 *Ibid.*
127 *Ibid.*
128 Minutes, CFL Meeting, April 29, 1986.
129 *Ibid.*
130 Minutes, CFL Meeting, November 28, 1986.
131 *Ibid.*
132 *Ibid.*
133 Minutes, CFL Meeting, April 29, 1986.
134 *Ibid.*
135 *Ibid.*, May 8, 1986.
136 *Ibid.*, June 11, 1986.
137 *Ibid.*, May 8, 1986.
138 *Ibid.*
139 *Ibid.*
140 *Winnipeg Free Press*, January 18, 1985.
141 *Toronto Star*, December 1, 1986.
142 *Ibid.*
143 *Ibid.*
144 *Ibid.*, November 26, 1986.
145 *Ibid.*
146 *Ibid.*
147 *Ibid.*
148 *Ibid.*
149 *Vancouver Sun*, November 22, 1986.
150 *Ibid.*
151 *Ibid.*
152 *Ibid.*

Chapter Ten

1 Minutes, CFL Meeting, February 20, 1987.
2 *Ibid.*
3 *Ibid.*
4 *Ibid.*
5 *Ibid.*

6 *Ibid.*
7 *Ibid.*
8 Minutes, CFL Meeting, January 5, 1988.
9 *Ibid.*
10 *Ibid.*
11 *Ibid.*
12 *Ibid.*
13 *Ibid.*
14 *Ibid.*
15 *Ibid.*
16 *Ibid.*
17 *Ibid.*
18 *Ibid.*
19 *Ibid.*
20 Minutes, CFL Meeting, June 11, 1986.
21 *Ibid.*
22 *Ibid.*
23 *Ibid.*
24 *Ibid.*
25 *CFL Report on Roster Considerations for 1987*, p. 1.
26 *Ibid.*
27 *Ibid.*
28 *Ibid.*
29 *Ibid.*
30 *Ibid.*
31 Minutes, CFL Meeting, November 28, 1986.
32 *Ibid.*
33 *Ibid.*
34 *Ibid.*
35 *Winnipeg Free Press*, January 10, 1987.
36 Minutes, CFL Meeting, January 7, 1987.
37 *Ibid.*
38 Minutes, CFL Meeting, February 17, 1987.
39 *Ibid.*
40 Minutes, CFL Meeting, October 30, 1987.
41 Minutes, CFL Meeting, January 23, 1987.
42 Minutes, CFL Meeting, January 21, 1987.
43 *Ibid.*
44 *Ibid.*

45 *Winnipeg Free Press,* January 28, 1987.

46 Minutes, CFL Meeting, January 23, 1987.

47 *Toronto Star*, February 18, 1987.

48 *Ibid.*

49 *Ibid.*, February 19, 1987.

50 *Winnipeg Free Press*, May 13, 1987.

51 *Ibid.*

52 *Ibid.*

53 *Ibid.*

54 *Ibid.*

55 *Ibid.*, May 20, 1987.

56 *Ibid.*

57 Minutes, CFL Meeting, February 20, 1987.

58 *Ibid.*

59 *Ibid.*

60 *Ibid.*

61 *Ibid.*

62 *Ibid.*

63 Minutes, CFL Meeting, April 12, 1987.

64 Minutes, CFL Meeting, June 23, 1987.

65 *Ibid.*

66 *Ibid.*

67 *Ibid.*

68 Minutes, CFL Meeting, September 17, 1987.

69 *Ibid.*

70 Minutes, CFL Meeting, July 28, 1987.

71 *Ibid.*

72 *Ibid.*

73 *Ibid.*

74 *Ibid.*

75 *Ibid.*

76 *Ibid.*

77 *Ibid.*

78 *Ibid.*

79 *Toronto Star*, February 21, 1987.

80 *Ibid.*

81 *Ibid.*

82 *Winnipeg Free Press*, July 29, 1987.

83 CFL Report, March 4, 1988.

84 *Toronto Star*, November 24, 1987.

85 Minutes, CFL Meeting, September 17, 1987.

86 *Toronto Star*. September 18, 1987.

87 *Ibid.*

88 *Toronto Star*, January 9, 1987.

89 *Winnipeg Free Press*, July 28, 1987.

90 Minutes, CFL Meeting, January 23, 1987.

91 Minutes, CFL Meeting, October 30, 1987.

92 *Ibid.*

93 *Ibid.*

94 *Toronto Star*, November 25, 1987.

95 *Ibid.*

96 *Ibid.*, November 30, 1987.

97 *Ibid.*

98 *Ibid.*

99 *Calgary Herald,* January 29, 1988.

100 *Toronto Star,* January 8, 1988.

101 *Ibid.*

102 *Calgary Herald*, January 29, 1988.

103 *Ibid.*

104 *Ibid.*

105 Minutes, CFL Meeting, March 2, 1988.

106 Minutes, CFL Meeting, January 29, 1988.

107 Minutes, CFL Meeting, March 2, 1988.

108 Minutes, CFL Meeting, June 9, 1988.

109 Minutes, CFL Meeting, January 8, 1988.

110 Minutes, CFL Meeting, January 5, 1988.

111 Minutes, CFL Meeting, January 26, 1988.

112 *Ibid.*

113 *Ibid.*

114 *Ibid.*

115 Minutes, CFL Meeting, January 26, 1988.

116 *Ibid.*

117 Minutes, CFL Meeting, January 5, 1988.

118 Minutes, CFL Meeting, January 8, 1988.

119 *Ibid.*

120 *Ibid.*

121 *Ibid.*

122 Minutes, CFL Meeting, March 2, 1988.

123 Minutes, CFL Meeting, May 18, 1988.

124 *Ibid.*

125 *Ibid.*

126 Minutes, CFL Meeting, September 16, 1988.

127 *Ibid.*

128 *Calgary Herald,* November 25, 1988.

129 *Ibid.*

130 *Ibid.*

131 *Ibid,* November 25, 1988.

132 *Ibid.*

133 Interview with Matt Dunigan, May 17, 1992.

134 *Calgary Herald,* November 26, 1988.

Chapter Eleven

1 Minutes, CFL Meeting, January 8, 1988.

2 Minutes, CFL Meeting, December 12, 1988.

3 *Ibid.*

4 *Ibid.*

5 *Ibid.*

6 *Ibid.*

7 *Calgary Herald,* December 13, 1988.

8 Minutes, CFL Meeting, December 12, 1988.

9 *Calgary Herald,* December 13, 1988.

10 *Calgary Herald,* January 26, 1989.

[11] *Toronto Star*, January 24, 1989.

[12] *Ibid.*, February 25, 1989.

[13] Minutes, CFL Meeting, February 23, 1989.

[14] *Ibid.*

[15] *Ibid.*

[16] *Calgary Herald*, May 11, 1989.

[17] Minutes, CFL Meeting, December 12, 1988.

[18] *Toronto Star*, May 23, 1989.

[19] *Ibid.*

[20] *Ibid.*

[21] *Ibid.*, October 14, 1989.

[22] *Ibid.*

[23] *Ibid.*

[24] Minutes, CFL Meeting, December 12, 1988.

[25] *Ibid.*

[26] *Ibid.*

[27] *Calgary Herald*, December 13, 1988.

[28] *Ibid.*

[29] *Ibid.*

[30] *Ibid.*, January 10, 1989.

[31] *Ibid.*, June 8, 1989.

[32] *Ibid.*

[33] *Ibid.*

[34] Minutes, CFL Meeting, September 10, 1990.

[35] *Ibid.*

[36] *Ibid.*

[37] *Ibid.*

[38] Minutes, CFL Meeting, January 25, 1989.

[39] *Ibid.*

[40] *Calgary Herald*, January 26, 1989.

[41] *Ibid.*

[42] Minutes, CFL Meeting, February 24, 1989.

[43] *Ibid.*

[44] *Ibid.*

[45] *Toronto Star*, February 25, 1989.

[46] *Hamilton Spectator*, May 13, 1989.

[47] *Ibid.*, May 13, 1989.

[48] Minutes, CFL Meeting, February 24, 1989.

[49] *Ibid.*, July 16, 1989.

[50] *Toronto Star*, July 17, 1989.

[51] Minutes, CFL Meeting, July 16, 1989.

[52] *Ottawa Citizen*, July 27, 1989.

[53] *Ibid.*

[54] *Ibid.*, July 27, 1989.

[55] *Ibid.*

[56] *Ibid.*

[57] *Ibid.*

[58] Minutes, CFL Meeting, July 16, 1989.

[59] *Ibid.*

[60] *Ibid.*

[61] *Ibid.*, May 10, 1989.

[62] *Ibid.*

[63] *Ibid.*

[64] *The Globe and Mail*, November 25, 1989.

[65] *Ibid.*

[66] Minutes, CFL Meeting, November 23, 1989.

[67] *CFLPA News*, March 1990, p. 1.

[68] *Ibid.* No names were given in the Players' Association reports which documented these cases.

[69] *Ibid.*

[70] *Ibid.*, March, 1989, p. 3.

[71] *Ibid.*, March, 1990, p. 5.

[72] *Ibid.*

[73] *Ibid.*, September 21, 1990.

[74] Minutes, CFL Meeting, January 25, 1989.

[75] *Ibid.*, February 24, 1989.

[76] *Ibid.*, January 25, 1989.

[77] *The Globe and Mail*, January 25, 1989.

[78] *Ibid.*, February 23, 1990.

[79] *The Globe and Mail*, November 24, 1989.

[80] *Ibid.*

[81] Minutes, CFL Meeting, August 15, 1989.

[82] *Ibid.*, June 8, 1989.

[83] *Ibid.*

[84] *Ibid.*, October 14, 1989.

[85] *Ibid.*

[86] *Star Week* (supplement to the *Toronto Star*), December 9, 1989.

[87] *The Globe and Mail*, November 24, 1989.

[88] *Ibid.*

[89] *Ibid.*, November 27, 1989.

[90] *Ibid.*

[91] *Ibid.*

[92] *Ibid.*

[93] *Ibid.*

[94] *Toronto Star*, November 28, 1989.

[95] *The Globe and Mail*, December 13, 1989.

[96] *Ibid.*

[97] *Ibid.*

[98] Canadian Football League Finacial Statements for the year ended December 31, 1989.

[99] *Toronto Star*, November 29, 1989.

[100] *Ibid.*

[101] *Toronto Star*, October 14, 1989.

[102] *Ibid.*, August 4, 1989.

[103] *Ibid.*

[104] *Ibid.*, October 15, 1989.

[105] Minutes, CFL Meeting, November 24, 1989.

[106] *Vancouver Sun*, January 6, 1990.

[107] *Ibid.*

[108] *Ibid.*

[109] *Ibid.*

[110] *Ibid.*, January 23, 1990.

[111] *Ibid.*

[112] *Ibid.*

[113] *Ibid.*

[114] *Ibid.*

[115] Minutes, CFL Meeting, February 23, 1989.

[116] *Toronto Star*, February 23, 1989.

117 *Toronto Star*, February 24, 1989.
118 *Calgary Herald*, January 25, 1989.
119 *Ibid.*
120 *Ibid.*
121 *Ibid.*
122 *Ibid.*, January 24, 1990.
123 *Toronto Star*, March 30, 1990.
124 *Ibid.*
125 *Ibid.*
126 *Ibid.*
127 *Ibid.*
128 *Ibid.*
129 *Ibid.*
130 *Ibid.*, March 29, 1990.
131 *Ibid.*, March 30, 1990.
132 *The Globe and Mail*, March 30, 1990.
133 *Toronto Star*, May 25, 1990.
134 *Vancouver Sun*, February 24, 1990.
135 *Ibid.*
136 *Vancouver Sun*, May 19, 1990.
137 *Ibid.*
138 *Ibid.*
139 *Winnipeg Free Press*, May 10, 1990.
140 *Ibid.*, May 19, 1990.
141 *The Globe and Mail*, January 24, 1990.
142 *Ibid.*
143 *Vancouver Sun*, January 26, 1990.
144 *Ibid.*, January 25, 1990.
145 *Ibid.*
146 *Ibid.*, January 25, 1989.
147 *Vancouver Sun*, May 17, 1990.
148 *Winnipeg Free Press*, May 18, 1990.
149 *Ibid.*, May 17, 1990.
150 *Ibid.*
151 *Ibid.*
152 *Vancouver Sun*, January 25, 1990.
153 *Ibid.*
154 *Ibid.*

155 *Toronto Star*, January 25, 1990.
156 *Vancouver Sun*, January 25, 1990.
157 *Ottawa Citizen*, September 25, 1990.
158 *Ibid.*
159 *Ibid.*
160 *The Globe and Mail*, November 25, 1989.
161 *Winnipeg Free Press*, May 19, 1990.
162 *Ibid.*
163 *Vancouver Sun*, May 2, 1990.
164 *Ibid.*
165 *Ibid.*
166 *Ibid.*, May 11, 1990.
167 *The Globe and Mail*, September 13, 1990.
168 *Ibid.*
169 *Ibid.*
170 *Ibid.*
171 *Ibid.*
172 *Ibid.*
173 *Ibid.*
174 *Ibid.*
175 *Ibid.*
176 Minutes, CFL Meeting, September 12, 1990.
177 *The Globe and Mail*, September 22, 1990.
178 *Ibid.*
179 *Ibid.*
180 *Ibid.*
181 *Ibid.*, September 20, 1990.
182 *Ibid.*, September 12, 1989.
183 *Ibid.*, October 6, 1990.
184 *Ibid.*, September 14, 1990.
185 *Ibid.*
186 *Vancouver Sun*, October 12, 1990.
187 *Ibid.*, January 1, 1991.
188 *Ibid.*, September 12, 1990.
189 *Ibid.*, January 25, 1990.
190 *Ibid.*

191 *Toronto Star*, TV Guide, October 20, 1990.
192 *Toronto Star*, November 21, 1990.
193 *Ibid.*, November 6, 1990.
194 *Ibid.*
195 *Ibid.*, November 26, 1990.
196 *Ibid.*
197 *Ibid.*
198 *Vancouver Sun*, November 21, 1990.
199 *Toronto Star*, November 21, 1990.
200 *CFL Financial Report*, February 14, 1991.

Chapter Twelve

1 *The Globe and Mail*, February 26, 1991.
2 *Ibid.*
3 *Ibid.*
4 *Ibid.*, October 2, 1991.
5 *Ibid.*
6 *Ibid.*
7 *Ibid.*
8 *Ibid.*, April 21, 1991.
9 *Ibid.*, April 23, 1991.
10 *Ibid.*, June 5, 1991.
11 *Ibid.*
12 *Ibid.*
13 *Ibid.*
14 *Ibid.*, September 23, 1991.
15 *Ibid.*, October 2, 1991.
16 *Ibid.*
17 *Ibid.*, October 30, 1991.
18 *Ibid.*
19 *Ibid.*
20 *Ibid.*
21 *Ottawa Citizen*, July 27, 1991.
22 *Ibid.*
23 *CFL Stabilization Fund*, December 31, 1990.
24 *CFL Financial Report*, February 14, 1991.

[25] Minutes, CFL Meeting, July 26, 1991.
[26] *Ibid.*
[27] *Ibid.*
[28] *Ottawa Citizen,* July 27, 1991.
[29] *Ibid.*
[30] *Ibid.*
[31] Minutes, CFL Meeting, September 23, 1991.
[32] *Ibid.*
[33] *Ibid.*
[34] *Toronto Sun,* October 15, 1991.
[35] *Ibid.*
[36] Minutes, CFL Meeting, October 18, 1991.
[37] *Ibid.*
[38] *Ibid.*
[39] *Ibid.*
[40] *The Globe and Mail,* November 28, 1991.
[41] *Ibid.*
[42] Minutes, CFL Meeting, July 26, 1991.
[43] *Ottawa Citizen,* July 27, 1991.
[44] Minutes, CFL Meeting, September 23, 1991.
[45] *Ibid.*
[46] *Ibid.*
[47] *Ibid.*
[48] *Ibid.*
[49] *Ibid.,* May 15, 1991.
[50] Minutes, CFL Meeting, January 3, 1992.
[51] *Ibid.*
[52] Minutes, CFL Meeting, January 29, 1992.
[53] *Ibid.*
[54] *Ibid.,* July 26, 1991.
[55] *Ibid.*
[56] *Ibid.*
[57] *Ibid.*
[58] *Ibid.*
[59] *Ibid.,* September 23, 1991.
[60] *Ibid.*
[61] *Ibid.*
[62] *Ibid.*
[63] *Ibid.*

[64] *Ibid.*
[65] *Ibid.*
[66] *The Globe and Mail,* October 17, 1991.
[67] *Toronto Star,* October 31, 1991.
[68] Minutes, CFL Meeting, November 22, 1991.
[69] *Ibid.*
[70] *Toronto Star,* January 11, 1991.
[71] *Ibid.,* January 24, 1991.
[72] *Ibid.*
[73] *Ibid.,* February 1, 1991.
[74] *CFL Financial Report, 1990,* February 14, 1991.
[75] *The Globe and Mail,* November 21, 1991.
[76] *Ibid.*
[77] *Ibid.*
[78] *Ibid.*
[79] *Ibid.*
[80] *Ibid.,* November 20, 1991.
[81] *Ibid.*
[82] *Ibid.*
[83] *Ibid.,* November 21, 1991.
[84] *Ibid.*
[85] *Ibid.,* November 2, 1991.
[86] *Ibid.*
[87] *Ibid.,* November 23, 1991.
[88] *Ibid.,* November 21, 1991.
[89] *Ibid.*
[90] *Ibid.,* November 22, 1991.
[91] *Toronto Star,* November 23, 1991.
[92] *Ibid.*
[93] *Ibid.*
[94] *The Globe and Mail,* December 18, 1991.
[95] *Ibid.* Nov. 22, 1992.
[96] *Ibid.* Nov. 27, 1991.
[97] *Ibid.*
[98] Minutes, CFL Meeting, January 7, 1991.
[99] *Ibid.*

[100] *Toronto Star,* November 23, 1991.
[101] *The Globe and Mail,* November 22, 1991.
[102] *Toronto Star,* November 23, 1991.
[103] *The Globe and Mail,* November 21, 1991.
[104] *Ibid.*
[105] *Ibid.*
[106] *Ibid.*
[107] *Ibid.,* December 12, 1991.
[108] Minutes, CFL Meeting, April 29, 1992.
[109] *Toronto Star,* January 7, 1992.
[110] *Ibid.*
[111] *Ibid.*
[112] *The Globe and Mail,* December 12, 1991.
[113] *Toronto Star,* January 7, 1992.
[114] *Ibid.*
[115] *Ibid.*
[116] *Ibid.*
[117] Minutes, CFL Meeting, January 3, 1992.
[118] *Ibid.*
[119] *Ibid.*
[120] *Ibid.*
[121] Minutes, CFL Meeting, January 29, 1992.
[122] *Toronto Sun,* February 28, 1992.
[123] *Ibid.*
[124] *The Globe and Mail,* February 28, 1992.
[125] *Toronto Sun,* February 28, 1992.
[126] *Ibid.*
[127] *Ibid.*
[128] *Ibid.*
[129] *Ibid.*
[130] Minutes, CFL Meeting, January 29, 1992.
[131] *Ibid.*
[132] Minutes, CFL Meeting, February 27, 1992.
[133] *Ibid.*
[134] *Ibid.*

[135] *Ibid.*
[136] Minutes, CFL Meeting, April 29, 1992.
[137] *Ibid.*
[138] *Ibid.*
[139] *Ibid.*
[140] *Ibid.*
[141] *Ibid.*
[142] *Ibid.*
[143] *The Globe and Mail,* February 28, 1992.
[144] *Ibid.*
[145] Minutes, CFL Meeting, January 29, 1992.
[146] *Ibid.*
[147] *Ibid.*
[148] *Ibid.*
[149] Minutes, CFL Meeting, January 29, 1992.
[150] *Ibid.*
[151] Minutes, CFL Meeting, February 27, 1992.
[152] *Ibid.*
[153] *Ibid.*
[154] *Ibid.*
[155] *Toronto Star,* June 4, 1992.
[156] *Ibid.*
[157] *Ibid.*
[158] *Ibid.*
[159] *Ibid.*
[160] *Ibid.*
[161] *Ibid.*
[162] Minutes, CFL Meeting, June 29, 1992.
[163] *Ibid.*
[164] *Ibid.*
[165] *Ibid.*
[166] *Ibid.*
[167] Minutes, CFL Meeting, June 2, 1992.
[168] *Ottawa Citizen,* June 13, 1992.
[169] *Ibid.,* July 4, 1992.
[170] *Ibid.*
[171] *Ibid.*
[172] *Hamilton Spectator,* July 7, 1992.
[173] *Toronto Sun,* January 7, 1992.
[174] *Toronto Star,* February 20, 1992.
[175] *Ibid.*
[176] *Toronto Sun,* March 24, 1992.
[177] *Ibid.*
[178] *Ibid.*
[179] *Ibid.*
[180] *The Globe and Mail,* March 25, 1992.
[181] *Toronto Star,* July 22, 1992.
[182] *Ibid.*
[183] *Ibid.*
[184] *Ibid.*
[185] *Toronto Star,* August 27, 1992.
[186] Minutes, CFL Meeting, August 26, 1992.
[187] *Ibid.*
[188] *Ibid.*
[189] *Ibid.*
[190] *Ibid.*
[191] Minutes, CFL Meeting, September 4, 1992.
[192] *Ibid.*
[193] Minutes, CFL Meeting, September 16, 1992.
[194] *Ibid.*
[195] *Ibid.*
[196] *Ibid.*
[197] *Ibid.*
[198] *Toronto Sun,* September 24, 1992.
[199] *The Globe and Mail,* September 24, 1992,.
[200] *Toronto Star,* April 16, 1992.
[201] *The Globe and Mail,* May 8, 1992.
[202] *Ibid.*
[203] *Ibid.*
[204] *Ibid.*
[205] Minutes, CFL Meeting, February 27, 1992.
[206] *The Globe and Mail,* January 25, 1992.
[207] *Ottawa Citizen,* June 25, 1992.
[208] *Ibid.*
[209] *Ibid.*
[210] *Ibid.*
[211] *Ibid.*
[212] Minutes, CFL Meeting, January 29, 1992.
[213] Minutes, CFL Meeting, February 27, 1992.
[214] *Ibid.*
[215] Minutes, CFL Meeting, June 2, 1992.
[216] *Ibid.*
[217] *Ibid.*
[218] *Ibid.*
[219] *Ibid.*
[220] Minutes, CFL Meeting, June 29, 1992.
[221] *The Globe and Mail,* November 27, 1992.
[222] *Ibid.*
[223] Minutes, CFL Meeting, February 27, 1992.
[224] Minutes, CFL Meeting, April 29, 1992.
[225] *Ibid.*
[226] *Toronto Star,* May 12, 1992.
[227] *Ibid.*
[228] *The Globe and Mail,* October 30, 1992.
[229] Minutes, CFL Meeting, November 26, 1992.
[230] *Ibid.*
[231] Minutes, CFL Meeting, December 3, 1992.
[232] *Ibid.*
[233] *Ibid.*

Chapter Thirteen

[1] Minutes, CFL Meetings, December 3, 1992.
[2] Minutes, CFL Meetings, June 2, 1992.
[3] *Ibid.*
[4] *Ibid.*
[5] Minutes, CFL Meetings, June 29, 1992.
[6] *Ibid.*
[7] *Ibid.*
[8] *Ibid.*
[9] *Ibid.*

[10] Minutes, CFL Meetings, October 19, 1992.
[11] *Ibid.*
[12] *Ibid.*
[13] *Ibid.*
[14] *Ibid.*
[15] *Ibid.*
[16] *Ibid.*
[17] *Ibid.*
[18] *Ibid.*
[19] *Ibid.*
[20] *Ibid.*
[21] *Ibid.*
[22] *The Globe and Mail,* November 11, 1992.
[23] CFL Press Conference, November 12, 1992.
[24] *The Globe and Mail,* November 14, 1992.
[25] *Ibid.,* November 10, 1992.
[26] *Ibid.,* November 11, 1992.
[27] *Ibid.*
[28] *Toronto Star,* November 29, 1992.
[29] *Ibid.*
[30] *Ibid.*
[31] *Star Week,* November 28, 1992.
[32] *Ibid.*
[33] *Ottawa Citizen,* November 28, 1992.
[34] *Ibid.*
[35] *Ibid.*
[36] *The Globe and Mail,* November 24, 30, December 7, 1992.
[37] *The Globe and Mail,* November 20, 1992.
[38] *Ibid.*
[39] *Ibid.*
[40] *Toronto Star,* November 26, 1992.
[41] *Ibid.*
[42] *Ibid.*
[43] *Ibid.*
[44] *Ibid.*
[45] *The Globe and Mail,* November 19, 1992.

[46] *Ibid.,* November 12, 1992.
[47] *Ibid.,* November 30, 1992.
[48] *Ibid.,* November 26, 1992.
[49] *Ibid.,* November 29, 1992.
[50] *Ibid.,* November 14, 1992.
[51] *Toronto Star,* February 25, 1993
[52] *Ibid.*
[53] *Ibid.*
[54] *Ibid.,* November 27, 1994
[55] *Ibid.*
[56] *The Globe and Mail,* November 30, 1992.
[57] *Ibid.,* November 27, 1992.
[58] *Ibid.*
[59] *Ibid.,* October 5, 1992.
[60] *Ibid.*
[61] *The Globe and Mail,* October 5, 1992.
[62] *Ibid.*
[63] *Ibid.*
[64] *Ibid.*
[65] *Ibid.*
[66] *Ibid.,* January 13, 1993.
[67] *Ibid.*
[68] *Toronto Star,* January 11, 1993.
[69] *Toronto Sun,* January 13, 1993.
[70] *Ibid.*
[71] *Ibid.*
[72] *Ibid.,* January 13, 1993.
[73] *The Globe and Mail,* January 15, 1993.
[74] *Ibid.*
[75] *Ibid.*
[76] *Ibid.*
[77] *Ibid.,* January 28, 1993.
[78] *Ibid.*
[79] *Ibid.,* January 30, 1993.
[80] *Ibid.,* February 2, 1993.
[81] *Toronto Star,* February 6, 1993.

[82] *The Globe and Mail,* February 3, 1993.
[83] *Ibid.,* March 4, 1993.
[84] *Ibid.,* February 9, 1993.
[85] Minutes, CFL Meetings, November 26, 1992.
[86] *Ibid.*
[87] *Ibid.*
[88] *Ibid.*
[89] *Toronto Sun,* December 30, 1992.
[90] *Ibid.*
[91] *Ibid.*
[92] Minutes, CFL Meetings, October 19, 1992.
[93] *Ibid.*
[94] *Toronto Star,* January 21, 1993.
[95] *Ibid.*
[96] *Ibid.*
[97] *Toronto Star,* January 8, 1993.
[98] *Ibid.,* January 13, 1993.
[99] *Ibid.,* January 30, 1993.
[100] *Winnipeg Free Press,* February 12, 1993.
[101] *Ibid.*
[102] *Ibid.*
[103] *Ibid.,* February 13, 1993.
[104] *Ibid.*
[105] *Ibid.,* February 15, 1993.
[106] *Ibid.*
[107] *Ibid.*
[108] *Ibid.*
[109] *Toronto Star,* February 27, 1993.
[110] *Ibid.*
[111] *Winnipeg Free Press,* June 18, 1993.
[112] *Ibid.*
[113] *Ibid.*
[114] *Ibid.*
[115] *Ottawa Citizen,* July 7, 1993.
[116] *Ibid.*
[117] *Winnipeg Free Press,* July 19, 1993.
[118] *Ibid.*
[119] *Ibid.*

120 *Ibid.*
121 *The Globe and Mail,* September 29, 1993.
122 *Ibid.*
123 *Ibid.,* September 29, 1993.
124 *Ibid.*
125 *Toronto Star,* August 28, 1993.
126 *The Globe and Mail,* September 9, 1993.
127 *Ibid.*
128 *Ibid.*
129 *Ibid.*
130 *Ibid.,* January 6, 1993.
131 *Toronto Star,* August 15, 1993.
132 *The Globe and Mail ,* July 6, 1993.
133 *Toronto Star,* March 6, 1993.
134 CFRB Interview, September 19, 1993.
135 *Toronto Star,* November 9, 1993.
136 *Toronto Sun,* November 2, 1993.
137 *Toronto Star,* November 9, 1993.
138 *Ibid.,* November 19, 1993.
139 *Ibid.,* November 23, 1993.
140 *Ottawa Citizen,* June 3, 1993.
141 *Ibid.*
142 *Ibid.,* August 17, 1993.
143 *Ibid.*
144 *Ibid.*
145 *Ibid.*
146 *Winnipeg Free Press,* October 31, 1993.
147 *Ibid.*
148 *Ibid.*
149 *The Globe and Mail,* October 30, 1993.
150 *Ibid.,* November 10, 1993.
151 *Ibid.*
152 *Ibid.*
153 *Ibid.,* November 15, 1993.
154 *Toronto Star,* November 23, 1993.
155 *The Globe and Mail,* September 30, 1993.
156 *Ibid.,* August 11, 1993.
157 *Toronto Star,* November 24, 1993.
158 *Calgary Herald,* November 12, 1993.
159 *Ibid.,* November 20, 1993
160 *Ibid.*
161 *The Globe and Mail,* November 27, 1993
162 *Calgary Herald,* November 22, 1993
163 *Ibid.* November 20, 1993
164 *The Globe and Mail,* November 24, 1993
165 *Ibid.*
166 *Ibid.,* November 24, 1993
167 *Toronto Sun,* November 29, 1993
168 *Ibid.*
169 *The Globe and Mail,* November 27, 1993
170 *Ibid.*
171 Canadian Press, cited in *Calgary Herald,* November 26, 1993
172 *The Globe and Mail,* November 25, 1993
173 *Toronto Star,* December 9, 1993
174 *Winnipeg Free Press,* July 27, 1993.
175 *Toronto Star,* July 30, 1993.
176 *Ibid.,* August 7, 1993.
177 Minutes, CFL Meetings, Calgary, October 2, 1991.
178 *The Globe and Mail,* January 14, 1994
179 *Toronto Sun,* January 24, 1994
180 *Ottawa Citizen,* January 27, 1994
181 *Ibid.*
182 *Ibid.*
183 *Edmonton Journal,* January 27, 94
184 *Ottawa Citizen,* February 1, 1994
185 *Ibid.*
186 *The Globe and Mail,* February 17, 1994
187 *Ibid.*
188 *CFL Facts and Figures and Records 1994,* p.26
189 *The Globe and Mail.* June 17, 1994
190 *Ibid.*
191 *Ibid.,* September 20, 1994
192 *Baltimore Sun,* January 23, 1994
193 *Winnipeg Free Press,* April 8, 1994.
194 *The Globe and Mail,* April 28, 1994
195 *Ibid.,* June 1, 1994
196 *Ottawa Citizen,* August 23, 1994
197 *Ibid.,* August 27, 1994.
198 *Toronto Sun,* September 1, 1994.
199 The Fan Radio, Toronto September 22, 1994
200 *Ottawa Citizen,* July 20, 1994
201 *Ibid.*
202 *Winnipeg Free Press,* October 22, 1994.
203 *The Globe and Mail,* January 11, 1994
204 *Ibid.,* March 5, 1994
205 *Winnipeg Free Press,* April 26, 1994
206 *Ibid.,* May 6, 1994.
207 *The Globe and Mail.* May 27, 1994
208 *Toronto Star,* June 3, 1994
209 *Ibid.*
210 *Winnipeg Free Press,* November 12, 1994

[211] *Ibid.*, January 28, 1994

[212] *Vancouver Sun*, February 23, 1994

[213] *Winnipeg Free Press*, February 24, 1994

[214] Sean Foudie, interview December 10, 1994

[215] *Winnipeg Free Press*, April 9, 1994

[216] *Ibid.*, March 8, 1994

[217] *Ibid.*, October 16, 1994

[218] *The Globe and Mail*, November 10, 1994

[219] *Ibid.*, January 6, 1994

[220] *Ibid.*

[221] *Ibid.*

[222] *Ibid.*, January 18, 1994

[223] *Ibid.*

[224] *Orlando Sentinel*, January 17, 1994

[225] *Ibid.*

[226] *Ibid.*, Jan. 19, 1994.

[227] *The Globe and Mail*, January 21, 1994

[228] *Ibid.*, January 20, 1994

[229] *Toronto Sun*, March 4, 1994

[230] *Ibid.*

[231] *Winnipeg Free Press*, March 16, 1994

[232] *The Globe and Mail*, April 1, 1994

[233] *Ottawa Citizen*, November 6, 1994

[234] *The Globe and Mail*, March 15, 1994

[235] *Ottawa Citizen*, July 23, 1994

[236] *Ottawa Sun*, August 19, 1994

[237] *Ibid.*, October 15, 1994

[238] *Winnipeg Free Press*, November 18, 1994

[239] *The Globe and Mail*, November 14, 1994

[240] *Ibid.*, November 22, 1994

[241] *Toronto Star*, November 22, 1994

[242] *Ibid.*

[243] *The Globe and Mail*, November 30, 1994

[244] *Baltimore Sun*, November 23, 1994

[245] *Vancouver Sun*, December 1, 1994

[246] *Ibid.*, November 23, 1994

[247] *Toronto Star*, November 26, 1994

[248] *The Globe and Mail*, November 25, 1994

[249] *Toronto Star*, November 27, 1994

[250] *Ibid.*, November 24, 1994

[251] *The Globe and Mail*, November 26, 1994

[252] *Toronto Star*, November 24, 1994

[253] *Ibid.*

[254] *The Globe and Mail*, November 26, 1994

[255] *Ibid.*

[256] *Toronto Star*, November 27, 1994

[257] *Ibid.*

[258] *The Globe and Mail*, November 26, 1994

[259] *Ibid.*, December 8, 1994

[260] *Ibid.*, December 1, 1994

[261] *Vancouver Sun*, November 30, 1994

[262] *The Globe and Mail*, November 28, 1994

[263] *Ibid.*

Epilogue

[1] *The Globe and Mail*, March 15, 1995

[2] *Toronto Star*, Feburary 4, 1995

[3] *The Globe and Mail*, April 13, 1995

[4] *Winnipeg Free Press*, March 4, 1994

[5] *Ibid.*

[6] Larry Smith, "Inside Sports," TSN, January 31, 1994

[7] *Ottawa Citizen*, July 12, 1994.

[8] *Ibid.*, August 10, 1994

[9] *Winnipeg Free Press*, October 19, 1994